Nutritional Anemia

Nutritional
Anemia

Edited by
Klaus Kraemer
SIGHT AND LIFE, Basel, Switzerland

Michael B. Zimmermann
Swiss Federal Institute of Technology, Zurich, Switzerland

 **SIGHT AND LIFE**
Press

SIGHT AND LIFE Mission Statement

SIGHT AND LIFE is a humanitarian initiative of DSM. It aims to ensure a sustainable and significant improvement in human nutrition and health by encouraging partnerships with universities and intergovernmental and governmental agencies, by generating and exchanging scientific information and by forming networks.

The paper used in this book is acid-free and falls within the guidelines established to ensure permanence and durability.

Cover photo by Ulla Lohmann, Germany
Cover illustration by graphic art studio, Grenzach-Wyhlen, Germany
Proofreading by transparent – translation & text services, Berlin, Germany
Typeset and print by Burger Druck, Waldkirch, Germany

ISBN 3-906412-33-4

PREFACE

For half a billion women in developing regions worldwide, anemia is a life-long burden, one which affects most of their infants and young children as well. Controlling anemia in these vulnerable groups could significantly reduce maternal and infant morbidity. It would also enhance intellectual and work capacity, thereby improving family, community and national socioeconomic development.

In May 2002, the General Assembly of the United Nations reemphasized that control of nutritional anemia should be one of the global Development Goals to be achieved in the early years of this new millennium. Despite this, the global prevalence of anemia has hardly declined in the past decade, although considerable programmatic experience exists and a vast amount of scientific data has been compiled on iron metabolism. Much is still unknown, however, and many new issues continue to emerge from the ongoing research, both basic and programmatic. The reasons for this lack of improvement include the multifactorial etiology of anemia, underfunding and poor program implementation, often designed on the assumption that the sole cause of anemia is iron deficiency.

It is increasingly clear that effective control of anemia requires integrated solutions that are tailored to the particular needs and opportunities in each country. Components of such an approach include food fortification, micronutrient supplementation of vulnerable groups (particularly children and women of childbearing age), education, and dietary diversification, as well as control of diseases such as malaria, worm infections, and other chronic endemic infections. While each of these can help reduce the burden of anemia, none is capable of doing the job on its own.

The chapters of this book offer an account of the information that was presented and comprehensively discussed at a workshop on Nutritional Anemia in Barcelona, Spain, on September 27, 2006, in which all the contributors to this volume themselves took part. This event was co-organized by the editors of this volume. We sought the timely publication of this book in order to provide the latest update on the complex causes and consequences of nutritional anemia, and the effectiveness of current control strategies. The field of anemia is clearly of great interest to scientists, policy makers and program mangers. We hope this volume will help point the way forward in controlling this major global health problem. The introductory chapters in this book give an overview of the global burden of anemia prevalence, the economic implications and functional consequences, and the significance of these factors for policy makers. Subsequent chapters provide basic scientific information on iron metabolism and interactions with macronutrients and micronutrients as well as the role of infections in fostering anemia. Other chapters address the information needs of program managers, detailing programmatic approaches and outlining the safety and technical aspects of interventions.

We are particularly grateful to the authors, who are all leading scholars from UN agencies and the wider academic world, for their excellent contributions. A special acknowledgement is also due to all reviewers whose valuable comments have helped to improve the quality of the chapters. We would like to give a very special thanks to the SIGHT AND LIFE team, Svenia Sayer-Ruehmann and Anne-Catherine Frey, for assisting with the workshop as well as for all their technical support in finalizing this book. Svenia devoted much of her time and energies to corresponding with the authors to ensure that our tight timeline was met. We would also like to express our deep appreciation to Jane Badham for her invaluable assistance with the editing of the chapters. Lastly, we wish to thank SIGHT AND LIFE and DSM, in particular its President and CEO, Feike Sijbesma, for his continuing support of our work and the publication of this book.

Klaus Kraemer
Michael B. Zimmermann

FOREWORD

Every year hunger and undernutrition claim more than 10 million lives – more than the deaths from AIDS, malaria and tuberculosis combined. Many of these people are affected by "hidden hunger," a lack of essential vitamins and minerals, known as micronutrient deficiencies, which do not necessarily result in the swollen bellies and stick-like limbs many associate with serious malnutrition.

The effects of poor nutrition are not always easy to spot. Undernourished children are less likely to attend school, more likely to have learning difficulties, are more susceptible to disease. They are more likely to die young. Undernourished adults are less capable of providing sufficient food and other necessities for their families. Their immune systems may be compromised. Their productivity and income is invariably lower.

Poor nutrition impacts the health and development of individuals. It also retards the economic and social development of nations. For instance, it is estimated that anemia alone causes US $50 billion in gross domestic product losses annually.[1] Reducing the number of hungry and malnourished people translates into a better quality of life for individuals, as well as narrowing national disparities in health, education, and wealth.

Infants, young children and women of childbearing age are those at greatest risk of nutritional anemia. This condition, which claims one million lives each year, is associated with increased child and maternal mortality, stillbirths, low-birth-weight and premature babies. It is one of the world's leading causes of disability and can cause mild mental retardation and decreased work performance.

Caused predominantly by iron-deficiency, anemia is inextricably linked with people's nutritional status and hunger. In 2000, the United Nations Sub-Committee on Nutrition reported that 43% of people in developing countries currently suffer from anemia[2]. In spite of the significant burden anemia places on health systems and economies, it has often been overlooked by the international and public health communities.

This book assembles some of the leading research on health and nutrition. The evidence clearly points to the benefits – and feasibility – of reducing the prevalence of anemia and combating undernutrition. This textbook also serves as a guide for how government, international agencies, and non-governmental organizations can work together to decrease rates of nutritional anemia worldwide. It reviews the most effective ways of measuring and monitoring the prevalence of nutritional anemia and the most successful program designs for public health interventions.

International organizations, such as the World Food Programme, depend on such research in order to deliver the best possible assistance to

---

[1] MacDonald B, Haddad L, Gross R, McLachlan M. A foundation for development.
  Administrative Committee on Coordination/Subcommittee on Nutrition. Accessed July 24, 2005.
   Available at: http://www.ifpri.org/pubs/books/intnut/intnut.pdf
[2] ibid

hungry and malnourished poor people. These are the people who have least choice in their diet, and who are at tremendous risk of anemia and other micronutrient deficiencies. The World Food Programme and its partners help to provide iron supplements and fortified foods in developing countries around the world.

Iron fortification is one of the most cost-effective interventions and nutrition education programs have reduced the prevalence of anemia among infants and young children by increasing their consumption of fortified foods. Presently, the World Food Programme is the world's largest purchaser of vitamin- and mineral-fortified blended foods.

Fortified foods alone are not enough. Successful delivery of such interventions requires the strengthening of health systems, increased awareness, and financial investment. An integrated approach – including better water and sanitation,

infectious disease control, nutrition education, food security, and poverty-reduction programs – is required.

Together with partners like DSM and SIGHT AND LIFE, we can and must do more to reduce micronutrient deficiencies such as nutritional anemia. This textbook, which focuses on reducing the prevalence of nutritional anemia, is key to reducing overall hunger and malnutrition rates. It is incumbent upon us to use this information to combat nutritional anemia, improve the nutritional status of those in developing countries, and mitigate one of today's greatest public health problems.

The health and well being of millions of hungry women and children depends on it.

James T. Morris
Executive Director
World Food Programme

Contributors

HAROLD ALDERMAN
Africa Region of the World Bank, Washington, DC, USA; halderman@worldbank.org

JANE BADHAM
JB Consultancy, Health Communication and Strategy Consultants, Johannesburg, South Africa; jbconsultancy@mweb.co.za

HANS-KONRAD BIESALSKI
Institute for Biological Chemistry and Nutrition at the University of Hohenheim, Hohenheim, Germany; biesal@uni-hohenheim.de

MARTIN BLOEM
World Food Programme (WFP), Rome, Italy; martin.bloem@wfp.org

TOMMASO CAVALLI-SFORZA
Nutrition and Food Safety, WHO Regional Office for the Western Pacific, Manila, Philippines; cavalli-sforzat@wpro.who.int

MARY COGSWELL
Division of Nutrition and Physical Activity, Centers for Disease Control and Prevention, Atlanta; USA

IAN DARNTON-HILL
Nutrition Section, UNICEF, New York, USA; idarntonhill@unicef.org

OMAR DARY
A2Z Project, Academy for Educational Development, Washington, DC, USA; odary@aed.org

BRUNO DE BENOIST
World Health Organization (WHO), Geneva, Switzerland; debenoistb@who.int

SASKIA DE PEE
World Food Programme (WFP), Rome, Italy; sdepee@compuserve.com

INES EGLI
Institute of Food Science and Nutrition, Swiss Federal Institute of Technology (ETH), Zurich, Switzerland; ines.egli@ilw.agrl.ethz.ch

JÜRGEN ERHARDT
University of Indonesia, SEAMEO-TROPMED, Jakarta, Indonesia; erhardtj@gmx.de

ALISON D. GERNAND
Bloomberg School of Public Health, Johns Hopkins University, Baltimore, USA; agernand@jhsph.edu

GARY R. GLEASON
Friedman School of Nutrition Science and Policy, Tufts University, Boston, USA; Gary.Gleason@tufts.edu

EVA HERTRAMPF DÍAZ
Institute of Nutrition and Food Technology (INTA), University of Chile, Santiago, Chile; ehertram@inta.cl

SUSAN HORTON
Wilfrid Laurier University, Waterloo, Canada; shorton@wlu.ca

RICHARD HURRELL
Institute of Food Science and Nutrition, Swiss Federal Institute of Technology (ETH), Zurich, Switzerland; richard.hurrell@ilw.agrl.ethz.ch

ALAN JACKSON
Institute of Human Nutrition, University of Southampton, Southampton, UK; aaj@soton.ac.uk

AFAF KAMAL-ELDIN
Department of Food Science, Swedish University of Agricultural Sciences, Uppsala, Sweden; afaf.kamal-eldin@lmv.slu.se

KLAUS KRAEMER
SIGHT AND LIFE, Basel, Switzerland; klaus.kraemer@sightandlife.org

SEAN LYNCH
Eastern Virginia Medical School, Norfolk, USA;
srlynch@visi.net

M.G. VENKATESH MANNAR
The Micronutrient Initiative, Ottawa, Canada;
vmannar@micronutrient.org

ERIN MCLEAN
World Health Organization (WHO), Geneva,
Switzerland; mcleane@who.int

REGINA MOENCH-PFANNER
Global Alliance for Improved Nutrition (GAIN),
Geneva, Switzerland; rmoenchpfanner@gain-
geneva.org

CHRISTINE A. NORTHROP-CLEWES
Northern Ireland Centre for Food and Health, University of Ulster, Coleraine, UK; c.clewes@ulster.ac.uk

MANUEL OLIVARES
Institute of Nutrition and Food Technology
(INTA), University of Chile, Santiago, Chile;
molivare@inta.cl

NEAL PARAGAS
Institute of Human Nutrition, Columbia University, New York, USA; np2014@columbia.edu

KLAUS SCHÜMANN
Technical University of Munich, Freising, Germany; kschuemann@schuemann-muc.de

JOHN M. SCOTT
School of Biochemistry & Immunology, Trinity
College Dublin, Dublin, Ireland; jscott@tcd.ie

NEVIN SCRIMSHAW
International Nutrition Foundation, Boston, USA;
nscrimshaw@inffoundation.org

RICHARD SEMBA
School of Medicine, Johns Hopkins University,
Baltimore, USA; rdsemba@jhmi.edu

NOEL SOLOMONS
Center for Studies of Sensory Impairment, Aging
and Metabolism (CeSSIAM), Guatemala City,
Guatemala; cessiam@guate.net.gt

ALFRED SOMMER
Bloomberg School of Public Health, Johns
Hopkins University, Baltimore, USA;
asommer@jhsph.edu

ELISABETH STOECKLIN
R & D Human Nutrition and Health, DSM Nutritional Products Ltd, Kaiseraugst, Switzerland;
elisabeth.stoeklin@dsm.com

BRIAN THOMPSON
Food and Agriculture Organization (FAO), Rome,
Italy; brian.thompson@fao.org

DAVID THURNHAM
Northern Ireland Centre for Food and Health,
University of Ulster, Coleraine, UK;
di.thurnham@ulster.ac.uk

MELODY C. TONDEUR
Division of Gastroenterology, Hepatology and
Nutrition, Hospital for Sick Children, Toronto,
Canada, melody.tondeur@sickkids.ca

MARET G. TRABER
Linus Pauling Institute & Department of Nutrition
and Exercise Sciences, Oregon State University,
Corvallis, USA; maret.traber@oregonstate.edu

RICARDO UAUY
Institute of Nutrition and Food Technology
(INTA), University of Chile, Santiago, Chile;
ricardo.uauy@lshtm.ac.uk

KEITH P. WEST
Bloomberg School of Public Health, Johns Hopkins
University, Baltimore, USA; kwest@jhsph.edu

DANIEL WOJDYLA
Escuela de Estadistica, Universidad Nacional de
Rosario, Argentina

MICHAEL ZIMMERMANN
Laboratory for Human Nutrition, Swiss Federal
Institute of Technology (ETH), Zurich, Switzer-
land; michael.zimmermann@ilw.agrl.ethz.ch

STANLEY ZLOTKIN
Departments of Paediatrics and Nutritional Scien-
ces and Public Health Sciences, University of
Toronto, Canada; stanley.zlotkin@sickkids.ca

Contents

Worldwide prevalence of anemia in pre-school aged children, pregnant women and non-pregnant women of reproductive age[*]

Erin McLean[1]

Ines Egli[2]

Bruno de Benoist[1]

Daniel Wojdyla[4]

and Mary Cogswell[3]

[1]Department of Nutrition for Health and Development, World Health Organization, Geneva, Switzerland
[2]Human Nutrition Laboratory, Swiss Federal Institute of Technology, Zurich, Switzerland
[3]Division of Nutrition and Physical Activity, Centers for Disease Control and Prevention, Atlanta, USA
[4]Escuela de Estadistica, Universidad Nacional de Rosario, Rosario, Argentina
Contact: debenoistb@who.int

[*] Two of the authors are staff member of the World health Organization. They alone are responsible for the views expressed in this publication and they do not necessarily represent the decisions, policy or views of the World Health Organization. Moreover the findings and conclusions in this report are those of the authors and do not necessarily represent the views of CDC.

ERIN MCLEAN

Erin obtained her PhD in Nutrition from the University of California, Davis, USA. She is currently working as a Technical Officer for the Micronutrient Program in the Department of Nutrition for Health and Development at the World Health Organization in Geneva, Switzerland. Erin's primary work is with the Micronutrient Deficiency Information System, developing regional and global prevalence estimates for anemia.

MARY COGSWELL

Mary obtained her PhD. in nutritional epidemiology from Johns Hopkins University, School of Hygiene and Public Health, Baltimore, USA. She is currently an epidemiologist with the Division of Nutrition and Physical Activity, Centers for Disease Control and Prevention. Mary collaborates with and provides consultation to state health departments, universities, international organizations, and other constituents on nutrition assessment, surveillance, and evaluation of programs. She has over 50 publications in peer-reviewed journals and has won awards for her research on perinatal nutrition and on the assessment and prevention of iron deficiency.

INES EGLI

Ines has a PhD in Nutrition from the Swiss Federal Institute of Technology (ETH), Zurich, Switzerland. She is currently a senior scientist and lecturer at the Human Nutrition Laboratory at ETH where she supervises research projects on mineral bioavailability and infant nutrition, and leads a postgraduate course in Nutrition and Health. She has also worked in the Nutrition Department of the World Health Organization in the area of micronutrient deficiencies with a special focus on iron, iodine, and vitamin A.

DANIEL WOJDYLA

Daniel has an MSc in Biostatistics from the University of North Carolina, Chapel Hill, USA. He is currently Adjunct Professor in the School of Statistics of the National University of Rosario, Rosario, Argentina and is also a statistician at the Rosario Center for Perinatal Studies (CREP), where he is in charge of statistical analyses for clinical trials and epidemiologic studies on reproductive health.

BRUNO DE BENOIST

Bruno is a paediatrician. He obtained his MD from the University of Paris, France, and an MSc in Nutrition from the London School of Hygiene and Tropical Medicine, UK. He is currently Coordinator of the Micronutrient Unit at the World Health Organization, Geneva, Switzerland. His special interest is micronutrient disorders and their relation to public health and food fortification.

INTRODUCTION

Anemia is a widespread public health problem associated with an increased risk of morbidity and mortality, especially in pregnant women and young children (1). Among the numerous factors, both nutritional (such as vitamin and mineral deficiencies) and non-nutritional (such as infection and hemoglobinopathies), that contribute to the onset of anemia, iron deficiency and malaria play an important role. Given the role of iron in oxygen transport and the low levels of available iron in the diets of a large proportion of the global population, it is assumed that iron deficiency is one of the biggest contributing factors to the global burden of anemia. Iron deficiency is considered one of the ten leading global risk factors in terms of its attributable disease burden.

One of the mandates of the World Health Organization (WHO) is to inform its Member States about the global health situation. Previous estimates of anemia prevalence were made for all population groups in 1985 (2) and 2001 (3), while estimates of anemia prevalence in women were made in 1982 (4) and 1992 (5). For these estimates, the data were collected prior to 1990, with the exception of the 2001 estimates, which included data up to 1995, but did not include detailed description of the methodology on how the estimates were derived (3). Thus, it is time to update the global anemia estimates and provide a current picture of the global situation, especially in the most affected groups – women and young children. The objective of this paper is to present estimates of anemia prevalence in preschool aged children, pregnant women and nonpregnant women at global and regional levels, using data collected by WHO for the Vitamin and Mineral Nutrition Information System (VMNIS) (http://www.who.int/vmnis). These estimates are based on the 192 Member States of WHO, which represent 99.8% of the global population.

METHODOLOGY

Data collection

We used data from the VMNIS, which are collected from scientific literature and from partners, including WHO Regional and Country offices, United Nations organizations, Ministries of Health, research and academic institutions, and non-governmental organizations. We searched MEDLINE and WHO Regional databases systematically, and manually searched for articles published in non-indexed medical and professional journals. We included surveys in the VMNIS only if hemoglobin was measured from capillary, venous, or cord blood using quantitative photometric methods or automated cell counters and if anemia prevalence or mean hemoglobin concentrations were reported, while we excluded surveys that measured only clinical signs of anemia or hematocrit. For the VMNIS, we included data representative of any administrative level within a country, including nationally representative data, surveys representative of a Region, the first administrative level boundary, second administrative level boundary, or local surveys.

Data selection for the estimates

We selected survey data from the VMNIS on hemoglobin concentration and/or anemia prevalence for each country using four criteria: the time frame in which the survey took place, the administrative level for which the survey was representative (national or sub-national), the survey sample size, and the population groups surveyed.

The time frame for the current estimates is 1993–2005. If no survey date was provided, we used the date of publication. Nationally representative surveys were used preferentially for country estimates. If two or more national surveys were available, we used the most recent. When a national survey was unavailable for a country, if two or more surveys representative of the first administrative boundary within a country (e.g., state, province, etc.) were available we pooled them, weighted by the population size of the area they represented and used them as representative of the entire country. A sample size of 100 or more was generally required although we made some exceptions. If the sample size was between 50 and 100 and the results were being extrapolated to fewer than 50,000 people or to pregnant women, for whom the number of women included is usually small, we used the data. When a country did not have data that met these criteria, we estimated the prevalence using prediction models.

Population

We defined the population groups as follows: preschool aged children (0–4.99 years), pregnant women (no age range defined), nonpregnant women (15.00–49.99 years). Wherever possible, children below 0.5 years of age were excluded from the estimate for preschool aged children since the cut-off for anemia is not defined in this age group. However, the estimate was applied to the entire population of children less than 5 years of age. Occasionally, in the nonpregnant women group, pregnant women could not be excluded because all women were included in the figure provided by the country report, but pregnant women usually made up a small proportion of the group and thus their exclusion would not be expected to change the figure significantly. If a survey reported results by physiological status, lactating women were combined with other nonpregnant nonlactating women to provide the estimate for nonpregnant women.

Hemoglobin threshold

The hemoglobin concentration cut-offs to define anemia are the WHO–recommended cut-offs for each population group (3): 110 g/L for preschool

aged children and pregnant women and 120 g/L for nonpregnant women. If anemia prevalence was adjusted for altitude or smoking in a survey, the adjusted figure was used since there is statistical and physiological evidence to support that hemoglobin distributions vary under these conditions (6, 7). However, we did not adjust data not already adjusted and we did not accept any other corrections.

Anemia prevalence from survey data

When the anemia prevalence was reported using the appropriate hemoglobin threshold, we used the data provided in the survey. However, if surveys provided mean hemoglobin concentration or only anemia prevalence for an alternative cut-off, we derived the prevalence by assuming a normal distribution of hemoglobin and utilizing other information provided about the population's hemoglobin concentration. We utilized, in order of preference: the mean and standard deviation provided in the survey, the mean hemoglobin concentration alongside the prevalence for an alternative cut-off to derive a standard deviation, or the prevalence for an alternative cut-off and an average standard deviation derived for the population group from data in the VMNIS. Since hemoglobin concentrations are likely to be skewed towards lower values in a population with a high prevalence of deficiency, we may have slightly overestimated anemia prevalence in some populations.

In cases where disaggregated data were provided or where subnational data were used, we pooled the data. For data disaggregated by age, physiological status or any other classification, we derived anemia prevalence by weighting each prevalence estimate by its sample size. For subnational data, we weighted the data by the general population estimate for that area using the most recently available census data for the country between 1993 and 2005.

We considered each estimate representative of the entire country whether from national or subnational data. For each estimate, we calculated the variance in the logit scale using the sample size and generated a 95% confidence interval as a measure of uncertainty, which was back-transformed to the original scale (8, 9). We used a design effect of two to calculate the confidence interval, since the majority of the surveys employed cluster sampling, but did not provide an estimate of their design effect.

Models to estimate anemia prevalence for countries with no eligible data

The level of development and the health of a population are closely related. For this reason, we developed regression models to predict anemia prevalence in countries with no eligible data, using health and development indicators. We started with the 2002 Human Development Index (HDI) score, a numerical reflection of development produced by the United Nations Development Programme (UNDP) and comprising indicators of life expectancy, education and wealth (10). For the 17 WHO Member States with no HDI score produced by UNDP, an estimate of the HDI score was generated using a regression model and the same indicators for life expectancy and wealth, but a proxy indicator for education (11-13). HDI explained 22.4–48.9% of the variation in anemia prevalence in countries with survey data for the three population groups. To further improve the model, we included other health indicators available from WHO statistics (available for ≥190 of 192 WHO Member States) as potential explanatory variables. Some of these additional indicators significantly improved the anemia prediction model and we kept them in the model. For preschool aged children (*n*=82), the additional variables were expenditure on health and adult female mortality, which together with HDI explained 55% of the variation in anemia prevalence. In pregnant women (*n*=60), immunization for DTP3 before 1 year of age,

expenditure on health and adult male mortality were utilized alongside HDI to predict anemia, explaining 32.3% of the variation in prevalence. To predict anemia prevalence for nonpregnant women, population growth rate and expenditure on health with HDI explained 45.3% of the variation. For these estimates, we calculated the variance based on the regression equations and produced 95% confidence intervals as a measure of uncertainty.

Classification of anemia as a public health problem

The prevalence of anemia as a public health problem is categorized as follows: <5%, no public health problem; 5–19.9%, mild public health problem; 20–39.9%, moderate public health problem; ≥40%, severe public health problem (3).

Population coverage, population proportion and number of individuals with anemia

We based these estimates on the 192 WHO Member States, which represent 99.8% of the global population. We calculated the population figures using the 2006 population projection from the 2004 revision of the United Nations Population Division (14). We calculated the population figures for pregnant women based on the total number of births (time period 2005–2010) by assuming one child per woman per year, not taking into account spontaneous and induced abortions (14). For 15 countries with a small population (0.01% of all women), birth data were unavailable and we estimated the population figure by applying the WHO regional birth average per reproductive age woman (15.00–49.99 years) to the number of reproductive age women in that country.

We estimated the population coverage by summing the population in countries with estimates based on survey data and dividing this figure by the total population of that population group.

Table 1.1: Percentage of the population covered by actual survey data globally and by UN Region.[1]

Population group[2]	Global	Africa	Asia	Europe	LAC	NA	Oceania
PreSAC	76.1	76.7	82.1	19.2	70.5	92.4	5.1
PW	69.0	65.3	80.9	0.9	38.4	92.8	4.7
NPW	73.5	63.6	88.8	23.9	37.5	89.9	16.5

[1] WHO Member States are stratified by United Nations Regions: Africa, Asia, Europe, Latin America and the Caribbean (LAC), Northern America (NA), and Oceania.
[2] Population groups: PreSAC, preschool aged children (0.00–4.99y); PW, pregnant women (no age range defined); NPW, non-pregnant women (15.00–49.99y).

Table 1.2: Anemia in preschool aged children, pregnant women and non-pregnant women globally and by Region.

Area	PreSAC[1]		PW		NPW	
	Prevalence (%)[3]	# affected (millions)	Prevalence (%)[3]	# affected (millions)	Prevalence (%)[3]	# affected (millions)
Global	47.4 (45.7–49.1)	293.1 (282.8–303.5)	41.8 (39.9–43.8)	56.4 (53.8–59.1)	30.2 (28.7–31.6)	468.4 (446.2–490.6)
UN Region[2]						
Africa	64.6 (61.7–67.5)	93.2 (89.1–97.4)	55.8 (51.9–59.6)	19.3 (18.0–20.7)	44.4 (40.9–47.8)	82.9 (76.5–89.4)
Asia	47.7 (45.2–50.3)	170.0 (161.0–178.9)	41.6 (39.0–44.2)	31.7 (29.7–33.6)	33.0 (31.3–34.7)	318.3 (302.0–334.6)
Europe	16.7 (10.5–23.0)	6.1 (3.8–8.4)	18.7 (12.3–25.1)	1.4 (0.9–1.8)	15.2 (10.5–19.9)	26.6 (18.4–34.9)
LAC	39.5 (36.0–43.0)	22.3 (20.3–24.3)	31.1 (21.8–40.4)	3.6 (2.5–4.7)	23.5 (15.9–31.0)	33.0 (22.4–43.6)
NA	3.4 (2.0–4.9)	0.8 (0.4–1.1)	6.1 (3.4–8.8)	0.3 (0.2–0.4)	7.6 (5.9–9.4)	6.0 (4.6–7.3)
Oceania	28.0 (15.8–40.2)	0.7 (0.4–1.0)	30.4 (17.0–43.9)	0.2 (0.1–0.2)	20.2 (9.5–30.9)	1.5 (0.7–2.4)

[1] Population groups: PreSAC, preschool aged children (0.00–4.99y); PW, pregnant women (no age range defined); NPW, non-pregnant women (15.00–49.99y).
[2] WHO Member States are stratified by United Nations Regions: Africa, Asia, Europe, Latin America and the Caribbean (LAC), Northern America (NA), and Oceania.
[3] 95% CI

We estimated the number of individuals with anemia for each country and grouping of countries for all population groups based on the estimated proportion of the population with anemia for every country and presented the 95% confidence intervals as a measure of uncertainty.

Combining national estimates
We combined country estimates to provide estimates at the global level as well as by United Nations Region by pooling the data and weighting it by the population that each estimate represented. We constructed a 95% confidence interval by using the estimated variance of the weighted average. For one country without data, no proxy indicators were available and so no country estimate was generated, but the UN subregional estimate had to be applied to that country to make regional and global estimates.

RESULTS

All three population groups were covered by a significant amount of actual data, which covered between 69.0–76.1% of the population in all groups (**Table 1.1**). Coverage varied by UN Region and was highest in Northern America, Asia, and Africa, while it was lower in Europe and Oceania. Only preschool children had eligible subnational data, which covered a small proportion of the population (3.7%) and the coverage of this group by national data remained high at 72.3%.

The global prevalence of anemia in preschool aged children, pregnant women and nonpregnant women is 47.4%, 41.8%, and 30.2% respectively. These estimates, the number of individuals affected, and the information from UN Regions are presented in **Table 1.2**. Globally, 818 million (95% CI; 751–885) women (both pregnant and nonpregnant) and young children suffer from anemia and over half of these, approximately 520 million (95% CI: 493–547), live in Asia. The highest prevalence of anemia is in Africa for all three population groups, but the greatest number of people affected are in Asia, where 58.0%, 56.1%, and 68.0% of the global anemia burden exists in preschool aged children, pregnant women and nonpregnant women respectively.

Anemia as a public health problem
Anemia is a worldwide public health problem. More than half the world's population of preschool aged children and pregnant women reside in countries where anemia is a severe public health problem (56.3% and 57.5% respectively) (**Table 1.3**). The proportion is lower for nonpregnant women of childbearing age, but still significant (29.6%). The degree of severity of the public health problem by country for preschool aged children, pregnant women, and nonpregnant women is presented in **Figures 1.1–1.3**. Countries with anemia as a severe public health problem were grouped in Africa, Asia, and Latin America and the Caribbean.

DISCUSSION

Globally, almost half of preschool aged children and pregnant women and close to one third of nonpregnant women suffer from anemia. Since a large segment of the population is covered by actual survey data (69.0–76.1%), these estimates are likely to reflect the actual global prevalence of anemia for these population groups. However, UN regional estimates may be more accurate for some populations and in some areas since the coverage varies significantly among regions. For all three groups, the coverage is the greatest in three UN regions: North America, Asia, and Africa. North America is the best covered, but the number of countries in this region is much lower (two countries) than in the African (53 countries) and Asian (47 countries) UN regions. The coverage in the European and Oceania

Table 1.3: Anemia as a public health problem[1] in WHO Member States.

Level of public health problem	PreSAC[2]		PW		NPW	
	# of countries	Total population 1000's (%)[3]	# of countries	Total population 1000's (%)	# of countries	Total population 1000's (%)
None	2	20570 (3.3)	0	0 (0.0)	1	4171 (0.3)
Mild	40	40921 (6.6)	33	11156 (8.3)	59	647857 (41.7)
Moderate	81	208472 (33.7)	91	46162 (34.2)	78	441285 (28.4)
Severe	69	348322 (56.3)	68	77466 (57.5)	54	459518 (29.6)
	192	618285	192	134783	192	1552831

[1] The prevalence of anemia as a public health problem is categorized as follows: <5%, no public health problem; 5–19.9%, mild public health problem; 20–39.9%, moderate public health problem; ≥40%, severe public health problem.

[2] Population groups: PreSAC, preschool aged children (0.00–4.99y); PW, pregnant women (no age range defined); NPW, nonpregnant women (15.00–49.99y).

[3] This is the percentage of preschool aged children who live in countries where anemia presents this level of a public health problem.

regions is low, where data are available for less than one quarter of the population in all groups. In Latin America and the Caribbean, coverage for preschool aged children is similar to coverage in Asia or Africa, but for pregnant and nonpregnant women it is about half the coverage found in Asia and Africa.

The pattern of anemia prevalence by region is similar for the three groups, Africa and Asia being the most affected. These regions are the poorest and this may therefore reflect the link between anemia and development. Compared to North America, anemia is three times more prevalent in Europe. One reason may be that the European region includes countries with a range of social and economic profiles, especially in the Eastern subregion. However, the difference remains when North America is compared to Western or Northern Europe, where the countries have more similar economic profiles to those in North America (data not shown). It may also be the result of the low coverage of anemia survey data in Europe compared to North America. Finally, it could be that in North America foods are widely fortified

with iron and a high proportion of iron intake comes from fortified foods (15).

The current estimates are the first to utilize nationally representative data for China, which accounts for 20% of the global population. Furthermore, the majority of the surveys used are nationally representative, which was not the case for previous estimates. Surveys are also based on larger sample sizes than many of the previous estimates. For example, the median sample size in our estimates was 2,580 preschool aged children, 611 pregnant women, and 4,265 nonpregnant women; while in the DeMaeyer estimates, the median number of subjects was 500 for all population groups (2). Finally, in these estimates, we used regression-based equations to generate estimates for countries with no eligible data, considering the country's health and development situation. In previous estimates, neighbouring country information or regional estimates were applied to countries without data.

These estimates are not quantitatively comparable to previous estimates since the methodolo-

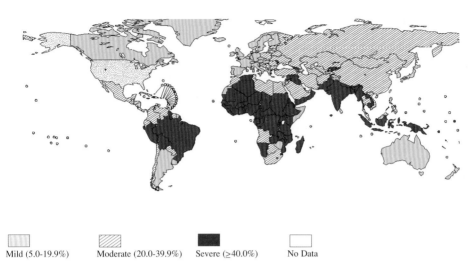

Mild (5.0-19.9%)   Moderate (20.0-39.9%)   Severe (≥40.0%)   No Data

Figure 1.1: Anemia as a public health problem in preschool aged children.

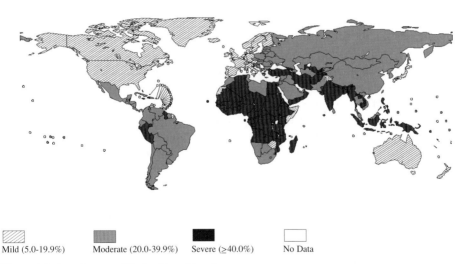

Mild (5.0-19.9%)   Moderate (20.0-39.9%)   Severe (≥40.0%)   No Data

Figure 1.2: Anemia as a public health problem in pregnant women.

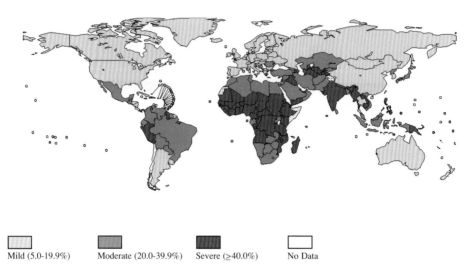

Mild (5.0-19.9%)   Moderate (20.0-39.9%)   Severe (≥40.0%)   No Data

Figure 1.3: Anemia prevelance in non-pregnant women.

The boundaries and names shown and the designations used on this map do not imply the expression of any opinion whatsoever on the part of the World Health Organization concerning the legal status of any country, territory, city or area or of its authorities, or concerning the delimitation of its frontiers or boundaries. Dotted lines on maps represent approximate border lines for which there may not yet be full agreement. © WHO 2005. All rights reserved

gies used are so different. However, it is interesting to note that DeMaeyer's anemia estimates (which excluded China) were 43% for preschool aged children, 51% in pregnant women, and 35% in all reproductive aged women. When we exclude China from our estimates, the prevalence of anemia is respectively 52%, 44%, and 34%. The variation in methods and a larger number of nationally representative surveys in the current estimates compared with previous estimates may be responsible for these differences.

In 1992, WHO published the anemia prevalence estimates of 37%, 51%, and 35% for all women, pregnant and nonpregnant respectively. These estimates included subnational data for China. Current estimates of 31%, 42%, and 30% are lower, but this change may be accounted for by the considerable difference in methods and coverage of national surveys.

The current estimates do have some limitations. Firstly, we treated all surveys as equal despite the fact that quality varies greatly and adjustments are made in some surveys for population representativeness, smoking or altitude, but not in others. Secondly, some surveys covered only a segment of the population group (e.g., 3.00–4.99 years for preschool aged children), but we used these data to make an estimate for the entire population group. Similarly, the estimates for pregnant women do not take into account the trimester assessed by the surveys since it is rarely reported. However, this could affect the estimate of anemia prevalence, since prevalence is likely to be lower early in pregnancy. Also, subnational data were treated equally to national data even though they may actually under- or over-estimate the prevalence of anemia depending on the reasons for which the survey was conducted. Finally, we had to adjust hemoglobin concentrations for country estimates which did not present the prevalence of anemia for the appropriate threshold and we based this adjustment on normal hemoglobin distribution. In fact, the distribution may be negatively skewed in populations with a high prevalence of anemia and we may have slightly over-estimated the anemia prevalence in these populations.

These data on anemia prevalence are based on the best available information and they are a good starting point to track progress in eliminating anemia. However, additional information would allow interventions to be more targeted and specific.

Anemia in children less than two years of age is of greatest concern since their rapid growth requires a high intake of iron which is frequently not covered by their diet. It was not possible to estimate the anemia prevalence in this group separately because of insufficient data. However, given that almost half the global population of preschool aged children suffer from anemia, with a prevalence as high as 64.6% in Africa and 47.7% in Asia, and that we know anemia prevalence is higher in the group of children less than two years old, we would expect that anemia in this age group is a major global public health problem, especially in low income countries.

Based on these estimates of anemia prevalence, the magnitude of nutritional anemia or even of iron deficiency anemia is difficult to assess since most anemia surveys in the WHO VMNIS do not address the causes of anemia and are restricted solely to measuring hemoglobin. More specifically, few surveys provide information on iron deficiency, on the relative proportions of anemia with concomitant iron deficiency, or on iron deficiency with concomitant anemia. The surveys that do provide information on iron deficiency often use different indicators and thresh-

olds. The assumption in designing anemia surveys is that iron deficiency is the main cause of anemia and therefore anemia prevalence can be used as a proxy for iron deficiency prevalence. Previously, the US NHANES 1976–80 data were utilized to estimate iron deficiency from the prevalence of anemia (3, 16) and it has been suggested that when anemia prevalence is 20%, iron deficiency exists in 50% of the population, and when anemia prevalence is greater than 40%, the entire population suffers from some degree of iron deficiency. This assumption may apply to countries with a high prevalence of anemia and iron deficiency where the primary cause of anemia is iron deficiency, but does not necessarily hold in situations where the prevalence of anemia and iron deficiency are low or where factors other than iron deficiency (other nutritional deficiencies, malaria, infections) cause anemia (17).

In spite of its limitations, anemia prevalence data remains an important indicator of public health since anemia is related to morbidity and mortality in the population groups usually considered the most vulnerable – preschool aged children and pregnant women. At a global level, anemia prevalence is a useful indicator to assess the impact of widespread or highly effective interventions and to track the progress made towards the goal of reducing anemia in pregnant women and preschool children by one third that was adopted by the UN Special Session on Children in 2002 (18). However, in order to make full use of these prevalence data, information on the cause of anemia should be collected in any anemia survey so that interventions for anemia control can be better adapted to the local situation and can therefore be more effective.

REFERENCES

1.   World Health Organization. The world health report 2002: reducing risks, promoting healthy life. Geneva: WHO, 2002.
2.   DeMaeyer E, Adiels-Tegman M. The prevalence of anaemia in the world. World Health Stat Q 1985;38:302–16.
3.   UNICEF/UNU/WHO. Iron deficiency anaemia: assessment, prevention, and control. A guide for programme managers. WHO/NHD, 2001 [report no. 01.3].
4.   Royston E. The prevalence of nutritional anaemia in women in developing countries: a critical review of available information. World Health Stat Q 1982;35:52–91.
5.   World Health Organization. The prevalence of anaemia in women: a tabulation of available information. WHO/MCH/MSM,1992 [report no. 92.2].
6.   Hurtado A, Merino C, Delgado E. Influence of anoxemia on haematopoietic activities. Arch Int Med 1945;75:284–323.
7.   Nordenberg D, Yip R, Binkin NJ. The effect of cigarette smoking on hemoglobin levels and anemia screening. JAMA 1990;264:1556–9.
8.   Lohr SL. Sampling: design and analysis. Pacific Grove, CA: Duxbury Press, 1998.
9.   Wackerly D, Mendenhall W, Scheaffer RL. Mathematical statistics with applications. Pacific Grove, CA: Duxbury Press, 2001.
10. United Nations Development Programme. Human development indicators. In: Murphy C, Ross-Larson B, eds. Human development report 2004. New York: UNDP, 2004:139–250.

11. World Health Organization. The world health report 2004 – changing history. Geneva: WHO, 2004.
12. World Health Organization. The world health report 2000 – health systems: improving performance. Geneva: WHO, 2000.
13. Mathers CD, Loncar D. Projections of global mortality and burden of disease from 2002 to 2030. PLoS Med. 2006;3:e442.
14. United Nations Population Division. World Population Prospects - the 2004 revision. New York: UN, 2005.
15. Hurrell RF, Jacob S. Role of the food industry in iron nutrition: iron intake from industrial food products. In: Hallberg L, Asp NG, eds. Iron nutrition in health and disease. London: John Libbey & Co., 1996:339–47.
16. Dallman PR, Yip R, Johnson C. Prevalence and causes of anemia in the United States, 1976 to 1980. Am J Clin Nutr 1984;39:437–45.
17. Asobayire FS, Adou P, Davidsson L, Cook JD, Hurrell RF. Prevalence of iron deficiency with and without concurrent anemia in population groups with high prevalences of malaria and other infections: a study in Cote d'Ivoire. Am J Clin Nutr 2001;74:776–82.
18. United Nations Children's Fund. A world fit for children: millennium development goals; special session on children documents; the convention on the rights of the child. New York: UNICEF, 2004.

2

The case for urgent action to address nutritional anemia

M.G. Venkatesh Mannar

The Micronutrient Initiative, Ottawa, Canada
Contact: vmannar@micronutrient.org

VENKATESH MANNAR
Venkatesh has a Master's degree in chemical engineering and extensive experience with planning and implementing programs to eliminate micronutrient deficiencies. He is currently President of the Micronutrient Initiative (MI), an international nonprofit agency based in Canada. His role is overseeing the implementation of MI's global mandate to support national actions to eliminate micronutrient malnutrition. He has a special interest in salt iodization and serves on the International Council for the Control of Iodine Deficiency Disorders, and the Network for the sustained Elimination of Iodine Deficiency, as well as being a member of the Leadership Group of the Flour Fortification Initiative.

INTRODUCTION

The continued persistence of anemia in many parts of the world at high levels is a challenge that needs to receive the highest priority for attention and action. Despite the magnitude of the anemia problem, and the constantly expanding body of research findings relating to pathogenesis, risk factors, and efficacious interventions, coverage of interventions remains poor.

In part this is because there is no easy solution and the approaches that are effective have considerable drawbacks. However, lack of priority may also be an underlying reason for the lack of progress. For many decades iron deficiency has been seen as a "women's problem." Moreover, it is so common, affecting up to three-quarters of pregnant women in some parts of Asia for example, that it has come to be regarded as normal. Among policy makers the unspoken view has seemed to be that women somehow cope and that iron deficiency is not enough of a problem to justify a major national effort to reduce it.

This view, never justifiable, must surely now give way under the weight of evidence linking iron deficiency in early childhood to substantial effects on physical and intellectual development. In most developing countries today, iron deficiency is estimated to be preventing 40 to 60% of the population from reaching their full mental potential.

Several recent global reviews have underscored the urgency to act to address iron deficiency and anemia:

- In the World Health Report 2002, which quantified the most important risks to health, iron deficiency was identified among the 10 most serious risks in countries with high infant mortality coupled with high adult mortality (1). The same study found that particular measures to address iron deficiency anemia are among the most cost-effective public health interventions.

- The Copenhagen Consensus 2004 panel of eminent economists, including several Nobel Laureates, concluded that the returns of investing in micronutrient programs (including iron), among a list of 17 possible development investments, are second only to those of fighting HIV/AIDS. The benefit-to-cost ratio of iron interventions based on resource savings, improvement in cognitive development and schooling, and physical productivity was estimated to be as high as 200:1 (2).

- The Disease Control Priorities Project (3) has also highlighted the cost-effectiveness of iron interventions (66 to 70 USD per DALY averted for iron fortification).

THE PROGRESS

Interventions to address nutritional anemias traditionally have focused on providing iron and folic acid supplements principally to pregnant women and, to a much lesser extent, children under 2 years of age. Iron supplementation in controlled experiments has proven highly efficacious where anemia is not exacerbated by parasitic infection or malaria. However, those analyses which have attempted to assess effectiveness in field settings have generally failed to show significant reductions in anemia prevalence. Further the effectiveness of large-scale food fortification programs has not been systematically documented so far, notwithstanding the fact that some of these programs have been ongoing for more than 50 years. Data on the conditions under which food fortification can reduce iron deficiency is still lacking. Overall the goal of reducing "…by one-third the prevalence of anaemia, including iron deficiency, by 2010…" (4) in women and children is unlikely to be met unless we strengthen field application of supplementation efforts coupled with other creative means of increasing the iron content of diets and enhancing its absorption.

Fortunately over the past 10 years there has been a significant scale-up and intensification of efforts in several countries to address anemia and particularly iron deficiency through supplementation and food fortification. These impart confidence that systematic application of known interventions can significantly reduce anemia in field settings and be sustained on a population-wide basis. Key developments are summarized below:

- There is as we will hear today a better technical consensus on key issues. There is a better understanding of the conditions under which supplementation programs can be effective. There is sufficient knowledge and experience with iron supplementation for pregnant women to design and implement effective national programs. Programmatic and technical guidelines (5) reflect a much larger body of experience to guide effective programming.
- In food fortification we have much better information and guidelines today regarding iron compounds that are stable and bioavailable (6). Work continues to refine our knowledge on what iron compounds work best under a specific set of conditions. WHO has just published comprehensive guidelines for food fortification with micronutrients, including iron (7).
- The food industry (especially the cereal flour industry) is aware of the problem and large-scale fortification has commenced in several parts of the world, especially Latin America, the Middle East/North Africa, and South East and Central Asia. More than 63 countries are fortifying all or some of their flour with iron, folic acid and other nutrients, covering 25% of the flour that is milled in large roller mills (8). Fortification with iron is also being extended on a large scale to cereal flour derivatives including processed baked products, complementary foods, noodles, and pastas.
- Workable strategies and interventions now exist to provide iron to children under two years of age through fortified complementary foods as well as multinutrient premixes for addition in the home (9).
- Considerable efforts have been invested by the Micronutrient Initiative, ETH Zurich, and other organizations in developing and recently taking to scale the double-fortification of salt. Technology is now available for a stable encapsulated iron premix that can be easily added to iodized salt. By using the capacity and delivery systems already established during the push for universal salt iodization, double-fortified salt is already being produced and distributed through commercial channels and also through public programs to reach economically weaker sections of the population. Double-fortified salt could potentially reach more than 1 billion people around the world (10).
- Since 1999 the Chilean National Supplementary Feeding Program (PNAC) has been providing 2 kg/month of iron-fortified full-fat powdered milk to 70% of infants 12 to 18 months of age, resulting in a significant decrease in anemia prevalence. Lactating mothers consume it until their infants are weaned.
- Condiments fortified with iron (soy and fish sauces) are emerging as a major vehicle in parts of Asia (China, Vietnam, and Thailand). In China, through a project supported by the Global Alliance for Improved Nutrition (GAIN), fortified soy sauce is already reaching nearly 12 million people.
- Technologies to fortify rice with iron and folic acid have been developed and successfully tested for acceptability and efficacy (11).
- There is a growing body of work led by the International Food Policy Research Institute (IFPRI) and HarvestPlus related to improved varieties of staple crops such as rice, wheat, and beans with high iron content. Polished rice with 8 ppm iron (16 times the level in current commercial varieties) and 20 ppm zinc has been identified in germplasm collections at the International Rice Research Institute in the Philippines. Initial studies using the rice showed efficacy in improving iron stores of women with iron-poor diets (12).

High-iron beans with iron levels up to 127 µg/g have been identified. The first set of selected materials combining high iron with superior agronomic attributes, e.g. drought tolerance, was recently distributed to African partners for local evaluation (13).

- The intersection between iron status and infection is also being given more attention today and public health measures are beginning to have an impact on anemia levels in a few parts of the world.

These efforts must be supported by an increase in the amount of attention given to communication, for example in the form of compelling advocacy to those policy makers capable of mobilizing resources. It is equally important to foster strategic alliances, reach agreement on priority target groups, and support behavioral change. The social marketing perspective is also critical for iron, particularly when new and affordable iron-containing products are introduced in a society or group.

WHAT WOULD IT TAKE TO FIGHT IDA MORE EFFECTIVELY?

A basic yet formidable challenge is putting iron on the agenda of policy makers and development agencies nationally and globally. Creating awareness, building alliances, and mobilizing actors at all levels and sectors is critical. Iron needs global champions to communicate the need and urgency for action.

While the starting point is to address key issues and propose consensus statements that provide clarity to policy makers and program planners in order to strengthen and expand programs, the information that a policy maker needs does not flow automatically from scientific consensus and technological feasibility. We need to build much better bridges between those that have the science and technology, those that deliver the services, and those that have the power to make the political and financial decisions.

The main challenge in food fortification is to enable universal fortification of staple foods or condiments with meaningful levels of iron. This involves systematic planning and collaboration with the food processing industry in addressing issues of coverage, cost, effectiveness, benefits, and risk in relation to gains, performance of the technology within the environmental, socioeconomic and cultural context of the recipient population, the identification of intended beneficiaries, their needs, and their social and economic circumstances. Parallel with improving bioavailability of iron compounds (including encapsulated forms of iron), development of other strategies to effectively improve iron utilization from the diet also needs increased attention. Gaining better knowledge of interactions among various micronutrients (e.g. iron and zinc, vitamins limiting iron absorption and mobilization) and other dietary compounds, and of other nutritional and non-nutritional causes of anemia, pose as challenges to be overcome for enhanced effectiveness of interventions.

In the area of iron supplementation, in addition to timely supply of good quality supplements and effective delivery systems, there is also the challenge of ensuring high compliance for the supplementation programs to be successful. Ensuring effectiveness through improved programming and assured provision of higher quality supplements to target groups and addressing factors that limit motivation to take supplements have the largest potential to improve program effectiveness.

The potential of the food industry to create nutritious complementary foods for young children has hardly been tapped and has yet to be developed. Industrially produced fortified complementary foods are recommended by pediatricians worldwide as an important part of a nutritionally adequate diet for infants (complementary to breast milk and home-prepared complementary foods)–especially to meet the micronutrient requirements of infants for iron and zinc. Beyond having a superior micronutrient content to that of home-prepared rice porridge and other traditional infant foods, industrially fortified complementary foods also have the advantages of delivering higher bioavailability of micronutrients, higher energy density, and higher protein quality, all in a safe and convenient manner. From the food technology perspective, the challenge is to increase both the energy density of complementary foods and levels of iron and other nutrients (and eliminate absorption-inhibiting factors) at an affordable price. From the public health perspective, we need a combination of proper regulation that protects infant health yet supports industrial innovation, and strong public education on appropriate practices of feeding and caring for infants and young children. Large and rapid growth in the production and consumption of fortified complementary foods will be possible only through an effective public-private social marketing partnership to increase the percentage of infants and young children who are fed fortified complementary foods and promote the use of fortified complementary foods only in the latter half of infancy and the second year of life.

While recent studies have questioned the safety of iron supplementation for young children in malaria-endemic areas, a preliminary statement from WHO has recommended that the conclusions not be extrapolated to fortification or food-based applications where patterns of iron absorption and metabolism may be substantially different (14).

The Way Forward

Clearly a more effective anemia strategy will involve concurrent efforts to address inadequate iron intake and to reduce concurrent infections,

particularly parasitic and malarial. Given the highly regulated nature of iron absorption, no single intervention will revert and prevent IDA in any given population. A combination of interventions need to be universally advocated and implemented including supplementation of at-risk groups, universal and targeted fortification, dietary modification, parasitic disease and malaria control, and vitamin A interventions, in addition to overall education of policy makers, professionals and the public. The proper combination of effective strategies will vary according to each country's epidemiological, socioeconomic, political and cultural context.

Programmatically, the priority in global efforts to increase the iron intakes of vulnerable populations almost certainly should be given to national scale programs for:

- Fortification of staple foods, condiments, and complementary foods with bioavailable forms of iron (care is needed in selecting the compound and the level of fortification);
- Iron supplementation programs for the highest priority population groups: pregnant women, children under two and adolescent girls.
- While biofortification of crops with iron is not yet ready for widespread application, it is clearly one of the interventions of the future and needs to be aligned with crop improvement efforts for key staples and promotion/adoption at the regulatory, farmer and consumer level.

Country strategies must be tailored to suit specific national paradigms, combining complementary and effective interventions that will result in the most cost-effective model. In the wider picture there is certainly need to establish and scale up effective technologies (especially in using iron compounds that do not impart color or react with food matrices while offering a good bioavailability). Beyond the technology we need to tackle on a parallel track the operational considerations related to making programs work in communities where iron-deficient people live. Issues of demand, supply and logistics, communications and community participation, partnership building across a wide spectrum of players – public and private – are equally important to ensure the success and sustainability of efforts to eliminate anemia and iron deficiency in large populations. Many of these needs interact and are mutually reinforcing.

REFERENCES

1. World Health Organization. The world health report 2002: reducing risks, promoting healthy life. Geneva, Switzerland: World Health Organization, 2002.
2. Behrmann JR, Alderman H, Hoddinott J. Hunger and malnutrition. Copenhagen Consensus Challenge Paper, 2004.
3. Disease Control Priorities in Developing Countries. 2nd ed. New York: Oxford University Press, 2006.
4. United Nations. Report of the 27th session of the UN General Assembly Special Session on Children. 2002.
5. USAID. Anemia guidance manual. 2003.
6. Flour Fortification Initiative. Wheat flour fortification: current knowledge and practical applications. Summary report of an International Technical Workshop: Cuernevaca (Mexico), 2004.
7. World Health Organization. Guidelines for food fortification with micronutrients. Geneva, Switzerland: World Health Organization, Department of Nutrition for Health and Development. 2006.
8. Flour Fortification Initiative. Tabular overview of progress in flour fortification. In press 2006.
9. Zlotkin SH, Schauer C, Christofides A, Sharieff W, Tondeur MC, Hyder SMZ. Micronutrient sprinkles to control childhood anemia. PLoS Med 1 (1):e1(2004)
10. The Micronutrient Initiative. Double fortification of salt: a technical breakthrough to alleviate iron and iodine deficiency disorders around the world. Ottawa: The Micronutrient Initiative, 2005.
11. Moretti D, Lee TC, Zimmerman MB, Nuessli J, Hurrell RE. Development and evaluation of iron-fortified extruded rice grains. J Food Sci 2005;70:4.
12. Haas Jere D, Beard JL, Murray-Kolb LE, del Mundo AM, Felix A, Gregorio GB. Iron-biofortified rice improves the iron stores of non-anemic Filipino women. J Nutr 2005;135:2823–2830.
13. HarvestPlus, www.harvestplus.org.
14. World Health Organization. Iron supplementation of young children in regions where malaria transmission is intense and infectious disease highly prevalent. WHO Statement. Geneva: World Health Organization, 2006.
15. Beaton GH, McCabe GP. Efficacy of intermittent iron supplementation in the control of iron deficiency anaemia: an analysis of experience in developing countries. Ottawa: The Micronutrient Initiative, 1999.
16. Horton S, Ross J. The economics of iron deficiency. Ottawa: The Micronutrient Initiative, 2000.
17. Committee on Micronutrient Deficiencies, Institute of Medicine. Prevention of micronutrient deficiencies: tools for policymakers and public health workers. Howson CP, Kennedy ET, Horwitz A, eds. Washington, DC: National Academy Press, 1998.

3

The economics of addressing nutritional anemia

Harold Alderman[1]

Susan Horton[2]

[1]World Bank, Washington DC, USA
[2]Wilfrid Laurier University, Ontario, Canada
Contact: halderman@worldbank.org

HAROLD ALDERMAN
Harold has a PhD in economics from Harvard University and an MS in Nutrition from Cornell University, both in the USA. He is currently Social Protection Advisor for the Africa Region of the World Bank where he has worked for the last 15 years. Harold's research focus has been on the economics of nutrition interventions and food pricing policies. Recent studies include estimates of the economic returns from investment in nutrition and evaluations of program impacts.

SUSAN HORTON
Susan has a PhD in economics from Harvard University, USA. She is currently Vice President: Academic at Laurier University in Canada. Susan's main area of specialization is in health and labor market issues in developing countries. These include economics of health, nutrition, household use of time, labor markets, and poverty and she has worked and researched extensively in developing countries across the world.

INTRODUCTION

There is abundant evidence that iron deficiency anemia is associated with a range of health consequences, as reviewed in the various chapters of this volume. Similarly, evidence from various clinical and field trials shows the potential for practical interventions to reduce some of these undesirable health outcomes. This chapter addresses the question of how programs aiming to diminish the risks of poor health associated with anemia can be evaluated in economic terms.

The first step in such an evaluation is to state the costs of the iron deficiency anemia in dollar terms so as to have the consequences in a unit of measurement that is in common with other claims on public resources. This differs from the calculation of effectiveness of an intervention in terms of natural units (such as increases in life expectancy) or in terms of disability adjusted life years (DALYs), a composite measure that combines years lived with disability and years lost to premature death in a single metric (1).

Using an economic denominator facilitates aggregation of different benefits from the same intervention, for example, with a deworming program that reduces anemia as well as facilitates ponderal growth and vitamin A absorption. More important in many contexts is the fact that such a metric permits the comparison of health programs with interventions outside the health area (2).

There are two general approaches to such estimates of economic benefits. First, one can calculate what the expected gains in economic terms would be if a case of anemia were prevented. Alternatively, one could estimate the impact on GNP if anemia could be reduced. The latter differs from the former in that it scales the individual gains by the prevalence rate of anemia, and has the strong advantage of motivating political will. However, the former is most amenable to comparisons of intervention costs and expected benefits, as discussed below.

The economic gains from reducing any micronutrient deficiency can come from both cost reductions (say, by reducing the costs associated with mortality or morbidity) or from enhanced productivity. At least six distinct categories of economic benefits from improved nutrition can be identified:

1) Reduced infant and child mortality.
2) Reduced costs of health care for neonates, infants, and children.
3) Productivity gain from improved physical capacity.
4) Productivity gain from increased cognitive ability.
5) Reduction in costs of chronic diseases.
6) Intergenerational benefits through improved health.

Placing precise numbers on the economic value from any one of these benefits involves a range of assumptions and adaptations to the country context. A particularly vexing problem is how to quantify the economic cost of early mortality. Most simply, this can be based on the expected lifetime earnings of the individual. Other approaches are linked to the revealed behavior of either individuals or governments. For example, the value of a statistical life (VSL) can be derived from the premium paid to a worker to induce him or her to accept employment that incrementally increases the risk of mortality (3). The magnitude of the higher wage relative to the decrease in life expectancy provides an estimate of how the employee values the risk. Typically, such estimates in dollar terms are in the seven digits range for a lifetime or over $100,000 (US) per year of life expectancy. Estimates are higher in wealthier countries, although the proportional increase in the VSL is generally less than the increase in national income. An alternative approach to valuing reduced mortality is based on the behavior of governments. In particular, the resources actually used in a society to avert a death provide an estimate of the average value that the public places on averting a death (4).

These two approaches generally result in estimates that are far apart, but as they measure different things they cannot be directly compared. Due in part to the inherent limitations of such methodologies, many approaches to estimating the economic benefits of nutrition interventions only indicate costs in terms of productivity – and they can be considerable in their own right, as discussed in Section 2. Other studies report sensitivity estimates and details on the underlying assumptions, so that it is possible to see if the economic rationale for an investment changes over a reasonable range of presumed values for deferred mortality (5). A further and flexible alternative is to provide results in terms of DALYs and then to convert the DALYs into dollar terms using a range of estimates. One study suggests a range between $1,000 and $5,000 (6, see also 7).

As with any analysis of causality, it is necessary to distinguish the specific consequences of anemia from its correlates when determining the expected benefits from a specific intervention. This is less of an issue with respect to contemporaneous impacts of anemia on productivity, since there are experimental approaches that have been used to directly assess changes in productivity. In such cases, however, it is still important to determine the incentive structure a beneficiary faces; a capacity for increased work does not necessarily translate into increased effort unless there are incentives for the worker to increase performance. Still, it is comparatively straightforward to assign a value to the output from increased effort, controlling for economic context.

The impact of improved iron status during childhood on subsequent adult productivity, however, is seldom obtained directly from experimental evidence. In the absence of longitudinal studies that track experimental interventions over decades, in order to estimate the economic impact of increased cognitive development due to supplementation or fortification in childhood, it is necessary to draw upon the general literature on productivity enhancement. For a given change in an indicator of cognitive ability, the change on subsequent earnings must be estimated using a maintained assumption that the relationship between IQ or similar cognitive measures and earnings is not affected by the type of intervention that influences the indicator.[1]

One such estimate of the impact of IQ on earnings, conditional on years of schooling, uses data from the United States (8). For men, the impact of a half standard deviation decline in IQ on the logarithm of wages was 0.05, or slightly more than the impact of an additional year of post-secondary schooling. Using the same data set, but a different measure of ability, another study shows that the net impact of ability is both the direct impact on wages as well as the impact that works through schooling choices (9). Using the methodology of the latter study disaggregated by gender and ethnic group, as well as including other background variables, but without schooling, a half standard deviation decline in cognitive ability leads to 8–12% lower wages.

A different measure of cognitive ability – performance on Raven's matrices – was used in a study of wages in rural Pakistan (10) that found a similar pattern in the effect of ability on wages with and without controlling for the impact of ability on schooling. This study found that a half standard deviation decline in this measure leads

---

[1] Non cognitive skills may have as much, or more, impact on earnings. However, while these may be influenced by developmental programs, it is less clear that they are malleable to micronutrient interventions.

to a 6.5% reduction in wages, in estimates that do not include schooling in the regression. The point estimate drops by two thirds in estimates that include both years of schooling as well as achievement in school, both of which are indirectly affected by ability. Overall, these and similar studies cited in Behrman, Alderman and Hoddinott (2) imply an impact of a half standard deviation change in IQ on earnings in the neighborhood of 5%.

Since improvements are the result of intervention in childhood, for any comparison of the program costs of such benefits, it is necessary to account for the time lag between the intervention and the stream of benefits. That is, unlike the direct productivity effects due to increased work capacity following iron fortification or supplementation, there is typically a 10–15 year lag between interventions that increase the cognitive capacity of children and the stream of benefits, which commences only when they enter the labor market and which continues for their whole working life. Benefits incurred at different times have to be given different economic values, due to the fact that monetary intervention carries a greater long-term impact if it takes effect early in life rather than later. This is also because the sooner it is obtained, then economic benefits can be reinvested and further productive returns gained.

Unfortunately, although the rationale for discounting future benefits is not in dispute, there is no unambiguous way to determine this discount rate. For example, DALYs are typically calculated using a fairly low discount of 3% per year (1) while rates of 10% have been proposed for World Bank investments (11). All discount rates reduce the present value of future benefits relative to current costs; the larger the discount rate, the greater the importance given to immediate returns.

A final consideration before discussing the potential economic benefits as well as the cost of interventions in addressing iron deficiency anemia is whether low income countries can expect that robust income growth will address the need for interventions at all. Even though it is currently widespread, if anemia were to decline rapidly in concurrence with progress in providing equitable growth, it might be a moot point to prioritize programs which tackle iron deficiency. Unfortunately, while such a viewpoint is often expressed in regards to malnutrition in general, the Millennium Development Goal (MDG) of reducing underweight is unlikely to be met with income growth (12): Iron deficiency anemia is even less responsive to economic growth.

For example, for every 10% increase in income per capita , the percentage of underweight children declines by 5%; a similar estimate undertaken for this paper using data from Mason, Rivers and Helwig (13) shows that a 10% increase in income per capita is associated with a decline of only 2.5% in prevalence rates of anemia in children 0–59 months old. This estimate also reveals a slight trend in lower rates of anemia over time, after controlling for national incomes.

Table 3.1 illustrates a similar difference between the rates at which underweight and anemia decline, using the example of India. As indicated, the share of children in the upper income quintile that are underweight is less that half the share in the lower income group. However, the percentage of children that are anemic declines by only 20%. There are few multivariate estimates of the determinants of anemia in the literature. One study, from Indonesia (14), looked at hemoglobin concentration, which admittedly is not synonymous with anemia rates. Still, this analysis found that for every 10% increase of household per capita expenditures, hemoglobin concentration in children increased by only 0.2%. Thus, it would take a fivefold increase of income to raise hemoglobin concentration by 1 g/dL, an improvement that is feasible in controlled trials of supplementation and fortification.

Table 3.1: Percentage of Indian children under 5 that are malnourished, presented by income quintiles (45).

Income quintiles	Percentage of children with weight-for-age below 2 standard deviations			Percentage of children with anemia (HB <11 g/dl)		
	Male	Female	Both	Male	Female	Both
Lowest	59.7	61.5	60.7	80.2	77.2	78.8
Second	51.7	56.5	54.0	80.0	77.8	79.0
Middle	47.2	51.3	49.2	75.0	75.1	75.1
Fourth	37.6	40.3	38.9	73.3	71.1	72.3
Highest	25.2	27.6	26.4	65.1	62.7	63.9

ESTIMATING THE COST OF ANEMIA

Section 1 identified six categories of costs of anemia. Of these, there are more estimates for three of the categories: 1) - infant and child and maternal mortality; 2) productivity gains from improved physical capacity; and 3) productivity gains from increased cognitive ability. The literature examining possible effects of iron on morbidity is very recent; there is little on chronic disease. We simply do not have results of iron intervention studies on young girls, which require us to track them longitudinally in order to look at pregnancy outcomes and intergenerational benefits.

There are two key groups for whom iron has been identified as affecting mortality, namely women in childbirth, and infants during the peri-natal period. In one study it is estimated that 20% of perinatal mortality, and 10% of maternal mor-tality in developing countries, is attributable to iron deficiency. The study suggests that "0.8 mil-lion (1.5%) of deaths worldwide are attributable to iron deficiency, 1.3% of male deaths and 1.8% of female deaths. Attributable DALYs are even greater, amounting to the loss of about 35 million health life years (2.4% of global DALYs). Of these DALYs, 12.5 million (36%) occurred in SEAR D, 4.3 million (12.4%) in WPR B, and 10.1

million (29%) in Africa" (15). (Note that SEAR refers to Southeast Asia Region, and WPR refers to Western Pacific Region, using the WHO categories). These estimates are based on the known relation between maternal and perinatal mortality rates and hemoglobin levels in blood. Thus nutritional anemia is associated with a significant health burden. This could be converted to an economic burden using methods suggested in Section 1.

The cost of lost adult productivity associated with anemia has been investigated intensively. Intervention studies both in the laboratory and in the field date back to the 1970s. Iron interventions in well-controlled studies have clear impacts on physical capacity (both maximal work capacity and endurance) and have been demonstrated to have productivity impacts in the order of 5% on light manual labor, and as high as 17% on heavy manual labor (16). A recent ongoing study in Indonesia confirms effects on the income of the self-employed as being as high as 20% for men and 6% for women, confirming the potentially large impact on productivity and, by inference, on income as well (17).

Productivity changes of this size have poten-tially important economic impacts in poor coun-tries where anemia levels are high, and manual labor is a significant proportion of employment. Estimates of the annual costs per person of the current levels of anemia in nine developing countries range from $0.62 to almost $4.00, using data from 1994. One caveat is that these are typically labor-surplus economies. Arguably, increased productivity might not be as important as in a labor-scarce country; on the other hand the loss of productivity in physical activity outside the market economy (carrying water, collecting wood, etc.) might have further effects on the quality of life that market statistics on GDP do not capture.

Estimates of the effects of iron intervention on children's cognitive ability and therefore subsequent adult economic productivity are more speculative, relying on linking iron interventions to mental and motor abilities in children under 2 and to cognitive ability in children over 2, and inferring the effects on adult productivity. Intervention studies suggest that there are adverse effects of iron deficiency in children, with deficiencies in the second year of life perhaps being very critical: When anemia levels are particularly high while growth is very rapid, there may potentially be irreversibilities. One can infer that the anemia potentially reduces adult earnings (due to cognitive effects) by 2.5%, based on a series of assumptions.

A recent study of an iron intervention with a longitudinal follow-up over a period of 18 years confirms that these estimates may be reasonable (18). Children were enrolled in the study between the ages of 1 and 2. Anemia was corrected with iron supplements for those children in the intervention group. All children received cognitive tests in early childhood (below age 2), and again at ages 5–8, 11–14, 15–18, and 19. (The specific tests included Bayley tests in infancy, and age-appropriate Wechsler tests and other cognitive tests at later ages.) The results were not reported for the intervention group versus the control group, but rather for those without anemia at the end of the

intervention (either because anemia was corrected, or because they had not been anemic), versus those whose anemia had not been corrected (i.e., a subset of the control group). The nonanemia group contained a higher proportion of higher socioeconomic status (SES) households (since anemia status is somewhat correlated with SES). The results are quite striking. In the middle SES group, those with adequate iron status scored 8–9 points above those who remained anemic in early childhood, a difference that was maintained up to age 19. In the lower SES group, those with adequate iron status scored 10 points higher in early childhood, a gap which widened to 25 points at age 19. These results suggest that iron deficiency below age 2 does indeed have significant effects on life course: a difference in cognitive score of this magnitude is known to have effects on schooling and on earnings.

The results are not as powerful as results which directly compare intervention and control, since the measure of SES used does not perfectly control for all other household factors which affect ability independent of iron status. Nevertheless, the results are intriguing.

The estimated effect of a 2.5% loss of earnings due to cognitive losses in childhood for nine developing countries implies an additional loss of per capita of GDP which ranges from $0.21–1.88 (these represent present values of discounted future lifetime losses (16). The total losses per capita (due to physical productivity as well as cognitive losses) amount to $0.83–4.81, or 0.37–1.86% of GDP. The range is from approximately 1–2% in the poor countries in South Asia, and 0.4–1% in the other developing countries considered (in sub-Saharan Africa, Latin America, and the Middle East). These losses amount to billions of dollars annually, which is very considerable, especially when compared to the modest costs of decreasing nutritional anemia discussed in the next section.

ECONOMIC COSTS OF ACHIEVING REDUCTIONS IN NUTRITIONAL ANEMIA

In this section we first discuss five conceptual and practical issues involved in calculating cost-effectiveness of interventions, before turning to the evidence. We focus largely on interventions affecting iron, as the most common nutrient whose deficiency is associated with anemia. Literature on the cost-effectiveness of other nutrients affecting anemia is extremely limited.

The first issue is that there may be more than one outcome of interest for interventions aimed at reducing anemia. Some interventions (those affecting pregnant women in particular) may improve maternal hemoglobin and hence reduce maternal and perinatal mortality. For these interventions, the DALY is a useful measure of outcome. Other interventions (for example affecting the iron status of children and working adults) may affect economic productivity. In the case of children, this occurs with a long lag mediated by improvements in cognitive development. For adults, this may occur very quickly via effects on endurance and on maximal work capacity, and hence on productivity, particularly in manual work. However, since these interventions do not have identical outcomes, cost-effectiveness rankings based on different outcome measures do not yield a unique ranking.

Section 1 discussed how one might assign a dollar value to a DALY, and hence combine outcomes measured in DALYs with those (related to economic productivity) in dollars. Even if one is willing to make the (very large) assumptions involved, there is no agreement on the value of human life in all countries over all time, and hence no unique ranking is possible either within or across countries.

A second issue is that in measuring cost-effectiveness, it is usually too costly or time-consuming to collect data on the ultimate outcomes of interest (i.e., DALYs or economic productivity). A study of the effects on economic productivity due to improved nutrition in children under 2 would take 20 or more years to complete. Instead, we usually rely on information from existing studies as to how a proximate indicator affects the ultimate outcome of interest, and then measure the effects of the intervention on the proximate indicator. The two most commonly used proximate indicators are proportion anemic (or severely anemic), and (more recently) hemoglobin (as measured in g/dL). There are also other indicators of iron status which are used, for iron deficiency anemia (serum ferritin, erythrocyte protoporphyrin, etc.).

These two proximate indicators do not yield identical results, since after all each is a summary measure of a distribution of hemoglobin levels. The older literature uses proportion anemic. For example, the early literature on mortality outcomes used maternal anemia as the predictor, and the early studies on adult productivity all use anemia. However, more recent literature suggests that this has some disadvantages. There may be functional impairments associated with iron deficiency not associated with anemia; and it is thought that only approximately half of measured anemia can be attributed to iron deficiency.

More recently, the literature has moved to using hemoglobin level as a proximate indicator, providing additional insights. For example, once hemoglobin level was used, a strong association with perinatal mortality was documented (19). Similarly, while anemia was found to be surprisingly invariant to supplementation, hemoglobin levels do respond. Unfortunately, many of the older studies on adult productivity used anemia and have not been replicated (or reinterpreted) using hemoglobin levels. This causes some difficulties in calculating cost-effectiveness.

A third issue is that some interventions affect not only nutritional anemia, but also other health and economic outcomes. For example, deworming (see Section 3.3 below for references) can be effective in improving hemoglobin levels, and one might assume that the major link is through decreased hookworm infestation. However, anthelmintic treatment usually targets a range of helminthes, and, as such, may improve not only the iron status but also other aspects of nutrition. Hence, if cost per DALY gained is used as an indicator for deworming, it may be that a proportion of the DALYs gained are not related to nutritional anemia. Deworming might appear cost-effective when considering DALY gained, but less cost-effective if only nutritional anemia is of interest.

A fourth issue is that cost-effectiveness varies with the scale of the program, since both the effectiveness in terms of changes in outcome indicators (different rates of adherence, for example) and cost structures may depend on coverage (20). Costs may decrease over time if there are start-up costs to establishing a program, such as investing in physical infrastructure, or if a targeting system needs to be put into place (21). Similarly, costs per beneficiary may decrease if there are appreciable fixed costs of administration that can be spread over larger programs without proportional increases in size. Cost, however, may also increase with scale, for example if capacity constraints are reached and new investments are required. Costs will also increase with program expansion if it is initiated in the most accessible communities and expanded into harder to reach target groups. In addition to these scale economies and diseconomies there may be economies of scope that come from linking services such as the addition of deworming to vitamin A supplementation programs, or the combination of health and nutrition services, as in a long term study of programmatic and economic synergies in Narangwal, India (22).

A study of vitamin A fortification in the Philippines illustrates the interplay of distribution objectives and rising marginal costs (23). The study notes that fortification was more cost-effective than supplementation for 70% of the population, but that cost-effective expansion beyond this base was better achieved with supplementation. This study is also one of the relatively few that attempts to indicate the value of the community volunteers' time, and not just that of staff, in health posts.

The fifth and final general point on the costs of interventions is the distinction between public and private costs. Since taxation generally creates economic distortions – often referred to as deadweight loss – the costs of a dollar of government revenues is generally more than a dollar to the economy (24). In a few cases, if a sector or department budget is fixed in the short run, program costs are a zero sum tradeoff for other budget items, but in most cases the economic rationale for a project is the full resource cost, including the cost of raising revenue. Note, however, that benefits that are expressed in terms of saving expenditures – for example, reduced hospital or outpatient costs or reduced school repetition – would also be expressed in terms of the costs of revenue.

In the rest of this section we summarize the evidence on cost-effectiveness of interventions to reduce nutritional anemia. We focus almost exclusively on interventions affecting iron status, since, "Other nutrient deficiencies, such as vitamin B_{12}, pyridoxine (PN) and copper are of little public health significance because of their infrequency" (25). In our discussion, we include not only interventions to increase intake of nutrients, but also anthelmintic treatment, which also directly affects nutrient status (via uptake and loss of ingested nutrients).

We also limit the discussion to interventions primarily aimed at nutritional anemia. Given that anemia is also related to infection (malaria being particularly important), interventions affecting infection will also reduce anemia; bednets appear particularly cost-effective: the 90% range for cost per DALY is $5.00–31.00 (26).

We consider in the next four subsections fortification (including home fortification), supplementation, deworming, and finally conclude with some discussion of longer-run solutions such as home gardening, dietary diversification and biofortification. Literature on the cost-effectiveness of the longer-run interventions is sparse. The summary tables **(Table 3.2, Table 3.3)** are not comprehensive, but rather include a selection of the more recent studies.

When interpreting the literature, the five issues discussed above should be borne in mind. The results may focus on outcomes (DALYs or dollars) or proximate indicators (anemia, hemoglobin). There may also be multiple outcomes, for example growth or reduction of schistosomiasis (particularly for interventions involving deworming). Care must also be taken to identify if cost-effectiveness estimates are based on program experience or simply ex ante calculations that depend crucially on the quality of the assumptions made. Costs depend on scale, and finally, the costs of a program which reduces other costs are different than those which require additional taxation.

Fortification

Table 3.2 summarizes some of the growing numbers of studies involving fortification. An issue with earlier studies of country-wide fortification programs was that there were no control groups. This has been remedied more recently. Most studies suggest that fortification is associated with reductions in anemia and increases in mean hemoglobin. In turn, studies have projected changes in these indicators to outcomes such as mortality (27) and economic productivity (16). When calculated by the cost per DALY saved or the Benefit-to-Cost Ratio (BCR), iron fortifica-

tion is one of the most attractive public health interventions available.

There is much literature on how fortification with iron can be deployed most effectively (for example, the type of iron compound used, the type of food vehicle used, the need for monitoring and quality assurance, the safe amount of fortification) (28). There are also limitations to fortification, as discussed elsewhere in this volume. For example, it requires some centralization of food processing. Moreover, many vehicles for fortification are consumed in small quantities by low income households, even when the fortified product is readily available, and often not at all by marginal populations mainly relying on subsistence production. There are additional limitations in reaching very young children. (Global Alliance for Improved Nutrition [GAIN]) is currently encouraging work on affordable fortification of weaning foods, using local production. Moreover, fortification alone does not meet the full needs of some population subgroups (pregnant and lactating women in particular).

The unit cost (cost per person per year) of fortification is generally in the range of $0.10–1.00 (the highest cost being for fortifying beverages, including milk). The costs of fortification are often passed on to the consumer, and thus do not incur the extra deadweight costs of raising revenue referred to above. However, some fortified products – for example milk used in school programs in many Latin American countries – would not be consumed in sufficient quantities by low income households in the absence of subsidies. These subsidies are on the cost of the product itself and not only on the relatively small cost of iron fortification.

The example of fortifying food in school feeding programs with iron illustrates the fact that, should a government decide on an in-kind transfer program, the additional or marginal costs of adding a supplement or fortification to that program is generally a small share of the total program costs and may be able to enhance the nutritional value of the program as indicated in a pilot fortification scheme of milk distribution in Mexico (29). Similarly, another pilot – still under evaluation – is investigating the impact and cost-effectiveness of distribution of multiple micronutrients, including iron syrup, Sprinkles or fortified complementary food (all three with identical micronutrient content) to the beneficiaries of

Table 3.2: Summary of cost-effectiveness information, fortification interventions.

Intervention type	Country, year published, reference	Cost-effectiveness or costs and effects	Comments
Fortification of food with elemental iron, 80% of population covered	Africa D, Southeast Asia D, 2004 (27)	$20/DALY (Afr D) $49/DALY (SEA D)	Hypothetical study
Fortification of wheat or maize with ferrous sulphate	Model, nine countries, 2003 (16)	Returns 6:1 (physical productivity only), 9:1 (including cognitive)	Hypothetical study, based on fortification program data
Fortification of soy sauce with NaFeEDTA, affected all households	China 2005 (46)	$0.007/capita/year; Increase in Hb 0.39 to 0.85 g/dL (varies by age/sex); Decrease in anemia 16–42% (varies by age/sex)	Household randomized controlled trial (RCT), 18 months Costs probably artificially low because of Chinese currency
Fortification of drinking water (iron sulphate and ascorbic acid), preschool children	Brazil 2005 (39)	$0.19/capita (for 8 months); Hb increase from 11.8 to 12.4 g/dL; Anemia fell from 43.2% to 21%	No control group, also tested for parasites and dewormed if positive at 1 and 4 months
Fortification of wheat/maize flour with iron and B vitamins, for whole population	Venezuela 1996 (47)	$0.12/capita/year; Anemia fell from 19% to 10% in school age children	No control group
Fortification of salt with iron and iodine for households	Morocco 2003 (48)	$0.22/capita/year; Anemia fell 22 percentage points more in treatment group after 9 months	RCT at household level
Fortification of subsidized milk with iron sulphate, zinc, vitamins A, C, B_{12} and folic acid	Mexico 2005 (29)	Anemia fell 10.6% points more in treatment than in control	Treatment/control communities

Note: D refers to a WHO categorization of countries based on disease profile

Oportunidades, a targeted poverty program that provides up to $250 per child per year, after noting that earlier beneficiaries had high levels of anemia. Yet another example of enhancing food distribution programs by inclusion of fortification is seen in a pilot program in the northeast of India that replaces the standard flour ration included in the public distribution system with fortified flour.

Although many of the benefits of fortification accrue to private individuals, few countries rely on market mechanisms alone to promote fortification. In addition to subsidies, regulatory means are used to increase coverage. Even in developed countries with varied diets, fortification with iron remains mandatory. For example, there is mandatory fortification with iron and other nutrients of eight different cereal products in the USA (30), three different cereal products in Canada, flour in the UK, and one or more cereal products in 16 countries in Latin America and the Caribbean, as well as in at least 10 other developing countries.

Home fortification (with products such as Sprinkles or Nutrasets) is a relatively new development, and lies somewhere between fortification and supplementation. Home fortification may entail a sachet of micronutrients designed to be sprinkled on the meal of a young child, or perhaps a fortified spread which can be used in conjunction with bread or another cereal product. These are generally more costly per capita than population-based fortification, because of the packaging and distribution costs. Nevertheless, for populations (refugees, isolated regions) or particular age groups (young children) which cannot be reached by population based fortification, or for groups who do not purchase sufficient quantities of fortified products, this may be a cost-effective alternative. In **Table 3.3** the results for one hypothetical example using Sprinkles (31) has a high (37:1) benefit-to-cost ratio, although this is predicated on the strong assumption that a 4 month intervention at crucial ages in childhood has a major impact on cognitive outcomes. This is probably

too optimistic, and it would be necessary to continue delivery of iron to children throughout a longer period.

Supplementation

There have been many supplementation studies, since iron supplementation during pregnancy and lactation is considered essential. Costs per person are estimated in the $2.00–5.00 range, although often such cited costs do not fully cover the costs of personnel. However, results in programs at scale have been disappointing (32). In efficacy trials, iron supplementation has been associated with reducing the prevalence of anemia at term and correcting maternal anemia, with longer-term smaller-dose supplementation being more effective than short-term, large-dose supplementation. Nevertheless, often the implementation of supplementation programs have not led to a significant decrease in anemia, with possible reasons being inefficiencies in supply, beneficiaries' lack of adherence to recommended dosage frequency (perhaps related to side-effects), and insufficient support and monitoring from front-line workers.

The type of personnel support provided in the efficacy trials would almost certainly make a program at scale quite expensive. In the successful efficacy trials, considerable supervision is required to ensure that supplements are consumed, and households are typically only given supplies for a month or less because of the possibility of small children ingesting a toxic dose. Thus, although trials find that supplementation has a favorable benefit-to-cost ratio (however, perhaps five times more costly than fortification in per DALY terms) (27), these have been difficult to realize in practice.

One promising field trial of supplementation with iron and folate took place in a community in Nepal characterized by both high rates of low birth weight (LBW) and anemia (33). The authors found that it was necessary to reach 11 women with the

Table 3.3: Summary of cost-effectiveness information, supplementation interventions, home fortification, deworming.

Intervention type	Country, year published, reference	Cost-effectiveness or costs and effects	Comments
Home fortification, Sprinkles for children mainly 6–12 months	Pakistan 2006 (31)	Present value of productivity gains $37 per $1.00 spent	Hypothetical model
Supplementation with iron, 80% population coverage	Africa D, Southeast Asia D, 2004 (27)	$105/DALY Africa, $182/DALY Asia (cost is higher in other regions)	Hypothetical, no use of any supplementation program outcomes
Supplementation for preschool children with daily iron; deworming (4-cell trial)	Tanzania 2004 (38)	Iron reduced risk of becoming severely anemic 29% (not significant); Mebendazole reduced moderate anemia 17% in children <24 months	RCT; positive effects of deworming on growth; positive effects of iron and deworming on appetite
Weekly supplementation for adults; deworming 1 and 6 months; 6 months results so far	Indonesia 2004 (17)	Average Hb 0.2 g/dL higher in treatment than in control (men) and 0.1 higher (women)	Also observed income increases 20% for men, 6% for women, primarily due to increases for self-employed
Deworming of school-age children (once, observed 12 months later)	Kenya 2004 (36)	Average Hb 0.16 g/dL higher in treatment than control, anemia 2 percentage points lower	$5.00/DALY averted, predominantly due to schistosomiasis

Note: D refers to a WHO categorization of countries based on disease profile

micronutrient supplements in order to prevent one case of LBW. While no cost data were provided in the published study, Christian and West (personal communication) estimated that the costs of $64 per pregnant woman reached during the experimental phase could be reduced to $13 in an ongoing program. Given the fact that one in 11 births would be a direct beneficiary in terms of averted LBW, the cost during the trial does not represent an economically efficient intervention using an estimate of $510 of benefits per low birth weight averted (34).

However, if at least one third of this possible cost reduction can be realized, the intervention would be efficient. Moreover, due to economies of scope, such a cost would also allow provision of vitamin A at little marginal cost and, thus, might reduce both infant and maternal mortality.

Deworming

Periodic deworming is known to be simple and safe, and can have significant effects on nutritional status (including iron status, particularly where hookworm is concerned) as well as on school attendance. One study estimated that it costs $3.50 to increase school participation by one child year via deworming of children in Kenya (35), presumably partially mediated through reduced anemia (though this was not assessed). Similarly, a combined program of deworming and supplementation was found to increase preschool participation in Delhi. Using a range of plausible assumptions, this was extrapolated to the estimated impact on earnings, with an additional $29 earned expected for a cost of $1.70 (36).

Few studies of deworming have measured iron status. One recent study found significant effects of deworming on anemia in children less than 2 years old in Tanzania (37), whereas the effect of iron supplementation in the trial was not significant. In the same study, deworming affected growth but iron supplementation did not. Another ongoing study in Indonesia publicizes the effect of iron supplementation in adults on wages and on anemia, but does not highlight the fact that some of the effects may be attributable to periodic (twice-yearly) deworming (17). Similarly, a study of iron fortification of drinking water in Brazil (38) does not highlight the possible importance of deworming infected children early in the supplementation trial. Moreover, deworming is probably five to 10 times less costly than supplementation; deworming might cost $0.50/year, compared to $2.00–5.00 for monitored supplementation.

Longer run interventions

In the longer run, increased dietary diversity is the main mechanism to improve nutritional quality of the diet. Home gardening approaches to addressing nutritional anemia, however, are somewhat problematic in low income countries due to the low bioavailability of nonheme iron and the relatively high cost of heme iron. There are efforts to increase home production of small animals, but almost no good cost-effectiveness data.

Biofortification – increasing nutrient density and availability through plant breeding using both conventional crop breeding and biotechnology – is a possible exception. These approaches are promising (39, 40) but involve extensive (and, to date, uncertain) fixed costs for technology generation. There are, however, few, if any, incremental variable costs of operation over the general costs of producing a crop which has increased iron availability.[2]

Given that mineral micronutrients comprise less than 10 parts per million in milled rice, it is unlikely that such amounts will affect the taste, appearance, or texture of rice or wheat in a manner that affects consumer demand. Thus, the fixed costs of research can potentially be spread over a large population base. Results from Bangladesh suggest that a 50% increase in iron intakes derived from fortified rice would reduce anemia by as much as 6% (42). Similar improvements in iron status have been obtained from trials with non anemic women in the Philippines (43).

Because improved cultivars that are denser in iron are still being developed, there are no *ex post* assessments of rates of return to these investments. One *ex ante* study (40) provides estimates of the benefit-to-cost ratios of the dissemination of iron dense varieties of rice and wheat in India and Bangladesh, assuming a 25 year time period

---

[2] In principle, if a cultivar had higher production costs this would lead either to lower adoption or to a possible subsidy (a recurrent cost). However, trials with varieties of rice and wheat that seem most promising for biofortification with iron suggest that these nutritionally enhanced cultivars are more resistant to disease and environmental stress: Their roots release chemical compounds that unbind trace minerals present in most soils, and thus they require less chemical inputs (41).

with no benefits in the first 10 years, with costs after that associated only with plant breeding and dissemination. Using a 3% discount rate and incorporating an allowance for maintenance costs over the following 15 years, the present value of these costs is estimated at $35.9 million. Benefits accrue from years 11 to 25. Conservatively, it is assumed that these improved varieties are adopted on only 10% of the area devoted to rice and wheat, and that they reduce anemia rates by only 3%, averting 44 million cases of anemia annually. The present discounted lifetime value of a case of anemia averted is $27.50 (16). Using these assumptions, the total present value of nutrition benefits is $694 million, giving a benefit-to-cost ratio of 19:1, or an internal rate of return of 29%.[3]

CONCLUSIONS AND NEXT STEPS

The first section pointed out some of the practical and conceptual issues involved in estimating the economic magnitude of costs both of iron deficiency and of interventions designed to reduce nutritional anemia. None of these issues are insuperable, and Section 2 provided some estimates of the costs of iron deficiency, through three of the key mechanisms. Current studies (looking at broader impact, for example self-employment earnings, and longitudinal studies of children who received iron interventions) serve to endorse still further the heavy costs of iron deficiency.

Policy-makers are not unaware of the costs of deficiency, but the key issue for policy has been the difficulties in finding cost-effective interventions which reduce iron deficiency, previously measured using anemia rates, and now preferably by blood hemoglobin level.

Given the very high proportion of the population with iron deficiency or anemia in most developing countries, mandatory fortification of some widely consumed foods should be considered in all countries. Although there is some leakage to non-deficient populations, these costs, in many situations, are likely less than that incurred by targeting and may not have a substantial effect on cost-effectiveness. The literature considers possible risks (in malarial areas, and to individuals with conditions such as thalassemia), but in general the good of the overall population is considered of overriding importance. Estimated costs are of the order of $0.10–$1.00 per person per year, with the benefit-to-cost ratio to the order of 6:1 (physical benefits to adults) or as high as 9:1 (also including estimated cognitive benefits to children).

Supplementation has an important role for selected population groups, particularly pregnant and lactating women, whose needs cannot be met by fortification; however continued operational research is required to design programs which work cost-effectively in the field. Home fortification (a kind of hybrid between fortification and supplementation) holds considerable promise for groups who cannot readily be reached by fortification, such as weaning-age children, and vulnerable groups in areas not reached by commercially-processed foods or who purchase only small quantities of such foods. Supplementation costs are of the order of $2.00-5.00 per person per year, and in favorable circumstances economic benefits may exceed costs. Home fortification targeted at small children at vulnerable ages might have a similar cost, but a better benefit-to-cost ratio.

The importance of deworming has probably been overlooked. Several recent studies of both

---

[3] The study only presents estimates for a discount rate of 3%. Under the assumption that the benefits are distributed evenly over the 11–25 year period, with a discount rate of 5% the benefit-to-cost ratio would be 11.6.

fortification and supplementation suggest that it works synergistically with fortification and supplementation, rendering both likely to be more cost-effective. While it has been primarily used for school-age children, it may be as important if not even more important for preschool children. One hypothesis is that although worm loads are lower in younger children, the impact on absorption in the gut is more disruptive (38). There are studies suggesting programs can cost-effectively reach preschool children (44). Costs are approximately $0.50/person/year, and the benefit-to-cost ratio may be comparable to that for fortification.

The interventions discussed above should not divert emphasis from long run solutions such as increased dietary diversity, agricultural improvements, and rising income. Biofortification is one possible way to enhance such long run efforts. This has potentially low costs per person (although the fixed costs are high, the benefits can reach millions of people), and potentially favorable benefit-to-cost ratios, although this remains to be proven.

REFERENCES

1. Jamison, D, et al. Disease control priorities in developing countries. 2nd ed. New York: Oxford University Press, 2006.

2. Behrman J, Alderman H, Hoddinott J. Hunger and malnutrition. In: Lomborg B, ed. Global crises, global solutions. Cambridge, UK: Cambridge University Press, 2004.

3. Viscusi WK, Aldy JE. The value of a statistical life: a critical review of market estimates throughout the world. J Risk Uncertain 2003;27:15–76.

4. Summers LH, Investing in all the people. Pak Dev Rev 1992;31(4):367–406.

5. Behrman J, Alderman H, Hoddinott J. Hunger and malnutrition. In: Lomborg B, ed. Global crises, global solutions. Cambridge, UK: Cambridge University Press, 2004.

6. Stokley, N. Expert comments. In: Lomborg B, ed. Global crises, global solutions. Cambridge, UK: Cambridge University Press, 2004.

7. Mill A, Shillcut S. Communicable disease. In: Lomborg B, ed. Global crises, global solutions. Cambridge, UK: Cambridge University Press, 2004.

8. Altonji J, Dunn T. The effects of family characteristics on the returns to education. Rev Econ Stat 1996;78(4):692–704.

9. Cawley J, Heckman J, Vytlacil E. Three observations on wages and measured cognitive ability. J Labor Econ 2001;8:419–42.

10. Alderman H, Behrman J, Ross D, Sabot R. The returns to endogenous human capital in Pakistan's rural wage labor market. Oxf Bull Econ Stat 1996;58(1):29–55.

11. Belli P, Anderson J, Barnum H, Dixon J, Tan JP. Handbook on economic analysis of investment operations. Washington, DC: World Bank, 1996.

12. Haddad L, Alderman H, Appleton S, Song L, Yohannes Y. Reducing child malnutrition: how far does income growth take us? World Bank Econ Rev 2003;17(1):107–31.

13. Mason J, Rivers J, Helwig C. Recent trends in malnutrition in developing regions: vitamin A deficiency, anemia, iodine deficiency, and child underweight. Food Nutr Bull 2005;26(1):57–162.

14. Block S, Webb P. Maternal nutrition knowledge versus schooling as determinants of child micronutrient status. Oxford Economic Papers, in press.

15. WHO (World Health Organization). The world health report 2002. Geneva: WHO, 2002.

16. Horton S, Ross R. The economics of iron deficiency. Food Policy 2003;28(1):51–75.

17. Thomas D, Frankenberg E, Habicht J-P, et al. Causal effect of health on labor market outcomes: evidence from a random assignment iron supplementation intervention. Presented at Population Association of America annual meeting, Boston, April 2004.

18. Lozoff B, Jimenez E, Smith JB. Double burden of iron deficiency in infancy and low socio-economic status: a longitudinal analysis of cognitive test scores to 19 years. Arch Pediatr Adolesc Med 2006;160(11):1108–13.

19. Stoltzfus RJ, Mullany L, Black RE. Iron deficiency anemia. In: Essazti M, Lopez AD, Rodgers A, Murray CJL, eds. Comparative quanitification of health risks: global and regional burden of disease attributable to selected major risk factors. Vol 1. Geneva: WHO, 2004:163–209.

20. Johns J, Tan Torres T. Costs of scaling up interventions: a systematic review. Health Policy Plan 2005;20(1):1–13.

21. Caldes N, Coady D, Malluccio J. A comparative analysis of program costs across three social safety net programs. World Development 2006;34(5):818–37.

22. Kielmann A, Taylor C, Parker R. The Narangwal nutrition study: a summary review. Am J Clin Nutr 1978;31:2040–57.

23. Fiedler J, Dado D, Maglalang H, Juban N, Capistrano M, Magpantay M. Cost analysis as a vitamin A program design and evaluation tool: a case study of the Philippines. Soc Sci Med 2000;51:223–42.

24. Feldstein M. Tax avoidance and the deadweight loss of the income tax. Rev Econ Stat 1999;81(4):674–80.

25. DeMaeyer EM, Dallman P, Gurney JM, Hallberg L, Sood SK, Srikantia SG. Preventing and controlling iron deficiency anaemia through primary health care: a guide for health administrators and programme managers. Geneva: WHO, 1989:5–58.

26. Breman JG, Mill A, Snow RW, et al. Conquering malaria. In: Jamison DR, Breman JG, Measham AR, et al., eds. Disease control priorities in developing countries. Washington DC: World Bank, 2006.

27. Baltussen R, Knai C, Sharan M. Iron fortification and iron supplementation are cost-effective interventions to reduce iron deficiency in four subregions of the world. J Nutr 2004;134:2678–84.

28. WHO (World Health Organization). Guidelines on food fortification with micronutrients for the control of micronutrient malnutrition. Geneva: WHO, 2004.

29. Villalpando S, Shamah T, Rivera JA, Lara Y, Monterubbio E. Fortifying milk with ferrous gluconate and zinc oxide in a public nutrition program reduced the prevalence of anemia in toddlers. J Nutr 2006;136:2633–7.

30. Bowley A. Nutriview. Special Issue, Mandatory Food Enrichment 2003. Basel: Roche Vitamins Europe Ltd, 2003.

31. Sharieff W, Horton SE, Zlotkin S. Economic gains of a home fortification program. Can J Public Health 2006;97:20–3.

32. Gillespie, S. Major issues in the control of iron deficiency. Ottawa: Micronutrient Initiative, 1998.

33. Christian P, Khatry S, Katz J, Pardhan E, LeClerq S, Shrestha S, Adhikari R, Sommer A, West K. Effects of alternative maternal micronutrient supplements on low birth weight in rural Nepal: double blind randomised community trial. BMJ 2003;326:571.

34. Alderman H, Behrman J. Reducing the incidence of low birth weight in low-income countries has substantial economic benefits. World Bank Res Obs 2006;21(1):25–48.

35. Miguel E, Kremer M. Worms: Identifying impacts on health and education in the presence of treatment externalities. Econometrica 2004;72(1):159–217.

36. Bobonis G, Miguel E, Puri-Sharma C. Iron Deficiency Anemia and School Participation. Journal of Human Resources (JHR) 2006;41(4):692–721.

37. Stoltzfus RJ, Chway HM, Montresor A, et al. Low dose daily iron supplementation improves iron status and appetite but not anemia, whereas quarterly anthelminthic treatment improves growth, appetite and anemia in Zanzibari preschool children. J Nutr 2004;134:348–56.

38. Beinner MA, Lamounier JA, Tomaz C. Effect of iron-fortified drinking water of daycare facilities

on the hemoglobin status of young children. J Am Coll Nutr 2005;24(2):107–14.

39. Bouis H. Plant breeding: a new tool for fighting micronutrient malnutrition, J Nutr 2002;132:491S–4S.

40. Nestel P, Bouis H, Meenakshi J, Pfeiffer W. Biofortification of staple food crops. J Nutr 2006;136:1064–7.

41. Welch RM. Breeding strategies for biofortified staple plant foods to reduce micronutrient malnutrition globally. J Nutr 2002;132:495S–9S.

42. Bhargava A, Bouis H, Scrimshaw N. Dietary intakes and socioeconomic factors are associated with the hemoglobin concentration of Bangladeshi women. J Nutr 2001; 131:758–64.

43. Haas J, Beard JL, Murray-Kolb LE, del Mundo AM, Felix A, Gregorio GB. Iron-biofortified rice improves the iron stores of nonanemic Filipino women. J Nutr 2005;135:2823–30.

44. Alderman H, Konde-Lule J, Sebuliba I, Bundy D, Hall A. Effect on weight gain of routinely giving albendazole to preschool children during child health days in Uganda: cluster randomized controlled trial. BMJ 2006;333:122.

45. Gwatkin D, Rutstein S, Johnson K, Suliman E, Wagstaff A. Initial country-level information about socio-economic differences in health, nutrition and population. 2nd ed. Washington DC: World Bank, 2003.

46. Chen J, Zhao X, Zhang S, et al. Studies on the effectiveness of NaFeEDTA-fortified soy sauce in controlling iron deficiency: a population-based intervention trial. Food Nutr Bull 2005;26(2):177–86.

47. Layrisse M, Cháves JF, Mendez-Castellano H, Bosch V, Tropper E, Bastardo B, González E. Early response to the effect of iron fortification in the Venezuelan population. Am J Clin Nutr 1996;64:903–7.

48. Zimmermann MB, Zeder C, Chaouki N, Saad A, Torresan T, Hurrell RF. Dual fortification of salt with iodine and encapsulated iron: a randomized, double blind, controlled trial in Moroccan school-children. Am J Clin Nutr 2003;77:425–32.

4

Diagnosis of nutritional anemia – laboratory assessment of iron status

Hans-Konrad Biesalski[1]   Jürgen G. Erhardt[2]

[1]*Department of Biological Chemistry and Nutrition at University of Hohenheim, Hohenheim, Germany*
[2]*University of Indonesia, SEAMEO-TROPMED, Jakarta, Indonesia*
Contact: mail@nurtrisurvey.de

HANS-KONRAD BIESALSKI
Hans obtained his MD and habilitation from the University of Mainz, Germany. He currently heads the Department of Biological Chemistry and Nutrition at the University of Hohenheim in Stuttgart, Germany. Hans has over 30 years of experience in research on retinoids and their actions on cellular growth and differentiation, vitamin A and human health, and the role of anti-oxidants and vitamins in human nutrition. He also holds several patents and has founded a biotech company (BioTeSys GmbH) which develops cell and organ culture models to test biological compounds and carries out clinical studies.

JÜRGEN ERHARDT
Juergen has a PhD in Nutrition Science from Hohenheim University in Stuttgart, Germany. He is currently working as a scientist at the University of Indonesia in Jakarta. Jürgen is researching the development of simple micromethods for evaluating micronutrient status, and the programming of software for dietetic calculations and nutrition surveys.

Introduction

Anemia, defined as a low concentration of hemoglobin (Hb) in blood, can be caused by several factors. Besides diseases which lead to losses of blood or impairment of the production of Hb, nutrition plays the most important role. Some vitamins like vitamin B_{12}, folic acid and riboflavin influence the formation of Hb but the most important nutritional factor is iron deficiency, the most frequently occurring micronutrient deficiency in both developed and less developed countries. Since iron deficiency usually responds to iron supplementation or fortification, the assessment of iron status is crucial in the evaluation of nutritional anemia. There are some clinical indicators for iron deficiency, with chronic fatigue the most important, but they are usually unspecific symptoms (1). The evaluation of the iron intake (differentiated in heme and non-heme iron) might also be helpful but the diagnosis relies mainly on biochemical indicators, especially for the early stages of iron deficiency. Usually iron deficiency occurs in three sequentially developing stages: depleted iron stores, iron deficient erythropoiesis and iron deficiency anemia. These stages can be analyzed biochemically (**Table 4.1**) and there is now an agreement that the measurement of Hb, ferritin and soluble transferrin receptor (sTfR), complemented with indicators of acute and chronic infections, is the best procedure for evaluating iron status. Unfortunately this is usually a difficult and costly procedure. Therefore part of this chapter will address the problem on how to make this measurement simple and inexpensive, with a focus on developing countries.

Assessment of the Various Biochemical Indicators

Hemoglobin

For the diagnosis of nutritional anemia, it is essential to measure Hb in blood. It is one of the most common and least expensive measurements done in a nutritional laboratory. Since it involves only the dilution of e.g. 20 μL whole blood with 5 mL Drabkin's reagent and measuring the absorption at 540 nm it is also one of the easiest measurements. Inexpensive kits, which are available from several manufactures, include controls which help in getting the correct values. The only critical step is to dilute exactly the EDTA or heparin-anticoagulated blood. To be able to measure Hb in the field and small offices portable hemoglobinometers are available. Probably the best known is Hemocue (www.hemocue.com). It uses disposable cuvettes which only need a drop of blood from the finger and cost around 1 USD per cuvette. Currently used cut off values and factors which influence them are shown in **Table 4.2** and **Table 4.3**. Unfortunately the measurement of Hb is

Table 4.1: Influence of the iron status on various indicators in absence of other diseases (modified from [4], for sTfR a method specific cut off value has to be used).

	Hb	Ferritin (μg/L)	sTfR
Iron overload	Above cut off	> 300	Low
Normal	Above cut off	100 ± 60	Normal
Depleted iron stores	Above cut off	20	Normal
Iron deficient erythropoiesis	Above cut off	10	High
Iron deficiency anemia	Below cut off	< 10	High

not very sensitive or specific for iron deficiency (1). Only the third stage of iron deficiency affects the Hb synthesis and there are a number of other conditions and diseases which influence the Hb concentration. To find out if iron deficiency is responsible for the anemia it is usually necessary to include other indicators which are more sensitive and specific for the iron status. If this is not possible, an alternative can be to compare the Hb distribution curve from young children, women in childbearing age and men. If the shift between men and the other groups is bigger than in a standard reference group it indicates that the iron supply is not enough for young children and women, who have a relative higher requirement than men (2).

Table 4.2: Normally used cut offs for hemoglobin to define anemia (4).

	Cut off
Children aged 0.5-5 years	<110 g/L
Children aged 5-11 years	<115 g/L
Children aged 12-13 years	<120 g/L
Men	<130 g/L
Non-pregnant women	<120 g/L
Pregnant women	<110 g/L

Ferritin

Currently the most important indicator for the iron status is the measurement of ferritin. The plasma content correlates well with the iron stores, and in the first stage of iron deficiency the concentration of ferritin already decreases, which makes it the most sensitive parameter. Low ferritin always indicates storage iron depletion. Since ferritin is increased by a number of factors, especially infection and inflammation, a high value is not inevitably a sign of a good iron status. To solve this problem it is helpful to also measure parameters for acute and chronic infection, to discover subjects in which the ferritin concentration might be increased by infection. Currently the

most used parameter for acute infections is C-reactive protein (CRP) and for chronic infections alpha-1 glycoprotein (AGP). Another solution is to measure an indicator like sTfR, which is less influenced by infection. Until now there are no clear cut off values for ferritin but they usually range between 10 and 30 μg/L. A ferritin value below 10 μg/L certainly shows iron deficiency. Because of its common use the cost for ferritin ELISA kits is quite low and starts at around 100 USD for a 96 well plate including standards and controls. The cost of the chemicals for immuno-turbidimetric measurements or radioimmunoassay are in the same range. By including a standard clinical chemistry control, which usually has values for ferritin in different concentrations, it is relatively easy to check the reliability of the fer-

Table 4.3: Influences of various factors on the Hb cut off (all values are approximated) (4).

		Effect
Race	African descent	5-10 g/L lower
Smoking		3-7 g/L higher
Living in altitude	1000 m	1 g/L higher
	1500 m	4 g/L higher
	2000 m	7 g/L higher
	2500 m	12 g/L higher
	3000 m	18 g/L higher

ritin measurement. Unfortunately the cut off of ferritin is near the detection limit of most methods, where the accuracy of the measurements is usually less reliable. The lowest ferritin concentration in the clinical controls is also mostly relatively high (around five times more than the cut off value) which can make the calculation of prevalence rates unreliable especially when a value of 10 µg/L is used.

Soluble transferrin receptor (sTfR)
In the last 10 to 15 years sTfR is increasingly used to detect iron deficiency anemia, mainly in situations where infection is a factor, which increases ferritin but has much less influence on the sTfR level. The sTfR is released from the cells into the blood stream depending on the iron requirements. The concentration is increased in the second stage of iron deficiency, after the iron stores are exhausted and the Hb concentration is still above the cut off level. It is therefore a less sensitive parameter than ferritin but more sensitive than Hb. Unfortunately there is still no international certified standard available and each method or kit has its own cut off value. Since the different methods correlate very well it is relatively easy to get the same prevalence rates when the appropriate cut off value is used. Usually an ELISA or turbidimetric technique is used to measure sTfR. The cost for these kits is still much more expensive than for ferritin (around four times higher). Therefore the measurement of sTfR is usually limited to small studies or well funded surveys. Something which may substantially reduce the cost of estimating iron deficiency in population groups is the combined measurement of ferritin and sTfR. The ratio of the two indicators enables the calculation of the iron stores in mg/kg body weight similar to the results of bone marrow staining, which is the gold standard in defining iron deficiency. Since this increases the sensitivity to detect iron deficiency by several times, with a much smaller sample size it is possible to obtain the same information (3).

VARIOUS OTHER PARAMETERS

Hematocrit
The hematocrit usually correlates well with Hb, but is even less sensitive for iron deficiency than Hb. Therefore it is not a very helpful indicator in the diagnosis of nutritional anemia.

Iron saturation of plasma transferrin (ratio of plasma iron to total iron binding capacity) and mean corpuscular volume (MCV)
Under clinical settings where automatic clinical/hematology analyzers are available, the iron saturation of plasma transferrin and MCV are well established indicators and relatively inexpensive to measure. A low saturation of transferrin with iron and a reduced size of the erythrocytes indicate iron deficiency, but the specificity of both indicators is not high. A large number of clinical disorders affect the transferrin saturation (1) and plasma iron has a marked diurnal variation. MCV is also a very late indicator for iron deficiency. In nutrition surveys or a standard nutrition lab where the automated analyzers are not available, the manual methods to measure these indicators are cumbersome and error prone (4). Therefore ferritin/sTfR are usually the more useful indicators under these circumstances.

Zinc protoporphyrin (ZnPP)
In iron deficiency the iron in protoporphyrin is substituted by zinc and can be measured selectively by hematoflourometry (4). This happens already in the second stage of iron deficiency before the Hb falls under the cut off levels, which makes ZnPP a more sensitive parameter than Hb. A special hematoflourometer costs around 10,000 USD and weighs less than 10 kg. It is a very simple and robust measurement and can be useful in screening for iron deficiency (5). The most critical factor to keep in mind when using ZnPP is the influence of lead, which increases ZnPP. In most cases it is probably not significant, but normal environmental exposure can influence the ZnPP in blood (1).

RESEARCH NEEDS AND NEW DEVELOPMENTS

It is now clear, and also recommended by a workshop of the WHO/CDC (6), that the combination of Hb, ferritin, sTfR and parameters of infection (e.g. CRP and AGP) are the best indicators to measure iron status. To implement this there is a great need for the following improvements, especially in developing countries:

- Reducing the cost: The measurement of Hb is simple and inexpensive, but the measurement of all other parameters is usually quite expensive. With the standard methods, the chemicals can cost more than 15 USD to measure one sample and together with the labor and fix cost of a lab the expenses can easily more than double.

- Improving the throughput: It is obvious that taking four independent measurements of the same sample is a very inefficient procedure. Therefore a combined measurement would be very helpful.

- Increasing the sensitivity: Very often only a small amount of blood is available, e.g. from a finger prick or a dried blood spot (DBS), which requires a very sensitive method, especially for ferritin where the cut off is below 30 μg/L.

- Increasing the robustness: In a standard clinical chemistry laboratory it may be expected that the results are reliable, but everyone who has to work under difficult environmental conditions knows that unreliable measurements are one of the biggest problems, resulting in wrong decisions and waste of resources.

Since ferritin, sTfR, CRP and AGP are proteins, immunological methods like ELISA, radial immunodiffusion (RID) or turbidimetry are possible methods to quantify them. Radioimmunoassays are still in use for the measurement of ferritin but they are replaced now by other methods, which create no problem with radioactive waste. Because of its high sensitivity and low technical

Figure 4.1: Collection of DBS (first vertically dried for some minutes and then horizontally stored overnight in the low humidity environment of the desiccant box).

requirements the ELISA technique is very often the method of choice for the measurement of these proteins. There are several companies which offer ELISA kits for these proteins. Since a kit with a 96 well plate costs between 100 and 400 USD for each protein, the easiest way to reduce the cost for an ELISA is to establish in-house ELISA methods. By a simple exchange of the antibodies it is also possible to make a combined measurement, and depending on the number of samples which are measured the cost for the chemicals can be reduced to less than 5 USD for all four proteins (7). Unfortunately ELISA techniques are not the most robust methods, and some experience is needed in order to get reliable results. RID is a very robust and simple method but the sensitivity is limited. Therefore there are currently no kits available to measure ferritin or sTfR with RID. Turbidimetric methods can be more robust and easier to automatize but until now conventional turbidimetry hasn't been tested for sufficient sensitivity and suitability for a combined measurement. In clinical settings the most convenient alternative approach to measure these proteins is via autoanalyzer, e.g. the machines from Roche/Hitachi which offer the measurement of all four proteins. They use a special turbidimetric procedure to increase the sensitivity but the machines are costly and the expenses for the chemicals are comparable with ELISA kits. The use of this method must therefore be justified by its higher convenience and potentially higher reliability.

Dried blood spots

Collecting blood samples in the field with centrifugation and freezing and sending them frozen to the laboratory is a laborious procedure and sometimes not possible. The best solution would be to have a robust method in the field to measure these indicators directly, but except for Hb and with some limitation ZnPP it is currently not possible. Therefore the collection of blood samples on filter paper can be an alternative **(Figures 4.1 and 4.2)**. It doesn't require the centrifugation of the blood samples and there is no freezing or frozen transport to the laboratory nec-

essary. Hb can be measured in DBS by directly extracting the Hb in Drabkin's reagent but usually the recovery of Hb is slightly reduced (3 to 4%). If this is not corrected it can have significant influence on the detection of anemia prevalence (8), especially when a large number of subjects have Hb values around the cut off value. Ferritin cannot be measured in DBS since erythrocytes have a high content of ferritin, which doesn't correlate well with ferritin in plasma. An alternative is to centrifuge the sample and to measure ferritin in dried plasma spots (9, 10). Unfortunately this makes only the storage and transport of the samples easier. Something that has to be kept in mind is the relative instability of sTfR. Therefore strict rules have to be followed (good drying overnight in a low humidity environment and storage below 20°C) to get reliable sTfR results from DBS.

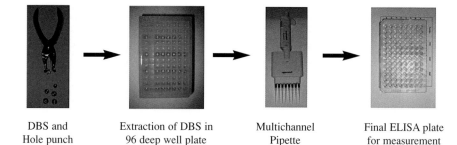

| DBS and | Extraction of DBS in | Multichannel | Final ELISA plate |
| Hole punch | 96 deep well plate | Pipette | for measurement |

Figure 4.2: Principle of DBS measurement (shown here for ferritin, sTfR, RBP and CRP).

REFERENCES

1.   Cook JD. Diagnosis and management of iron-deficiency anaemia. Best Pract Res Clin Haematol 2005;18(2):319–32.

2.   Yip R, Stoltzfus RJ, Simmons WK. Assessment of the prevalence and the nature of iron deficiency for populations: the utility of comparing hemoglobin distribution. In: Hallberg L, Asp NG, eds. Iron Nutrition in Health and Disease. London: John Libbey and Co, 1996:31–48.

3.   Cook JD, Flowers CH, Skikne BS. The quantitative assessment of body iron. Blood 2003;101(9): 3359–64.

4.   Gibson R. Principles of Nutritional Assessment. 2nd ed. New York: Oxford University Press, 2005.

5.   Mei Z, Parvanta I, Cogswell ME, Gunter EW, Grummer-Strawn LM. Erythrocyte protoporphyrin or hemoglobin: which is a better screening test for iron deficiency in children and women? Am J Clin Nutr 2003;77(5):1229–33.

6.   Joint WHO/CDC technical consultation on assessment of iron status at population level. Geneva, 2004 Apr 6-8.

7.   Erhardt JG, Estes JE, Pfeiffer CM, Biesalski HK, Craft NE. Combined measurement of ferritin, soluble transferrin receptor, retinol binding protein, and C-reactive protein by an inexpensive, sensitive, and simple sandwich enzyme-linked immunosorbent assay technique. J Nutr 2004;134(11):3127–32.

8.   Sari M, de Pee S, Martini E, Herman S, Sugiatmi, Bloem MW, Yip R. Estimating the prevalence of anaemia: a comparison of three methods. Bull World Health Organ 2001;79(6):506–11.

9.   Flowers CH, Cook JD. Dried plasma spot measurements of ferritin and transferrin receptor for assessing iron status. Clin Chem 1999;45(10):1826–32.

10.   Ahluwalia N, de Silva A, Atukorala S, Weaver V, Molls R. Ferritin concentrations in dried serum spots from capillary and venous blood in children in Sri Lanka: a validation study. Am J Clin Nutr 2002;75(2):289–94.

5

An overview of the functional significance of iron deficiency

Gary Gleason[1]　　　　　Nevin S. Scrimshaw[2]

[1]Friedman School of Nutrition Science and Policy, Tufts University, Boston, USA
[2]International Nutrition Foundation, United Nations University, Boston, USA
Contact: Gary.Gleason@tufts.edu

GARY GLEASON
Gary has a PhD in Mass Media and Communication from the University of Iowa, USA. He is currently an Associate Professor at the Friedman School of Nutrition Science and Policy at Tufts University, Boston USA. He is also the Director of the Iron Deficiency Project Advisory Service (IDPAS) which is a proactive international project that provides technical and research information in areas mainly related to iron nutrition to developing country projects and researchers. He is also a co-chair of the United Nations Standing Committee on Nutrition Working Group on Micronutrients and coordinates an annual report working group on activities related to improving micronnutreint nutrition from developing countries, researchers, international organizations, NGOs and private sector sources.

NEVIN SCRIMSHAW
Nevin obtained his PhD and MPH from Harvard University and his MD from the University of Rochester, both in the USA. He is a clinical and public health nutritionist, founded the Institute of Nutrition of Central America and Panama (INCAP), and was for many years Head of the Department of Nutrition and Food Science at the Massachusetts Institute of Technology, USA, where he is now Professor Emeritus. Nevin is the founder and President of the International Nutrition Foundation and Senior Advisor for the UNU Food and Nutrition Program. His current interests, amongst many, relate to the functional consequences of iron deficiency and rapid assessment procedures for the evaluation and improvement of nutrition programs. Nevin has over 650 publications to his name and has authored or edited more than 20 books. In 1991 he was named the World Food Prize Laureate.

INTRODUCTION

As noted elsewhere in this volume, on a global basis iron deficiency is the most widespread micronutrient and overall nutritional deficiency. As stated by the World Health Organization (WHO), "the numbers are staggering: 2 billion people – over 30% of the world's population – are anemic with about 1 billion suffering from iron deficiency anemia. In many developing countries one out of two pregnant woman and more than one out of every three preschool children are estimated to be anemic" (1). In countries where meat consumption is low, such as India and many in sub-Saharan Africa, up to 90% of women are or become anemic during pregnancy.(2)

WHO estimates that some 800,000 deaths worldwide are attributable to iron deficiency anemia (3) and this disease remains among the 15 leading contributors to the global burden of disease. As measured in disability adjusted life years (DALYs), iron deficiency anemia accounts for 25 million, or 2.4%, of the total (4). This summary of the functional consequences of iron deficiency begins with a brief outline of the iron status in humans in general, and the variations that are normal at different life stages for males and females. The iron status of individuals ranges from iron excess to degrees of iron deficiency anemia. Although iron needs vary for different groups based on such factors as rapid growth (late infancy, adolescence, pregnancy) and differences in normal iron losses (menstruation, childbirth), a relatively powerful self regulatory process in the intestinal tract increases iron absorption progressively with iron depletion and decreases absorption with repletion over a wide range of intakes.

Women tend to have substantially lower iron stores than men (one eighth of total body iron in women compared to one third in men), making them more vulnerable to iron deficiency when iron intake is lowered or need increases. Women of reproductive age lose iron during menses and have a substantially higher need for iron during pregnancy, because of the increase in red cell volume of the mother and placental and fetal growth (5). This substantially increases their risk of iron deficiency anemia. The rapid growth of infants, especially between 6–24 months, includes a major increase in overall red blood cell and tissue volume. Their need for iron during this period is proportionately nearly as great as that of pregnant women, and is difficult to meet through breast-feeding and common complementary feeding practices alone.

If there is too little iron in the diet, if the iron consumed is poorly bioavailable or if the overall meal contents interact to curtail availability beyond the range of the body's ability to upregulate absorption to meet iron needs, stored iron will be used up and iron deficiency will occur.

The stages of iron deficiency for various population age and sex groups are shown in **Figure 5.1** (6). The first stage, depletion of iron stores, has no functional changes. Where iron stores are exhausted, and tissues begin to have insufficient iron, the resulting condition is iron deficiency. Negative effects, which have been found among those who are iron deficient but not outright anemic, include cognitive impairment, decreased physical capacity, and reduced immunity, and are more serious with iron deficiency anemia (7). Anemia severity increases as hemoglobin concentration or hematocrit values decrease below the range for the healthy reference sample of the same age and sex as set by WHO **(see Table 5.1 and 5.2)**. Severe iron deficiency anemia can be fatal.

A normal male body has in total approximately 4.0 g of iron and a normal woman an average of 2.5 g. Approximately 65% of the body's iron is in hemoglobin in circulating red cells and in the muscle protein myoglobin. In men, about a

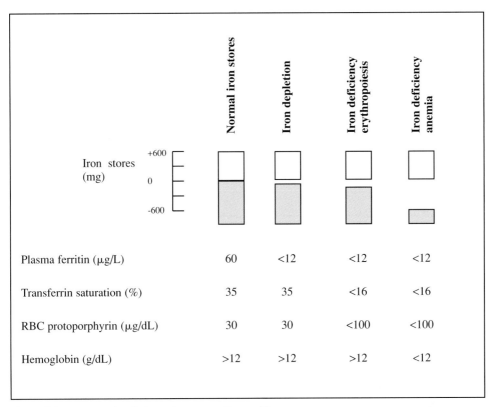

Figure 5.1: Iron status in relation to iron stores. Source (6).

Measurements of iron status in realtionship to body iron stores (mg). Negative iron stores indicate the amount of iron that must be replaced in circulating red cells before iron reserves can re-accumulate.

Table 5.1: Hemoglobin and hematocrit cutoffs used to define anemia in people living at sea level (48).

Age or sex group	Hemoglobin below g/dL	Hematocrit below (%)
Children 6 months to 5 years	11.0	33
Children 5–11 years	11.5	34
Children 12–13 years	12.0	36
Non-pregnant women	12.0	36
Pregnant women	11.0	33
Men	13.0	39

Table 5.2: Stages of anemia. Source (48) and values used in demographic and health surveys.

	Anemia measured by hemoglobin (g/dL)			
	Anemia	Mild	Moderate	Severe
Children 6–59 months	<11.0	10–10.9	7.0–9.9	<7.0
Children 5–11 years	<11.5	10–11.4	7.0–9.9	<7.0
Children 12–14 years	<12.0	10–11.9	7.0–9.9	<7.0
Non-pregnant women above 15 years	<12.0	10–11.9	7.0–9.9	<7.0
Pregnant women	<11.0	10–10.9	7.0–9.9	<7.0
Men (above 15 years)	<13.0	12–12.9	9.0–11.9	<9.0

Note: Hemoglobin values change with altitude and formulas are available to adjust hemoglobin values at different altitudes to define anemia.

third of total body iron is stored in ferritin and hemosiderin in the liver, and for women the stored proportion is considerably lower, about one eighth. Iron is also found in many essential iron dependent enzymes and other biochemically active iron compounds.

IRON DEFICIENCY ANEMIA AND ITS CONSEQUENCES

Weakness and fatigue have long been associated with the pallor that reflects anemia, and current science points to adverse functional consequences from iron deficiency even before anemia is present. Studies have shown that mild iron deficiency anemia among those who are not physically active

may have relatively few consequences because compensatory mechanisms function to more completely extract oxygen from hemoglobin in tissues, increase cardiac output and redirect blood flow to the heart muscles and brain (8) .

The risk of iron deficiency anemia during pregnancy is high because additional iron is needed to supply the mother's expanding blood volume (an approximate 20% increase) and to support the rapid growth of the fetus and placenta (5). During the second half of pregnancy the iron required cannot be easily met by diet (9). Even most healthy women do not have sufficient body stores of iron only to support an average pregnancy. Only about 0.3 mg of the approximately 85 mg of iron (10) needed can be mobilized from stores. The additional amount is essential and is very often well beyond that made available through common diets, especially those common for women in many developing countries. Even though pregnant women have been shown to absorb more iron from foods, a high prevalence of anemia during the third trimester of pregnancy has been consistently shown. In the United States approximately 30% of pregnant women from lower income groups are found to be anemic (11).

Moderate (Hb 70–90 g/L) and severe (Hb <70 g/L) anemia are associated with increased maternal and child mortality and infectious diseases (12). Increased risk of maternal death may be related to several factors, including cardiac failure during labor with severe anemia to lower tolerance of hemorrhagic blood loss during childbirth. Moderate to severely anemic pregnant women also appear to have slower healing times and increased risk of infection. All of these factors require further research.

Based on epidemiologic studies, anemia during early pregnancy has been associated with preterm (13, 14) and low birth weight; both factors are associated with greater risk of fetal and neonatal death. Favorable pregnancy outcomes occur 30–45% less often in anemic mothers, and infants of anemic mothers are less likely to have normal iron reserves (5).

In summary, a pregnant woman who is anemic has a significantly higher risk of maternal mortality, prenatal infant loss, and prematurity. Her infant is at greater risk of death, and is more likely to be below normal birth weight and to be born with poorer iron stores. Such an infant is more likely to become iron deficient and anemic before six months of age.

IRON DEFICIENCY IN INFANCY AND EARLY CHILDHOOD

Considerable emphasis is placed on reducing the prevalence of iron deficiency in infancy and early childhood, because a large body of evidence indicates that poor iron status negatively affects cognitive, motor and social development during this period of rapid growth and development (14) Iron deficiency anemia has been shown to have significant adverse effects on infants between 6 months and 24 years of age, that include decreases in responsiveness and activity, as well as increases in body tension and fatigue. Depending on the age at which anemia occurs and its severity, some developmental deficits can be improved or even corrected with iron treatment, but with iron deficiency in infancy some cognitive and social differences can remain permanent (15).

The risk of iron deficiency is high during infancy because only about 50% of the iron requirement of a normal six month old can be obtained from breast milk, and by this age the stores received at birth are likely to have been used to support normal functions and growth even in children born at term of well nourished mothers. If the mother is anemic and/or the child is of low birth weight, the stores are depleted much earlier. Continued breastfeeding alone will supply only half of the infant's iron needs, while the other half, approximately 4 mg/day, must come from complementary foods or an iron containing supplement if iron deficiency anemia is to be avoided. Where well fortified infant cereals are available and affordable, they provide the required iron, as does iron fortified infant formula.[1]

The high risk of iron deficiency anemia in children 6–24 months of age is clearly shown in

---

[1] The major benefits to breastfeeding are well recognized and strategies to prevent iron deficiency in infants and young children should in no way discourage exclusive breastfeeding for about six months, but rather assure that additional and adequate levels of absorbable iron are part of the nutrition of normal birth weight children 6–24 months of age.

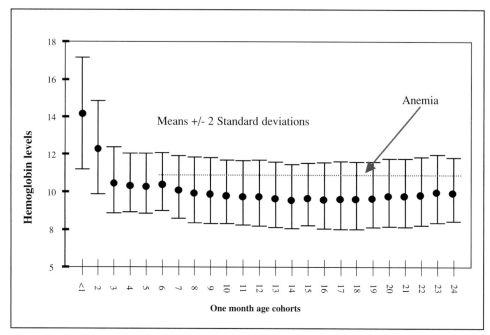

Figure 5.2: Mean hemoglobin levels (g/dL) of children. Grouped by age in months from 19 population surveys (total n=31,859). Source (49).

analysis of pooled data from 18 Demographic and Health Surveys (DHS) from 11 developing countries. Cohorts of children selected by months of age from 6–24 months from more than 31,000 children for which hemoglobin had been measured found approximately 50% anemia among cohorts of children in each montly age group **(see Figure 5.2)**.

For infants younger than six months, especially in developing countries, several factors may lead to an iron status inadequate for normal growth and development. Studies have also found the infants of mothers suffering from anemia during pregnancy have lower iron stores at birth. Cutting the pulsing umbilical cord before iron rich cord blood is transferred to the newborn also results in lower iron in the infant at birth. Low birth weights account for up to 20% of infants in poorly nourished populations, and these infants receive low levels of iron stores based on lower

overall tissue and blood volume at birth. These facts, compounded by the increased iron needs associated with the rapid weight gain of low birth weight infants, are the basis for the WHO and UNICEF recommendation that low birth weight infants receive supplementary iron beginning at two months (16, 17), and continuing up to 24 months of age (18).

IRON DEFICIENCY IN SCHOOLCHILDREN

Iron deficient schoolchildren in Indonesia and India have been found to have poorer performance than those with normal iron status, and lower performance could be substantially improved after 12 weeks of iron supplementation (19, 20). A positive association between iron status and performance was also found in a large double blind study of 1,358 children 9–11 years old in Thailand (21), where schoolchildren who were anemic had significantly lower scores in Thai language mathematics and other subjects than iron replete children. However, in this study there was no significant improvement following 14 weeks of daily iron supplementation that restored hemoglobin levels to normal. It was suggested that their iron deficiency as schoolchildren reflected the iron deficiency that they had suffered in infancy.

Iron deficiency is disadvantageous to achievement of schoolchildren in various environments and across cultural groups, with serious implication for the effectiveness of education in many developing countries.

IRON DEFICIENCY AND TEMPERATURE REGULATION

Iron deficient rats are unable to maintain their body temperatures when exposed to low environmental temperatures (22, 23). Severe iron deficiency anemia lowered the ability to maintain body temperature in subjects exposed to environment without protective clothing.

IRON DEFICIENCY AND PHYSICAL CAPACITY

Iron deficiency decreases physical performance. The treadmill performance of Guatemalan agricultural workers was found linearly related to their hemoglobin status (**Figure 5.3**). It returned to normal with iron supplementation (24).

Among Indonesian rubber tappers, hemoglobin status was shown to affect work output and productivity-linked take home pay. When rubber tappers were given iron supplementation for 60 days, their pay increased by more than 30% (25). In the same study, for a task where productivity was not linked to pay, workers employed to weed crops who were not anemic covered more area than anemic workers. The area weeded by formerly anemic workers increased with the iron supplementation (**see Figure 5.4**). Among women in Indonesia and men in Sri Lanka (26) working on tea plantations the productivity of iron deficient individuals was significantly less than those with normal hemoglobin concentrations. After supplementation with iron, the iron deficient subjects collected more tea and thereby increased their take home pay.

Once work capacity has been reduced by iron deficiency anemia, blood transfusion that restores blood hemoglobin levels does not improve performance, suggesting that deficient iron-dependent muscle enzymes are responsible (26). This is confirmed by experiments with rats showing that dietary iron deficiency causes marked impairment in oxidative energy production in skeletal muscle (27) that manifests as less efficient glucose oxidation and decreased capacity for physical exercise.

IRON AND MORBIDITY FROM INFECTION

A study as early as the 1920s reported that London infants given an iron supplement had less bronchitis and gastroenteritis (28). Infants receiving a formula fortified with iron and vitamins in a 1966 study had about 50% fewer respiratory infections than infants who received an unfortified version of the same formula (29). Iron deficiency was reported to be associated with increased diarrheal and respiratory diseases in a study of Alaskan Inuit children (30), and meningitis was observed to be fatal only among those who were anemic (31). Morbidity from infections among anemic rubber tappers decreased after iron supplementation in an Indonesia study (9, 32), and decreases in diarrheal and respiratory infections were observed in family members receiving iron supplementation in field studies in Egypt (33) and women tea pickers in Indonesia.

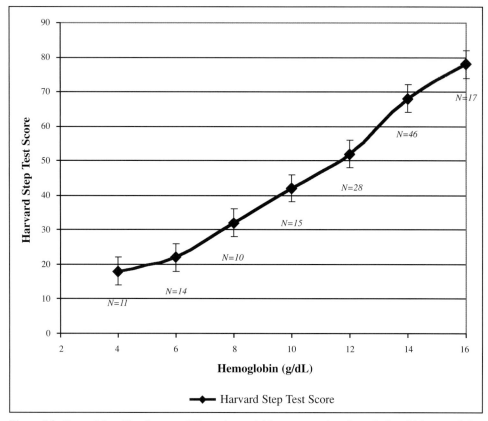

Figure 5.3: Harvard Step Test Score at different hemoglobin concentrations in agricultural labourers living in the lowlands of Guatamala. Source (24).

These results are supported by research related to the need for and the role of iron in a number of biological mechanisms involved in the immune response to infections. However, there are other studies that have found no positive effect on lowering infectious disease prevalence by providing iron. Differences in iron needs, iron status and the immune functions of various individuals and groups during different lifecycle stages are complicating factors as well as disease exposure. A review of interactions of iron and infection for a meeting to reassess the public health importance of iron deficiency in 2000 found some issues relating to iron deficiency and infection still unresolved (34).

The most common area of debate regarding the positive or negative impact of providing iron as a public health intervention is related to the interaction of iron and malaria (35). The dietary and environmental factors associated with high malaria prevalence in children lead many to a concurrent condition of iron deficiency anemia. There is near universal agreement among researchers and clinicians, and it is as a recommendation by WHO, that all children found to be suffering from iron deficiency anemia in areas of high malaria prevalence should be given supplementary iron as a component of a proactive intervention that also includes provision of treated bed nets and anti-malarial drugs.

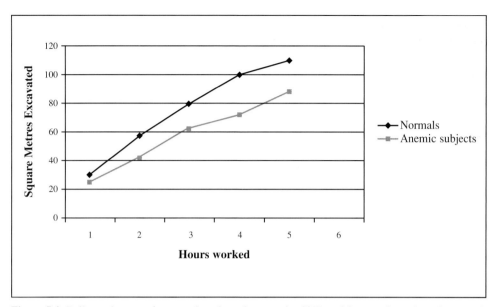

Figure 5.4: Daily work output for normal workers (hematocrit ≥38%) and for anemic workers (hematocrit <38%). The major cause of anemia was iron deficiency. Source (9).

However, a recent study in Zanzibar, Tanzania has resulted in changes in the former UNICEF recommendations on iron supplementation. It was found that in an area with stable, perennial and intense transmission of *Plasmodium falciparum* malaria, iron supplements given to children who were iron replete, with or without zinc, resulted in an increased rate of severe adverse events in children (morbidity and mortality) (36). This outcome led to a WHO consultation that recommended that universal iron supplementation not be used in areas of high malaria transmission. It should be noted that a substudy in the same area found that iron supplementation of children who were not iron replete had better health outcomes than those who did not receive a supplement.

There is agreement among clinicians and researchers that adequate iron is needed to support immune system functioning. However, public health recommendations for implementation of a practical, low cost intervention package to correct iron deficiency anemia and promote healthy iron status among infants and young children in environments where *P. falciparum* malaria is hyperendemic remains in debate.

There is less controversy regarding the functional consequences of iron deficiency anemia and other types of infections. In developing countries, iron deficiency anemia and infections are common, and experimental evidence shows that there is a decreased resistance to infection in iron deficient humans and experimental animals.

While adequate iron status is essential for preventing and overcoming infections, pathogenic microorganisms also require iron to grow and reproduce. Thus, the body must continually maintain its overall supply of iron in forms that are unusable by pathogens and that are not free to create compounds that cause cellular and other damage. This is accomplished by binding iron strongly in forms that withhold it from the replication of pathogenic organisms. However, if the immune system has been damaged by severe protein deficiency or other nutrient deficiencies and iron supplementation is given therapeutically in large doses of iron that overwhelm the body's ability to withhold iron from pathogens, the consequences can be disastrous.

Thus, in severely malnourished subjects exposed to serious acute infection, too much iron, particularly when administered parenterally, can enhance the growth of pathogenic organisms before immunity is restored. Serious illness and death have been seen where children with kwashiorkor were given parental iron (37), and seriously malnourished refugees administered therapeutic doses of iron because of severe anemia (38).

IRON EXCESS AND CHRONIC DISEASE

A final area of the functional consequences of iron deficiency is that of chronic disease. There has been some concern raised about the possible relationship between high iron stores and heart disease or cancer (39). A 2001 review focusing on research over a 15 year period concluded that there was no convincing evidence of iron stores affecting heart disease (40, 41) in adults despite some evidence suggesting that high body iron stores, as judged from serum ferritin levels, may be associated with such a risk (42). A 1988 study found that high iron stores could increase a risk of lung cancer development (43). These reports suggest that the mechanism is the prooxidant activity of iron. Although these studies are inconclusive, they indicate the need for further research on this issue.

Iron intake may be important for individuals homozygous for the relatively rare hereditary disorder of hemochromatosis. The only strong evidence linking iron overload with cancer is the increased risk of hepatic carcinoma among individuals with this disorder. This association is attributed to chronic injury to hepatic tissues from extremely high levels of iron in the liver.

CONCLUSION

In summary, iron deficiency has been shown to affect adversely the physical capacity and work performance of adolescents and adults and the immune status, and morbidity from infections of all age groups. Severe iron deficiency anemia impairs the maintenance of body temperature in adults exposed to a cool environment. It also impairs cognitive performance and behavior at any age. In general, these effects are corrected by iron supplementation, but, if moderate to severe iron deficiency occurs in infancy, the effects on cognition may not be reversible (44).

Nevertheless, iron is a two edged sword. Iron given to a severely malnourished individual with impaired immunity can benefit the replication of a pathogen before the immune system can be rebuilt. Iron overload in individuals homozygous for the genetic disorder hemochromatosis can lead to hepatic fibrosis, and even death. There is also concern, but not strong evidence, that iron supplementation of replete individuals can cause oxidative stress that may increase the risk of heart disease and cancer in some persons.

Reviews from leading agencies working internationally on nutrition and child development, organizations including the United Nation Children's Fund (UNICEF), the United Nations Education, Scientific and Cultural Organization (UNESCO), the Untied Nations Population Fund (UNFPA), the World Food Programme (WFP), the Development Programme (UNDP), the Joint United Nations Programme on HIV/AIDS (UNAIDS), the World Health Organization (WHO) and the World Bank, all strongly support the conclusion that even mild anemia in infants and young children can impair intellectual development and that priority should be given to the prevention of iron deficiency in this age group (45).

The concerns raised by studies on the functional consequences of iron deficiency and their longer term economic and social impacts, led in 2001 to the setting of an international target to reduce anemia prevalence including iron deficiency, by 30% in each member country by 2010 from 2000 levels. This target was agreed upon by UN member countries at the 2002 Special Session of the General Assembly (46).

References

1. World Health Organization (WHO). Nutrition. Geneva: WHO, www.who.int/nutrition/en: WHO 2007.
2. Allen L, de Benoist B, Dary O, Hurrell R. Guidelines on food fortification with micronutrients. Geneva: WHO, 2006.
3. World Health Organization (WHO). World Health Report 2002: reducing risks, promoting healthy life: overview. Geneva: WHO, 2002.
4. Stoltzfus R, Stiefel H. Iron deficiency and the global burden on disease. Audiovisual materials from a presentation given at the 2003 INACG Symposium: Integrating programs to move iron deficiency and anemia control forward. Marrakesch, Morocco, 6 February 2003.
5. Bothwell TH, Charlton RW. Iron deficiency in women. Washington DC: INACG, 1981.
6. DeMaeyer, EM. Preventing and controlling iron deficiency anemia through primary health care: a guide for health administrators and program managers. Geneva: WHO, 1989.
7. UNICEF/UNU/WHO/MI. Preventing iron deficiency in women and children. Technical consensus on key issues. UNICEF/UNU/WHO/MI technical workshop, 7–9 October 1998. Boston and Ottawa: International Nutrition Foundation and The Micronutrient Initiative, 1998.
8. Varat, MA, Adolph RJ, Fowler NO. Cardiovascular effects of anemia. Am Heart J 1972;83:416–26.
9. Earl R, Woteki CE. Iron deficiency anemia: recommended guidelines for prevention, detection and management among US children and women of childbearing age. Washington, DC: National Academy Press, 1993.
10. Hallberg L. Iron balance in pregnancy. In: Berger H, ed. Vitamins and minerals in pregnancy and lactation. Nestle Nutrition Workshop Series No. 16. New York: Raven Press, 1989:115–27.
11. Perry G, Yip R, Zyrkowski C. Nutritional risk factors among low-income US women. Semin Perinatol 1995;19:211–21.
12. Elder L. Issues in programming for maternal anemia. Arlington, VA: MotherCare/ILSI, 2002.
13. Scholl TO, Hediger ML, Fischer RL, Shearer JW. Anemia vs iron deficiency: increased risk of preterm delivery in a prospective study. Am J Clin Nutr 1992;55:985–8.
14. Lozoff B. Iron deficiency in infancy: impact on behavior and development. UN SCN Annual Meeting, Chennai, India, 3–7, unpublished presentation, March 2003.
15. Lozoff B, Hagen, Mollen E, Wolf A. Poorer behavioral and developmental outcome more than 10 years after treatment for iron deficiency in infancy. Pediatrics 2000;105:11.
16. Llewelyn-Jones D. Severe anaemia in pregnancy as seen in KualaLumpur. Aust N Z J Obstet Gynaecol 1965;5:191–7.
17. Beischer NA, Holsman M, Kitchen WH. Relation of various forms of anemia to placental weight. Amer J Obstet Gyn 1968;101:801–9.
18. Stoltzfus R. Guidelines for the use of iron supplementation to prevent and treat iron deficiency anemia. Geneva: INACG/WHO/UNICEF, 1998.

19. Soemantri AG, Pollitt E, Kim I. Iron deficiency anemia and educational achievement. Am J Clin Nutr 1985;42:1221–8.

20. Seshadri S, Gopaidas T. Impact of iron supplementation on cognitive functions in preschool and school-aged children: the Indian experience. Am J Clin Nutr 1989;50:675–86.

21. Pollitt E, Hathirat P, Kotchabhakdi NJ, Missell L, Valyasevi A. Iron deficiency and educational achievement in Thailand. Am J Clin Nutr 1989;50:687–97.

22. Dillman E, et al. Effect of iron deficiency on catecholamine metabolism and body temperature regulation. In: Pollitt E, Leibel RL, eds. Iron deficiency: brain biochemistry and behavior. Raven Press, New York, 1982:57–63.

23. Martinez-Torres C, Cubeddu L, Dillmann E, Brengelmann GL, Leets I, Layrisse M, Johnson DG, Finch C. Effect of exposure to low temperature on normal and iron-deficient subjects. Am J Physiol 1984;246:R380–3.

24. Viteri F, Torum B. Anemia and physical work capacity. Clin Hematol 1974;3:609–26.

25. Basta SS, Soekirman, Karyadi D, Scrimshaw NS. Iron deficiency anemia and the productivity of adult males in Indonesia. Am J Clin Nutr 1979;32:916–25.

26. Edgerton VR, Gardner GW, Ohira Y, Gunawardena KA, Senewiratne B. Iron-deficiency anemia and its effect on worker productivity and activity patterns. BMJ 1979;2:1546–9.

27. Finch C, Miller L, Inamdar A. Iron deficiency in the rat: physiological and biochemical studies of muscle dysfunction. J Clin Invest 1976; 59:447–53

28. MacKay HM. Anemia in infancy: its prevalence and prevention. Arch Dis Child 1928;3:117–47.

29. Andelman MB, Sered BR. Utilization of dietary iron by term infants. A study of 1,048 infants from a low socioeconomic population. Am J Dis Child 1966;111:45–55.

30. Brown CV, Brown GW, Bonrhill B. Iron deficiency and its functional consequences. Alaska Med 1967;9:93–9.

31. Fortuine R. Acute purulent meningitis in Alaska natives: epidemiology, diagnosis and prognosis. Can Med Assoc J 1966;94(1):19–22.

32. Hussein MA, Hassan HA, Abdel-Ghaffar AA, Salem S. Effect of iron supplements on the occurrence of diarrhoea among children in rural Egypt. Food and Nutr Bull 1999;10(2):35.

33. Husaini KHD, Gunadi H. Evaluation of nutritional anemia intervention among anemic female workers on a tea plantation. In: Iron deficiency and work performance. Washington, DC: The Nutrition Foundation, 1981:73

34. Beard J, Stolzfus R, eds. Iron Deficiency Anemia. J Nutr 2001;131S Supplement II:2001: 131S.5. Oppenheimer SJ. Iron and Its relation to immunity and infectious disease. J Nutr 2001;131:616S–35S.

35. Mwangi T, Bethony J, Brooker S. Malaria and helminth interactions in humans: an epidemiological viewpoint. Annals of Tropical Medicine and Parasitology (2006) 100: 551-570.

36. Sazawal S, Black RE, Ramsan M, et al. Effects of routine prophylactic supplementation with iron and folic acid on admission to hospital and mortality in preschool children in a high malaria transmission setting: community based, randomised, placebo-controlled trial. Lancet 2006:367:133–43.

37. Murray MJ, Murray AB, Murray CJ, Murray MB. The effect of iron status of Nigerian mothers on that of their infants at birth and 6 months, and on the concentration of Fe in breastmilk. Br J Nutr 1978;39:627–30.

38. Murray MJ, Murray AB, Murray MB, Murray CJ. The adverse effect of iron repletion on the course of certain infections. Br Med J 1978;2(6145):1113–5.

39. van Asperen IA, Feskens EJ, Bowles CH, Kromhout D. Body iron stores and mortality due to cancer and ischaemic heart disease: a 17-year follow-up study of elderly men and women. Int J Epidemiol 1995;24:665–70.

40. Ma J, Stampfer M. Body iron stores and coronary heart disease. Clin Chem 2002;48:601–3.

41. Sempos C, Looker AC, Gillum RF, McGee DL, Vuong CV, Johnson CL. Serum ferritin and death

from all causes and cardiovascular disease: the NHANES II Mortality Study. Ann Epidemiol 2000;10: 441–8.

42. Ramakrishnan U, Kuklina E, Stein A. Iron stores and cardiovascular disease risk factors in women of reproductive age in the United States. Am J Clin Nutr 2002;76:1256–60.

43. Selby J, Friedman G. Epidemiologic evidence of an association between body iron stores and risk of cancer. Int J Cancer 1988;41:677–82.

44. Working Group Report, SCN Working Group on Micronutrients. In: 29th Session UN SCN Meeting, 11–15 March 2002.

45. UNICEF. Facts for Life. New York: UNICEF/WHO/UNESCO/UNFPA/UNDP/UNAIDS/WFP/World Bank, 2002:153.

46. UNICEF. World Fit for Children. United Nations General Assembly, New York, 2001.

47. WHO/UNICEF/UNU. Indicators for assessing iron deficiency and strategies for its prevention. Geneva: WHO, 2002.

48. WHO/UNICEF/UNU (2001). Iron deficiency anaemia. Assessment prevention and control. A guide for programme managers. Geneva, WHO/UNICEF/UNU.

49. Gleason G, Carter H, Amed I. Anemia Levels in Monthly Age Cohorts of Children (0-24 months) Accumulated from 18 Demographic and Health Surveys. Unpublished Presentation, Workshop on prevention of Anemia in Children 6-24 Months of Age, International Nutrition Foundation, Micronutrient Initiative, Ottawa, 2003.

6

Iron metabolism

Sean Lynch

Eastern Virginia Medical School, Norfolk, USA
Contact: srlynch@visi.net

SEAN LYNCH

Sean obtained his MD from the University of the Witwatersrand, Johannesburg, South Africa. He is currently Professor of Clinical Medicine at the Eastern Virginia Medical School in Norfolk, Virginia, USA. His research interests have focused on iron absorption, factors that control dietary and fortification iron bioavailability, the assessment of iron status in populations, and the pathophysiological consequences of iron deficiency. Recently Sean has concentrated his attention on the application of research findings related to iron nutrition and iron bioavailability to fortification programs aimed at reducing the prevalence of iron deficiency anemia in developing countries.

INTRODUCTION

Iron plays a vital role in oxygen transport and storage, oxidative metabolism, cellular proliferation and many other physiological processes. Its most important property is the reversible one-electron oxidation-reduction reaction between the two common oxidation states, Fe^{2+} and Fe^{3+}, allowing it to coordinate electron donors and to participate in redox processes (1). This property also accounts for its greatest potential for causing toxic effects. Reactions with oxygen can lead to the formation of unstable intermediates with unpaired electrons. These free radicals, particularly the hydroxyl radical OH·, react with most organic molecules with very high rate constants, causing their destruction. Cell membranes and DNA are particularly vulnerable.

Iron is also an essential nutrient for all known pathogens, many of which have developed complex mechanisms for acquiring it, permitting successful multiplication in iron restricted environments (2). Freely available iron may greatly increase virulence. The human body has developed complicated metabolic processes to absorb, transport and store iron ensuring a ready supply for cellular growth and function, but limiting its participation in reactions that produce free radicals and its availability to invading pathogens.

PHYSIOLOGY OF IRON HOMEOSTASIS

Human beings normally have 40–50 mg Fe/kg body weight **(Table 6.1)**. Approximately 75% is present in metabolically active compounds. The remaining 25% constitutes a dynamic store that is turned over constantly. It ensures an adequate supply for normal physiological functions despite short term variations in absorption or loss from the body. The store also supplies the immediate needs when requirements are increased (e.g., by rapid growth or pregnancy). Iron reserves that have been utilized are then gradually replaced by increased absorption.

Ferritin is the major iron storage protein. It is located predominantly in the cells that function as the storage sites, the macrophages of the spleen, liver, bone marrow and skeletal muscle (3). However, all nucleated cells synthesize ferritin to manage their intracellular iron economy. Apoferritin is a large spherical protein shell (M_r 440000) composed of varying mixtures of 24 subunits of two types (L, M_r 19700 and H, M_r 21100) (4). Each ferritin molecule can reversibly store as many as 4,500 iron atoms within the protein shell. Channels that connect the interior with the surface provide routes for iron to move in and out in concert with cellular

Table 6.1: Distribution of body iron in adults (approximate estimates for Western countries). Adapted from Bothwell et al. (3) and Finch and Huebers (6).

Type of iron	Men (mg)	Women (mg)
Functional iron		
Hemoglobin	2300	1680
Myoglobin	320	205
Heme and nonheme enzymes	160	128
Storage iron		
Ferritin and hemosiderin	1000	300

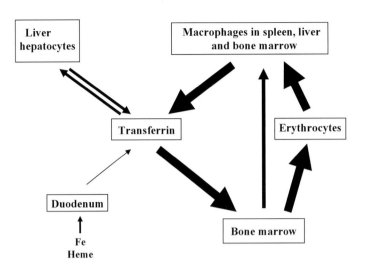

Figure 6.1: Iron homeostasis and storage.

requirements. Catabolism of ferritin may result in the utilization of the iron core or conversion to hemosiderin which is an amorphous form of iron that is water insoluble and less rapidly available (5).

Internal iron exchange

The cells in most body organs are turning over constantly, necessitating a steady supply of nutrients, including iron. The iron requirements of the bone marrow for hemoglobin synthesis outweigh those of all other tissues from a quantitative point of view. Kinetic studies have therefore focused on the relationship between iron and red blood cell production, but it is important to remember that a reduction in iron supply has functional consequences for all body cells that may be unrelated to anemia and oxygen delivery.

Almost all functional requirements are supplied from the circulating transferrin bound pool. It contains only about 3 mg iron in adults (3, 6), but ten times as much iron, approximately 35 mg, moves through the compartment each day, roughly 80% destined for red blood cell production (**Figure 6.1**).

A small proportion of the iron passing through the plasma transferrin pool, about 1 mg, is absorbed iron. The largest fraction is iron recovered from the turnover of erythrocytes and defective erythrocyte precursors (7, 8). At the end of their 120 day life spans, red blood cells are catabolized by specialized macrophages in the spleen, liver and bone marrow. Depending on the body's immediate requirements, the recovered iron is either released to transferrin within a few hours or temporarily placed in the cellular store (9, 10). Finally, a variable but much smaller quantity of iron is derived from liver hepatocytes, which constitute another important storage site.

Transfer of iron from macrophages and hepatocyte iron stores to transferrin

Iron is exported from macrophages and liver hepatocytes by the transmembrane protein and only known cellular iron exporter in humans, ferroportin (Fpn), with the aid of the ferroxidase, ceruloplasmin (11–13). As described below, the rate of release is closely matched to tissue (primarily erythroid) requirements so that the iron saturation of transferrin is maintained at approximately 35% (3). The capacity for augmenting the iron supply is considerable if stores are adequate. In the face of an increased demand resulting from blood loss, an individual with a store of about 1000 mg can mobilize an additional 40 mg of iron each day. An individual with a 200 mg store can mobilize about 20 mg per day, although this rate can only be sustained for a few days (6). Iron can be recycled through macrophages at an even greater rate (as much as 80–160 mg/day) in conditions such as thalassemia major, because the defective red cells and their precursors have very short life spans and almost all of the iron derived from heme catabolism is returned to the plasma immediately (6, 9, 10, 14). Sturgeon and Finch have demonstrated erythroid marrow production levels that are six to ten times normal (15).

The body's ability to provide additional iron by increasing absorption is very different. It is limited to about 2–4 mg per day unless iron supplements are provided (6). If iron stores are depleted by significant blood loss it may take two to three months for accelerated absorption to restore normal hemoglobin levels.

When iron requirements are reduced, transfer from macrophages to transferrin is downregulated, allowing a greater proportion of iron derived from erythrocyte catabolism to enter the storage pool (9, 10). However the capacity to downregulate iron release is not unlimited. A minimum of 20% of the heme iron load is returned to the plasma in individuals whose bone marrow requirements are low (e.g., in aplastic anemia) even if they do not suffer from a genetic iron loading disorder (3, 14). As a result, the plasma iron and transferrin saturation rise. More iron is delivered to the liver and other tissues, exceeding the capacity of cells to regulate their internal iron economy. The consequence is damage to various organs, including the liver, heart, and pancreas, which is characteristic of secondary iron overload in patients requiring repeated blood transfusions for conditions such as aplastic anemia and thalassemia.

The release of iron from macrophages is regulated by a recently discovered small, cysteine-rich cationic peptide, hepcidin (16–18), which is produced in liver hepatocytes, circulates in the plasma and is excreted in the urine. It acts as a negative regulator of macrophage iron release and intestinal iron absorption by binding to Fpn causing it to be internalized and degraded in lysosomes (19, 20). Hepatocyte iron release may also be regulated by this mechanism, at least in part. Hepcidin expression is induced independently by the accumulation of storage iron and by inflammation. It is suppressed when iron stores are depleted and by anemia, hypoxemia and accelerated erythropoiesis (17, 21–24) The details of the sensing mechanisms responsible for regulating its production, particularly in relation to changes in iron status, and anemia, hypoxemia and erythropoietic rate, are still being determined.

We also need to know much more about the functions and regulation of Fpn. It is likely that factors other than hepcidin have a significant role (e.g., messenger RNA (mRNA) for Fpn contains an iron responsive element (discussed below), the functional importance of which has not been established) (25). Nevertheless, there is an accumulating body of experimental evidence indicating that the hepcidin-Fpn mechanism ensures a steady supply of iron to all body cells in a form and concentration range that permits the control of internal cellular iron economy (see next section). Circulating iron in its more stable ferric form is tightly bound to transferrin, preventing free radicals from being generated and making iron less available to invading pathogens.

Cellular iron uptake

Transferrin has two binding sites for iron that have different chemical characteristics in vitro, but function identically in vivo (1, 6). Iron loading occurs in a random fashion so that the relative amounts of apoferric, monoferric and diferric transferrin are a function of transferrin saturation.

In most cells a cell surface transmembrane glycoprotein dimer, transferrin receptor 1 (TfR 1), plays the major role in iron uptake by binding and internalizing diferric and monoferric transferrin (26). The di- and monoferric transferrin/TfR 1 complexes enter clathrin coated pits and are internalized within the cell as vesicles or endosomes. The endosomes then fuse with acidic vesicles (internal pH <5.5). Iron is released and transported across the endosomal membrane by a transmembrane iron transporter, divalent metal transporter 1 (DMT 1). The affinity of TfR 1 for apotransferrin increases in the acidic environment and the apotransferrin/TfR 1 complexes are transported back to the cell surface where apotransferrin loses its affinity for the receptor once exposed to the neutral pH of the plasma. Apotransferrin is released into the plasma transferrin pool and the receptors are available to be reutilized for additional iron uptake.

Individual cells control their iron uptake by modulating the expression of TfR 1 on the cell membrane **(Figure 6.2)** and storing iron not immediately required for metabolic functions in ferritin. It is then readily available to meet future needs. Coordinated regulation of uptake and storage occurs primarily at a translational level in most cells. Two iron regulatory proteins, IRP 1 and IRP 2, sense cellular requirements and control uptake and storage (27, 28). They are RNA binding proteins that modulate the expression of five cis-acting iron-responsive elements (IREs) located on the 3′ untranslated region (UTR) of transferrin receptor messenger RNA (mRNA) and a single IRE on the 5′ UTR of ferritin mRNA. The binding of IRPs to TfR 1 mRNA IREs retards cytoplasmic degradation, increasing the number of receptors on the cell surface and iron uptake. When an IRP is bound to the ferritin mRNA IRE, ferritin synthesis is interrupted. Less iron is placed in stores, making it available for incorporation into functional compounds.

The binding of the IRPs to IREs therefore accelerates cellular iron acquisition and reduces its transfer to stores. When intracellular iron supply is sufficient to meet functional needs, IRP 1 affinity for the IREs is lost and it becomes active as cytosolic aconitase. With iron deprivation, IRE binding activity is restored. IRP 2 undergoes proteosome-mediated degradation in iron replete cells. Iron deprivation stimulates the synthesis of new IRP 2. The IRP regulation of intracellular iron economy is more complicated than the simplified outline given above might suggest. Both IRPs also respond to other intracellular events, although the responses are different for each IRP in some cases. Inflammation, oxidative stress, nitric oxide and several other factors influence the IRP-IRE regulation and cellular iron economy (29–31).

Iron uptake in three cell types (erythroid precursors, hepatocytes and macrophages that process senescent erythrocytes) is more complex. Transferrin receptor mediated uptake accounts for most of the iron acquired by erythroid precursors (32). However it must accommodate the large amounts necessary for heme synthesis. Transcriptional control overrides the primary translational regulation characteristic of other cells that have lower requirements (33). The uptake and release of iron by hepatocytes is also more complex. They express both TfR 1 and a homologue, transferrin receptor 2 (TfR 2), the latter being present in greater amounts (34, 35). Neither appears to be essential for iron uptake. Mutations of TfR 2 result in iron overload, not iron deficiency (36) and low circulating transferrin concentrations in a rare inherited disorder, atransferrinemia, are associated with marked hepatic iron overload (37). The liver hepatocyte has been shown to take up non-transferrin-bound iron efficiently in animal models (38, 39) and is also involved in the retrieval of iron from haptoglobin bound hemoglobin and heme bound to hemopexin (40) Finally, as described above, the specialized macrophages responsible for recycling hemoglobin iron derive most of their iron from senescent erythrocytes (41). Macrophages also have transferrin receptors, but increased cellular iron raises, rather than lowers, transferrin receptor expression (33).

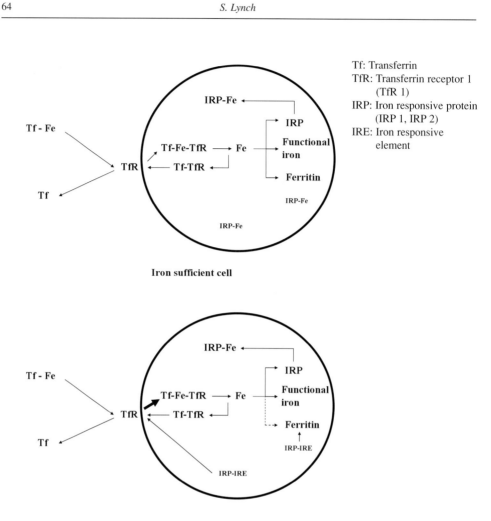

Tf: Transferrin
TfR: Transferrin receptor 1
      (TfR 1)
IRP: Iron responsive protein
      (IRP 1, IRP 2)
IRE: Iron responsive
      element

Iron sufficient cell

Iron deficient cell

Figure 6.2: Regulation of cellular iron supply and storage.

Absorption and Excretion

Absorption

Iron is a constituent of most foods. Consumption is therefore a function of caloric intake (3). However, its availability for absorption is quite variable and poor bioavailability is the major reason for the high prevalence of nutritional iron deficiency anemia in developing countries. Absorption occurs primarily in the proximal small intestine through mature enterocytes located on the tips of the intestinal villi. Two transporters appear to mediate the entry of most if not all dietary iron into the mucosal cells; one transfers intact heme molecules derived from hemoglobin or myoglobin in meat (heme carrier protein 1 (HCP 1)) (42), and the other (DMT 1) (43–45) all other iron that is rendered soluble in gastric juice and remains in solution in the upper small intestine (nonheme iron). Absorption of nonheme iron requires reduction to the ferrous state by dietary components such as ascorbic acid and/or mucosal ferric reductases, duodenal cytochrome b (Dcytb) being considered the most important (46). Only a small proportion of dietary iron is heme, even in countries where meat consumption is high, but 20–30% is absorbed (47). The availability for absorption of nonheme, often the only form of iron in developing countries, is more variable and depends on meal composition. Some dietary components, particularly ascorbic acid and animal tissue, promote absorption while others such as phytates, polyphenols, calcium, and certain proteins found in cow's milk and legumes such as soy beans are inhibitory (48).

The possibility that receptors for other forms of dietary iron have a significant role in absorption awaits further clarification. Receptors for lactoferrin have been demonstrated in infants (49, 50), although their importance for iron absorption is uncertain (51). Recent claims for the high bioavailability of phytoferritin iron (52), the predominant form of storage iron in cereal grains and other foods (53, 54), need to be confirmed. It has been postulated that the mechanism for absorption is different from that for the common nonheme pool iron. One recent study did demonstrate improved iron status among women eating high iron rice (55). If corroborated by other trials, these observations could have very important implications for efforts to reduce the prevalence of nutritional iron deficiency in developing countries.

Heme iron is released by heme oxygenase within the enterocytes (47) and enters a pathway common to both heme and nonheme iron. Although the details of its movement across the cell are still incompletely understood (56), some iron is stored in ferritin and lost to the body when the enterocyte exfoliates. The rest is transported across the basolateral membrane to become bound to circulating transferrin for delivery to transferrin receptors as described above for recycled iron. Transfer from the enterocyte to transferrin is also mediated by the specific exporter found on macrophages and hepatocytes,

Fpn (11, 13, 57, 58), which functions in conjunction with the ferroxidase activity of a membrane bound ceruloplasmin homologue, hephaestin (59, 60), and possibly ceruloplasmin itself (61).

Absorption is regulated according to the body's needs. As with macrophage and hepatic iron release, hepcidin is now considered to be the most important factor controlling absorption. It regulates transfer to transferrin by Fpn in a manner similar to that described above for macrophages (22). Nonheme iron absorption is also regulated during uptake from the duodenal lumen into mucosal cells by DMT 1. The DMT 1 gene in enterocytes generates two alternatively spliced mRNAs that differ in the 3´ UTR by the presence or absence of an IRE in animal models. Isoform 1 has an IRE, isoform 2 does not. The expression of isoform 1 is markedly upregulated, specifically in the duodenum, by dietary iron starvation. It is then located in the apical two thirds of the enterocytes, particularly in the brush border (62). Other studies have shown that DMT 1 expression is also rapidly modified in response to an oral iron load (detectable within one hour) and by the rate of iron acquisition by duodenal enterocytes during their early development in the crypts of Lieberkuhn (63) These observations indicate that enterocyte iron status has an important role in controlling nonheme iron absorption by regulating its transfer from the lumen into these cells.

The integration of hepcidin regulation with enterocyte iron concentration and DMT 1 isoform 1 expression are unclear. Hepcidin could influence DMT 1 either directly, or indirectly by causing intracellular iron levels to rise because exit via Fpn is reduced (64, 65). The entry of heme into duodenal enterocytes appears to be unregulated (66).

Excretion
Iron is lost from the body through the exfoliation of skin cells, in sweat and urine and through

the gastrointestinal tract (67). These daily basal losses account for about 1.0 mg and 0.9 mg in men and women respectively (14 μg/kg). Menstrual losses (averaged over 30 days) add a mean of 0.60–0.70 mg in women of childbearing age (3). While no mechanism for the regulation of iron excretion has been identified in human beings, passive compensatory changes do occur. Basal losses may drop to 0.50 mg in iron deficiency and be as high as 2.0 mg in iron overload (3, 67). Menstrual losses are also reduced in anemic women because, with their lower hemoglobin values, there is less iron in the menstrual blood (68).

IRON REQUIREMENTS AND THE HUMAN LIFE CYCLE

Dietary iron requirements are highest in the second and third trimesters of pregnancy and in the rapidly growing infant between 6 and 18 months of age **(Figure 6.3)**. The next high risk period for nutritional iron deficiency is the adolescent growth spurt and the onset of menstruation in girls (69). The needs of women of childbearing age are much higher than those of men, but quite variable because of the wide range in monthly menstrual blood loss (70), a pattern that is remarkably consistent in several different surveys (71, 72). Estimates of the iron requirements for women of childbearing age living in the United States indicate that about 5% have high menstrual rates and must absorb as much as 2.5 mg each day to replace their losses (73). Iron requirements are least in adult men and postmenopausal women.

The high iron requirements in pregnancy are met by both maternal stores that are accumulated prior to conception and during the first trimester

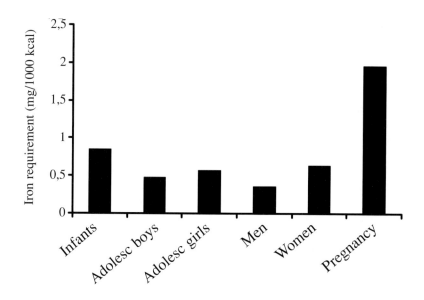

Figure 6.3: Relationship between estimated average requirement for absorbed iron and energy consumption at different stages of the human life cycle. Data from Institute of Medicine Dietary Reference Intakes (73).

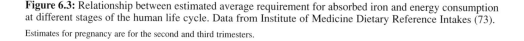

Estimates for pregnancy are for the second and third trimesters.

as the result of the cessation of menstruation, and by accelerating absorption during the second and third trimesters (3, 74). The critical importance of maternal iron sufficiency for ensuring an optimal supply for the developing fetus has only recently been appreciated (75). Iron supplementation during the latter part of pregnancy may benefit the infant even if the mother is neither iron deficient nor anemic at 20 weeks of gestation (76).

While all children and women of childbearing age in developing countries are at risk for nutritional iron deficiency, the risk is highest in infants aged 4–18 months and during pregnancy. Once the birth iron endowment is exhausted, infants depend on weaning foods for their iron because the iron content of human milk is low. This is a period of particular vulnerability because requirements are high and, under ideal circumstances, a significant part of the nutritional and energy need comes from human milk. Weaning foods must provide relatively more iron than energy without compromising breast milk consumption (77). Unfortunately, traditional weaning foods in developing countries are often poor sources of bioavailable iron.

As indicated above, iron stores have the dominant role in regulating the rate of absorption in the absence of diseases that cause inflammation, disorders that accelerate erythropoiesis, severe anemia and inherited iron loading conditions. There is a close inverse relationship between serum ferritin and nonheme absorption (3). Uptake from heme is also inversely correlated with serum ferritin, but the proportional effect of increasing iron stores is much smaller (78). These relationships have implications for the prevention of nutritional iron deficiency in women and children when requirements rise. Iron stores are always the first source for the increased need. Since absorption is inversely correlated with stores, upregulation of absorption, sufficient to restore iron balance, may only be achievable when there is very little storage iron left. The

body lacks the capacity to accelerate absorption, and concurrently accumulate iron for later use.

The increasing importance of bioavailable nonheme iron for individuals with high requirements, even when the diet contains generous quantities of meat, is illustrated in **Figure 6.4** (79, 80). This model assumes a daily iron intake of 11 mg (2.2 mg from heme) for women and 16 mg (3.2 mg from heme) for men. The absorption of iron from the two dietary forms was calculated for women with depleted iron stores, women of childbearing age with a serum ferritin of 30 μg/L (iron store approximately 300 mg), men with a serum ferritin of 100 μg/L (iron store approximately 1000 mg), both characteristic of the population of the United States and men with increased stores. The men with normal iron stores get two thirds of their iron from heme. The women's requirements are higher and their intakes lower; they get approximately equal proportions from heme and nonheme. The critical importance of nonheme bioavailability is evident in women with depleted stores. They derive almost two thirds of their requirements from nonheme because the quantity of heme is relatively limited and its absorption rate little increased by iron deficiency. Women in developing countries who eat little meat are even more dependent on nonheme sources. At the other end of the spectrum, men with high iron stores have modestly reduced heme and markedly decreased nonheme iron uptake. They no longer accumulate iron (81).

The control of absorption in children appears to parallel that in adults. The distribution of stores in children matched that of their mothers in a recent study (82) and dietary factors have similar quantitative effects (83). However, the results of one study suggest that absorption in infants less than six to nine months of age may be independent of iron status and controlled primarily by erythropoietic drive (84).

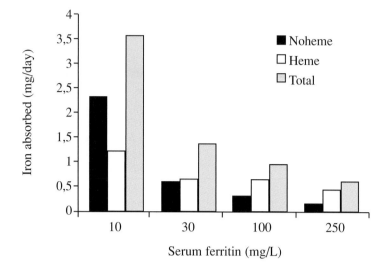

Figure 6.4: Effect of iron status on absorption of heme and nonheme iron. Data from Lynch (80) as adapted from Cook (79).

DISORDERS OF IRON BALANCE

Iron deficiency

Iron deficiency remains the most prevalent micronutrient deficiency state worldwide (85). It is estimated that two billion individuals are iron deficient; most of them are women or children in developing countries. Diets with an inadequate content of bioavailable iron are the primary cause, but disorders that increase iron loss as a result of pathological bleeding, particularly hookworm, have a very important role.

Malabsorption due to disorders that affect the upper small intestine can also cause iron deficiency. The most common appear to be celiac disease (86, 87) and *Helicobacter pylori* infections (88–91). Celiac disease may be more prevalent in some Mediterranean and south Asian countries than previously realized (92–94). It is also important to note that inadequate absorption of multiple nutrients associated with histological abnormalities of the intestinal mucosa was thought to contribute to the high prevalence of iron deficiency in

countries such as India, Pakistan, Bangladesh and Haiti in earlier studies (3). The prevalence of "tropical sprue" appears to be declining and the specificity of this entity, as well as the overlap with tropical enteropathy, has been questioned recently (95). The possible relevance of these entities to nutritional iron deficiency is unclear and further research is needed. Finally, surgical procedures that alter the anatomy of the stomach and duodenum may also decrease iron absorption.

Impaired iron absorption resulting from mutations in genes encoding proteins involved in iron transport appears to be rare, although a G $\rightarrow$ A mutation at cDNA nucleotide 829 (G277S) has been reported to be a risk factor for iron deficiency anemia in homozygous women (96).

Iron overload

Iron overload is far less prevalent than iron deficiency. It can be considered under three headings, primary systemic iron overload, secondary iron overload, both of which affect several different

Table 6.2: Primary systemic iron overload disorders. Adapted from Pietrangelo (105).

HFE – related hereditary hemochromatosis (Type 1)
Gene and chromosomal location: HFE, 6p21.3 Autosomal recessive High transferrin saturation Parenchymal iron accumulation in liver, heart, endocrine organs Low clinical penetrance, variable organ damage
Juvenile hereditary hemochromatosis (Types 2A and 2B)
Gene and chromosomal locations: Type 2A: HJV, 1q21 Type 2B: HAMP, 19q13.1 Autosomal recessive High transferrin saturation Parenchymal iron accumulation in liver, heart, endocrine organs Early onset, severe organ damage
TfR 2 related hereditary hemochromatosis (Type 3)
Gene and chromosomal location: TfR 2, 7q22 Autosomal recessive High transferrin saturation Parenchymal iron accumulation in liver, heart, endocrine organs Variable organ damage
Ferroportin related iron overload (Type 4)
Gene and chromosomal location: SLC40A1, 2q32 Autosomal dominant High transferrin saturation only in late disease Predominant reticuloendothelial iron overload in early stages Organ damage later in the clinical course

organs and are the result of excessive absorption and abnormal release from stores, and organ/tissue specific iron overload.

The regulation of iron absorption as iron stores increase in human beings with normal mucosal function is remarkable effective. There are only isolated case reports of clinically significant iron overload resulting from the ingestion of large quantities of supplemental iron over extended periods of time (3). In contrast to iron deficiency, primary systemic iron overload appears virtually always to result from the phenotypic expression of an inherited abnormality related to the regulation of iron transport. In the past, sub-Saharan iron overload was considered

to be an exception (3). Men who are at greatest risk for the disorder consume large quantities of highly bioavailable iron (97, 98) and there is little doubt that this excessive intake is an important contributory factor (99). However more recent observations have provided strong circumstantial evidence for an underlying genetic mutation (100) suspected of affecting the function of Fpn (101–104).

Dysregulation of hepcidin and abnormal function of its receptor Fpn, resulting in inappropriate iron release from stores and excessive absorption, are now considered to be the most important etiological factors in patients with primary systemic iron overload (**Table 6.2**) (22,

105). HFE related hemochromatosis Type 1, an autosomal recessive trait, is by far the most common genetic disorder of iron metabolism in populations originating in Northern Europe, affecting one in 300 individuals (106). Hepcidin levels are inappropriately low, but not as severely decreased as they are in other related disorders (22). Beutler et al. have estimated that only 1% of homozygotes living in the Unites States develop frank clinical manifestations despite their high bioavailability diet (107). However, a report from Australia demonstrates that many more may have laboratory evidence of organ damage (108). If unrecognized, a small minority of individuals, particularly men, will develop signs and symptoms, usually in middle age when the body iron content has reached 15–40 g. The mechanism of action of the HFE gene is unknown, but it is suspected of being a modulator of signaling for the iron sensor for hepcidin (22).

Two much rarer types of hemochromatosis have their clinical onset in the second or third decades of life and present a more severe phenotype (juvenile hereditary hemochromatosis). One, type 2A, is associated with a mutation in the hemojuvelin (HJV) gene. The mechanism of action of HJV is unclear. However, it directly regulates hepcidin expression in vitro (109). Rare cases of juvenile hereditary hemochromatosis (Type 2B) have been linked to mutations in the gene for hepcidin itself, the hepcidin antimicrobial peptide (HAMP) gene (110, 111).

The phenotype associated with the gene encoding TfR 2 (Type 3) occurs early in life, but is milder than Type 2 juvenile hereditary hemochromatosis (112). The function of TfR2 is unknown, although recent observations indicate that it also modulates hepcidin production (113).

Finally, mutations of the hepcidin target, Fpn, may affect its functionality or responsiveness to hepcidin (114–116). The resulting

phenotype may be similar to Type 1 HFE hemochromatosis or characteristic of ferroportin related iron overload (Type 4), with predominant reticuloendothelial iron accumulation in the initial stages and an onset in the fourth or fifth decades (105).

Secondary iron overload leads to severe morbidity in patients with thalassemia and sideroblastic anemia who have accelerated ineffective erythropoiesis (117). They continue to absorb excessive quantities of iron despite increasing iron stores if they are anemic (118). Finch proposed the existence of two regulators of iron absorption, a "stores regulator" and an "erythropoietic regulator" (119). The "erythropoietic regulator" was postulated to override the control exerted by the "stores regulator" in these conditions. Recent studies point to a common mediator, hepcidin, for both regulators (22), but also provide support for the apparent dominance of erythropoietic rate in the control of iron absorption. Hepcidin production has been reported to be decreased despite elevated serum ferritin levels (indicative of increased iron stores) in the presence of accelerated erythropoiesis (120, 121), leading to continued iron accumulation. Repeated blood transfusions also contribute significantly to the iron overload in these patients.

There are several other rarer causes of iron overload. They include atransferrinemia as well as conditions that lead to organ/tissue specific iron overload. They are beyond the scope of this review. Examples include abnormalities of iron trafficking in the mitochondrion (122) and aceruloplasminemia (123, 124).

Anemia of inflammation
(anemia of chronic disease)
The anemia of inflammation is a mild or moderate anemia that is characterized by decreased iron release from macrophage stores, reduced absorption, restriction of the supply available for red cell production and reduced plasma iron and transfer-

rin concentrations (125). Many investigators have postulated that it is a vital host response that evolved to deprive pathogens of iron, and that it is one of the mechanisms that constitute "nutritional immunity" (126, 127).

The accumulating body of experimental evidence related to hepcidin indicates that increased hepcidin production, induced by the inflammatory cytokine IL6, accounts for almost all of the clinical and laboratory features of the anemia of inflammation (128, 129). The hepcidin response to inflammation appears to be independent of iron status.

Although the former name of the anemia of inflammation, "anemia of chronic disease," suggested slow evolution of the characteristic laboratory findings, the fall in plasma iron concentration was well known to occur rapidly after the onset of infection or inflammation. Recent studies demonstrate that synthetic hepcidin administered to mice causes hypoferremia within hours of a single intraperitoneal injection (130).

CONCLUSION

Major advances have been made in understanding the physiology of human iron metabolism over the past fifty years, although many questions remain to be answered. The scientific knowledge base has provided a sound foundation for approaches to combating nutritional iron deficiency. I have provided only a brief overview of some of the highlights that are relevant to nutrition and nutritional anemia.

REFERENCES

1. Aisen P. Iron metabolism: an evolutionary perspective. In: Brock JH, Halliday JW, Pippard MJ, Powell LW, eds. Iron metabolism in health and disease. London: W.B. Saunders Company Ltd, 1994:1–30.
2. Bullen JJ, Griffiths E, eds. Iron and infection. Molecular, physiological and clinical aspects. 2nd ed. New York: John Wiley & Sons, 1999.
3. Bothwell TH, Charlton RW, Cook J, Finch C. Iron metabolism in man. Oxford: Blackwell Scientific Publications, 1979.
4. Halliday JW, Ramm GA, Powell LW. Cellular iron processing and storage: the role of ferritin. In: Brock JH, Halliday JW, Pippard MJ, Powell LW, eds. Iron metabolism in health and disease. London: W.B. Saunders Company Ltd, 1994:97–121.
5. Wixom RL, Prutkin L, Munro HN. Hemosiderin: nature, formation, and significance. Int Rev Exp Pathol 1980;22:193–225.
6. Finch CA, Huebers H. Perspectives in iron metabolism. N Engl J Med 1982;306:1520–8.
7. Cook JD, Marsaglia G, Eschbach JW, Funk DD, Finch CA. Ferrokinetics: a biologic model for plasma iron exchange in man. J Clin Invest 1970;49:197–205.
8. Finch CA, Deubelbeiss K, Cook JD, et al. Ferrokinetics in man. Medicine (Baltimore) 1970;49:17–53.
9. Fillet G, Cook JD, Finch CA. Storage iron kinetics. VII. A biologic model for reticuloendothelial iron transport. J Clin Invest 1974;53:1527–33.
10. Fillet G, Beguin Y, Baldelli L. Model of reticuloendothelial iron metabolism in humans: abnormal behavior in idiopathic hemochromatosis and in inflammation. Blood 1989;74(2):844–51.
11. Donovan A, Brownlie A, Zhou Y, Shepard J, Pratt SJ, Moynihan J, Paw BH, Drejer A, Barut B, et al. Positional cloning of zebrafish ferroportin 1 iden-

tifies a conserved vertebrate iron exporter. Nature 2000;403:776–81.

12. Knutson MD, Vafa MR, Haile DJ, Wessling-Resnick M. Iron loading and erythrophagocytosis increase ferroportin 1 (FPN1) expression in J774 macrophages. Blood 2003;102:4191–7.

13. Donovan A, Lima CA, Pinkus JL, Pinkus GS, Zon LI, Robine S, Andrews NC. The iron exporter ferroportin/Slc40a1 is essential for iron homeostasis. Cell Metab 2005;1:191–200.

14. Hillman RS, Henderson PA. Control of marrow production by the level of iron supply. J Clin Invest 1969;48:454–60.

15. Sturgeon P, Finch CA. Erythrokinetics in Cooley's anemia. Blood 1957;12:64–73.

16. Krause A, Neitz S, Magert HJ, Schulz A, Forssmann WG, Schulz-Knappe P, Adermann K. LEAP-1, a novel highly disulfide-bonded human peptide, exhibits antimicrobial activity. FEBS Lett 2000;480:147–50.

17. Pigeon C, Ilyin G, Courselaud B, Leroyer P, Turlin B, Brissot P, Loreal O. A new mouse liver-specific gene, encoding a protein homologous to human antimicrobial peptide hepcidin, is overexpressed during iron overload. J Biol Chem 2001;276:7811–9.

18. Park CH, Valore EV, Waring AJ, Ganz T. Hepcidin, a urinary antimicrobial peptide synthesized in the liver. J Biol Chem 2001;276:7806–10.

19. Nemeth E, Tuttle MS, Powelson J, Vaughn MB, Donovan A, Ward DM, Ganz T, Kaplan J. Hepcidin regulates cellular iron efflux by binding to ferroportin and inducing its internalization. Science 2004;306:2090–3.

20. Delaby C, Pilard N, Goncalves AS, Beaumont C, Canonne-Hergaux F. Presence of the iron exporter ferroportin at the plasma membrane of macrophages is enhanced by iron loading and down-regulated by hepcidin. Blood 2005;106:3979–84.

21. Ganz T. Hepcidin – a peptide hormone at the interface of innate immunity and iron metabolism. Curr Top Microbiol Immunol 2006;306:183–98.

22. Nemeth E, Ganz T. Regulation of iron metabolism by hepcidin. Annu Rev Nutr 2006;26:323–42.

23. Ganz T, Nemeth E. Regulation of iron acquisition and iron distribution in mammals. Biochim Biophys Acta 2006;1763:690–9.

24. Ganz T, Nemeth E. Iron imports. IV. Hepcidin and regulation of body iron metabolism. Am J Physiol Gastrointest Liver Physiol 2006;290:G199–203.

25. Liu XB, Hill P, Haile DJ. Role of the ferroportin iron-responsive element in iron and nitric oxide dependent gene regulation. Blood Cells Mol Dis 2002;29:315–26.

26. Irie S, Tavassoli M. Transferrin-mediated cellular iron uptake. Am J Med Sci 1987;293:103–11.

27. Kim HY, Klausner RD, Rouault TA. Translational repressor activity is equivalent and is quantitatively predicted by in vitro RNA binding for two iron-responsive element- binding proteins, IRP1 and IRP2. J Biol Chem 1995;270:4983–6.

28. Hentze MW, Muckenthaler MU, Andrews NC. Balancing acts: molecular control of mammalian iron metabolism. Cell 2004;117:285–97.

29. Recalcati S, Pometta R, Levi S, Conte D, Cairo G. Response of monocyte iron regulatory protein activity to inflammation: abnormal behavior in genetic hemochromatosis. Blood 1998;91:2565–72.

30. Recalcati S, Taramelli D, Conte D, Cairo G. Nitric oxide-mediated induction of ferritin synthesis in J774 macrophages by inflammatory cytokines: role of selective iron regulatory protein-2 downregulation. Blood 1998;91:1059–66.

31. Theil EC. Integrating iron and oxygen/antioxidant signals via a combinatorial array of DNA - (antioxidant response elements) and mRNA (iron responsive elements) sequences. J Inorg Biochem 2006;100:2074–8.

32. Iacopetta BJ, Morgan EH, Yeoh GC. Transferrin receptors and iron uptake during erythroid cell development. Biochim Biophys Acta 1982;687:204–10.

33. Ponka P, Lok CN. The transferrin receptor: role in health and disease. Int J Biochem Cell Biol 1999;31:1111–37.

34. Kawabata H, Yang R, Hirama T, Vuong PT, Kawano S, Gombart AF, Koeffler HP. Molecular cloning of transferrin receptor 2. A new member of the transferrin receptor-like family. J Biol Chem 1999;274:20826–32.

35. Andrews NC. Molecular control of iron metabolism. Best Pract Res Clin Haematol 2005;18:159–69.
36. Camaschella C, Roetto A, Cali A, et al. The gene TFR2 is mutated in a new type of haemochromatosis mapping to 7q22. Nat Genet 2000;25:14–5.
37. Hamill RL, Woods JC, Cook BA. Congenital atransferrinemia. A case report and review of the literature. Am J Clin Pathol 1991;96:215–8.
38. Wright TL, Brissot P, Ma WL, Weisiger RA. Characterization of non-transferrin-bound iron clearance by rat liver. J Biol Chem 1986;261:10909–14.
39. Brissot P, Wright TL, Ma WL, Weisiger RA. Efficient clearance of non-transferrin-bound iron by rat liver. Implications for hepatic iron loading in iron overload states. J Clin Invest 1985;76:1463–70.
40. Hershko C, Cook JD, Finch CA. Storage iron kinetics. II. The uptake of hemoglobin iron by hepatic parenchymal cells. J Lab Clin Med 1972;80:624–34.
41. Bratosin D, Mazurier J, Tissier JP, et al. Cellular and molecular mechanisms of senescent erythrocyte phagocytosis by macrophages. A review. Biochimie 1998;80:173–95.
42. Shayeghi M, Latunde-Dada GO, Oakhill JS, et al. Identification of an intestinal heme transporter. Cell 2005;122:789–801.
43. Fleming MD, Trenor CC, 3rd, Su MA, Foernzler D, Beier DR, Dietrich WF, Andrews NC. Microcytic anaemia mice have a mutation in Nramp2, a candidate iron transporter gene. Nat Genet 1997;16:383–6.
44. Gunshin H, Mackenzie B, Berger UV, et al. Cloning and characterization of a mammalian proton-coupled metal-ion transporter. Nature 1997;388:482–8.
45. Anderson GJ, Frazer DM. Recent advances in intestinal iron transport. Curr Gastroenterol Rep 2005;7:365–72.
46. McKie AT, Barrow D, Latunde-Dada GO, et al. An iron-regulated ferric reductase associated with the absorption of dietary iron. Science 2001;291:1755–9.
47. Uzel C, Conrad ME. Absorption of heme iron. Semin Hematol 1998;35:27–34.
48. Skikne B, Baynes RD. Iron absorption. In: Brock JH, Halliday JW, Pippard MJ, Powell LW, eds. Iron metabolism in health and disease. London: W. B. Saunders Company Ltd, 1994:151–87.

49. Kawakami H, Lonnerdal B. Isolation and function of a receptor for human lactoferrin in human fetal intestinal brush-border membranes. Am J Physiol 1991;261:G841–6.
50. Lonnerdal B. Lactoferrin receptors in intestinal brush border membranes. Adv Exp Med Biol 1994;357:171–5.
51. Davidsson L, Kastenmayer P, Yuen M, Lonnerdal B, Hurrell RF. Influence of lactoferrin on iron absorption from human milk in infants. Pediatr Res 1994;35:117–24.
52. Davila-Hicks P, Theil EC, Lonnerdal B. Iron in ferritin or in salts (ferrous sulfate) is equally bioavailable in nonanemic women. Am J Clin Nutr 2004;80:936–40.
53. Sczekan SR, Joshi JG. Isolation and characterization of ferritin from soyabeans (glycine max). J Biol Chem 1987;262:13780–8.
54. Graham RD, Stangoulis JC. Trace element uptake and distribution in plants. J Nutr 2003;133:1502S–5S.
55. Haas JD, Beard JL, Murray-Kolb LE, del Mundo AM, Felix A, Gregorio GB. Iron-biofortified rice improves the iron stores of nonanemic Filipino women. J Nutr 2005;135:2823–30.
56. Ma Y, Specian RD, Yeh KY, Yeh M, Rodriguez-Paris J, Glass J. The transcytosis of divalent metal transporter 1 and apo-transferrin during iron uptake in intestinal epithelium. Am J Physiol Gastrointest Liver Physiol 2002;283:G965–74.
57. Ganz T. Cellular iron: ferroportin is the only way out. Cell Metab 2005;1:155–7.
58. Canonne-Hergaux F, Donovan A, Delaby C, Wang HJ, Gros P. Comparative studies of duodenal and macrophage ferroportin proteins. Am J Physiol Gastrointest Liver Physiol 2006;290:G156–63.
59. Han O, Wessling-Resnick M. Copper repletion enhances apical iron uptake and transepithelial iron transport by Caco-2 cells. Am J Physiol Gastrointest Liver Physiol 2002;282:G527–33.
60. Vulpe CD, Kuo YM, Murphy TL, et al. Hephaestin, a ceruloplasmin homologue implicated in intestinal iron transport, is defective in the sla mouse. Nat Genet 1999;21:195–9.
61. Cherukuri S, Potla R, Sarkar J, Nurko S,

Harris ZL, Fox PL. Unexpected role of cerulo-plasmin in intestinal iron absorption. Cell Metab 2005;2:309–19.

62. Canonne-Hergaux F, Gruenheid S, Ponka P, Gros P. Cellular and subcellular localization of the Nramp2 iron transporter in the intestinal brush border and regulation by dietary iron. Blood 1999;93:4406–17.

63. Morgan EH, Oates PS. Mechanisms and regulation of intestinal iron absorption. Blood Cells Mol Dis 2002;29:384–99.

64. Frazer DM, Wilkins SJ, Becker EM, Vulpe CD, McKie AT, Trinder D, Anderson GJ. Hepcidin expression inversely correlates with the expression of duodenal iron transporters and iron absorption in rats. Gastroenterology 2002;123:835–44.

65. Frazer DM, Wilkins SJ, Becker EM, Murphy TL, Vulpe CD, McKie AT, Anderson GJ. A rapid decrease in the expression of DMT1 and Dcytb but not Ireg1 or hephaestin explains the mucosal block phenomenon of iron absorption. Gut 2003;52:340–6.

66. Powell LW, Campbell CB, Wilson E. Intestinal mucosal uptake of iron and iron retention in idiopathic haemochromatosis as evidence for a mucosal abnormality. Gut 1970;11:727–31.

67. Green R, Charlton R, Seftel H, Bothwell T, Mayet F, Adams B, Finch C, Layrisse M. Body iron excretion in man: a collaborative study. Am J Med 1968;45:336–53.

68. Hallberg L. Iron requirements. Comments on methods and some crucial concepts in iron nutrition. Biol Trace Elem Res 1992;35:25–45.

69. Dallman PR. Changing iron needs from birth through adolescence. New York: Nestec Ltd., Vevy/Raven Press, Ltd., 1992.

70. Hallberg L, Hogdahl AM, Nilsson L, Rybo G. Menstrual blood loss--a population study. Variation at different ages and attempts to define normality. Acta Obstet Gynecol Scand 1966;45:320–51.

71. Cole SK, Billewicz WZ, Thomson AM. Sources of variation in menstrual blood loss. J Obstet Gynaecol Br Commonw 1971;78:933–9.

72. Hefnawi F, El-Zayat AF, Yacout MM. Physiologic studies of menstrual blood loss. I.

Range and consistency of menstrual blood loss in and iron requirements of menstruating Egyptian women. Int J Gynaecol Obstet 1980;17:343–8.

73. Institute of Medicine. Dietary reference intakes for vitamin A, vitamin K, arsenic, boron, chromium, copper, iodine, iron, manganese, molybdenum, nickel, silicon, vanadium, and zinc. Washington, DC: National Academy Press, 2001.

74. Lynch SR. The potential impact of iron supplementation during adolescence on iron status in pregnancy. J Nutr 2000;130:448S–51S.

75. Preziosi P, Prual A, Galan P, Daouda H, Boureima H, Hercberg S. Effect of iron supplementation on the iron status of pregnant women: consequences for newborns. Am J Clin Nutr 1997;66:1178–82.

76. Cogswell ME, Parvanta I, Ickes L, Yip R, Brittenham GM. Iron supplementation during pregnancy, anemia, and birth weight: a randomized controlled trial. Am J Clin Nutr 2003;78:773–81.

77. Lynch SR, Stoltzfus RJ. Iron and ascorbic Acid: proposed fortification levels and recommended iron compounds. J Nutr 2003;133:2978S–84S.

78. Lynch SR, Skikne BS, Cook JD. Food iron absorption in idiopathic hemochromatosis. Blood 1989;74:2187–93.

79. Cook JD. Adaptation in iron metabolism. Am J Clin Nutr 1990;51:301–8.

80. Lynch SR. Overview of the relationship of iron to health. Contemporary Nutrition 1994;19:1–4.

81. Garry PJ, Hunt WC, Baumgartner RN. Effects of iron intake on iron stores in elderly men and women: longitudinal and cross-sectional results. J Am Coll Nutr 2000;19:262–9.

82. Cook JD, Boy E, Flowers C, Daroca Mdel C. The influence of high-altitude living on body iron. Blood 2005;106:1441–6.

83. Hurrell RF, Davidsson L, Reddy M, Kastenmayer P, Cook JD. A comparison of iron absorption in adults and infants consuming identical infant formulas. Br J Nutr 1998;79:31–6.

84. Domellof M, Lonnerdal B, Abrams SA, Hernell O. Iron absorption in breast-fed infants: effects of age, iron status, iron supplements, and complementary foods. Am J Clin Nutr 2002;76:198–204.

85. WHO/UNICEF/UNU. Iron deficiency anemia

assessment, prevention, and control. Geneva: World Health Organization, 2001.

86. Lombardo T, Ximenes B, Ferro G. Hypochromic microcytic anemia as a clinical presentation of celiac disease. Clin Lab 2006;52:231–6.

87. Cook HB, Burt MJ, Collett JA, Whitehead MR, Frampton CM, Chapman BA. Adult coeliac disease: prevalence and clinical significance. J Gastroenterol Hepatol 2000;15:1032–6.

88. Annibale B, Capurso G, Chistolini A, D'Ambra G, DiGiulio E, Monarca B, DelleFave G. Gastrointestinal causes of refractory iron deficiency anemia in patients without gastrointestinal symptoms. Am J Med 2001;111:439–45.

89. Annibale B, Capurso G, Delle Fave G. The stomach and iron deficiency anaemia: a forgotten link. Dig Liver Dis 2003;35:288–95.

90. Ciacci C, Sabbatini F, Cavallaro R, et al. Helicobacter pylori impairs iron absorption in infected individuals. Dig Liver Dis 2004;36:455–60.

91. Hershko C, Ronson A, Souroujon M, Maschler I, Heyd J, Patz J. Variable hematologic presentation of autoimmune gastritis: age-related progression from iron deficiency to cobalamin depletion. Blood 2006;107:1673–9.

92. Ertekin V, Selimoglu MA, Doneray H, Orbak Z, Ozkan B. Prevalence of celiac disease in a sample of Turkish children and adolescents with type 1 diabetes mellitus. J Clin Gastroenterol 2006;40:655–7.

93. Sood A, Midha V, Sood N, Avasthi G, Sehgal A. Prevalence of celiac disease among school children in Punjab, North India. J Gastroenterol Hepatol 2006;21:1622–5.

94. Mankai A, Landolsi H, Chahed A, et al. Celiac disease in Tunisia: serological screening in healthy blood donors. Pathol Biol (Paris) 2006;54:10–3.

95. Walker MM. What is tropical sprue? J Gastroenterol Hepatol 2003;18:887–90.

96. Lee PL, Halloran C, Trevino R, Felitti V, Beutler E. Human transferrin G277S mutation: a risk factor for iron deficiency anaemia. Br J Haematol 2001;115:329–33.

97. Walker ARP, Arvidsson UB. Iron 'overload' in the South African Bantu. Tran R Soc Trop Med Hyg 1953;47:536–48.

98. Bothwell TH, Seftel H, Jacobs P, Torrance JD, Baumslag N. Iron overload in Bantu subjects. Studies on the availability of iron in Bantu beer. Am J Clin Nutr 1964;14:45–71.

99. MacPhail AP, Simon MO, Torrance JD, Charlton RW, Bothwell TH, Isaacson C. Changing patterns of dietary iron overload in black South Africans. Am J Clin Nutr 1979;32:1272–8.

100. Gordeuk VR. African iron overload. Semin Hematol 2002;39:263–9.

101. McNamara L, Gordeuk VR, MacPhail AP. Ferroportin (Q248H) mutations in African families with dietary iron overload. J Gastroenterol Hepatol 2005;20:1855–8.

102. Barton JC, Acton RT, Rivers CA, Bertoli LF, Gelbart T, West C, Beutler E. Genotypic and phenotypic heterogeneity of African Americans with primary iron overload. Blood Cells Mol Dis 2003;31:310–9.

103. Beutler E, Barton JC, Felitti VJ, Gelbart T, West C, Lee PL, Waalen J, Vulpe C. Ferroportin 1 (SCL40A1) variant associated with iron overload in African-Americans. Blood Cells Mol Dis 2003;31:305–9.

104. Gordeuk VR, Caleffi A, Corradini E, et al. Iron overload in Africans and African-Americans and a common mutation in the SCL40A1 (ferroportin 1) gene. Blood Cells Mol Dis 2003;31:299–304.

105. Pietrangelo A. Hereditary hemochromatosis – a new look at an old disease. N Engl J Med 2004;350:2383–97.

106. Powell LW, Jazwinska E, Halliday JW. Primary iron overload. In: Brock JH, Halliday JW, Pippard MJ, Powell LW, eds. Iron metabolism in health and disease. London: W.B. Saunders Company Ltd, 1994:227–70.

107. Beutler E, Felitti VJ, Koziol JA, Ho NJ, Gelbart T. Penetrance of 845G–> A (C282Y) HFE hereditary haemochromatosis mutation in the USA. Lancet 2002;359:211–8.

108. Olynyk JK, Cullen DJ, Aquilia S, Rossi E, Summerville L, Powell LW. A population-based study of the clinical expression of the hemochromatosis gene. N Engl J Med 1999;341:718–24.

109. Lin L, Goldberg YP, Ganz T. Competitive regulation of hepcidin mRNA by soluble and cell-asso-

ciated hemojuvelin. Blood 2005;106:2884–9.

110. Roetto A, Papanikolaou G, Politou M, Alberti F, Girelli D, Christakis J, Loukopoulos D, Camaschella C. Mutant antimicrobial peptide hepcidin is associated with severe juvenile hemochromatosis. Nat Genet 2003;33:21–2.

111. Roetto A, Daraio F, Porporato P, Caruso R, Cox TM, Cazzola M, Gasparini P, Piperno A, Camaschella C. Screening hepcidin for mutations in juvenile hemochromatosis: identification of a new mutation (C70R). Blood 2004;103:2407–9.

112. Piperno A, Roetto A, Mariani R, et al. Homozygosity for transferrin receptor-2 Y250X mutation induces early iron overload. Haematologica 2004;89:359–60.

113. Nemeth E, Roetto A, Garozzo G, Ganz T, Camaschella C. Hepcidin is decreased in TFR2 hemochromatosis. Blood 2005;105:1803–6.

114. De Domenico I, Ward DM, Nemeth E, Vaughn MB, Musci G, Ganz T, Kaplan J. The molecular basis of ferroportin-linked hemochromatosis. Proc Natl Acad Sci U S A 2005;102:8955–60.

115. Drakesmith H, Schimanski LM, Ormerod E, et al. Resistance to hepcidin is conferred by hemochromatosis-associated mutations of ferroportin. Blood 2005;106(3):1092–7.

116. Schimanski LM, Drakesmith H, Merryweather-Clarke AT, et al. In vitro functional analysis of human ferroportin (FPN) and hemochromatosis-associated FPN mutations. Blood 2005;105:4096–102.

117. Pippard MJ. Secondary iron overload. In: Brock JH, Halliday JW, Pippard MJ, Powell LW, eds. Iron metabolism in health and disease. London: W. B. Saunders Company Ltd, 1994:271–309.

118. de Alarcon PA, Donovan ME, Forbes GB, Landaw SA, Stockman JA, 3rd. Iron absorption in the thalassemia syndromes and its inhibition by tea. N Engl J Med 1979;300:5–8.

119. Finch C. Regulators of iron balance in humans.

Blood 1994;84:1697–702.

120. Papanikolaou G, Tzilianos M, Christakis JI, et al. Hepcidin in iron overload disorders. Blood 2005;105:4103–5.

121. Kearney SL, Nemeth E, Neufeld EJ, Thapa D, Ganz T, Weinstein DA, Cunningham MJ. Urinary hepcidin in congenital chronic anemias. Pediatr Blood Cancer 2007;48(1):57–63.

122. Napier I, Ponka P, Richardson DR. Iron trafficking in the mitochondrion: novel pathways revealed by disease. Blood 2005;105:1867–74.

123. Harris ZL, Takahashi Y, Miyajima H, Serizawa M, MacGillivray RT, Gitlin JD. Aceruloplasminemia: molecular characterization of this disorder of iron metabolism. Proc Natl Acad Sci U S A 1995;92:2539–43.

124. Okamoto N, Wada S, Oga T, et al. Hereditary ceruloplasmin deficiency with hemosiderosis. Hum Genet 1996;97:755–8.

125. Finch CA. Anemia of chronic disease. Postgrad Med 1978;64:107–13.

126. Kochan I. The role of iron in bacterial infections, with special consideration of host-tubercle bacillus interaction. Curr Top Microbiol Immunol 1973;60:1–30.

127. Weinberg ED. Iron withholding: a defense against infection and neoplasia. Physiol Rev 1984;64:65–102.

128. Nemeth E, Rivera S, Gabayan V, Keller C, Taudorf S, Pedersen BK, Ganz T. IL-6 mediates hypoferremia of inflammation by inducing the synthesis of the iron regulatory hormone hepcidin. J Clin Invest 2004;113:1271–6.

129. Andrews NC. Anemia of inflammation: the cytokine-hepcidin link. J Clin Invest 2004;113:1251–3.

130. Rivera S, Nemeth E, Gabayan V, Lopez MA, Farshidi D, Ganz T. Synthetic hepcidin causes rapid dose-dependent hypoferremia and is concentrated in ferroportin-containing organs. Blood 2005;106:2196–9.

7

Optimizing the bioavailability of iron compounds for food fortification

Richard Hurrell

Ines Egli

*Institute of Food Science and Nutrition, Swiss
Federal Institute of Technology, Zurich, Switzerland
Contact: richard.hurrell@ilw.agrl.ethz.ch*

RICHARD HURRELL
Richard has a PhD in Nutrition from Cambridge University in the UK. He is currently Professor of Human Nutrition at the Swiss Federal Institute of Technology, Zurich, Switzerland. Richard's specialist area is the field of stable isotope techniques for human bioavailability of iron, calcium, zinc, magnesium, and selenium absorption. He also focuses on iron fortification and biofortification strategies. Richard has more than 150 publications to his name, is a Board Member of the Global Alliance for Improved Nutrition, and is the joint author of the recent WHO Guidelines on Food Fortification.

INES EGLI
Ines has a PhD in Nutrition from the Swiss Federal Institute of Technology (ETH), Zurich, Switzerland. She is currently a senior scientist and lecturer at the Human Nutrition Laboratory at ETH where she supervises research projects on mineral bioavailability and infant nutrition, and leads a postgraduate course in Nutrition and Health. She has also worked in the Nutrition Department of the World Health Organization in the area of micronutrient deficiencies with a special focus on iron, iodine, and vitamin A.

INTRODUCTION

Determining the bioavailability of iron compounds relative to ferrous sulfate (relative bioavailability value, [RBV]) has proven useful in ranking their potential for food fortification. The efficacy of iron fortified foods, however, depends on the absolute absorption of the iron compound, which is influenced by its RBV, but is also determined by the amount of fortification compound added, by the iron status of the consumers and by the presence of inhibitors or enhancers of iron absorption in the meal. Phytic acid and phenolic compounds, commonly present in cereal and legume foods, are the major inhibitors of iron absorption, whereas ascorbic acid from fruits, vegetables and muscle tissue are the major enhancers of iron absorption. Ascorbic acid is commonly added to iron fortified foods to optimize iron absorption.

The World Health Organization (1) has recently published guidelines on food fortification with micronutrients, which include recommendations for iron fortification compounds and a method to define the iron fortification level. Recent efficacy studies, which have to a large extent followed these guidelines, have shown good efficacy of iron fortified salt, fish sauce, wheat flour and rice in improving the iron status of target populations. This review will first summarize the WHO guidelines on iron compounds, and present the method used to define the iron fortification levels. This is followed by an update on the RBVs of different iron fortification compounds and an update on the ways to enhance the bioavailability of fortification iron.

WORLD HEALTH ORGANIZATION GUIDELINES ON RECOMMENDED IRON COMPOUNDS (1)

WHO has recently released new guidelines for food fortification, which include recommendations for preferred iron compounds and a proce-

dure by which the iron fortification level can be defined. The order of preference for iron fortification compounds is ferrous sulfate, ferrous fumarate, encapsulated ferrous sulfate, encapsulated ferrous fumarate, electrolytic iron at twice the level of ferrous sulfate, ferric pyrophosphate at twice the level of ferrous sulfate, and NaFeEDTA (sodium iron ethylene diamine tetraacetic acid). Electrolytic iron and ferric pyrophosphate should be added at twice the level of ferrous sulfate to allow for their lower RBVs. Additionally, specific recommendations are given detailing which iron compounds are most appropriate to add to the different food vehicles. These are shown in **Table 7.1**. There are recommendations for cereal flours and different cereal based foods, rice, milk products, cocoa products, and condiments. NaFeEDTA is recommended for high phytate cereal flours and for sauces such as fish sauce and soy sauce which are rich in peptides. Ferrous bisglycinate or micronized dispersible ferric pyrophosphate (2) are recommended for liquid milk products and other beverages.

Electrolytic iron is the only elemental iron powder recommended for cereal flour and breakfast cereal fortification. Atomized iron and carbon dioxide reduced iron powders are specifically not recommended because of their low RBV (3). Hydrogen-reduced (H-reduced) iron and carbonyl iron powders may be recommended at a later date as more information becomes available on these compounds. Ferrous sulfate and ferrous fumarate encapsulated with hydrogenated lipids can also be used for the fortification of cereal flours and cereal based complementary foods. The resulting iron absorption is generally believed to be as good as the nonencapsulated compounds, provided that the capsule to iron compound ratio does not exceed 60:40 (4).

When the fortified foods are suitably packaged and do not undergo further harsh heat treatments, ascorbic acid can be added to enhance iron absorption. The addition of ascorbic acid is recommended for complementary foods, dried milks and cocoa products. NaFeEDTA is not recommended for complementary food fortification at this time, as too few studies in young children have been made with this compound, and the amounts of iron as NaFeEDTA that can be added are limited by the recommendations of the Joint FAO/WHO Expert Committee on Food Additives (5).

Table 7.1: Suggested iron fortification compounds for different food vehicles (1).

Food vehicle	Fortificant
Low extraction (white) wheat flour or degermed corn flour	Dry ferrous sulfate Ferrous fumarate Electrolytic iron (2x amount) Encapsulated ferrous sulfate Encapsulated ferrous fumarate
High extraction wheat flour, corn flour, corn masa flour	NaFeEDTA Ferrous fumarate (2x amount) Encapsulated ferrous sulfate (2x amount) Encapsulated ferrous fumarate (2x amount)
Pasta	Dry ferrous sulfate
Rice	Ferric pyrophosphate (2x amount)
Dry milk	Ferrous sulfate plus ascorbic acid
Fluid milk	Ferric ammonium citrate Ferrous bisglycinate Micronized dispersible ferric pyrophosphate
Cocoa products	Ferrous fumarate plus ascorbic acid Ferric pyrophosphate (2x amount) plus ascorbic acid
Salt	Encapsulated ferrous sulfate Ferric pyrophosphate (2x amount)
Sugar	NaFeEDTA
Soy sauce, fish sauce	NaFeEDTA Ferrous sulfate plus citric acid
Juice, soft drinks	Ferrous bisglycinate, ferrous lactate Micronized dispersible ferric pyrophosphate
Bouillon cubes	Micronized dispersible ferric pyrophosphate
Cereal based complementary foods	Ferrous sulfate Encapsulated ferrous sulfate Ferrous fumarate Electrolytic iron (2x amount) All with ascorbic acid (≥2:1 molar ratio of ascorbic acid: iron)
Breakfast cereals	Electrolytic iron (2x amount)

WORLD HEALTH ORGANIZATION GUIDELINES FOR DEFINING THE LEVEL OF IRON FORTIFICATION (1)

In order to define the level of iron fortification, it is necessary to know the composition of the usual diet. This is needed to estimate dietary iron bioavailability at 5%, 10% or 15%. In addition, it is necessary to have detailed information on the iron intake of the target population. In reality, there is a wide range of iron intakes within each population subgroup, and the goal of the fortification program is to shift the iron intake distribution in the target population upwards, so that only a small proportion of that population is at risk of inadequate intake. For most nutrients, the process is to calculate the amount of extra daily nutrient required so that only 2.5% of the target population has an intake below the estimated average requirement (EAR) (6). The EAR cut-point method, however, cannot be used to estimate the prevalence of inadequate iron intakes since the iron requirements of some population subgroups, notably children, menstruating adolescents and menstruating adult women are not normally distributed. These groups would be the expected target populations of an iron fortification program.

For such population groups, it is recommended to use the full probability approach to define the iron fortification level. WHO (1) provides tables giving the probability of inadequacy of each target population at different iron intakes in relation to the expected iron bioavailability from the regular diet. An abbreviated table is shown for menstruating women (**Table 7.2**). By combining these values with a detailed knowledge of iron intake in the target population, it is possible to calculate the prevalence of inadequate intakes within the population subgroup (**Table 7.3**). For each intake range, a prevalence of inadequacy is obtained by multiplying the percentage of the group with intakes in that range by the probability of inadequacy. The example given in **Table 7.3** is for adult menstruating women consuming a 5% bioavailability diet. For these women, the overall prevalence of inadequacy is about 60%. The next step is to calculate the amount of extra daily iron intake necessary to decrease the esti-

Table 7.2: Probability of inadequate iron status in menstruating women consuming different amounts of iron daily (modified from WHO 2006) (1).

Usual mean iron intake	Probability of inadequacy for women consuming diets of different iron bioavailability*		
mg	15%	10%	5%
<5	1.0	1.0	1.0
5-10	0.71	0.93	1.0
10-15	0.30	0.65	1.0
15-20	0.09	0.35	0.91
20-25	0	0.16	0.70
25-30	0	0.04	0.50
30-35	0	0	0.35
35-40	0	0	0.25
40-45	0	0	0.15
45-50	0	0	0.08
50-55	0	0	0.04
55-60	0	0	0.04
>60	0	0	0

* These values have been recalculated from the original table. Users are advised to consult WHO guidelines, 2006, for more precise numbers.

mated prevalence of inadequacy to 2–3%. In this example, it would be around 35 mg iron extra per day. This amount needs to be provided by the fortified food vehicle. Knowing that these women consumed an average of 300 g of wheat flour per day, the flour could be fortified with 120 mg iron/kg as ferrous sulfate, 60 mg iron/kg of NaFeEDTA or 240 mg iron/kg as electrolytic iron; the different amounts calculated according to the different RBV values of the iron compounds. This is an extreme example of women consuming a whole grain cereal diet and, because of the very low iron bioavailability of this diet, large amounts of fortification iron are necessary to bring iron intake in line with iron requirements. The best choice of compound in this example would be NaFeEDTA at 60 ppm, although cost and possible sensory changes could still be an issue. Care should be taken that other population groups do not exceed the upper limit of iron intake at these high levels of fortification (7).

RELATIVE BIOAVAILABILITY OF IRON FORTIFICATION COMPOUNDS

Much has been published on the relative bioavailability (RBV) of different iron compounds (8–10). A large selection of potential iron fortification compounds have been ranked in relation to ferrous sulfate, whose RBV is set at 100. The ranking is based either on the ability of the iron compound to replete hemoglobin in anemic rats (11) or more recently, directly in relation to fractional iron absorption in humans as measured by either radioactive or stable isotope techniques (12, 13). These rat and human studies have subdivided the iron fortification compounds into four categories. The data from human isotope studies are shown in **Table 7.4**. Category 1 contains iron compounds that are readily soluble in water. All have an RBV close to 100 in adults, but their disadvantage is that they often cause unacceptable color and flavor changes in food. Category 2 contains the poorly water soluble iron compounds, which readily dissolve in the dilute acid of the gastric juice. These compounds, which include ferrous fumarate, also have an RBV of 100 since they dissolve completely during gastric digestion. Because they are poorly soluble in water, these compounds cause far fewer adverse organoleptic changes than ferrous sulfate (12). Category 3 contains those iron compounds which are insoluble in water and poorly soluble in dilute acid. Included in this category are two of the most widely used iron fortification compounds, the different elemental iron powders and ferric pyrophosphate. Because they are water insoluble, these com-

Table 7.3: Examples for the calculation of the prevalence of inadequate iron intakes by menstruating women consuming a 5% bioavailability diet (adapted from WHO 2006) (1).

Usual daily iron intake	% of women	Probability of inadequacy*	% prevalence of inadequate intakes
mg	A	B	A x B
<15	2	1.0	2.0
15-20	20	0.91	18.2
20-25	25	0.70	17.5
25-30	30	0.50	15.0
30-35	13	0.35	4.6
35-45	8	0.20	1.6
45-60	2	0.05	0.1
>60	0	0	0
Total prevalence of inadequate iron intake			59.0

* from Table 7.2.

Table 7.4: Relative bioavailability of commonly used iron fortification compounds from human isotope absorption studies (adapted from Hurrell 2002) (110).

Compound	Iron content (%)	Relative bioavailability (relative to ferrous sulfate)
Category 1: Water soluble		
Ferrous sulfate 7H$_2$O	20	100
Ferrous sulfate, dried	33	100
Ferrous gluconate	12	89
Ferrous lactate	19	67/106*
Ferric ammonium citrate	17	50-70
Category 2: Poorly water soluble, soluble in dilute acid		
Ferrous fumarate	33	30/100**
Ferrous succinate	33	92
Category 3: Water insoluble, poorly soluble in dilute acid		
Ferric pyrophosphate	25	21-75
Micronized dispersible ferric pyrophosphate	1.2	15-93
Ferric orthophosphate	29	25-32
Elemental iron		
Hydrogen-reduced	96	13-148
Electrolytic	97	75
Carbonyl	99	5-20
Category 4: Chelates		
Ferrous bisglycinate	20	90-350
NaFeEDTA	13	200-400

* RBV of 106 was with pharmaceutical doses with added ascorbic acid (23).
** Adult studies give RBV values close to 100; some infant studies have given RBV values as low as 30 (12, 37–42).

pounds cause few if any sensory changes in the food vehicle; however they do not completely dissolve in the gastric acid during digestion and have lower and more variable RBVs (**Table 7.4**). The physical characteristics of the five different elemental iron powders vary according to their method of manufacture. This influences their solubility in gastric acid and thus their RBVs (10). Additionally, the RBVs of these poorly soluble iron compounds may be influenced by the food vehicle (14) and by the iron status of the subject (15), which can sometimes result in unexpectedly low RBV values. Category 4 contains the iron chelates, NaFeEDTA (16) and ferrous bisglycinate (17). The advantage of these compounds is

that, in the presence of phytic acid, they have an RBV two to threefold that of ferrous sulfate. They are, however, more susceptible to adverse sensory changes than Category 2 or Category 3 compounds. This section reviews individual iron fortificants in respect to RBV in human isotope studies and, when available, efficacy studies.

Category 1: Water soluble iron compounds

Ferrous sulfate

Ferrous sulfate, as the reference compound, has an RBV of 100 in both rats and humans. It has been successfully used to fortify infant formula, dried milk, bread and pasta (9) and can be used to fortify low extraction wheat flour that is stored for no more than a few months (18). It may, however, provoke fat oxidation and rancidity in cereal flours stored for longer periods (9) and has been reported to cause unacceptable color changes in cocoa products (19), infant cereals (20), salt (21) and extruded rice (22). It often causes a metallic taste in liquid products and can precipitate peptides from soy sauce and fish sauce. Dried ferrous sulfate is somewhat less soluble, and is preferred to the heptahydrate form as it is less prooxidant (12).

Ferrous gluconate

This compound has been reported to have a similar RBV to ferrous sulfate both in rats and humans, although the human isotope study was made in the 1960s with pharmaceutical doses (23). It is soluble in water, so would be expected to cause similar sensory problems as ferrous sulfate. It has been less frequently used in food fortification, as it costs about five times more than ferrous sulfate. It has been used to fortify infant formula (24), grape juice and malt extract (25), but rapidly causes fat oxidation and off colors in stored cereal based complementary foods (20). Recently it has been shown to be a highly efficacious iron fortificant for whole milk powder reconstituted for consumption. Low income Mexican children aged 10–30 months were fed 400 mL reconstituted milk per day that was fortified with 5.8 mg iron as ferrous gluconate and ascorbic acid at a molar ratio to iron of 2.5:1. After six months feeding, the prevalence of anemia decreased from 41% to 12%, with no change in control children receiving nonfortified milk (26).

Ferrous lactate

This water soluble iron compound has been reported to give slight off flavors in liquid whole milk and skim milk (27) and to cause a darkening of color of chocolate milks (19). In rats, it has been reported to have a similar RBV to ferrous sulfate, and was shown to replete hemoglobin in a similar way as ferrous sulfate in anemic rats fed fortified infant formulas that had been heat processed and freeze dried (28, 29). Although in earlier human studies with pharmaceutical doses (30 mg) it was reported to have an RBV equivalent to ferrous sulfate (23), in a recent study with fish sauce it was found to have an RBV of only 67 (13). In this study, volunteer subjects were fed a meal of rice and vegetable soup seasoned with fish sauce fortified with ^{57}Fe-labeled ferrous lactate. The authors suggested that ferrous lactate was unstable in the aqueous fish sauce and degraded in a few days to less well absorbed ferric compounds.

Ferric ammonium citrate

This iron compound has been used to fortify infant formula and fruit flavored beverages (18) and has been reported to be organoleptically acceptable in fluid skim milk (30). Although ferric ammonium citrate has been reported to be as well absorbed as ferrous sulfate by anemic rats (31), several studies in human volunteers have shown it to be less well absorbed than ferrous sulfate when fed either as pharmacological preparations or used to fortify foods. Using erythrocyte incorporation of radioiron to measure iron absorption, Hahn et al. (32) reported a threefold higher iron absorption from 10 mg of iron as ferrous sulfate than as ferrous ammonium citrate and, after a review of several studies, it was concluded that humans absorb pharmacological doses of soluble ferrous iron about five times better than soluble ferric iron (33). More recently, the RBV of ferric ammonium citrate was reported to be only 23 in subjects administered 60 mg of radiolabeled iron supplements (34). In fortified foods, isotopically labeled ferric ammonium citrate has been reported to have an RBV of 50–70. Layrisse et al. (35) used ferric ammonium citrate to fortify sugar added to soft drinks, and found it to be about 70% as well absorbed as native food iron in two separate studies. Similarly, when ferric ammonium citrate was used to fortify fish sauce, which was fed to volunteers with rice and vegetable soup, iron was only 50% as well absorbed as from the same meal fortified with ferrous sulfate (13). The lower absorption of soluble ferric iron compared to soluble ferrous iron is presumably related to the more ready formation of insoluble, unabsorbable ferric hydroxides in the duodenum. This may perhaps be prevented by the addition of ascorbic acid to the iron fortified food.

Category 2: Poorly water soluble iron compounds which are soluble in dilute acid

Ferrous fumarate

Ferrous fumarate has been used mostly to fortify cereal based complementary foods for young children, but it has also been added to maize flour in Venezuela with some success (36) and to chocolate drinks (9). It is, however, a dark red color and may cause sensory problems in some applications. Because of its insolubility in water it causes fewer sensory changes than ferrous sulfate. It does not cause fat oxidation during storage of cereal based complementary foods, but may cause color changes during preparation for feeding, particularly if fruits are present. Similarly, if added to chocolate drink powders, which are reconstituted with boiling water, sufficient iron may dissolve to cause color changes (37). In radio and stable isotope studies, ferrous fumarate has been reported to have a similar RBV to ferrous sulfate in adults (12, 37-40). When making the recommendations for the choice of iron fortificant for infant foods, it has been assumed that ferrous fumarate will also be as well absorbed as ferrous sulfate. Two recent studies in infants and young children, however, have cast doubt on the use of ferrous fumarate for complementary food fortification (41, 42), at least at the currently used fortification level. In young children in Mexico and Bangladesh, many with low iron status, the RBV of ferrous fumarate was only 30–35% that of

ferrous sulfate. One would imagine that ferrous fumarate could still be a useful iron compound to fortify complementary foods, provided that the level of iron and ascorbic acid is adjusted so that the amount of iron absorbed is sufficient to meet the child's needs. The reasons for lower iron absorption from ferrous fumarate than from ferrous sulfate in young children are unclear. Lower gastric acid secretion has been suggested (41) although poor iron status is another possibility (15), with iron absorption from ferrous sulfate being upregulated to a greater extent than from ferrous fumarate. In a recent stable isotope study from Mexico, iron absorption from ferrous fumarate and ferrous sulfate were similar in women, preschool children and infants fed a maize based complementary food (Harrington et al., unpublished).

Ferrous succinate

Ferrous succinate, like ferrous fumarate, is insoluble in water but readily soluble in dilute acids. It has the advantage of being a pale brownish yellow color but, unlike ferrous fumarate, it has not been widely used for food fortification. It has been suggested for fortification of infant cereals and chocolate drinks (12, 37) and has shown equivalent bioavailability to ferrous sulfate in both rats and humans (12).

Category 3: Water insoluble compounds which are poorly soluble in dilute acid

Ferric pyrophosphate

This iron compound is an off-white, water insoluble powder which causes few if any sensory changes when added to different food vehicles. It is widely used to fortify chocolate drink powders and has been used extensively to fortify cereal based complementary foods. Its RBV is reported to vary from 45–58 in rats and from 25–75 in humans (9). More recently, Fidler et al. (43) reported an RBV of 36% for ferric pyrophosphate fed in a fortified infant cereal to young women and, in a stable isotope study in infants, fractional iron absorption from ferric pyrophosphate added to a wheat-soy complementary food was also about one third of iron absorption from ferrous fumarate (44). The variability in the RBV could be due to several factors. These include the physical characteristics of the compound and the composition of the meal. Both can influence the dissolution of iron in the gastric juice. In addition, it has been proposed that ferrous sulfate absorption may be more influenced by phytate and ascorbic acid than ferric pyrophosphate absorption (15, 43), and that iron deficient individuals may upregulate absorption from ferrous sulfate to a greater extent than from ferric pyrophosphate (15). Any factor which influences iron absorption from ferrous sulfate in a different way than iron absorption from ferric pyrophosphate will influence the RBV value of ferric pyrophosphate.

Despite these uncertainties, and despite a lower absorption than from ferrous sulfate, ferric pyrophosphate has proven efficacious in improving the iron status of schoolchildren fed iron fortified salt (45) and iron fortified extruded rice (46) when added at an increased level of fortification. A breakthrough in food fortification was the iron fortification of extruded rice grains with small particle size ferric pyrophosphate, without causing adverse color formation (22). The extruded grains were not detectable from normal rice grains, and were mixed 1:50 with normal grains and fed as part of a school lunch program to children in Bangalore, India (46). The children, aged 4–14 years, were consuming 4–7 mg iron/day in a diet estimated to be at 10% iron bioavailability. According to WHO (1), these children should consume 15–17 mg iron/day to have a 4% probability of inadequacy. Thus, it was necessary to provide an extra 10 mg iron/day in fortified food. As ferric pyrophosphate with an RBV of about 50 was used as the iron fortificant, the level of fortification was increased to provide 20 mg extra iron per day. A seven month long randomized double blind efficacy trial was made in two groups of 90

schoolchildren. They were fed the iron fortified rice for lunch six days per week and iron status was monitored with serum ferritin, CRP, serum transferrin receptor, and hemoglobin. All the children were dewormed, and the prevalence of iron deficiency in the dewormed control children decreased from around 80% to 50%. The prevalence of iron deficiency in the dewormed children receiving the iron fortified rice decreased from 80% to 25%, significantly lower (P<0.01) than the control children.

In this study and in the salt study of Zimmermann et al. (45), the pyrophosphate was ground to reduce its particle size from around 20 μm to 2.5 μm, and was added to the food vehicle at a twofold higher concentration to allow for its lower RBV. It is unlikely that the grinding of the ferric pyrophosphate had any significant effect on its bioavailability, as in rat studies the RBV value of the 2.5 μm ground ferric pyrophosphate was 69, compared to 59 for the regular pyrophosphate (P>0.05) (47). In the same study, micronized, dispersible ferric pyrophosphate with a particle size of 0.5 μm had an RBV of 95.

Micronized, dispersible ferric pyrophosphate (MDFP)

This innovative compound (SunActive iron, Taiyo Kagaku, Japan) is produced from ferric chloride and sodium pyrophosphate, using a dispersion technique which results in a particle size of approximately 0.3 μm. By adding emulsifiers, the formation of agglomerates is prevented and the aqueous form can be added to liquid food products such as milks and beverages with few sensory problems. A dried form is also available. MDFP has been reported to have a similar bioavailability to ferrous sulfate in hemoglobin repletion studies in rats (47, 48), and in human studies was reported to have an RBV of 93 in a yoghurt drink and 83 in a cereal based complementary food, although neither was significantly different from ferrous sulfate (2). It is suggested that the small particle size of MDFP causes it to dissolve more readily in gastric juice. The demonstration that ascorbic acid enhances iron absorption from MDFP (2) confirms that this iron compound dissolves in the gastric juice. In this recent study, the RBV of an experimental MDFP, with a particle size of 0.8 μm, was 62 in a wheat-milk complementary food, decreased to 39 on addition of ascorbic acid and was only 15 when added to a rice meal (46). The interesting observation from these studies is that iron absorption from MDFP varied from 2–4%, whereas iron absorption from ferrous sulfate varied from 3% in the wheat meals to 12% in the rice meals, being more influenced by both meal composition and the iron status of the subject. In the rice meals, due to the changes in ferrous sulfate absorption, the RBV of MDFP varied from around 15 in subjects of low iron status to almost 100 in subjects of normal iron status. This study indicates that, although RBV values of MDFP (and perhaps other poorly soluble iron compounds) can be variable, their absorption is relatively constant. Therefore, when designing a fortified food, the expected level of absorption, and not the RBV, should be considered. MDFP would seem a useful iron compound for liquid milk products and beverages, and has been recommended for this purpose by WHO (1).

Ferric orthophosphate

This compound would appear to be similar to ferric pyrophosphate both in color and solubility, and has been used to fortify infant foods, chocolate drinks and salt (8). Although much less studied, somewhat lower RBV values have been reported for ferric orthophosphate than for ferric pyrophosphate. Harrison et al. (49) tested five commercial samples in studies with rats, and reported RBV values varying from 6–46. In a study with infants fed fortified infant cereal, Rios et al. (50) reported an RBV of 26, which is similar to the value of 31 found by Cook et al. (51) when feeding adults isotopically labeled ferric orthophosphate baked into bread rolls.

Elemental iron compounds

Even though elemental iron powders have been used to fortify wheat flour for more than 50 years, it was not until recently that certain forms of elemental iron were shown to be efficacious fortificants in this vehicle (52). This study, made in Thailand, was the first fortification efficacy trial to use the body iron method of Cook et al. (53) to monitor iron status. The study was a randomized double blind controlled trial in 330 women of child bearing age with serum ferritin <25 μg/L. The women, working in clothing factories, were divided into four groups and, at break time six days per week over 35 weeks, they consumed a wheat flour snack fortified with 12 mg iron as either ferrous sulfate, electrolytic iron, H-reduced iron, or with no iron. The mean baseline body iron status of the women was 1.0–1.5 mg/kg body weight. This increased to 5.3 mg/kg body weight in the women consuming the snack fortified with ferrous sulfate, 4.2 mg/kg body weight in the women consuming the snack fortified with electrolytic iron, and 3.2 mg/kg body weight in the women consuming the snack fortified with H-reduced iron. There was no change in the body iron status in the women consuming the non iron fortified snack. The relative efficacy of electrolytic iron was 79% and H-reduced iron was 49%. The electrolytic iron powder was A131, and the H-reduced iron powder was AC-325, both compounds from North American Höganäs, Pennsylvania, USA.

The quantity of iron added to a fortified food is fundamental to the success of a program. Adding too little iron will not lead to an improvement of iron status, as will not conducting the efficacy study for a sufficient length of time. This is demonstrated by a recent study in which iron deficient schoolchildren (serum ferritin <20 μg/L) were fed electrolytic iron fortified bread containing an average of 3.7 mg iron on school days. No improvement in iron status was found after 7.5 months, which included only 137 days (circa 20 weeks) of feeding (54). The length of the study was shorter than previous studies and the amount of iron per day about one third that fed in studies which reported an improvement in iron status (45, 52, 55). The authors failed to take into account that electrolytic iron is only about half as well absorbed as ferrous sulfate, and that its level of fortification should be increased accordingly (10).

There are many elemental iron powders, manufactured by five different manufacturing procedures. These powders are mostly used for molding components of cars, such as gear wheels, and those supplied to the food industry have not been specifically manufactured for the purpose of food fortification. Food manufactures should therefore check carefully the origin of the elemental iron powders supplied for food fortification. Of the five types of elemental iron powders that are manufactured, WHO (1) recommends only the use of electrolytic iron powder. H-reduced iron and carbonyl iron powders were considered to require further study. Atomized iron (Quebec Metal Powders) and carbon monoxide-reduced iron were not recommended because of their much lower RBV (3, 56). These recommendations were largely based on a SUSTAIN Task Force report on the usefulness of elemental iron for cereal flour fortification (10). This report was based a review of in vitro studies, rat assays, human bioavailability studies with isotopically labeled compounds, and efficacy studies monitoring iron status in human subjects. It was concluded that, at the present time, only electrolytic iron powder can be recommended as an iron fortificant. As it is only approximately half as well absorbed as ferrous sulfate, it was recommended that the amount added should provide double the amount of iron. This conclusion for electrolytic iron was based on the following evidence: an improvement in iron status of infants consuming an electrolytic iron fortified infant cereal (57); a human bioavailability study with radiolabeled electrolytic iron having similar but not identical characteristics to the commercial powders, having an absorption of 75% of that of ferrous sulfate (58); and a series of

rat hemoglobin repletion studies with electrolytic iron powders similar to those being marketed today showing an RBV approximately 50% of that of ferrous sulfate. As with ferric pyrophosphate, ascorbic acid enhances iron absorption from electrolytic iron to a lesser extent than from ferrous sulfate (59).

Category 4: Iron chelates

Amino acid chelates

Ferrous bisglycinate is the major amino acid chelate produced commercially, although ferrous trisglycinate and ferric glycinate are also available. A patented ferrous bisglycinate compound, manufactured by Albion Laboratories, Utah, USA, has been used in most published studies. The chelate is reported to be formed by two glycine molecules combining with ferrous iron in a double heterocyclic ring structure (60). Evidence would suggest that iron is protected from inhibitors by the structure, since iron absorption is one to 3.5 times higher than from ferrous sulfate when added to bread rolls and milk products containing inhibitors such as phytate and calcium (17). Ferrous bisglycinate is more bioavailable than ferrous trisglycinate (61).

Amino acid chelates are recommended for milk and beverage products (1). Ferrous bisglycinate has Generally Recognized as Safe (GRAS) status but is relatively expensive and readily promotes fat oxidation in cereal foods (62) unless an anti-oxidant is added (63), and causes undesirable color reactions in some foods. Four non controlled efficacy studies with ferrous bisglycinate fortified foods have reported a marked decrease in the prevalence of anemia or iron deficiency anemia in children or adolescents. Three studies made in Brazil reported good efficacy in fortified liquid milk (64), sweetened bread rolls (65) and a whey based beverage (66), and a fourth study in Saudi Arabia reported good efficacy in an iron fortified flavored milk drink (67). Recently, ferrous bisglycinate fortified bread made from high extraction flour resulted in small but significant increases in both hemoglobin and serum ferritin when fed in a randomized controlled design to South African schoolchildren (54). A longer feeding period with higher iron concentrations would probably have given more impressive results. The influence of ferrous bisglycinate on stored flour was not investigated in this study. The main disadvantage of ferrous bisglycinate is its high cost. A recent cost analysis showed the cost of ferrous bisglycinate, taking bioavailability into account, to be 7–18 times that of ferrous sulfate (68).

NaFeEDTA

Evidence suggests that NaFeEDTA is a highly effective iron fortificant, being two to four times better absorbed than ferrous sulfate from inhibitory meals (16), and causing fewer organoleptic problems than freely water soluble compounds. Its recent acceptance by the Joint FAO/WHO Expert Committee on Food Additives (JECFA) for use in supervised food fortification programs where iron deficiency anemia is endemic (5) has led to two large iron fortification programs in China with soy sauce and wheat flour, and an upcoming wheat flour fortification program in Pakistan. The compound was recently awarded GRAS status in the United States.

EDTA binds strongly to iron at the pH level of gastric juice, and then exchanges ferric iron for other metals as the pH rises in the duodenum. In this way, it protects iron from phytate and polyphenol binding in the stomach and releases it for absorption in the duodenum (69). Such properties make it an ideal fortificant for high phytate cereal flours. In addition, it is highly useful in fermented sauces such as fish or soy, where most soluble compounds cause peptide precipitation in storage. In whole grain wheat flour rolls, iron absorption from NaFeEDTA was 4%, compared to only 1% with ferrous sulfate, whereas in wheat rolls made from low extraction flour, the corresponding values were

12% and 6% (38). On the other hand, iron absorption from ferrous sulfate or NaFeEDTA was similar to low phytate meals such as white rice and vegetables (70). Unlike ferrous bisglycinate, NaFeEDTA does not appear to cause fat oxidation reactions in stored cereal flours (71).

The cost of iron fortification with NaFeEDTA, adjusted for bioavailability, was estimated as being 5–15 times higher than ferrous sulfate (68), so it is somewhat less expensive than ferrous bisglycinate. It can, however be degraded in some liquid products by ultraviolet rays from the sun. Fidler et al. (72) reported 35% losses of EDTA from NaFeEDTA fortified fish sauce stored in clear class bottles under daily sunlight for 2–6 weeks. It has, however, been consistently shown to improve the iron status of targeted populations when added to a variety of condiments. These include fish sauce in Thailand (73) and Vietnam (74, 75), sugar in Guatemala (76), curry powder in South Africa (77) and soy sauce in China (78), although there has been no demonstration yet of its efficacy when added to cereal flours. In addition, it is not recommended for cereal based complementary foods for children less than three years of age, because the amount required to supply sufficient iron would approach or surpass the acceptable daily intake for iron as NaFeEDTA, of 0.2 mg/kg body weight/day. A way around this restraint might be a mixture of ferrous sulfate and NaFeEDTA, as lower molar ratios of EDTA to iron also strongly enhance iron absorption (79).

Encapsulated iron compounds

Microencapsulation is a process whereby the iron compound is encapsulated with a continuous layer of coating material that separates it physically from the food matrix. Its main advantage is that it should allow the addition of iron compounds of high relative bioavailability, such as ferrous sulfate and ferrous fumarate, to difficult food vehicles such as cereal flours or salt without causing any adverse sensory changes. Encapsulated iron compounds are suitable for most dry products such as infant foods, dry beverage mixes, condiment sachets and Sprinkles sachets for mixing with complementary foods. As they protect against fat oxidation, they are recommended for cereal flour fortification (1), however, widespread use in wheat flour fortification is prevented at the present time by the large size of the capsules, which are removed during the final sieving process.

The coatings are commonly hydrogenated palm oil or hydrogenated soy bean oil, although maltodextrin and celluloses have also been used. The hydrogenated oils protect against moisture but melt at 52–70 °C, and the released iron may then cause adverse color reactions. Maltodextrin and the celluloses are water soluble, and offer less protection against adverse color reactions or against lipid oxidation during storage if moisture is present. When the ratio of the coating material to the iron compound is close to 1:1, there is no change in the bioavailability of ferrous sulfate in rat assays (12). Ferrous sulfate encapsulated in hydrogenated soy bean oil added to salt (1:1) was efficacious in improving the iron status of Moroccan schoolchildren (55) and [57]Fe-labeled ferrous fumarate added (40:60) with Sprinkles to a maize based complementary food was well absorbed by infants (80). Amounts of coating material greater than 60:40, or the inclusion of other compounds, such as waxes, into the coating, may decrease bioavailability (4). Encapsulation increases the cost of ferrous sulfate from two to eightfold (68).

ENHANCING THE BIOAVAILABILITY OF FORTIFICATION IRON

Addition of ascorbic acid

Ascorbic acid is the most commonly added compound for the enhancement of iron absorption from iron fortified foods. It is routinely added to infant formulas and commercial infant cereals, to iron fortified chocolate drink powders and a variety of dietetic products. It enhances the absorption of fortification iron (with the exception of the chelates) and intrinsic food iron in a dose dependent way (81). The enhancing effect has been attributed to its reducing and chelating properties during the digestion of the food (82). The addition of ascorbic acid overcomes the negative effects of all major inhibitors of iron absorption, including phytate, polyphenols (83), calcium and casein from milk products (84), and can increase iron absorption two to threefold, although recent studies indicate that insoluble iron compounds such as elemental iron and ferric pyrophosphate are less enhanced by ascorbic acid than ferrous sulfate (43, 59). A 2:1 molar ratio of ascorbic acid to iron is recommended for low phytate products and powdered milk, and a 4:1 ratio is recommended for high phytate products (85).

The use of ascorbic acid as an enhancing agent is limited by its instability in aqueous solutions, during storage of powdered foods, and during prolonged heat processing or cooking. Adequate packaging to exclude oxygen can help preserve ascorbic acid during storage, however, almost all will be destroyed during heat treatments such as baking or during preparation for consumption if extensive cooking is required (e.g. non precooked cereal based complementary foods). A possible solution is the use of ascorbyl palmitate, a synthetic ester composed of palmitic acid and ascorbic acid. This compound is thermostable and its reductive and vitamin properties are reported to be maintained during baking (86). When baked with ferrous sulfate into bread, it increased iron absorption in women from 10.5% to 14.6% at a 2:1 molar ratio, and to 20.2% at a 4:1 molar ratio (87).

Addition of erythorbic acid

Erythorbic acid is a stereoisomer of ascorbic acid which appears to have a better enhancing effect on iron absorption but to be more sensitive to oxidation (88). It has strong reducing properties and is a common additive in processed foods (89), but has limited antiscorbutic activity in guinea pigs (90). Its antiscorbutic activity in humans has not been investigated. When added to a ferrous sulfate fortified cereal porridge, iron absorption by women increased from 4.1% to 10.8% at a 2:1 molar ratio, and to 18.8% at a 4:1 molar ratio (91). The addition of ascorbic acid to the same meal at a 4:1 molar ratio increased iron absorption from 4.1% to 11.7%. Although erythorbic acid was 1.6 fold more potent as an enhancer of iron absorption than ascorbic acid (P<0.0002) in this study, its lack of antiscorbutic activity and sensitivity to oxidation may limit its usefulness in iron fortification programs.

Addition of other organic acids

With the possible exception of fruit drinks, the addition of other organic acids does not appear to be an option, as the large quantities of organic acids which are required to enhance iron absorption will cause unacceptable flavor changes in most vehicles (92). Although citric, lactic, tartaric and malic acids do enhance iron absorption and are commonly used food additives, they effectively enhance iron absorption only at molar ratios in excess of 100:1. One gram or more of citric, malic or tartaric acid was necessary to increase iron absorption by two to threefold, from 3 mg ferrous sulfate iron added to a rice meal (93).

Addition of EDTA complexes

Na_2EDTA and $CaNa_2EDTA$ are permitted food additives and could be used as enhancers of fortification iron absorption. Na_2EDTA has been demonstrated to substantially increase iron absorption in human subjects from a ferrous sulfate fortified rice meal (79) and from a ferrous sulfate fortified wheat-soy infant cereal (38) even at molar ratios below 1:1. However, unlike with NaFeEDTA, the mixture of ferrous sulfate and Na_2EDTA promoted fat oxidation reactions in stored wheat flour (71). Unfortunately, Na_2EDTA does not appear to increase the absorption of the more insoluble iron compounds that cause fewer organoleptic problems. Na_2EDTA at a 1:1 molar ratio did not increase iron absorption in adolescent girls consuming ferrous fumarate fortified tortillas (94), or by adults consuming either a ferrous fumarate or a ferric pyrophosphate fortified cereal porridge (38, 40), or an elemental iron fortified breakfast cereal (95).

Phytic acid degradation

Phytic acid in cereal and legume based foods is a potent inhibitor of iron absorption from iron fortification compounds and from native food iron (96). It can, however, be degraded in an aqueous environment by the addition of exogenous phytases or by the activation of native phytases in the cereal grains under controlled pH and temperature conditions (97). To obtain a meaningful increase in iron absorption, it is necessary to achieve near complete degradation of phytate from meals containing few or no enhancers of iron absorption (98, 99) although, when enhancers of iron absorption are present in a meal, even a 50% phytate reduction can considerably improve iron absorption (100).

Low cost cereal and legume based complementary foods would be appropriate foods for dephytinization, as it is usually not possible to add ascorbic acid to these products without expensive packaging. In single meal studies, complete dephytinization of cereal porridges with added phytase under controlled temperature and pH conditions increased fractional iron absorption from two to twelvefold (101). In such porridges, with no enhancers of iron absorption, it has been recommended that the phytate to iron molar ratio should be reduced to <1:1 and, if possible, to <0.4:1 (85). When commercial phytases are not available, native cereal phytases can be activated by a similar wet processing methodology. Egli et al. (102) screened 26 cereals, pseudocereals, legumes and oilseeds for phytase activity.

Legumes and oilseeds had low phytase activity, as did sorghum, maize and rice. Rye, triticale, wheat, buckwheat and barley had the highest phytase levels and whole wheat, whole rye and buckwheat were considered useful sources of phytase for dephytinizing complementary foods. When 10% whole wheat or rye was added to a cereal and legume based complementary food mixture, phytate could be degraded completely after one to two hours of wet processing (103). While sophisticated industrial processing methods may be too expensive and complicated for developing countries, phytate degradation by traditional fermentation processes (104) or germination processes (105) would seem to be a possibility. In industrialized countries, it is probably simpler and less expensive to add ascorbic acid than to degrade phytate.

ENSURING THE EFFICACY OF IRON FORTIFIED FOODS

When designing an iron fortified food, the food manufacturer must choose the iron compound with the highest RBV that causes no sensory changes in the food vehicle. Cost may be an issue, and sensory trials checking for off colors and off flavors during storage of the fortified food or during the preparation of the meal should confirm the suitability of the compound. The level of fortification should be based on the needs of the consumer, the estimated or measured iron absorption and the consumption of the food vehicle by the target population. If the level of absorption is considered too low due to the presence of inhibitors such as phytic acid or polyphenols, ascorbic acid is the most suitable enhancer of iron absorption that can be added to iron fortified foods. The iron chelates NaFeEDTA and ferrous bisglycinate are also possible, as is the dephytinization of the food using added or native phytases. If an insoluble iron compound of lower RBV is chosen as the fortificant, it is essential that the level of fortification is increased accordingly.

Several studies have been made in recent years which have to a large extent followed the WHO guidelines both for the choice of food fortification compounds and for the choice of the methods to monitor iron status (1, 106). With only one exception, the iron fortified foods tested greatly improved the iron status of the target population. Two studies in Morocco with fortified salt clearly demonstrate how relative bioavailability of the iron compound can be linked to the efficacy of the iron fortified food (45, 55). In the first study (55), sensory studies demonstrated that ferrous sulfate encapsulated in hydrogenated soy bean oil was an acceptable fortification compound for the local salt. The dietary iron intake of schoolchildren consuming a diet based on wheat bread was 9–15 mg, and the iron bioavailability from the diet was estimated at 5%. Salt intake was 7–12 g/day. Based on this information, the fortification level was set at 1 mg iron/g salt so as to provide an extra 7–12 mg iron/day and an estimated 0.5 mg of extra absorbed iron per day. The salt was provided monthly to individual households and was added primarily to bread, bean paste and olives. The efficacy study was made by following schoolchildren from these households. It was a nine month randomized double blind controlled trial in two groups of 180 6–15 year old schoolchildren. Hemoglobin, serum ferritin, serum transferrin receptor and zinc protoporphyrin were measured at baseline, 20 weeks and 40 weeks. Iron deficiency anemia (IDA) was defined as low hemoglobin, and two out of three iron status parameters outside the normal range. After 40 weeks, IDA in the children consuming the iron fortified salt had decreased from 35% to 8% (P<0.001) with no significant change in IDA in the children receiving the nonfortified salt.

Although the Moroccan salt fortified with encapsulated ferrous sulfate was satisfactory from a sensory viewpoint during the dry season, it deve-loped a slight yellow color during the wet season. To overcome the color formation, the salt was fortified with ferric pyrophosphate, which was additionally ground to a mean particle size of about 2.5 μm (45). Because the RBV of ferric pyrophosphate is only about half that of ferrous sulfate both in rats (47) and humans (12, 37), the quantity of iron added to the salt was increased from 1 mg iron/g to 2 mg iron/g. The efficacy study was repeated exactly as before, but over 10 months in two groups of 80 6–15 year old school-children. IDA in the children receiving the forti-fied salt decreased from 30% at baseline to 5% after 10 months (P<0.001) with no significant changes in the group receiving the nonfortified salt.

Other recent studies which have shown good efficacy of iron fortified foods are studies with NaFeEDTA fortified fish sauce in Vietnam (74), elemental iron fortified wheat snacks in Thailand (52), and fortified extruded rice in India (46). In the fortified fish sauce study, young women con-suming a mean of 9 mg iron/day from a rice based diet of an estimated 10–15% iron bioavailability were provided daily with 10 mL fish sauce con-taining 1 mg iron/mL as NaFeEDTA. In a ran-domized double blind controlled trial, two groups of 60 anemic women factory workers consumed rice or noodles with vegetables and 10 mL fish sauce with or without iron six times per week for six months. IDA, defined as low hemoglobin plus either low ferritin or high transferrin receptor, decreased from around 70% to 20% in those women receiving the fortified sauce, with no change in the women receiving the nonfortified sauce.

Based on these studies, we can now claim that we know technically how to design an effective iron fortified food. The success of the program, however, depends not only on the iron fortified food. It depends on an efficient manufacturing and distribution system with well planned quality control and monitoring procedures, good social marketing, and especially on the nutritional status and general health of the target population. Efficacy may be blunted by other micronutrient deficiencies (107, 108) and by widespread infec-tions such as malaria or intestinal worms (109). In these situations, multiple micronutrient forti-fication and other public health measures to con-trol infections may be necessary before the iron fortification program is successful.

REFERENCES

1.   World Health Organization. Guidelines on food fortification with micronutrients. Geneva: World Health Organization, 2006.

2.   Fidler MC, Walczyk T, Davidsson L, et al. A micronised, dispersible ferric pyrophosphate with high relative bioavailability in man. Br J Nutr 2004;91:107–12.

3.   Swain JH, Newman SM, Hunt JR. Bioavailability of elemental iron powders to rats is less than bakery-grade ferrous sulfate and predicted by iron solubility and particle surface area. J Nutr 2003;133:3546–52.

4.   Zimmermann MB. The potential of encapsula-ted iron compounds in food fortification: a review. Int J Vitam Nutr Res 2004;74:453–461.

5.   FAO/WHO JECFA. Fifty-third meeting. Summary and conclusions. Geneva, 1999.

6.   Food and Nutrition Board, Institute of Medicine. Dietary reference intakes: applications for dietary assess-ment. Washington DC: National Academy Press, 2000.

7.   Institute of Medicine. Dietary reference intakes for vitamin A, vitamin K, arsenic, boron, chromium, copper, iodine, iron, manganese, molybdenum, nick-el, silicon, vanadium and zinc. Washington DC:

National Academy Press, 2001.

8.   Hurrell R. Types of iron fortificants. Nonelemental sources. In: Clydesdale F, Wiemer K, eds. Iron fortification of foods. Orlando: Academic Press, 1985:39–53.

9.   Hurrell R. Iron. In: Hurrell R, ed. The mineral fortification of foods. First ed. Surrey: Leatherhead Food RA, 1999:54–93.

10.   Hurrell R, Bothwell T, Cook JD, et al. The usefulness of elemental iron for cereal flour fortification: a SUSTAIN Task Force report. Sharing United States technology to aid in the improvement of nutrition. Nutr Rev 2002;60:391–406.

11.   Fritz JC, Pla GW, Roberts T, Boehne JW, Hove EL. Biological availability in animals of iron from common dietary sources. J Agr Food Chem 1970;18:647–51.

12.   Hurrell RF, Furniss DE, Burri J, Whittaker P, Lynch SR, Cook JD. Iron fortification of infant cereals: a proposal for the use of ferrous fumarate or ferrous succinate. Am J Clin Nutr 1989;49:1274–82.

13.   Walczyk T, Tuntipopipat S, Zeder C, Sirichakwal P, Wasantwisut E, Hurrell RF. Iron absorption by human subjects from different iron fortification compounds added to Thai fish sauce. Eur J Clin Nutr 2005; 59:668-74.

14.   Hallberg L, Brune M, Rossander L. Low bioavailability of carbonyl iron in man: studies on iron fortification of wheat flour. Am J Clin Nutr 1986;43:59–67.

15.   Moretti D, Zimmermann MB, Wegmuller R, Walczyk T, Zeder C, Hurrell RF. Iron status and food matrix strongly affect the relative bioavailability of ferric pyrophosphate in humans. Am J Clin Nutr 2006;83:632–8.

16.   Bothwell TH, MacPhail AP. The potential role of NaFeEDTA as an iron fortificant. Int J Vitam Nutr Res 2004;74:421–34.

17.   Hertrampf E, Olivares M. Iron amino acid chelates. Int J Vitam Nutr Res 2004;74:435–43.

18.   Cook JD, Reusser ME. Iron fortification: an update. Am J Clin Nutr 1983;38:648–59.

19.   Douglas FW, Rainey NH, Wong NP, Edmondson LF, LaCroix DE. Color, flavor, and iron bioavailability in iron-fortified chocolate milk. J Dairy Sci 1981;64:1785–93.

20.   Hurrell RF. Bioavailability of different iron compounds used to fortify formulas and cereals: technological problems. In: Stekel A, ed. Iron nutrition in infancy and childhood. New York: Raven Press, 1984:147–78.

21.   Rao BS. Salt. In: Clydesdale FM, Wiemer KL, eds. Iron fortification of foods. Orlando: Academic Press Inc., 1985:155–63.

22.   Moretti D, Lee TC, Zimmermann MB, Nuessli J, Hurrell RF. Development and evaluation of iron-fortified extruded rice grains. J Food Sci 2005;70:330–6.

23.   Brise H, Hallberg L. A method for comparative studies on iron absorption in man using two radio-iron isotopes. Acta Med Scand 1962;376:7–22.

24.   Saarinen UM, Siimes MA. Iron absorption from breast milk, cow's milk and iron-supplemented formula: an opportunistic use of changes in total body iron determined by hemoglobin, ferritin and body weight in 132 infants. Pediatr Res 1979;13:143–147.

25.   Kaltwasser J, Werner E. Bioavailability of iron enriched dietetic foods. INSERM 1983;113:309–20.

26.   Villalpando S, Shamah T, Rivera JA, Laria Y, Monterrubio E. Fortifying milk with ferrous gluconate and zinc oxide in a public nutrition program reduced the prevalence of anemia in toddlers. J Nutr 2006;136:2633–7.

27.   Demott BJ. Effects on flavor of fortifying milk with iron and absorption of the iron from intestinal tract of rats. J Dairy Sci 1971;54:1609–14.

28.   Theuer RC, Kemmerer KS, Martin WH, Zoumas BL, Sarett HP. Effect of processing on availability of iron salts in liquid infant formula products. Experimental soy isolate formulas. J Agric Food Chem 1971;19:555–8.

29.   Theuer RC, Martin WH, Wallander JF, Sarett HP. Effect of processing on availability of iron salts in liquid infant cereal formula products. Experimental milk-based formulas. J Agric Food Chem 1973;21:482–5.

30.   Borenstein B. Rationale for food fortification with vitamins, minerals and amino acids. CRC Crit Rev Food Technol 1971;2:171–86.

31.   Fritz JC, Pla GW. Vitamins and other nutrients.

Application of the animal hemoglobin repletion test to measurement of iron availability in foods. J Assoc Off Anal Chem 1972;55:1128–32.

32. Hahn PF, Jones E, Lowe RC, Meneely GR, Peacock WE. The relative absorption and utilization of ferrous and ferric iron in anemia as determined with the radioactive isotope. Am J Physiol 1945;143:191–202.

33. Heinrich HC, Gabbe EE, Bruggemann J, Oppitz KH. Effects of fructose on ferric and ferrous iron absorption in man. Nutr Metab 1974;17:236–48.

34. Gonzalez H, Mendoza C, Viteri FE. Absorption of unlabeled reduced iron of small particle size from a commercial source. A method to predict absorption of unlabeled iron compounds in humans. Arch Latinoam Nutr 2001;51:217–24.

35. Layrisse M, Martinez-Torres C, Renzi M. Sugar as a vehicle for iron fortification: further studies. Am J Clin Nutr 1976;29:274–9.

36. Garcia-Casal MN, Layrisse M. Iron fortification of flours in Venezuela. Nutr Rev 2002;60:26–9.

37. Hurrell RF, Reddy MB, Dassenko SA, Cook JD. Ferrous fumarate fortification of a chocolate drink powder. Br J Nutr 1991;65:271–83.

38. Hurrell RF, Reddy MB, Burri J, Cook JD. An evaluation of EDTA compounds for iron fortification of cereal-based foods. Br J Nutr 2000;84:903–10.

39. Davidsson L, Dimitriou T, Boy E, Walczyk T, Hurrell RF. Iron bioavailability from iron-fortified Guatemalan meals based on corn tortillas and black bean paste. Am J Clin Nutr 2002;75:535–9.

40. Fidler MC, Davidsson L, Zeder C, Walczyk T, Hurrell RF. Iron absorption from ferrous fumarate in adult women is influenced by ascorbic acid but not by Na2EDTA. Br J Nutr 2003;90:1081–5.

41. Sarker SA, Davidsson L, Mahmud H, et al. Helicobacter pylori infection, iron absorption, and gastric acid secretion in Bangladeshi children. Am J Clin Nutr 2004;80:149–53.

42. Perez-Exposito AB, Villalpando S, Rivera JA, Griffin IJ, Abrams SA. Ferrous sulfate is more bioavailable among preschoolers than other forms of iron in a milk-based weaning food distributed by PROGRESA, a national program in Mexico. J Nutr 2005;135:64–9.

43. Fidler MC, Davidsson L, Zeder C, Walczyk T, Marti I, Hurrell RF. Effect of ascorbic acid and particle size on iron absorption from ferric pyrophosphate in adult women. Int J Vitam Nutr Res 2004;74:294–300.

44. Davidsson L, Kastenmayer P, Szajewska H, Hurrell RF, Barclay D. Iron bioavailability in infants from an infant cereal fortified with ferric pyrophosphate or ferrous fumarate. Am J Clin Nutr 2000;71:1597–602.

45. Zimmermann MB, Wegmueller R, Zeder C, et al. Dual fortification of salt with iodine and micronized ferric pyrophosphate: a randomized, double-blind, controlled trial. Am J Clin Nutr 2004;80:952–9.

46. Moretti D, Zimmermann MB, Muthayya S, et al. Extruded rice fortified with micronized ground ferric pyrophosphate reduces iron deficiency in Indian schoolchildren: a double-blind randomized controlled trial. Am J Clin Nutr 2006;84:822–9.

47. Wegmüller R, Zimmermann MB, Moretti D, Arnold M, Langhans W, Hurrell RF. Particle size reduction and encapsulation affect the bioavailability of ferric pyrophosphate in rats. J Nutr 2004;134:3301–4.

48. Sakaguchi N, Rao TP, Nakata K, Nanbu H, Juneja LR. Iron absorption and bioavailability in rats of micronized dispersible ferric pyrophosphate. Int J Vitam Nutr Res 2004;74:3–9.

49. Harrison BN, Pla GW, Clark GA, Fritz JC. Selection of iron sources for cereal enrichment. Cereal Chem 1976;53:78–84.

50. Rios E, Hunter RE, Cook JD, Smith NJ, Finch CA. The absorption of iron as supplements in infant cereal and infant formulas. Pediatrics 1975;55:686–93.

51. Cook JD, Minnich V, Moore CV, Rasmussen A, Bradley WB, Finch CA. Absorption of fortification iron in bread. Am J Clin Nutr 1973;26:861–72.

52. Zimmermann MB, Winichagoon P, Gowachirapant S, et al. Comparison of the efficacy of wheat-based snacks fortified with ferrous sulfate, electrolytic iron, or hydrogen-reduced elemental

iron: randomized, double-blind, controlled trial in Thai women. Am J Clin Nutr 2005;82:1276–82.

53. Cook JD, Flowers CH, Skikne BS. The quantitative assessment of body iron. Blood 2003;135:452-8.

54. van Stuijvenberg ME, Smuts CM, Wolmarans P, Lombard CJ, Dhansay MA. The efficacy of ferrous bisglycinate and electrolytic iron as fortificants in bread in iron-deficient schoolchildren. Brit J Nutr 2006;95:532–8.

55. Zimmermann MB, Zeder C, Chaouki N, Saad A, Torresani T, Hurrell RF. Dual fortification of salt with iodine and microencapsulated iron: a randomized, double-blind, controlled trial in Moroccan schoolchildren. Am J Clin Nutr 2003;77:425–32.

56. Hoppe M, Hulthen L, Hallberg L. The relative bioavailability in humans of elemental iron powders for use in food fortification. Eur J Nutr 2006;45:37–44.

57. Walter T, Dallman PR, Pizarro F, et al. Effectiveness of iron-fortified infant cereal in prevention of iron deficiency anemia. Pediatrics 1993;91:976–82.

58. Forbes AL, Adams CE, Arnaud MJ, et al. Comparison of in vitro, animal, and clinical determinations of iron bioavailability: International Nutritional Anemia Consultative Group Task Force report on iron bioavailability. Am J Clin Nutr 1989;49:225–38.

59. Swain JH, Johnson LK, Hunt JR. An irradiated electrolytic iron fortificant is poorly absorbed by humans and is less responsive than FeSO4 to the enhancing effect of ascorbic acid. J Nutr 2006;136:2167–74.

60. Ashmead HD, Graff DJ, Ashmead HH. Intestinal absorption of metal ions and chelates. Springfield, IL: Charles C. Thomas, 1985.

61. Bovell-Benjamin A, Viteri F, Allen L. Iron absorption from ferrous bisglycinate and ferric trisglycinate in whole maize is regulated by iron status. Am J Clin Nutr 2000;71:1563–9.

62. Bovell-Benjamin A, Allen L, Frankel E, Guinard J-X. Sensory quality and lipid oxidation of maize porridge as affected by iron amino acid chelates and EDTA. J Food Sci 1999;64:371–6.

63. Allen LH. Advantages and limitations of iron amino acid chelates as iron fortificants. Nutr Rev 2002;60:18–21; discussion 45.

64. Iost C, Name JJ, Jeppsen RB, DeWayne Ashmead H. Repleting hemoglobin in iron deficiency anemia in young children through liquid milk fortification with bioavailable iron amino acid chelate. J Am Coll Nutr 1998;17:187–94.

65. Giorgini E, Fisberg M, De Paula RAC, Ferreira AMA, Valle J, Braga JAP. The use of sweet rolls fortified with iron bis-glycinate chelate in the prevention of iron deficiency anemia in preschool children. Arch Latinoam Nutr 2001;51:48–53.

66. Miglioranza LH, Matsuo T, Caballero-Cordoba GM, et al. Effect of long-term fortification of whey drink with ferrous bisglycinate on anemia prevalence in children and adolescents from deprived areas in Londrina, Parana, Brazil. Nutrition 2003;19:419–21.

67. Osman AK, Al-Othaimeen A. Experience with ferrous bis-glycine chelate as an iron fortificant in milk. Int J Vitam Nutr Res 2002;72:257–63.

68. Moore W, Grant F, Kratky Z, et al. A model for calculating the cost of employing iron absorption enhancement strategies in fortification programs. Int J Vitam Nutr Res 2004;74:463–6.

69. INACG International Nutritional Anemia Consultative Group. Iron EDTA for food fortification. Washington DC: The Nutrition Foundation, 1993.

70. Fidler MC, Davidsson L, Walczyk T, Hurrell RF. Iron absorption from fish sauce and soy sauce fortified with sodium iron EDTA. Am J Clin Nutr 2003;78:274–8.

71. Hurrell RF. Preventing iron deficiency through food fortification. Nutr Rev 1997;55:210–22.

72. Fidler MC, Krzystek A, Walczyk T, Hurrell RF. Photostability of NaFeEDTA in stored fish sauce and soy sauce. J Food Sci 2004;96:380–3.

73. Garby L, Areekul S. Iron supplementation in Thai fish-sauce. Ann Trop Med Parasitol 1974;68:467–76.

74. Thuy PV, Berger J, Davidsson L, et al. Regular consumption of NaFeEDTA-fortified fish sauce improves iron status and reduces the prevalence of anemia in anemic Vietnamese women. Am J Clin Nutr 2003;78:284–90.

75. Van Thuy P, Berger J, Nakanishi Y, Khan NC, Lynch S, Dixon P. The use of NaFeEDTA-fortified fish sauce is an effective tool for controlling iron deficiency in women of childbearing age in rural Vietnam. J Nutr 2005;135:2596–601.

76. Viteri FE, Alvarez E, Batres R, et al. Fortification of sugar with iron sodium ethylenedi-aminotetraacetate (FeNaEDTA) improves iron status in semirural Guatemalan populations. Am J Clin Nutr 1995;61:1153–63.

77. Ballot DE, MacPhail AP, Bothwell TH, Gillooly M, Mayet FG. Fortification of curry powder with NaFe(III)EDTA in an iron-deficient population: report of a controlled iron-fortification trial. Am J Clin Nutr 1989;49:162–9.

78. Mannar V, Gallego EB. Iron fortification: country level experiences and lessons learned. J Nutr 2002;132:856–8.

79. MacPhail AP, Patel RC, Bothwell TH, Lamparelli RD. EDTA and the absorption of iron from food. Am J Clin Nutr 1994;59:644–8.

80. Tondeur WC, Schauer CS, Christofides AL, et al. Determination of iron absorption from intrinsically labeled microencapsulated ferrous fumarate (Sprinkles) in infants with different iron and hematologic status by using a dual-stable-isotope method. Am J Clin Nutr 2004;80:1436–44.

81. Cook J, Monsen E. Vitamin C, the common cold, and iron absorption. Am J Clin Nutr 1977;30:235–241.

82. Conrad ME, Schade SG. Ascorbic acid chelates in iron absorption: a role for hydrochloric acid and bile. Gastroenterology 1968;55:35–45.

83. Siegenberg D, Baynes RD, Bothwell TH, et al. Ascorbic acid prevents the dose-dependent inhibitory effects of polyphenols and phytates on nonheme-iron absorption. Am J Clin Nutr 1991;53:537–41.

84. Stekel A, Olivares M, Pizarro F, Chadud P, Lopez I, Amar M. Absorption of fortification iron from milk formulas in infants. Am J Clin Nutr 1986;43:917–22.

85. Hurrell RF. How to ensure adequate iron absorption from iron-fortified food. Nutr Rev 2002;60:7–15.

86. Mauro DJ, Wetzel DL, Seib PA, Hoseney RC. Determination of a surfactant (sodium 6-0-palmotyl-L-ascorbate) in bread by high performance liquid chromatography. Cereal Chem 1979;56:152–5.

87. Pizarro F, Olivares M, Hertrampf E, et al. Ascorbyl palmitate enhances iron bioavailability in iron-fortified bread. Am J Clin Nutr 2006;84:830–4.

88. Yourga FJ, Esselen WB, Fellers CR. Some antioxidant properties of D-iso ascorbic acid and sodium salt. Food Res 1944;9:188–96.

89. Rehwoldt R. Tracking the use of antioxidants through industry surveys. Food Chem Toxicol 1986;24:1039–41.

90. Fabianek J, Herp A. Antiscorbutic activity of D-araboascorbic acid. Proc Soc Exp Biol Med 1967;125:462–5.

91. Fidler MC, Davidsson L, Zeder C, Hurrell RF. Erythorbic acid is a potent enhancer of nonheme-iron absorption. Am J Clin Nutr 2004;79:99–102.

92. Hurrell RF, Lynch S, Bothwell T, et al. Enhancing the absorption of fortification iron - A SUSTAIN Task Force report. Int J Vitam Nutr Res 2004;74:387–401.

93. Gillooly M, Bothwell TH, Torrance JD, et al. The effects of organic acids, phytates and polyphenols on the absorption of iron from vegetables. Br J Nutr 1983;49:331–42.

94. Davidsson L, Walczyk T, Zavaleta N, Hurrell RF. Improving iron absorption from a Peruvian school breakfast meal by adding ascorbic acid or Na2EDTA. Am J Clin Nutr 2001;73:283–7.

95. Fairweather-Tait SJ, Wortley GM, Teucher B, Dainty J. Iron absorption from a breakfast cereal: effects of EDTA compounds and ascorbic acid. Int J Vitam Nutr Res 2001;71:117–22.

96. Hurrell RF. Influence of vegetable protein sources on trace element and mineral bioavailability. J Nutr 2003;133:2973–7.

97. Hurrell RF. Phytic acid degradation as a means of improving iron absorption. Int J Vitam and Nutr Res 2004;74:445–52.

98. Hallberg L, Rossander-Hulthen L, Gramatkovski E. Iron fortification of flour with a complex ferric orthophosphate. Am J Clin Nutr 1989;50:129–35.

99. Hurrell RF, Juillerat MA, Reddy MB, Lynch SR, Dassenko SA, Cook JD. Soy protein, phytate,

and iron absorption in humans. Am J Clin Nutr 1992;56:573–8.

100. Tuntawiroon M, Sritongkul N, Rossander-Hulten L, et al. Rice and iron absorption in man. Eur J Clin Nutr 1990;44:489–97.

101. Hurrell RF, Reddy MB, Juillerat MA, Cook JD. Degradation of phytic acid in cereal porridges improves iron absorption by human subjects. Am J Clin Nutr 2003;77:1213–9.

102. Egli I, Davidsson L, Juillerat MA, Barclay D, Hurrell RF. The influence of soaking and germination on the phytase activity and phytic acid content of grains and seeds potentially useful for complementary feeding. J Food Sci 2002;67:3484–8.

103. Egli I, Davidsson D, Juillerat MA, Barclay D, Hurrell R. Phytic acid degradation in complementary foods using phytase naturally occurring in whole grain cereals. J Food Sci 2003;68:1855–9.

104. Sharma A, Kapoor AC. Levels of antinutritional factors in pearl millet as affected by processing treatments and various types of fermentation. Plant Food Hum Nutr 1996;49:241–52.

105. Marero L, Payumo E, Aguinaldo A, Matsumoto I, Homma S. The antinutritional factors in weaning foods prepared from germinated legumes and cereals. Lebensm Wiss Technol 1991;24:177–81.

106. World Health Organization (WHO), Centers for Disease Control and Prevention (CDC). Assessing the iron status of populations. Geneva: World Health Organization, 2004:1–31.

107. Suharno D, West CE, Muhilal, Karyadi D, Hautvast JG. Supplementation with vitamin A and iron for nutritional amemia in pregnant women in West Java, Indonesia. Lancet 1993;342:1325–8.

108. Powers HJ. Riboflavin-iron interactions with particular emphasis on the gastrointestinal tract. P Nutr Soc 1995;54:509–17.

109. Wegmueller R, Fatoumata C, Zimmermann MB, Adou P, Hurrell RF. Salt dual fortified with iodine and micronized ground ferric pyrophosphate affects iron status but not hemoglobin in children in Côte d'Ivoire. J Nutr 2006;136:1–7.

110. Hurrell RF. Fortification: overcoming technical and practical barriers. J Nutr 2002;132:806–12.

8

Copper and zinc interactions in anemia: a public health perspective

Manuel Olivares[1]   Eva Hertrampf[1]   Ricardo Uauy[1,2]

[1]*Institute of Nutrition and Food Technology (INTA), University of Chile, Chile*
[2]*London School of Hygiene and Tropical Medicine, London University, United Kingdom*
Contact: molivare@inta.cl

MANUEL OLIVARES

Manuel obtained his MD from the University of Chile. He is currently Head of the Micronutrients Laboratory and Program for Micronutrients at the Institute of Nutrition and Food Technology (INTA) in Chile, as well as Professor of Pediatrics and Hematology at the University of Chile. Manuel has served as a consultant to the Pan American Health Organization, World Health Organization, UNICEF, International Atomic Energy Agency, Micronutrient Initiative, and Chilean Copper Commission (COCHILCO).

EVA HERTRAMPF DÍAZ

Eva obtained her MD and MSc in Human Nutrition from the University of Chile. She is currently an Associate Professor at the Institute of Nutrition and Food Technology (INTA) in Chile. Eva's special interest is the field of nutritional anemia and the prevention of iron and zinc deficiency in populations.

RICARDO UAUY

Ricardo obtained his PhD from the Massachusetts Institute of Technology, USA, and is a member of the Chilean Academy of Medicine. He is currently the Chair of Public Health Nutrition at the London School of Hygiene and Tropical Medicine, as well as being the President of the International Union of Nutrition Science (IUNS). Ricardo is one of the most eminent and distinguished scientists in international nutrition and a highly respected advisor to the UN, WHO, and FAO. His expertise includes basic nutritional science, applied biomedical research, and population based intervention programs. Ricardo was recently awarded the Chilean Presidential Award in Science for his research into the effects of fatty acids on gene expression during retinal and brain development.

COPPER AND ZINC IN RELATION TO ANEMIA

Copper metabolism

Copper is an essential nutrient that is important for appropriate functional, structural, and catalytic activity of cuproproteins. Most of them are enzymes that display oxidative-reductase activity in which copper is essential to the electron transfer process (1). Copper body content in humans relative to other trace minerals follows iron and zinc in importance. Total copper content of a 70 kg adult is around 110 mg (1). The brain and liver comprise only 5% of body weight, yet contain 25% of total body copper content (1). The major site of copper absorption is the duodenum, although a smaller fraction is also absorbed in the stomach and in the jejunum (2). The mechanisms by which copper is absorbed are not fully understood. There is evidence suggesting that at low dietary copper levels, absorption occurs by a saturable active transport mechanism, whereas at higher levels, passive diffusion plays a role (3). Both the copper transporter 1 (Ctr 1) and the divalent metal transporter 1 (DMT1) are involved in copper uptake by the enterocyte (4, 5). Within the enterocyte, copper is stored bound to metallothionein, and another fraction is delivered by chaperones to specific molecules (6). One of these molecules is ATP7A, or MNK (the protein defective in Menkes disease), which is involved in copper efflux in most cells, except the hepatocyte in which ATP7B, or WND (the protein defective in Wilson disease), performs this role (7, 8)

Copper is transferred from the intestinal mucosa to portal blood mainly as a copper-albumin complex. After liver uptake it is secreted from the liver into the bloodstream bound to ceruloplasmin (2). Biliary copper excretion is the main form of endogenous copper elimination (2). Only ~15% of the copper excreted in the bile is reabsorbed by the enterohepatic circulation. Apparent copper absorption may vary from 15 to 80%, with the usual range being 40 to 60%, and is determined by host and dietary related factors, some of which are not fully defined. Copper absorption is influenced by copper intake and by copper nutritional status (9, 10). When dietary copper is low, the fraction absorbed increases and endogenous losses decline, whereas the contrary occurs at high copper intake (9, 10). The evidence suggests that the up-regulation of absorption in response to a decrease in dietary copper intake is faster than the down-regulation in response to high intakes. The chemical form in which copper is found in the lumen markedly affects its absorption. As solubility of copper compounds increases, copper is absorbed more efficiently (11). Cow's milk, zinc, ascorbic acid, and phytates all diminish copper absorption, whereas animal protein, human milk, and histidine enhance absorption (3, 9, 11-13).

Copper deficiency

Acquired copper deficiency is a clinical syndrome that occurs mainly in infants, although it has also been described in children and in adults. Copper deficiency is usually the consequence of low copper stores at birth, inadequate dietary copper intake, poor absorption, and elevated requirements induced by rapid growth or increased copper losses (14). The multiple factors that condition deficiency commonly coexist in copper-deficient subjects. Copper deficiency is more frequent in preterm infants (15), especially of very low birth weight, due to their reduced copper stores at birth and given the smaller relative size of the liver and higher requirements determined by their faster growth. Infants fed exclusively cow's milk-based diets are more prone to develop copper deficiency because of its low copper content and its limited absorption in that matrix (13). In contrast, breast-fed infants absorb more copper (13), perhaps due to the lower casein content of human milk or to absortion-enhancing factors present in human milk. In developing countries, where infant feeding is often based on cow's milk and enriched with a high concentration of refined

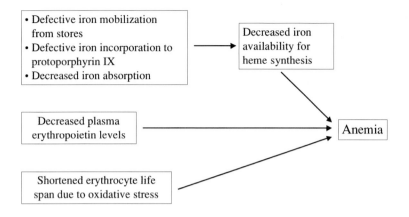

Figure 8.1: Potential mechanisms by which copper deficiency can induce anemia.

carbohydrates, copper deficit may be more preva-lent since fructose and other refined sugars lower copper absorption. Copper deficiency has also been reported in subjects with malabsorption syn-dromes such as celiac disease, tropical and non-tropical sprue, cystic fibrosis, or short bowel syn-drome due to intestinal resection. Copper deficit should be suspected in infants with prolonged or recurrent diarrheal episodes, abnormal bile loss, intestinal resections, or loss of intestinal contents from intestinal fistula (14). High oral intakes of zinc and iron decrease copper absorption and may predispose to copper deficiency (16).

The available information indicates that the most common cause of overt, clinical copper defi-ciency is insufficient copper supply during the nutritional recovery of malnourished children (14, 17, 18). These infants present several factors that are frequently associated to copper defi-ciency. These include a history of low weight at birth with consequently low liver reserves; short duration of breast-feeding; consuming diets based on cow's milk and high-refined carbohydrates; increased losses of the nutrient due to diarrheal disease; and frequent/recurrent infections. During nutritional recovery, they may grow at 10 to 20 times the normal rate for their age, thus increasing the requirements imposed by tissue gain.

The Anemia of Copper Deficiency. Common clinical manifestations of acquired copper defi-ciency include anemia, neutropenia, and bone abnormalities (14, 17). Reported anemia and neu-tropenia prevalence in copper deficient infants was 92% and 84%, respectively (18). The hema-tological changes are characterized by anemia of variable hypochromia, with normocytic or macro-cytic red cells, and are accompanied by a reduced reticulocyte count, hypoferremia, neutropenia, and thrombocytopenia (14, 17-19). In a small number of cases there is a microcytic anemia. Megaloblatic changes, vacuolization of the ery-throid and myeloid progenitors, arrest in the matur-ation of myeloid precursors and the existence of ringed sideroblasts may be found upon examina-tion of the bone marrow (14).These alterations are fully reversed by copper supplementation and are unresponsive to iron therapy alone (17, 20).

It has been hypothesized that this anemia is due to a defective iron mobilization **(Figure 8.1)** resulting from reduced ceruloplasmin activity (14, 18, 21). This enzyme, through its ferroxidase action, is fundamental for the transformation of the Fe^{2+} to Fe^{3+} (22), a step indispensable for the incorporation of iron into the circulating transferrin. Reduced ceruloplasmin activity explains why iron remains trapped in the reticuloendothelial system and thus unavailable for erythropoiesis. In addition, there may also be a reduction in the synthesis of heme due to decreased activities of ferrochelatase, cytochrome c or both (23). These copper-dependent enzymes are critical for the reduction of Fe^{3+} to Fe^{2+} in the mitochondria and for the subsequent incorporation of iron into protoporphyrin IX.

Recently, an anchored homologue of ceruloplasmin, hephaestin, has been found in enterocytes and other cells. This molecule also plays a role in tissue iron efflux and therefore serves to regulate dietary iron absorption (24). Ferrous iron is transported across the basolateral membrane by ferroportin in a process coupled with hephaestin, responsible for oxidizing Fe^{2+} to Fe^{3+}. Copper-deficient rats have a decreased expression of ceruloplasmin in the liver, and, in the enterocytes, a decreased expression of hephaestin coupled with an increased expression of ferroportin. This translates into systemic iron deficiency and decreased iron absorption, thus accounting for the refractory nature of anemia and the lack of response to iron treatment (24, 25).

Additional mechanisms for the development of anemia in copper deficiency are presented in **Figure 8.1**. They include a reduction of the erythropoietin demonstrated in rodents and humans (14, 26, 27), and a decrease in erythrocyte copper/zinc superoxide dismutase, a key red cell antioxidant enzyme; this may shorten the life span of erythrocytes in response to oxidative stress induced by various causes (28).

Zinc metabolism

Zinc is ubiquitous within cells, thus limiting the study of zinc-dependent mechanisms that determine physiological functions. Its role in biology

is defined in three functional classes: a) catalytic, influencing properties of multiple enzyme systems and intracellular signaling; b) structural, constituting strong complexes with organic molecules, thereby enabling the structural modification of specific proteins, nucleic acids, and cellular membranes; and c) regulatory, affecting the level of expression of zinc-responsive transcription factors and specific genes. These roles explain why zinc plays a central role in cellular growth, differentiation, and metabolism. Zinc is especially important during periods of rapid growth, both pre- and postnatally for tissues such as those of the immune system and the gastrointestinal tract that undergo continuous cell renewal. Critical functions that are affected by zinc nutriture include pregnancy outcome, fetal growth and development, linear growth, susceptibility to infection, and neurobehavioral development, among others (29).

Zinc is absorbed into the body throughout the small intestine, which also regulates whole-body homeostasis through changes in both the fractional absorption of dietary zinc and excretion of endogenous zinc in gastrointestinal tract secretions. Absorption adapts to physiological needs, increasing during lactation and decreasing with aging. Stress conditions such as infectious disease may alter absorption efficiency. Intestinal excretion and urinary losses can also be affected by zinc status (29). Total body zinc content is 1.5 to 2.5 g. Approximately 90% of the zinc turns over slowly, and therefore is not readily available for metabolism. The remaining zinc comprises the so-called "rapidly exchangeable pool of zinc," which is thought to be particularly important in maintaining zinc-dependent functions. The size of this pool is sensitive to the amounts of zinc absorbed from the diet. A stable dietary influx is considered to be necessary to satisfy the normal requirements of zinc for maintenance and growth (30). The total content in the diet, zinc nutritional status, and bioavailability of zinc from food all influence the efficiency of its absorption. Zinc

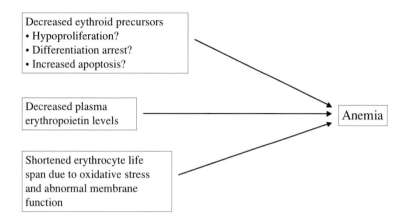

Figure 8.2: Potential mechanisms by which zinc deficiency can induce anemia.

absorption is determined largely by its solubility in the intestinal lumen, which in turn is affected by its chemical form and the presence of inhibitors or enhancers of uptake. An example of a specific inhibitor is phytate (inositol phosphate), which is present in many plants and binds zinc under conditions present in the intestinal lumen.

Zinc deficiency
The main causes of deficiency are low intake, increased requirements, malabsorption, increased losses, and impaired utilization. When intake of absorbable zinc is inadequate, diet-induced zinc deficiency occurs. Low intakes are exacerbated by life stage (infants, children, adolescents, and pregnant and lactating women) or pathological conditions (preterm birth, low birth weight, and diarrheal disorders) that increase zinc losses or enhance needs (31).

Anemia and zinc deficiency
The first descriptions of severely zinc-deficient subjects included an anemia as a presenting sign, possibly due to combined iron deficiency or to the specific effect of zinc on red cell maturation (32). Studies of animals deficient in zinc showed a reduction of bone marrow erythroid precursors and in plasma erythropoietin in mice and rats,

respectively (33–35). The mechanism by which zinc alters erythropoiesis is not fully understood **(Figure 8.2)**. Whether erythroid proliferation is compromised or there is an arrest on precursor differentiation with an increase in the rate of apoptosis requires further research. Alternatively, deficiency of this mineral may shorten the RBC lifespan since zinc is a cofactor for RBC-SOD contributing to protection from oxidative stress and to cell integrity (36, 37).

INTERACTIONS BETWEEN COPPER, ZINC AND IRON WITH ANEMIA AS AN ENDPOINT

Copper and zinc interaction affects iron's availability for erythropoeisis
Experimental studies performed in humans have shown an inhibitory effect of zinc on Fe absorption **(Figure 8.3)**. However, conflicting results have been obtained when this interaction has been evaluated using different delivery systems or food matrices. The negative interaction has been found solely when both microminerals were supplied in an aqueous or saline solution (38–41). However, the threshold dose at which zinc impairs iron absorption has not been well established. Mixed

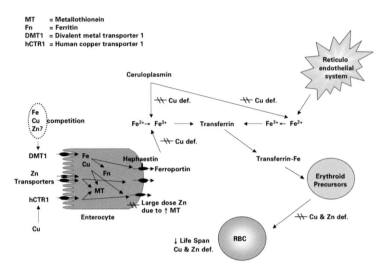

Figure 8.3: Potential mechanisms by which high-dose zinc supplementation could induce anemia. For further details and interpretation of the figure see body of chapter.

results were obtained in wheat flour co-fortified with Fe and zinc (42, 43). It has been proposed that zinc and Fe compete for a shared absorptive pathway. Thus, the negative interaction could be explained by a competitive binding to DMT1 (44). However, some recent studies performed in Caco-2 cells have questioned the role of DMT1 on zinc uptake (45). It has recently been postulated that iron and zinc compete for a common pathway other than DMT1, located in the apical membrane of the intestinal cell (46). We conclude that the mechanisms involved in the interaction between zinc and Fe at the absorption level are not fully understood. It has also been demonstrated that large doses of zinc inhibit copper absorption and may produce copper deficit, which indirectly could affect iron status leading to anemia **(Figure 8.3)** (16, 47, 48). However, a dose response curve for the effect of zinc has not been established at the usual level of exposure and it is unlikely that zinc conditions copper deficiency at low doses. However, zinc and copper have an antagonistic interaction within the enterocyte; this is mediated by their binding to metallothionein as a storage protein, a low-molecular-

weight cysteine-rich protein that has a higher capacity to bind copper than zinc (49). Metallothionein expression is regulated by dietary intake of zinc. When large doses of zinc are provided there is a mucosal block in copper transport and metallothionein expression is induced leading to a higher proportion of dietary copper being bound to metallothionein and stored within the enterocyte. Conversely, a lower fraction of copper is transferred to the plasma (50, 51). Copper bound to metallothionein lost in the gut through mucosal cell shedding may thus represent a protective mechanism to prevent toxicity from high copper exposure.

The public health relevance of these interactions may have been considered of limited relevance in the past. However recent studies have shown that combined Fe and zinc supplementation was less efficacious than single supplementation with Fe in reducing the prevalence of anemia and in improving Fe status (52–54). On the one hand, it should be noted that other studies have not confirmed this potentially detrimental effect (55–57). On the other hand, three studies performed in subjects presumably deficient in Fe and zinc demonstrated a larger increase in hemoglobin after combined Fe and zinc supplementation than with either Fe or zinc supplementation alone (58–60).

The role of copper and zinc in anemia of infectious disease

Acute infections are a well-recognized cause of mild to moderate anemia. Resistance to infections depends on healthy immune function. Zinc and copper are necessary for the normal function of the immune system (61). Nonspecific, cell-mediated and humoral immunity are depressed even in mild zinc deficiency (61–63). Main findings include a decrease in natural killer cell activity and depressed function of monocytes and macrophages and alteration of neutrophil phagocytosis. T and B lymphocyte counts (peripheral and central tissues) can be depressed and proliferative response to mitogens, TH1 cell and TH2 cell function, and cytokine production (interferon-β, tumor necrosis factor-α, interleukin-2) impaired (61–63). In addition to alterations to the immune system, zinc deficiency may also contribute to an increased susceptibility to pathogens by changing the morphology, integrity, and function of the intestinal and respiratory mucosa. Several studies have demonstrated an increased incidence of diarrhea and acute lower respiratory infection in zinc deficiency (64). Zinc supplementation improved immunity, reduced morbidity and mortality, and shortened the time to recovery from these acute infectious diseases (62–65). Additional studies suggest that zinc supplementation probably reduces the incidence of malaria (65). Lower rates of infectious diseases among infants born to zinc-supplemented mothers have been demonstrated (66). In vitro studies have suggested that zinc inhibits the replication and/or binding of several viruses to cells, yet there is no conclusive evidence that zinc deficiency increases the incidence, duration or severity of viral infections including common cold (64, 67) **(Figure 8.4)**. The immunosuppressive effect observed at very high doses of supplemental zinc may be explained in part by secondary copper deficiency induced by excess zinc (68).

Neutropenia is a frequent clinical manifestation of copper deficiency (14, 18, 24, 69). Studies in

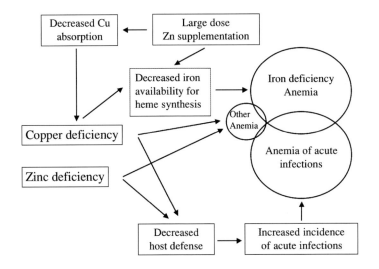

Figure 8.4: Potential mechanisms by which copper and zinc deficits could contribute to the occurrence of anemia.

humans have demonstrated that copper deficiency induces impaired phagocytic activity of neutrophils, decreases the proliferative response of peripheral blood mononuclear cells to mitogens, and reduces interleukin-2 production. It also restricts secretion of interleukin-2 receptors, a marker of early T cell activation (69–72). An increased frequency of severe lower respiratory infections has been described in copper-deficient infants (73).

In the developing world iron deficiency coexists with micronutrient deficiencies and infection, and zinc and copper deficiencies could be a contributor factor in the increased frequency of infections **(Figure 8.4)**, which would in turn contribute to infection-associated erythropoeisis impairment. Even mild infections that do not warrant medical attention induce a significant decrease in hemoglobin, serum iron, TIBC, and transferrin saturation, whereas free erythrocyte protoporhyrin and serum ferritin increase significantly (74, 75). Most of the laboratory changes in indices of iron nutrition persist for 2 to 3 weeks after the appearance of fever while some may become abnormal during the incubation period of the illness (74, 75). The modifications of laboratory indices of iron status are related to the severity of the infectious process. This knowledge has lead to the use of the serum transferrin receptor as an aid in the interpretation of iron status in individuals or populations with high frequency of acute infection since common minor acute infections do not modify this marker (76).

CONCLUSIONS AND RESEARCH NEEDS

1. Dietary copper deficit and genetic defects of copper metabolism have significant effects on iron metabolism and red cell resistance to oxidative stress and thus may contribute to the burden of anemia. Copper deficit should be included in the differential diagnosis of anemia unresponsive to iron supplementation. Copper excess may also contribute to anemia by inducing hemolysis.
2. Zinc deficit may contribute to the burden of anemia by altering erythropoiesis in the bone marrow or by decreasing red cell resistance to oxidative stress.
3. High-dose zinc supplementation interferes with copper and iron absorption. It may also interfere with iron mobilization and impair immune responses thus contributing to the anemia burden.
4. Both copper and zinc deficiency are associated with impaired host defenses and thus increase the burden of anemia secondary to infection.
5. The potential public health relevance of zinc and copper interactions with iron remains undefined. However, results of intervention trials to prevent anemia using iron supplementation in combination with zinc, or iron by itself, indicate the need to assess the significance of this possibility under different circumstances. In addition to considering the significant effects of copper and zinc intake on childhood infections, it is important to assure nutritional adequacy of these metals in order to maximize the possibility of iron being effective in preventing anemia.

REFERENCES

1. Uauy R, Olivares M, González M. Essentiality of copper in humans. Am J Clin Nutr 1998;67:952S–9S.
2. Linder MC, Hazegh-Azam M. Copper biochemistry and molecular biology. Am J Clin Nutr 1996;63:797S–811S.

3. Lönnerdal B. Bioavailability of copper. Am J Clin Nutr 1996;63:821S–9S.
4. Lee J, Prohaska J, Thiele D. Essential role for mammalian copper transporter Ctr1 in copper homeostasis and embryonic development. Proc Natl Acad Sci USA 2001;98:6842–7.

5.   Arredondo M, Muñoz P, Mura C, Núñez MT. DMT1, a physiologically relevant apical Cu1+ transporter of intestinal cells. Am J Physiol 2003;284: C1525–C30.

6.   Bertinato J, L'Abbé MR. Maintaining copper homeostasis: regulation of copper-trafficking proteins in response to copper deficiency or overload. J Nutr Biochem 2004;15:316–22.

7.   Mercer JRB, Livingston J, Hall B. Isolation of a partial candidate gene for Menkes disease by positional cloning. Nat Genet 1993;3:20–5.

8.   Bull PC, Thomas GR, Rommens JM, Forbes JR, Cox DW. The Wilson disease gene is a putative copper transporting P-type ATPase similar to the Menkes gene. Nat Genet 1993;5:327–36.

9.   Turnlund JR, Keyes WR, Anderson HL, Acord LL. Copper absorption and retention in young men at three levels of dietary copper by use of the stable isotope 65Cu. Am J Clin Nutr 1989;49:870–8.

10.   Milne DB, Johnson PE, Klevay LM, Sandstead H. Effect of copper intake on balance, absorption, and status indices of copper in man. Nutr Res 1990;10: 975–86.

11.   Mills CF. Dietary interactions involving the trace elements. Annu Rev Nutr 1985;5:173–93.

12.   Wapnir RA. Copper absorption and bioavailability. Am J Clin Nutr 1998;67:1054S–60S.

13.   Olivares M, Lonnerdal B, Abrams S, Pizarro F, Uauy R. Effects of age and copper intake on copper absorption in young infants measured using 65Cu as a tracer. Am J Clin Nutr 2002;76:641–5.

14.   Olivares M, Uauy R. Copper as an essential nutrient. Am J Clin Nutr 1996;63:791S–6S.

15.   Sutton AM, Harvie A, Cockburn A, Farquharson J, Logan RW. Copper deficiency in the preterm infant of very low birthweight: four cases and a reference range for plasma copper. Arch Dis Child 1985;60: 644–51.

16.   Willis MS, Monaghan SA, Miller ML, et al. Zinc-induced copper deficiency: a report of three cases initially recognized on bone marrow examination. Am J Clin Pathol 2005;123:125–31.

17.   Cordano A. Clinical manifestations of nutritional copper deficiency in infants and children. Am J Clin Nutr 1998;67:1012S–6S.

18.   Shaw JCL. Copper deficiency in term and preterm infants. In: Fomon SJ, Zlotkin S, eds. Nutritional Anemias. Nestlé Nutrition Workshop Series. Vol 30. New York: Raven Press, 1992:105–19.

19.   Ashkenazi A, Levine S, Dialjetti M, Fishel E, Benvenisty O. The syndrome of neonatal copper deficiency. Pediatrics 1973;52:525–33.

20.   Schubert WK, Lahey ME. Copper and protein depletion complicating hypoferric anemia of infancy. Pediatrics 1959;24:710–33.

21.   Lee GE, Williams DM, Cartwright GE. Role of copper in iron metabolism and heme biosynthesis. In: Prasad AS, Oberleas D, eds. Trace elements in human health and disease. Vol. 1. New York: Academic Press, 1976:373–90.

22.   Frieden E, Hsieh HS. Ceruloplasmin: the copper transport protein with essential oxidase activity. Adv Enzymol Relat Areas Mol Biol 1976;44:187–236

23.   Tephly TR, Wagner G, Sedman R, Piper W. Effects of metals on heme biosynthesis and metabolism. Fed Proc 1978;37:35-9.

24.   Chen H, Huang G, Su T, et al. Decreased hephaestin activity in the intestine of copper-deficient mice causes systemic iron deficiency. J Nutr 2006;136:1236–41.

25.   Reeves PG, DeMars LCS, Johnson WT, Lukaski HC. Dietary copper deficiency reduces iron absorption and duodenal enterocyte hephaestin protein in male and female rats. J Nutr 2005;135:92–8.

26.   Zidar BL, Shadduck RK, Zeigler Z, Winkelstein A. Observations on the anemia and neutropenia of human copper deficiency. Am J Hematol 1977;3:177–85.

27.   Higuchi T, Matsukawa Y, Okada K, et al. Correction of copper deficiency improves erythropoietin unresponsiveness in hemodialysis patients with anemia. Intern Med 2006;46:271–3.

28.   Hirase N, Abe Y, Sadamura S, et al. Anemia and neutropenia in a case of copper deficiency: role of copper in normal hematopoiesis. Acta Hematol 1992;87:195–7.

29.   King JC, Cousins RJ. Zinc. 10th ed. In: Shils M, Shike M, Ross AC, Caballero B, Cousins RJ, eds. Modern nutrition in health and disease. Baltimore: Lippincott Williams & Wilkins, 2006:271–85

30.   Hambidge KM. Zinc and health: current status and

future directions. J Nutr 2000;130:1341S–3S.

31. Black RE. Zinc deficiency, infectious disease and mortality in the developing world. J Nutr 2003;133:1485S–9S.

32. Prasad A, Miale A, Farid Z, Schubert A, Sandstead H. Zinc metabolism in patients with the syndrome of iron deficiencies, anemia, hypogonadism, and dwarfism. J Lab Clin Med 1963;61:537–45.

33. King LE, Fraker PJ. Zinc deficiency in mice alters myelopoiesis and hematopoiesis. J Nutr 2002;132: 3301–7.

34. King LE, Frentzel JW, Mann JJ, Fraker PJ. Chronic zinc deficiency in mice disrupted T cell lymphopoiesis and erythropoiesis while B cell lymphopoiesis and myelopoiesis were maintained. J Am Coll Nutr 2005;24:494–502.

35. Konomi A, Yokoi K. Zinc deficiency decreases plasma erythropoietin concentration in rats. Biol Trace Elem Res 2005;107:289–92.

36. Powell SR. The antioxidant properties of zinc. J Nutr 2000;130:1447S-54S.

37. O'Dell BL. Role of zinc in plasma membrane function. J Nutr 2000;130:1432S–6S.

38. Crofton RW, Gvozdanovic D, Gvozdanovic S, et al. Inorganic zinc and the intestinal absorption of ferrous iron. Am J Clin Nutr 1989;50:141–4.

39. Rossander-Hultén L, Brune M, Sandström B, Lönnerdal B, Hallberg L. Competitive inhibition of iron absorption by manganese and zinc in humans. Am J Clin Nutr 1991;54:152–6.

40. Friel JK, Serfass RE, Fennessey PV, et al. Elevated intakes of zinc in infant formulas do not interfere with iron absorption in premature infants. J Pediatr Gastroenterol Nutr 1998;27:312–6.

41. Olivares M, Pizarro F, Ruz M. Inhibition of iron absorption by zinc. Pediatr Res 2005;57:924 (abstr).

42. Herman S, Griffin I, Suwarti S, et al. Cofortification with zinc sulfate, but not zinc oxide, decreases iron absorption in Indonesian children. Am J Clin Nutr 2002;76:813–7.

43. López de Romaña D, Salazar M, Hambidge M, et al. Iron absorption by Peruvian children consuming wheat products fortified with iron only or iron and one of two levels of zinc. Proceedings of FASEB Experimental Biology; 2005 April 2–6; San Diego (abstr 274.23).

44. Gunshin H, Mackenzie B, Berger UV, Gunshin Y, Romero MF, Boron WF. Cloning and characterization of a mammalian proton-coupled metal-ion transporter. Nature 1997;388:482–8.

45. Kordas K, Stoltzfus RJ. New evidence of iron and zinc interplay at the enterocyte and neural tissues. J Nutr 2004;134:1295–8.

46. Yamaji S, Tennant J, Tandy S, Williams M, Srai SKS, Sharp P. Zinc regulates the function and expression of the iron transporters DMT1 and IREG1 in human intestinal Caco-2 cells. FEBS Lett 2001; 507:137–41.

47. Broun ER, Greist A, Tricot G, Hoffman R. Excessive zinc ingestion. JAMA 1990;264:1441–3.

48. Igic PG, Lee E, Harper W, Roach KW. Toxic effects associated with consumption of zinc. Mayo Clin Proc 2002;77:713-6.

49. Sone T, Yamaoka K, Minami Y, Tsunoo H. Induction of metallothionein synthesis in Menkes' and normal lymphoblastoid cells is controlled by the level of intracellular copper. J Biol Chem 1987;262: 5878–85.

50. Yuzbasiyan-Gurkan V, Grider A, Nostrant T, Cousins RJ, Brewer GJ. Treatment of Wilson's disease with zinc. X. Intestinal metallothionein induction. J Lab Clin Med 1992;120:380–6.

51. Fischer PW, Giroux A, L'Abbé, MR. Effects of zinc on mucosal copper binding and on the kinetics of copper absorption. J Nutr 1983;113:462–9.

52. Dijkhuizen MA, Wieringa FT, West CE, Martuti S, Muhilal. Effects of iron and zinc supplementation in Indonesian infants on micronutrient status and growth. J Nutr 2001;131:2860–5.

53. Lind T, Lonnerdal B, Stenlund H, et al. A community-based randomized controlled trial of iron and zinc supplementation in Indonesian infants: interactions between iron and zinc. Am J Clin Nutr 2003;77:883–90.

54. Schultink W, Merzenich M, Gross R, Shrimpton R, Dillon D. Effects of iron-zinc supplementation on the iron, zinc, and vitamin A status of anaemic pre-school children. Food Nutr Bull 1997;18:311–6.

55. Munoz EC, Rosado JL, Lopez P, Furr HC, Allen LH. Iron and zinc supplementation improves indicators of vitamin A status of Mexican preschoolers. Am J Clin Nutr 2000;71:789–94.

56. Berger J, Ninh NX, Khan NC, et al. Efficacy of combined iron and zinc supplementation on micronutrient status and growth in Vietnamese infants. Eur J Clin Nutr 2006;60:443–54.

57. Baqui AH, Zaman K, Persson LA, et al. Simultaneous weekly supplementation of iron and zinc is associated with lower morbidity due to diarrhea and acute lower respiratory infection in Bangladeshi infants. J Nutr 2003;133:4150–7.

58. Nishiyama S, Irisa K, Matsubasa T, Higashi A, Matsuda I. Zinc status relates to hematological deficits in middle-aged women. J Am Coll Nutr 1998;17:291–5.

59. Nishiyama S, Kiwaki K, Miyazaki Y, Hasuda T. Zinc and IGF-I concentrations in pregnant women with anemia before and after supplementation with iron and/or zinc. J Am Coll Nutr 1999;18:261–7.

60. Nishiyama S, Inomoto T, Nakamura T, Higashi A, Matsuda I. Zinc status relates to hematological deficits in women endurance runners. J Am Coll Nutr 1996;15:359–63.

61. Failla ML. Trace elements and host defense: recent advances and continuing challenges. J Nutr 2003;133:1443S–7S

62. Rink L, Kirchner H. Zinc-altered immune function and cytokine production. J Nutr 2000;130:1407S–11S.

63. Fraker PJ, King LE. Reprogramming of the immune system during zinc deficiency. Annu Rev Nutr 2004;24:277–98.

64. Fischer Walker C, Black RE. Zinc and the risk for infectious disease. Annu Rev Nutr 2004;24:255-75.

65. Bhutta ZA, Black RE, Brown KH, et al. Prevention of diarrhea and pneumonia by zinc supplementation in children in developing countries: pooled analysis of randomized controlled trials. Zinc Investigators' Collaborative Group. J Pediatr 1999;135:689–97.

66. Osendarp SJ, West CE, Black RE. The need for maternal zinc supplementation in developing countries: an unresolved issue. J Nutr 2003;133:817S–27S.

67. Chaturvedi UC, Shrivastava R, Upreti RK. Viral infections and trace elements: a complex interaction. Curr Sci 2004;87:1536–54.

68. Chandra RK. Excessive intake of zinc impairs immune responses. JAMA 1984;252:1443–6.

69. Percival SS. Copper and immunity. Am J Clin Nutr 1998;67:1064S–8S.

70. Heresi G, Castillo-Durán C, Muñoz C, Arevalo M, Schlesinger L. Phagocytosis and immunoglobulin levels in hypocupremic infants. Nutr Res 1985;5:1327–34.

71. Kelley DS, Daudu PA, Taylor PC, Mackey BE, Turlund JR. Effects of low-copper diets on human immune response. Am J Clin Nutr 1995;62:412–6.

72. Hopkins RG, Failla ML. Cu deficiency reduces interleukin-2 production and mRNA levels in human T-lymphocytes. J Nutr 1997;127:257–62.

73. Castillo-Durán C, Fisberg M, Valenzuela A, Egaña JI, Uauy R. Controlled trial of copper supplementation during the recovery of marasmus. Am J Clin Nutr 1983;37:898–903.

74. Olivares M, Walter T, Osorio M, Chadud P, Schlesinger L. The anemia of a mild viral infection: the measles vaccine as a model. Pediatrics 1989;84:851–5.

75. Olivares M, Walter T, Llaguno S, Osorio M, Chadud P, Velozo L. Modificaciones del hemograma y de los parámetros de laboratorio indicadores del metabolismo en infecciones virales leves (in Spanish) (Changes of blood cell counts and laboratory indices related to iron metabolism in mild viral infections). Sangre 1993;38:211-6.

76. Olivares M, Walter T, Cook JD, Llaguno S. Effect of acute infection on measurement of iron status: usefulness of the serum transferrin receptor. Int J Pediatr Hematol Oncol 1995;2:31–3.

9

Nutritional anemia: B-vitamins

John M. Scott

School of Biochemistry and Immunology at Trinity College Dublin, Dublin, Ireland
Contact: jscott@tcd.ie

JOHN M. SCOTT
John has a PhD in Biochemistry from Trinity College, Dublin, Ireland. He is currently a Senior Fellow at Trinity College, Dublin, Associate Professor of Biochemistry, and Professor of Experimental Nutrition. John is a world renowned expert in folate metabolism and has been on advisory boards for bodies such as the UK Department of Health, the UK Committee on Medical Aspects of Food and Nutrition Policy (COMA) Folic Acid Group, the Irish Food Safety Authority, and the FAO/WHO Consideration of Human Vitamin and Mineral Requirements.

INTRODUCTION

A very obvious outcome of inadequate intake of micronutrients is a reduction in hemoglobin biosynthesis, present as nutritional anemia. Anemia may be diagnosed through its signs and symptoms, such as fatigue, lethargy or breathlessness. Such clinical outcomes are progressive and if the deficiency is severe enough, can lead ultimately to death. However, appropriate treatment with the deficient nutrient or nutrients would be expected to lead to normal hemostasis and a full recovery. Of course, these nutrients fulfill many more functions than maintaining adequate rates of hemoglobin biosynthesis. Some of these other sequelae may in some well documented cases be irreversible, for example the neuropathy that arises in vitamin B_{12} deficiency which, if left undiagnosed, is largely irreversible (1). The impact of under-provision of nutrients in utero upon the developing embryo/fetus may be irreversible and have consequences on the health of the child or even, according to the Barker hypothesis, on the subsequent health of the adult (2). Thus, concerning nutrition adequacy, during pregnancy there are really three interrelated issues. Firstly, there is the health of the mother. Any extra risk as a result of being pregnant will not be expected to persist unless it is followed by further pregnancies in rapid succession. Secondly, there are the possibilities that under-nutrition during embryonic and fetal development may have lasting health indications for the child and/or adult. Such births give rise to children with a stunted growth pattern and perhaps impaired cognition development. The Barker hypothesis claims that under-nutrition in utero affects the development of the major organs and such systems as the heart, kidney and pancreas. Subsequently, in adult life this could lead to premature mortality and mortality through an increased prevalence of heart disease, diabetes, etc. Thirdly, as well as the proven case of increased NTD risk, there are a wide-range of claims, with varying degrees of supporting evidence, that poor mater-

nal nutrition can lead to an increased risk of other birth defects (oral-facial clefts, heart, etc.) or to adverse pregnancy outcomes (pregnancy loss, preeclampsia, etc.). Thus, concerns exist about inadequate provision of micronutrients, both for people of all ages but in particular for meeting the extra demands of pregnancy.

Some nutrients are not at risk of being deficient, because of their adequate levels in most diets. Some other micronutrients will be particularly at risk in some subjects. Iron deficiency is the most common deficiency because of its extremely high prevalence in women of childbearing age, due to blood loss. There is a wide spectrum of risk for the B complex of vitamins. Thus, biotin or panthothenic acid are essential nutrients but never deficient in humans, because the amount provided even in the most inadequate diet exceeds requirements. Extremes of poor intake of other nutrients can cause deficiency, as in these clinical conditions: thiamine (beri beri); niacin (pellagra); pyridoxal (sideroblastic anemia) riboflavin (ariboflavinosis). However, within the B complex the prevention and the consequence of deficiency or under-provision of two particular nutrients, folate and vitamin B_{12}, are by far the most important considerations. Thus, most of this review will concern these two nutrients. As mentioned later, deficiency of these nutrients becomes most apparent through their functions in maintaining purine and pyrimidine biosynthesis. A reduction in ability to synthesize DNA and maintain cell division is most easily seen in the synthesis of red cells, expressed as a very characteristic macrocytic megaloblastic anemia. However, it must be recognized that impaired DNA biosynthesis affects all replication cells with different sequalae. Less obvious still is reduction in the activity of some four dozen methyltransferases with a wide variety of functions, present in all cells. Reductions in these activities have wide ranging effects, the most apparent being that

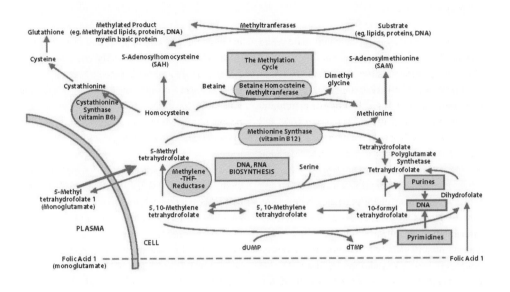

Figure 9.1: The metabolic and clinical functions of folic acid/folate and vitamin B_{12}.

vitamin B_{12}, deficiency also causes a very characteristic anemia, resulting as well in an equally well documented neuropathy, probably not due to impaired methylation.

FOLATE AND VITAMIN B_{12}:
MEGALOBLASTIC ANEMIA

By the end of the nineteenth century it was recognized that a particular type of anemia was associated with larger than normal red cells in the circulation (3). Furthermore, this macrocytic anemia was in many instances seen to be accompanied by the presence of abnormal red cell precursors in patients' bone marrow aspirates. These so-called megaloblasts were characterized as being different from the usual red cell normoblast precursors, in they had a large, poorly differentiated nuclei. It subsequently became clear that such megaloblastic anemia was due to either folate or vitamin B_{12} deficiency (3).

BIOCHEMICAL BASIS OF MEGALOBLASTIC ANEMIA OF FOLATE AND VITAMIN B_{12} DEFICIENCY

Examination of the folate pathway described in **Figure 9.1** shows that the folate cofactors in their reduced forms are necessary for purine and pyrimidine biosynthesis. Thus, the so-called carbon one folate derivatives of 10-formyl and 5,10-methylenetetrahydrofolate (MTHF) donate respectively in the former instance the carbon 2 and the carbon 8 of the purine ring. The latter folate, 5,10-methylene THF, is a cofactor for the very important enzyme, thymidylate synthase, and is responsible for the conversion of the uracil type base found in RNA to the thymine type base which is characteristic of DNA (**Figure 9.1**). It can thus be anticipated that the folate deficiency or even reduced folate status will diminish and compromise a cell's ability to synthesize purines and pyrimidines and thus DNA. This would reduce the ability of any cell to divide appropriately but would be most obvious clinically in the rapidly dividing cells of the bone marrow, which causes an anemia. It also causes a reduction in the white cells, platelets, etc. Such reduced ability to make DNA at the appropriate rate during the maturation of red cells in the bone marrow causes a less than normal number of cell divisions ingoing from the pluripotent stem cell to the erythrocytes. As red cells divide in the bone marrow compartment, the resultant two daughter cells after each division are slightly smaller than the parent cell. The reduction in the number of such divisions results in the eventual erythrocytes being larger than usual, or macrocytic, with a raised mean corpuscular volume (MCV). Of course, the overall reduction in cell division would also result in a reduction in hemoglobin biosynthesis and also be reflected as an anemia seen in a Full Blood Count (FBC). The reduced rate of cell division results in nuclei that are larger and more poorly differentiated than normal. Such megaloblasts are diagnostic of folate deficiency anemia. What is also clear is that an identical megaloblastic anemia occurs in vitamin B_{12} deficiency. It is identical in every respect morphologically to that seen in folate deficiency and there is a similar rise in MCV. The biochemical explanation for this is set out in the methyl trap hypothesis (4). There are only two vitamin B_{12} dependent enzymes in man. One of them, methionine synthase, uses the folate cofactor 5 methyl THF and is part of the methylation cycle (**Figure 9.1**). The enzyme that synthesizes 5 methyl THF, namely 5,10-methyltenetrahydrofolate reductase (MTHFR) is known to be irreversible in vivo. Once 5 methyl THF has been formed in a cell, the only way that it can participate in future purine or pyrimidine biosynthesis is by being used by methionine synthase, whose activity is absent or severely compromised if its essential cofactor, vitamin B_{12}, is deficient. This resultant trapping of folate in a cell as 5 methyl THF eventually reduces the folate cofactors involved in purines and pyrimidine biosynthesis to where this reduction produces the exact same megaloblastic anemia as that seen in folate

deficiency (1). In other words, while vitamin B_{12} deficient cells have adequate folate, it is trapped in a particular metabolic form and results in a sort of pseudo folate deficiency. The cell has adequate 5 methyl THF and one might thus anticipate that it would have a normal methylation cycle (**Figure 9.1**). However, this cycle is compromised because it also needs vitamin B_{12} dependent methionine synthase. The latter causes the very dramatic neuropathy seen in B_{12} deficiency. This is due to a reduction in the activity of one of the many methyltransferase in the cell that must, in a way that is as yet unclear, be involved in the maintenance of the myelin sheath (4). This neuropathy initially affects the peripheral nerves, but will eventually result in degeneration of the spinal column. The clinical manifestation of this is in an initial peripheral neuropathy progressing to ataxia, paralysis and if left untreated, ultimately death. The fully developed condition is called subacute combined degeneration (SCD). The change in the peripheral nerves and central nervous system are seen as a progression to demyelination, described in its latter stages in the spinal tracts as a "field of holes." Such demyelination can only be demonstrated at post mortem. The signs and symptoms in early stages of SCD are somewhat nonspecific and overlap to a significant extent with similar problems seen with advancing years. The features common to both would be memory loss, impaired mobility and general cognitive decline. The neuropathy can be detected clinically by a careful medical examination of neurological responses. Mostly from earlier examples of descriptions of patients with PA, it is estimated that about one third present the neuropathy only, one third the anemia and one third both. The concern is thus: if the anemia is treated or masked by an inappropriate administration of folic acid, as discussed below, its diagnosis, based on the neuropathy, will be absent in some patients until it has progressed to where it may be irreversible. In addition, it will be difficult to diagnose in many patients because its signs and symptoms will be confused with those of advancing years.

One would anticipate that folate deficiency would also compromise the methylation cycle and produce a similar neuropathy **(Figure 9.1)**, but for reasons that are unclear the neuropathy is not a usual presenting feature of folate deficiency. This may be because nerve tissue concentrates folate over other cell types. Only one study found this neuropathy characteric of vitamin B_{12} deficiency in a group of patients that had severe and prolonged folate deficiency (5).

Appropriate treatment of folate deficiency, either with food folate but more usually with the synthetic form of the vitamin folic acid, produces a complete remission of the anemia. Likewise, treatment of vitamin B_{12} deficiency with vitamin B_{12} produces a complete remission of the anemia. The neuropathy will also respond, but if it is very advanced some of the neural damage to the spinal column may not completely redress, leaving some residual neurological damage. If the vitamin B_{12} deficiency is nutritional, as in a vegan's, additional vitamin B_{12}, either by way of fortification or more usually by supplements, can be effective. If the malabsorption is due to absence of the intrinsic factor needed for absorption, then vitamin B_{12} treatment must be parenteral. A potentially serious issue arises if folic acid is used inappropriately to treat what in fact is vitamin B_{12} deficiency. What is seen to happen clinically is that the continuous ingestion of folic acid produces the folate cofactors needed for purine and pyrimidine biosynthesis. Thus, in such subjects DNA biosynthesis will be normalized and an anemia will appear to be successfully treated. However, the methylation cycle will continue to be compromised with a continuation of the neuropathy, to where it will present later at a much more advanced stage and at a point where it may largely be irreversible. This so-called masking of the anemia of vitamin B_{12} deficiency results in an anemia where the most easily recognizable signs and symptoms of vitamin B_{12} deficiency do not emerge. The neuropathy is much more difficult to diagnose and its presence is frequently confused

with the advancement in years, where of course the problem of vitamin B_{12} deficiency is most prevalent. Thus, such vitamin B_{12} deficient patients inappropriately receiving folic acid treatments may go undiagnosed (1).

The interaction of folic acid on the diagnosis of vitamin B_{12} deficiency as documented above is universally accepted. What is more controversial is the suggestion that the administration of folic acid may exacerbate the neuropathy, accelerating its rate of progression. This contention comes from the clinical description of the progression of the neuropathy described in the earlier case reports, where folic acid had been administered inappropriately (3, 4). Phrases such as an "explosive" progression of the neuropathy are used. Since the clinicians involved were some of the leaders of the day in the study of PA, it is very credible that they would have been able to recognize such a phenomenon. However since they were not blinded to the presence or absence of the alternative treatment, it is really impossible to say.

INADEQUATE FOLATE STATUS

While intestinal malabsorption of folate produces deficiency resulting in coeliac disease and tropical sprue, dietary deficiency, rather than malabsorption is the real issue in folate deficiency. Folate in nature is unstable, not fully bioavailable and is not found in any great density in most foods except liver, which is not a large part of any diet. Vegetables are good sources of folate, but because of their low abundance even in what are considered good sources, a significant food intake is not always available in developing countries to ensure an adequate status. Recently it has become clear that there is a common polymorphism named 677 C → T in the folate dependent enzyme methylenetetrahydrofolate reductase that increases folate requirement by as much as 30% (6). This polymorphism has a high prevalence of up to

25% in some communities. In some communities, high alcohol intake, displacing as it does, food intakes, can exacerbate folate deficiency.

There is a large increase in requirement during pregnancy and lactation. There is good evidence that this is associated with the rapid extra demand for DNA synthesis during which a significant extra amount of folate is catabolised (broken down). This is particularly true during the latter stages of pregnancy and during lactation (7). Thus, one might expect folate deficiency and reduced status to be a general problem in developing countries, with this problem exacerbated by pregnancy.

PREVALENCE OF REDUCED FOLATE STATUS

Looking at two examples from the older literature, one can already see the likely problem that was to emerge with respect to folate status worldwide in the subsequent decades. Two studies in the 1980s showed a marked contrast in prevalence. In Benin in rural central Africa, it was reported that of 586 adults, over 42% had overt anemia, and that over 20% of this was due to folate deficiency (8). This was contrasted with a study from southern Algeria by the same group, where only 7% of 254 young adult women were found to be anemic, with none of the anemia caused by folate deficiency (9). Thus, in contrast to vitamin B_{12} deficiency where specific intestinal (perncious anemia and gastric atrophy) or regional (veganism) factors contributed in a reasonable identifiable way to reduced status, severe folate deficiency worldwide may be very localized, apart from circumstances like pregnancy where there is a specific increased requirement which is frequently not met. The overall pattern that one sees with folate status is that even in developed countries such as the USA the diet as it has currently evolved has been inadequate for optimum folate status. This is perhaps best illustrated by the paper by Jacques et. al. (10), which

found that in the USA prior to fortification of flour with folic acid in 1998, over 22% of the population had impaired folate status, which fell to 1.7% post fortification. A pattern of general under-provision of folate right through to overt deficiency is seen in developing countries. This could be expected to depend upon the source and amounts of food available, mindful that folate is found in vegetable based diets, but as mentioned above, not really abundant in any particular food. In addition, amounts consumed will be subject to methods of preparation, in that natural folate is labile and easily destroyed during cooking (11). Folate also deteriorates during storage, a good example being the large difference in status found between northern and southern China due to lack of availability of fresh food during the long winter in the former (12). Taking a number of status studies by way of examples one sees, for example, a study of 278 randomly selected adults in Zimbabwe found 30% had low folate levels (13). By contrast, in 250 elderly women in New Zealand, only 3 and 5% have low serum and red cell folate (14). In a study of 567 school children in Thailand, hemoglobinopathies, vitamin A status and age were the major predictors of hemoglobin status. Only about 1% had biochemical evidence of reduced folate status, either by RCF or plasma folate (15).

In Sri Lanka in 945 schoolchildren, nearly half of females and over half of males had anemia. Iron deficiency was the cause of the anemia in 30% of the males and 48% of the females. However, impaired folate status were reported to be present in over half of either group (16).

Recent large studies continue to show reduced status as an issue. For example in a mixed group of 5,658 samples in Venezuela taken during 2001–2005, some 30% were considered to be folate deficient (17). However, as discussed below, Venezuela has now opted for mandatory fortification with folic acid, so this once serious problem has now probably largely disappeared.

Pregnancy has long been known to put extra pressure on folate status. While initially this was thought to be due simply to transfer of maternal folate to the fetus, it is now clear that the rapid cell proliferation associated with pregnancy greatly increases the rate of folate breakdown (catabolism) and thus increases in requirement (7). The topic of folate and pregnancy has recently been extensively reviewed by Tamura and Picciano (18). Historically, the pattern that has emerged in developed countries was that some decades ago, the latter stages of pregnancy were often associated with overt deficiency. This was less and less observed as the food supply improved (19). The picture emerged in developed countries that if a woman entered pregnancy with sufficiently adequate stores they would be adequate to meet the extra burden required, and there would be no emergence of deficiency and certainly no anemia. This has resulted in different practices in developed countries, where some obstetricians recommend folic acid supplements in late pregnancy and others do not. Of course, this all depends on the mother entering the pregnancy with adequate stores, and this expectation clearly would not be met in many developing countries.

There is thus a long established role of inadequate folate status in the megaloblastic anemia of pregnant women (3). However such anemia was associated with poor maternal stores entering pregnancy, and was only seen late in pregnancy. More recently, a completely different role for folate/folic acid has been described. It is now established that women taking extra folic acid, before during and after conception (periconceptionally), can reduce the prevalence of spina bifida and other neural tube defects (NTDs) by certainly over a half and possibly as much as three-quarters.

It is now clear that the prevention of NTDs by women taking extra folic acid prior to the crucial period of the closure of the neural tube between days 21 and 27 only happens in less than a quarter

of pregnancies, despite intensive public awareness campaigns in many developed countries. This is largely due to the fact that in all communities where it has been examined, over half of pregnancies are unplanned. Even in the planned pregnancies the message is difficult to get across, and there is also the issue of compliance, even where women understand the benefit. This has led many developed countries to turn to the mandatory fortification of a staple such as flour with folic acid, with an impressive reduction of NTD prevalence, for example in Canada, where perhaps as much as half are prevented. It seems appropriate, as discussed elsewhere, that such fortification might be extended to developing countries. The dilemma with such a public health policy is that one has to balance the amount of the nutrient, in this instance, folic acid, so as to produce an optimal benefit but still not expose those who benefit or, of even greater concern, the general population, to risks associated with high intakes of the vitamin. With respect to folic acid, the most commonly discussed adverse effect is the masking of vitamin B_{12} deficiency. Such masking is very dose-dependent, and it is considered that it does not happen at intakes of less than 1,000 µg (or 1.0 mg) of folic acid per day. This concern is the basis for setting the Upper Tolerable Intake Level (UL) for folic acid at that amount. There is, however, a different concern, namely that the addition of folic acid might accelerate the growth of existing tumors. This is most often cited with respect to colorectal cancer (CRC), but it could also be true of other cancers. Most studies would consider that improving folate status and increased intake of folic acid are associated with a reduction in the occurrence of CRC. The concern, however, relates not to causing a new cancer to emerge, but to its subsequent more rapid growth and progression. This would have a particular and obvious disadvantage with CRC, where all such cancers, before they become adenomas requiring surgery and chemotherapy, go through a stage where they exist as a polyp. If such polyps are suspected to be present, as they

Table 9.1: Forty-two countries have mandatory folic acid food fortification programs (see dark shaded areas in **Figure 9.2**).

Country	Fortification Position	Information on Food Fortified and Fortification Level
North America		
USA	Mandatory	140µg/100g grain in food as consumed
Canada	Mandatory	150µg/100g white flour in foods as consumed 200µg/100g enriched uncooked pasta (estimated to provide 150µg/100g cooked pasta)
	Voluntary	150 - 220µg/10g cornflour
Australia and New Zealand		
Australia New Zealand	Voluntary	Folic acid can be added to a maximum claim of 50% recommended dietary intake for adults (100µg) per reference quantity of the following foods: flour; savoury biscuits; breads; breakfast cereals; pasta; fruit and vegetable juices and drinks; fruit cordial; beverages derived from legumes (currently Australia and New Zealand are exploring the option of mandatory folic acid food fortification for the prevention of birth defects)
South America and Caribbean		
Chile	Mandatory	220µg/100g flour
Brazil Argentina Bolivia Colombia Costa Rica Dominican Republic Ecuador El Salvador Guatemala Honduras Mexico Nicaragua Panama Paraguay	Mandatory	150µg/100g wheat and maize flour
Barbados Belize Grenada Guadalupe Guyana Peru Puerto Rico St. Vincent Surinam Trinidad Tobago	Mandatory	All fortify wheat flour (extended to corn flour, rice and milk in some countries). Fortification levels range from 40-300µg/100g

Table 9.1 (continued): Forty-two countries have mandatory folic acid food fortification programs (see dark shaded areas in **Figure 9.2**).

Country	Fortification Position	Information on Food Fortified and Fortification Level
Venezuela	Mandatory	Details of food and fortification levels unavailable
Europe		
Belgium	Voluntary	Foods and food supplements are fortified. For the product to be labelled as fortified with folic acid, a daily portion must contain between 15 and 200% of 200µg
France	Voluntary	Breakfast cereals: only fortified if they are planned to be consumed by children or women (levels unavailable) Goat's milk: 4.5µg folic acid/100g milk
Germany	Voluntary	Breakfast cereals (mainly), beverages, cereal bars and salt (levels unavailable)
Greece	Voluntary	Details of food and fortification levels unavailable
Hungary	Voluntary	In 1998, through a voluntary fortification programme, a bread to prevent birth defects, which was fortified with folic acid and vitamins B_2, B_6 and B_{12}, was introduced. This was unsuccessful due to being a higher priced product. In 2005, a group of mill workers have introduced two fortified flours:
1. for women who potentially could become pregnant (fortified with 350µg folic acid, 10µg B_{12}, 500µg B_2, and 1600µg B_6 per 100g flour;		
2. for prevention of cardiovascular disease (fortified with 250µg folic acid, 10µg B_{12}, 500µg B_2, and 1600µg B_6 per 100g flour.		
Iceland	Voluntary	Breakfast cereals: 30-700µg/100g Flour and rice: 30-100µg/100g
Ireland	Voluntary	Various products fortified under the 'Folic Acid Flash Labelling Scheme' including: milk (70µg/100ml); yogurt (36µg/90g serving); breads 50-263µg/100g bread; flour used to make bread (140µg/100g flour)
UK	Voluntary	Breakfast cereal and breakfast-type products (8-643µg/100g) Some yellow fat spreads: 1mg/100g (currently the UK are re-examining mandatory folic acid food fortification for the prevention of birth defects)
Middle East and Africa		
Israel	Mandatory	Fortifies wheat flour with folic acid and vitamin B_{12} (levels unavailable)
Saudi Arabia	Mandatory	Enriched wheat and enriched treated flour (150µg/100g)

Table 9.1 (continued): Forty-two countries have mandatory folic acid food fortification programs (see dark shaded areas in **Figure 9.2**).

Country	Fortification Position	Information on Food Fortified and Fortification Level
Malawi South Africa Zambia	Mandatory	Maize flour (206µg/100g) Maize meal (189 -194µg/100g) White wheat flour (136µg/100g) Brown wheat flour (124µg/100g) White and brown bread (74µg/100g) Enriched maize meal (240µg/100g)
Bahrain Morocco Nigeria Oman Qatar Yemen	Mandatory	Details of food and fortification levels unavailable
Asia		
Indonesia	Mandatory	Enriched wheat flour (200µg/100g)
Kazakhstan Kyrgyzstan	Mandatory	Details of food and fortification levels unavailable
Table adapted from various sources: General information (31,40,114), USA (55,101), Canada (15,72,98,104,105); Chile (52,53), Hungary (22), Australia and New Zealand (40,70, 95;96,120)		

frequently are as a result of bleeding or irregular bowel habits, they can be identified and removed at colonoscopy without further difficulty. It is estimated from various strands of evidence that such polyps may be there for perhaps a decade prior to their conversion to an adenoma, but a conservative estimate is that in most instances they are present for in excess of three years. Clearly if this conversion to full cancer took place more rapidly, as is suggested could be brought about by folic acid, particularly high levels of folic acid, this diagnostic window of opportunity is decreased. The evidence that such acceleration of CRC and other cancers does occur is generally seen in the first instance by the fact that one of the most effective drugs in treating and retarding the tumor growth is the anti-folate methotrexate. In addition, the front line drug in treating CRC, 5-fluorouracil, acts by inhibiting the folate dependent enzyme thymidylate synthase. In addition,

some animal tumor implants have their growth rate accelerated by folic acid. Further concerns relate to an intervention trial that found that folic acid ingestion over a three year period compared to placebo, while it did not cause an increase in the number of patients recurring with polyps, did show more polyps in those that did have such a recurrence. Finally, there was an apparent increase in the prevalence of CRC in North America that appears to have occured simultaneously or shortly after fortification was introduced in 1998. The arguments for and against the involvement of folic acid in CRC has been discussed at length by the Scientific Advisory Committee in the UK. They, in conjunction with a special committee on cancer, concluded that the evidence that folic acid advances the growth of existing tumors to be unproved and have recommended unreservedly that fortification with folic acid proceed in the UK.

FORTIFICATION WITH FOLIC ACID

A major new consideration in the last decade is that over 40 countries have followed the USA and Canada in setting a policy of fortification (**Table 9.1**). Several other countries, such as Ireland, Austria, Australia and New Zealand, are very close to adopting such a policy. Viewing this as a figure one can see that the issue of global folate deficiency or reduced status must now be considered in parallel with the policy of widespread mandatory folic acid fortification (**Figure 9.2**). It should be emphasized that as with the USA and Canada nearly a decade ago, these mandatory fortification policies are been driven almost exclusively by public health policies to prevent NTDs. The levels of fortification chosen would deliver a mean daily intake of folic acid of 100 μg/d in the USA and Canada. Other countries, such as Israel, have used higher levels. It is clear that levels of this order while not perhaps optimally preventing all folate related NTDs (20, 21), would have a major impact on normalising folate status (10). Recent data particularly from Canada (22) show that this fortification has been largely but not completely successful with a prevalence of 50% and 70% in reductions of NTDs being achieved (**Figure 9.3**).

INTERVENTION TRIALS

As discussed in the abstract and in the introduction, the prevalence of megaloblastic anemia in developing countries may be significantly under-detected because of the very common concomitant prevalence of iron deficiency. Iron deficiency would result in a microcytic anemia. However, a combination of iron with folate or vitamin B_{12} deficiency results frequently in a normocytic anemia and not a macrocytic anemia, frequently used as the first indication of folate or vitamin B_{12} deficiency. The unravelling of combined deficiencies, which together produce a normocytic anemia, makes identifying deficiency of folate or vitamin B_{12} difficult. The true prevalence of folate or serum vitamin B_{12} deficiency, as discussed in the previous section, is difficult to establish in a secure way. One can of course use vitamin levels of folate in serum or even better,

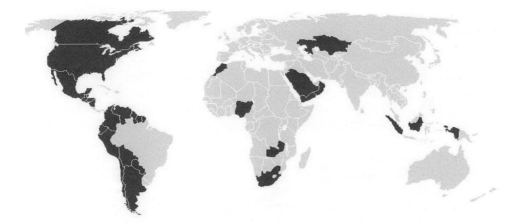

Figure 9.2: Forty-two countries have mandatory folic acid food fortification programmes (see dark shaded areas).

the red cell folate, or for vitamin B_{12}, serum, and more recently, holotranscobalamin. This could of course support an etiology due to folate and or vitamin B_{12} deficiency, however such levels need to be very low to be diagnostic. Likewise, the use of biomarkers of the status of these two nutrients, such as serum homocysteine (t Hcy) or methylmalonic acid (MMA) are helpful but not capable of a definite conclusion and are usually not available. Unravelling the presence of the anemia as being due to iron or folate or B_{12} deficiency can alternatively be advanced from the result of intervention trials, where iron and either folic acid and/or vitamin B_{12} is administered separately.

A comprehensive overview of nutritional interventions in pregnancy was undertaken by Villar et al. (23). They make many valid and important points in this study. They suggest that "results from observational studies or uncontrolled evaluations are likely to be confounded by the effect of several covariates and a population selection bias." They suggest that such selection bias will preselect for better-off populations,

making it likely that intervention groups will have better outcomes. Hence, one needs a control group for proper comparison, ideally with a placebo group. Their review looked only at such randomized interventions, and they concluded that while folic acid intervention had no apparent benefit in preventing gestational hypertension, it might have other benefits such as prevention of anemia.

As mentioned by Allen and Shrimpton (24) the International Research on Infant Supplementation Study (IRIS) was undertaken in four developing countries and recognized that multiple micronutrient deficiencies were probably present, as well as a more pervasive iron deficiency. These studies are ongoing in Indonesia, Peru, Vietnam and South Africa (25). They seek to compare placebo (P) with daily iron (DI), daily iron plus multiple micronutrient (DMM), or weekly iron plus micronutrients (WMM). Encouraging results from the South African arm are already available. DMM was most effective in improving anemia (26). It is not possible of course to say which of the 13 micronutrients

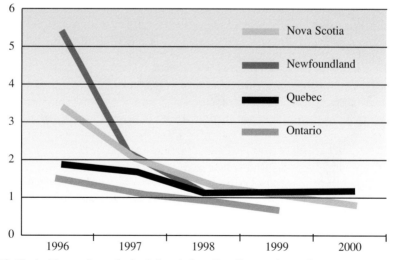

Figure 9.3: The incidence of neural tube defects in four Canadian provinces after mandatory folic acid food fortification was begun in 1996 and fully in place in 1998.

was responsible for this reduction in anemia including which, if any, of the B complexes of B_1, B_2, B_6, B_{12}, niacin or folic acid. In addition, it cannot be ruled out that the effect of such other micronutrients was not acting through improving the response to iron, as suggested in other studies (see later).

An excellent review of a number of intervention trials was carried out by Fishman et al. (27) who comprehensively researched the literature for such interventions. Little has emerged since this review to alter the picture. In this chapter, the emphasis is more on trying to resolve the issue of evidence for concommant combined deficiency of iron with folate and/or vitamin B_{12}, with a view to seeing if supplementation or, more probably, fortification with one or both of these vitamins would be warranted as a widespread endeavour.

INTERVENTION TRIALS WITH FOLIC ACID

While several intervention trials have taken place, emphasis is given in this review to ones that were placebo controlled, due to difficulty of interpretation of such a complex issue in the other studies. Batu et al. (28) in a short trial of four weeks' duration in an intervention on 112 pregnant women, found some support for a graded response in hemoglobin (Hb) in women given folic acid and iron as against those given iron alone. A further study found that folic acid alone showed no improvement in a reduction in hemoglobin while the combination of folic acid and iron seemed to be more effective than iron alone (29). Iyengar and Apte (30) found no difference in hemoglobin (Hb) over a 12–16 week intervention in 768 pregnant Indian women, whether iron was given separately or together with folic acid. In 146 Australian pregnancies Fleming et al. (31) found that when folic acid was given on its own or with iron it did not enhance the effect of iron on

its own. Sood et al. (32), in a large pregnant population of 647, found that while folic acid on its own or even in combination with vitamin B_{12} was similar with respect to Hb changes over 10–12 weeks, these two vitamins did seem to enhance the benefit of giving iron alone. Charoenlarp et al. (33) found in pregnant and non-pregnant women in Thailand and Burma that while supplements with iron were of benefit with respect to Hb there was again no real evidence that the addition of folic had any further benefit. Fleming et al. (34) in 200 Nigerian women treated for 16 weeks, found that iron appeared to have a benefit that was not enhanced further by folic acid. Thus using altered Hb during pregnancy as an outcome would seem to indicate a very clear benefit for iron intervention. However, there appeared to be little extra benefit for this outcome with folic acid intervention on its own, but it may enhance the iron response. An earlier indication of compromised folate status than overt anemia is the presence of hyper-segmented neurophils. These are an early sign of an impaired rate of folate dependent DNA biosynthesis on the maturation of the nucleus. One of the studies discussed above (31) did find that such hyper-segmentation was reduced by the time of delivery by folic acid intervention. Folic acid intervention also seemed to have improved red cell morphology in the study in Nigerian pregnant women by folic acid intervention (34).

A preparation containing 15 micronutrients was compared to the same with added iron from around 13 weeks gestation in pregnant women in Mexico. There was no reduction in anemia compared to iron alone (35).

Scholl et al. found pregnancy outcome in low income pregnant adolescents in New Jersey was better in those who took supplements than those who did not (36).

It is considered that premature and low birth weight infants are at considerable increased risk if they have a reduced folate status. Several poorly designed interventions have not added any great conclusions in this area, as summarized by Fishman et al. (27). Some responses to interventionsin to low birth weight infants were reported on iron alone in a large trial in the UK (37). However, the trial was neither randomized or double blind. Folic acid seemed to have a transient benefit in a further intervention trial in infants in the USA at six months, but there was no difference after one year between the folic acid treated or the placebo group (38).

Christian et al. (39) conducted a randomized trial in rural Nepal, where nearly half of all babies are usually underweight. They found a marked decline in low birth weight by a combination of iron-folic acid, which was not improved by adding other micronutrients. Also, folic acid alone had no effect, so the authors attribute the benefits to iron.

Two intervention trials have been conducted in non-pregnant women using improvement in Hb response as an indication of response. Mackey and Picciano (40) conducted a small trial on 21 women on multivitamins, compared to the same multivitamin plus 1.0 mg/d of folic acid. They found a significant increase in Hb concentration. The hemocit also improved over the 12 week period. The women seemed to have normal hemoglobin status to begin with, in that they were not anaemic or folate deficient. This study, though small, would seem to indicate some added benefit for folic acid. However, no obvious benefit was found in a large study of 624 non-pregnant Thai or Malaysian women (41).

Two Cochrane Database reviews were conducted on pregnancies some years back. Mahomed (42) reviewed eight trials involving 5,449 women, and concluded that such supplements "had no detectable effect on any sustained measures of either maternal or fetal outcome." However they did "prevent low hemoglobin at delivery." A further review by Mahomed (43) included 21 trials of more variable quality. Again, there was no measurable effect on pregnancy outcome but again, there was an improvement in hemoglobin levels.

The above studies in developing countries correspond to earlier experience in developed countries. Megaloblastic anemia in pregnancy, while recognized in earlier studies, became less and less obvious as diet and social conditions improved (3, 35). However, most studies would indicate that women who enter pregnancy with good stores have sufficient folate to show no signs or symptoms of megaloblastic anemia before delivery (3, 7).

VITAMIN B_{12}

The biochemical interdependence of vitamin B_{12} (cobalamin) and folate has been described above. It is clear how the identical anemia seen in both deficiencies arises. It is less clear why vitamin B_{12} deficiency leads to obvious cognitive or neurological sequale which seem to be absent in folate deficiency.

Another obvious difference between the two vitamins is their prevalence, and reasons why they become deficient. Folate in its natural form is unstable, has significantly reduced bioavailability and is not abundant in almost any diet even in affluent countries. By contrast, most diets have levels of vitamin B_{12} that will exceed the recommended daily allowance (RDA) (1, 44). The evidence of a widespread prevalence of reduced status, even in those on excellent diets is ascribed to the presence of hypochlorhydria in significant proportions of all populations. This is due to gastric atrophy, with the absence of acid preventing the liberation of vitamin B_{12} from the bound form that it is present in foods. While it is less well documented, one could anticipate equally high prevalence of such malabsorption in developing countries. There are circumstances where reduced status can be anticipated (i.e., in vegans, strict vegetarians who take no animal products such as eggs or milk products in their diet). It is simply a fact that the enzymes necessary to assemble this very large vitamin are only present in bacteria and some algae. Its synthesis is completely absent in plant and vegetables of all kinds, being only present in such foods by way of bacterial contamination. Vitamin B_{12} enters the human food chain exclusively through animal products, either as meat or animal products such as milk or milk products or eggs. Some strict vegans do consume products which would contain some of the vitamins via bacteria or algal synthesis. Thus, in general, vegetarians or more particularly, vegan communities are a high-risk group of being vitamin B_{12} deficient.

This topic has recently been the subject of an extensive review by Stabler and Allen (45). They draw the distinction between those at risk from insufficient dietary intake and those who have impaired malabsorption. In the latter instance, there are two sub-categories, those with true pernicious anemia and subjects at risk of vitamin B_{12} malabsorption, because of gastric atrophy.

DIETARY DEFICIENCY OF VITAMIN B_{12}

Dietary deficiency is a severe problem on the Indian subcontinent, Mexico, Central and South America and certain areas of Africa (45). Vitamin B_{12} is only found in food of animal origin or in fermented foods of vegetable origin. Many developing countries have relatively poor intake of such foods because of lack of accessibility and high cost. Of greater risk are populations, where because of cultural and religious beliefs are either vegetarian (with ingestion of eggs and milk products) or vegans where the diet contains no items of animal foods, with vitamin B_{12} being provided only by fermented foods or through bacterial contamination. It is thus not unexpected that defi-

ciency will exist in many sectors, as reported by studies on vitamin levels as a reflection of status. The following are examples of percentages of impaired status: urban India 60% (46); Nepal 49% (47); rural Kenya 31% (48); Venezuelan children and women 11% (49); Guatemalan elderly 38% (50); and Chilean men 50% and women 31% (51). A study by Black et al. (52) in Mexican adults found prevalence of 19–30% deficiency, depending upon gender and lactation, etc. Other studies have used vitamin B_{12} levels have to assess the likelihood of impaired B12 status, with varying results. Thus, a study on 1,650 adults in Bangladesh attributed 5% of low homocysteine to low B_{12} intake (53). Ongoing studies on a group of Kenyan children are very illustrative of the risk of poor vitamin B_{12} status, even in non-vegetarian communities where animal sourced foods (ASF) are in poor supply (48). This large cohort, of some 555 children aged 5–14 years, had vitamin B_{12} levels measured at baseline and after intervention. After a year of intervention on a meat or milk meal supplement the prevalence had fallen from baseline to post intervention values of 80.7% to 64.1% and 71.6% to 45.1% respectively.

The above illustrates that the under-provision of ASF through lack of availability for whatever reason, puts communities at risk but this is of course most graphically illustrated in strict vegan communities. As reviewed by Stabler and Allen (45) vitamin B_{12} deficiency in vegans emerged initially as an issue in the 1970s in the UK in African Indians, but similar experiences had also been categorized in several countries such as Holland. Strict vegans in their countries of origin have not usually been found to be as deficient, perhaps through ingestion of fermented or contaminated foods (45). However, infants born to vitamin B_{12} deficient vegan mothers are at high risk of developing deficiency because of their poor body stores at birth (54). This is particularly the case where they are breast-fed for longer periods as would happen more often in developing countries, because human breast milk is a much poorer source of vitamin B_{12} than the cows' milk found in formula foods (55).

MALABSORPTION OF VITAMIN B_{12}

Pernicious anemia (PA) is a specific autoimmune disease, where in response to immune penetration of the gastrointestinal tract, usually with increasing age, antibodies are present in either the parietal cells or to gastric intrinsic factor, or both (45). While such antibodies are detectable only in about half of patients with PA, this abnormal immune reaction in PA reduces or eventually eliminates the active absorption of vitamin B_{12} from the diet. Various studies have reported different prevalences of PA, from being a fraction of a percent to as high as 4.3% in developed countries, as reviewed by Baik and Russell (56).

Malabsorption of vitamin B_{12} due to gastric atrophy in the elderly is now thought to be very common, and helps to explain why in the face of apparently normal levels of food vitamin B_{12} in the diet at perhaps five times the RDA, many elderly subjects show biochemical and even clinical signs of having impaired status. As reviewed by Carmel (57), the reduction or absence of acid as a result of gastric atrophy prevents the absorption of food bound vitamin B_{12}. The absorption of free vitamin B_{12} present in supplements or in fortified foods would be unimpaired, an important consideration since a fortification program would go towards solving this issue. Various estimates have put the prevalence of this gastric atrophy as high as 30% in the elderly (57). There is also a suggestion that such gastric atrophy might be higher in some ethnic groups. In a study on an elderly Latino cohort in the USA nearly half were found to have evidence of gastric atrophy with malabsorption food bound vitamin B_{12} but not free vitamin B_{12} (58).

In summary, while classical pernicious anemia is a problem, it has a low prevalence. By contrast, gastric atrophy may be a cause of malabsorption of vitamin B_{12} in a large sector of the elderly in both developed and developing countries. Most importantly, the latter, unlike the former, would be remedied by fortification of a food staple such as flour, with synthetic (free) vitamin B_{12}.

As summarized by Allen (59) in a recent review, more attention needs to be given to vitamin B_{12} status. She points out that a recent study shows that a review of data from Latin America shows that more than 40% of the subjects of all ages have low plasma vitamin B_{12} (60). A high prevalence of impaired vitamin B_{12} status is also seen in Kenyan school-children (48) and pregnant Nepalese women (47) and amongst Indian adults (64). Traditionally the problem was assumed to be due to strict vegetarianism, however it is now apparent that it is also an issue in lacto-ovo vegetarians (61) and in those with low meat consumption (62).

Maternal vitamin B_{12} status is also important in lactation, because as pointed out earlier, the effect on the infant is exacerbated by the low level of vitamin B_{12} in human milk. Low breast milk samples have been reported in Mexico (63) and Guatemala (64) with a knock-on deficiency in their infants.

INTERVENTION TRIALS WITH VITAMIN B_{12}

While vitamin B_{12} has been used in various intervention trials it has almost without exception been used in combination with folic acid with or without iron (27). As discussed earlier, under folic acid intervention trials, one can see that folic acid interventions apparently had no very extensive benefit. One can in some of the studies see that even when combined with vitamin B_{12} there was no apparent benefit. This, by inference can lead to the conclusion that vitamin B_{12} on its own would not have produced a response. Thus, the study of Iyengar and Apte (65) in pregnant women reported no benefit in Hb concentration for the combined vitamins. A similar conclusion was reached by the study of Basu et al. (66).

RIBOFLAVIN (VITAMIN B$_2$)

Riboflavin is widely abundant in most diets so long as they have a component of milk or milk products, meat, fish, or vegetables or fruit. However, in common with thiamine deficiency, which causes pellagra, riboflavin is not abundant in rice based diets (67). While overt deficiency with classical signs and symptoms of ariboflavinosis are probably not common, large sectors of the developing world are at risk of at least having reduced status (67). A wide range of enzymes involved in oxidation/reduction reactions use either adenine mononucleotide (FMM) or flavin adenine dinucleotide (FAD) as a cofactor. A central component of these cofactors is riboflavin, which must be provided in the diet as a vitamin (67). One could thus anticipate that deficiency, or even a reduced status of riboflavin could have a wide range of effects. Deficiency, if severe and prolonged enough is known to produce a normocytic normochronic anemia, although it is not clear which particular enzyme or enzymes give(s) rise to this clinical manifestation. Such overt anemia is really only associated with severe deficiency. However, what is perhaps of more general interest is the suggestion that even quite modest reductions in riboflavin status are widespread (68, 69), and that this may interfere with iron metabolism or absorption (67). A small study in Yugoslavia on 58 children given either no supplement or no riboflavin seemed to show a response in Hb over three months, although the design was neither placebo controlled nor randomized (70). A more recent trial in Croatia found no benefit in Hb response in riboflavin given above that of a placebo (70). In a small but well controlled study in 27 Nigerian adults, evidence emerged for a benefit of riboflavin alone in improving Hb concentration over an eight week period (72). Powers et al. (73) found an enhancing effect of Hb con-

centration in pregnant women on riboflavin given alone compared to placebo, although this effect was absent in lactating women.

Other trials have sought to show an enhancing effect of the addition of riboflavin to an iron supplement, in line with the putative biochemical interaction between the two discussed above. Decker et al. (74) produced evidence of an enhancement in pregnant women in Austria. Similarly, Charoenlarp et al. (75) found a significant enhancement in Hb concentration over five months in young children given riboflavin plus iron greater than seen with iron alone. .

PYRIDOXAL (VITAMIN B$_6$)

As with riboflavin, this vitamin is involved in the active site at numerous enzymes. Effects of its deficiency would be hard to predict. There does appear to be a well-documented sideroblastic anemia associated with its severe deficiency. Its role as a cofactor for rate-limiting enzyme in heme biosynthesis, namely α-aminolevulinic acid synthase, is an obvious candidate.

A small intervention trial in Germany on 32 anaemic children seems to show that vitamin B$_6$ gave greater acceleration in Hb synthesis than when iron was given alone (76). A normal population of 115 children in Croatia showed no benefits over placebo (71). Thaver et al. (77) conducted a review of five trials during pregnancy involving 1,646 women from the literature in 2006. They concluded that there was "no evidence that routine supplementation with vitamin B$_6$ during pregnancy is of any benefit and it may cause harm if too much is taken."

NIACIN (VITAMIN B$_1$)

This cofactor is involved in several key enzymes. Its deficiency is well documented as causing the deficiency condition pellagra. Anemia is not a pronounced feature of pellagra. There are no reported intervention trials.

THIAMINE

This is an essential cofactor for a number of key enzymes in biochemical pathways. Overt thiamine deficiency is associated with the well documented disease beri beri. This is associated with progressive neurological dysfunction rather than an anemia. While rare and not of great public health significance, it is worth noting that an isolated syndrome located to a genetic variant on the long arm of chromosome one which gives rise to a very specific type of megaloblastic anemia and is responsive to thiamine (78).

PANTHOTHENIC ACID

This vitamin is a constituent of coenzyme A, involved in metabolism. It has other functions, such

as being part of a cofactor in fatty acid synthase. While there is no doubt that it is an essential nutrient, its deficiency or signs and symptoms of such deficiency have not been documented as occurring in humans.

MULTIVITAMIN INTERVENTIONS

By their very nature, one cannot unravel which components in a multivitamin preparation may be the one to elicit a response. However, one of the main issues to be addressed in this chapter is the issue of whether any of the B complex of vitamins have an additional effect over the well documented effect of iron and the treatment of nutritional anemia. Trials that address this issue specifically are worth mentioning. Thus, a study in children in Peru showed no added benefit from a multivitamin containing several of the B complex over iron alone (79). A contrary experience was found in a small study of 28 children in Germany (80).

REFERENCES

1. Scott JM, Browne P. Anaemia/Megaloblastic anaemia. In: Sadler MJ, B.Caballero B, Strain JJ, eds. Encyclopedia of Human Nutrition. 2nd ed, London: Academic Press, 2005:109–17
2. Barker D. The midwife, the coincidence and the hypothesis. BMJ 2003;327:1428–30.
3. Chanarin I. The megaloblastic anaemias. 2nd ed. Oxford: Blackwell Scientific Publications, 1979:1–3.
4. Weir DG, Scott JM. The biochemical basis of the neuropathy in cobalamin deficiency Baillieres Clin Haematol 1995;8(3):479–97.
5. Manzoor M, Runcie, J. Folate-responsive neuropathy: report of 10 cases. BMJ 1976;1(6019):1176–8.
6. Molloy AM, Daly S, Mills J, et al.

Thermolabile variant of 5,10-methylenetetrahydrofolate reductase associated with low red cell folates: implications for folate intake recommendations. Lancet 1997;350(9075):445–6.
7. Higgins JR, Quinlivan EP, McPartlin J, Scott JM, Weir DG, Darling RN. The relationship between increased folate catabolism and the increased requirement for folate in pregnancy. Br J Obstet and Gynaecol 2000;107:1149–54.
8. Hercberg S, Chauliac M, Galan P, et al. Relationship between anaemia, iron and folacin deficiency, haemoglobinopathies and parasitic infection. Hum Nutr Clin Nutr 1986;40(5):371–9.
9. Hercberg S, Galan P, Assami M, Assami S.

Evaluation of the frequency of anaemia and iron-deficiency anaemia in a group of Algerian menstruating women by a mixed distribution analysis: contribution of folate deficiency and inflammatory processes in the determination of anaemia. Int J Epidemiol 1988;17(1):136–41.

10. Jacques PF, Selhub J, Bostom AG, Wilson PW, Rosenberg IH. The effect of folic acid fortification on plasma folate and total homocysteine concentrations. N Eng J Med 1999;340(19):1449–54.

11. McKillop DJ, Pentieva K, Daly S, et al. The effect of different cooking methods on folate retention in various foods that are amongst the major contributors to folate intake in the UK diet. Br J Nutr 2002;88(6):681–8.

12. Berry RJ, Li Z, Erickson JD, et al. Prevention of neural tube defects with folic acid in China. China-U.S. collaborative project for neural tube defect prevention. N Engl J Med 1999;341(20):1485–90.

13. Allain TJ, Gomo Z, Wilson AO, Ndemera B, Adamchak DJ, Matenga JA. Anaemia, macrocytosis, vitamin B12 and folate levels in elderly Zimbabweans. Cent Afr J Med 1997;43(11):325–8.

14. de Jong N, Green TJ, Skeaff CM, et al. Vitamin B12 and folate status of older New Zealand women. Asia Pac J Clin Nutr 2003;12(1):85–91.

15. Thurlow RA, Winichagoon P, Green T, et al. Only a small proportion of anaemia in northeast Thai schoolchildren is associated with iron deficiency. Am J Clin Nutr 2005;82(2):380–7.

16. Hettiarachchi M, Liyanage C, Wickremasinghe R, Hilmers DC, Abrahams SA. Prevalence and severity of micronutrient deficiency: a cross-sectional study among adolescents in Sri Lanka. Asia Pac J Clin Nutr 2006;15(1):56–63.

17. Garcia-Casal MN, Osorio C, Landaeta M, et al. High prevalence of folic acid and vitamin B12 deficiencies in infants, pregnant women in Venezuela. Eur J Clin Nutr 2005;59:1064–70.

18. Tamura T, Picciano MF. Folate and human reproduction. Am J Clin Nutr 2006;83:993–1016.

19. Kirke PN, Scott JM. Pre-conception nutrition and prevention of neural tube defects. In: Sadler JM, Caballero B, Strain JJ, eds. Encyclopedia of Human Nutrition. 2nd ed, London: Academic Press, 2005.

20. Daly LE, Kirke PM, Molloy A, Weir DG, Scott JM, Folate levels and neural tube defects. Implications for prevention. JAMA 1995;274:1698–702.

21. Daly S, Molloy AM, Mills JL, et al. Minimum effective dose of folic acid for food fortification to prevent neural tube defects, Lancet 1997; 350(9052):1666–9.

22. Report of national committee on folic acid fortification. Dublin: Food Safety Authority of Ireland, 2006.www.fsai.ie/publications/reports/folic_acid.pdf

23. Villar J, Merialdi M, Gulmezoglu AM, et al. Characteristics of randomized controlled trials included in systematic reviews of nutritional interventions reporting maternal morbidity, mortality, preterm delivery, intrauterine growth restriction and small for gestational age and birth weight outcomes. J Nutr 2003;133(5 Suppl 2):1632S–9S.

24. Allen L, Shrimpton R, The international Research on infant supplementation study: implications for programs and further research. Am J Clin Nutr 2005;135;666S–9S.

25. Gross R, Benade S, Lopez G, The international research on infant supplementation initiative. J Nutr 2005;135(3):628S–30S.

26. Smuts CM, Dhansay MA, Faber M, et al. Efficacy of multiple micronutrient supplementation for improving anaemia, micronutrient status, and growth in South African infants. Am J Clin Nutr 2005;135(3):653S–9S.

27. Fishman SM, Christian P, West KP. The role of vitamins in the prevention and control of anaemia. Public Health Nutrition 2000;3(2)125–50.

28. Batu AT, Toe T, Pe H, Nyunt KK. A prophylactic trial of iron and folic acid supplements in pregnant Burmese women. Isr J Med Sci 1976;12:1410–7.

29. Basu RN, Sood SK, Ramachandran K, Mathur M, Ramalingaswami V. Ethiopathogenesis of nutritional anaemia in pregnancy: a therapeutic approach. Am J Clin Nutr 1973;26(6):591–4.

30. Iyengar L, Apte SV. Prophylaxis of anaemia of pregnancy. Am J Clin Nutr 1970;2(6)3:725–30.

31. Fleming AF, Martin JD, Hahnel R, Westlake AJ. Effects of iron and folic acid antenatal supple-

ments on maternal haematology and fetal wellbeing. Med J Austr 1974;2:429–36.

32.   Sood SK, Ramachandran K, Mathur M, et al. WHO sponsored collaborative studies on nutritional anaemia in India: 1 the effects of supplemental oral iron administration to pregnant women. Q J Med 1975;44(174):241–58.

33.   Charoenlarp P, Dhanamitta S, Kaewvichit R, et al. A WHO collaborative study on iron supplementation in Burma and in Thailand. Am J Clin Nutr 1988;47(2):280–97.

34.   Fleming AF, Ghatoura GB, Harrison KA, Briggs ND, Dunn DT. The prevention of anaemia in pregnancy in primigravidae in the guinea savanna of Nigeria. Ann Trop Med Parasitol 1986;80(2):211–33.

35.   Ramakrishnan U, Neufeld LM, Gonzalez-Cossio T, et al. Multiple micronutrient supplements during pregnancy do not reduce anaemia or improve iron status compared to iron-only supplements in semirural Mexico. J Nutr 2004;134:898–903.

36.   Scholl TO, Hediger ML, Bendich A, Schall JI, Smith WK, Krueger PM. Use of multivitamin/mineral prenatal supplements: influence on the outcome of pregnancy. Am J Epidemiol 1997;146(2):134–41.

37.   Stevens D, Burman D, Strelling MK, Morris A. Folic acid supplementation in low birth weight infants. Pediatrics 1979;64:333–5.

38.   Worthington-White DA, Behnke M, Gross S. Premature infants require additional folate and vitamin B-12 to reduce the severity of the anaemia of prematurity. Am J Clin Nutr 1994;60:930–5.

39.   Christian P, Khatry SK, Katz J, et al. Effects of alternative maternal micronutrient supplements on low birth weight in rural Nepal: double blind randomised community trial. BMJ 2003;326(7389):571.

40.   Mackey AD, Picciano MF. Maternal folate status during extended lactation and the effect of supplemental folic acid. Am J Clin Nutr 1999;69(2):285–92.

41.   Tee ES, Kandiah M, Awin N, et al. School-administered weekly iron-folate supplements improve hemoglobin and ferriting concentrations in Malaysian adolescent girls. Am J Clin Nutr 1999;69:1249–56.

42.   Mahomed K. Iron and folate supplementation in pregnancy. Cochrane Database Sys Rev 2000;(2):CD001135.

43.   Mahomed K. Folate supplementation in pregnancy. Cochrane Database Sys Rev 2000;(2):CD000183.

44.   Weir DG, Scott JM. Cobalamins: Physiology dietary sources and requirements, In: Sadler MT, Caballero B, Strain JJ, eds. Encyclopedia of Human Nutrition. London: Academic Press, 1998:394–401.

45.   Stabler SP, Allen RH. Vitamin B12 deficiency as a worldwide problem. Ann Rev Nutr 2004;24:299–326.

46.   Refsum H, Yajnik CS, Gadkari M, et al. Hyperhomocysteinemia and elevated methylmalonic acid indicate a high prevalence of cobalamin deficiency in Asian Indians. Am J Clin Nutr 2001;84:233–41.

47.   Bondevik, GT, Schneede J, Refsum H, Lie RT, Ulstein M, Kvale G, Homocysteine and methylmalonic acid levels in pregnant Nepali women. Should cobalamin supplementation be considered? Eur J Clin Nutr 2001;74:55(10):856–64.

48.   Siekmann JH, Allen LH, Bwibo NO, Dement, MW, Murphy SP, Neumann CG. Kenyan school children have multiple micronutrient deficiencies, but increased plasma vitamin B-12 is the only detectable micronutrient response to meat or milk supplementation. J Nutr 2003;133:3972S–80S.

49.   Garcia-Casel, MN, Osorio C, Landaeta M, Leets I, Matus P, Fazzino F, Marcos E. High prevalence of folic acid and vitamin B12 deficiencies in infants, children, adolescents and pregnant women in Venezuela. Eur J Clin Nutr 2005);59(9):1064–70.

50.   King JE, Mazariegos M, Valdez C, Castaneda C, Solomons NW. Nutritional status indicators and their interactions in rural Guatemalan elderly: a study in San Pedro Ayampuc. Am J Clin Nutr 1997;66;795–802.

51.   Olivares M, Hertrampf E, Capurro MT, Wegner D, Prevalence of anaemia in elderly subjects living at home: role of micronutrient deficiency and inflammation. Eur J Clin Nutr 2000;54:834–9.

52.   Black AK, Allen LH, Pelto GH, de Mata MP, Chavez A. Iron, vitamin B-12 and folate status in

Mexico: associated factors in men and women and during pregnancy and lactation. J Nutr 1994;124:1179–88.

53. Gamble MV, Ahsan H, Liu X, et al. Folate and cobalamin deficiencies and hyperhomocysteinemia in Bangladesh. Am J Clin Nutr 2005;81(6):1372–7.

54. Allen LH. Vitamin B12 metabolism and status during pregnancy, lactation and infancy. Adv Exp Med Biol 1994;352:173–86.

55. Anaya M, Begin F, Brown KH, Peerson JM, Torun B, Allen L. The high prevalence of vitamin B12 deficiency in Guatemalan infants is associated with a higher intake of breast milk, and with poor quality complementary foods. FASEB J 2004;18:844A.

56. Baik HW, Russell RM. Vitamin B12 deficiency in the elderly, Annu Rev Nutr 1999;19:357–77.

57. Carmel R. Colabamin, the stomach and ageing, Am J Clin Nutr 1997;66:750–9.

58. Campbell AK, Miller JW, Green R, Haan MN Allen LH. Plasma vitamin B-12 concentrations in an elderly Latino population are predicted by serum gastrin concentrations and crystalline vitamin B-12 intake. J Nutr 2003;133(9):2770–6.

59. Allen LH, Multiple micronutrients in pregnancy and lactation: an overview. Am J Clin Nutr 2005;81(5):1206S–12S.

60. Allen LH, Folate and vitamin B12 status in the Americas. Nutr Rev 2004;62:29S–33S.

61. Helman AD, Darnton-Hill I. Vitamin and iron status in new vegetarians. Am J Clin Nutr 1987;45:785–9.

62. Hermann W, Schorr H, Purschwitz K, Rassoul F, Richter V. Total homocysteine, vitamin B(12), and total antioxidant status in vegetarians. Clin Chem 2001;47(6):1094–101.

63. Allen LH, Rosado JL, Casterline JE, Martinez H, Lopez P, Munoz E, Black AK. Vitamin B-12 deficiency and malabsorption are highly prevalent in rural Mexican communities. Am J Clin Nutr 1995;62:1013–9.

64. Casterline, JE, Allen LH and Ruel MT. Vitamin B-12 deficiency is very prevalent in lactating Guatemalan women and their infants at three months postpartum. J Nutr 1997;127:1966–72.

65. Iyengar I, Apte SV. Prophylaxis of anaemia of pregnancy. Am J Clin Nutr 1970;23:725–30.

66. Basu RN, Sood SK, Ramachandran K, Mathur M, Ramalingaswami V. Etiopathogenesis of nutritional anaemia in pregnancy: a therapeutic approach. Am J Clin Nutr 1973;26:591–4.

67. Power JH. Riboflavin (vitamin B-2) and health. Amer J Clin Nutr 2003;77:1352–60.

68. Powers HJ, Bates CJ, Lamb WH. Haematological response to supplement of iron and riboflavin to pregnant and lactating women in rural Gambia. Hum Nutr Clin Nutr 1985;39C:117–29.

69. Prasad PA, Bamji MS, Kakshmi AV, Satyanarayama K. Functional impact of riboflavin supplementation in urban school children. Nutr Res 1990;10: 275–81.

70. Buzina R, Jusic M, Milanovic N, Sapunar J, Brubacher G. The effects of riboflavin administration on iron metabolism parameters in a school-going population. Int J Vitam Nutr Res 1979;49:136–43.

71. Suboticanec K, Stavljenic A, Schalch W, Buzina R. Effects of pyridoxine and riboflavin supplementation on physical fitness in young adolescents. Int J Vitam Nutr Res 1990;60(1):81–8.

72. Ajayi OA, Okike OC, Yusuf Y. Haematological response to supplements of riboflavin and ascorbic acid in Nigerian young adults. Eur J Haematol 1990;44:209–12.

73. Powers HJ, Bates CJ, Lamb WH. Haematological response to supplements of iron and riboflavin to pregnant and lactating women in rural Gambia. Hum Nutr Clin Nutr 1985;39(2):117–29.

74. Decker K, Dotis B, Glatzle D, Hinselmann M. Riboflavin status and anaemia in pregnant women. Nutr Metab 1977;21:17S–9S.

75. Charoenlarp P, Pholpothi T, Chatpunyaporn P, Schelp FP. Effect of riboflavin on the hematologic changes in iron supplementation of schoolchildren. Southeast Asian J Trop Med Public Health 1980;11:97–103.

76. Reinken I, Kurz R, [Activity studies of an iron-vitamin B6 preparation for enteral treatment of iron deficiency anaemia.] Int J Vitam Nutr Res 1975;44:411–18. German.

77   Thaver D, Saeed MA, Bhutta ZA, Pyridoxine (vitamin B6) supplementation in pregnancy. Cochrane Database Syst Rev 2006;(2):CD000179.
78   Ricketts CJ, Minton JA, Samuel J, Ariyawansa I, Wales JK, Lo IF, Barrett TG. Thiamine-responsive megaloblastic anaemia syndrome: long-term follow-up and mutation analysis of seven families. Acta Paediatr 2006;95(1):99–104.

79   Bradfield RB, Jensen MV, Gonzales L, Garrayar C. Effect of low-level iron and vitamin supplementation on a tropical anaemia, Am J Clin Nutr 1968;21:57–67.
80   Reinken I, Kurz R. [The treatment of anaemia due to iron deficiency with iron combined with vitamins.] Klin Padiatr 1978;190:163–7.

10

Vitamin A in nutritional anemia

Keith P. West, Jr.

Alison D. Gernand

Alfred Sommer

Bloomberg School of Public Health, Johns Hopkins University, Baltimore, USA
Contact: kwest@jhsph.edu

KEITH P. WEST, JR.
Keith earned his PhD from the Johns Hopkins School of Hygiene and Public Health in the USA. He is currently the inaugural George G. Graham Professor of Infant and Child Nutrition in the Department of International Health at the Johns Hopkins Bloomberg School of Public Health, holds a joint appointment in the Department of Ophthalmology at the Johns Hopkins School of Medicine, and is a Registered Dietitian. He is presently directing collaborative research projects that are evaluating effects of micronutrient interventions on the health and survival of mothers and children in Bangladesh and Nepal. Keith has worked extensively in Southern Asia over the past three decades to prevent vitamin A deficiency.

ALISON D. GERNAND
Alison has a MPH in International and Family Health from the University of Texas School of Public Health, Houston, and is a Registered Dietitian. She worked as a Program Manager to develop, implement, and evaluate a bilingual, community-based nutrition intervention for Hispanics on the US-Mexico border region of El Paso, Texas and Juarez, Mexico. She is currently a PhD student and a Research Assistant at the Center for Human Nutrition, Department of International Health, Johns Hopkins Bloomberg School of Public Health, Baltimore.

ALFRED SOMMER
Alfred obtained his MD from Harvard Medical School, Boston, and holds an MHS in Epidemiology from the Johns Hopkins School of Hygiene and Public Health, Baltimore, USA. He is currently Dean Emeritus and Professor of Epidemiology and International Health at the Johns Hopkins Bloomberg School of Public Health as well as Professor of Ophthalmology at the Wilmer Eye Institute at Johns Hopkins University School of Medicine. Alfred has won numerous awards for his work, is a member of many professional associations, and is an honorary lecturer at a number of universities.

INTRODUCTION

There are many possible causes of anemia; including iron deficiency, hookworm, malaria, chronic diseases and other nutritional deficiencies. Iron deficiency is a major form of nutritional anemia that results from a depletion of the body's iron stores and plasma levels, depriving the erthyroid bone marrow of essential iron for hemoglobin synthesis (1). Iron-deficient erythropoiesis, however, may also occur in the presence of normal or elevated iron stores that are sequestered as a result of inflammation from infection (2, 3) or chronic disease (1). Other nutritional deficiencies, such as those of folic acid, vitamins B_{12}, C or vitamin A may also adversely affect hematopoiesis and lead to anemia (4). In particular, vitamin A deficiency may increase the risk of iron deficient-erythropoiesis and anemia as a result of altering the absorption, storage, release or transport of iron to the marrow (5). Because vitamin A is essential for an adequate innate and acquired immune response, vitamin A deficiency may also contribute to inflammation-induced sequestration of iron and other responses to infection that increase risk of anemia (6, 7). Interventions that control vitamin A deficiency therefore have the potential to help control anemia induced by either malnutrition or infection. The importance to public health of the interaction between anemia - vitamin A deficiency can be gauged by the extent to which both co-occur within populations.

While developing countries provide context for a modern public health focus on vitamin A deficiency as a cause of anemia, historically its role in nutritional anemia has been a global one (8). Nearly a hundred years ago, Danish orphans with xerophthalmia were noted to be "weak, thin and markedly anemic" (9). In China, Berglund described an anemia that responded to treatment with cod liver oil (10). Nearly all infants in a case series reported from the United States in the 1930s who had died with histopathologic evidence of vitamin A deficiency had, on autopsy, sequestered deposits of iron in the liver and spleen (11). In early rat experiments, progressive vitamin A deficiency was noted to cause a fall in

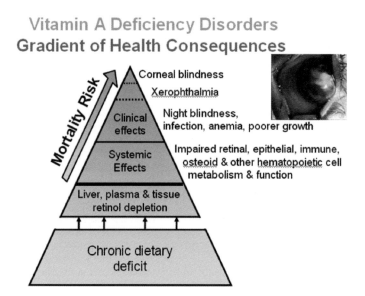

Figure 10.1: Vitamin A Deficiency Disorders (VADD): Adapted from (28).

hemoglobin prior to developing xerophthalmia (12), degenerative changes in the bone marrow (13) and heavy deposits of hemosiderin (14). However, a biphasic hematologic response was also apparent in early studies, with hemoglobin concentration initially falling, followed by a polycythemia in the presence of severe vitamin A deficiency (15). The finding of hemoconcentration in late-stage vitamin A deficiency, attributed to a disturbance in water balance and reduced water intake, has since been repeatedly observed in different species (12, 16-18). Over the ensuing decades anemia was routinely noted as a potential consequence of human vitamin A deficiency (19, 20).

From the mid-fifties onward, multiple population based surveys among children and adults consistently noted an interdependence between serum retinol and blood hemoglobin levels, serving to strengthen evidence of this biological linkage (8). In the seventies Hodges and colleagues carried out a small but seminal study in which the hemoglobin concentration of 5 of 8 male volunteers on a chronic, vitamin A-deficient diet dropped 30% (from a mean of 161 to 114 g/L), despite receiving adequate dietary iron. Their hemoglobin returned to normal following either daily vitamin A or β-carotene supplementation (21), suggesting that vitamin A is required for an adequate hematologic response to iron. Subsequent studies have revealed blunted responses to iron when vitamin A status is marginal or deficient (22) or improved responses to iron when provided with vitamin A (23-26). Over the past thirty years the metabolic connection of vitamin A and iron in affecting risk of anemia, and the potential of vitamin A to enhance effects of iron or alone to alleviate part of the burden of anemia have been areas of intense research, review and program interest (4, 5, 8, 27).

After briefly reviewing the extent and broad health consequences of vitamin A deficiency, this review focuses on anemia as a potential disorder of vitamin A deficiency, the hematologic response to vitamin A under varying conditions, and plau-

sible metabolic pathways that may respond to shifts in vitamin A nutriture. As childhood and pregnancy represent life stages of greatest risk for vitamin A deficiency (27, 28), iron deficiency and anemia (8), the chapter focuses on evidence in these vulnerable groups.

VITAMIN A DEFICIENCY DISORDERS (VADD)

Vitamin A deficiency is the leading cause of pediatric blindness and a major nutritional determinant of severe infection and mortality among children in the developing world (27). There are an estimated 125-130 million preschool aged children with vitamin A deficiency, defined by a serum retinol concentration less than 0.70 µmol/L (20 µg/dL) or equivalently, by abnormal conjunctival impression cytology (28–30). Mild to moderate vitamin A deficiency appears to be a problem in school-aged and adolescent years, although its health consequences at these ages remain unclear (31). In adulthood, there is growing evidence of widespread maternal vitamin A deficiency in undernourished settings, where an estimated 20 million pregnant women at a given time are believed to be of marginal to deficient status, of whom six million have night blindness (28), the most common clinical manifestation of deficiency (32).

Conceptually, the diverse health consequences of vitamin A deficiency (VAD) have been grouped as a class of disorders (or VADD) among which anemia is one that, depending on conditions of risk, respond to vitamin A repletion (33). Illustrated in **Figure 10.1**, vitamin A deficiency disorders as a public health problem arise from a diet that is chronically insufficient in vitamin A or provitamin A carotenoids to meet physiologic needs (27). Food sources of preformed vitamin A include liver, cod liver oil, milk, cheese and fortified foods, while common food sources of provitamin A carotenoids (especially β-carotene)

Table 10.1: Differences in blood hemoglobin per unit increment in serum retinol; surveys and observational studies.

Country (reference)	Age (yr) / sex	Number	Difference in Hb (Δ g/L) per µg/dL (µmol/L) increment in serum retinol	Prevalence (%)	
				VAD	Anemia[1]
Eight countries[2] (21)	15–45 / F (NPNL)	NR	0.71 (20.5)	Varied	Varied
Thailand (51)	1–8 / M & F	1060	0.54 (15.5	44	100
Bangladesh (52)	5–12/ M & F	242	0.17 (4.9)	<3	NR
Pakistan (53)	4–8 / M & F	120	0.77 (22.0)	17	100
Bangladesh (54)	5–15 / F	225	0.34 (9.9)	11	22
Kazakhstan (50)	8–17 / M & F	159	0.18 (5.1)	1	27
Nepal (46, West et al., unpublished, 2006)	15–44 / F (pregnant, placebo)	349	0.38 (11.0)	19	73[3]
	15–44 / F (pregnant, β-carotene)	479	0.29 (8.4)	14	67
	15–44 / F (pregnant, vitamin A)	405	0.18 (5.2)	3	68

[1] VAD = vitamin A deficiency defined as plasma/serum retinol <0.70 µmol/L (20 µg/dL); anemia defined as Hb <110 g/L; NPNL = non-pregnant, non-lactating women, NR = not reported.

[2] Paraguay, Chile, Northeast Brazil, Uruguay, Ecuador, Venezuela, Guatemala and Ethiopia.

[3] Anemia prevalence in a population with a 73% prevalence of hookworm (60).

include soft yellow fruits, orange and yellow tubers and dark green leafy vegetables (34, 35). Vitamin A is known to have two basic functions: It enables proper functioning of rod photoreceptors in the retina of the eye to permit vision under conditions of low light. Absence of dietary vitamin A leads to the condition of night blindness (36). Secondly, through nuclear retinoid recep-tors, retinoic acid metabolites of vitamin A are involved in regulating synthesis of proteins that affect cell growth, differentiation, function or longevity, consequences of which have been well studied in epithelial, immune, osteoid and other hematopoietic cell systems (37). Depending on numerous host factors, progressive vitamin A deficiency can lead to increased severity of infection such as measles (38), malaria (39) and diarrhea (40), anemia (27), poorer growth (41, 42) and advanced stages of xerophthalmia that include conjunctival xerosis with "Bitot's spots," and xerosis, ulceration and necrosis of the cornea **(shown in Figure 10.1)** (27). Underlying vitamin A deficiency increases risk of death from severe illness, reflected by a demonstrated ability of vitamin A supplementation to reduce child mortality by 25-35% in many settings (27, 43-45) and, in high risk populations, maternal mortality (46).

ANEMIA AS A VADD

Anemia has many causes, including those of nutritional origin, of which iron deficiency dominates, infectious origin (eg, due to hookworm, malaria, HIV and other infectious diseases), and those due to inflammation of chronic disease. While iron deficiency is the leading cause of nutritional anemia, vitamin A joins several hematinic nutrients including vitamins C, E, and B_{12} and folic acid that, when deficient, can adversely affect iron-dependent erythropoiesis and contribute to anemia (4). Vitamin A deficiency, for example, may compromise iron absorption, storage, transport and delivery to bone marrow through several paths (4, 5, 8), reduce erythrocytosis by lowering erythropoietin production (47-49), or may induce iron sequestration due to increased severity of infection (7). The classic study by Hodges et al was likely reflecting some of these blunted effects of vitamin A deficiency on iron metabolism (21) as have other studies. For example, in South Africa vitamin A deficiency appeared to blunt serum iron and transferrin saturation responses in school children who were given a soup fortified with iron (20 mg) and vitamin C (100 mg) for nearly four months (22). Increased serum ferritin concentrations suggested that iron had been absorbed and stored, but not released in children with poorer vitamin A status. In the evidence that follows, from studies of association, treatment trials, animal experiments and

in vitro studies, it seems apparent that a fraction of anemia in undernourished populations may be a consequence of vitamin A deficiency and reparable following vitamin A intervention.

Evidence of association: vitamin A deficiency and anemia

Vitamin A and hematologic status covary, as do risks of vitamin A deficiency and anemia in undernourished populations. In many settings serum retinol and hemoglobin concentrations are correlated, whether expressed on an ecological basis, as reported by Hodges et al from eight country surveys of non-pregnant, non-lactating women in 1978 (r=0.77, n=8, p<0.05) or as seen in populations of children, adolescents and pregnant women among which correlation coefficients have ranged from r=0.18 to 0.90 (8, 21, 50). Since then a number of studies have correlated and quantified the linear association between serum retinol and blood hemoglobin concentrations in different populations (50-54). From these studies it is possible to calculate the change that might be expected in hemoglobin if vitamin A status (ie, serum retinol) were to increase in a population, as presented in **Table 10.1**. Estimates of hemoglobin change vary from 0.2 g/L to 0.8 g/L for each microgram per liter increase in plasma retinol. Thus, a vitamin A intervention that maintains a plasma retinol increment of, say, 5 µg/dL (0.175 µmol/L) might expect to raise hemoglobin by up to 4 g/L, with presumably larger increments expected to occur in vitamin A-deficient populations, and smaller ones seen in groups exhibiting higher, homeostatically controlled levels of plasma retinol. This was seen in a randomized trial population in Nepal where women were supplemented weekly with placebo, β-carotene (42 mg) or vitamin A (7000 µg retinol equivalents) for at least several months prior to a mid-gestational phlebotomy (46). Vitamin A status was lowest among placebo recipients and highest in those given preformed vitamin A supplements (46, 55). Under these experimentally achieved conditions, a larger hemoglobin difference per unit increase in serum retinol was observed in the placebo group (0.39 g/L) while the shallowest slope occurred among mothers whose vitamin A status was adequate (due to their routine receipt of preformed vitamin A) (0.18 g/L) (West KP et al, unpublished data, 2006). These data would predict a stronger effect for vitamin A in preventing anemia in more vitamin A-deficient populations.

The extent to which vitamin A deficiency and anemia co-occur or cluster is of interest as it reflects the extent to which biologic interdependence may exist under extant population conditions (5). Several surveys in recent years reveal overlap in children and pregnant women. For example, in the Marshall Islands where 60% of children 1 to 5 years of age had vitamin A deficiency (serum <0.70 µmol/L) and 36% had anemia (Hb <110 g/L), one-third had both conditions. The relative odds of having anemia given that a child was vitamin A-deficient was 1.45 (odds ratio, p <0.01) (56). Nearly the same situation was observed in Micronesia, where 57% of Chuukese preschoolers were vitamin A-deficient (based on impression cytology), 41% were anemic based on a hematocrit of <33 and 33% had both conditions (57). In less-deficient Honduras, where 48% and 40% of 1 to 2 year olds were marginal or worse in vitamin A status (serum retinol <1.05 µmol/L) and anemic (Hb <110 g/L), 22% were classified with both (58). In Venezuela where only 22% of 2 to 6 year old children were vitamin A-deficient (<0.70 µmol/L) and 38% anemic, both conditions were found in only 8% (59). Among undernourished, pregnant women in Nepal, the prevalences of marginal-to-deficient vitamin A status (serum retinol <1.05 µmol/L), anemia and both were 54%, 73% and 43% (60), among whom the odds ratio of having anemia if vitamin A status was poor was 2.5 (95% confidence interval: 1.2 to 5.0). Thus, while findings on co-occurrence of anemia and vitamin A deficiency suggest both conditions overlap, especially where individual burdens of each are high, they also substantially occur independently, meriting their own assessments and approaches to prevention.

Effects of vitamin A supplementation on hematologic status

Clinical trials carried out in populations of children (**Table 10.2**) and women of reproductive age (**Table 10.3**) have tended to show improvement in indices of iron metabolism and erythropoiesis in response to vitamin A interventions, despite variation in nutritional risk, and in the dosage, frequency, duration and form of supplementation.

1. Children

Initial studies in Southeast Asia and Central America were directed toward discerning effects of vitamin A delivered via fortification. In Indonesia, preschool consumption of vitamin A-fortified monosodium glutamate (MSG) that provided ~240 µg of vitamin A per day (or ~80% of the new Recommended Dietary Allowance (35) led to a mean increase of 10 g/L vs. a 2 g/L change in controls after almost a year of test program exposure (61) (**Table 10.2**). These findings supported an earlier study in Guatemala where iron indicators favorably shifted and stabilized in the first two years after a national sugar fortification program that enabled children's daily vitamin A intake to reach ~350 retinol equivalents per day (62). After six months serum retinol and iron increased, serum ferritin decreased, and total iron-binding capacity (TIBC) and transferrin saturation (%TS) increased, suggesting that tissue iron had been mobilized following improved vitamin A status. After two years, there had been a sustained increase in serum concentrations of retinol (+2.5 µg/dL), iron (+9 µg/dL) and ferritin (+5 µg/dL) and a consistent, lower TIBC (-14 µg/dL) suggesting that iron stores and iron delivered, presumably for erythropoiesis, had increased over time.

Two trials in Latin America and one in East Africa have tested effects of daily, semi-weekly or weekly small-dose vitamin A supplementation, alone and with iron or zinc, for periods of up to six months **(Table 10.2)**. In Guatemala, a daily supplement of 3 mg of vitamin A per day among children 1 to 8 years of age led to ~6 g/L increase in hemoglobin over controls after two months (23). Adding vitamin A to iron was no more efficacious than giving iron alone **(Figure 10.2a)**. A similar, randomized, factorial design was implemented in Tanzania among 9 to 12 year old children to test the effects of 1.5 mg (5000 IU) of vitamin A alone and with 60 mg of iron given 3 days per week. Over the course of three months, vitamin A supplementation significantly increased the mean hemoglobin concentration by ~10 g/L over the change in controls, with further significant increments of 4.0 and 8.6 g/L obtained with iron alone and vitamin A plus iron **(Figure 10.2b)**. No other hematologic indices were assessed (24). The comparability of these two trials in their design and rigor offer an opportunity to view their consistency of effects related to vitamin A, iron and both nutrients combined. In Belize, a weekly oral dose of vitamin A increased hemoglobin whereas adding a weekly dose of zinc had no additional hematologic effect (63).

Several trials in Latin America, Southern Asia and Africa have focused on discerning effects of single, high-potency vitamin A supplementation in anemic and/or vitamin A deficient children **(Table 10.2)**. These tests are relevant where periodic vitamin A supplementation remains a major prophylaxis strategy in the developing world. Among anemic Peruvian infants and toddlers, giving a 30 mg (100,000 IU) oral dose of vitamin A at the outset of the two-month trial, that also evaluated added zinc to iron alone, conferred no additional benefit over that seen with daily zinc (64). Vitamin A status of the children, however, was not reported and may have been adequate.

In Thailand, giving children a single 60 mg (200,000 IU) dose of vitamin A led to, after two weeks, increases in serum iron, %TS, hemoglobin and hematocrit compared to controls (65). In another trial by the same investigators, serum iron and %TS were higher in the treatment group after two months, but these effects had disappeared four months after dosing (51). In mildly xerophthalmic cases and biochemically deficient controls in Indonesia, a 60 mg oral dose of vitamin A increased serum ferritin (iron stores) after five weeks. While there was no overall hematologic response, among initially anemic children (Hb < 110 g/L) high potency vitamin A appeared to stimulate a 7 g/L increase in hemoglobin (66). Children were not followed up longer, however, as they had been in the Thai study.

A trial in Morocco **(Table 10.2)** compared the efficacy of two, consecutive 5-monthly rounds of vitamin A (60 mg) in mildly vitamin A-deficient and anemic school aged children. Because of its randomized design, placebo use, extended duration and choice of indicators, the trial provides the most complete findings to date on the hematologic responses to periodic vitamin A supplementation in a population unaffected by endemic infectious disease (49). Compared to controls, whose status remained constant, sequential doses of vitamin A had cumulative effects: serum retinol and its carrier proteins gradually increased as percentages of vitamin A-deficient children decreased, reflecting the intended nutritional effect. Hemoglobin gradually increased, reaching a difference of 7 g/L from controls after 10 months, and the prevalence of anemia decreased (38% vs. 59% in controls). Plasma erythropoietin (EPO) concentration gradually increased (by 3.7 mIU/mL over controls by 10 months), supported by a decrease in the log10 EPO regression slope on hemoglobin which can be interpreted as reflecting a physiologic adjustment in hemoglobin (ie, hypoxia)-induced regulation of EPO production (67), supporting a view that hematopoiesis may have been mediated by improved

Table 10.2: Clinical trials of vitamin A on anemia in children.

Country (reference)	Description of study			Baseline prevalence[1]		Changes in:[2]		
	Subjects' age (n)	Length of trial	Treatment groups and regimen	Anemia (%)	VAD (%)	Hb[3] (g/L)	Serum retinol (μmol/L)	Serum ferritin (μg/L)
Indonesia (61)	0–5 yr (445)	5 mo	Unfortified MSG ~240 μg RAE VA/d fortified MSG	NR	39 38	-2.0 10.0[a,b]	-0.70 0.11	NR
Guatemala (23)	1–8 yr (115)	2 mo	Placebo 3 mg VA/d 3 mg/kg iron/d 3 mg VA/d + 3 mg/kg iron/d	80 80 83 71	NR	3.2 9.3[a] 13.8[a,b] 14.2[a,b]	0.10 0.35[a,b] 0.13 0.36[a,b]	-4.9 0.1 5.5[a] 5.4[a]
Tanzania (24)	9–12 yr (136)	3 mo	Placebo 3 d/wk 1.5 mg VA 3 d/wk 60 mg iron 3 d/wk 1.5 mg VA 3 d/wk + 60 mg iron 3 d/wk	100	NR	3.6[a] 13.5[a,b] 17.5[a,b] 22.1[a,b]	NR	NR
Belize (63)	2–6 yr (43)	6 mo	Placebo 70 mg zinc/wk 3030 RAE VA/wk 70 mg zinc/wk + 3030 RAE VA/wk	NR	NR	4.0 8.0[a,b] 12.0[a,b] 11.0[a,b]	0.05 0.16 0.18 0.12	NR
Peru (64)	6–35 mo (323)	18 wk	3 mg/kg iron/d 3 mg/kg iron/d + 3 mg/kg zinc/d 3 mg/kg iron/d + 3 mg/kg zinc/d + 100,000 IU VA (single dose)	100	NR	19.5[a] 24.0[a,b] 23.8[a,b]	NR	24.5[a] 33.0[a,b] 30.8[a,b]
Thailand (51)	1–8 yr (166)	4 mo	No supplement 60 mg VA + 40 mg VE (single dose)	100	NR	2.4[a] 2.0[a]	0.13[a] 0.15[a]	12.5[a] 6.6[a]

Country (reference)	Subjects' age (n)	Length of trial	Treatment groups and regimen	Anemia (%)	VAD (%)	Hb[3] (g/L)	Serum retinol (μmol/L)	Serum ferritin (μg/L)
Thailand (65)	3–9 yr (134)	2 wk	No supplement 60 mg VA (single dose)	100	NR	-0.8 2.2[b]	-0.07[a] 0.15[a,b]	6.1 5.0
Indonesia (66)	3–6 yr (236)	5 wk	*Xerophthalmic children:* Placebo 60 mg VA (single dose) *Clinically normal children:* Placebo 60,000 μg RAE VA (single dose) *All children with Hb <11.0 g/L:* Placebo 60 mg VA (single dose)	NR	100 100 50 37	5.0 5.0 5.0 5.0 14.0[a] 21.0[a,b]	0.1 1.1[a,b] 0.1 0.9[a,b] NR	4.0 16.8[a,b] 3.1 12.9[a,b] NR
Morocco (49)	5–13 yr (81)	10 mo	Placebo (sunflower oil) at baseline & 5 mo 60 mg VA at baseline & 5 mo	54 54	20 15	1 7[a,b]	0.06 0.21[a,b]	1 -7[a,b]

[1] VAD = vitamin A deficiency defined as plasma/serum retinol <0.70 μmol/L (20 μg/dL); anemia defined per Hb cutoff used in study.

[2] Superscripts: a denotes significantly different from baseline, P<0.05; b denotes significantly different from control at follow up. P<0.05.

[3] Abbreviations: Hb, hemoglobin; yr, year; mo, month; wk, week; d, day; MSG, monosodium glutamate; NR, not reported; RAE, retinol activity equivalents; VA, vitamin A; IU, international units; VE, vitamin E.

NR = not reported

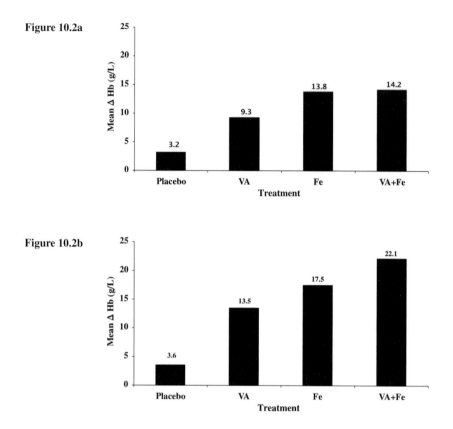

Figure 10.2: (a) Effects of daily vitamin A (3 mg), iron (3 mg/kg) or both vitamin A and iron supplementation versus a placebo on blood hemoglobin after 2 months in 1–8 year old Guatemalan children. Vitamin A also raised serum iron and %TS (23). (b) Effects of thrice weekly vitamin A (1.5 mg), iron (60 mg) or both vitamin A and iron versus a placebo on blood hemoglobin after 3months in 9-12 year old Tanzanian schoolchildren (24).

vitamin A nutriture (68). Concentrations of transferrin receptor and serum ferritin both steadily declined while their ratio remained unchanged, suggesting that while total body iron remained unchanged, hepatic iron had been mobilized to support erythropoiesis. Given a lack of measurable change in estimated body iron stores, these findings do not suggest there had been an increase in iron absorption.

High potency vitamin A appears to stimulate iron metabolism, reduce iron-deficient erythropoieisis and improve hematologic health. Overall,

interventions in children suggest that a ~3 to 10 g/L increase in hemoglobin can be expected when dosing anemic and, at least mildly vitamin A deficient individuals (8). Based on trials in South Asia, the duration of effect may be less than four months, perhaps affected by seasonality and limits of dosage efficacy. In populations less stressed by seasonality and infectious diseases, as may exist in Morocco, the duration of effect appears to be at least five months. The latter trial also suggests that repeated, periodic doses of vitamin A may confer additive hematologic benefit.

2. Women of reproductive age

Research on the roles of vitamin A to prevent anemia has maintained a focus on the reproductive years, when during pregnancy 40% to 60% of women may have iron deficiency and anemia (69) and, in undernourished populations, 10% or more may become night blind due to vitamin A deficiency (32, 70). In a factorial trial among 251 pregnant Indonesian women in the early nineties, Suharno and colleagues observed that daily vitamin A supplementation (2.4 mg retinol) of mothers for eight weeks significantly raised hemoglobin concentration by 3.7 g/L over that of placebo

recipients, an effect that explained 35% of pregnancy-related anemia (**Table 10.3**) (25). Several other status indicators improved including packed cell volume, TIBC, %TS and serum retinol and iron concentrations, suggestive of iron mobilization into circulation. The maximal effects were observed in women receiving both vitamin A and iron, among whom virtually all (97%) anemia had resolved. These findings are re-expressed across ratios in **Figure 10.3a** which shows a gradient of decreased risk of anemia among women given vitamin A, iron, or both nutrients, relative to placebo recipients. Another trial among pregnant

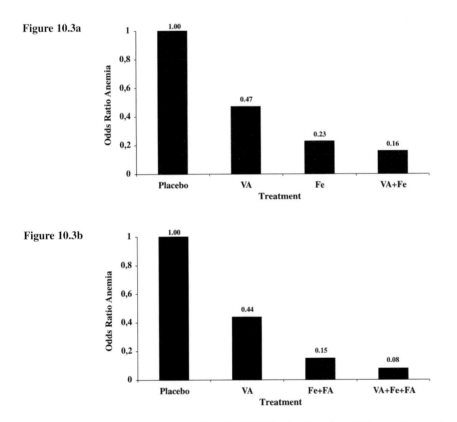

Figure 10.3a

Figure 10.3b

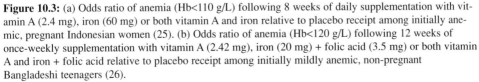

Figure 10.3: (a) Odds ratio of anemia (Hb<110 g/L) following 8 weeks of daily supplementation with vitamin A (2.4 mg), iron (60 mg) or both vitamin A and iron relative to placebo receipt among initially anemic, pregnant Indonesian women (25). (b) Odds ratio of anemia (Hb<120 g/L) following 12 weeks of once-weekly supplementation with vitamin A (2.42 mg), iron (20 mg) + folic acid (3.5 mg) or both vitamin A and iron + folic acid relative to placebo receipt among initially mildly anemic, non-pregnant Bangladeshi teenagers (26).

Table 10.3: Clinical trials of vitamin A on anemia in women of reproductive age.

Country (reference)	Description of study			Baseline prevalence[1]		Changes in:[2]		
	Subjects' age (n)	Length of trial	Treatment groups and regimen	Anemia (%)	VAD (%)	Hb[3] (g/L)	Serum retinol (µmol/L)	Serum ferritin (µg/L)
Indonesia (25)	17–35 yr Pregnant (251)	8 wk	Placebo 2.4 mg VA/d 60 mg iron/d 2.4 mg VA/d + 60 mg iron/d	100	10	2.0 6.0b 10.0b 15.0b	-0.01 0.18b 0.00 0.23b	-0.2 0.0 0.6b 0.4b
Indonesia (71)	17–35 yr Pregnant (190)	14-20 wk	120 mg iron/wk + 500 µg folic acid/wk 120 mg iron/wk + 500 µg folic acid/wk + 4,800 RE VA/wk	19	13 17	2.1 3.7a	-0.12 0.01	-3.0 -7.1a
Bangladesh (26)	14–19 yr F (480)	12 wk	Placebo 2.42 mg retinol palmate/wk 120 mg iron/wk + 3.5 mg folic acid/wk 120 mg iron/wk + 3.5 mg folic acid/wk + 2.42 mg retinol palmate/wk	96 82 82 92	27	1.2 3.3a,b 9.1a,b 12.2a,b	-0.01 0.15b -0.01 0.13b	-2.9 -3.9 2.3b 5.0b
Bangladesh (78)	15–45 yr Non-pregnant (216)	60 d	60 mg iron/d 60 mg iron/d + 200,000 IU VA (single dose) 60 mg iron/d + 15 mg zinc/d + 200,000 IU VA (single dose)	100	6	13.4a 15.9a 17.9a,b	-0.03 0.09 0.04	20.0a 13.8a 16.0a
Malawi (79)	Pregnant (203)	Enrollment to delivery	30 mg iron/d + 400 µg folic acid/d 30 mg iron/d + 400 µg folic acid/d + 3000 µg RE VA/d	49 51	25 35	7.3a 4.7a	-0.11a 0.07	NR
Malawi (80)	Pregnant (700)	Enrollment to delivery	60 mg iron/d + 250 µg folic acid/d 60 mg iron/d + 250 µg folic acid/d + 5,000 IU VA/d 60 mg iron/d + 250 µg folic acid/d + 10,000 IU VA/d	100	<5	0.9a 0.8a 1.0a	-0.86 0.62 1.69	NR

[1] VAD = vitamin A deficiency defined as plasma/serum retinol <0.70 µmol/L (20 µg/dL); anemia defined per Hb cutoff used in study.

[2] Superscripts: a denotes significantly different from baseline, P<0.05; b denotes significantly different from control at follow up, P<0.05.

[3] Abbreviations: Hb, hemoglobin; yr, year; mo, month; wk, week; d, day; MSG, monosodium glutamate; NR, not reported; RE, retinol equivalents; VA, vitamin A; IU, international units; VE, vitamin E.

Indonesian women that added 4800 retinol equivalents of vitamin A to iron (120 mg) + folic acid
(500 µg) on a weekly dose schedule observed, relative to iron alone, a slight improvement in hemoglobin and a drop of 4 µg/dL in serum ferritin,
likely reflecting mobilized iron stores (**Table
10.3**) (71). On stratification, however, the entire
effect on hemoglobin occurred in women who
were anemic at baseline. The vitamin A supplement also increased vitamin A but not iron levels
in breast milk (72).

Indian studies among pregnant women generally show similar effects as in Southeast Asia.
One early study found a hematinic effect of
adding ~2 mg of vitamin A daily to iron (73)
while another did not (74), but both trials experienced 50% loses to follow-up making their different results difficult to resolve. A third trial among
81 women tested effects of adding, to daily iron,
vitamin A as a single, oral 200,000 IU dose at
mid-pregnancy (a practice usually recommended
for treatment (75). After 16 weeks there were
small but significant increases in hemoglobin,
packed cell volume, red blood cell count, %TS
and serum iron (76).

Another approach to preventing both vitamin
A and iron deficiencies is to do so earlier in life,
before pregnancy, as advanced by Ahmed and
colleagues in Bangladesh who randomized non-
pregnant, anemic teenage women to receive weekly
vitamin A, iron + folic acid or both versus placebo
receipt for three months. As seen in Indonesian
gravida, the odds of anemia (Hb <120 g/L) relative to placebo recipients decreased monotoni-
cally to 0.44, 0.15 and 0.08, respectively (26, 77)
(**Figure 10.3b**). Consistent with other studies,
vitamin A supplement use was associated with
increases in hemoglobin, serum retinol, iron, and
TIBC and % TS, while there was a decrease in
serum ferritin (**Table 10.3**). The lost iron storage
seen with vitamin A only did not occur in women
taking iron and vitamin A, reflecting a more complete response when both nutrients are given

together (26). A second trial among non-pregnant,
anemic Bangladeshi women found that a single
large dose of vitamin A (60 mg) plus daily iron
did not improve hemoglobin status after 2 months
beyond the use of daily iron (78). It is possible
that a single, large dose of vitamin A is not as
efficacious as daily, smaller doses given with iron
for raising hemoglobin. On the other hand, the
study was underpowered and the study population
had a normal vitamin A status with a mean serum
retinol of ~1.4 µmol/L and a low prevalence of
deficiency (6% with serum retinol < 0.70 µmol/L).

Finally, in Malawi, two different trials supplemented pregnant women with daily vitamin A
in addition to daily iron and folic acid (**Table 10.3**),
similar to other studies during pregnancy, and did
not observe differences in hemoglobin change between those receiving vitamin A and the controls
(79, 80). Although the earlier trial in 2001 was
conducted in a vitamin A-deficient group of mothers (~30% <0.70 µmol/L), the dosage of 3 mg of
retinol equivalency that started from mid-pregnancy onward did not change serum retinol levels
(79). The more recent study tested two higher doses
of vitamin A (5000 and 10,000 IU) and also found
no response in serum retinol, although baseline
prevalence of vitamin A deficiency was less than 5
percent (80). These findings are in agreement with
the general premise that vitamin A interventions
may not measurably affect erythropoiesis in the
absence of deficiency or when there is no effect on
indicators of vitamin A status.

MECHANISMS AND PATHWAYS OF INTERACTION

Based on what has been said before and previous
reviews, it appears that variation in vitamin A
nutriture can mediate iron metabolism at several
points along the internal iron and reticuloendothelial circuitry, simply depicted in **Figure 10.4**.
While controversial, four plausible mechanisms
can be posited for how variation in vitamin A

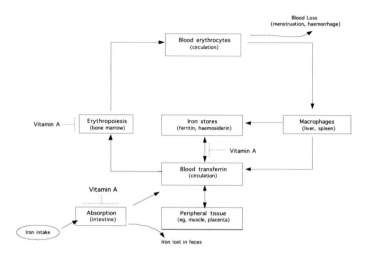

Figure 10.4: Potential sites of hematopoietic effects of vitamin A. Adapted from (4).

nutriture might affect hematopoiesis and hematologic status. These relate to (a) influencing the dynamics of tissue storage and release of iron into circulation, (b) having a direct regulatory effect on erythropoiesis, (c) modifying the sequestration and release of tissue iron associated with responses to infection, and (d) exerting an effect on iron absorption.

Mobilization of tissue iron stores

Under normal conditions, iron not required for erythropoiesis or other iron-dependent functions is delivered by circulating transferrin to iron storage (as ferritin or hemosiderin). Mobilization is achieved when iron is released from ferritin into the circulation (**Figure 10.4**). As a general rule, an 8 to 10 mg change in ferritin storage can be inferred for each 1 µg per liter change in serum ferritin concentration (1). Where measured, supplementation with vitamin A alone has usually, though not always (66), led to a modest fall in serum ferritin (49, 71). This could reflect, in part, a reduction in the acute phase reaction of serum ferritin to infection (1) mediated by vitamin A (6,

7). However, in the absence of reported evidence of infections (e.g., elevated acute phase proteins or other clinical morbidity), a decreased serum ferritin is more likely to reflect the release of utilizable iron into the bloodstream. An increase in %TS or decrease in TIBC further support increased entry of iron into the circulation for delivery to the bone marrow (1). The response of serum ferritin in these studies generally finds support from animal studies that show increased storage iron and lower femur or tibial iron in progressive vitamin A depletion (17, 81) that responds to vitamin A supplementation with lower hepatic or spleen iron concentrations. However, such responses have not been as clear in animals with marginal-to-mild vitamin A deficient states (82).

Erythropoiesis

In bone marrow, the formation of red blood cells requires differentiation and commitment of stem cells toward erythroblast development, a process that requires erythropoietin (EPO) in the latter stages of red cell development (47). EPO is a regulatory glycoprotein hormone that is produced in the peritubular cells of the adult kidney in response to hypoxia to stimulate red cell production and longevity. In cell culture, EPO has increased in response to retinoic acid, independently of oxygen tension (83). Few human studies have to date examined effects of vitamin A supplementation on EPO production. Among three studies to date, one in pregnant women failed to change circulating EPO levels with a vitamin A supplement regimen that also did not change vitamin A status (79). This study did not examine the independent effects of vitamin A, solely adding it to iron and folic acid. Among severely anemic Zanzibari preschoolers, high potency vitamin A intake (those under 12 months and those ≥12 months, received 30 mg or 60 mg respectively) induced an unexpected, precipitous decline in serum EPO levels, along with marked reductions in C-reactive protein and serum ferritin within 72 hours (84). EPO production tends to be sharply diminished in subjects with *falciparum* malaria, which may exacerbate anemia and make short term treatment responses difficult to interpret (85). In mildly vitamin A-deficient and anemic Morrocan school-aged children, vitamin A supplementation stimulated a sustained increase in EPO synthesis and erythropoieisis (49). Although data are currently conflicting, they are sufficient to implicate a role for vitamin A in stimulating erythropoiesis via the regulatory influence on EPO (68).

Anemia of infection

The anemia of infection is characterized by a set of cytokine-induced mechanisms that lead to shortened red blood cell survival, impaired red blood cell production, and decreased mobilization and utilization of iron. This form of iron-deficient erythropoiesis is also accompanied by up-regulation of ferritin and down-regulation of transferrin as part of the acute phase response (2). Vitamin A status can influence mechanisms of host resistance and severity of infection (6), but its effects on anemia risk may be obscured or altered during infection. For example, among Tanzanian children with pneumonia and variably with malaria and HIV infection, receipt of a vitamin A supplement (60 mg) had no significant effect on risk of anemia (86).

Other examples of where vitamin A may have uncertain effects on anemia include malaria, HIV and tuberculosis. The anemia of malaria is frequent and can be severe, especially during early childhood and pregnancy (87, 88). Factors that complicate the risk of anemia during malaria include host-parasite competition for essential micronutrients, including iron and vitamin A (39). Vitamin A deficiency is common during malaria, and while vitamin A deficiency is often associated with the risk of anemia, this link may be less evident in the presence of malaria (89). Further, hemoglobin may not respond to vitamin A that still reduces the severity of malaria episodes, as was seen in a vitamin A trial among preschoolers in Papua New Guinea (90). In populations affected by the human immunodeficiency virus (HIV), anemia is common and associated with progression to more severe disease (8). Micronutrient deficiencies, including vitamin A deficiency, are also common in HIV-infected individuals (91). In pregnant HIV-infected women an association exists between serum retinol and blood hemoglobin levels, as it does in non-HIV-infected populations (92). However, there are few studies that have tested effects of vitamin A supplementation on anemia under conditions of HIV infection. For example, six week old infants of Malawian HIV-infected pregnant women supplemented daily with vitamin A (3 mg) from mid-pregnancy onward, had a mean hemoglobin level that was 4g/L higher (93). In Zimbabwe, however, neither maternal nor infant receipt of high potency vitamin A affected infant hemoglobin or risk of anemia (94). A well-known trial in Tanzania that tested effects of vitamin A and multivitamins on many health outcomes was unable to assess effects of either supplement on hemoglobin clearly, as all women were given iron + folate supplements (95). Finally, while patients with pulmonary tuberculosis tend to be quite vitamin A deficient, irrespective of age, only one trial has reported a non-significant change in hemoglobin with a combination of vitamin A and zinc supplementation (96). While vitamin A is known to reduce the severity of infection (27), its effect on reducing the anemia of infection still merits research.

Iron absorption

It is plausible that vitamin A or β-carotene intake or status in the gut might influence iron absorption, although the data are presently conflicting and mechanisms unclear. Several studies in rats, fed vitamin A-deficient diets, showed increased absorption of iron as vitamin A was depleted (81, 97, 98); however one study in a similarly controlled trial did not observe this effect (17). *In vitro*, Caco-2 cells responded to β-carotene by increasing the absorption of iron by twofold (99). In humans, three studies have been conducted to date, two in developing countries (Venezuela and the Ivory Coast), and one in an industrialized setting (Switzerland) that evaluated iron absorption by dietary vitamin A intake based on erythrocyte incorporation of labeled iron, a surrogate for absorption. Among Venezuelan subjects (some of whom were anemic), low dose vitamin A (0.37 to 2.78 μmol) or β-carotene (0.58 to 2.06 μmol) supplementation of a rice, wheat, or corn meal containing 2–5 mg of iron increased non-heme iron (radiolabeled ^{59}Fe or [55]Fe) uptake by 0.8–3.0 times (100). The studies in Switzerland (healthy adults) and the Ivory Coast (school-children with poor iron status) had different methods to the one in Venezuela and found a very slight decrease in iron absorption that could not be explained (101, 102). Although a postulated mechanism includes a chelating effect of vitamin A to protect iron

from the inhibitory effects of phytates, polyphenols, and tannic acid in the gut, there is not sufficient evidence *in vivo* for this effect (99, 103).

Conclusions

In those areas where vitamin A deficiency poses a problem to public health, it is likely to contribute to iron-deficient erythropoiesis and therefore be a cause of responsive, mild or mild-to-moderate anemia. The effect is clearest when both the deficiency and anemia are uncomplicated by chronic infectious disease. It is important to note that most studies, however, have been undertaken in groups selected for anemia, vitamin A deficiency or both. Under such conditions, adequate vitamin A supplementation can be expected to raise hemoglobin concentrations by, on average, 2–10 g/L over a period of two weeks or longer. The range of impact on hemoglobin generally agrees with predictions from observational studies. The impact of vitamin A may be achieved by (1) enhancing hepatic tissue mobilization and delivery of iron to bone marrow, (2) improving erythropoiesis, possibly by upregulating erythropoietin production and extending red blood cell longevity, (3) reducing sequestration of tissue iron by reducing the severity infection, and (4) facilitating iron absorption. The greatest body of evidence supports the first two mechanisms. The nutritional influence of vitamin A, however, on the internal iron circuit may be obscured by the type and severity of concurrent infection, such as malaria, HIV or tuberculosis, which may alter distributions of both vitamin A and iron independently, or directly impact on vitamin A-iron pathways. Finally, while vitamin A deficiency can be a cause of anemia, the effect can be expected to be modest compared to the roles of iron deficiency, hookworm or malaria infections, where they are endemic (104).

REFERENCES

1. Cook JD. Diagnosis and management of iron-deficiency anaemia. Best Pract Res Clin Haematol 2005;18:319–32.

2. Means RT, Jr. The anaemia of infection. Baillieres Best Pract Res Clin Haematol 2000;13:151–62.

3. Semba RD, Broadhead R, Taha TE, Totin D, Ricks MO, Kumwenda N. Erythropoietin response to anemia among human immunodeficiency virus-infected infants in Malawi. Haematologica 2001;86:1221–2.

4. Fishman SM, Christian P, West KP. The role of vitamins in the prevention and control of anaemia. Public Health Nutr 2000;3:125–50.

5. Bloem MW. Interdependence of vitamin A and iron: an important association for programmes of anaemia control. Proc Nutr Soc 1995;54:501–8.

6. Ross, A. C. The relationship between immunocompetence and vitamin A status. Sommer, A. and West, K. P., Jr. Vitamin A deficiency: health, survival, and vision. (9), 251–273. 1996. New York, Oxford University Press.

7. Beisel WR, Black RE, West KP, Jr., Sommer A. Micronutrients in infection. In: Guerrant RL, Walker DH, Weller PF, eds. Tropical infectious diseases: principles, pathogens, & practice. Philadelphia: Churchill Livingstone 1999:76–87.

8. Semba RD, Bloem MW. The anemia of vitamin A deficiency: epidemiology and pathogenesis. Eur J Clin Nutr 2002;56:271–81.

9. Bloch CE. Clinical investigation of xerophthalmia and dystrophy in infants and young children (xerophthalmia et dystrophia alipogenetica). J Hygiene 1921;19:283–304.

10. Berglund H, Keefer CS, Yang CS. Deficiency anemia in Chinese, responding to cod liver oil. Proc Soc Exper Biol Med 1929;26:418–21.

11. Blackfan KD, Wolbach SB. Vitamin A deficiency in infants. A clinical and pathological study. J Pediatr 1933;3:679–706.

12. Sure B, Kik MC, Walker DJ. The effect of avitaminosis on hematopoietic function. I. Vitamin A deficiency. J Biol Chem 1929;83:375–85.

13. Findley GM, Mackenzie RD. The bone marrow in deficiency diseases. J Pathol Bacteriol 1922;25:402-3.

14. Wolbach SB, Howe PR. Tissue changes following deprivation of fat-soluble A vitamin. J Exp Med 1925;42:753–77.

15. Koessler KK, Maurer S, Loughlin R. The relation of anemia, primary and secondary, to vitamin A deficiency. JAMA 1926;87:476–82.

16. McLaren DS, Tchalian M, Ajans ZA. Biochemical and hematologic changes in the vitamin A-deficient rat. Am J Clin Nutr 1965;17:131–8.

17. Mejia LA, Hodges RE, Rucker RB. Role of vitamin A in the absorption, retention and distribution of iron in the rat. J Nutr 1979;109:129–37.

18. Pedersen S, Saeed I, Jensen SK, Michaelsen KF, Friis H. Haemoconcentration associated with low vitamin A status can mask anaemia. Acta Trop 2002;84:55–8.

19. Abbott OD, Ahmann CF, Overstreet MR. Effect of avitaminosis A on the human blood picture. Am J Physiol 1939;126:254–60.

20. Wagner KH. Die experimentelle Avitaminose A beim Menschen. Z Physiol Chem 1940;264:153–89.

21. Hodges RE, Sauberlich HE, Canham JE, Wallace DL, Rucker RB, Mejia LA, Mohanram M. Hematopoietic studies in vitamin A deficiency. Am J Clin Nutr 1978;31:876–85.

22. van Stuijvenberg ME, Kruger M, Badenhorst CJ, Mansvelt EP, Laubscher JA. Response to an iron fortification programme in relation to vitamin A status in 6-12-year-old school children. Int J Food Sci Nutr 1997;48:41–9.

23. Mejia LA, Chew F. Hematological effect of supplementing anemic children with vitamin A alone and in combination with iron. Am J Clin Nutr 1988;48:595–600.

24. Mwanri L, Worsley A, Ryan P, Masika J. Supplemental vitamin A improves anemia and growth in anemic school children in Tanzania. J Nutr 2000;130:2691–6.

25. Suharno D, West CE, Muhilal, Karyadi D, Hautvast JG. Supplementation with vitamin A and iron for nutritional anaemia in pregnant women in West Java, Indonesia. Lancet 1993;342:1325–8.

26. Ahmed F, Khan MR, Jackson AA. Concomitant

supplemental vitamin A enhances the response to
weekly supplemental iron and folic acid in anemic
teenagers in urban Bangladesh. Am J Clin Nutr
2001;74:108–15.

27. Sommer A, West KP, Jr. Vitamin A deficiency:
health, survival, and vision. New York: Oxford
University Press, 1996.

28. West KP, Jr. Extent of vitamin A deficiency
among preschool children and women of reproductive age. J Nutr 2002;132:2857S–66S.

29. de Pee S, Dary O. Biochemical indicators of
vitamin A deficiency: serum retinol and serum retinol
binding protein. J Nutr 2002;132:2895S-901S.

30. Congdon NG, West KP, Jr. Physiologic indicators
of vitamin A status. J Nutr 2002;132:2889S–94S.

31. Singh V, West KP, Jr. Vitamin A deficiency and
xerophthalmia among school-aged children in South-
eastern Asia. Eur J Clin Nutr 2004;58:1342–9.

32. Christian P. Recommendations for indicators:
night blindness during pregnancy--a simple tool to
assess vitamin A deficiency in a population. J Nutr
2002;132:2884S–8S.

33. Sommer A, Davidson FR. Assessment and control of vitamin A deficiency: the Annecy Accords. J
Nutr 2002;132:2845S–50S.

34. Hands ES. Nutrients in Food. Philadelphia:
Lippincott Williams & Wilkins, 2000.

35. Food and Nutrition Board, Institute of Medicine.
Dietary reference intakes for vitamin A, vitamin K,
arsenic, boron, chromium, copper, iodine, iron, manganese, molybdenum, nickel, silicon, vanadium, and
zinc. Washington D.C.: National Academy Press, 2001.

36. Sommer A. Vitamin A deficiency and its consequences. Geneva: World Health Organization, 1995.

37. Gudas LJ, Sporn MB, Roberts AB. Cellular
biology and biochemistry of the retinoids. In: Sporn
MB, Roberts AB, Goodman DS, eds. The retinoids:
biology, chemistry, and medicine. New York: Raven
Press 1994:443–520.

38. Barclay AJ, Foster A, Sommer A. Vitamin A
supplements and mortality related to measles: a randomised clinical trial. Br Med J (Clin Res Ed)
1987;294:294–6.

39. Shankar AH. Nutritional modulation of malaria
morbidity and mortality. J Infect Dis 2000;182

Suppl 1:S37–S53.

40. Barreto ML, Santos LM, Assis AM, Araujo MP,
Farenzena GG, Santos PA, Fiaccone RL. Effect of
vitamin A supplementation on diarrhoea and acute
lower-respiratory-tract infections in young children
in Brazil. Lancet 1994;344:228–31.

41. West KP, Jr., Djunaedi E, Pandji A, Kusdiono,
Tarwotjo I, Sommer A. Vitamin A supplementation
and growth: a randomized community trial. Am J
Clin Nutr 1988;48:1257–64.

42. West KP Jr, LeClerq SC, Shrestha SR, Wu LS-F,
Pradhan EK, Khatry SK, Katz J, Adhikari R, Sommer
A. Effects of vitamin A on growth of vitamin A-deficient children: field studies in Nepal. J Nutr
1997;127:1957-65.

43. Sommer A, Tarwotjo I, Djunaedi E, West KP Jr,
Loeden AA, Tilden R, Mele L. Impact of vitamin A
supplementation on childhood mortality. A randomised
controlled community trial. Lancet 1986;1:1169–73.

44. West KP Jr, Pokhrel RP, Katz J, LeClerq SC,
Khatry SK, Shrestha SR, Pradhan EK, Tielsch JM,
Pandey MR, Sommer A. Efficacy of vitamin A in
reducing preschool child mortality in Nepal. Lancet
1991;338:67–71.

45. Fawzi WW, Chalmers TC, Herrera MG,
Mosteller F. Vitamin A supplementation and child
mortality. A meta-analysis. JAMA 1993;269:898–903.

46. West KP Jr, Katz J, Khatry SK, LeClerq SC,
Pradhan EK, Shrestha SR, Connor PB,Dali SM,
Christian P, Pokhrel RP, Sommer A. Double blind,
cluster randomised trial of low dose supplementation with vitamin A or beta carotene on mortality
related to pregnancy in Nepal. The NNIPS-2 Study
Group. BMJ 1999;318:570–5.

47. Fisher JW. Erythropoietin: physiology and
pharmacology update. Exp Biol Med (Maywood)
2003;228:1–14.

48. Jelkmann W, Pagel H, Hellwig T, Fandrey J.
Effects of antioxidant vitamins on renal and hepatic erythropoietin production. Kidney Int 1997;51:497–501.

49. Zimmermann MB, Biebinger R, Rohner F, Dib
A, Zeder C, Hurrell RF, Chaouki N. Vitamin A supplementation in children with poor vitamin A and
iron status increases erythropoietin and hemoglobin
concentrations without changing total body iron. Am

J Clin Nutr 2006;84:580–6.

50. Hashizume M, Chiba M, Shinohara A, Iwabuchi S, Sasaki S, Shimoda T, Kunii O, Caypil W, Dauletbaev D, Alnazarova A. Anaemia, iron deficiency and vitamin A status among school-aged children in rural Kazakhstan. Public Health Nutr 2005;8:564–71.

51. Bloem MW, Wedel M, Egger RJ, Speek AJ, Chusilp K, Saowakontha S, Schreurs WH. Iron metabolism and vitamin A deficiency in children in northeast Thailand. Am J Clin Nutr 1989;50:332–8.

52. Ahmed F, Barua S, Mohiduzzaman M, Shaheen N, Bhuyan MA, Margetts BM, Jackson AA. Interactions between growth and nutrient status in school-age children of urban Bangladesh. Am J Clin Nutr 1993;58:334–8.

53. Khan I, Baseer A. Hematologic effect of vitamin A supplementation in anemic Pakistani children. J Pak Med Assoc 1996;46:34–8.

54. Ahmed F, Khan MR, Karim R, Taj S, Hyderi T, Faruque MO, Margetts BM, Jackson AA. Serum retinol and biochemical measures of iron status in adolescent schoolgirls in urban Bangladesh. Eur J Clin Nutr 1996;50:346–51.

55. Yamini S, West KP, Jr., Wu L, Dreyfuss ML, Yang DX, Khatry SK. Circulating levels of retinol, tocopherol and carotenoid in Nepali pregnant and postpartum women following long-term beta-carotene and vitamin A supplementation. Eur J Clin Nutr 2001;55:252–9.

56. Palafox NA, Gamble MV, Dancheck B, Ricks MO, Briand K, Semba RD. Vitamin A deficiency, iron deficiency, and anemia among preschool children in the Republic of the Marshall Islands. Nutrition 2003;19:405–8.

57. Loyd-Puryear M, Humphrey JH, West KP Jr, Aniol K, Mahoney F, Kennum DG. Vitamin A deficiency and anemia in Micronesian children. Nutr Res 1989;9:1007-1016.

58. Albalak R, Ramakrishnan U, Stein AD, Van der Haar F, Haber MJ, Schroeder D, Martorell R. Co-occurrence of nutrition problems in Honduran children. J Nutr 2000;130:2271–3.

59. Castejon HV, Ortega P, Amaya D, Gomez G, Leal J, Castejon OJ. Co-existence of anemia, vitamin A deficiency and growth retardation among children 24-84 months old in Maracaibo, Venezuela. Nutr Neurosci 2004;7:113–9.

60. Dreyfuss ML, Stoltzfus RJ, Shrestha JB, Pradhan EK, LeClerq SC, Khatry SK, Shrestha SR, Katz J, Albonico M, West KP Jr. Hookworms, malaria and vitamin A deficiency contribute to anemia and iron deficiency among pregnant women in the plains of Nepal. J Nutr 2000;130:2527–36.

61. Muhilal, Permeisih D, Idjradinata YR, Muherdiyantiningsih, Karyadi D. Vitamin A-fortified monosodium glutamate and health, growth, and survival of children: a controlled field trial. Am J Clin Nutr 1988;48:1271–6.

62. Mejia LA, Arroyave G. The effect of vitamin A fortification of sugar on iron metabolism in preschool children in Guatemala. Am J Clin Nutr 1982;36:87–93.

63. Smith JC, Makdani D, Hegar A, Rao D, Douglass LW. Vitamin A and zinc supplementation of preschool children. J Am Coll Nutr 1999;18:213–22.

64. Alarcon K, Kolsteren PW, Prada AM, Chian AM, Velarde RE, Pecho IL, Hoeree TF. Effects of separate delivery of zinc or zinc and vitamin A on hemoglobin response, growth, and diarrhea in young Peruvian children receiving iron therapy for anemia. Am J Clin Nutr 2004;80:1276–82.

65. Bloem MW, Wedel M, van Agtmaal EJ, Speek AJ, Saowakontha S, Schreurs WH. Vitamin A intervention: short-term effects of a single, oral, massive dose on iron metabolism. Am J Clin Nutr 1990;51:76–9.

66. Semba RD, Muhilal, West KP, Winget M, Natadisastra G, Scott A, Sommer A. Impact of vitamin A supplementation on hematological indicators of iron metabolism and protein status in children. Nutr Res 1992;12:469-478.

67. Barosi G. Inadequate erythropoietin response to anemia: definition and clinical relevance. Ann Hematol 1994;68:215–23.

68. Evans T. Regulation of hematopoiesis by retinoid signaling. Exp Hematol 2005;33:1055–61.

69. ACC/SCN. Fourth report on the world nutrition situation. 2000. Geneva, ACC/SCN in collaboration with IFPRI.

70. Christian P, West KP Jr, Khatry SK, Katz J, Shrestha SR, Pradhan EK, LeClerq SC, Pokhrel RP. Night blindness of pregnancy in rural Nepal-nutritional and health risks. Int J Epidemiol 1998;27:231–7.

71. Muslimatun S, Schmidt MK, Schultink W, West CE, Hautvast JA, Gross R, Muhilal. Weekly supplementation with iron and vitamin A during pregnancy increases hemoglobin concentration but decreases serum ferritin concentration in Indonesian pregnant women. J Nutr 2001;131:85–90.

72. Muslimatun S, Schmidt MK, West CE, Schultink W, Hautvast JG, Karyadi D. Weekly vitamin A and iron supplementation during pregnancy increases vitamin A concentration of breast milk but not iron status in Indonesian lactating women. J Nutr 2001;131:2664–9.

73. Panth M, Shatrugna V, Yasodhara P, Sivakumar B. Effect of vitamin A supplementation on haemoglobin and vitamin A levels during pregnancy. Br J Nutr 1990;64:351–8.

74. Shatrugna V, Raman L, Uma K, Sujatha T. Interaction between vitamin A and iron: effects of supplements in pregnancy. Int J Vitam Nutr Res 1997;67:145–8.

75. Ross DA. Recommendations for vitamin A supplementation. J Nutr 2002;132:2902S–6S.

76. Chawla PK, Puri R. Impact of nutritional supplements on hematological profile of pregnant women. Indian Pediatr 1995;32:876–80.

77. Ahmed F, Khan MR, Islam M, Kabir I, Fuchs GJ. Anaemia and iron deficiency among adolescent schoolgirls in peri-urban Bangladesh. Eur J Clin Nutr 2000;54:678–83.

78. Kolsteren P, Rahman SR, Hilderbrand K, Diniz A. Treatment for iron deficiency anaemia with a combined supplementation of iron, vitamin A and zinc in women of Dinajpur, Bangladesh. Eur J Clin Nutr 1999;53:102–6.

79. Semba RD, Kumwenda N, Taha TE, Mtimavalye L, Broadhead R, Garrett E, Miotti PG,Chiphangwi JD. Impact of vitamin A supplementation on anaemia and plasma erythropoietin concentrations in pregnant women: a controlled clinical trial. Eur J Haematol 2001;66:389–95.

80. van den Broek NR, White SA, Flowers C, Cook JD, Letsky EA, Tanumihardjo SA, Mhango C, Molyneux M, Neilson JP. Randomised trial of vitamin A supplementation in pregnant women in rural Malawi found to be anaemic on screening by HemoCue. BJOG 2006;113:569–76.

81. Strube YNJ, Beard JL, Ross AC. Iron deficiency and marginal vitamin A deficiency affect growth, hematological indices and regulation of iron metabolism genes in rats. J Nutr 2002;132:3607-15.

82. Beynen AC, Sijtsma KW, Van Den Berg GJ, Lemmens AG, West CE. Iron status in rats fed a purified diet without vitamin A. Biol Trace Elem Res 1992;35:81–4.

83. Neumcke I, Schneider B, Fandrey J, Pagel H. Effects of pro- and antioxidative compounds on renal production of erythropoietin. Endocrinology 1999;140:641–5.

84. Cusick SE, Tielsch JM, Ramsan M, Jape JK, Sazawal S, Black RE, Stoltzfus RJ. Short-term effects of vitamin A and antimalarial treatment on erythropoiesis in severely anemic Zanzibari preschool children. Am J Clin Nutr 2005;82:406–12.

85. Burgmann H, Looareesuwan S, Kapiotis S, Viravan C, Vanijanonta S, Hollenstein U, Wiesinger E, Presterl E, Winkler S, Graninger W. Serum levels of erythropoietin in acute Plasmodium falciparum malaria. Am J Trop Med Hyg 1996;54:280–3.

86. Villamor E, Mbise R, Spiegelman D, Ndossi G, Fawzi WW. Vitamin A supplementation and other predictors of anemia among children from Dar Es Salaam, Tanzania. Am J Trop Med Hyg 2000;62:590–7.

87. Nussenblatt V, Semba RD. Micronutrient malnutrition and the pathogenesis of malarial anemia. Acta Tropica 2002;82:321–37.

88. Ekvall H. Malaria and anemia. Curr Opin Hematol 2003;10:108–14.

89. Nabakwe EC, Lichtenbelt WV, Ngare DK, Wierik M, Westerterp KR, Owino OC. Vitamin a deficiency and anaemia in young children living in a malaria endemic district of western Kenya. East Afr Med J 2005;82:300–6.

90. Shankar AH, Genton B, Semba RD, Baisor M, Paino J, Tamja S, Adiguma T, Wu L, Rare L, Tielsch

JM, Alpers MP, West KP Jr. Effect of vitamin A supplementation on morbidity due to plasmodium falciparum in young children in Papua New Guinea: a randomised trial. Lancet 1999;354:203–9.

91. Semba RD, Tang AM. Micronutrients and the pathogenesis of human immunodeficiency virus infection. Br J Nutr 1999;81:181–9.

92. Friis H, Gomo E, Koestel P, Ndhlovu P, Nyazema N, Krarup H, Michaelsen KF. HIV and other predictors of serum folate, serum ferritin, and hemoglobin in pregnancy: a cross-sectional study in Zimbabwe. Am J Clin Nutr 2001;73:1066–73.

93. Kumwenda N, Miotti PG, Taha TE, Broadhead R, Biggar RJ, Jackson JB, Melikian G, Semba RD. Antenatal vitamin A supplementation increases birth weight and decreases anemia among infants born to human immunodeficiency virus-infected women in Malawi. Clin Infect Dis 2002;35:618–24.

94. Miller MF, Stoltzfus RJ, Iliff PJ, Malaba LC, Mbuya NV, Humphrey JH. Effect of maternal and neonatal vitamin A supplementation and other postnatal factors on anemia in Zimbabwean infants: a prospective, randomized study. Am J Clin Nutr 2006;84:212–22.

95. Fawzi WW, Msamanga GI, Spiegelman D, Urassa EJ, McGrath N, Mwakagile D, Antelman G, Mbise R, Herrera G, Kapiga S, Willett W, Hunter DJ. Randomised trial of effects of vitamin supplements on pregnancy outcomes and T cell counts in HIV-1-infected women in Tanzania. Lancet 1998;351:1477–82.

96. Karyadi E, West CE, Schultink W, Nelwan RH, Gross R, Amin Z, Dolmans WM, Schlebusch H, van der Meer JW. A double-blind, placebo-controlled study of vitamin A and zinc supplementation in persons with tuberculosis in Indonesia: effects on clinical response and nutritional status. Am J Clin Nutr 2002;75:720–7.

97. Amine EK, Corey J, Hegsted DM, Hayes KC. Comparative hematology during deficiencies of iron and vitamin A in the rat. J Nutr 1970;100:1033–40.

98. Roodenburg AJ, West CE, Yu S, Beynen AC. Comparison between time-dependent changes in iron metabolism of rats as induced by marginal deficiency of either vitamin A or iron. Br J Nutr 1994;71:687–99.

99. Garcia-Casal MN, Leets I, Layrisse M. Beta-carotene and inhibitors of iron absorption modify iron uptake by Caco-2 cells. J Nutr 2000;130:5–9.

100. Garcia-Casal MN, Layrisse M, Solano L, Baron MA, Arguello F, Llovera D, Ramirez J, Leets I, Tropper E. Vitamin A and beta-carotene can improve nonheme iron absorption from rice, wheat and corn by humans. J Nutr 1998;128:646–50.

101. Walczyk T, Davidsson L, Rossander-Hulthen L, Hallberg L, Hurrell RF. No enhancing effect of vitamin A on iron absorption in humans. Am J Clin Nutr 2003;77:144–9.

102. Davidsson L, Adou P, Zeder C, Walczyk T, Hurrell R. The effect of retinyl palmitate added to iron-fortified maize porridge on erythrocyte incorporation of iron in African children with vitamin A deficiency. Br J Nutr 2003;90:337–43.

103. Layrisse M, Garcia-Casal MN, Solano L, Baron MA, Arguello F, Llovera D, Ramirez J, Leets I, Tropper E. New property of vitamin A and beta-carotene on human iron absorption: effect on phytate and polyphenols as inhibitors of iron absorption. Arch Latinoam Nutr 2000;50:243–8.

104. International Vitamin A Consultative Group (IVACG). IVACG statement: vitamin A and iron interactions. 1998.

11

Oxidative stress and vitamin E in anemia

Maret G. Traber[1]   Afaf Kamal-Eldin[2]

[1]Linus Pauling Institute and Department of Nutrition and Exercise Sciences, Oregon State University, Corvallis, Oregon, USA
[2]Department of Food Science, Swedish University of Agricultural Sciences, Uppsala, Sweden
Contact: maret.traber@oregonstate.edu

MARET TRABER

Maret obtained her PhD in Nutrition from the University of California, Berkeley, USA, and is considered to be one of the world's leading experts in vitamin E. She is Principal Investigator in the Linus Pauling Institute at Oregon State University, USA, where her research is focused on human vitamin E kinetics and the factors that modulate human vitamin E requirements. Maret has written over 195 scientific publications and served on the National Academy of Sciences, Institute of Medicine Panel on Dietary Anti-oxidant and Related Compounds that established the dietary requirements for the antioxidant vitamins C and E, selenium, and carotenoids.

AFAF KAMAL-ELDIN

Afaf has a PhD and is currently Associate Professor at the Department of Food Science at the Swedish University of Agricultural Sciences. Afaf's special research field is in biologically active compounds in plant foods and their health benefits, focusing on the chemistry of compounds, analytical methods, absorption and metabolism, bioactivities, and the use of biomarkers of intake.

Introduction

Anemia (hemoglobin level less than 11 g/dL compared with 12–15.5 g/dL in healthy people) refers to situations where the number of healthy erythrocytes (RBCs) in the circulation is minimized as a result of inadequate production or excessive destruction. It can result from nutritional deficiencies (iron deficiency anemia and megaloblastic or vitamin B_{12} deficiency anemia), inherited disorders (hemolytic anemia), and/or from infections or exposure to certain toxins and medications (aplastic anemia). Hemolytic anemia, prevalent in inherited diseases such as sickle cell anemia, thalassemia, and glucose-6-phosphate dehydrogenase deficiency, occurs as a result of destruction of premature or defective RBCs. Aplastic anemia occurs when the bone marrow capacity to produce RBCs is compromised due to viral infections and/or exposure to toxic chemicals, radiation, or medications (such as antibiotics, antiseizure drugs, and some cancer treatments). In fatigued individuals, anemia may result as a combination of these etiological factors.

Anemia can lead to a variety of health problems since the oxygen required by the body is carried by RBCs and because oxidative stress can be generated by the iron released from damaged RBCs. Oxidative stress, overproduction of reactive oxygen species and impaired antioxidant potential are associated with anemia (1). Moreover, the major site of antioxidant defense in blood is the erythrocyte, especially its intracellular enzymatic antioxidants, including superoxide dismutase (SOD), catalase (CAT), and glutathione peroxidase (GSH-px)) with glutathione (GSH) as a major partner (2). Importantly, low molecular weight antioxidants, especially vitamin E and vitamin C, also provide significant protection (3).

In this review, we discuss the prevalence of oxidative stress and low vitamin E levels in various types of anemias including iron deficiency anemia, thalassemia and sickle cell anemias, glucose-6-phosphate dehydrogenase (G6PD, EC 1.1.1.49) deficiency anemia, malaria, and human immunodeficiency virus/acquired immunodeficiency syndrome (HIV/AIDS). We also discuss the relationship between extremely poor diets and vitamin E status, especially anemia or neurologic abnormalities arising from frank vitamin E deficiency. The role of α-tocopherol in amelioration of symptoms associated with anemia is also discussed. The term vitamin E refers to the group of eight phytochemicals exhibiting the antioxidant activity of α-tocopherol, which are provided by dietary intakes. In this review, the specific chemical form, α-tocopherol, is used for measured plasma and tissue concentrations, or the specific chemical form, α-tocopherol, needed by the body. These definitions are consistent with the report by the Food and Nutrition Board of the Institute of Medicine, when they defined vitamin E for the purpose of meeting human vitamin E requirements (4).

Oxidative stress

Oxidative stress represents an imbalance between the generation of free radicals and reactive oxygen species (ROS) and protection by antioxidant enzymes along with a low cellular content of antioxidants such as GSH, vitamin C, vitamin E, etc. (5). A free radical is any chemical species that contains one or more unpaired electrons capable of independent existence, however brief (6). A radical can be formed either by loss (oxidation) or gain (reduction) of an electron by a non-radical molecule. Oxygen is a special case because it has two unpaired electrons. A species with an unpaired electron has the tendency to react very rapidly with other molecules, and thus cause free radical damage. Radicals can damage virtually all molecules, including protein, DNA, carbohydrates, and lipids. It is beyond the scope of this review to discuss this topic in detail, but some limited examples are given below.

ROS are defined as free radical and non-radical compounds that may cause oxidative injury. Examples include: triplet oxygen ($\cdot^{\uparrow}O=O^{\uparrow}\cdot$), singlet oxygen ($\cdot^{\uparrow}O=O_{\downarrow}\cdot$), superoxide anion ($O_2^{\cdot-}$), hydrogen peroxide ($H_2O_2$), and hydroxyl radicals (HO·). HO· are especially dangerous because of their high reactivity with molecules that are adjacent to the location where they are formed. Transition metal ions, such as iron and/or copper, can act as catalysts, catalyzing redox reactions via the Fenton reaction:

$$Fe^{2+} + H_2O_2 \longrightarrow Fe^{3+} + OH^{\cdot} + OH^-$$

Free radicals and ROS react with various molecules, causing damage and dysfunction. Proteins and DNA nucleotides are especially susceptible to damage (6). A peptide chain can be cleaved by oxidants, potentially inactivating a protein. Additionally, specific amino acids can be oxidized. The two amino acids most prone to oxidative attack are cysteine and methionine. Other amino acids that are often modified during oxidative stress include arginine, proline, threonine, tyrosine, histidine, tryptophan, valine, and lysine. Protein oxidation is measured most commonly by detection of modified groups (carbonyl groups) or specific oxidized amino acids. The most important mechanisms of DNA damage involve direct attack of oxidants on individual nucleotides in DNA (6). Guanine is the DNA base most susceptible to oxidative attack. The nucleotide oxidation product is 8-hydroxyguanine (8OHG or 8-oxoG) and the nucleoside deri-vative is 8-hydroxy-2-deoxyguanosine (8OHdG or 8-oxodG). DNA can also be damaged by reactive nitrogen species, some of which can be derived from nitrosamines. ROS and reactive nitrogen species (RNS) can cause DNA strand breaks and point mutations.

Sugars and their oxidized products can react with lysine to form advanced glycation end prod-ucts; other substrates, such as amino groups on phospholipids, can contribute to these products (6). Ascorbate itself has been proposed to be a substrate for some advanced glycation end products via oxidation and glyoxal formation, especially in the aging lens of the eye (6).

Unlike the previous examples where a single or a few molecules are damaged by ROS, lipid peroxidation is especially dangerous because it is a chain reaction and can damage numerous polyunsaturated fatty acids (PUFA) (7). Assessment of lipid peroxidation is an important means to evaluate oxidative stress. Thiobarbituric acid reactive substances (TBARS) are believed to re-present production of malondialdehyde, a lipid peroxidation product of the PUFA, linoleic acid. However, because many compounds interfere with this assay, results from this colorimetric assay are not widely accepted. However, if chromatographic/mass spectrometric measurements are used for malondialdehyde analysis, the data can be reliable (8). A much more promising biomarker of lipid peroxidation are the F_2-isoprostanes and their metabolites (9, 10). These compounds are stable products of radical mediated peroxidation of arachidonic acid. The F_2-isoprostanes are frequently touted as the most reliable markers of lipid peroxidation and can be measured either in plasma or urine. Importantly, these free radical-produced breakdown products of arachidonic acid are increased in association with a number of atherosclerotic risk factors, such as cigarette smoking, hypercholesterolemia, diabetes, and obesity. Importantly, a reduction in cardiovascular disease risk is also associated with a decrease in isoprostanes (11).

VITAMIN E BACKGROUND

1. Vitamin E definitions
Vitamin E is the collective name for the eight molecules synthesized by plants that have a chromanol head group and a phytyl tail (tocopherols)

or an isoprenoid tail (tocotrienols) and that exhibit the antioxidant activity of a-tocopherol (12). These eight molecules, α-, β-, γ-, and δ-tocopherols, and α-, β-, γ-, and δ-tocotrienols, vary in the number of methyl groups on the chromanol ring, but are all potent lipid-soluble antioxidants. Despite their antioxidant activities, the Food and Nutrition Board (4), however, concluded that humans require only α-tocopherol to meet their vitamin E needs. This conclusion was based on the observation that the hepatic α-tocopherol transfer protein (α-TTP) preferentially recognizes α-tocopherol, that defects in the α-TTP gene are associated with vitamin E deficiency in humans, and that high α-tocopherol intakes (daily supplements of 1 g or more) can reverse or prevent the progression of the peripheral neurologic disease, a vitamin E deficiency symptom in humans, as discussed further below. Although vitamin E biological activity has traditionally been based on the rat fetal resorption assay, previously it was not apparent that the pregnant rodent uterus expresses α-TTP (13, 14), thus α-TTP preferentially accumulate α-tocopherol and compromise the assessment of the importance of the physiological role of non-α-tocopherol forms.

Unlike most other vitamins, chemically synthesized α-tocopherol is not identical to the naturally occurring form. The α-tocopherol synthesized by plants has three chiral centers, at positions 2,4 ', and 8', that are all in the R-conformation, while chemically synthesized α-tocopherol contains eight stereoisomers, either R- or S- in equal proportion at the three chiral centers in the molecule, and is designated *all-rac*-α-tocopherol (on labels: *d,l*-α-tocopherol). The form synthesized by plants, RRR-α-tocopherol (on labels: d-α-tocopherol) constitutes only one of the eight stereoisomers present in *all-rac*-α-tocopherol. The Food and Nutrition Board (4) further defined vitamin E for human requirements as only *2R*-α-tocopherol; thus, only half of the stereoisomers in *all-rac*-α-tocopherol meet the

vitamin E requirement. With regard to human nutrition, natural α-tocopherol (*RRR* or *d* form) is provided by foods or supplements while *all-rac*-α-tocopherol (or *d,l*-α-tocopherol) is obtained by food fortification or supplementation.

2. Antioxidant functions

Vitamin E, particularly α-tocopherol, functions in vivo as a lipid soluble, chain breaking antioxidant (15–18); and is a potent peroxyl radical scavenger (19). When lipid hydroperoxides are oxidized to peroxyl radicals (ROO·), these react 1000-times faster with α-tocopherol (TOH) than with PUFA (RH). The phenolic hydroxyl group of the chromanol ring reacts with an organic peroxyl radical to form the corresponding organic hydroperoxide and the vitamin E radical (TO·) (20):

In the presence of vitamin E:
$$ROO· + TOH \longrightarrow ROOH + TO·$$
In the absence of vitamin E:
$$ROO· + RH \longrightarrow ROOH + R·$$
$$R· + O_2 \longrightarrow ROO·$$

In this way, α-tocopherol, for example, acts as a chain-breaking antioxidant, preventing the further auto-oxidation of PUFA. The tocopheroxyl radical (TO·) reacts with vitamin C (or other reductants serving as hydrogen donors, AH), thereby oxidizing the latter and returning vitamin E to its reduced state (21).

$$TO· + AH \longrightarrow TOH + A·$$

Biologically important hydrogen donors, which have been demonstrated in vitro to regenerate tocopherol from the tocopheroxyl radical, include ascorbate (vitamin C) and thiols (22), especially glutathione (23–26). Importantly, this interaction between vitamins E and C has been demonstrated in humans; cigarette smokers have faster vitamin E turnover than can be normalized by vitamin C supplementation (27, 28).

The regeneration of tocopherol from the tocopheroxyl radical in the RBC membrane **(Figure 11.1)** is especially relevant to the discussion of oxidative stress causing RBC damage, thereby leading to RBC destruction and ultimately anemia. Besides vitamins E and C and thiols, a number of antioxidant enzymes, including SOD, GSH-px, and CAT, are involved in the protection of RBCs against oxidative stress and the sparing of vitamin E (29).

FACTORS IN HUMAN VITAMIN E STATUS

1. Digestion, intestinal absorption, and lipoprotein transport

The absorption of vitamin E from the intestinal lumen is dependent upon processes necessary for fat digestion and uptake into enterocytes. Pancreatic esterases and bile acids are required for release of free fatty acids from dietary triglycerides and the formation of micelles for absorption of fat and fat soluble compounds, including vitamin E (30). Thus, vitamin E deficiency occurs as a result of fat malabsorption. Vitamin E absorption is also dependent on the fat content of the food, with little absorption from vitamin E supplements in the absence of fat (31–33). Importantly, various forms of vitamin E, such as a- and g-tocopherols (34, 35), or *RRR*- and *SRR*-α-tocopherols (36, 37), have similar apparent efficiencies of intestinal absorption and secretion in chylomicrons. Thus, there is no discrimination between various vitamin E forms during absorption.

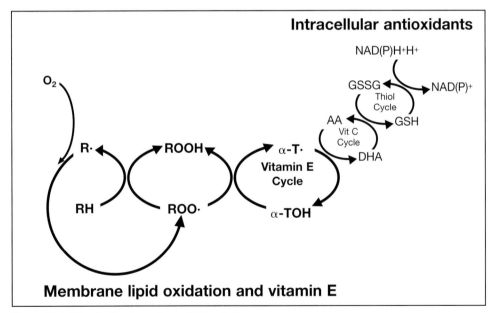

Figure 11.1: Vitamin E and membrane lipid oxidation.

As part of the antioxidant network, α-tocopherol (α-TOH) forms a tocopheroxyl radical (α-TO·) when it intercepts a peroxyl radical (ROO·) in a cell membrane. In the absence of vitamin E, these ROO· can abstract a hydrogen from PUFA (RH) and generate both a hydroperoxide (ROOH) and another carbon-centered radical (R·), which in the presence of oxygen (O_2) will form a ROO· and thus a lipid peroxidation chain reac-tion occurs. If α-tocopherol (α-TOH) is present it intercepts the radical 1000 times faster than the radical reacts with PUFA, and both a ROOH and an α-TO· are formed. This α-TO· radical can be detoxified and α-TOH regenerated by intracellular antioxidants including vitamin C, glutathione, and reducing equivalents (NAD(P)H) derived from oxidative metabolism.

During chylomicron catabolism in the circulation, some of the newly absorbed vitamin E is transferred to circulating lipoproteins and some remains with the chylomicron remnants. During this process, vitamin E is also transferred to high density lipoproteins (HDL). Because HDL readily transfer vitamin E to other lipoproteins, vitamin E is distributed to all of the circulating lipoproteins. Kostner et al. (38) have demonstrated that the phospholipid transfer protein (PLTP) catalyzes vitamin E exchange between lipoproteins. Once chylomicron remnants reach the liver, the dietary fats are repackaged and secreted into the plasma in very low density lipoproteins (VLDL) (39).

Plasma α-tocopherol concentrations are dependent upon the hepatic α-TTP (40–43) and in humans, a genetic defect in α-TTP results in severe vitamin E deficiency (44). A loss ofα-TTP also impairs the ability to discriminate between RRR- and SRR-a-tocopherols (43, 45). α-TTP is necessary for facilitated hepatic α-tocopherol transfer to plasma; in its absence α-tocopherol plasma concentrations fall rapidly (46). Studies in subjects with "ataxia with isolated vitamin E deficiency (AVED)" demonstrated that the subjects can absorb the vitamin E, but α-tocopherol leaves the plasma in less than one third the time observed in control subjects (47). α-Tocopherol is secreted from hepatocytes into VLDL under α-TTP control (48, 49). This protein preferentially transfers *RRR*-α-tocopherol (40) and mediates its secretion from the liver (50), but a study in rats demonstrated that the incorporation of *RRR*-α-tocopherol into VLDL did not occur inside the liver (51). These data were consistent with those of Arita et al. (52), who showed that so long as there was a lipoprotein acceptor in the media, VLDL production by cells was not required. Moreover, Qian et al. (53) demonstrated that over expression of α-TTP increased α-tocopherol secretion by cells and that α-TTP facilitated transfer of α-tocopherol to acceptor lipoproteins, specifically apolipoprotein A-I, an apolipoprotein found in HDL. The precise steps by which α-TTP transfers α-tocopherol from the hepatocyte to plasma lipoproteins remains under intense investigation.

Unlike other fat soluble vitamins, which have specific plasma transport proteins, the various dietary forms of vitamin E are transported non specifically in lipoproteins in the plasma. The mechanisms of lipid and lipoprotein metabolism determine the delivery of vitamin E to tissues. There are various routes by which tissues likely acquire vitamin E: 1) via lipase mediated lipo-protein catabolism (54); 2) via the various lipoprotein receptors, including the low density lipoprotein (LDL) receptor (55); or via HDL lipid uptake by the scavenger receptor-B1 (SR-B1) (this latter route is important for vitamin E delivery to lung (56–59), brain (60, 61) and liver (62)); as well as 3) mediated by various transporters, such as ABCA1 (63). In addition, vitamin E rapidly exchanges between lipoproteins and between lipoproteins and membranes, and may enrich membranes with vitamin E. PLTP has an important role in moving vitamin E between such lipoproteins and between lipoproteins and membranes (64). Recent studies have suggested that PLTP may be very important in transferring a-tocopherol between membranes in the brain (65).

2. Vitamin E pharmacokinetics

Deuterated α-tocopherol has been used to assess the kinetics and distribution of α-tocopherol into various tissues in rats (66), guinea pigs (67), mice (43), and humans (68). From these studies it is apparent that a group of tissues is in rapid equilibrium with the plasma α-tocopherol pool. Erythrocytes, liver, and spleen quickly replace "old" with "new" α-tocopherol while other tissues, such as heart or muscle, have slower α-tocopherol turnover times (69). By far the tissues with the slowest α-tocopherol turnover times appear to be the brain and spinal cord. In general, the a-tocopherol content of the central nervous system is spared during α-tocopherol depletion (70–72). However, the peripheral nerves (73), especially the sensory neurons, are the most susceptible to vitamin E deficiency (74).

Plasma vitamin E kinetics has been studied in humans using deuterium-labeled stereo-isomers of α-tocopherol (*RRR-* and *SRR-*) (47) and using differently deuterated α- and γ-tocopherols (75). In normal subjects, the fractional disappearance rates of *RRR*-α-tocopherol (0.4 ± 0.1 pools per day) compared with *SRR-* (1.2 ± 0.6) were significantly greater (P<0.01). Thus, *RRR*-α-tocopherol halflife in normal subjects was approximately 48 h, consistent with the "slow" disappearance of *RRR*-α-tocopherol from the plasma (47). This hepatic recirculation of *RRR*-α-tocopherol results in the daily replacement of nearly all of the circulating *RRR*-α-tocopherol. Like *SRR-* α-tocopherol, plasma g-tocopherol fractional disappearance rates (1.4 ± 0.4 pools per day) were greater than those of α-tocopherol (0.3 ± 0.1). In this study, γ-tocopherol half-lives were 13 ± 4 h compared with 57 ± 19 h for α-tocopherol. These data suggest that non-*RRR*-α-tocopherols are quickly removed from plasma.

3. Tissue vitamin E storage sites

The mechanisms for the release of α-tocopherol from tissues are unknown and no organ is known to function as a storage organ for α-tocopherol, releasing it on demand. The bulk of vitamin E in the body is localized in the adipose tissue (76). Thus, the analysis of adipose tissue α-tocopherol content is a useful estimate of long term vitamin E status (77, 78). Also, unlike other fat soluble vitamins, vitamin E is not accumulated in the liver to toxic levels, suggesting that excretion and metabolism are important in preventing adverse effects.

The eye is of special interest with respect to vitamin E nutrition. AREDS (Age-Related Eye Disease Study) found that an intervention with vitamin E, β-carotene, and zinc in patients with macular degeneration was beneficial in delaying the progression of symptoms (79). Importantly, the cocktail of antioxidants provided both vitamin E and a source of vitamin A. Similarly, recent studies in mice lacking α-TTP suggest that this protein may be involved in the maintenance of retinal α-tocopherol (80).

4. Metabolism and excretion

The vitamin E metabolites, α-CEHC (2,5,7,8-tetramethyl-2-(2-carboxyethyl)-6-hydroxy-chroman) and γ-CEHC (2,7,8-trimethyl-2-(2carbo-xyethyl)-6-hydroxychroman) are derived from α-tocopherol and α-tocotrienol, and from γ-tocopherol and γ-tocotrienol, respectively (81, 82). Vitamin E forms appear to be metabolized similarly to xenobiotics, in that they are ω-oxidized by cytochrome P450s (CYPs), then conjugated and excreted in urine (83) or bile (84). Hepatic CYP 4F2 catalyzes the ω-oxidation of α- and γ-tocopherols (85) but CYP 3A may also be involved (82, 86–88). Similarly to other xenobiotics, CEHCs are sulfated or glucuronidated (89–91). Xenobiotic transporters are likely candidates for mediating hepatic CEHC excretion because CEHCs are found in plasma, urine, and bile. Additionally, α-tocopherol is excreted into bile via MDR2 (p-glycoprotein) (92), an ATP-binding cassette phospholipid transporter that facilitates bilia-ry phospholipid excretion.

VITAMIN E DEFICIENCY IN HUMANS

Low serum or plasma vitamin E concentrations are indicative of vitamin E deficiency (**Figure 11.2**). The Food and Nutrition Board

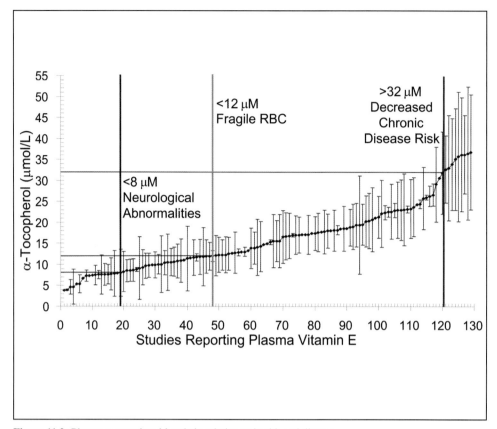

Figure 11.2: Plasma α-tocopherol levels in relation to health and disease.

Plasma α-tocopherol concentrations less than 8 μmol/L are associated with neurologic disease (117, 118), less than 12 μmol/L with increased RBC fragility (4) and over 32 μmol/L with decreased risk of chronic diseases (225). Reported plasma or serum α-tocopherol concentrations have been used to generate the figure. The x-axis value is an identification number that associates the concentrations with their corresponding publication shown in the reference list. Some articles contain multiple values and may appear multiple times in the reference list.

Identification numbers shown on the x-axis are: 1. (119), 2. (182), 3. (181), 4. (121), 5. (119), 6. (226), 7. (119), 8. (227), 9. (192), 10. (119), 11. (202), 12. (120), 13. (228), 14. (201), 15. (202), 16. (203), 17. (226), 18. (229), 19. (228), 20. (223), 21. (202), 22. (201), 23. (202), 24. (120), 25. (228), 26. (121), 27. (217), 28. (217), 29. (230), 30. (217), 31. (181), 32. (231), 33. (217), 34. (228), 35. (223), 36. (120), 37. (232), 38. (231), 39. (233), 40. (228), 41. (192), 42. (121), 43. (194), 44. (229), 45. (228), 46. (229), 47. (180), 48. (194), 49. (223), 50. (229), 51. (229), 52. (229), 53. (223), 54. (230), 55. (234), 56. (194), 57. (235), 58. (194), 59. (230), 60. (183), 61. (180), 62. (232), 63. (234), 64. (235), 65. (235), 66. (146), 67. (203), 68. (232), 69. (232), 70. (236), 71. (236), 72. (237), 73. (238), 74. (223), 75. (239), 76. (240), 77. (240), 78. (239), 79. (240), 80. (120), 81. (241), 82. (192), 83. (236), 84. (241), 85. (242), 86. (236), 87. (146), 88. (242), 89. (243), 90. (230), 91. (232), 92. (236), 93. (243), 94. (244), 95. (245), 96. (236), 97. (236), 98. (237), 99. (246), 100. (245), 101. (237), 102. (215), 103. (214), 104. (247), 105. (215), 106. (247), 107. (236), 108. (183), 109. (248), 110. (247), 111. (247), 112. (246), 113. (248), 114. (183), 115. (238), 116. (215), 117. (214), 118. (237), 119. (246), 120. (249), 121. (237), 122. (249), 123. (249), 124. (249), 125. (232), 126. (249), 127. (249), 128. (232), 129. (232).

(4) defined the lower limit of plasma α-tocopherol at 12 μmol/L for normal, healthy, adult humans. If subjects have altered lipid levels, then measurements of plasma concentrations may be insufficient and both serum total cholesterol and triglycerides should also be mea-sured. For example, measurements of plasma α-tocopherol levels are insufficient for pa-tients with cholestatic liver disease because they have elevated serum lipids. Calculation of effective plasma vitamin E concentrations needs to take into account these high lipid (sum of plasma total cholesterol and triglyceride) levels (93). When only plasma α-tocopherol is considered, patients with elevated cholesterol or triglyceride concentrations may have α-tocopherol concentrations in the apparently "normal" range, but these may not be sufficient to protect tissues. Specifically, Sokol et al. (94) showed in patients with cholestatic liver disease characterized by extraordinarily high lipid levels, who also had neurologic symptoms related to vitamin E deficiency, that plasma α-tocopherol concentrations were in the normal range. Thus, it was necessary to calculate the α-tocopherol/lipids ratio to show that the apparently high plasma α-tocopherol was in fact at deficient levels.

There is also a great deal of controversy with respect to the idea that α-tocopherol/lipids may be adequate if circulating lipid levels are low. However, if low nutrient intakes lead to abnormally low plasma lipid levels, then there is ansufficient lipoprotein carrier for the vitamin E. In which case, the absolute plasma α-tocopherol concentrations may be a more reliable biomarker of vitamin E status than the lipid ratio (93). Certainly, it is worthwhile to present both forms of the data.

1. Deficiency symptoms
Vitamin E deficiency was first described in rats in 1922 by Evans and Bishop (95). Deficiency symptoms in various animal species were described by Machlin in his comprehensive book on vitamin E

(96). Necrotizing myopathy, fetal death and resorption, anemia, and tissue accumulation of lipofuscin (a fluorescent pigment of "aging") were symptoms described in various vitamin E-deficient animals. Vitamin E deficiency symptoms in target tissues are dependent not only upon α-tocopherol content, uptake, and turnover, but also on the degree of oxidative stress, as well as the PUFA content.

Horwitt (97, 98) attempted to induce vitamin E deficiency in men by feeding a diet low in vitamin E for 6 years to volunteers at the Elgin State Hospital in Illinois. After about two years, their serum vitamin E levels decreased into the deficient range. Although their erythrocytes were more sensitive to peroxide-induced hemolysis, overt anemia did not develop. The data from the Horwitt study was used both in 1968 and again in 2000 to set the recommended daily allowances (RDA) for vitamin E (4). These latest RDAs are discussed further below. It was not until the mid-1960s that vitamin E deficiency was described in children with fat malabsorption syndromes, principally abetalipoproteinemia and cholestatic liver disease (99). By the mid-1980s, it was clear that the major vitamin E deficiency symptom in humans was a peripheral neuropathy characterized by the degeneration of the large caliber axons in the sensory neurons (99). This neurodegeneration is apparent as a cause of the ataxia that is observed in these subjects. Subsequently, AVED patients were identified; these were patients with peripheral neuropathies without fat malabsorption, who were vitamin E deficient (73). Studies in AVED patients opened new avenues in vitamin E investigations because these patients were found to have a genetic defect in the hepatic α-TTP (44, 100).

Overt vitamin E deficiency occurs only rarely in humans. Vitamin E deficiency does occur as a result of genetic abnormalities in α-TTP and as a result of various fat malabsorption syndromes. In α-tocopherol deficiency, anemia occurs as a result of free radical damage to erythrocyte membranes (101). Similarly, peripheral neuropathy likely occurs due to free radical damage to the nerves (74). Chronic under consumption of vitamin E will lead to overt vitamin E deficiency symptoms if the α-tocopherol levels in target tissues (e.g., peripheral nerves) become depleted. Thus, children historically have been the susceptible population in which vitamin E deficiency has been observed. Elderly have been suggested to suffer vitamin E inadequacy, causing immune dysfunction (102).

It should be emphasized that subjects with peripheral neuropathies, especially those with ataxia or retinitis pigmentosa, should be evaluated to assess if they are vitamin E deficient because these are recognized symptoms that occur with vitamin E deficiency. The ataxia of Friedreich's ataxia is so remarkably similar to that of AVED patients (103, 104) that plasma concentrations of vitamin E in all patients with ataxia should definitely be measured.

2. Vitamin E deficiency caused by genetic defects in α-TTP

Genetic defects in α-TTP are associated with a characteristic syndrome, AVED (previously called familial-isolated vitamin E (FIVE) deficiency). AVED patients have neurologic abnormalities, which are similar to those of patients with Friedreich's ataxia (103, 104). The symptoms are characterized by a progressive peripheral neuropathy with a specific "dying back" of the large caliber axons of the sensory neurons, which results in ataxia (105). Retinitis pigmentosa, also a symptom of vitamin E deficiency in humans (106), has been described in patients with AVED (107, 108). The defect in the α-TTP gene in three AVED patients with retinitis pigmentosa was described; they all had the histidine 101 transfer defect (108). Importantly, vitamin E supplementation stops or slows the progression of retinitis pigmentosa caused by vitamin E deficiency (108).

3. Vitamin E deficiency caused by genetic defects in lipoprotein synthesis

Vitamin E deficiency is also caused by genetic defects in lipoprotein synthesis that result in fat malabsorption. Studies of patients with hypobetalipoproteinemia or abetalipoproteinemia (low to non detectable circulating chylomicrons, VLDL or LDL) have demonstrated that lipoproteins containing apolipoprotein B are necessary for effective absorption and plasma transport of lipids, especially vitamin E (109). These patients have steatorrhea from birth because of the impaired ability to absorb dietary fat, which also contributes to their poor vitamin E status. Clinical features also include retarded growth, acanthocytosis, retinitis pigmentosa and a chronic progressive neurological disorder with ataxia. The acanthocytosis is a spicular shape to the erythrocytes, likely due to abnormal cholesterol distribution in the membrane. Nonetheless, it is important to note that this disorder, which is associated with poor vitamin E status, is also associated with abnormalities in erythrocyte function. Clinically, both hypobetalipoproteinemic or abetalipoproteinemic subjects become vitamin E deficient and develop a characteristic neurologic syndrome, a progressive peripheral neuropathy, if they are not given large vitamin E supplements (approximately 10 g per day) (109, 110). Despite low plasma concentrations, adipose tissue α-tocopherol concentrations reach normal levels in patients given large (10 g/day) vitamin E doses (110).

4. Vitamin E deficiency caused by fat malabsorption

Vitamin E deficiency also occurs secondary to fat malabsorption because vitamin E absorption requires biliary and pancreatic secretions. Failure of micellar solubilization and malabsorption of dietary lipids leads to vitamin E deficiency in children with chronic cholestatic hepatobiliary disorders, including disease of the liver and anomalies of intrahepatic and extrahepatic bile ducts (73). Children with cholestatic liver disease, who have impaired secretion of bile into the small intestine, have severe fat malabsorption. Neurologic abnormalities, which appear as early as the second year of life, become irreversible if the vitamin E deficiency is uncorrected (30, 73, 111). Children with cystic fibrosis can also become vitamin E deficient because the impaired secretion of pancreatic digestive enzymes causes steatorrhea and vitamin E malabsorption, even when pancreatic enzyme supplements are administered orally (73). More severe vitamin E deficiency occurs if bile secretion is impaired (112–115). It should be emphasized that any disorder that causes chronic fat malabsorption can lead to vitamin E deficiency. Thus, generally poor intake of nutrients in combination with chronic diarrhea in children could lead to vitamin E deficiency, if the fat malabsorption is sufficiently severe and the child has low α-tocopherol body stores.

VITAMIN E STATUS IN MALNOURISHED STATES

Vitamin E status in humans can be compromised during anemia as a result of the oxidative stress caused by erythrocyte hemolysis. Despite the wide range of anemia types (e.g., iron deficiency anemia, vitamin B_{12} and folate deficiency anemias, thalassemia and sickle cell anemias, G6PD deficiency anemia, aplastic anemia, idiopathic autoimmune hemolytic anemia, chronic disease anemias, drug-induced immune hemolytic anemia, immune hemolytic anemia, megaloblastic anemia, pernicious anemia), oxidative stress is a common denominator. Antioxidant molecules and enzymes mentioned *vide supra* critically maintain the redox balance in the erythrocytes that contain high hemoglobin-bound iron concentrations. Anemia, especially during release of free iron in hemolytic anemia, increases the oxidative stress and iron toxicity (116).

1. Protein energy malnutrition (PEM)

The hepatic α-TTP protein is required to maintain normal plasma α-tocopherol concentrations (100). It is, therefore, not surprising that vitamin E deficiency symptoms have been reported in children with severely limited food intake, which not only might be limiting in vitamin E, but limiting the protein necessary to synthesize the hepatic α-TTP necessary for regulation of plasma α-tocopherol. Kalra et al. (117) reported in 100 PEM patients, who had low plasma α-tocopherol concentrations and low α-tocopherol/lipid ratios, that they also had neurologic abnormalities characteristic of vitamin E deficiency. Remarkably, 92% of the children with neurologic abnormalities had plasma α-tocopherol concentrations of 8 γmol/L or less, a value observed in many children with PEM (**Table 11.1**). In a follow up study with 6 weeks of vitamin E supplementation, not only were the subjects' circulating α-tocopherol levels normalized, but there was also improvement in their neurologic abnormalities (118). This pair of reports (117, 118) clearly identifies vitamin E deficiency as a cause of the neurologic abnorma-lities in children with PEM.

Brainstem auditory evoked potentials (BAEPs) may be associated with vitamin E deficiency in children with cystic fibrosis, as well as those with malnutrition (124–126). It should be noted, however, that AVED patients who do not malabsorb other nutrients do not have hearing difficulties, so it is not clear as to the role of vitamin E deficiency in abnormal BAEP responses.

There are several examples from studies around the world (**Table 11.1**) that have demonstrated the existence of children at various stages of malnutrition who have plasma α-tocopherol concentrations that are at, or well below, those of the minimum concentration of 12 γmol/L for adults set by the Food and Nutrition Board (4). However, fat malabsorption has been reported as a confounding clinical observation during recovery from extreme malnutrition (127). Therefore,

Table 11.1: Plasma α-tocopherol in children with protein energy malnutrition (PEM, e.g., kwashiorkor or marasmus).

Country (median, mean, or range, error)	Age, n	Status	α-Tocopherol (µmol/L)	α-Tocopherol/ Lipids (units)		Ref.
India	3–8 years, n=50	Control	9.5 ± 2.1	0.72 ± 0.12	mg/g	(117)
(mean ± SD)	3–8 years, n=100	PEM	6.0 ± 2.6	0.47 ± 0.14	mg/g	(117)
Nigeria	22 months, n=18	Control	7.4 -	0.70 -	mg/g	(119)
(median)	24 months, n=12	Kwashiorkor	3.8 -	0.48 -	mg/g	(119)
	14 months, n=8	Severe marasmus	6.9 -	0.70 -	mg/g	(119)
	17 months, n=15	Marasmus	5.3 -	0.66 -	mg/g	(119)
Nigeria	24 months,1–4 years, n=10	Control	17.4 ± 4.0	1.8 ± 0.4	mg/g	(120)
(mean ± SD)	15 months, 1–4 years, n=26	Marasmus	8.8 ± 0.5	1.0 ± 0.2	mg/g	(120)
	28 months, 1–4 years, n=11	Marasmic-kwashiorkor	7.9 ± 1.0	0.8 ± 0.2	mg/g	(120)
	36 months, 1–4 years, n=10	Kwashiorkor	10.7 ± 3.4	1.2 ± 0.4	mg/g	(120)
Kenya	3.4 ± 1.3 years, n=39	Control	11.6 ± 4.2	1.6 ± 0.3	mmol/mol	(121)
(mean ± SD)	3.1 ± 1.5 years, n=30	Kwashiorkor	4.6 ± 4.2	1.1 ± 0.7	mmol/mol	(121)
	2.5 ± 1.1 years, n=16	Marasmus	9.3 ± 4.2	1.4 ± 0.8	mmol/mol	(121)
Sudan	21 months, n=14	Marasmus	9.4 (5.0–17.7)	1.0 (0.5–1.7)	mg/g	(122)
(median, range)	24 months, n=11	Marasmic-kwashiorkor	8.5 (1.6–9.9)	0.86 (0.2–1.3)	mg/g	(122)
	24 months, n=5	Kwashiorkor	9.1 (4.9–26.5)	0.87 (0.4–3.0)	mg/g	(122)
Egypt	13 ± 2 months, n=22	Control	16.5 ± 0.8	- -	-	(123)
(mean ± SE)	13 ± 2 months, n=26	Kwashiorkor	11.6 ± 0.7	- -	-	(123)
	12 ± 1 months, n=20	Marasmus	11.5 ± 1	- -	-	(123)

some reports also include the ratio of α-tocopherol per total lipids because vitamin E is transported in the plasma lipoproteins. Often this calculation results in a value for α-tocopherol/lipids for many PEM children that puts them into the normal range of equal to or greater than 0.6 mg/g total lipids (128). However, this calculation is generally used when circulating lipids are high and thus retaining α-tocopherol in the circulation. It is not clear that the calculation is valid when plasma lipids are low because the α-tocopherol concentration would then appear higher than reflected in a target tissue, such as the peripheral nerve.

The degree to which vitamin E deficiency is associated with kwashiorkor and/or marasmus is not clear because evaluation of vitamin E status in malnourished children is difficult. Although plasma triglycerides are sometimes increased and sometimes not, children with kwashiorkor uniformly appear to have low plasma cholesterol concentrations (129–133). Moreover, elevated circulating triglycerides and fatty liver of PEM appear to be a result of dysregulation of lipid metabolism (130). Reportedly, the fatty liver is not likely a failure in hepatic VLDL synthesis, assembly or secretion (134), but the abnormality, rather, appears to be an inability for tissue or plasma triglycerides to undergo lipolysis (129, 135). Protein depletion in PEM can be so severe that there is insufficient protein for synthesis of lipolytic enzymes to digest fat. This metabolic abnormality thus complicates evaluation of vitamin E nutriture. The transport and delivery of vitamin E is critically dependent on the hepatic secretion of lipoproteins and their uptake by peripheral tissues. Indeed, if α-tocopherol is trapped in triglyceride-rich lipoproteins that cannot be effectively catabolized, then the α-tocopherol is not available to the target tissues and oxidative stress can ensue. Indeed, lipid peroxidation can lead to further damage and a damaging chain reaction can occur in membranes.

It is not clear that vitamin E supplementation would be beneficial until the underlying metabolic problem is resolved. Fat must be consumed with supplemental α-tocopherol, and vitamin E absorption is impaired during fat malabsorption. Moreover, if α-tocopherol were absorbed, it may not be released from chylomicrons, if lipolysis is impaired. Finally, following α-tocopherol uptake by the liver, α-TTP function is required for α-tocopherol secretion back into the plasma. Moreover, elevated VLDL may contain α-tocopherol, but not allow its release until lipolysis is normalized. Thus, it is critical to normalize metabolic abnormalities caused by PEM.

2. Iron deficiency anemia

Inadequate food intake is also associated with iron deficiency anemia. This disorder is associated with decreased production of hemoglobin (Hb) and other iron-containing proteins such as myoglobin, catalase, peroxidase, and cytochromes. The erythrocyte membranes, with their high PUFA concentration, are more susceptible to oxidative damage in the case of iron deficiency anemia (136, 137).

Iron supplementation to deficient individuals was found to increase the oxidative stress (i.e., increased malnodialdehyde (MDA) levels and compromised antioxidant enzyme activities) (138). Indeed, as discussed above, high levels of free iron may enhance radical production via the Fenton and Haber-Weiss reactions (6, 139). Importantly, treatment of iron-deficient patients with a combination of iron and vitamins A, C, and E proved effective in normalizing the oxidative stress (138).

ANEMIA IN THALASSEMIA AND SICKLE CELL DISEASES

Thalassemia and sickle cell diseases are two inherited blood Hb disorders that cause anemia.

To understand the etiology of these diseases, it is important to review some basic aspects of RBC hematology. In healthy humans, about 95% of the Hb is Hb A ($\alpha_2\beta_2$) with small amounts of Hb A_2 ($\alpha_2\delta_2$) and Hb F ($\alpha2\gamma2$) with the α-globin chain encoded in duplicate on chromosome 16 and the non α-globlin chains (β, δ, γ) encoded in a cluster on chromosome 11. A mutation in the β-chains of HbA, where a lysyl residue substitutes the normal glutamyl residue in the 26th position, gives HbE. Thalassemia is a collective name for a number of disease variants characterized by a failure of one or more of the four α-globin genes and two β-globin genes to produce normal Hb. About 90 million people worldwide carry defective genes leading to thalassemia. The condition is classified into α- or β-thalassemia depending on the defect.

In α-thalassemias, a single α-globin gene defect is clinically silent, a two α-globin gene defect produces normal or mild Hb reduction, while a three α-globin gene defect produces moderately severe hemolytic anemia. A defect in one β-globin gene leads to β-thalassemia minor while defects in both β-globin genes lead to β-thalassemia major (or Cooley's anemia). A third type of thalassemia, the Eβ-thalassemia, results when the patient inherits β-thalassemia from one parent and HbE from the other parent. The heterogenity of thalassemias leads to a wide variability in the degree of anemia associated with the disease (140). In the homozygous state of sickle cell disease, glutamine is changed to valine at the sixth position of the Hb β-chains yielding the Hb S variant (141, 142).

1. Oxidative stress and antioxidant supplementation

The mild to severe anemia associated with the different types of thalassemias results from oxidative stress (143-145) that damages erythrocyte membranes resulting in decreased deformability and hemolysis, as well as to increased recognition and removal by immune cells (146). There is strong evidence for oxidative stress in thalassemic patients, especially those receiving transfusion therapy. A lower ratio of unsaturated-to-saturated fatty acids (147), a 50 % decrease in titratable-SH groups (148), as well as decreased plasma concentrations of vitamins A, C, E and carotenoids have been reported (149–153). Specifically α-thalassemic patients compared with healthy controls had lower plasma vitamin C (6.7 ± 1.4 compared with 13.2 ± 1.2 μg/ml, $P<0.001$), vitamin E (6.6 ± 0.2 compared with 7.8 ± 0.5 μg/ml, $P<0.001$) and vitamin A concentrations (56 ± 4 compared with 76 ± 5 μg/dl, $P<0.001$) (146). Moreover, erythrocyte vitamin E in α-thalassemic patients was also lower than in controls (56 compared with 67 μg/dl, respectively). Moreover, in both Eβ- and β-thalassemic patients, increased protein oxidation leads to protein degradation, as reflected by increased tyrosine release (154).

Thalassemia is also characterized by low enzyme activities of CAT, GSH-px, and glutathione reductase and elevated SOD activity (154). Remarkably, these enzyme concentrations were all normalized by vitamin E treatment (154).

Oxidative stress is also manifested in sickle cell disease. Sickle cell disease is a chronic inflammatory disease characterized during crisis by elevated levels of tumor necrosis factor-α (TNF-α) and interlukin-6 (IL-6) (155–158). Sickle cell RBCs are unstable (159) and produce large amounts of $O_2\cdot$-, H_2O_2 and $\cdot OH$ as a result of Hb deoxygenation and subsequent RBC rupture (158, 160–163). Compared with healthy controls, sickle cell diseased individuals may have higher levels of homocysteine (164, 165), which also contributes to oxidative stress.

As a result of the oxidative stressors associated with sickle cell disease, low levels of antioxidant nutrients, vitamins C and E and carotenoids have been reported (166–170). Notably, patients with sickle cell anemia (171) and β-thalassemia (172) both have lower serum lipids than healthy controls. Nonetheless, low plasma vitamin E levels are highlighted here because vitamin E supplements appear to counteract the sickling process (173–175). Several groups have reported that thalassemic and sickle cell disease patients would benefit from vitamin E therapy (154, 176, 177). For example, Jaja et al. (178) posited that low plasma concentrations of vitamin E are related to elevated levels of irreversibly sickled cells and to the pathogenesis of painful crisis, and tested whether vitamin E supplementation (100 mg per day for 6 w) would improve hematological parameters in ten children with sickle cell anemia (4 to 10 y). They found that vitamin E supplementation affected several parameters related to Hb status and RBCs, for example it increased packed cell volume ($P<0.001$), Hb concentration ($P<0.01$) and percent fetal Hb ($P<0.001$), but significantly reduced mean corpuscular Hb concentration ($P<0.01$) and percent irreversibly sickled cells ($P<0.001$). Thus, there may be benefit to vitamin E supplementation in children with sickle cell disease.

Vitamin E supplementation raises plasma α-tocopherol concentrations, but the extent of the increase is largely dependent upon the starting vitamin E status (**Table 11.2**). If the subject is severely nutritionally compromised, then vitamin E supplementation may have to be accompanied

by a strong dietary program to achieve the optimal outcome (179).

Thalassemia and sickle cell disease are treated in some cases by blood transfusion, which leads to iron overload and to oxidative stress *inter alia* in RBCs (184). A study from Thailand showed that 20 children with β-thalassemia major who received packed red cells blood transfusions without iron chelation therapy had low vitamin C and vitamin E levels and high oxidative stress (185). They recommended supplementation of β-thalassemia patients with both nutrients (185).

GLUCOSE-6-PHOSPHATE DEHYDROGENASE DEFICIENCY

G6PD is the enzyme that catalyzes the rate-limiting step in the hexose monophosphate pathway. G6PD is an important enzyme for the functionality of the red blood cell. G6PD deficiency is an inherited defect with a great variability that affects about 400 million people worldwide, mainly in tropical areas (186). G6PD deficiency is an inherited response to malaria, and has been suggested to be one of the major evolutionary changes in the human genome (187).

G6PD is involved in the production of NAD(P)H, which is important for maintaining

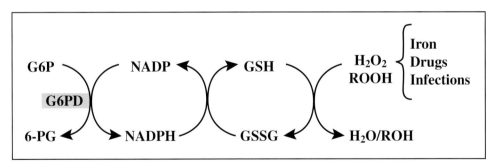

Figure 11.3: Role of glucose-6-phosphate dehydrogenase in oxidative stress.

G6PD regenerates NAD(P)H using GSH and therefore is important in the deactivation of reactive oxygen species such as hydrogen peroxide (H_2O_2) and other ROOH.

Table 11.2: Plasma α-tocopherol in children and adults with thalassemia and sickle cell disease.

Country (median, mean, or range, error)	Age, n	Status	α-Tocopherol (μmol/L)	Ref.
India	n=6	Normal	4.0 ± 0.4	(154)
(mean ± SE)	n=9	Eβ-thalassemia	2.7 ± 0.4	(154)
		4 week vitamin E supplementation	5.1 ± 0.4	(154)
	n=8	β-thalassemia	2.9 ± 1.5	(154)
		4 week vitamin E supplementation	2.9 ± 1.4	(154)
Egypt	9 ± 4 years, 2–18 years, n=63	Control	14.0 ± 3.8	(180)
(mean ± SD)	9 ± 5 years, 2–18 years, n=64	Thalassemia	11.9 ± 3.3	(180)
Saudi Arabia	30 ± 13 years, n=25	Severe sickle cell anemia	4.7 ± 1.7	(181)
(mean ± SD)	29 ± 8 years, n=25	Control	10.0 ± 2.3	(181)
Nigeria (mean ± SE)	23 ± 1 years, n=10	Sickle cell anemia	4.0 ± 0.2	(182)
Netherlands	9 ± 5 years, n=13	Sickle cell disease, baseline	13.9 ± 4.8	(183)
(mean ± SD)		8 month supplementation 1 (460 mg α-tocopherol + others),	23.1 ± 8.5	(183)
		followed by 7 month supplementation 2 (400 mg mixed α-tocopherol + others)	25.7 ± 7.4	(183)

adequate redox levels of glutathione and other sulfydryl groups **(Figure 11.3)**. GSH is essential for the detoxification of ROS and lipid hydroper-oxides. Thus, G6PD deficiency is associated with oxidative stress. The disorder leads to oxidation of Hb to methemoglobin, heinz body formation, membrane damage, and anemia due to increased removal of damaged erythrocytes from the cir-culation. Vitamin E administration restored the inactivation of G6PD activity due to nicotine admini-stration in various rat tissues in vivo and in vitro (188). In G6PD-deficient subjects with a history of hemolysis, a 16-week course of oral vitamin E therapy (800 IU/day) increased plasma vitamin E concentrations, improved blood Hb levels, and decreased reticulocytosis and hemolysis (189). Thus, vitamin E supple-ments may be helpful to alleviate oxidative stress due to G6PD deficiency.

MALARIA

Malaria is a common disease in the tropics, annu-ally accounting for 500 million episodes and about 2.7 million deaths (190). According to the World Health Organization (http://www.who.int/topics/malaria/en), malaria is "a protozoan disease caused in humans by four species of the genus *Plasmodium* (*P. falciparum, P. vivax, P. ovale*, and *P. malariae*) and transmitted by the bite of an infected female mosquito of the genus *Anopheles*. Malaria is endemic in parts of Asia, Africa, Central and South America, Oceania, and certain Caribbean islands. It is characterized by extreme exhaustion associated with paroxysms of high fever, sweating, shaking chills, and anemia."

Elevated biomarkers of oxidative stress have been reported in malaria-infected erythrocytes; as the subject recovered, the oxidative stress decreased (191). Das et al. (192) reported in 50 children with severe and 50 with mild malaria, along with 50 age- and sex-matched control sub-jects, that glutathione, α-tocopherol, retinol, and

all carotenoid concentrations were lower in the patients than in the control subjects (*P*<0.001). They concluded that the disease caused a marked reduction in plasma cholesterol and thus α-toco-pherol concentrations were normalized if repor-ted as α-tocopherol/cholesterol. Adelekan et al. (193) reported that malaria alone exerts a greater influence on plasma antioxidants than does mal-nutrition. While Griffiths et al. (194) demonstrated that plasma α-tocopherol concentrations may not change, but erythrocyte α-tocopherol concentra-tions are markedly depleted during malarial episodes. Similarly, plasma ascorbic acid has been reported to be lower in children infected with malaria compared with healthy children (195).

According to Sherman et al. (196) the human malaria parasite, *P. falciparum*, causes the ery-throcyte to age and during this process "the para-sitized cell becomes less dense and deformable, its biconcave disc shape becomes more spherical and is covered with microscopic protuberances (knobs); the amounts of membrane cholesterol and phospholipids are altered and phosphatidyl serine (PS) is externalized. The malaria-infected cell is osmotically fragile, more permeable to a wide variety of molecules. There are declines in sialic acid, reduced glutathione, α-tocopherol, and ATP. These time-dependent changes result from oxidative assault and a combination of fac-tors, including a decline in levels of antioxidants and ATP coupled with an enhanced flux of ions especially calcium." Interestingly, α-tocopherol may have a critical role in regulating cell responses because α-tocopherol appears to regu-late the externalization of phosphatidyl serine, a key step in the initiation of apoptosis (197). Although, antioxidants, such as ascorbic acid or α-tocopherol, do not inhibit *P. falciparum* growth in vitro (198); remarkably, Hemmer et al. (199) report that cultured endothelial cells are damaged by neutrophil secretory products from cells exposed to malaria. Moreover, they found that the antioxidants, ascorbic acid and α-tocopherol, can reduce malaria-associated endothelial apoptosis in vitro (199). Paradoxically, in mice malaria resistance is increased with vitamin E deficiency (200), while the opposite appears to occur in people. That is, in humans antioxidant status decreases with increased disease severity and, generally, the severity of the decrease in plasma α-tocopherol declines with recovery from disease, as illustrated in the two studies from Uganda **(Table 11.3)**, (201, 202).

A potential explanation for the decline in plasma α-tocopherol observed in many studies during malarial episodes arises from studies by Guha et al. (204). They found that malarial infection induces hepatic apoptosis through augmentation of oxidative stress. It is therefore not surprising that oxidative stress caused by the malarial infection depletes plasma antioxidants. Importantly, the hepatic dysfunction will further cause diminution of the secretion of α-tocopherol from the liver into the plasma, and thus, with increasing severity of the disease, cause a further limitation in the plasma and tissue antioxidant defenses (205, 206). These findings suggest that improved antioxidant defenses will be beneficial in mounting appropriate immune responses.

Interestingly, antimalarial drugs, such as chloroquine, function by forming complexes with free heme; these complexes disturb the redox equilibrium and can kill the parasite (207). Moreover, chloroquine treatment not only increases oxidative stress, it also diminishes antioxidant enzymes (208). The parasite reacts by producing extra glutathione to counter the oxidative stress (207). Drugs that reduce cellular glutathione levels enhanced the antimalarial action of chloroquine in mice (209). Hence, a level of oxidative stress may be important during treatment, although it contributes negatively to the general health, possibly inducing anemia as a result of destruction of red blood cells. The infected individual, suffering from enhanced oxidative stress during the incubation period and the malaria episode as well as during treatment, may benefit from a post-treatment vitamin E supplementation.

HIV AND AIDS

Human immunodeficiency virus/acquired immunodeficiency syndrome (HIV/AIDS) is associated with numerous hematologic disorders, especially anemia (210), and severe anemia in this syndrome is associated with increased risk of mortality (211). A recent review of clinical trials suggested that currently there are no useful therapeutic strategies to decrease anemia in HIV/AIDS patients (212).

Reactive oxygen species (ROS) are believed to play a critical role in the activation of NF-κB transcription factor and the stimulation of HIV infections (213, 214). Allard et al. (214) showed that HIV-positive patients in Toronto, Canada, had both an increase in oxidative stress biomarkers and lower plasma antioxidants compared with healthy volunteers. Lipid peroxides (50.7 ± 8.2 compared with 4.5 ± 0.8 μmol/L, $P<0.005$), breath pentane (9.05 ± 1.23 compared with 6.06 ± 0.56 pmol/kg/min, $P<0.05$), and ethane output (28.1 ± 3.4 compared with 11.4 ± 0.6 pmol/kg/min, $P<0.05$) were higher in the HIV-positive patients. Moreover, plasma antioxidant concentrations, including ascorbic acid (40.7 ± 3.0 compared with 75.7 ± 4.3 μmol/L, $P<0.005$), α-tocopherol (22.5 ± 1.2 compared with 26.6 ± 2.6 μmol/L, $P<0.05$), β-carotene (0.23 ± 0.04 compared with 0.38 ± 0.04 μmol/L, $P<0.05$), and selenium (0.37 ± 0.05 compared with 0.85 ± 0.09 μmol/L, $P<0.005$) were lower in the HIV-positive patients. Allard et al. (214) suggested that the lower plasma antioxidant concentrations resulted from chronic oxidative stress caused by their infection that could lead to further enhancement in lipid peroxidation. When Allard et al. (215) provided vitamin E and C supplementation in HIV-infected individuals, there was decreased oxidative stress, as well as a trend toward decreased viral load. Spada et al. (216) also reported that vitamin E decreased viral load, as well as increased hematocrit and Hb concentrations.

Table 11.3: Plasma α-tocopherol in children and adults with malaria.

Country (median, mean, or range, error)	Age, n	Status	α-Tocopherol (µmol/L)		Ref.
India	7.8 ± 3.0 years, n=50	Control	17.7	–	(192)
(median)	7.7 ± 2.7 years, n=50	Mild malaria	11.5	–	(192)
	7.7 ± 2.9 years, n=50	Severe malaria	7.3	–	(192)
Kenya	1.8 ± 2.3 years, n=30	Control	11.7 ± 0.8		(194)
(mean ± SE)	2.2 ± 0.36 years, n=18	Complicated malaria	12.0 ± 1.3		(194)
	2.3 ± 0.53 years, n=21	Malarial anemia	13.0 ± 1.1		(194)
	2.3 ± 0.33 years, n=39	Non-stratified malaria	12.9 ± 0.8		(194)
Uganda	39 ± 26 months, n=273	Malaria	7.6 ± 2.6		(201)
(mean ± SD)	39 ± 26 months, n=187	7 day follow up	8.6 ± 2.6		(201)
	30 ± 22 months, n=39	Baseline severely anemic	7.7 ± 2.3		(202)
	30 ± 22 months, n=39	7 day follow up	8.5 ± 2.6		(202)
	40 ± 26 months, n=148	Baseline not severely anemic	7.5 ± 2.3		(202)
	40 ± 26 months, n=148	7 day follow up	8.6 ± 2.6		(202)
Thailand	25.2 years, n=58	Control with DDT exposure	7.7 ± 3.8		(203)
(mean ± SD)	24.7 years, n=50	Malaria with DDT exposure	15.6 ± 6.3		(203)

Additional benefits of multivitamins and antioxidants were reported during pregnancy. Supplementation of HIV-infected women with vitamin B complex, vitamin C, and vitamin E during pregnancy and lactation was shown to be an effective intervention for improving ponderal growth in children (217). Despite these positive reports, there are relatively few antioxidant intervention trials in the literature, suggesting that there was relatively limited success in the ten years since these first trials were reported.

The role of malnutrition in immune function has been suggested to be important in viral infections, not only for the health of the person, but also as a critical factor influencing virus virulence (218). Importantly, vitamin E supplementation has improved host immune response. For example, immune function has been found to improve with vitamin E supplementation in elderly nursing home residents (219, 220); moreover, higher vitamin E levels were associated with improved immune function (220). Therefore, it is also reasonable to consider if vitamin E and C supplementation would be of benefit to support immune function during various infectious diseases.

CONCLUDING REMARKS

Based on the summary of the findings presented here, it is clear that many malnourished children have low plasma α-tocopherol concentrations. Moreover, in some cases low plasma α-tocopherol concentrations have been demonstrated to be associated with the classic neurologic abnormalities seen in AVED subjects who have a genetic defect in the hepatic α-TTP. Thus, it is likely that if neurologic testing were carried out in more children, then more children would be found with frank vitamin E deficiency. Although anemia was an early classic symptom of vitamin E deficiency in children (221), it is clear that neurologic abnormalities, especially ataxia, are now considered the first unequivocal symptom of vitamin E deficiency in humans (4).

This observation, however, does not negate the importance of α-tocopherol in maintaining erythrocyte membranes and the susceptibility of α-tocopherol-depleted membranes to rupture and hemolysis.

"Antioxidant nutrients" is a rubric that covers a wide variety of dietary components in addition to vitamin E discussed in this review. Vitamin C and a range of dietary antioxidants are relatively abundant in a variety of fruits and vegetables. By contrast, α-tocopherol is more difficult to acquire from the diet because it is present in appreciable amounts only in foods such as nuts, some seeds, and vegetable oils. The complication in evaluating vitamin E status during malnutrition is the difficulty in evaluating α-tocopherol intakes. The quality of the diet and the amounts of vitamin E consumed do not appear to have been studied in many investigations of kwashiorkor or marasmus. For example, one study noted that antioxidant intakes were limited based on their observation that few tomatoes were consumed (222). It is often difficult to assess the α-tocopherol contents of diets because of the variability of vitamin E in oil, as well as the limitation in accurate food vitamin E measurements (4).

Moreover, it can be postulated that the product of low vitamin E status may not be solely due to a limitation in α-tocopherol intakes. For example, severe PEM is associated not only with poor vitamin E status, but also with essential fatty acid deficiency (223). Also as was discussed previously, the expression of the hepatic α-TTP may be sensitive to dietary protein intake. It certainly would seem likely that if plasma albumin concentrations are not maintained, then the hepatic α-TTP might be expendable in the short term and thus not synthesized in the liver if protein intakes are inadequate. Additionally, a subject could consume a vitamin E-containing supplement, but if no dietary fat is consumed with the supplement, the vitamin E will not be absorbed (33). If the α-tocopherol were absorbed, and secreted in chylomicrons, or if lipo-lysis is limiting (135), α-tocopherol may not be available to the tissues. However, if the chylomicron remnants containing α-tocopherol are taken up by the liver, the α-tocopherol may not be secreted by the hepatic α-TTP into the plasma, if the α-TTP is limiting or perhaps not even synthesized. These various steps in α-tocopherol absorption and deli-very to the liver all seem quite dependent upon dietary factors that are not likely to be available or functional during severe malnutrition. Thus, vitamin E deficiency at the RBC and tissue level may occur.

The formulation of a nutritional supplement containing α-tocopherol may be critical because vitamin E is not well absorbed in the absence of dietary fat (33). Remarkably, Faber et al. (224) reported on anemia in infants aged 6–12 mo (n=361), who were randomly assigned to receive maize-meal porridge for 6 months that was either unfortified (control group) or fortified with β-carotene, iron, zinc, ascorbic acid, copper, selenium, riboflavin, vitamin B_6, vitamin B_{12}, and vitamin E. The proportion of infants with anemia decreased from 45% to 17% in the fortified-porridge group, whereas it remained >40% in the control group. These findings suggest that the combination of nutrients as a supplement to food may be the best strategy for ameliorating anemia in at-risk children.

Taken together, many of the various types of anemia reported herein seem to be accompanied by low vitamin E status that may be also associated with neurologic symptoms characteristic of α-tocopherol deficiency. While the α-tocopherol deficiency in malnutrition may be caused by inadequate food intakes, other anemias related to genetic malfunctions or viral infections may result in a α-tocopherol deficiency caused either by impaired vitamin E absorption or increased oxidative stress. In the latter cases, α-tocopherol deficiency may occur in the absence of deficiencies of other nutrients. In any case, the severity of the neurologic abnormalities that result from α-tocopherol deficiency, as well as the immunologic dysregulation reported to occur with inadequate α-tocopherol intakes, emphasizes the critical need not only for vitamin E supplementation but also adequate dietary support with respect to all nutrients.

ABBREVIATIONS

8- hydroxyguanine (80HG ar 8-oxoG)
8-hydroxy-2-deoxyguanosine (80HdG or 8-oxodG)
α-tocopherol (α-TOH)
α-tocopheroxyl radical (αc-TO·)
α-tocopherol transfer protein (α-TTP)
ataxia with isolated vitamin E deficiency (AVED)
catalase (CAT)
carboxyethyl-6-hydroxychroman (CEHC)
carbon centered radical (R·)
cytochrome P450 (CYP)
erythrocyte (RBC)
glutathione peroxidase (GSH-px)
glucose-6-phosphate dehydrogenase (G6PD, EC 1.1.1.49)
hemoglobin (Hb)
high density lipoprotein (HDL)

human immunodeficiency virus/acquired immunodeficiency syndrome (HIV/AIDS)
lipid hydroperoxides (ROOH)
low density lipoprotein (LDL)
oxygen (0_2)
peroxyl radical (ROO·)
phospholipid transfer protein (PLTP)
polyunsaturated fatty acids (PUFA, RH)
protein energy malnutrition (PEM)
reactive oxygen species (ROS)
reactive nitrogen species (RNS)
recommended daily allowance (RDA)
reducing equivalents (NAD(P)H)
scavenger receptor-B1 (SR-B1)
superoxide dismutase (SOD)
thiobarbituric acid reactive substances (TBARS)
verly low density lipoprotein (VLDL)

REFERENCES

1. Grune T, Sommerburg O, Siems WG. Oxidative stress in anemia. Clin Nephrol 2000;53:18S–22S.
2. Stern A. Red cell oxidative damage. In: Sies H, ed. Oxidative stress. London: Academic Press, 1986:331–49.
3. Chan AC. Partners in defense, vitamin E and vitamin C. Can J Physiol Pharmacol 1993;71:725–31.
4. Food and Nutrition Board, Institute of Medicine. Dietary reference intakes for vitamin C, vitamin E, selenium, and carotenoids. Washington: National Academy Press, 2000.
5. Sies H. Oxidative stress: introductory remarks. In: Sies H, ed. Oxidative stress. London: Academic Press, 1986:1–8.
6. Halliwell B, Gutteridge JMC. Free radicals in biology and medicine. 3rd ed. Oxford: Oxford University Press, 1999.
7. Burton GW, Traber MG. Vitamin E: antioxidant activity, biokinetics, and bioavailability. Annu Rev Nutr 1990;10:357–82.
8. Kadiiska MB, Gladen BC, Baird DD, et al. Biomarkers of oxidative stress study II: are oxidation products of lipids, proteins, and DNA markers of CCl4 poisoning? Free Radic Biol Med 2005;38:698–710.
9. Roberts LJ 2nd, Fessel JP. The biochemistry of the isoprostane, neuroprostane, and isofuran pathways of lipid peroxidation. Chem Phys Lipids 2004;128:173–86.
10. Davies SS, Zackert W, Luo Y, Cunningham CC, Frisard M, Roberts LJ 2nd. Quantification of dinor, dihydro metabolites of F(2)-isoprostanes in urine by liquid chromatography/tandem mass spectrometry. Anal Biochem 2006;348:185–91.
11. Morrow JD. Quantification of isoprostanes as indices of oxidant stress and the risk of atherosclerosis in humans. Arterioscler Thromb Vasc Biol 2005;25:279–86.
12. Sheppard AJ, Pennington JAT, Weihrauch JL. Analysis and distribution of vitamin E in vegetable oils and foods. In: Packer L, Fuchs J, eds. Vitamin E in health and disease. New York, NY: Marcel Dekker, Inc., 1993:9–31.
13. Kaempf-Rotzoll DE, Horiguchi M, Hashiguchi K, et al. Human placental trophoblast cells express alpha-tocopherol transfer protein. Placenta 2003;24:439–44.
14. Kaempf-Rotzoll DE, Igarashi K, Aoki J, et al. Alpha-tocopherol transfer protein is specifically localized at the implantation site of pregnant mouse uterus. Biol Reprod. 2002;67:599–604.
15. Tappel AL. Vitamin E as the biological lipid antioxidant. Vitam Horm 1962;20:493–510.
16. Ingold KU, Burton GW, Foster DO, et al. A new vitamin E analogue more active than alpha-tocopherol in the rat curative myopathy bioassay. FEBS Lett 1986;205(1):117–20 1986.
17. Burton GW, Joyce A, Ingold KU. Is vitamin E the only lipid-soluble, chain-breaking antioxidant in human blood plasma and erythrocyte membranes? Arch Biochem Biophys 1983;221:281–90.
18. Ingold KU, Webb AC, Witter D, Burton GW, Metcalfe TA, Muller DP. Vitamin E remains the major lipid-soluble, chain-breaking antioxidant in human plasma even in individuals suffering severe vitamin E deficiency. Arch Biochem Biophys 1987;259:224–5.
19. Burton GW, Cheeseman KH, Doba T, Ingold KU, Slater TF. Vitamin E as an antioxidant in vitro and in vivo. Ciba Found Symp 1983;101:4–18.
20. Burton GW, Doba T, Gabe EJ, et al. Autoxidation of biological molecules. 4. Maximizing the antioxidant activity of phenols. J Am Chem Soc 1985;107:7053–65.
21. Buettner GR. The pecking order of free radicals and antioxidants: lipid peroxidation, alpha-tocopherol, and ascorbate. Arch Biochem Biophys 1993;300:535–43.
22. Wefers H, Sies H. The protection by ascorbate and glutathione against microsomal lipid peroxidation is dependent on vitamin E. Eur J Biochem 1988;174:353–7.
23. McCay PB. Vitamin E: interactions with free radicals and ascorbate. Ann Rev Nutr 1985;5:323–40.

24. Niki E. Antioxidants in relation to lipid peroxidation. Chem Phys Lipids 1987;44:227–53.

25. Sies H, Murphy ME. Role of tocopherols in the protection of biological systems against oxidative damage. Photochem Photobiol 1991;8:211–24.

26. Sies H, Stahl W, Sundquist AR. Antioxidant functions of vitamins Vitamins E and C, beta-carotene, and other carotenoids. Ann NY Acad Sci 1992;669:7–20.

27. Bruno RS, Ramakrishnan R, Montine TJ, Bray TM, Traber MG. α-Tocopherol disappearance is faster in cigarette smokers and is inversely related to their ascorbic acid status. Am J Clin Nutr 2005;81:95–103.

28. Bruno RS, Leonard SW, Atkinson JK, et al. Faster vitamin E disappearance in smokers is normalized by vitamin C supplementation. Free Radic Biol Med 2006;40:689–97.

29. Attri S, Sharma N, Jahagirdar S, Thapa BR, Prasad R. Erythrocyte metabolism and antioxidant status of patients with Wilson disease with hemolytic anemia. Pediatr Res 2006;59:593–7.

30. Sokol RJ, Heubi JE, Iannaccone S, Bove KE, Harris RE, Balistreri WF. The mechanism causing vitamin E deficiency during chronic childhood cholestasis. Gastroenterology 1983;85:1172–82.

31. Hayes KC, Pronczuk A, Perlman D. Vitamin E in fortified cow milk uniquely enriches human plasma lipoproteins. Am J Clin Nutr 2001;74:211–8.

32. Borel P, Pasquier B, Armand M, et al. Processing of vitamin A and E in the human gastrointestinal tract. Am J Physiol Gastrointest Liver Physiol 2001;280:95G–103G.

33. Bruno RS, Leonard SW, Park S-I, Zhao Y, Traber MG. Human vitamin E requirements assessed with the use of apples fortified with deuterium-labeled α-tocopheryl acetate. Am J Clin Nutr 2006;83:299–304.

34. Traber MG, Kayden HJ. Preferential incorporation of α-tocopherol vs γ-tocopherol in human lipoproteins. Am J Clin Nutr 1989;49:517–26.

35. Meydani M, Cohn JS, Macauley JB, McNamara JR, Blumberg JB, Schaefer EJ. Postprandial changes in the plasma concentration of α- and γ-tocopherol in human subjects fed a fat-rich meal supplemented with fat-soluble vitamins. J Nutr 1989;119:1252–58.

36. Traber MG, Burton GW, Ingold KU, Kayden HJ. *RRR*- and *SRR*-α-tocopherols are secreted without discrimination in human chylomicrons, but *RRR*-α-tocopherol is preferentially secreted in very low density lipoproteins. J Lipid Res 1990;31:675–85.

37. Traber MG, Burton GW, Hughes L, et al. Discrimination between forms of vitamin E by humans with and without genetic abnormalities of lipoprotein metabolism. J Lipid Res 1992;33:1171–82.

38. Kostner GM, Oettl K, Jauhiainen M, Ehnholm C, Esterbauer H, Dieplinger H. Human plasma phospholipid transfer protein accelerates exchange/transfer of alpha-tocopherol between lipoproteins and cells. Biochem J 1995;305:659–67.

39. Havel R. McCollum Award Lecture, 1993: Triglyceride-rich lipoproteins and atherosclerosis – new perspectives. Am J Clin Nutr 1994;59:795–9.

40. Hosomi A, Arita M, Sato Y, et al. Affinity for alpha-tocopherol transfer protein as a determinant of the biological activities of vitamin E analogs. FEBS Lett 1997;409:105–8.

41. Terasawa Y, Ladha Z, Leonard SW, et al. Increased atherosclerosis in hyperlipidemic mice deficient in alpha-tocopherol transfer protein and vitamin E. Proc Natl Acad Sci USA 2000;97:13830–4.

42. Yokota T, Igarashi K, Uchihara T, et al. Delayed-onset ataxia in mice lacking alpha-tocopherol transfer protein: model for neuronal degeneration caused by chronic oxidative stress. Proc Natl Acad Sci USA 2001;98:15185–90.

43. Leonard SW, Terasawa Y, Farese RV, Jr., Traber MG. Incorporation of deuterated *RRR*- or *all rac* α-tocopherol into plasma and tissues of α-tocopherol transfer protein null mice. Am J Clin Nutr 2002;75:555–60.

44. Cavalier L, Ouahchi K, Kayden HJ, et al. Ataxia with isolated vitamin E deficiency: heterogeneity of mutations and phenotypic variability in a large number of families. Am J Hum Genet 1998;62:301–10.

45. Traber MG, Sokol RJ, Kohlschütter A, et al. Impaired discrimination between stereoisomers of

α-tocopherol in patients with familial isolated vitamin E deficiency. J. Lipid Res 1993;34:201–10.

46. Traber MG, Sokol RJ, Burton GW, et al. Impaired ability of patients with familial isolated vitamin E deficiency to incorporate alpha-tocopherol into lipoproteins secreted by the liver. J Clin Invest 1990;85:397–407.

47. Traber MG, Ramakrishnan R, Kayden HJ. Human plasma vitamin E kinetics demonstrate rapid recycling of plasma *RRR*-α-tocopherol. Proc Natl Acad Sci USA 1994;91:10005–8.

48. Cohn W, Loechleiter F, Weber F. α-Tocopherol is secreted from rat liver in very low density lipoproteins. J Lipid Res 1988;29:1359–66.

49. Bjørneboe A, Bjørneboe G-EA, Hagen BF, Nossen JO, Drevon CA. Secretion of α-tocopherol from cultured rat hepatocytes. Biochim Biophys Acta 1987;922:199–205.

50. Traber MG, Rudel LL, Burton GW, Hughes L, Ingold KU, Kayden HJ. Nascent VLDL from liver perfusions of cynomolgus monkeys are preferentially enriched in *RRR*- compared with *SRR*-α tocopherol: studies using deuterated tocopherols. J Lipid Res 1990;31:687–94.

51. Traber MG, Burton GW, Hamilton RL. Vitamin E trafficking. Ann NY Acad Sci 2005;1031:1–12.

52. Arita M, Nomura K, Arai H, Inoue K. alpha-tocopherol transfer protein stimulates the secretion of alpha-tocopherol from a cultured liver cell line through a brefeldin A-insensitive pathway. Proc Natl Acad Sci USA 1997;94:12437–41.

53. Qian J, Morley S, Wilson K, Nava P, Atkinson J, Manor D. Intracellular trafficking of vitamin E in hepatocytes: role of tocopherol transfer protein. J Lipid Res 2005;46:2072–82.

54. Traber MG, Olivecrona T, Kayden HJ. Bovine milk lipoprotein lipase transfers tocopherol to human fibroblasts during triglyceride hydrolysis in vitro. J Clin Invest 1985;75:1729–34.

55. Traber MG, Kayden HJ. Vitamin E is delivered to cells via the high affinity receptor for low density lipoprotein. Am J Clin Nutr 1984;40:747–51.

56. Guthmann F, Harrach-Ruprecht B, Looman AC, Stevens PA, Robenek H, Rustow B. Interaction of lipoproteins with type II pneumocytes in vitro: mor-phological studies, uptake kinetics and secretion rate of cholesterol. Eur J Cell Biol 1997;74:197–207.

57. Kolleck I, Witt W, Wissel H, Sinha P, Rustow B. HDL and vitamin E in plasma and the expression of SR-BI on lung cells during rat perinatal development. Lung 2000;178:191–200.

58. Kolleck I, Sinha P, Rustow B. Vitamin E as an antioxidant of the lung: mechanisms of vitamin E delivery to alveolar type II cells. Am J Respir Crit Care Med 2002;166:62S–6S.

59. Rustow B, Haupt R, Stevens PA, Kunze D. Type II pneumocytes secrete vitamin E together with surfactant lipids. Am J Physiol 1993;265:133L–9L.

60. Goti D, Hrzenjak A, Levak-Frank S, et al. Scavenger receptor class B, type I is expressed in porcine brain capillary endothelial cells and contributes to selective uptake of HDL-associated vitamin E. J Neurochem 2001;76:498–508.

61. Goti D, Hammer A, Galla HJ, Malle E, Sattler W. Uptake of lipoprotein-associated alpha-tocopherol by primary porcine brain capillary endothelial cells. J Neurochem 2000;74:1374–83.

62. Witt W, Kolleck I, Fechner H, et al. Regulation by vitamin E of the scavenger receptor BI in rat liver and HepG2 cells. J Lipid Res 2000;41:2009–16.

63. Oram JF, Vaughan AM, Stocker R. ATP-binding cassette transporter A1 mediates cellular secretion of alpha-tocopherol. J Biol Chem 2001;276:39898–902.

64. Jiang XC, Tall AR, Qin S, et al. Phospholipid transfer protein deficiency protects circulating lipoproteins from oxidation due to the enhanced accumulation of vitamin E. J Biol Chem 2002;277:31850–6.

65. Desrumaux C, Risold PY, Schroeder H, et al. Phospholipid transfer protein (PLTP) deficiency reduces brain vitamin E content and increases anxiety in mice. FASEB J 2005;19:296–7.

66. Ingold KU, Burton GW, Foster DO, Hughes L, Lindsay DA, Webb A. Biokinetics of and discrimination between dietary *RRR*- and *SRR*-α-tocopherols in the male rat. Lipids 1987;22:163–72.

67. Burton GW, Wronska U, Stone L, Foster DO, Ingold KU. Biokinetics of dietary *RRR*-α-tocopherol in the male guinea pig at three dietary levels of vita-

min C and two levels of vitamin E. Evidence that vitamin C does not "spare" vitamin E in vivo. Lipids 1990;25:199–210.

68. Burton GW, Traber MG, Acuff RV, et al. Human plasma and tissue alpha-tocopherol concentrations in response to supplementation with deuterated natural and synthetic vitamin E. Am J Clin Nutr 1998;67:669–84.

69. Burton GW, Traber MG. Vitamin E: antioxidant activity, biokinetics and bioavailability. Annu Rev Nutr 1990;10:357–82.

70. Bourre J, Clement M. Kinetics of rat peripheral nerve, forebrain and cerebellum a-tocopherol depletion: comparison with different organs. J Nutr 1991;121:1204–7.

71. Vatassery GT. Alpha-tocopherol levels in various regions of the central nervous systems of the rat and guinea pig. Lipids 1978;13:828–31.

72. Meydani M, Macauley JB, Blumberg JB. Influence of dietary vitamin E, selenium and age on regional distribution of alpha-tocopherol in the rat brain. Lipids 1986;21:786–91.

73. Sokol RJ. Vitamin E deficiency and neurological disorders. In: Packer L, Fuchs J, eds. Vitamin E in health and disease. New York, NY: Marcel Dekker, Inc., 1993:815–49.

74. Traber MG, Sokol RJ, Ringel SP, Neville HE, Thellman CA, Kayden HJ. Lack of tocopherol in peripheral nerves of vitamin E-deficient patients with peripheral neuropathy. N Engl J Med 1987;317:262–5.

75. Leonard SW, Paterson E, Atkinson JK, Ramakrishnan R, Cross CE, Traber MG. Studies in humans using deuterium-labeled α- and γ-tocopherol demonstrate faster plasma γ-tocopherol disappearance and greater γ-metabolite production. Free Radic Biol Med 2005;38:857–66.

76. Traber MG, Kayden HJ. Tocopherol distribution and intracellular localization in human adipose tissue. Am J Clin Nutr 1987;46:488–95.

77. Kayden HJ, Hatam LJ, Traber MG. The measurement of nanograms of tocopherol from needle aspiration biopsies of adipose tissue: normal and abetalipoproteinemic subjects. J Lipid Res 1983; 24:652–6.

78. Handelman GJ, Epstein WL, Machlin LJ, van Kuijk FJGM, Dratz EA. Biopsy method for human adipose with vitamin E and lipid measurements. Lipids 1988;23:598–604.

79. Age-Related Eye Disease Study Research Group. A randomized, placebo-controlled, clinical trial of high-dose supplementation with vitamins C and E, beta carotene, and zinc for age-related macular degeneration and vision loss: AREDS report no. 8. Arch Ophthalmol 2001;119:1417–36.

80. Tanito M, Yoshida Y, Kaidzu S, et al. Acceleration of age-related changes in the retina in alpha-tocopherol transfer protein null mice fed a vitamin E-deficient diet. Invest Ophthalmol Vis Sci 2007;48:396–404.

81. Lodge JK, Ridlington J, Vaule H, Leonard SW, Traber MG. α- and γ-Tocotrienols are metabolized to carboxyethyl-hydroxychroman (CEHC) derivatives and excreted in human urine. Lipids 2001;36:43–8.

82. Birringer M, Pfluger P, Kluth D, Landes N, Brigelius-Flohe R. Identities and differences in the metabolism of tocotrienols and tocopherols in HepG2 cells. J Nutr 2002;132:3113–8.

83. Brigelius-Flohé R, Traber MG. Vitamin E: function and metabolism. FASEB J 1999;13:1145–55.

84. Kiyose C, Saito H, Kaneko K, et al. Alpha-tocopherol affects the urinary and biliary excretion of 2,7,8-trimethyl-2 (2'-carboxyethyl)-6-hydroxychroman, gamma-tocopherol metabolite, in rats. Lipids 2001;36:467–72.

85. Sontag TJ, Parker RS. Cytochrome P450 omega-hydroxylase pathway of tocopherol catabolism: novel mechanism of regulation of vitamin E status. J Biol Chem 2002;277:25290–6.

86. Birringer M, Drogan D, Brigelius-Flohe R. Tocopherols are metabolized in HepG2 cells by side chain omega-oxidation and consecutive beta-oxidation. Free Radic Biol Med 2001;31:226–32.

87. Parker RS, Sontag TJ, Swanson JE. Cytochrome P4503A-dependent metabolism of tocopherols and inhibition by sesamin. Biochem Biophys Res Commun 2000;277:531–4.

88. Ikeda S, Tohyama T, Yamashita K. Dietary sesame seed and its lignans inhibit 2,7,8-trimethyl-

2(2'-carboxyethyl)-6-hydroxychroman excretion into urine of rats fed gamma-tocopherol. J Nutr 2002;132:961–6.

89. Swanson JE, Ben RN, Burton GW, Parker RS. Urinary excretion of 2,7, 8-trimethyl-2-(beta-carboxyethyl)-6-hydroxychroman is a major route of elimination of gamma-tocopherol in humans. J Lipid Res 1999;40:665–71.

90. Stahl W, Graf P, Brigelius-Flohe R, Wechter W, Sies H. Quantification of the alpha- and gamma-tocopherol metabolites 2,5,7,8-tetramethyl-2-(2'-carboxyethyl)-6-hydroxychroman and 2,7,8-trimethyl-2-(2'-carboxyethyl)-6-hydroxychroman in human serum. Anal Biochem 1999;275:254–9.

91. Pope SA, Burtin GE, Clayton PT, Madge DJ, Muller DP. Synthesis and analysis of conjugates of the major vitamin E metabolite, alpha-CEHC. Free Radic Biol Med. 2002;33:807–17.

92. Mustacich DJ, Shields J, Horton RA, Brown MK, Reed DJ. Biliary secretion of alpha-tocopherol and the role of the mdr2 P-glycoprotein in rats and mice. Arch Biochem Biophys 1998;350:183–92.

93. Traber MG, Jialal I. Measurement of lipid-soluble vitamins—further adjustment needed? Lancet 2000;355:2013–4.

94. Sokol RJ, Heubi JE, Iannaccone ST, Bove KE, Balistreri WF. Vitamin E deficiency with normal serum vitamin E concentrations in children with chronic cholestasis. N Engl J Med 1984;310:1209–12.

95. Evans HM, Bishop KS. On the existence of a hitherto unrecognized dietary factor essential for reproduction. Science 1922;56:650–1.

96. Machlin LJ. Vitamin E. In: Machlin LJ, ed. Handbook of vitamins. New York: Marcel Dekker, 1991:99–144.

97. Horwitt MK, Harvey CC, Duncan GD, Wilson WC. Effects of limited tocopherol intake in man with relationships to erythrocyte hemolysis and lipid oxidations. Am J Clin Nutr 1956;4:408–19.

98. Horwitt MK. Vitamin E and lipid metabolism in man. Am J Clin Nutr 1960;8:451–61.

99. Sokol RJ. Vitamin E deficiency and neurologic disease. Annu Rev Nutr 1988;8:351–73.

100. Ouahchi K, Arita M, Kayden H, et al. Ataxia with isolated vitamin E deficiency is caused by mutations in the alpha-tocopherol transfer protein. Nature Genetics 1995;9:141–5.

101. Kayden HJ, Silber R, Kossmann CE. The role of vitamin E deficiency in the abnormal autohemo-lysis of acanthocytosis. Trans Assoc Am Physicians 1965;78:334–42.

102. Meydani SN, Han SN, Wu D. Vitamin E and immune response in the aged: molecular mechanisms and clinical implications. Immunol Rev 2005;205:269–84.

103. Ben Hamida M, Belal S, Sirugo G, et al. Friedreich's ataxia phenotype not linked to chromosome 9 and associated with selective autosomal recessive vitamin E deficiency in two inbred Tunisian families. Neurology 1993;43:2179–83.

104. Ben Hamida C, Doerflinger N, Belal S, et al. Localization of Friedreich ataxia phenotype with selective vitamin E deficiency to chromosome 8q by homozygosity mapping. Nat Genet 1993;5:195–200.

105. Sokol RJ, Kayden HJ, Bettis DB, et al. Isolated vitamin E deficiency in the absence of fat malabsorption - familial and sporadic cases: characterization and investigation of causes. J Lab Clin Med 1988;111:548–59.

106. Trevithick JR, Robertson JM, Mitton KP. Vitamin E and the eye. In: Packer L, Fuchs J, eds. Vitamin E in health and disease. New York, NY: Marcel Dekker, Inc., 1993:873–926.

107. Matsuya M, Matsumoto H, Chiba S, Kashiwagi M, Kasahara M. [A sporadic case of essential vitamin E deficiency manifested by sensory-dominant polyneuropathy and retinitis pigmentosa.] No To Shinkei 1994;46:989–94. Japanese.

108. Yokota T, Shiojiri T, Gotoda T, Arai H. Retinitis pigmentosa and ataxia caused by a mutation in the gene for the α-tocopherol-transfer protein. N Engl J Med 1996;335:1769–70.

109. Rader DJ, Brewer HB. Abetalipoproteinemia - new insights into lipoprotein assembly and vitamin-E metabolism from a rare genetic disease. JAMA 1993;270:865–9.

110. Traber MG, Rader D, Acuff R, Brewer HB, Kayden HJ. Discrimination between RRR- and all

racemic-α-tocopherols labeled with deuterium by patients with abetalipoproteinemia. Atherosclerosis 1994;108:27–37.

111. Sokol RJ, Heubi JE, Butler-Simon N, McClung HJ, Lilly JR, Silverman A. Treatment of vitamin E deficiency during chronic childhood cholestasis with oral d-α-tocopheryl polyethylene glycol 1000 succinate (TPGS). I. Intestinal absorption, efficacy and safety. Gastroenterology 1987;93:975–85.

112. Elias E, Muller DPR, Scott J. Association of spinocerebellar disorders with cystic fibrosis or chronic childhood cholestasis and very low serum vitamin E. Lancet 1981;2(8259):1319–21.

113. Cynamon HA, Milov DE, Valenstein E, Wagner M. Effect of vitamin E deficiency on neurologic function in patients with cystic fibrosis. J Pediatr 1988;113:637–40.

114. Sokol RJ, Reardon MC, Accurso FJ, et al. Fat-soluble-vitamin status during the first year of life in infants with cystic fibrosis identified by screening of newborns. Am J Clin Nutr 1989;50:1064–71.

115. Stead RJ, Muller DP, Matthews S, Hodson ME, Batten JC. Effect of abnormal liver function on vitamin E status and supplementation in adults with cystic fibrosis. Gut 1986;27:714–8.

116. Andrews NC. Disorders of iron metabolism. N Engl J Med 1999;341:1986–95.

117. Kalra V, Grover J, Ahuja GK, Rathi S, Khurana DS. Vitamin E deficiency and associated neurological deficits in children with protein-energy malnutrition. J Trop Pediatr 1998;44:291–5.

118. Kalra V, Grover JK, Ahuja GK, Rathi S, Gulati S, Kalra N. Vitamin E administration and reversal of neurological deficits in protein-energy malnutrition. J Trop Pediatr 2001;47:39–45.

119. Becker K, Botticher D, Leichsenring M. Antioxidant vitamins in malnourished Nigerian children. Int J Vitam Nutr Res 1994;64:306–10.

120. Laditan AA, Ette SI. Plasma alpha-tocopherol (vitamin E) levels and tocopherol-lipid ratio among children with protein-energy malnutrition (PEM). Ann Trop Paediatr 1982;2:85–8.

121. Sauerwein RW, Mulder JA, Mulder L, et al. Inflammatory mediators in children with protein-energy malnutrition. Am J Clin Nutr 1997;65:1534–9.

122. Ahmed HM, Laryea MD, el-Karib AO, et al. Vitamin E status in Sudanese children with protein-energy malnutrition. Z Ernahrungswiss 1990;29: 47–53.

123. Ashour MN, Salem SI, El-Gadban HM, Elwan NM, Basu TK. Antioxidant status in children with protein-energy malnutrition (PEM) living in Cairo, Egypt. Eur J Clin Nutr 1999; 53:669–73.

124. Vaisman N, Tabachnik E, Shahar E, Gilai A. Impaired brainstem auditory evoked potentials in patients with cystic fibrosis. Dev Med Child Neurol 1996;38:59–64.

125. Odabas D, Caksen H, Sar S, et al. Auditory brainstem potentials in children with protein energy malnutrition. Int J Pediatr Otorhinolaryngol 2005;69:923–8.

126. Durmaz S, Karagol U, Deda G, Onal MZ. Brainstem auditory and visual evoked potentials in children with protein-energy malnutrition. Pediatr Int 1999;41:615–9.

127. Murphy JL, Badaloo AV, Chambers B, Forrester TE, Wootton SA, Jackson AA. Maldigestion and malabsorption of dietary lipid during severe childhood malnutrition. Arch Dis Child 2002;87:522–5.

128. Sokol RJ, Butler-Simon N, Conner C, et al. Multicenter trial of d-alpha-tocopheryl polyethylene glycol 1000 succinate for treatment of vitamin E deficiency in children with chronic cholestasis. Gastroenterology 1993;104:1727–35.

129. Agbedana EO, Johnson AO, Taylor GO. Selective deficiency of hepatic triglyceride lipase and hypertriglyceridaemia in kwashiorkor. Br J Nutr 1979;42:351–6.

130. Dhansay MA, Benade AJ, Donald PR. Plasma lecithin-cholesterol acyltransferase activity and plasma lipoprotein composition and concentrations in kwashiorkor. Am J Clin Nutr 1991;53:512–9.

131. Ibrahim SA, Eltom AM, Abdul-Rahman AM, Saeed BO. Correlation of some biochemical parameters with clinical features of protein energy malnutrition. East Afr Med J 1994;71:77–83.

132. Feillet F, Parra HJ, Kamian K, Bard JM, Fruchart JC, Vidailhet M. Lipoprotein metabolism in

marasmic children of northern Mauritania. Am J Clin Nutr 1993;58:484–8.

133. Etukudo MH, Agbedana EO, Akinyinka OO, Osifo BO. Plasma electrolytes, total cholesterol, liver enzymes, and selected antioxidant status in protein energy malnutrition. Afr J Med Med Sci 1999;28:81–5.

134. Badaloo A, Reid M, Soares D, Forrester T, Jahoor F. Relation between liver fat content and the rate of VLDL apolipoprotein B-100 synthesis in children with protein-energy malnutrition. Am J Clin Nutr 2005;81:1126–32.

135. Badaloo AV, Forrester T, Reid M, Jahoor F. Lipid kinetic differences between children with kwashiorkor and those with marasmus. Am J Clin Nutr 2006;83:1283–8.

136. Acharya J, Punchard NA, Taylor JA, Thompson RP, Pearson TC. Red cell lipid peroxidation and antioxidant enzymes in iron deficiency. Eur J Haematol 1991;47:287–91.

137. Kumerova A, Lece A, Skesters A, Silova A, Petuhovs V. Anaemia and antioxidant defence of the red blood cells. Mater Med Pol 1998;30:12–5.

138. Gadjeva V, Kuchukova D, Georgieva R. Vitamin combinations reduce oxidative stress and improve antioxidant status in patients with iron deficiency anemia. Comp Clin Path 2005;14:99–104.

139. Gutteridge JM. Biological origin of free radicals, and mechanisms of antioxidant protection. Chem Biol Interact 1994;91:133–40.

140. Schrier SL. Pathophysiology of thalassemia. Curr Opin Hematol 2002;9:123–6.

141. Pauling L, Itano HA, et al. Sickle cell anemia a molecular disease. Science 1949;110:543–8.

142. Ingram VM. Gene mutations in human haemoglobin: the chemical difference between normal and sickle cell haemoglobin. Nature 1957;180:326–8.

143. Kahane I, Shifter A, Rachmilewitz EA. Cross-linking of red blood cell membrane proteins induced by oxidative stress in beta thalassemia. FEBS Lett 1978;85:267–70.

144. Shinar E, Rachmilewitz EA. Oxidative denaturation of red blood cells in thalassemia. Semin Hematol 1990;27:70–82.

145. Kattamis C, Kattamis AC. Oxidative stress disturbances in erythrocytes of beta-thalassemia. Pediatr Hematol Oncol 2001;18:85–8.

146. Cheng ML, Ho HY, Tseng HC, Lee CH, Shih LY, Chiu DT. Antioxidant deficit and enhanced susceptibility to oxidative damage in individuals with different forms of alpha-thalassaemia. Br J Haematol 2005;128:119–27.

147. Rachmilewitz EA, Shohet SB, Lubin BH. Lipid membrane peroxidation in beta-thalassemia major. Blood 1976;47:495–505.

148. Kahane I, Rachmilewitz EA. Alterations in the red blood cell membrane and the effect of vitamin E on osmotic fragility in beta-thalassemia major. Isr J Med Sci 1976;12:11–5.

149. Giardini O, Cantani A, Donfrancesco A. Vitamin E therapy in homozygous beta-thalassemia. N Engl J Med 1981;305:644.

150. Giardini O, Cantani A, Donfrancesco A, et al. Biochemical and clinical effects of vitamin E administration in homozygous beta-thalassemia. Acta Vitaminol Enzymol 1985;7:55–60.

151. Livrea MA, Tesoriere L, Pintaudi AM, et al. Oxidative stress and antioxidant status in beta-thalassemia major: iron overload and depletion of lipid-soluble antioxidants. Blood 1996;88:3608–14.

152. Tesoriere L, D'Arpa D, Butera D, et al. Oral supplements of vitamin E improve measures of oxidative stress in plasma and reduce oxidative damage to LDL and erythrocytes in beta-thalassemia intermedia patients. Free Radic Res 2001;34: 529–40.

153. Dhawan V, Kumar Kh R, Marwaha RK, Ganguly NK. Antioxidant status in children with homozygous thalassemia. Indian Pediatr 2005;42: 1141–5.

154. Das N, Das Chowdhury T, Chattopadhyay A, Datta AG. Attenuation of oxidative stress-induced changes in thalassemic erythrocytes by vitamin E. Pol J Pharmacol 2004;56:85–96.

155. Hebbel RP. Beyond hemoglobin polymerization: the red blood cell membrane and sickle disease pathophysiology. Blood 1991;77:214–37.

156. Amer J, Ghoti H, Rachmilewitz E, Koren A, Levin C, Fibach E. Red blood cells, platelets and poly-

morphonuclear neutrophils of patients with sickle cell disease exhibit oxidative stress that can be ameliorated by antioxidants. Br J Haematol 2006;132:108–13.

157. Jison ML, Munson PJ, Barb JJ, et al. Blood mononuclear cell gene expression profiles characterize the oxidant, hemolytic, and inflammatory stress of sickle cell disease. Blood 2004;104: 270–80.

158. Rice-Evans C, Omorphos SC, Baysal E. Sickle cell membranes and oxidative damage. Biochem J 1986;237:265–9.

159. Klings ES, Farber HW. Role of free radicals in the pathogenesis of acute chest syndrome in sickle cell disease. Respir Res 2001;2:280–5.

160. Hebbel RP, Eaton JW, Balasingam M, Steinberg MH. Spontaneous oxygen radical generation by sickle erythrocytes. J Clin Invest 1982;70: 1253–9.

161. Misra HP, Fridovich I. The generation of superoxide radical during the autoxidation of hemoglobin. J Biol Chem 1972;247:6960–2.

162. Lux SE, John KM, Karnovsky MJ. Irreversible deformation of the spectrin-actin lattice in irreversibly sickled cells. J Clin Invest 1976;58:955–63.

163. Repka T, Hebbel RP. Hydroxyl radical formation by sickle erythrocyte membranes: role of pathologic iron deposits and cytoplasmic reducing agents. Blood 1991;78:2753–8.

164. Lowenthal EA, Mayo MS, Cornwell PE, Thornley-Brown D. Homocysteine elevation in sickle cell disease. J Am Coll Nutr 2000;19:608–12.

165. Dhar M, Bellevue R, Brar S, Carmel R. Mild hyperhomocysteinemia in adult patients with sickle cell disease: a common finding unrelated to folate and cobalamin status. Am J Hematol 2004;76: 114–20.

166. Tangney CC, Phillips G, Bell RA, Fernandes P, Hopkins R, Wu SM. Selected indices of micronutrient status in adult patients with sickle cell anemia (SCA). Am J Hematol 1989;32:161–6.

167. Chiu D, Vichinsky E, Ho SL, Liu T, Lubin BH. Vitamin C deficiency in patients with sickle cell anemia. Am J Pediatr Hematol Oncol 1990;12:262–7.

168. Jain SK, Williams DM. Reduced levels of plasma ascorbic acid (vitamin C) in sickle cell disease

patients: its possible role in the oxidant damage to sickle cells in vivo. Clin Chim Acta 1985;149: 257–61.

169. Natta C, Stacewicz-Sapuntzakis M, Bhagavan H, Bowen P. Low serum levels of carotenoids in sickle cell anemia. Eur J Haematol 1988;41:131–5.

170. Essien EU. Plasma levels of retinol, ascorbic acid and alpha-tocopherol in sickle cell anaemia. Cent Afr J Med 1995;41:48–50.

171. Rahimi Z, Merat A, Haghshenass M, Madani H, Rezaei M, Nagel RL. Plasma lipids in Iranians with sickle cell disease: hypocholesterolemia in sickle cell anemia and increase of HDL-cholesterol in sickle cell trait. Clin Chim Acta 2006;365: 217–20.

172. Zannos-Mariolea L, Papagregoriou-Theodoridou M, Costantzas N, Matsaniotis N. Relationship between tocopherols and serum lipid levels in children with beta-thalassemia major. Am J Clin Nutr 1978;31:259–63.

173. Ndombi IO, Kinoti SN. Serum vitamin E and the sickling status in children with sickle cell anaemia. East Afr Med J 1990;67:720–5.

174. Phillips G, Tangney CC. Relationship of plasma alpha tocopherol to index of clinical severity in individuals with sickle cell anemia. Am J Hematol 1992;41:227–31.

175. Natta CL, Machlin LJ, Brin M. A decrease in irreversibly sickled erythrocytes in sickle cell anemia patients given vitamin E. Am J Clin Nutr 1980;33:968–71.

176. Miniero R, Canducci E, Ghigo D, Saracco P, Vullo C. Vitamin E in beta-thalassemia. Acta Vitaminol Enzymol 1982;4:21–5.

177. Suthutvoravut U, Hathirat P, Sirichakwal P, Sasanakul W, Tassaneeyakul A, Feungpean B. Vitamin E status, glutathione peroxidase activity and the effect of vitamin E supplementation in children with thalassemia. J Med Assoc Thai 1993;76: 146S–52S.

178. Jaja SI, Aigbe PE, Gbenebitse S, Temiye EO. Changes in erythrocytes following supplementation with alpha-tocopherol in children suffering from sickle cell anaemia. Niger Postgrad Med J 2005;12:110–4.

179. Rachmilewitz E, Shifter A, Kahane I. Vitamin E deficiency in beta-thalassemia major: changes in hematological and biochemical parameters after a therapeutic trial with alpha-tocopherol. Am J Clin Nutr 1979;32:1850–8.

180. Nasr MR, Ali S, Shaker M, Elgabry E. Antioxidant micronutrients in children with thalassaemia in Egypt. East Mediterr Health J 2002;8:490–5.

181. Hasanato RM. Zinc and antioxidant vitamin deficiency in patients with severe sickle cell anemia. Ann Saudi Med 2006;26:17–21.

182. Gbenebitse S, Jaja SI, Kehinde MO. Effect of changes in plasma vitamin E level of vascular responses and lipid peroxidation in sickle cell anaemia subjects. Niger Postgrad Med J 2005;12:81–4.

183. Muskiet FA, Muskiet FD, Meiborg G, Schermer JG. Supplementation of patients with homozygous sickle cell disease with zinc, alpha-tocopherol, vitamin C, soybean oil, and fish oil. Am J Clin Nutr 1991;54:736–44.

184. Sadrzadeh SM, Graf E, Panter SS, Hallaway PE, Eaton JW. Hemoglobin. A biologic fenton reagent. J Biol Chem 1984;259:14354–6.

185. Dissayabutra T, Tosukhowong P, Seksan P. The benefits of vitamin C and vitamin E in children with beta-thalassemia with high oxidative stress. J Med Assoc Thai 2005;88:317S–21S.

186. Beutler E. Glucose-6-phosphate dehydrogenase deficiency. N Engl J Med 1991;324:169–74.

187. Kwiatkowski DP. How malaria has affected the human genome and what human genetics can teach us about malaria. Am J Hum Genet 2005;77:171–92.

188. Gumustekin K, Ciftci M, Coban A, et al. Effects of nicotine and vitamin E on glucose 6-phosphate dehydrogenase activity in some rat tissues in vivo and in vitro. J Enzyme Inhib Med Chem 2005;20:497–502.

189. Eldamhougy S, Elhelw Z, Yamamah G, Hussein L, Fayyad I, Fawzy D. The vitamin E status among glucose-6 phosphate dehydrogenase deficient patients and effectivenes of oral vitamin E. Int J Vitam Nutr Res 1988;58:184–8.

190. Snow RW, Guerra CA, Noor AM, Myint HY, Hay SI. The global distribution of clinical episodes of Plasmodium falciparum malaria. Nature 2005;434:214–7.

191. Das BS, Nanda NK. Evidence for erythrocyte lipid peroxidation in acute falciparum malaria. Trans R Soc Trop Med Hyg 1999;93:58–62.

192. Das BS, Thurnham DI, Das DB. Plasma alpha-tocopherol, retinol, and carotenoids in children with falciparum malaria. Am J Clin Nutr 1996;64:94–100.

193. Adelekan DA, Adeodu OO, Thurnham DI. Comparative effects of malaria and malnutrition on plasma concentrations of antioxidant micronutrients in children. Ann Trop Paediatr 1997;17:223–7.

194. Griffiths MJ, Ndungu F, Baird KL, Muller DP, Marsh K, Newton CR. Oxidative stress and erythrocyte damage in Kenyan children with severe Plasmodium falciparum malaria. Br J Haematol 2001;113:486–91.

195. Hassan GI, Gregory U, Maryam H. Serum ascorbic acid concentration in patients with acute Falciparum malaria infection: possible significance. Braz J Infect Dis 2004;8:378–81.

196. Sherman IW, Eda S, Winograd E. Erythrocyte aging and malaria. Cell Mol Biol (Noisy-le-grand) 2004;50:159–69.

197. Klein A, Deckert V, Schneider M, et al. Alpha-tocopherol modulates phosphatidylserine externalization in erythrocytes. Relevance in phospholipid transfer protein-deficient mice. Arterioscler Thromb Vasc Biol 2006;26(9):2160–7.

198. Geary TG, Boland MT, Jensen JB. Antioxidants do not prevent the in vitro induction of Plasmodium falciparum crisis forms by human malaria-immune, TB or rabbit TNF serum. Am J Trop Med Hyg 1986;35:704–7.

199. Hemmer CJ, Lehr HA, Westphal K, Unverricht M, Kratzius M, Reisinger EC. Plasmodium falciparum malaria: reduction of endothelial cell apoptosis in vitro. Infect Immun 2005;73:1764–70.

200. Levander OA, Ager ALJ, Morris VC, May RG. Menhaden-fish oil in a vitamin E-deficient diet: protection against chloroquine-resistant malaria in mice. Am J Clin Nutr 1989;50:1237–9.

201. Metzger A, Mukasa G, Shankar AH, Ndeezi G, Melikian G, Semba RD. Antioxidant status and acute malaria in children in Kampala, Uganda. Am J Trop Med Hyg 2001;65:115–9.

202. Nussenblatt V, Mukasa G, Metzger A, Ndeezi G, Eisinger W, Semba RD. Relationship between carotenoids and anaemia during acute uncomplicated Plasmodium falciparum malaria in children. J Health Popul Nutr 2002;20:205–14.

203. Stuetz W, McGready R, Cho T, et al. Relation of DDT residues to plasma retinol, alpha-tocopherol, and beta-carotene during pregnancy and malaria infection: A case-control study in Karen women in northern Thailand. Sci Total Environ 2006;363: 78–86.

204. Guha M, Kumar S, Choubey V, Maity P, Bandyopadhyay U. Apoptosis in liver during malaria: role of oxidative stress and implication of mitochondrial pathway. FASEB J 2006;20:1224–6.

205. Simoes AP, van den Berg JJ, Roelofsen B, Op den Kamp JA. Lipid peroxidation in Plasmodium falciparum-parasitized human erythrocytes. Arch Biochem Biophys 1992;298:651–7.

206. Mohan K, Ganguly NK, Dubey ML, Mahajan RC. Oxidative damage of erythrocytes infected with Plasmodium falciparum. An in vitro study. Ann Hematol 1992;65:131–4.

207. Becker K, Tilley L, Vennerstrom JL, Roberts D, Rogerson S, Ginsburg H. Oxidative stress in malaria parasite-infected erythrocytes: host-parasite interactions. Int J Parasitol 2004;34:163–89.

208. Magwere T, Naik YS, Hasler JA. Effects of chloroquine treatment on antioxidant enzymes in rat liver and kidney. Free Radic Biol Med 1997;22: 321–7.

209. Deharo E, Barkan D, Krugliak M, Golenser J, Ginsburg H. Potentiation of the antimalarial action of chloroquine in rodent malaria by drugs known to reduce cellular glutathione levels. Biochem Pharmacol 2003;66:809–17.

210. Adias TC, Uko E, Erhabor O. Anaemia in human immunodeficiency virus infection: a review. Niger J Med 2006;15:203–6.

211. Stringer JS, Zulu I, Levy J, et al. Rapid scale-up of antiretroviral therapy at primary care sites in Zambia: feasibility and early outcomes. JAMA 2006;296:782–93.

212. Marti-Carvajal Aj Sola I. Treatment for anemia in people with AIDS. Cochrane Database Syst Rev 2007;24:CD004776.

213. Schreck R, Rieber P, Baeuerle PA. Reactive oxygen intermediates as apparently widely used messengers in the activation of the NF-kappa B transcription factor and HIV-1. EMBO J 1991;10: 2247–58.

214. Allard JP, Aghdassi E, Chau J, Salit I, Walmsley S. Oxidative stress and plasma antioxidant micronutrients in humans with HIV infection. Am J Clin Nutr 1998;67:143–7.

215. Allard JP, Aghdassi E, Chau J, et al. Effects of vitamin E and C supplementation on oxidative stress and viral load in HIV-infected subjects. AIDS 1998;12:1653–9.

216. Spada C, Treitinger A, Reis M, et al. An evaluation of antiretroviral therapy associated with alpha-tocopherol supplementation in HIV-infected patients. Clin Chem Lab Med 2002;40:456–9.

217. Villamor E, Saathoff E, Bosch RJ, et al. Vitamin supplementation of HIV-infected women improves postnatal child growth. Am J Clin Nutr 2005;81:880–8.

218. Beck MA, Handy J, Levander OA. Host nutritional status: the neglected virulence factor. Trends Microbiol 2004;12:417–23.

219. Meydani SN, Meydani M, Blumberg JB, et al. Vitamin E supplementation and in vivo immune response in healthy elderly subjects. A randomized controlled trial. JAMA 1997;277:1380–6.

220. Meydani SN, Leka LS, Fine BC, et al. Vitamin E and respiratory tract infections in elderly nursing home residents: a randomized controlled trial. JAMA 2004;292:828–36.

221. Farrell P, Bieri J, Fratantoni J, Wood R, Di Sant'Agnese P. The occurrence and effects of human vitamin E deficiency. J Clin Invest 1977;60:233–41.

222. Sullivan J, Ndekha M, Maker D, Hotz C, Manary MJ. The quality of the diet in Malawian children with kwashiorkor and marasmus. Matern Child Nutr 2006;2:14–22.

223. Squali Houssaini FZ, Foulon T, Payen N, Iraqi MR, Arnaud J, Groslambert P. Plasma fatty acid status in Moroccan children: increased lipid peroxidation and impaired polyunsaturated fatty acid metabolism in protein-calorie malnutrition. Biomed Pharmacother 2001;55:155–62.

224. Faber M, Kvalsvig JD, Lombard CJ, Benade AJ. Effect of a fortified maize-meal porridge on anemia, micronutrient status, and motor development of infants. Am J Clin Nutr 2005:1032–9.

225. Wright ME, Lawson KA, Weinstein SJ, et al. Higher baseline serum vitamin E concentrations are associated with lower total and cause-specific mortality in the alpha-tocopherol, beta-carotene cancer prevention study. Am J Clin Nutr 2006;84:1200–7.

226. Drewel BT, Giraud DW, Davy SR, Driskell JA. Less than adequate vitamin E status observed in a group of preschool boys and girls living in the United States. J Nutr Biochem 2006;17:132–8.

227. Laryea MD, Mayatepek E, Brunninger P, Doehring-Schwerdtfeger E, Leichsenring M, Bremer HJ. Vitamin E status of Congolese children in a rural area. Int J Vitam Nutr Res 1990;60:107–11.

228. Allen LH, Rosado JL, Casterline JE, et al. Lack of hemoglobin response to iron supplementation in anemic Mexican preschoolers with multiple micronutrient deficiencies. Am J Clin Nutr 2000;71:1485–94.

229. Christian P, Jiang T, Khatry SK, LeClerq SC, Shrestha SR, West KP, Jr. Antenatal supplementation with micronutrients and biochemical indicators of status and subclinical infection in rural Nepal. Am J Clin Nutr 2006;83:788–94.

230. Thurnham DI, Singkamani R, Kaewichit R, Wongworapat K. Influence of malaria infection on peroxyl-radical trapping capacity in plasma from rural and urban Thai adults. Br J Nutr 1990;64:257–71.

231. Kim YN, Lora KR, Giraud DW, Driskell JA. Nonsupplemented children of Latino immigrants have low vitamin E intakes and plasma concentrations and normal vitamin C, selenium, and carotenoid intakes and plasma concentrations. J Am Diet Assoc 2006;106:385–91.

232. de Souza Junior O, Treitinger A, Baggio GL, et al. alpha-Tocopherol as an antiretroviral therapy supplement for HIV-1-infected patients for increased lymphocyte viability. Clin Chem Lab Med 2005;43:376–82.

233. Jayaram S, Soman A, Tarvade S, Londhe V. Cerebellar ataxia due to isolated vitamin E deficiency. Indian J Med Sci 2005;59:20–3.

234. Monarque-Favard C, Garcia I, Abidi H, et al. Malnourished elderly people and lipid status. J Nutr Health Aging 2002;6:370–4.

235. Kom GD, Schwedhelm E, Nielsen P, Boger RH. Increased urinary excretion of 8-iso-prostaglandin F2alpha in patients with HFE-related hemochromatosis: a case-control study. Free Radic Biol Med 2006;40:1194–200.

236. Hop LT, Berger J. Multiple micronutrient supplementation improves anemia, micronutrient nutrient status, and growth of Vietnamese infants: double-blind, randomized, placebo-controlled trial. J Nutr 2005;135:660S–5S.

237. Jaruga P, Jaruga B, Gackowski D, et al. Supplementation with antioxidant vitamins prevents oxidative modification of DNA in lymphocytes of HIV-infected patients. Free Radic Biol Med 2002;32:414–20.

238. Kabagambe EK, Baylin A, Irwig MS, et al. Costa Rican adolescents have a deleterious nutritional profile as compared to adults in terms of lower dietary and plasma concentrations of antioxidant micronutrients. J Am Coll Nutr 2005;24:122–8.

239. Andert CU, Sanchaisuriya P, Sanchaisuriya K, Schelp FP, Schweigert FJ. Nutritional status of pregnant women in Northeast Thailand. Asia Pac J Clin Nutr 2006;15:329–34.

240. Molnar D, Decsi T, Koletzko B. Reduced antioxidant status in obese children with multimetabolic syndrome. Int J Obes Relat Metab Disord 2004;28:1197–202.

241. Strauss RS. Comparison of serum concentrations of alpha-tocopherol and beta-carotene in a cross-sectional sample of obese and nonobese chil-

dren (NHANES III). National Health and Nutrition Examination Survey. J Pediatr 1999;134:160–5.

242. Stephensen CB, Marquis GS, Jacob RA, Kruzich LA, Douglas SD, Wilson CM. Vitamins C and E in adolescents and young adults with HIV infection. Am J Clin Nutr 2006;83:870–9.

243. Laryea MD, Biggemann B, Cieslicki P, Wendel U. Plasma tocopherol and tocopherol to lipid ratios in a normal population of infants and children. Int J Vitam Nutr Res 1989;59:269–72.

244. Tang AM, Graham NM, Semba RD, Saah AJ. Association between serum vitamin A and E levels and HIV-1 disease progression. AIDS 1997;11: 613–20.

245. Kuno T, Hozumi M, Morinobu T, Murata T, Mingci Z, Tamai H. Antioxidant vitamin levels in plasma and low density lipoprotein of obese girls. Free Radic Res 1998;28:81–6.

246. Madebo T, Lindtjorn B, Aukrust P, Berge RK. Circulating antioxidants and lipid peroxidation products in untreated tuberculosis patients in Ethiopia. Am J Clin Nutr 2003;78:117–22.

247. Baylin A, Villamor E, Rifai N, Msamanga G, Fawzi WW. Effect of vitamin supplementation to HIV-infected pregnant women on the micronutrient status of their infants. Eur J Clin Nutr 2005;59: 960–8.

248. Martin-Gallan P, Carrascosa A, Gussinye M, Dominguez C. Estimation of lipoperoxidative damage and antioxidant status in diabetic children: relationship with individual antioxidants. Free Radic Res 2005;39:933–42.

249. Van Campenhout A, Van Campenhout C, Lagrou AR, et al. Impact of diabetes mellitus on the relationships between iron-, inflammatory- and oxidative stress status. Diabetes Metab Res Rev 2006;22(6):444–54.

Selenium

Richard D. Semba

School of Medicine, Johns Hopkins University, Baltimore, USA
Contact: rdsemba@jhmi.edu

RICHARD SEMBA
Richard obtained his MD from Stanford University and MPH from Johns Hopkins University, both in the USA. He is currently Professor of Ophthalmology at the Johns Hopkins School of Medicine, and holds joint appointments in International Health and in Molecular Microbiology and Immunology in the Johns Hopkins Bloomberg School of Public Health. Richard has conducted research in anemia in different populations around the world and is currently studying the role of hepcidin and other factors in the pathogenesis of anemia of chronic inflammation. He has published widely and served on the editorial boards of the Journal of Nutrition and Nutrition.

INTRODUCTION

Anemia is common in older adults, and the prevalence of anemia increases with advancing age (1, 2). Among older adults, anemia has been associated with a wide spectrum of adverse outcomes (3), including reduced quality of life (4, 5), decreased muscle strength (6), increased disability (7), higher risk of Alzheimer's disease (8), and increased all-cause mortality among nursing home residents (9) and among moderately to severely disabled women living in the community (10). Anemia has also been linked with congestive heart failure (11) and impaired cognitive function (12). The reduction of oxygen-carrying capacity of the blood that occurs with anemia may account for fatigue, cardiovascular complications, and impaired physical performance (3). Anemia among older adults is caused by renal failure, chronic inflammation, and nutritional deficiencies, and about one-third of the anemia is unexplained (13). Selenium deficiency may potentially explain a portion of the unexplained anemia that occurs in some populations at high risk for anemia.

Recently, low circulating selenium levels have been associated with anemia in older adults living in the community (14). Selenium deficiency may contribute to anemia among dialysis patients (15) and adults with pulmonary tuberculosis (16). Lower serum selenium levels have also been described in anemic compared with nonanemic adults in Vietnam (17). These observations in humans are consistent with previous studies, which have shown that selenium deficiency is associated with anemia in animals (18, 19). The relationship between selenium status and anemia has not been well characterized in humans, and at present, selenium deficiency should be considered a possible cause of anemia that requires further investigation and confirmation. The purpose of this chapter is to provide a succinct review of the role of selenium in human health, the epidemiology of selenium deficiency, the potential role of selenium in the pathogenesis of anemia, and directions for future research.

HISTORICAL BACKGROUND

Selenium was identified as a new chemical element by Jöns Jacob Berzelius (1779–1848) in 1817 (20, 21). Well over a century later, selenium was recognized to be an essential nutrient by Klaus Schwarz and Calvin Foltz in 1957, when they observed that selenium prevented liver necrosis in vitamin E-deficient rats (22). Lack of selenium was soon noted to contribute to nutritional deficiency syndromes among animals, such as white muscle disease in sheep, goats, and cattle, gizzard myopathy in turkeys, exudative diathesis in chickens, and mulberry heart disease in swine. Selenium was found to be a constituent of the enzyme glutathione peroxidase by John Rotruck and colleagues in 1973 (23). The importance of selenium to human health was recognized in 1979, when Chinese scientists discovered that selenium supplementation protected against Keshan disease, an endemic cardiomyopathy that occurs primarily among children living in areas of China with selenium-poor soils (24). In 1984, selenium deficiency was shown to be associated with widespread anemia among cattle grazing in selenium-poor areas in the Florida Everglades, and selenium supplementation prevented the anemia (19). The Recommended Dietary Allowance for selenium was first established in 1989 (26), and dietary recommendations for selenium were established by the World Health Organization in 1996 (26).

ROLE OF SELENIUM IN HUMAN HEALTH

Selenium is an essential trace element and a normal constituent of the diet. Most selenium is present in human tissues in the form of two selenium-containing amino acids, selenocysteine and selenomethionine. Selenomethionine cannot be synthesized by humans and is found in plant proteins, where selenomethionine is incorporated randomly in varying amounts in place of methionine. The biochemical functions of selenium are related to its role in selenoproteins, and several of these selenoproteins are antioxidant enzymes. As of 2006, 25 selenoenzymes or selenoproteins have been identified in humans (27), and these include glutathione peroxidase, phosopholipid hydroperoxide glutathione peroxidase, selenoprotein P, iodothyronine deiodinases, and thioredoxin reductase. Glutathione peroxidase (GPX1), the most abundant member of the glutathione peroxidases, protects against oxidative stress (28), and phospholipid hydroperoxide glutathione peroxidase reduces phospholipid hydroperoxide (29). Selenoprotein P is a regulator of selenium hemostasis (30). Iodothyronine deiodinases regulate thyroid hormone metabolism by catalyzing the deiodination of thyroxine, triiodothyronine, and reverse triiodothyronine (31, 32). Thioredoxin reductase is involved in antioxidant defenses and redox regulation of cellular function (33).

The richest dietary sources of selenium are organ meats and seafood (0.4–1.5 µg/g) (34). Cereals and grains contain variable amounts of selenium (<0.1 to >0.8 µg/g) (34) depending upon the selenium content of the soil where the plants were grown. The selenium content of muscle meats, in turn, depends upon the selenium content of plants upon which the animals fed or the level of fortification of animal feed with selenium. More than 90% of dietary selenium is in the form of selenomethionine (35), with the remaining portion consisting of selenocysteine in animal selenoproteins and inorganic forms of selenium. Selenium absorption is not regulated, and 50–100% of dietary selenium is absorbed (34). There are two major selenium compartments in the body: the unregulated selenomethionine compartment that changes in proportion to selenium intake, and the well-regulated selenocysteine-inorganic selenium compartment that consists of the biochemically active pool of selenium in the body. Selenocysteine-containing proteins, with the exception of selenoprotein P, are thought to have

enzymatic activity in which the selenocysteine residue is located at the catalytic site (29). Mammalian selenoproteins contain selenocysteine, which is synthesized and incorporated into selenoproteins via a complex pathway that is still incompletely understood in animals.

Clinically overt selenium deficiency occurs in the form of Keshan disease, as noted above, and an additional stress such as Coxsackie B virus infection may be involved in the pathogenesis of this syndrome (36). Insufficient selenium intake usually does not have obvious clinical manifestations. Selenium deficiency can limit the synthesis of selenoproteins, and thus low serum or plasma selenium concentrations have been associated with increased susceptibility to oxidative stress (37) and increased risk of cancer (38, 39). A serum/plasma selenium level of >0.8–1.1 µmol/L is associated with maximization of plasma selenoproteins (40). The current dietary requirements for selenium provided by the Food and Nutrition Board of the Institute of Medicine are based in part upon maintenance of optimal levels of selenoproteins in blood, especially plasma glutathione peroxidase (41). Activity of selenoprotein P has also been used as an indicator of selenium sufficiency (41). The selenium requirement for prevention of chronic disease has not yet been definitively determined (41). Low serum selenium concentrations have been associated with increased mortality from cancer (42, 43) and increased all-cause mortality among community-dwelling older men and women in France (44) and women in Baltimore, Maryland (45). Low activity of glutathione peroxidase, a major selenoenzyme, was associated with increased risk of cardiovascular events among adults with suspected coronary artery disease (46).

EPIDEMIOLOGY OF SELENIUM DEFICIENCY

The dietary intake of selenium varies widely worldwide, as selenium concentrations in plant-based foods reflect the concentrations of selenium in the soil where the plants were grown. The selenium concentrations in animal sources of food, in turn, depend upon the selenium content of the plants used for forage, or whether animal feed was fortified with selenium. Serum selenium concentrations seem to decrease with age (47, 48) and are lower in persons with chronic diseases (48). Risk factors for low serum selenium levels in older adults include smoking (49, 50) and low meat and fish intake (49, 51). Lower serum selenium concentrations have been reported among obese women (49). The global distribution of selenium deficiency has not been well characterized and data are sporadic. China (52), Tibet, Africa (53), New Zealand (54), Europe (55), Russia (56), and the United States (57) have some geographic areas where the selenium content of the soil is low and selenium intake may be more limited.

SELENIUM AND THE PATHOGENESIS OF ANEMIA

Low serum selenium levels were independently associated with anemia among adults age 65 and older in phase 2 of the Third National Health and Nutrition Examination Survey (NHANES III), (R.D. Semba, 1991–1994, unpublished) and among women aged 70–79 years living in the community in the Women's Health and Aging Studies (WHAS) I and II (14). In WHAS, the prevalence of anemia decreased from the lowest to the highest quartile of serum selenium (**Figure 12.1**). An increase in loge selenium was associated with a reduced risk of anemia (Odds ratio per 1 SD increase=0.63, 95%; CI=0.47–0.84), adjusting for age, education, chronic diseases, iron status, and serum interleukin-6 (IL-6) (14). A similar relationship was noted between quartiles of serum selenium and the prevalence of anemia in NHANES III (R.D. Semba, 1991–1994, unpublished). A strong correlation between low plasma selenium concentrations and low hemoglobin was observed in the British National Diet and Nutri-

tion Survey among 1,134 men and women aged 65 years and older (48). Although these findings show that low serum/plasma selenium levels are associated with anemia, the direction of the association is not clear. Data from animal studies suggest that the association is in the direction of low serum/plasma selenium causing anemia. Alternatively, it is possible that anemia could cause low serum/plasma selenium levels, but such a biological mechanism to explain this direction of the association is not readily apparent.

A potential biological mechanism by which selenium could contribute to anemia is through maintenance of an optimal concentration of glutathione peroxidase, a key antioxidant selenoenzyme, in erythrocytes (58). Glutathione peroxidase protects hemoglobin against oxidation in erythrocytes (59). Although there is still no direct evidence that serum selenium is related to erythrocyte and hemoglobin stability in humans, there is a possible relevant example of erythrocyte damage due to increased oxidative stress in animals (60) with protection by selenium. Livestock that forage on *Brassica* (mustard, rape) are susceptible to brassica anemia in which oxidative stress causes excessive erythrocyte damage (61), and selenium supplementation has been shown to protect animals against erythrocyte damage (62–64). If low serum selenium levels are associated with reduced life span of erythrocytes in humans, then selenium deficiency would likely be associated with an increased reticulocyte count and high erythro-poietin levels. Studies in selenium-deficient pigs suggest that selenium deficiency limits erythropoiesis but does not affect red cell half-life (65).

Low selenium status can upregulate the activity of hepatic heme oxygenase-1, which catalyzes the initial step of heme catabolism and reduces heme to biliverdin, carbon monoxide, and free divalent iron (66, 67). Whether upregulation of heme oxygenase-1 plays a role in the relationship of selenium deficiency to anemia is not known.

Another potential mechanism by which selenium could contribute to anemia is through increased inflammation and oxidative stress. Low serum selenium concentrations have been described in adults with anemia of chronic inflammation (R.D. Semba, unpublished). Low serum selenium concentrations among disabled older women living in the community were predictive of subsequent rises in IL-6 (68). Thus, selenium could potentially play a role in the anemia of chronic inflammation through its relationship with the upregulation of IL-6 through the redox-sensitive transcription factor nuclear factor-kappaB. In turn, IL-6 has been implicated in the upregulation of hepcidin, the iron regulatory hormone that blocks iron absorption in the gut and iron release from macrophages and the liver (69). The role of hepcidin in the anemia of chronic inflammation is not well understood, and little is known is about the relationship between selenium levels, hepcidin, and anemia.

FUTURE DIRECTIONS FOR RESEARCH

Low serum selenium levels are associated with anemia among older men and women living in the community. These observations raise potentially important public health questions. Has selenium deficiency been overlooked as a cause of anemia among older adults? Does selenium deficiency contribute to anemia in other populations at high risk for anemia, such as young children and pregnant women? It is not known whether improving dietary selenium intake will increase hemoglobin concentrations among older adults with low serum selenium concentrations. Further work is

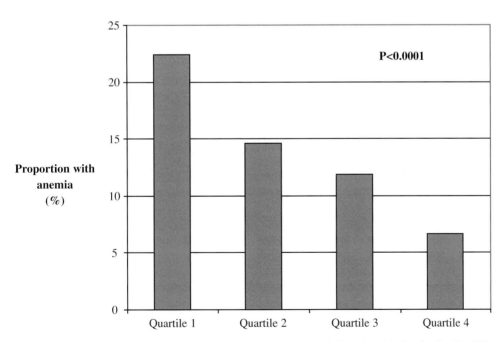

Figure 12.1.: Proportion of women, aged 70–79 years, in the Women's Health and Aging Studies I and II, with anemia by quartile of serum selenium.

needed to gain insight into the potential role of selenium in the pathogenesis of anemia. Investigations are needed that corroborate these findings in other populations at high risk for anemia, that identify underlying biological mechanisms, and that determine whether improving selenium status has an impact upon anemia in older adults. Well-designed clinical trials will provide the strongest evidence for a causal role of selenium in anemia in human populations.

REFERENCES

1. Beghé C, Wilson A, Ershler WB. Prevalence and outcomes of anemia in geriatrics: a systematic review of the literature. Am J Med 2004;116(7A):3S–10S.

2. Woodman R, Ferrucci L, Guralnik J. Anemia in older adults. Curr Opin Hematol 2005;12:123–8.

3. Lipschitz D. Medical and functional consequences of anemia in the elderly. J Am Geriatr Soc 2003;51:10S–13S.

4. Thomas ML. Impact of anemia and fatigue on quality of life in cancer patients: a brief review. Med Oncol 1998;15(1):3S–7S.

5. Valderrabano F. Quality of life benefits of early anaemia treatment. Nephrol Dial Transplant 2000;15(3);23–8.

6. Cesari M, Penninx BW, Lauretani F, Russo CR, Carter C, Bandinelli S, et al. Hemoglobin levels and skeletal muscle: results from the InCHIANTI study. J Gerontol A Biol Sci Med Sci 2004;59:238–41.

7. Penninx BWJH, Pahor M, Cesari M, Corsi AM, Woodman RC, Bandinelli S, et al. Anemia is associated with disability and decreased physical performance and muscle strength in the elderly. J Am Geriatr Soc 2004;52:719–24.

8. Beard CM, Kokmen E, O'Brien PC, Anía BJ, Melton LJ III. Risk of Alzheimer's disease among elderly patients with anemia: population-based investigations in Olmsted County, Minnesota. Ann Epidemiol 1997;7:219–24.

9. Kikuchi M, Inagaki T, Shinagawa N. Five-year survival of older people with anemia: variation with hemoglobin concentration. J Am Geriatr Soc 2001;49:1226–8.

10. Chaves PHM, Xue QL, Guralnik JM, Ferrucci L, Volpato S, Fried LP. What constitutes normal hemoglobin concentration in community-dwelling disabled older women? J Am Geriatr Soc 2004;52:1811–6.

11. Silverberg DS, Wexler D, Blum M, Keren G, Sheps D, Leibovitch E, et al. The use of subcutaneous erythropoietin and intravenous iron for the treatment of anemia of severe, resistant congestive heart failure improves cardiac and renal function and functional cardiac class, and markedly reduces hospitalizations. J Am Coll Cardiol 2000;35:1737–44.

12. Nissenson AR. Epoietin and cognitive function. Am J Kidney Dis 1992;20(1):21–4.

13. Guralnik JM, Eisenstaedt RS, Ferrucci L, Klein HG, Woodman RC. Prevalence of anemia in persons 65 years and older in the United States: evidence for a high rate of unexplained anemia. Blood 2004;104:2263–8.

14. Semba RD, Ferrucci L, Cappola AR, Ricks MO, Ray AL, Xue QL, et al. Low serum selenium is associated with anemia among older women living in the community. Biol Trace Elem Res 2006;112:97–108.

15. Hampel G, Schaller KH, Rosenmüller M, Oefele C. Selenium-deficiency as contributing factor to anemia and thrombocytopenia in dialysis patients. Life Support Syst 1985; 3(1):36–40.

16. van Lettow M, West CE, van der Meer JWM, Wieringa FT, Semba RD. Low plasma selenium concentrations, high plasma human immunodeficiency virus load and high interleukin-6 concentrations are risk factors associated with anemia in adults presenting with pulmonary tuberculosis in Zomba district, Malawi. Eur J Clin Nutr 2005;59:526–32.

17. van Nhien N, Khan NC, Yabutani T, Ninh NX, Kassu A, Houng BT, et al. Serum levels of trace elements and iron-deficiency anemia in adult Vietnamese. Biol Trace Elem Res 2006;111:1–9.

18. Latshaw JD, Ort JF, Diesem CD. The selenium requirements of the hen and effects of a deficiency. Poultry Sci 1977:56:1876–81.

19. Morris JG, W.S. Cripe WS, Chapman HL Jr, Walker DF, Armstrong JB, Alexander JD Jr, et al. Selenium deficiency in cattle associated with Heinz bodies and anemia. Science 1984;223:491–3.

20. Berzelius JJ. Lettre de M. Berzelius à M. Berthollet sur deux métaux nouveaux. Ann Chim Phys 1817;7:199–207.

21. Berzelius JJ. Chemische Entdeckungen im Mineralreiche gemacht zu Fahlun in Schweden: Selenium, ein neuer metallartiger Körper, Lithon, ein neues Alkali, Thorina, eine neue Erde. Ann Physik 1818;29:229–54.

22. Schwarz K, Foltz CM. Selenium as an integral part of factor 3 against dietary necrotic liver degeneration. J Am Chem Soc 1957;79:3292–3.

23. Rotruck JT, Pope AL, Ganther HE, Swanson AB, Hafeman DG, Hoekstra WG. Selenium: biochemical role as a component of glutathione peroxidase. Science 1973;179: 588–90.

24. Keshan Disease Research Group. Observations on the effect of sodium selenite in the prevention of Keshan disease. Chin Med J 1979;92:471–6.

25. National Research Council. Recommended Dietary Allowances. 10th ed. Washington, DC: National Academy of Sciences, 1989.

26. World Health Organization. Trace elements in human nutrition and health. Geneva: WHO, 1996.

27. Moghadaszadeh B, Beggs AH. Selenoproteins and their impact on human health through diverse physiological pathways. Physiology (Bethesda) 2006;21:307–15.

28. Lei XG. Glutathione peroxidase-1 gene knockout on body antioxidant defense in mice. Biofactors 2001;14:93–9.

29. Imai H, Nakagawa Y. Biological significance of phospholipid hydroperoxide glutathione peroxidase (PHGPx, GPx4) in mammalian cells. Free Radic Biol Med 2003;34:145–69.

30. Burk RF, Hill KE. Selenoprotein P: an extracellular protein with unique physical characteristics and a role in selenium homeostasis. Annu Rev Nutr 2005;25:215–35.

31. Galton VA. The roles of the iodothyronine deiodinases in mammalian development. Thyroid 2005;15:823–34.

32. Beckett GJ, Arthur JR. Selenium and endocrine systems. J Endocrinol 2005;184:455–65.

33. Rundlöf AK, Arnér ESJ. Regulation of the mammalian selenoprotein thioredoxin reductase 1 in relation to cellular phenotype, growth, and signaling events. Antioxid Redox Signal 2004;6:41–52.

34. Burk RF, Levander OA. Selenium. In: Shils ME, Shike M, Ross AC, Caballero B, Cousins RJ, eds. Modern nutrition in health and disease. 10th ed. Philadelphia: Lippincott Williams & Wilkins, 2006:312–25.

35. Food and Nutrition Board, Institute of Medicine. Dietary Reference Intakes for vitamin C, vitamin E, selenium, and carotenoids. Washington, DC: National Academy Press, 2000.

36. Beck MA, Levander OA, Handy J. Selenium deficiency and viral infection. J Nutr 2003;133 (5 Suppl 1):1463S–7S.

37. Brenneisen P, Steinbrenner H, Sies H. Selenium, oxidative stress, and health aspects. Mol Aspects Med 2005;26:256–67.

38. Etminan M, FitzGerald JM, Gleave M, Chambers K. Intake of selenium in the prevention of prostate cancer: a systematic review and meta-analysis. Cancer Causes Control 2005;16:1125–31.

39. Rayman MP. Selenium in cancer prevention: a review of the evidence and mechanism of action. Proc Nutr Soc 2005;64:527–42.

40. Hill KE, Xia Y, Åkesson B, Boeglin ME, Burk RF. Selenoprotein P concentration in plasma in an index of selenium status in selenium-deficient and selenium-supplemented Chinese subjects. J Nutr 1996;126:138–45.

41 Thomson CD. Assessment of requirements for selenium and adequacy of selenium status: a review. Eur J Clin Nutr 2004;58:391–402.

42. Kok FJ, de Bruijn AM, Vermeeren R, Hofman A, van Laar A, de Bruin M, et al. Serum selenium, vitamin antioxidants, and cardiovascular mortality: a 9-year follow-up study in the Netherlands. Am J Clin Nut 1987;45:462–8.

43. Kornitzer M, Valente F, De Bacquer D, Neve J, De Backer G. Serum selenium and cancer mortality: a nested case-control study within an age- and sex-stratified sample of the Belgian adult population. Eur J Clin Nutr 2004;58:98–104.

44. Akbaraly NT, Arnaud J, Hininger-Favier I, Gourlet V, Roussel AM, Berr C. Selenium and mortality in the elderly: results from the EVA study. Clin Chem 2005;51:2117–23.

45. Ray AL, Semba RD, Walston J, Ferrucci L, Cappola AR, Ricks MO, et al. Low serum selenium and total carotenoids predict mortality among older women living in the community: the Women's Health and Aging Studies. J Nutr 2006;136:172–6.

46. Blankenberg S, Rupprecht HJ, Bickel C, Torzewski M, Hafner G, Tiret L, et al. Glutathione peroxidase 1 activity and cardiovascular events in patients with coronary artery disease. N Engl J Med 2003;349:1605–13.

47. Savarino L, Granchi D, Ciapetti G, Cenni E, Ravaglia G, Forti P, et al. Serum concentrations of zinc and selenium in elderly people: results in healthy nonagenarians/centenarians. Exp Gerontol 2001;36:327–39.

48. Bates CJ, Thane CW, Prentice A, Delves HT. Selenium status and its correlates in a British national diet and nutrition survey: people aged 65 years and over. J Trace Elem Med Biol 2002;16:1–8.

49. Arnaud J, Bertrais S, Roussel AM, Arnault N, Ruffieux D, Favier A, et al. Serum selenium determinants in French adults: the SU.VI.M.AX study. Br J Nutr 2006;95:313–20.

50. Kafai MR, Ganji V. Sex, age, geographical location, smoking, and alcohol consumption influence serum selenium concentrations in the USA: Third National Health and Nutrition Examination Survey, 1988–1994. J Trace Elem Med Biol 2003;17:13–8.

51. Hansen JC, Deutch B, Pedersen HS. Selenium status in Greenland Inuit. Sci Total Environ 2004;331:207–14.

52. Tan J, Zhu W, Wang W, Li R, Hou S, Wang D, et al. Selenium in soil and endemic diseases in China. Sci Total Environ 2002; 284:227–35.

53. Vanderpas JB, Contempre B, Duale NL, Goossens W, Bebe N, Thorpe R, et al. Iodine and selenium deficiency associated with cretinism in northern Zaire. Am J Clin Nutr 1990;52:1087–93.

54. Thomson CD. Selenium and iodine intakes and status in New Zealand and Australia. Br J Nutr 2004;91:661–72.

55. Thorling EB, Overvad K, Geboers J. Selenium status in Europe – human data. A multicenter study. Ann Clin Res 1986;18:3–7.

56. Golubkina NA, Alfthan GV. The human selenium status in 27 regions of Russia. J Trace Elem Med Biol 1999;13:15–20.

57. Jackson ML. Selenium: geochemical distribution and associations with human heart and cancer death rates and longevity in China and the United States. Biol Trace Elem Res 1988;15:13–21.

58. Chow CK, Chen CJ. Dietary selenium and age-related susceptibility of rat erythrocytes to oxidative damage. J Nutr 1980;110:2460–6.

59. Nagababu E, Chrest FJ, Rifkind JM. Hydrogen-peroxide-induced heme degradation in red blood cells: the protective roles of catalase and glutathione peroxidase. Biochim Biophys Acta 2003; 1620:211–7.

60. McPhail DB, Sibbald AM. The role of free radicals in brassica-induced anaemia of sheep: an ESR spin trapping study. Free Radic Res Commun 1992;16:277–84.

61. Prache S. Haemolytic anaemia in ruminants fed forage brassicas: a review. Vet Res 1994; 25:497–520.

62. Rotruck JT, Pope AL, Ganther HE, Hoekstra WG. Prevention of oxidative damage to rat erythrocytes by dietary selenium. J Nutr 1972;102: 689–96.

63 Gutzwiller A. Einfluss der Selenversorgungslage der Ziege auf die Resistenz der Erythrozyten gegen oxidative Schädigung. Schweiz Arch Tierheilkd 1991;133:157–61.

64. Gutzwiller A. "Erythrocyte resistance to oxidative damage and leucocyte capacity to reduce nitroblue tetrazolium in selenium-deficient cattle" (in German). Zentralbl Veterinarmed A 1998; 45:271–78.

65. Fontaine M, Valli VE, Young LG. Studies on vitamin E and selenium deficiency in young pigs. III. Effects on kinetics of erythrocyte production and destruction. Can J Comp Med 1977;41:57–63.

66. Mostert V, Hill KE, Burk RF. Loss of activity of the selenoenzyme thioredoxin reductase causes induction of hepatic heme oxygenase-1. FEBS Lett 2003;541:85–8.

67. Tron K, Novosyadlyy R, Dudas J, Samoylenko A, Kietzmann T, Ramadori G. Upregulation of heme oxygenase-1 gene by turpentine oil-induced localized inflammation: involvement of interleukin-6. Lab Invest 2005;85:376–87.

68. Walston J, Xue Q, Semba RD, Ferrucci L, Cappola A, Ricks M, et al. Serum antioxidants, inflammation, and total mortality in older women. Am J Epi 2006;163:18–26.

69. Roy CN, Andrews NC. Anemia of inflammation: the hepcidin link. Curr Opin Hematol 2005;12:107–11.

13

Interactions between iron and vitamin A, riboflavin, copper, and zinc in the etiology of anemia

Michael B. Zimmermann

Laboratory for Human Nutrition, Swiss Federal Institute of Technology, Zurich, Switzerland
Contact: michael.zimmermann@ilw.agrl.ethz.ch

MICHAEL ZIMMERMANN
Michael obtained his MD from Vanderbilt University School of Medicine and his MSc in Nutritional Science at the University of California in Berkeley, both in the USA. He is currently Senior Scientist in the Laboratory for Human Nutrition at the Swiss Federal Institute of Technology in Zurich (ETHZ), visiting Professor at Wageningen University in the Netherlands, and holds the Unilever Endowed Chair in International Health and Micronutrients. Michael's research focus is nutrition and metabolism, including the effects of micronutrient deficiencies on thyroid function, and he has won many awards for his work.

INTRODUCTION

The prevalence of anemia is particularly high in developing countries, where 39% of children under five years old, 48% of 5-14 year old children, 42% of all women, and 52% of pregnant women are anemic (1). It is estimated that about half of the anemia is due to iron deficiency (2), and the remainder due to other causes, such as nutritional deficiencies (e.g., deficiencies of vitamin A, riboflavin, folic acid and vitamin B_{12}), infectious disorders (particularly malaria, HIV and tuberculosis), hemoglobinopathies, and ethnic differences in normal Hb distributions (3, 4). In sub-Saharan Africa, anemia affects 50-80% of children (1, 5). In Côte d'Ivoire, using specific indicators of iron status, iron deficiency was detected in approximately 50% of anemic children (6). Although iron deficiency is often assumed to be the cause of most anemia in children in developing regions, a recent Thai study demonstrated that this is not always the case; among 567 6-12 year old children in the rural Northeast, the prevalence of anemia was 31%. Hemoglobinopathies, suboptimal vitamin A status, and age were the major predictors of hemoglobin concentrations (7). Only a small proportion of anemia in the children was associated with iron deficiency. In a study in Sri Lankan children (8), the prevalence of anemia was 50% in males and 58% in females, but among the anemic children, only 30% of males and 48% of females were iron deficient.

Multiple micronutrient deficiencies often coexist in populations in developing countries. Concurrent deficiencies of vitamin A and iron are common in African schoolchildren (9, 10). In a recent survey of Sri Lankan adolescents, iron deficiency was found in 30% of males and 48% of females; folate and zinc deficiencies were found in 54% and 55% of the children, respectively (8). The relative risks of having at least two deficiencies of iron, folate and/or zinc among the anemic children were 1.6 (95% CI; 0.6-4.2) among boys

and 0.8 (95% CI; 0.5-1.5) among girls. A deficiency of one micronutrient may influence the absorption, metabolism and/or excretion of another micronutrient. An example is the aggravation of iodine deficiency goiter by iron deficiency anemia (10), an effect mediated through impairment of the iron dependent thyroid enzyme, thyroperoxidase. This review will focus on interactions between iron deficiency and four other micronutrients – vitamin A, riboflavin, copper, and zinc – in the etiology of anemia (**Table 13.1**).

VITAMIN A

Vitamin A (VA) deficiency (VAD) affects less than 30% of the global population (11). The most vulnerable groups are women of reproductive age, infants and children (12), the same age groups at highest risk for anemia (13, 14). The link between VAD and anemia has been recognized for many years. Surveys in developing countries have generally reported positive correlations between serum retinol (SR) and hemoglobin (Hb) concentrations, with stronger associations in populations with poorer VA status. These include studies in Central American schoolchildren (r=0.21, P<0.05) (15); Indian children (r=0.52, P<0.001) (16); Malawian adolescents (r=0.16, P=0.08) (17) and Austrian adults (r=0.56, P<0.001) (18). In pooled data from Vietnam, Chile, Brazil, Uruguay, Ecuador, Venezuela, Guatemala and Ethiopia, VA status and Hb were highly correlated (r=0.77, P<0.0001) (19). In Indonesia, infants and their mothers with SR <0.7 µmol/L had a 2.4 fold increased risk for iron deficiency anemia (IDA) (20). In Tanzania, pregnant women with Hb values <90 g/L were 2.2 fold more likely to have VAD (21).

Hodges, et al. (19) fed adults three different VA deficient diets together with mineral and vitamin supplements for 1-2 years. Despite daily

Table 13.1: Overview of potential interactions of iron and vitamin A, riboflavin, copper and zinc in the etiology of anemia.

Micronutrient interaction	Effect	Mechanism
Vitamin A (VA) – iron	VA repletion in combined iron- and VA-deficient populations improves Hb	May increase resistance to infection, and thereby reduce circulating hepcidin levels triggered by inflammation, increasing dietary iron absorption and mobilization to the marrow
		May improve dietary iron absorption
		May directly stimulate erythropoiesis by increasing renal erythropoietin synthesis
Riboflavin – iron	Compared to iron supplements given alone, riboflavin and iron supplementation produce a greater increase in Hb	May improve mobilization of iron from stores
		May increase dietary iron absorption
Copper – iron	Copper deficiency produces a "functional" iron deficiency anemia, that is responsive to copper but not iron	Reduced hephaestin activity impairs dietary iron absorption by reducing iron efflux from the enterocyte
		Reduced ceruloplasmin activity decreases iron availability to the marrow by reducing iron efflux from the liver and spleen
Zinc – iron	Concurrent zinc and iron supplementation may reduced the efficacy of the iron to increase Hb	May compete at the divalent metal transporter 1 (DMT 1) for transfer from the lumen into the enterocyte

intakes of 18-19 mg iron, mild anemia developed after approximately six months. As SR levels fell from adequate (>30 µg/dL), to 20-30 µg/dL, to low (<20µg/dL), mean Hb values fell from 156 to 129 to 119 g/L. The anemia was not responsive to iron therapy until the subjects were repleted with VA. Children receiving a soup fortified with iron and vitamin C increased serum iron levels and transferrin saturation to a greater extent when SR levels were >40 µg/dL as compared to <20 µg/dL (22) suggesting VA status affects mobilization of storage iron.

Data from human studies investigating the influence of VA on absorption are equivocal. In Venezuela, iron absorption from fortified bread meals was increased in the presence of VA or β-carotene (23, 24). Iron absorption from a wheat bread based meal increased from 6.9% to 8.3% when the bread was consumed with 300 µg retinol equivalent (RE) added to drinking water (23). In the second study, iron absorption increased from 3.0 to 8.5% when maize based bread contained 40 µg RE as β-carotene; from 3.0 to 8.3% when a wheat bread contained 51 µg RE as β-carotene; and from 2.1 to 8.8% when a rice meal contained 56 µg RE as β-carotene (24). The authors suggested that VA or β-carotene forms a complex with iron in the digestive tract, and that this complex protects iron from reacting with inhibitors of iron absorption such as phytic acid or phenolic compounds. This seems unlikely, however, since the molar ratios of VA to iron used in their studies were <0.04. In a later report (25), β-carotene, but not retinol, increased iron uptake in a Caco-2 cell system. This suggests that the effect of retinol on iron incorporation into erythrocytes seen in the earlier studies may not be due to increased iron absorption from the gut but rather on improved mobilization of stored iron for erythropoiesis. In contrast, there was no effect of VA on iron absorption when similar meals were fed to Swiss and Swedish subjects (26). The authors suggested that the contradictory results may be due to lower VA status, and possibly lower over-

all nutritional status, in the Venezuelan subjects who were from a lower socioeconomic population compared to the subjects from Switzerland and Sweden. Another study suggested that iron absorption was inhibited when VA was added to a maize meal fed to VA deficient children in the Côte d'Ivoire, and VA supplementation for three weeks did not affect iron absorption (27). These contradictory data suggest that further research is needed to clarify the effect of VA status on iron absorption.

In pre-school and school-age children (28-32) as well as in nonpregnant and pregnant women (33-36), improving VA status usually increases Hb and reduces anemia, although not all studies agree (37, 38). Provision of VA fortified monosodium glutamate not only improved VA status of preschool children in Indonesia but also increased Hb by 10 g/L over a five month period (28). In Indonesia, anemic pregnant women with marginal VA status were given a placebo, VA (2.4 mg RE/d), iron (60 mg/d) or iron plus VA (60 mg iron/d, 2.4 mg RE/d) (33). After eight weeks, the percentage of women no longer anemic was 16%, 35%, 68% and 97%, respectively. In a similar design, anemic school children in Tanzania received daily a placebo, VA (1.5 mg RE), iron (40 mg), or iron plus VA; the Hb increase in the four groups was 3.6 g/L, 13 g/L, 17.5 g/L, and 22.1 g/L, respectively, after three months (32). Overall, these studies suggest that, in areas where VA and iron intakes are poor, dual fortification or supplementation will likely be more effective in controlling anemia than providing VA or iron alone.

The mechanism by which vitamin A exerts its effect on erythropoiesis remains unclear. Several mechanisms may explain the effect of VA status on anemia (39): 1) decreased resistance to infection in VAD, and, hence, an increase in the anemia of infection; 2) effects on iron absorption and/or metabolism; and 3) direct modulation of erythropoiesis. In developing countries with a high prevalence of infectious diseases, because VA status modulates immune function, VAD may increase risk for infection, and thereby, the anemia of infection (40). There is little data available to directly support this hypothesis (39). Moreover, in a recent controlled study in North African children free of malaria and hookworm, VA repletion clearly improved Hb, suggesting that this mechanism may not be important in some regions (62).

In animals with VA deficiency, iron is retained in the liver and spleen, and is less available for erythropoiesis (41-44). In VA deficient rats, iron uptake by the bone marrow is impaired (45) and erythrocyte incorporation of ^{59}Fe is decreased (46, 47). In deficient animals, repletion with VA increases utilization of iron in bone and spleen (48). In humans, VA deficiency is associated with a low proportion of transferrin saturation and low iron binding capacity (29, 49). In children, consumption of VA fortified sugar increases serum iron, serum ferritin and the proportion of transferrin saturation (50). Roodenburg, et al. (48, 51) suggested that VAD impairs erythropoiesis and speculated that iron accumulation in the reticuloendothelial system may be due to reduced iron transport due to an inhibition of transferrin synthesis. However, Mejia and Arroyave (49) did not find a decrease in circulating transferrin concentrations in rats with VAD.

Retinoids may stimulate erythropoiesis through a direct effect on the later stages of red cell development (52, 53). In vitro, retinoic acid, synergistically with erythropoietin (EPO), stimulates the formation of erythroid burst-forming unit (BFU-E) colonies (54) and d16 (early) erythroid colonies (55). EPO is a 30400 dalton glycoprotein, produced mainly by renal peritubular cells. It acts on the late stages of erythropoiesis, primarily on colony-forming unit erythroid (CFU-E) cells, and stimulates maturation through the normoblast into reticulocytes and mature erythrocytes (56). The enhancer region of the EPO gene contains a response element that is regulated by retinoic acid (57). In vitro and in animal models, VA treatment stimulates production of EPO (57). In VA deficient rats, treatment with retinoic acid transiently increases circulating EPO concentrations, which return to original levels after 24 hours (58). Retinoids increase EPO gene transcription in an oxygen dependent manner (59).

It is unclear if vitamin A supplementation increases EPO concentrations in humans. Two studies in malnourished populations have examined the effect of VA supplementation on circulating EPO (38, 60). Compared to iron and folate supplementation, VA, iron and folate supplementation did not affect EPO concentrations in Malawian pregnant women (38). In Tanzanian children, a single dose of VA decreased serum ferritin and EPO concentrations measured after 72 hours (60). However, these studies did not have true controls, and were done in regions endemic for malaria, which influences EPO concentrations (61).

A recent intervention trial in malaria-free school-age children with poor VA and iron status investigated the effect of VA repletion on Hb, iron status, and EPO concentrations (62). Using a double blind, randomized design, Moroccan school-children (n=81) were given either VA (200,000 IU) or a placebo at baseline and at five months. At baseline, five and 10 months, Hb, indicators of iron and vitamin A status, and EPO were measured. At baseline, 54% of children were anemic and 77% had low VA status. In the VA group at 10 months, serum retinol improved significantly compared to the control. VA treatment increased mean Hb by 7 g/L and reduced the prevalence of anemia from 54% to 38%. VA treatment increased mean corpuscular volume and decreased serum transferrin receptor, indicating improved iron deficient erythropoiesis. VA decreased serum ferritin, suggesting mobilization of hepatic iron stores. Calculated from the TfR to serum ferritin ratio (TfR/SF), overall body iron stores remained

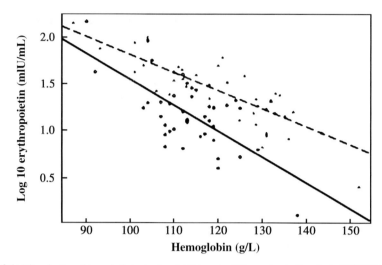

Figure 13.1: Vitamin A and iron deficient schoolchildren (n=81) received vitamin A (200,000 IU) or a placebo at baseline and at five months. Compared to placebo (—) vitamin A repletion (- - -) increased circulating erythropoietin (EPO) concentrations and decreased the slope of the regression line of log(10) EPO on Hb at 10 months. This effect is likely explained by a direct VA-mediated stimulus of erythropoiesis that downregulated the EPO response to lower Hb concentrations.

unchanged. These findings argue against a VA-mediated increase in iron absorption. Rather, they suggest VA repletion causes redistribution of iron from stores to the marrow for erythropoiesis. In the VA group at 10 months, there was an increase in EPO and a decrease in the slope of the regression line of log(10) EPO on Hb (**Figure 13.1**). Several mechanisms may explain the change in the slope of the regression line. It may represent physiologically appropriate EPO levels for children with Hb at the lower range of the distribution after improvements in iron deficient erythropoiesis. Alternatively, a direct VA-mediated stimulus of erythropoiesis may have downregulated the EPO response to lower Hb concentrations. Enhanced erythropoiesis may lower circulating EPO levels in anemia (63), due to internalization and degradation of the EPO-EPO receptor complex in maturing erythroid cells (64). In summary, in children deficient in VA and iron, VA supplementation mobilizes iron from existing stores to support increased erythropoiesis, an effect likely mediated by increases in circulating EPO (62).

RIBOFLAVIN

Riboflavin (vitamin B_2) is required for many metabolic pathways, usually as a precursor of the flavin coenzyme, NAD, in oxidation reactions (65). Riboflavin deficiency is particularly common in regions where intakes of dairy products and meat are low (66). Deficiency causes impaired growth, cheilosis, angular stomatitis, glossitis and dermatitis, and impaired vision (67). Schoolchildren, in both developing and industrialized countries, are an age group at high risk for riboflavin deficiency (68).

Riboflavin deficiency may also impair erthryopoiesis and contribute to anemia (69, 70). Suggested mechanisms for this effect of riboflavin deficiency are decreased mobilization of iron from stores (71, 72), decreased iron absorption, and increased iron losses (73-75). Although these mechanisms have been investigated in animals, there is little data from humans. A stable isotope study in adult Gambian men showed a greater increase in hemoglobin with riboflavin supplementation compared to controls' (both groups received iron supplements) (76). But this study did not demonstrate an increase in iron absorption, suggesting the improvement in hemoglobin may have been due to iron mobilization from stores (76). In three trials in children and pregnant women, compared to iron supplements given alone, riboflavin and iron supplementation produced a greater increase in hemoglobin, although the results may have been confounded by concomitant folic acid supplementation (77-79). A study in pregnant women reported that the combination of iron and riboflavin supplementation, or riboflavin supplementation alone, did not prevent a decrease in hemoglobin, although the decrease was less in the treated groups than the control group (80). Riboflavin supplementation given concurrently with iron improves the response to iron supplementation in adult males and schoolchildren (81, 82). Another trial reported no additional benefit of riboflavin plus iron compared to iron supplementation alone in young adults (83). Similarly, no effect could be found in a riboflavin supplementation trial in Croatian schoolchildren with adequate hemoglobin levels (84). Taken together, these data suggest that the effect of riboflavin status on hemoglobin is variable, and may be confounded by the multifactorial etiology of anemia, particularly in countries in sub-Saharan Africa.

The few published studies investigating riboflavin status in African children suggest that riboflavin deficiency may be widespread. A study in Botswanan children reported that 33-40% of children had an erythrocyte glutathione reductase activation coefficient (EGRAC) ≥1.4 (85). In a study in Kenya, approximately one third of children were riboflavin deficient, as measured as red blood cell riboflavin (86). In a survey of 2-5 year old South African children, intakes of riboflavin were less than half of the recommended daily allowance (RDA) (87). A food survey in central Côte d'Ivoire found low consumption of dairy products and meat, the usual major dietary sources of riboflavin, but riboflavin intakes were not reported (88).

A recent study in 5-15 year old children in south-central Côte d'Ivoire examined the prevalence of riboflavin deficiency in children, estimated the riboflavin content of the local diet and determined if riboflavin deficiency predicts anemia and/or iron deficiency (89). Three-day weighed food records were done to determine riboflavin intakes. Prevalence of anemia in the sample was 52%; 59% were iron deficient, and 36% suffered from iron deficiency anemia. Only 2% of children were VA deficient. Plasmodium parasitemia was found in 49% of the children. Milk and meat intakes were low, and the median intake of riboflavin was 0.42 mg/day, only 47% of the estimated average requirement for this age group. The prevalence of riboflavin deficiency was 65%. Age, elevated C-reactive protein (CRP) and iron deficiency were significant predictors of hemoglobin. Riboflavin deficient children free of malaria were more likely to be iron deficient (odds ratio; 3.07; 1.12-8.41), but riboflavin deficiency did not predict hemoglobin and/or anemia in this age group (89). Thus, these data did not support a detrimental effect of riboflavin deficiency on anemia, as suggested by earlier studies (69, 90).

COPPER

Copper deficiency is a rare cause of anemia (91, 92), which is usually microcytic (93), but also normocytic and macrocytic anemia have also been reported (94). It may be associated with neutropenia and thrombocytopenia (95), and is responsive to dietary supplementation with copper but not with iron (96). How copper deficiency causes anemia is uncertain. The divalent metal transporter 1 (DMT1), the duodenal iron transporter, is also a physiologically relevant copper transporter, and these metals could potentially compete with each other for uptake into enterocytes (97). Mild copper deficiency alters gene expression of proteins involved in iron metabolism (98). Copper dependent enzymes are necessary for red cell maturation: Ferroxidase II is responsible for the oxidation of iron during erythropoiesis (99), and copper deficient animals with low levels of cytochrome oxidase only poorly synthesize heme from ferric iron and protoporphyrin (100).

Copper deficiency impairs dietary iron absorption in animals (101) and humans (102). Moreover, animals and humans consuming copper deficient diets develop iron deficiency anemia in addition to accumulating iron in the gut, liver, and spleen (103, 104). These effects are likely mediated through the copper-containing ferroxidases, ceruloplasmin (105) and hephaestin (106) that modulate iron efflux from cells. Ceruloplasmin is found primarily in the circulation, and modulates iron homeostasis in the liver and other tissues. Hephaestin is found at the basolateral membrane of enterocytes in the small intestine, and required for efficient dietary iron absorption (107). Iron absorption in sex-linked anemic mice (sla) is impaired due to a defect in the (108). Sla mice take up iron normally from the intestinal lumen into enterocytes, but are unable to transfer it adequately to the circulation. In a study by Chen, et al. (109), mice were fed a copper deficient diet or a control diet for six weeks. In the copper deficient mice, ceruloplasmin ferroxidase activity was circa 50% that of the controls', and enterocyte hephaestin was also significantly reduced. Efflux of iron from the enterocyte to the circulation involves ferroportin 1, the basolateral iron exporter (110) and hephaestin, a process that is regulated systemically by the liver derived peptide hepcidin (111). In the Chen, et al. study (109), in copper deficient mice, hepatic hepcidin expression was 40% of controls' and enterocyte ferroportin 1 levels were increased tenfold, suggesting systemic iron deficiency. However, although copper deficiency impairs dietary iron absorption and results in iron deficiency anemia,

copper deficiency in the general population is rare, so this interaction is not likely to be of public health importance.

ZINC

Iron deficiency anemia is frequently the result of low dietary iron absorption due to low intakes of meat and high intakes of inhibitors, such as phytate and polyphenols. These same dietary factors decrease bioavailability of zinc (112). Although the data do not suggest that zinc deficiency plays a role in anemia, deficiencies of iron and zinc often coexist, and supplements containing both iron and zinc could be of value in vulnerable populations. However, several studies have suggested concurrent zinc supplementation may reduce the efficacy of iron, possibly by impairing iron absorption. However, high intake of nonheme iron inhibits the absorption of zinc (113-115), and conversely, a high ratio of dietary zinc to iron can inhibit iron absorption (116, 117). These interactions have been reported when the micronutrients were given in a water solution in adults (116, 117), but not when given in infant formula or meals (115, 117-120). The mechanism of this interaction is not clear, but may involve competition for absorption in the small intestine. The DMT 1 transports both iron and zinc ions (121). It is possible that high concentrations of zinc reduce absorption of iron into the enterocyte, although this has not been demonstrated in mammalian systems. The effects of zinc supplementation during mid and late infancy on intestinal iron transport mechanisms were recently investigated using a suckling rat model (122). Earlier in infancy, zinc supplementation was associated with increased enterocyte iron retention, decreased hephaestin, and increased ferroportin 1 expression. During late infancy, these effects were absent. The data suggest that zinc supplementation may reduce iron absorption through increased enterocyte iron retention, possibly due to reduced hephaestin levels (122).

In a recent six month randomized controlled supplementation trial in Vietnam, infants received daily either 10 mg iron, 10 mg zinc, 10 mg iron plus 10 mg zinc, or a placebo. The combined iron–zinc supplementation was as effective as iron supplements to control iron deficiency and anemia (123). Similar efficiency of combined iron–zinc and iron supplementation alone on iron status was also reported in Mexican children (124-126). In contrast, in studies in Indonesian infants (127, 128) with the same doses and duration of zinc and iron supplementation used in the Vietnam study (123), the combined iron–zinc supplementation was less effective than iron alone on improvement of iron status. These data suggest that concurrent zinc supplementation

reduced the efficacy of the iron (128). Differences in baseline iron status between the studies may help explain the differing results; in the Vietnam study (123) there was a greater severity of anemia and iron deficiency than in the Indonesian studies (128).

In a recent review, Fischer Walker, et al. (129) concluded that zinc supplementation alone does not appear to have negative effects on iron status that are clinically relevant. However, the review also suggested that when zinc supplements are given with iron supplements, iron status does not improve as much as when iron is given alone. Further research is needed to clarify the effects of joint zinc and iron supplementation.

REFERENCES

1. WHO/U CF/UNU. Iron deficiency anemia assessment, prevention, and control. Geneva: World Health Organization, 2001.
2. Zimmermann MB, Hurrell RF. Nutritional iron deficiency. Lancet 2006 (in press).
3. Nestel P. Adjusting hemoglobin values in program surveys. Washington, DC: International Nutritional Anemia Consultative Group (INACG), 2002.
4. Lynch SR. The impact of iron fortification on nutritional anaemia. Best Pract Res Clin Haematol. 2005;18(2):333–46.
5. United Nations ACC/SCN. Fourth report on the World nutrition situation. Geneva: UN ACC/SCN in collaboration with The International Food Policy Research Institute (IFPRI), 2000:132.
6. Asobayire FS, Adou P, Davidsson L, Cook JD, Hurrell RF. Prevalence of iron deficiency with and without concurrent anemia in population groups with high prevalences of malaria and other infections: a study in Cote d'Ivoire. Am J Clin Nutr. 2001; 74(6):776–82.

7. Thurlow RA, Winichagoon P, Green T, Wasantwisut E, Pongcharoen T, Bailey KB, Gibson RS. Only a small proportion of anemia in northeast Thai schoolchildren is associated with iron deficiency. Am J Clin Nutr 2005;82(2):380–7.
8. Hettiarachchi M, Liyanage C, Wickremasinghe R, Hilmers DC, Abrahams SA. Prevalence and severity of micronutrient deficiency: a cross-sectional study among adolescents in Sri Lanka. Asia Pac J Clin Nutr. 2006;15(1):56–63.
9. Zimmermann MB, Wegmüller R, Zeder C, Chaouki N, Biebinger R, Hurrell RF, Windhab E. Triple fortification of salt with microcapsules of iodine, iron and vitamin A. Am J Clin Nutr 2004;80:1283–90.
10. Zimmermann MB, Adou P, Zeder C, Torresani T, Hurrell RF. Persistence of goiter despite oral iodine supplementation in goitrous children with iron deficiency anemia in the Côte d'Ivoire. Am J Clin Nutr 2000;71:88–93.
11. WHO. Vitamin A deficiency and iodine deficiency disorders: prevalence estimates for the glob-

al burden of disease. Micronutrient Deficiency Information System (MDIS). Geneva: World Health Organization, 2001.

12. West KP. Extent of vitamin A deficiency among preschool children and women of reproductive age. J Nutr 2002;132:2857S–66S.

13. WHO/UNICEF/UNU (United Nations Children's Fund, United Nations University). IDA: prevention, assessment and control. Report of a joint WHO/UNICEF/UNU consultation. Geneva: World Health Organization, 1998:1–9.

14. Cook JD. Diagnosis and management of iron-deficiency anaemia. Best Pract Res Clin Haematol 2005;18(2):319–32.

15. Majia LA, Hodges RE, Arroyave G, Viteri F, Torun B. Vitamin A deficiency and anemia in Central American children. Am J Clin Nutr 1977;30:1175–84.

16. Mohanram M, Kulkarni KA, Reddy V. Hematological studies in vitamin A deficient children. Int J Vitam Nutr Res 1977;47:389–93.

17. Fazio-Tirrozzo G, Brabin L, Brabin B, Agbaje O, Harper G, Broadhead R. A community based study of vitamin A and vitamin E status of adolescent girls living in the Shire Valley, southern Malawi. Eur J Clin Nutr 1998;52:637–42.

18. Wenger R, Ziegler B, Kruspl W, Syre B, Brubacher G, Pillat B. [Relationship between vitamin status (A, B1, B2, B6, and C), clinical features and nutritional habits in a population of old people (author's transl)]. Wien Klin Wochenschr 1979; 91:557–63.

19. Hodges RE, Sauberlich HE, Canham JE, et al. Hematopoietic studies in vitamin A deficiency. Am J Clin Nutr 1978;31:876–85.

20. Dijkhuizen MA, Wieringa FT, West CE, Muherdiyantiningsih, Muhilal. Concurrent micronutrient deficiencies in lactating mothers and their infants in Indonesia. Am J Clin Nutr 2001;73:786–91.

21. Hinderaker SG, Olsen BE, Lie RT, et al. Anemia in pregnancy in rural Tanzania: associations with micronutrients status and infections. Eur J Clin Nutr 2002;56:192–9.

22. van Stuijvenberg ME, Kruger M, Badenhorst CJ, Mansvelt EPG, Laubscher JA. Response to an iron fortification programme in relation to vitamin A status in 6-12-year-old schoolchildren. Int J Food Sci Nutr 1997;48:41–9.

23. Layrisse M, Garcia-Casal MN, Solano L, et al. The role of vitamin A on the inhibitors of nonheme iron absorption: preliminary results. J Nutr Biochem 1997;8:61–7.

24. Garcia-Casal MN, Layrisse M, Solano L, Baron MA, Arguello F, Llovera D, Ramirez J, Leets I, Tropper E. Vitamin A and beta-carotene can improve nonheme iron absorption from rice, wheat and corn by humans. J Nutr 1998; 128:646–50.

25. Garcia-Casal MN, Leets I, Layrisse M. Beta-carotene and inhibitors of iron absorption modify iron uptake by Caco-2 cells. J Nutr 2000;130:5–9.

26. Walczyk T, Davidsson L, Rossander-Hulthen L, Hallberg L, Hurrell RF. No enhancing effect of vitamin A on iron absorption in humans. Am J Clin Nutr 2003;77:144–9.

27. Davidsson L, Adou P, Zeder C, Walczyk T, Hurrell R. The effect of retinyl palmitate added to iron-fortified maize porridge on erythrocyte incorporation of iron in African children with vitamin A deficiency. Brit J Nutr 2003;90:337–43.

28. Muhilal, Permeisih D, Idjradinata YR, Muherdiyantiningsih, Karyadi D. Vitamin A-fortified monosodium glutamate and health, growth, and survival of children: a controlled field trial. Am J Clin Nutr 1988;48:1271–6.

29. Mejia LA, Chew F. Hematological effect of supplementing anemic children with vitamin A alone and in combination with iron. Am J Clin Nutr 1988;48:595–600.

30. Bloem MW, Wede lM, Egger RJ, Speek AJ, Schrijver J, Saowakontha S, Schreurs WHP. Iron metabolism and vitamin A deficiency in children in Northeast Thailand. Am J Clin Nutr 1989;50:332–8.

31. Semba RD, Muhilal, West KP Jr, Winget M, Natadisastra G, Scott A, Sommer A. Impact of vitamin A supplementation on hematological indicators of iron metabolism and protein status in children. Nutr Res 1992;12:469–78.

32. Mwanri L, Worsley A, Ryan P, Masika J. Supplemental vitamin A improves anemia and

growth in anemic school children in Tanzania. J Nutr 2000;130:2691–6.

33. Suharno D, West CE, Muhilal, Karyadi D, Hautvast GAJ. Supplementation with vitamin A and iron for nutritional anaemia in pregnant women in West Java, Indonesia. Lancet 1993;342:1325–8.

34. Chawla PK, Puri R. Impact of nutritional supplements on hematological profile of pregnant women. Indian Pediatr 1995;32:876–80.

35. Kolsteren P, Rahman SR, Hilderbrand K, Diniz A. Treatment for iron deficiency anaemia with a combined supplementation of iron, vitamin A and zinc in women of Dinajpur, Bangladesh. Eur J Clin Nutr 1999;53:102–6.

36. Muslimatun S, Schmidt MK, Schultink W, West CE, Hautvast JGAJ, Gross R, Muhilal. Weekly supplementation with iron and vitamin A during pregnancy increases hemoglobin concentration but decreases serum ferritin concentration in Indonesian pregnant women. J Nutr 2001;131:85–90.

37. Fawzi WW, Msamanga GI, Spiegelman D, Urassa EJ, McGrath N, Mwakagile D, Antelman G, Mbise R, Herrera G, Kapiga S, Willett W, Hunter DJ. Randomised trial of effects of vitamin supplements on pregnancy outcomes and T cell counts in HIV-1-infected women in Tanzania. Lancet 1998; 351:1477–82.

38. Semba RD, Kumwenda N, Taha TE, Mtimavalye L, Broadhead R, Garrett E, Miotti PG, Chiphangwi JD. Impact of vitamin A supplementation on anaemia and plasma erythropoietin concentrations in pregnant women: a controlled clinical trial. Eur J Haematol 2001;66,389–95.

39. Semba RD, Bloem MW. The anemia of vitamin A deficiency: epidemiology and pathogenesis. Eur J Clin Nutr 2002;56:271–81.

40. Means RT, Jr. The anaemia of infection. Baillieres Best Pract Res Clin Haematol 2000;13:151–162.

41. Staab DB, Hodges RE, Metcalf WK, Smith JL. Relationship between vitamin A and iron in the liver. J Nutr 1984;114:840–4.

42. Sklan D, Halevy O, Donaghue S. The effect of different dietary levels of vitamin A on metabolism of copper, iron and zinc in the chick. Int J Vit Nutr Res 1987;57:11–18.

43. Beynen AC, Sijtsma KW, van den Berg GJ, Lemmens AG, West CE. Iron status in rats fed a purified diet without vitamin A. Biol Trace Elem Res 1992;35:81–4.

44. Roodenburg AJC, West CE, Yu S, Beynen AC. Comparison between time-dependent changes in iron metabolism of rats as induced by marginal deficiency of either vitamin A or iron. Br J Nutr 1994;71:687–99.

45. Sijtsma KW, van den Berg GJ, Lemmens AG, West CE, Beynen A. Iron status in rats fed on diets containing marginal amounts of vitamin A. Br J Nutr 1993;70:777–85.

46. Mejia LA, Hodges RE, Rucker RB. Clinical signs of anemia in vitamin A-deficient rats. Am J Clin Nutr 1979;32:1439–44.

47. Gardner R, Hodges R, Rucker R. Fate of erythrocyte iron in vitamin A deficient rats. Fed Proc 1979;38:762.

48. Roodenburg AJC, West CE, Hovenier R, Beynen AC. Supplemental vitamin A enhances the recovery from iron deficiency in rats with chronic vitamin A deficiency. Br J Nutr 1996;75:623–36.

49. Mejia LA, Arroyave G. Lack of direct association between serum transferrin and serum biochemical indicators of vitamin A nutriture. Acta Vitaminol Enzymol 1983;5:179–84.

50. Mejia LA, Arroyave G. The effect of vitamin A fortification of sugar on iron metabolism in preschool children in Guatemala. Am J Clin Nutr 1982;36:87–93.

51. Roodenburg AJ, West CE, Beguin Y, et al. Indicators of erythrocyte formation and degradation in rats with either vitamin A or iron deficiency. J Nutr 2000;11:223–30.

52. Rusten LS, Dybedal I, Blomhoff HK, Blomhoff R, Smeland EB, Jacobsen SE. The RAR-RXR as well as the RXR-RXR pathway is involved in signaling growth inhibition of CD34β erythroid progenitor cells. Blood 1996;87:1728–36.

53. Perrin MC, Blanchet JP, Mouchiroud G. Modulation of human and mouse erythropoiesis by thyroid hormone and retinoic acid: evidence for specific effects at different steps of the erythroid pathway. Hematol Cell Ther 1997;39:19–26.

54. Douer D, Koeffler HP. Retinoic acid enhances growth of human early erythroid progenitor cells in vitro. J Clin Invest 1982;69:1039–41.

55. Correa PN, Axelrad AA. Retinyl acetate and all-trans-retinoic acid enhance erythroid colony formation in vitro by circulating human progenitors in an improved serum-free medium. Int J Cell Cloning 1992;10:286–91.

56. Fisher JW. Erythropoetin: physiology and pharmacology update. Exp Biol Med 2003;228:1–14.

57. Evans, T. Regulation of hematopoiesis by retinoid signalling. Exp Hematol 2005;33:105–61.

58. Okano M, Masuda S, Narita H, Masushige S, Kato S, Imagawa S, Sasaki R. Retinoic acid up-regulates erythropoietin production in hepatoma cells and in vitamin A-depletion rats. FEBS Lett 1994;349:229–33.

59. Kambe T, Tada-Kambe J, Kuge Y, Yamaguchi-Iwai Y, Nagao M, Sasaki R. Retinoic acid stimulates erythropoietin gene transcription in embryonal carcinoma cells through the direct repeat of a steroid=thyroid hormone receptor response element half-site in the hypoxia-response enhancer. Blood 2000;96:3265–71.

60. Cusick SE, Tielsch JM, Ramsan M, Jape JK, Sazawal S, Black RE, Stoltzfus RJ. Short-term effects of vitamin A and antimalarial treatment on erythropoiesis in severely anemic Zanzibari preschool children. Am J Clin Nutr 2005;82:406–12.

61. Burgmann H, Looareesuwan S, Kapiotis S, Viravan C, Vanijanonta S, Hollenstein U, Wiesinger E, Presterl E, Winkler S, Graninger W. Serum levels of erythropoietin in acute Plasmodium falciparum malaria. Am J Trop Med Hyg 1996;54:280–3.

62. Zimmermann MB, Biebinger R, Rohner F, Dib A, Zeder C, Hurrell RF, Chaouki N. Vitamin A supplementation in children with poor vitamin A and iron status increases erythropoietin and hemoglobin concentrations without changing total body iron. Am J Clin Nutr 2006;84:580–6.

63. Bray GL, Taylor B, O'Donnell R. Comparison of the erythropoietin response in children with aplastic anemia, transient erythroblastpenia, and iron deficiency. J Pediatr 1992;120:528–32.

64. Gross AW, Lodish HF. Cellular trafficking and degradation of erythropoietin and novel erythro-

poiesis stimulating protein (NESP). J Biol Chem 2006;281:2024–32.

65. McCormick DB. Co-enzymes, biochemistry. In: R Dulbecco, ed. Encyclopedia of human biology. San Diego: Academic Press, 1997:847–64.

66. Neumann CG, Bwibo NO, Murphy SP, Sigman M, Whaley S, Allen LH, Guthrie D, Weiss RE, Demment MW. Animal source foods improve dietary quality, micronutrient status, growth and cognitive function in Kenyan school children: background, study design and baseline findings. J Nutr 2003;133:3941S-9S.

67. FAO/WHO. Thiamin, riboflavin, niacin, vitamin B6, pantothenic acid and biotin. In: Human vitamin and mineral requirements. Rome: FAO, 2001:27–51.

68. Powers HJ. Riboflavin (vitamin B-2) and health. Am J Clin Nutr 2003;77:1352–60.

69. Foy H, Kondi A. A case of true red cell aplastic anaemia successfully treated with riboflavin. J Pathol Bacteriol 1953;65:559–64.

70. Foy H, Kondi A, Mbaya V. Effect of riboflavine deficiency on bone marrow function and protein metabolism in baboons. Preliminary Report. Br J Nutr 1964;18:307–18.

71. Sirivech S, Frieden E, Osaki S. The release of iron from horse spleen ferritin by reduced flavins. J Biochem 1974;143:311–5.

72. Powers HJ. Riboflavin-iron interactions with particular emphasis on the gastrointestinal tract. Proc Nutr Soc 1995;54:509–17.

73. Adelekan DA, Thurnham DI. The influence of riboflavin deficiency on absorption and liver storage of iron in the growing rat. Br J Nutr 1986;56,171–9.

74. Powers HJ, Wright AJ, Fairweather-Tait SJ. The effect of riboflavin deficiency in rats on the absorption and distribution of iron. Br J Nutr 1988;59:381–7.

75. Butler BF, Topham RW. Comparison of changes in the uptake and mucosal processing of iron in riboflavin-deficient rats. Biochem Mol Biol Int 1993;30:53–61.

76. Fairweather-Tait SJ, Powers HJ, Minski MJ, Whitehead J, Downes R. Riboflavin deficiency and iron absorption in adult Gambian men. Ann Nutr Metab 1992;36:34–40.

77. Charoenlarp P, Pholpothi T, Chatpunyaporn P, Schelp FP. The effect of riboflavin on the hematologic changes in iron supplementation of schoolchildren. Southeast Asian J Trop Med Public Health 1980;11:97–103.

78. Powers HJ, Bates CJ, Prentice AM, Lamb WH, Jepson M, Bowman H. The relative effectiveness of iron and iron with riboflavin in correcting a microcytic anaemia in men and children in rural Gambia. Hum Nutr-Clin Nutr 1983;37:413–25.

79. Suprapto B, Widardo, Suhanantyo. Effect of low-dosage vitamin A and riboflavin on iron-folate supplementation in anaemic pregnant women. Asia Pac J Clin Nutr 2002;11:263–7.

80. Powers HJ, Bates CJ, Lamb WH. Haematological response to supplements of iron and riboflavin to pregnant and lactating women in rural Gambia. Hum Nutr Clin Nutr 1985;39:117–29.

81. Buzina R, Jusic M, Milanovic N, Sapunar J, Brubacher G. The effects of riboflavin administration on iron metabolism parameters in a schoolgoing population. Int J Vitam Nutr Res 1979;49:136–43.

82. Ajayi OA, Okike OC, Yusuf Y. Haematological response to supplements of riboflavin and ascorbic acid in Nigerian young adults. Eur J Haematol 1990;44:209–12.

83. Powers HJ, Bates CJ. Micronutrient deficiencies in the aetiology of anaemia in a rural area in the Gambia. Trans R Soc Trop Med Hyg 1987;81:421–5.

84. Suboticanec K, Stavljenic A, Schalch W, Buzina R. Effects of pyridoxine and riboflavin supplementation on physical fitness in young adolescents. Int J Vitam Nutr Res 1990;60:81–8.

85. Abrams SA, Mushi A, Hilmers DC, Griffin IJ, Davila P, Allen L. A multinutrient-fortified beverage enhances the nutritional status of children in Botswana. J Nutr 2003;133:1834–40.

86. Siekmann JH, Allen LH, Bwibo NO, Demment MW, Murphy SP, Neumann CG. Kenyan school children have multiple micronutrient deficiencies, but increased plasma vitamin B-12 is the only detectable micronutrient response to meat or milk supplementation. J Nutr 2003;133:3972S–80S.

87. Faber M, Jogessar VB, Benade AJ. Nutritional status and dietary intakes of children aged 2-5 years and their caregivers in a rural South African community. Int J Food Sci Nutr 2001;52:401–11.

88. Staubli-Asobayire F. Development of a food fortification strategy to combat iron deficiency in the Ivory Coast. Zurich: Die Eidgenössische Technische Hochschule Zürich (ETH), 2000.

89. Rohner F, Zimmermann MB, Wegmueller R, Tschannen AB, Hurrell RF. Riboflavin deficiency is highly prevalent in school-age children in Côte d'Ivoire but does not increase risk for anaemia. Br J Nutr 2006 (in press).

90. Foy H; Kondi A. Anaemias of the Tropics: East Africa; with special reference to proteins and liver damage. Trans R Soc Trop Med Hyg 1958;52:46–70.

91. Todd L, Godber I, Gunn I. Iatrogenic copper deficiency causing anaemia and neutropenia. Ann Clin Biochem 2004;41:414–6.

92. Harless W, Crowell E, Abraham J. Anemia and neutropenia associated with copper deficiency of unclear etiology. Am J Hematol 2006;81(7):546–9.

93. Kahn MJ, Leissinger C. Underproduction anemias. In: Williams ME, Kahn MJ, eds. American Society of Hematology self-assessment program. 2nd ed. Massachusetts: Blackwell Publishing, 2005:71–85.

94. Miyoshi I, Saito T, Iwahara Y. Copper deficiency anaemia. Br J Haematol 2004;125:106.

95. Fuhrman MP, Herrmann V, Masidonski P, Eby C. Pancytopenia after removal of copper from total parenteral nutrition. Jpen-Parenter Nutr 2000;24:361–6.

96. Reeves PG, Demars LC. Signs of iron deficiency in copper-deficient rats are not affected by iron supplements administered by diet or by injection. J Nutr Biochem 2006;17:635–42.

97. Sharp P.The molecular basis of copper and iron interactions. Proc Nutr Soc 2004;63(4):563–9.

98. Auclair S, Feillet-Coudray C, Coudray C, Schneider S, Muckenthaler MU, Mazur A. Mild copper deficiency alters gene expression of proteins involved in iron metabolism. Blood Cells Mol Dis 2006;36(1):15–20.

99. Linder M, Hazegh-Azam M. Copper biochem-

istry and molecular biology. Am J Clin Nutr 1996;63:797S–811S.

100. Cizewski Culotta V, Gitlin JD. Disorders of copper metabolism. In: Scriver CR, Beaudett A, et al., eds. Metabolic and molecular bases of inherited disorders, 8th ed. New York: McGraw-Hill, 2001:3105–26.

101. Reeves PG, DeMars LC. Copper deficiency reduces iron absorption and biological half-life in male rats. J Nutr 2004;134:1953–57.

102. Chirulescu Z, Suciu A, et al., Possible correlation between the zinc and copper concentrations involved in the pathogenesis of various forms of anemia. Internal Med 1990;28:31–5.

103. Lee GR, Nacht S, Lukens JN, Cartwright GE. Iron metabolism in copper-deficient swine. J Clin Invest 1968;47:2058–69.

104. Danks DM. Copper deficiency in humans. Ciba Found Symp 1980;79:209–25.

105. Harris ZL, Durley AP, Man TK, Gitlin JD. Targeted gene disruption reveals an essential role for ceruloplasmin in cellular iron efflux. Proc Natl Acad Sci USA 1999;96:10812–7.

106. Chen H, Attieh ZK, Su T, Syed BA, Gao H, Alaeddine RM, Fox TC, Usta J, Naylor CE, et al. Hephaestin is a ferroxidase that maintains partial activity in sex-linked anemia mice. Blood 2004;103:3933–9.

107. Petrak J, Vyoral D. Hephaestin – a ferroxidase of cellular iron export. Int J Biochem Cell Biol 2005;37:1173–8.

108. Vulpe CD, Kuo YM, et al. Hephaestin, a ceruloplasmin homologue implicated in intestinal iron transport, is defective in the sla mouse. Nat Genet 1999;21:195–9.

109. Chen H, Huang G, Su T, Gao H, Attieh ZK, McKie AT, Anderson GJ, Vulpe CD. Decreased hephaestin activity in the intestine of copper-deficient mice causes systemic iron deficiency. J Nutr 2006;136(5):1236-41.

110. McKie AT, Marciani P, Rolfs A, Brennan K, Wehr K, Barrow D, Miret S, Bomford A, Peters TJ, et al. A novel duodenal iron-regulated transporter, IREG1, implicated in the basolateral transfer of iron to the circulation. Mol Cell 2000;5:299–309.

111. Frazer DM, Wilkins SJ, Becker EM, Vulpe CD, McKie AT, Trinder D, Anderson GJ. Hepcidin expression inversely correlates with the expression of duodenal iron transporters and iron absorption in rats. Gastroenterology 2002;123:835–44.

112. Lonnerdal B. Dietary factors influencing zinc absorption. J Nutr 2000;130(5S):1378S–83S.

113. Solomons NW, Jacob RA. Studies on the bioavailability of zinc in humans: effects of heme and nonheme iron on the absorption of zinc. Am J Clin Nutr 1981;34:475–82.

114. Valberg LS, Flanagan PR, Chamberlain MJ. Effects of iron, tin, and copper on zinc absorption in humans. Am J Clin Nutr 1984;40:536–41.

115. Sandstrom B, Davidsson L, Cederblad A, Lonnerdal B. Oral iron, dietary ligands and zinc absorption. J Nutr 1985;115:411–4.

116. Crofton RW, Gvozdanovic D, Gvozdanovic S, et al. Inorganic zinc and the intestinal absorption of ferrous iron. Am J Clin Nutr 1989;50:141–4.

117. Rossander-Hulten L, Brune M, Sandstrom B, Lonnerdal B, Hallberg L. Competitive inhibition of iron absorption by manganese and zinc in humans. Am J Clin Nutr 1991;54:152–6.

118. Davidsson L, Mackenzie J, Kastenmayer P, et al. Dietary fiber in weaning cereals: a study of the effect on stool characteristics and absorption of energy, nitrogen, and minerals in healthy infants. J Pediatr Gastroenterol Nutr 1996;22:167–79.

119. Haschke F, Ziegler EE, Edwards BB, Fomon SJ. Effect of iron fortification of infant formula on trace mineral absorption. J Pediatr Gastroenterol Nutr 1986;5:768–73.

120. Fairweather-Tait SJ, Wharf SG, Fox TE. Zinc absorption in infants fed iron-fortified weaning food. Am J Clin Nutr 1995;62:785–9.

121. Gunshin H, Mackenzie B, Berger UV, Gunshin Y, Romero MF, Boron WF, Nussberger S, Gollan JL, Hediger MA. Cloning and characterization of a mammalian proton-coupled metal-ion transporter. Nature 1997;388:482–8.

122. Kelleher SL, Lonnerdal B. Zinc supplementation reduces iron absorption through age-dependent changes in small intestine iron transporter expression in suckling rat pups. J Nutr 2006;136(5):1185–91.

123. Berger J, Ninh NX, Khan NC, Nhien NV, Lien DK, Trung NQ, Khoi HH, Efficacy of combined iron and zinc supplementation on micronutrient status and growth in Vietnamese infants. Eur J Clin Nutr 2006;60(4):443–54.

124. Rosado JL, Lopez P, Munoz E, Martinez H, Allen LH Zinc supplementation reduced morbidity, but neither zinc nor iron supplementation affected growth or body composition of Mexican preschoolers. Am J Clin Nutr 1997;65:13–9.

125. Allen LH, Rosado JL, Casterline JE, et al. Lack of hemoglobin response to iron supplementation in anemic Mexican preschoolers with multiple micronutrient deficiencies. Am J Clin Nutr 2000;71:1485–94.

126. Munoz EC, Rosado JL, Lopez P, Furr HC, Allen LH. Iron and zinc supplementation improves indicators of vitamin A status of Mexican preschoolers. Am J Clin Nutr 2000;71:789–94.

127. Dijkhuizen MA, Wieringa FT, West CE, Martuti S, Muhilal. Effects of iron and zinc supplementation in Indonesian infants on micronutrient status and growth. J Nutr 2001;131,2860–5.

128. Lind T, Lonnerdal B, Stenlund H, Ismail D, Seswandhana R, Ekstrom EC, et al. A community-based randomized controlled trial of iron and zinc supplementation in Indonesian infants: interactions between iron and zinc. Am J Clin Nutr 2003;77:883–90.

129. Fischer Walker C, Kordas K, Stoltzfus RJ, Black RE. Interactive effects of iron and zinc on biochemical and functional outcomes in supplementation trials. Am J Clin Nutr 2005;82:5–12.

14

Anemia in severe undernutrition (malnutrition)

Alan A. Jackson

Institute of Human Nutrition, University of Southampton, Southampton, UK
Contact: aaj@soton.ac.uk

ALAN JACKSON

Alan trained in pediatrics at the University of Cambridge and University College Hospital in London, UK and was a Wellcome Research Fellow and subsequently Director of Tropical Metabolism Unit at the University of the West Indies. He is currently Director of the Institute of Human Nutrition, University of Southampton, UK. Alan is a member of many professional societies and is the foundation Chairman of the Scientific Advisory Committee on Nutrition to the Department of Health and the Food Standards Agency in the UK. He is also a member of the Advisory Panel for the second Expert Report on Diet and Cancer of the World Cancer Research Fund.

INTRODUCTION

Anemia is commonly found at all ages as an associated feature of many pathological conditions, and a broad range of pathologies are often associated with poor nutritional status. Thus anemia might be the consequence of wasting syndromes, directly associated with poor diets or specific nutrient deficiencies, or a consequence of chronic inflammatory or other related disease processes. For this reason the anemia associated with established severe undernutrition, or malnutrition with edema, during childhood or adulthood is not specific but can present with a widely varied picture, containing elements of any of the factors described in some detail in the other chapters in this book (1, 2). The detailed characteristics of the clinical presentation will vary with the particular circumstances and the specific pattern of factors present in an individual. Given the complexity of the possible interactions, in the established condition it can be very difficult to determine the sequence in which one factor might have acted as a primary exposure, subsequently interacting with other factors which go on to make a later contribution and play their part as secondary contributing considerations. Nevertheless, regardless of the origin or basic cause, there are patterns of change which are important and that can be identified and characterized as a common feature of the response to severe malnutrition.

There are limited opportunities to follow in any detail the progressive development of anemia in groups of individuals or populations who have been systematically exposed to limited food intake over extended periods of time. Therefore, the descriptions provided in the experimental situation of the Minnesota studies of semistarvation around the time of the Second World War (3, 4), and the careful records maintained by physicians in the Warsaw Ghetto during the imposed famine in the Second World War (5), are of substantial significance in informing ideas about the etiopathology of the anemia as it develops. The

clinical syndrome providing the clearest picture of wasting as a consequence of relatively uncomplicated food deficiency is anorexia nervosa, but detailed investigation is usually only available at a very late stage of the disorder, by which time severe marrow failure may have supervened.

One of the difficulties in drawing comparisons between studies in different locations is that the terminology used to describe the condition and its associations and complications has been very varied, with little consistency over the years. There has been a rich lexicon of terms used to characterize the clinical syndromes which are currently captured by the definitions of severe undernutrition with or without edema (6). Many of the earlier terms were found wanting because they placed undue emphasis on one or another aspect of a complex clinical picture or because they implied an unhelpful value judgment in terms of the etiopathophysiology. Thus the terms marasmus, kwashiorkor, marasmic kwashiorkor, protein deficiency, energy deficiency, and protein energy deficiency have all been used at different times (1, 2, 7, 8). Frequently, the use of the terms has been purely descriptive and vague. At other times, in attempts to bring clarity to the area, the terms have been defined using more objective criteria. From this has emerged increasing consensus that, regardless of the context, there are two features which capture the essence of the underlying processes leading to the state of malnutrition, without necessarily being specific about the detailed aspects of multiple complex underlying causes (9, 10). An inadequate food intake, due to either a poor appetite or limited availability of food, leads to a wasting syndrome, best captured as a relative loss of weight and associated with a range of complex adaptive changes in all tissues and organs. Thus, reduced weight marks this process of reductive adaptation which can be determined functionally at the molecular, cellular and tissue levels as a reduction in the capacity of many metabolic processes, impaired regulation and control, a loss of reserve capacity, and a state of metabolic brittleness. Underlying specific pathologies, such as infection or a poor quality diet, might separately and together predispose to a reduced intake of food, but in addition they challenge metabolic integrity **(Figure 14.1)**. The development of edema identifies a state in which the ability to maintain the normal distribution of fluid amongst the body compartments indicates inadequate membrane function or cellular regulation. This compromised function reflects a failure of the integrity of fundamental aspects of the system, either because of poor dietary quality, the effect of other stressors such as infection, or more complex interactions. Despite many differences, there are commonalities to the underlying processes of metabolic change and increased susceptibility to additional stress, whether the loss of weight and deranged metabolic processes were initially due to an inadequate intake of food, or the quality of the dietary intake as a primary consideration, or secondary to an infective or other disease process.

APPEARANCE OF THE BLOOD PICTURE

Based on the experience in Minnesota and Warsaw, there is a progressive reduction in red cell mass during the process leading to severe malnutrition. During the early stages of malnutrition, the fall in hemoglobin may be more rapid than in later stages. However, some caution is required as it can be difficult to extrapolate directly from hemoglobin concentration or hematocrit to red cell mass because of the propensity to expansion of the plasma volume during malnutrition (11–13). Towards the end of 24 weeks of semi-starvation, the number of red blood cells had decreased by 27.6%, and hemoglobin decreased by 23.4% (4). Thus, a moderate macrocytic anemia developed. The percentage loss in total hemoglobin was slightly less than the percentage loss in body weight, but when allowance was made for changes in body composition there was an increase in hemoglobin per unit of active body tissue (4). The importance of the timing of investigations as the anemia evolves has been emphasized, with more rapid changes during the earlier period (2, 4, 14). In identifying the progressive nature of the disorder, Fondu (14, 15) suggested

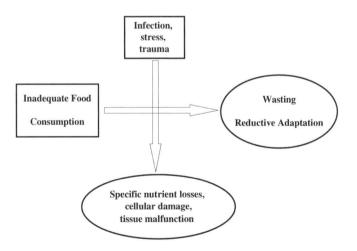

Figure 14.1: Factors leading to wasting and tissue malfunction.

that the anemia should be considered part of the adaptation to reduced metabolic activity, and should be differentiated from the anemia associated with chronic disorders. He identified two stages, with erythropoiesis being normal or increased in the first stage and low hemoglobin resulting from a reduction in the life span of the red cell. In the later, more advanced stage, tissue metabolism falls, erythropoiesis is no longer stimulated, and there is a decrease in erythrocyte volume.

As reviewed by Waterlow (2), infants and children suffering from severe forms of malnutrition frequently have a moderately reduced hemoglobin, 80 to 100 g/L, or reduced hematocrit, 30 to 35%. The reduction in red cell volume in the acute state of severe malnutrition, 16.9 mL/kg, shows some increase, 20 mL/kg, during recovery, but there is an extended delay in reaching that of control children from the same population, 23 mL/kg, and much less than the reference for age, 30 mL/kg. The red cells are frequently normal in size, but slightly hypochromic. Despite the tendency to a normocytic picture for the red cells, a wide range of changes has been described, in terms of the shape and size of the red cells or their relative fragility (1, 2, 4, 5). This range of different appearances is determined by the individual situation. There may be varying degrees of reticulocytosis, but in more severe cases reticulocytosis may be absent.

Anemia represents a reduction in the circulating red cell mass, which must be the result of blood loss or a change in the balance between the rates of red cell synthesis and red cell degradation. Altered red cell synthesis may be part of a general adaptive response or may be due to a specific constraint on the availability of energy, a macronutrient or other nutrient (16–20). Alterations in the rate of degradation are most likely to lead to a shortened life span of the red cell, either because the cells are of poor quality and more vulnerable, or because they exist in a challenging environment produced by infection or nutritional

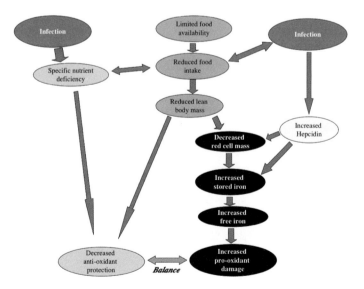

Figure 14.2: Metabolic derangement caused by infection and limited food supply.

or metabolic derangement. Fondu considered that the diminished erythrocyte survival time resulting from increased hemolysis was more likely to be due to poor vitamin E or selenium status than to a limitation of standard hematinics such as iron, folate, or B_{12} (1, 2, 15) **(Figure 14.2)**.

Malnourished individuals are highly susceptible to infection and also frequently have multiple deficiencies of specific nutrients. It is not easy to determine the extent to which this variability can be accounted for by adaptive responses, more complex nutrient deficiencies or the impact of concurrent infection. Therefore, in an established case of severe malnutrition, with or without edema, it can be difficult to differentiate the relative contribution of these multiple potential causes or the extent to which the relative overall effect represents some more complex interaction. Notwithstanding these complexities, an appreciation of the role of different components is of considerable importance since an injudicious approach to the treatment of anemia is one of the principle causes of excess mortality (22). During the early stages of treatment of severe undernutrition, the administration of supplemental iron can contribute to a significant increase in mortality (6, 7, 8).

RED CELL SYNTHESIS: MARROW

Specimens of marrow are not taken routinely and therefore descriptions of the changes seen in the marrow reflect a concern for either an underlying blood dyscrasia, or the consequence of occasional postmortem studies where other supervening pathologies have to be considered. For example, the systematic autopsies carried out where possible for those who died in the Warsaw Ghetto (5) identify that, in the most severely malnourished, marrow changes might be varied. This picture is in many respects similar to that reported for individuals with severe anorexia as a result of psychological disturbances, or the more complex

etiopathologies associated with severe undernutrition and edematous syndromes from parts of the developing world (1, 2). In more extreme situations, the adipose tissue in marrow is lost and is replaced with gelatinous, ground substance or mucopolysaccharides. Erythroid precursors are maintained to a varying extent and may appear to be more active than usual in some situations, but may show a preterminal decrease in activity.

A series of case reports characterizes the abnormal marrow in patients with anorexia nervosa. The most marked changes are seen in those with the most marked degree of weight loss, and are unusual (22–35). The main characteristic is serous or gelatinous change in which atrophy of fat is associated with an increase in ground substance or acid mucopolysaccharides. This gelatinous change may be associated with atrophy and significant reduction of erythroblasts and hypocellularity of the other blood forming tissues. The drive to erythropoiesis might be enhanced, as determined by increased levels of erythropoietin (24), and there may be evidence of increased iron storage, despite a low hemoglobin level (30). The pattern of change is similar to that in severe undernutrition under other circumstances. Although the changes can be severe, it appears that they are potentially completely reversible with successful treatment and recovery (30, 34, 35).

The drive to erythropoiesis in childhood malnutrition may be normal or increased, depending on the level of erythropoietin in blood or urine (15, 19, 36–38). The erythropoietin level tends to be higher than normal during the acute stages, and reduces towards normal with recovery. Nevertheless, even when other measures such as the regaining of weight indicate recovery, this does not necessarily mean that there is complete recovery of the red cells or a higher than usual drive to red cell formation. In some studies, an indirect relationship can be found between the concentration of erythropoietin and the hemoglobin level, but this is not always the case (19, 38). There are only a few reports of the synthesis of hemoglobin or red cells and these do not provide a clear picture, and the reticulocyte response is varied (37–41). If, in the absence of evident blood loss, and despite increased levels of erythropoietin, the red cell mass remains lower than would be expected, this strongly suggests a limitation to red cell production. Thus, a demonstrated increase in the stored iron in the marrow, liver and spleen, despite the increased erythropoietin providing a drive to utilization of this iron for enhanced red cell formation, suggests a constraint on the effective utilization of the available iron (37, 42, 43). And the other possibility remains: an increased rate of red cell loss or excessive red cell breakdown.

The marrow changes are usually reflected in changes in peripheral blood where, although the erythrocytes often appear normocytic with a near normal hemoglobin content, they may appear hypochromic, microcytic or megaloblastic. With successful treatment even the most severe changes appear to be reversible, although the timescale of improvement lags behind that of other systems. The changes in anorexia nervosa are similar to those noted in the experimental starvation studies (4), and also to those noted with the enforced starvation associated with severe food deprivation. One important feature which needs to be emphasized and which is consistent across many studies is the notable presence of iron deposits in the reticuloendothelium, including marrow, liver and spleen. This may be visible as hemosiderin or identifiable as free iron using appropriate techniques (1, 2, 42, 43). The increase in iron marks an inability to effectively utilize available iron for red cell synthesis, rather than an increase in the total body burden. This makes the identification and characterization of iron deficiency problematic, and has important implications for therapy (44).

RED CELL TURNOVER: BREAKDOWN

The normal life span of the red cell is around 120 days on average, but may be shorter in children. As red cells age and are exposed to circulatory stresses over a longer period of time, they progressively lose their metabolic competence and cellular integrity, ultimately leading to their removal from the circulation (47). As older or less competent cells are removed from the circulation, any inherent structural or functional limitation, or an increase in the stresses experienced in the circulation, will lead to removal of the more vulnerable cells with survival of the more robust ones (48, 49). Therefore, those cells remaining in the circulation will tend to be the more healthy ones and any interpretation based on the characteristics of circulating cells will tend to suggest a better state, representative of the healthier, surviving cells (47). Specific deficiencies of nutrients such as vitamin B_{12} or riboflavin reduce the life span of the cells and enhance breakdown of effete cells at a younger age. Changes in the structure of the cell (50) or its membrane, due to altered fatty acid or cholesterol composition (51–56), altered vitamin E or other antioxidant protection (57–64), or altered cellular or membrane function such as the activity of the Na,K-ATPase or other membrane pumps (65–68), could separately and together contribute to greater susceptibility to removal from the circulation and hence reduced life span. One common process through which all of these factors might operate in protecting or damaging cellular function is the ability to generate adequate antioxidant protection.

PROCESSES LEADING TO ANEMIA: REDUCTIVE ADAPTATION

Maintaining the delivery of oxygen to the tissues of the body represents one critically fundamental aspect of life which ensures the capability to generate energy efficiently from the macronutrients contained in food through oxidative processes.

The ability of the red cell to enhance the delivery of oxygen and the removal of carbon dioxide places it at the centre of function and health.

Survival in an uncertain environment requires the flexibility to cope with challenges from and changes within the external environment. Success in this regard is more likely when there is a reserve capacity for essential functions which can be drawn on as and when needed (6, 10). During harsh times, when resources are meager, this reserve might have to be sacrificed. Maintaining red cell mass as an essential function is a high priority for the body and is protected where possible. However, when food is limited and wasting of tissues progresses, the metabolic demands fall, the need for energy and oxygen is reduced, and the red cell mass required to deliver that oxygen is less (1, 2, 4, 5). Therefore, a decrease in red cell mass is a normal consequence of wasting and of reduced lean body mass.

Under normal circumstances, most of the iron in the body is maintained within red cells. When the red cell mass is decreased, the need for iron in this form is reduced. There are no regulated mechanisms in the body for the excretion of iron in excess of immediate requirements. Any iron which is not needed for the formation of red cells has to be held in a nontoxic form, bound to ferritin, but more obvious as hemosiderin when present in larger amounts, within the body's reticuloendothelial system (42–47).

PROCESSES LEADING TO ANEMIA: SPECIFIC NUTRIENT DEFICIENCIES

Bound or free iron may accumulate in the body as a sequela to wasting, but storage iron might also be increased if there is a metabolic block to its effective utilization (43–47). An increase in stored iron which cannot be effectively utilized for metabolic function can occur when the availability of another nutrient, such as vitamin A, riboflavin or copper, is limiting for red cell formation, or if red cell formation is downregulated in response to an inflammatory state (69). Therefore, there is a need to determine whether a seeming iron deficient anemia is the result of the absence of iron from the body or of an inability to effectively utilize iron that may be present but is not accessible to metabolic processes in a normal way (7, 43).

As with all other cells, the multiplication and differentiation of red cell precursors with the formation of mature erythrocytes which eventually appear in the circulation represent a complex process integrated in time and requiring ongoing availability of a full complement of nutrients and metabolic intermediates. Any limitation in one or more of these nutrients will challenge the ability to maintain red cell formation. Over and above the needs of other cells, there is the demand for those nutrients which are directly involved in the formation of hemoglobin, the recognized hematinics. The regulated requirements for iron, the particular needs for heme formation, and the unusual amino acid profile of globin all represent particular demands directly related to red cell production, which are a less obvious feature for the formation and maintenance of other cell lines (70). Iron status will be determined by all the factors associated with iron deficiency or excess and will also include the impact of reductive adaptation. Therefore, it is possible to identify situations where potentially available iron is reduced, normal or increased. Heme is formed from porphyrin, synthesized from glycine in a molar ratio of 1:4, thereby placing a disproportionate demand on glycine availability. Although glycine can be formed in the body, the capacity is finite and dependent upon micronutrient status (71). Limited glycine availability leads to an increase in urinary excretion of 5-L-oxoproline, indicating a probable limitation in the availability of glycine for the formation of both heme and glutathione (72). Red cell glutathione is substantially reduced in edematous malnutrition, associated with increased vulnerability to oxidative stress (43, 73–77). Competitive demand for the available glycine for a range of structural and functional purposes is likely to be particularly marked where there are increased losses of glycine as bile salt conjugates in diarrhea (9). In severely malnourished infants, the excretion of 5-OP is substantially increased. Any limitation in the availability of glycine is likely to reflect further effects on the metabolism of its associated amino acids, serine and cysteine (76, 78). The demands for serine for the formation of a balanced pattern of membrane phospholipids has implications for membrane stability and function, and cysteine availability will impact fundamentally on the ability of proteins to maintain their structure and functionality.

It is clear that the structural integrity of red cells is directly related to their functional capability (70). There is evidence that many aspects of the structure and function of red cells are determined by the availability in the body of specific nutrients derived from the diet, and their utilization both as substrate and as cofactors for a range of cellular functions. Any one of these factors, alone or in combination, can lead to loss of cellular integrity and premature removal of the red cell from the circulation, with consequent anemia (**see also Figure 14.1**). Alterations have been reported for its cholesterol content, fatty acid composition,

and antioxidant defense capability, which will all contribute to increased vulnerability, for example to osmotic shock, and greater susceptibility to any stressful exposure, such as infection, leading to a shortening in the red cell life span.

PROCESSES LEADING TO ANEMIA: INFECTION

Infection is a major feature of severe malnutrition, either as the primary etiological factor, for example in AIDS or tuberculosis, or as a secondary feature consequent upon the nutritionally driven impaired immune response (79). Most frequently, there is a complex interaction with infection leading to poor nutrition which in turn predisposes to more frequent infection. As the inflammatory response is impaired in the severest forms of malnutrition, the signs of infection may not be evident, and multiple foci of silent infection are not infrequent (6, 80–85). Therefore, in the context of severe malnutrition, the effects of infection on anemia might be indirect or direct, and either part of a specific effect of a particular infection, or an aspect of a more general response (**Figure 14.3**).

The usual response to infection is an inflammatory response marked by fever and with a widespread reordering of metabolic function, including sequestration of iron and zinc in the

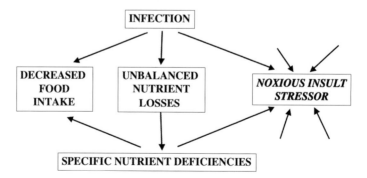

Figure 14.3: Interaction between infection and malnutrion.

liver and an increase in circulating acute phase proteins such as the copper- containing protein, ceruloplasmin (6, 43). This marks a shift in the pattern of proteins being synthesized and secreted by the liver with enhanced formation of acute phase proteins at the expense of the formation of nutrient transport proteins such as transferring, retinol-binding protein and albumin. Thus the potential for making hematinics available to the marrow is compromised. In childhood, any infection is likely to be associated with vomiting and diarrhea, which will in itself result in an increased loss of specific nutrients from the body, including zinc, vitamin A, vitamin B_{12}, and folate, increasing the likelihood of a specific deficiency. A diet that might have been marginally adequate is more likely to be inadequate against the background of nutrient depletion caused by increased losses in the stool. It has been known for many years that there is an important direct effect of infection blocking the absorption of iron in malnourished children. It is becoming increasingly clear that this is due to an effect of hepcidin secreted by the liver as an acute phase protein and part of the inflammatory response (69). Hepcidin blocks the gastrointestinal absorption of iron and increases the uptake of iron by macrophages, limiting its availability for red cell formation. All of these effects will limit the availability of nutrients for red cell formation and increase the likelihood of anemia.

Specific infections will increase the utilization of red cells or their loss from the body. Malaria clearly increases red cell turnover, and gastrointestinal blood loss will be increased with dysentery or intestinal helminthiasis (84–89). This introduces a specific difficulty in terms of differential diagnosis because increased losses of red cells can lead to an increased loss of iron from the body. Thus, without increased losses, malnutrition is more likely to be associated with an increase in iron as ferritin or hemosiderin in the reticuloendothelial system. With increased losses of iron, the reserve pool of iron might be completely drained. The presence or absence of increased iron in reserves will considerably affect the decision on the administration of iron during the early period of treatment of the acute severely ill individual (6). The extent to which the level of hemoglobin can be used as a reliable indicator to guide judgments in this situation, and the extent to which very low hemoglobin can be used to indicate the potential degree of exhaustion of iron reserves (90a), are not clear.

PROCESSES LEADING TO ANEMIA: HEMOLYSIS, PROOXIDANT DAMAGE

More than any other conceptual approach to the etiopathology of edematous malnutrition, the free radical theory of kwashiorkor has enabled the development of understanding of the complex interaction amongst micronutrients, macronutrients and energy balance, especially where reductive adaptation in severe undernutrition has lead to brittleness in metabolic regulation and control (6–8, 10, 43, 73). A serendipitous observation was the fact that in edematous malnutrition the whole blood or red cell glutathion content is significantly reduced, and that the magnitude of the reduction relates to the severity of the clinical presentation while seeking a marker for glycine status (73). However, this observation clearly indicated the importance of the balanced adequacy of micronutrients in resisting potentially toxic environmental challenge (7, 8). Further, it made clear the way in which the multiple layers of protection against free radical induced damage are fundamental to maintaining cellular protection, its structure and its function. Of critical importance, it raised the question of the extent to which the red cell plays an important, if not central and specific role, in the progressive pathophysiology of edematous malnutrition.

To an extent, the pathology of the red cell can be taken to mark the pathology of other cells in the body. However, in addition, the red cell's enhanced susceptibility to prooxidant damage will predispose it to a shortened life span, a critical basis for an increase in stored and/or free intracellular iron and the establishment of ensuing cellular pathology. An increased loss of red cells in the face of any limitation on red cell production inevitably leads to a reduction in red cell mass. The lowered hemoglobin will be one important, potential consequence, but of much greater significance is the fate of the iron which can no longer be returned to the synthesis of red cells and has to be handled and stored. Moreover, it has to be stored in a form in which free iron is unlikely to be generated to act catalytically as a centre for Fenton and Haber-Weiss reactions, the focus of radical induced molecular and cellular damage (43). The evidence from studies where the excess burden of iron has been removed by chelation therapy provides support for the proposal that free iron is causative for some of the features of severe malnutrition, and contributes directly to enhanced mortality (7, 8, 45).

The demonstration that reduced glutathione is usually, if not always, associated with edematous malnutrition, and that this is directly associated with increased susceptibility to free radical induced damage, has been demonstrated in many but not all studies. The cellular content of reduced glutathione plays a fundamental role in normal cellular function and it is critically involved in a range of functions related to cellular integrity. If the glutathione content of cells cannot be maintained then cells fail to survive. Antioxidant protection is one important function and, importantly, free radical challenge is a major process through which cellular glutathione can be depleted (7, 8). Thus, cellular glutathione has to be placed in the context of the other cellular antioxidant protective mechanisms and processes. For these reasons, single or multiple micronutrient deficiencies or altered membrane structure and function interact with impaired ability to maintain cellular glutathione status in determining cellular survival (77). The formation and maintenance of glutathione itself is sensitive to the dietary intake of total nitrogen and specific

amino acids (75–78). Although glutamic acid, cysteine and glycine, the three amino acids which go on to form glutathione, are not essential dietary components, the ability to maintain their synthesis at an adequate level is of critical importance (75, 76, 78). This is determined by the integrity of the control and regulatory systems on cells and tissues, the adequacy of dietary micronutrients, and the amount and quality of dietary nitrogen or protein (75, 76, 78). Thus, the quality of red cell synthesis and the life span of the red cell in a harsh circulatory environment mark the wider stresses placed upon the cells of the body in the undernourished state.

The effectiveness of antioxidant protection is directly related to the magnitude of the challenges imposed, either as a consequence of normal cellular metabolism, the oxidant burst associated with infection, or other pathological processes. The increase in stored iron as an integral feature of reductive adaptation may well go on to play a critical role in determining the magnitude of prooxidant stress in severe malnutrition. Thus, a range of factors contributing either to antioxidant protection or to free radical induced damage may play their part, leading to major changes in other regulatory systems such as the balance and extent of nitric oxide generation (90–94). A randomized controlled trial of a supplement of antioxidants in children at risk of developing edematous malnutrition failed to demonstrate any protective effect (95). It is important to determine whether this should be taken as evidence to support rejection of the idea that free radical damage plays a role in the etiology and pathogenesis of the process, or whether the particular choice of intervention was not suitable for the context (94).

PROCESSES LEADING TO ANEMIA: CLUES FROM TREATMENT/INTERVENTION

The condition which has been characterized as protein energy malnutrition comprises a clinical entity in which inadequate energy and macronutrient intake is associated with a diet of poor quality in which the availability of multiple micronutrients is limiting. Infection adds to the problem by increasing specific nutrient losses and the associated reductive adaptation increases individual vulnerability. Anemia is one manifestation of this complex process, and is usually associated with an inability to effectively utilize iron, leading to enhanced iron both in stored and free form. One of the early observations of importance was that diets based on cow's milk are relatively poor in copper, leading to copper deficiency which can present as severe microcytic anemia (96).

The likelihood of an individual dying from a period of severe undernutrition, or surviving with a reasonable chance of recovery, not only depends upon what is done in terms of immediate care but, critically, on the order in which different interventions are carried out (97). The systems for classifying malnutrition place emphasis on two characteristics: loss of relative weight and the presence of edema (6). Based on standard approaches in nutrition, the impetus is to correct the edema directly, frequently by the use of diuretics, to correct wasting through the generous provision of food, and to treat abnormal blood biochemistry by direct provision of single nutrients. Each treatment runs the risk of contributing to increased mortality unless at least equal attention is given to correcting the associated cellular damage, the result of multiple nutrient deficiencies (21). Although anemia might be a common presenting feature, and has many of the characteristics of an iron-deficient picture, the problem in the short term is an inability to effectively utilize the iron that is in the body, rather than any immediate shortage. Therapy with iron at this time increases mortality (7, 8, 43). With appropriate treatment, as infections are treated and specific nutrient deficiencies corrected, cellular competence returns. Lean body mass can be progressively restored and the red cell mass expanded to draw on the iron held as hemosiderin and ferritin. At some stage during this recovery process the

iron in storage is likely to be insufficient to meet demand and, as a more classic picture of iron deficiency emerges, iron supplementation becomes needed and is appropriate (47).

Many authors have observed that, following a bout of severe undernutrition, the reduced red cell mass can take a considerable time to return to normal levels, and may account for the prolonged period of convalescence which follows very severe bouts of illness. The drive to increased erythropoiesis may remain, as marked by increased levels of circulating erythropoietin. Therefore, the cause has to be sought elsewhere. It seems unlikely that any of the usual hematinics are limiting for this process. It may be that the delayed return of red cell mass to normal is a reflection of the delay in achieving a normal lean body mass. Even when body weight has recovered, body composition is likely to be abnormal, with relative adiposity and limited restoration of lean body mass (98). This might indicate that the delayed recovery of hemoglobin simply reflects this more general constraint. A further possibility is that the ability to adequately meet the needs for nonessential amino acids is constrained. For example, the ability to synthesize adequate amounts of glycine appears constrained during malnutrition. The demands for glycine during growth are high, and not all of these competing demands can be adequately met. It needs to be determined whether, under these circumstances, the availability of glycine constrains the formation of hemoglobin. If so, this would have important implications for the maintenance of red cell mass in other situations in which the ability to maintain the availability of all amino acids might be constrained. The implications for individual care and for a range of public health programs would be substantial. Similar considerations apply to the availability of fatty acids in general and specific unsaturated amino acids to meet the needs for cell membrane formation. Any limitation in metabolic interconversion to form the longer chain polyunsaturated fatty acids might limit the formation of red cells or their survival within the circulation.

There have recently been reports of a series of randomized controlled trials supported by UNICEF on the effect on growth and anemia of multiple micronutrient supplements during the second six months of life (99). Randomized controlled trials were carried out in four centers, Indonesia, Peru, South Africa, and Tanzania. Those who received multiple micronutrients, including iron and other hematinics, had a different response to those who received the placebo. In those receiving the placebo there was progressive deterioration in growth and hemoglobin status, which was ameliorated in those receiving the active supplement.

CONCLUSION

The accumulated experience and evidence suggests that the anemia associated with severe malnutrition is the consequence of multiple factors and represents an interaction between adaptation to inadequate food intake and the impact of other stresses associated with infection or dietary imbalance. In this situation, the effect of the additional stress is exaggerated compared with a normally nourished individual. One critical difference is the extent and nature of the body burden of iron. Constraints on the effective utilization of iron which cannot be effectively excreted leads to an increase in unutilized iron, despite no increase in the total body burden of iron. In this context, further supplementation of iron is hazardous, and the increase in potentially available, but unused, iron has its own negative impact on the system through the promotion of unbalanced prooxidant damage. An assumption that anemia found in malnourished individuals is a simple consequence of a poor or inadequate dietary intake of iron, without a critical consideration of the broader context, gives rise to the potential for serious error in care with inappropriate interventions.

REFERENCES

1.   Alleyne GAO, Hay RW, Picou DI, Stanfield JP, Whitehead RG. Protein-energy malnutrition. London: Edward Arnold, 1977.
2.   Waterlow JC. Protein-energy malnutrition. 2nd ed. London: Edward Arnold, 1992.
3.   Kalm LM, Semba RD. They starved so that others be better fed: remembering Ancel Keys and the Minnesota experiment. J Nutr 2005;135:1347–52.
4.   Keys A, Brozek J, Henschel A, Mickelsen O, Longstreet Taylor H. The biology of human starvation. Minneapolis, USA: University of Minnesota Press, 1950.
5.   Winick M. Hunger disease: studies by the Jewish physicians in the Warsaw ghetto. New York: John Wiley & Sons, 1979.
6.   Jackson AA. Severe malnutrition. In: Wareell DA, Cox TM, Firth JD, eds. Oxford Textbook of Medicine. 4th ed. 2003;10.4:1054–61.
7.   Golden MHN. Oedematous malnutrition. British Medical Bulletin 1998;54:433–44.
8.   Golden MHN. The development of concepts of malnutrition. J Nutr 2002;132:2117S–22S.
9.   Jackson AA. Severe undernutrition in Jamaica. Kwashiorkor and marasmus: the disease of the weanling. Acta Paediatr Scand Suppl 1986;323:43–51.
10. Jackson AA. The aetiology of kwashiorkor. In: Harrison GA, Waterlow JC, Diet and disease in traditional and developing societies. Society for the Study of Human Biology, Symposium 30. Cambridge University Press, 1990.
11. Viart P. Blood volume changes during treat-

ment of protein-calorie malnutrition. Am J Clin Nutr 1977;30(3):349–54

12. Fondu P. A reassessment of intravascular volume measurements in protein-calorie malnutrition. Eur J Clin Invest 1977;7(3):161–5.

13. Viart P. Hemodynamic findings during treatment of protein-calorie malnutrition. Am J Clin Nutr 1978;31(6):911–26.

14. Fondu P, Mandelbaum IM. Marasmic kwashiorkor anemia. III. Hemoglobin oxygen affinity. Biomedicine 1975;22(4):291–7.

15. Fondu P, Haga P, Halvorsen S. The regulation of erythropoiesis in protein-energy-malnutrition. Br J Haematol 1978;38(1):29–36.

16. Halsted CH, Sourial N, Guindi S, et al. Anemia of kwashiorkor in Cairo: deficiencies of protein, iron and folic acid. Am J Clin Nutr 1969;22(10):1371–82.

17. Kurnick JE, Ward HP, Pickett JC. Mechanism of the anemia of chronic disorders: correlation of hematocrit value with albumin, vitamin B12, transferrin, and iron stores. Arch Intern Med 1972;130(3):323–6.

18. Khalil M, Tanios A, Moghazy M, Aref MK, Mahmoud S, el-Lozy M. Serum and red cell folates, and serum vitamin B 12 in protein calorie malnutrition. Arch Dis Child 1973;48(5):366–9.

19. Macdougall LG, Moodley G, Eyberg C, Quirk M. Mechanisms of anemia in protein-energy malnutrition in Johannesburg. Am J Clin Nutr 1982;35(2):229–35.

20. Beard JL, Gomez LH, Haas JD. Functional anemia of complicated protein-energy malnutrition at high altitude. Am J Clin Nutr 1986;44(2):181–7.

21. Schofield C, Ashworth A. Why have mortality rates for severe malnutrition remained so high? Bull World Health Organ 1996;74(2):223–9.

22. Pearson HA. Marrow hypoplasia in anorexia nervosa. J Pediatr 1967;71(2):211–5.

23. Lampert F, Lau B. Bone marrow hypoplasia in anorexia nervosa. Eur J Pediatr 1976;124(1):65–71.

24. Kubanek B, Heimpel H, Paar G, Schoengen A. Haematological features of anorexia nervosa. Blut 1977;35(2):115–24.

25. Cornbleet PJ, Moir RC, Wolf PL. A histochemical study of bone marrow hypoplasia in anorexia

nervosa. Virchows Arch A Pathol Anat Histol 1977;374(3):239–47.

26. Smith RR, Spivak JL. Marrow cell necrosis in anorexia nervosa and involuntary starvation. Br J Haematol 1985;60:525–30.

27. Larrain C, Ampuero R, Pumarino H. Hematologic changes in anorexia nervosa. Rev Med Chil 1989;117(5):534–43.

28. Lambert M, Hubert C, Depresseux G, et al. Hematological changes in anorexia nervosa are correlated with total body fat mass depletion. Int J Eat Disord 1997;21(4):329–34.

29. Nonaka D, Tanaka M, Takaki K, Umeno M, Okamura T, Taketa H. Gelatinous bone marrow transformation complicated by self-induced malnutrition. Acta Haematol 1998;100(2):88–90.

30. Orlandi E, Boselli P, Covezzi R, Bonaccorsi G, Guaraldi GP. Reversal of bone marrow hypoplasia in anorexia nervosa: case report. Int J Eat Disord 2000;27(4): 480–2.

31. Nishio S, Yamada H, Yamada K, et al. Severe neutropenia with gelatinous bone marrow transformation in anorexia nervosa: a case report. Int J Eat Disord 2003;33(3):360–3.

32. Kennedy A, Kohn M, Lammi A, Clarke S. Iron status and haematological changes in adolescent female inpatients with anorexia nervosa. J Paediatr Child Health 2004;40(8):430–2.

33. Chen SH, Hung IJ, Jaing TH, Sun CF. Gelatinous degeneration of the bone marrow in anorexia nervosa. Chang Gung Med J 2004;27(11):845–9.

34. Marechaud R, Abadie JC, Babin P, Lessart M, Sudre Y. Reversible bone marrow hypoplasia in a case of male anorexia nervosa. Ann Med Interne (Paris) 1985;136(1):36–40.

35. Steinberg SE, Nasraway S, Peterson L. Reversal of severe serous atrophy of the bone marrow in anorexia nervosa. JPEN J Parenter Enteral Nutr 1987;11(4):422–3.

36. Ward HP, Kurnick JE, Pisarczyk MJ. Serum level of erythropoietin in anemias associated with chronic infection, malignancy, and primary hematopoietic disease. J Clin Invest 1971;50(2):332–5.

37. el-Nawawy A, Barakat S, Elwalily T, Abdel-Moneim Deghady A, Hussein M. Evaluation of ery-

thropoiesis in protein energy malnutrition. East Mediterr Health J 2002;8(2-3):281–9.

38. Wickramasinghe SN, Cotes PM, Gill DS, Tam RC, Grange A, Akinyanju OO. Serum immunoreactive erythropoietin and erythropoiesis in protein-energy malnutrition. Br J Haematol 1985;60(3):515–24.

39. Lanzkowsky P, McKenzie D, Katz S, Hoffenberg R, Friedman R, Black E. Erythrocyte abnormality induced by protein malnutrition. II. 51-chromium labelled erythrocyte studies. Br J Haematol 1967;13(5):639–49.

40. Stekel A, Smith NJ. Hematologic studies of severe undernutrition of infancy. 3. Erythrocyte survival in marasmic infants and calorie-deprived pigs. Am J Clin Nutr 1970;23(7):896–904.

41. Read WW, McLaren DS, Saboundjian A, Schultz GO. Nitrogen - 15 studies of erythropoiesis during recovery from marasmus. Am J Clin Nutr 1974;27:230–3.

42. Waterlow JC. Fatty Liver Disease in Infants in the British West Indies. Medical Research Council Special Report Series. No 263. London: HMSO, 1948.

43. Golden MH, Ramdath D. Free radicals in the pathogenesis of kwashiorkor. Proc Nutr Soc 1987;46(1):53–68.

44. Dempster WS, Sive AA, Rosseau S, Malan H, Heese HV. Misplaced iron in kwashiorkor. Eur J Clin Nutr 1995;49(3):208–10.

45. Sive AA, Dempster WS, Rosseau S, Kelly M, Malan H, Heese HD. Bone marrow and chelatable iron in patients with protein energy malnutrition. S Afr Med J 1996;86(11):1410–3.

46. Sive AA, Dempster WS, Malan H, Rosseau S, Heese HD. Plasma free iron: a possible cause of oedema in kwashiorkor. Arch Dis Child 1997;76(1):54–6.

46. Viteri FE. Primary protein-energy malnutrition: clinical, biochemical, and metabolic changes. In: Suskind RM, ed. Textbook of Pediatric Nutrition, New York: Raven Press, 1991:189–215.

47. Powers HJ, Thurnham DI. Riboflavin deficiency in man: effects on haemoglobin and reduced glutathione in erythrocytes of different ages. Br J Nutr 1981;46(2):257–66.

48. Rao A, Onuora CU, Cherian A. Detergent induced lysis of erythrocytes in kwashiorkor. Clin Chim Acta 1987;168(1):1–5.

49. Vertongen F, Heyder-Bruckner C, Fondu P, Mandelbaum I. Oxidative haemolysis in protein malnutrition. Clin Chim Acta 1981;116(2):217–22.

50. Wickramasinghe SN, Akinyanju OO, Grange A. Ultrastructure and cell cycle distribution of bone marrow cells in protein-energy malnutrition. Clin Lab Haematol 1988;10(2):135–47.

51. Wolff JA, Margolis S, Bujdoso-Wolff K, Matusick E, MacLean WC Jr. Plasma and red blood cell fatty acid composition in children with protein-calorie malnutrition. Pediatr Res 1984;18(2):162–7.

52. Koletzko B, Abiodun PO, Laryea MD, Bremer HJ. Fatty acid composition of plasma lipids in Nigerian children with protein-energy malnutrition. Eur J Pediatr 1986;145(1-2):109–15

53. Vajreswari A, Narayanareddy K, Rao PS. Fatty acid composition of erythrocyte membrane lipid obtained from children suffering from kwashiorkor and marasmus. Metabolism 1990;39(8):779–82.

54. el Harim I, Befort JJ, Balafrej A, Lahrichi M, Girard-Globa A. Lipids and lipoproteins of malnourished children during early renutrition: apolipoprotein A-IV as a potential index of recovery. Am J Clin Nutr 1993;58(3):407–11.

55. Franco VH, Hotta JK, Jorge SM, dos Santos JE. Plasma fatty acids in children with grade III protein-energy malnutrition in its different clinical forms: marasmus, marasmic kwashiorkor, and kwashiorkor. J Trop Pediatr 1999;45(2):71–5.

56. Squali Houssaini FZ, Foulon T, Payen N, Iraqi MR, Arnaud J, Groslambert P. Plasma fatty acid status in Moroccan children: increased lipid peroxidation and impaired polyunsaturated fatty acid metabolism in protein-calorie malnutrition. Biomed Pharmacother 2001;55(3):155–62.

57. Etukudo MH, Agbedana EO, Akinyinka OO, Osifo BO. Plasma electrolytes, total cholesterol, liver enzymes, and selected antioxidant status in protein energy malnutrition. Afr J Med Med Sci 1999;28(1-2):81–5.

58. Ahmed HM, Laryea MD, el-Karib AO, et al. Vitamin E status in Sudanese children with

protein-energy malnutrition. Z Ernahrungswiss 1990;29(1):47–53.

59. Laditan AA, Ette SI. Plasma alpha-tocopherol (vitamin E) levels and tocopherol-lipid ratio among children with protein-energy malnutrition (PEM). Ann Trop Paediatr 1982;2(2):85–8

60. Kwena AM, Nyandieka HS. Diagnostic potential of serum vitamin E tocopherol and cholesterol levels in children with protein energy malnutrition in western Kenya. East Afr Med J 2003;80(8):419–23.

61. Sempertegui F, Estrella B, Vallejo W, et al. Selenium serum concentrations in malnourished Ecuadorian children: a case-control study. Int J Vitam Nutr Res 2003;73:181–6.

62. Manary MJ, MacPherson GD, Mcardle F, Jackson MJ, Hart CA. Selenium status, kwashiorkor and congestive heart failure. Acta Paediatr 2001;90:950–2.

63. Salih MA, Mohamed EF, Galgan V, et al. Selenium in malnourished Sudanese children: status and interaction with clinical features. Ann Nutr Metab 1994;38(2):68–74.

64. Subotzky EF, Heese HD, Sive AA, Dempster WS, Sacks R, Malan H. Plasma zinc, copper, selenium, ferritin and whole blood manganese concentrations in children with kwashiorkor in the acute stage and during refeeding. Ann Trop Paediatr 1992;12(1):13–22.

65. Verjee ZH, Behal R. Protein-calorie malnutrition: a study of red blood cell and serum enzymes during and after crisis. Clin Chim Acta 1976;70(1):139–47.

66. Mandelbaum IM, Mozes N, Fondu P. Erythrocyte glycolysis in protein-energy malnutrition. Clin Chim Acta 1982;124(3):263–75.

67. Okunade WG, Olorunsogo OO. Effect of reactive oxygen species on the erythrocyte calcium-pump function in protein-energy malnutrition. Biosci Rep 1992;12(6):433–43.

68. Forrester T, Golden M, Brand S, Swales J. Reduction in vitro of red cell glutathione reproduces defects of cellular sodium transport seen in oedematous malnutrition. Eur J Clin Nutr 1990;44(5):363–9.

69. Nemeth E, Ganz T. Regulation of iron metabolism by hepcidin. Annu Rev Nutr 2006;26:323–42.

70. Jackson AA. The use of stable isotopes to study nitrogen metabolism in homozygous sickle cell disease. In: Velazquez A, Bourges H, eds. Genetic factors in nutrition. London: Academic Press, 1984:297–315.

71. Jackson AA. The glycine story. Eur J Clin Nutr 1991;45(2):59–65.

72. Persaud C, Forrester T, Jackson AA. Urinary excretion of 5-L-oxoproline (pyroglutamic acid) is increased during recovery from severe childhood malnutrition and responds to supplemental glycine. J Nutr 1996;126(11):2823–30.

73. Jackson AA. Blood glutathione in severe malnutrition in childhood. Trans R Soc Trop Med Hyg 1986;80(6):911–3.

74. Becker K, Leichsenring M, Gana L, Bremer HJ, Schirmer RH. Glutathione and association antioxidant systems in protein energy malnutrition: results of a study in Nigeria. Free Radic Biol Med 1995;18(2):257–63.

75. Reid M, Badaloo A, Forrester T, et al. In vivo rates of erythrocyte glutathione synthesis in children with severe protein-energy malnutrition. Am J Physiol Endocrinol Metab 2000;278(3):E405–12.

76. Badaloo A, Reid M, Forrester T, Heird WC, Jahoor F. Cysteine supplementation improves the erythrocyte glutathione synthesis rate in children with severe edematous malnutrition. Am J Clin Nutr 2002;76(3):646–52.

77. Becker K, Pons-Kuhnemann J, Fechner A, et al. Effects of antioxidants on glutathione levels and clinical recovery from the malnutrition syndrome kwashiorkor – a pilot study. Redox Rep 2005;10(4):215–26.

78. Jackson AA, Gibson NR, Lu Y, Jahoor F. Synthesis of erythrocyte glutathione in healthy adults consuming the safe amount of dietary protein. Am J Clin Nutr 2004;80(1):101–7.

79. Jackson AA, Calder PC. Severe undernutrition and immunity. In: Gershwin ME, Nestel P, Keen CLH, eds. Handbook of nutrition and immunity. New Jersey: Humana Press, 2004:71–92.

80. Sauerwein RW, Mulder JA, Mulder L, et al. Inflammatory mediators in children with protein-energy malnutrition. Am J Clin Nutr 1997;65(5):1534–9.

81. Reid M, Badaloo A, Forrester T, Morlese JF, Heird WC, Jahoor F. The acute-phase protein response to infection in edematous and nonedematous protein-energy malnutrition. Am J Clin Nutr 2002;76(6):1409–15.

82. Christie CD, Heikens GT, Golden MH. Coagulase-negative staphylococcal bacteremia in severely malnourished Jamaican children. Pediatr Infect Dis J 1992;11(12):1030–6.

83. Christie CD, Heikens GT, Black FL. Acute respiratory infections in ambulatory malnourished children: a serological study. Trans R Soc Trop Med Hyg 1990;8491):160–1.

84. Christie CD, Heikens GT, McFarlane DE. Nosocomial and community-acquired infections in malnourished children. J Trop Med Hyg 1988;91(4):173–80.

85. Geerligs PD, Brabin BJ, Eggelte TA. Analysis of the effects of malaria chemoprophylaxis in children on haematological responses, morbidity and mortality. Bull World Health Organ 2003;81(3):205–16.

86. van Eijk AM, Ayisi JG, Ter Kuile FO, et al. Malaria and human immunodeficiency virus infection as risk factors for anemia in infants in Kisumu, western Kenya. Am J Trop Med Hyg 2002;67(1):44–53.

87. Bundy DA, de Silva NR. Can we deworm this wormy world? Br Med Bull 1998;54(2):421–32.

88. Stoltzfus RJ, Chway HM, Montresor A, et al. Low dose daily iron supplementation improves iron status and appetite but not anemia, whereas quarterly anthelminthic treatment improves growth, appetite and anemia in Zanzibari preschool children. J Nutr 2004;134(2):348–56.

89. Stoltzfus RJ, Chwaya HM, Montresor A, Albonico M, Savioli L, Tielsch JM. Malaria, hookworms and recent fever are related to anemia and iron status indicators in 0- to 5-y old Zanzibari children and these relationships change with age. J Nutr 2000;130(7):1724–33.

90. Sive AA, Subotzky EF, Malan H, Dempster WS, Heese HD. Red blood cell antioxidant enzyme concentrations in kwashiorkor and marasmus. Ann Trop Paediatr 1993;13(1):33–8.

90a Cook JD, Baynes RD, Skikne BS. Iron deficiency and the measurement of iron status. Nutrition Research Reviews 1992;5:189-202

91. Lenhartz H, Ndasi R, Anninos A, et al. The clinical manifestation of the kwashiorkor syndrome is related to increased lipid peroxidation. J Pediatr 1998;132(5):879–81.

92. Ashour MN, Salem SI, El-Gadban HM, Elwan NM, Basu TK. Antioxidant status in children with protein-energy malnutrition (PEM) living in Cairo, Egypt. Eur J Clin Nutr 1999;53(8):669–73.

93. Fechner A, Bohme C, Gromer S, Funk M, Schirmer R, Becker K. Antioxidant status and nitric oxide in the malnutrition syndrome kwashiorkor. Pediatr Res 2001;49(2):237–43.

94. Shaaban SY, Nassar MF, Ibrahim SA, Mahmoud SE. Impact of nutritional rehabilitation on enzymatic antioxidant levels in protein energy malnutrition. East Mediterr Health J 2002;8(2-3):290–7.

95. Ciliberto H, Ciliberto M, Briend A, Ashorn P, Bier D, Manary M. Antioxidant supplementation for the prevention of kwashiorkor in Malawian children: randomised, double blind, placebo controlled trial. BMJ 2005;330(7500):1109.

96. Graham GG, Cordano A. Copper depletion and deficiency in the malnourished infant. Johns Hopkins Med J 1969;124(3):139–50.

97. World Health Organization, Hospital Care for Children: guidelines for the management of common illnesses with limited resources. Geneva: WHO, 2005.

98. Jackson AA, Golden BE, Golden MHN, Robinson HMR. Muscle growth during recovery from severe protein-energy malnutrition. In: Anderson W, Sadler W., eds. Perspectives in differentiation and hypertrophy. North Holland: Elsevier, 1982:379–83.

99. Smuts CM, Lombard CJ, Benade AJ, et al. International Research on Infant Supplementation (IRIS) Study Group. Efficacy of a foodlet-based multiple micronutrient supplement for preventing growth faltering, anemia, and micronutrient deficiency of infants: the four country IRIS trial pooled data analysis. J Nutr 2005;135(3):631S–8S.

15

Infection and the etiology of anemia

David I. Thurnham   Christine A. Northrop-Clewes

Northern Ireland Centre for Food and Health, School of Biomedical Sciences,
University of Ulster, UK
Contact: di.thurnham@ulster.ac.uk

DAVID THURNHAM

David has a PhD in Biochemistry from the School of Tropical Medicine, Liverpool University, UK. He is currently Emeritus Professor of Human Nutrition at the University of Ulster in Northern Ireland, UK, and an Honorary Senior Scientist at the MRC Human Nutrition Research Laboratories in Cambridge, UK. He has published widely on micronutrients but currently has a special interest in the influence of inflammation on micronutrients, especially vitamin A and iron.

CHRISTINE NORTHROP-CLEWES

Christine has a PhD in Biomedical Sciences from the University of Ulster, Northern Ireland, UK. She is currently the Chief Biomedical Scientist at the MRC Human Nutrition Laboratories in Cambridge, UK. Prior to this, she spent three years as an ORISE Research Fellow at the Centers for Disease Control and Prevention in Atlanta in the USA. Christine was part of the WHO/CDC Working Group that in 2004 produced the document "Assessing the iron status of populations." She has published extensively on micronutrients and factors affecting the growth of infants in developing countries.

BACKGROUND

Anemia is reported to be one of the most common and intractable nutritional problems in the world today. The World Health Organization (WHO) (1) estimates that some 2 billion people are anemic as defined by hemoglobin thresholds. The main causes of anemia, according to the report, are dietary iron deficiency; infectious diseases such as malaria, hookworm infections, and schistosomiasis; deficiencies of other key micronutrients including folate, vitamin B_{12}, and vitamin A; and inherited conditions that affect red cell stability such as thalassemia, sickle cell anemia, etc. There have been many attempts to reduce the prevalence of anemia over the last two decades but despite these efforts, the condition is still common. One of the reasons for the apparent failure to reduce the prevalence of anemia is that many programs and interventions have been designed on the assumption that iron deficiency is the only

cause (2). It is now more widely recognized that infection is a much more important cause of anemia than previously thought and that anemia is a consequence of a synergy of inflammation and insufficient bioavailable dietary iron to meet iron requirements. **Figure 15.1** summarizes the three main exogenous causes of anemia (disease, blood loss, and diet), but illustrates the central role of inflammation in all three. Thus, solving the problem of anemia, especially in the developing world, will not be successful without addressing the causes of disease and understanding how inflammation impairs the proper utilization of dietary iron.

Poverty, unsanitary conditions, and inadequate health care encourage the spread of disease and increases exposure of infants and children to disease. It is not surprising therefore that diarrhea,

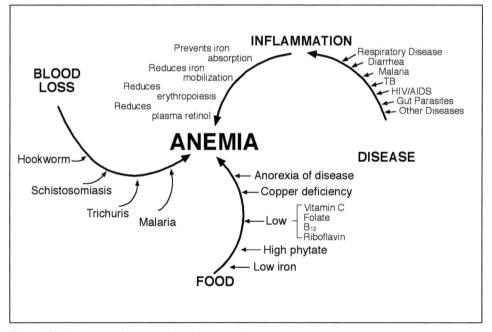

Figure 15.1: Exogenous factors contributing to anemia.

respiratory diseases, skin diseases, malaria, and helminth infestations are common in developing countries. Children are born with very little protection against pathogens but need exposure to pathogens in order to develop their own immune defenses. Infants acquire some protection from immunoglobulins and other factors in their mother's milk, and in time they acquire their own immune defenses. They do, however, spend a very large part of their early lives being sick (3–5).

It was noted more than 30 years ago that serum iron is depressed during the incubation period of most generalized infectious processes, in some instances several days before the onset of fever or any symptoms of clinical illness (6). In volunteers given endotoxin or live attenuated virus vaccine to induce therapeutic fever, depression of serum iron concentrations began within several hours, reached maximum at 24 hours, and were greatest in those developing severe fever (6). Administration of iron to such patients by oral or parenteral routes had little effect on serum iron or other indices of iron status probably because iron absorption is inhibited by the inflammatory process (7, 8) irrespective of iron status (9). The hypoferremia of inflammation does not represent a genuine (i.e., dietary) iron deficiency, but rather a redistribution of iron that can prevail in the face of normal iron stores (10). Chronic illnesses like cancer or rheumatoid arthritis are frequently accompanied by anemia of chronic inflammation (ACI), as the continuous presence of the inflammatory stimulus maintains a continuous hypoferremia and suppresses erythropoiesis. ACI was previously called anemia of chronic disease, but the importance of inflammation will be emphasized in this chapter and the newer term ACI will be used. With the wider recognition that infection is responsible for a large part of the anemias in children and adults in developing countries comes the realization that infection and the inflammatory response may also play an important role in the initial cause. Frequent exposure to endemic diseases will promote the inflammatory response and the hypoferremia, and

increase the risk of anemia by impairing erythrocyte synthesis and/or a shortening red cell life span. Whether this is also accompanied by a metabolic iron deficiency will depend on the ability to maintain iron stores. Thus iron absorption, iron loss, and bioavailability of dietary iron become the critical factors to maintain normal hemoglobin.

Vitamin A deficiency is frequently found with anemia (11) and supplements of iron and vitamin A have been shown to independently reduce the prevalence of anemia in preschool children (12–14) and adults (15). Data from the study by Suharno, et al. (15), where treating Indonesian women with both iron plus vitamin A for 8 weeks almost doubles the increase in hemoglobin compared with giving iron alone, are shown in **Table 15.1**. To date it has not been possible to demonstrate a mechanism by which vitamin A deficiency interferes directly in red cell synthesis to cause anemia. A prevalence study to investigate the association of inflammatory markers with anemia and iron and vitamin A deficiencies in preschool children in the Republic of the Marshall Islands found no evidence that inflammation was a risk factor for anemia (16). However, recent work in Zanzibar showed that hemoglobin synthesis followed a reduction in inflammation when vitamin A was given to pre-school children (17), which supports the hypothesis suggested earlier that the hemopoietic effect of vitamin A supplements was due to the reduction in morbidity (i.e., inflammation) (18).

As **Figure 15.1** indicates, there are a number of other dietary factors in addition to deficiencies of vitamin A and iron that can contribute to anemia. These factors are only summarized here, as their roles and importance are discussed in other chapters. In addition, and in contrast to vitamin A, there is less evidence to suggest that supplements of other micronutrients reduce the prevalence of morbidity or mortality, that is, influence the infectious etiology of anemia. Vitamin C has been shown to promote the absorption of vegetable sources of iron by reducing ferric to ferrous forms and increasing its solubility (19). Vitamin C status is often marginal, as dietary sources are usually dependent on seasonal supplies of vegetables and fruit. Folate and vitamin B_{12} are necessary for erythropoiesis and the synthesis of DNA. Green vegetables are also an important source of folate (20), and animal products, which are often in short supply in developing countries, are the main source of vitamin B_{12}. Riboflavin deficiency is often extensive in countries where dairy foods are poorly available, and may impose limitations on absorption and utilization of iron (21). Vitamin B_6, or pyridoxine, is also required in erythropoiesis for the synthesis of heme. Several forms of vitamin B_6 exist in the diet, so the supply is not usually limiting. Obviously, adequate supplies of protein and energy are needed for the proper growth and development of both children and adults, but very often the foods providing these nutrients also contain the main dietary component that reduces the bioavailability of dietary iron, namely phytate (19). Cereals frequently contain large amounts of phytate that bind to divalent cations like iron and zinc, making them largely unavailable for absorption. Overlying all these factors, however, is the fact that disease reduces appetite. The more frequently a child is sick, the more likely he is to be malnourished.

Anemia is very common in the developing world from an early age. However, infants are rarely anemic at birth. The relatively hypoxic conditions *in utero* results in high hemoglobin concentrations at birth, but as the oxygenation of infant blood improves, erythropoiesis ceases and hemoglobin concentrations drop over the first 2 months of life, mainly due to hemodilution as infants grow and natural red cell senescence (22). Thus by the age of 4 to 6 months, iron stores are marginal or depleted and the supply and bioavailability of dietary iron becomes critical. Up to 4 months of age, breast milk is the main source of dietary iron and protective immune factors for growing infants but, as intake of complementary foods increases so does exposure to environmental pathogens and the frequency of bouts of illness (4, 23). Such infants are dependent on good sources of dietary iron to maintain hematological status since iron absorption will be minimal during periods of anorexia and is blocked by fever and inflammation (7, 8). The greatest risk of iron deficiency occurs in those areas where dietary

Table 15.1: Impact of vitamin A and iron on hemoglobin in Indonesian women. Data from Suharno et al. (15).

Treatment	Number	Start	Mean Hb g/L 8 weeks	Increase
Placebo	62	103	105	
Vitamin A*	63	103	109	3.7***
Iron**	63	103	113	7.7***
Vitamin A and iron	63	103	118	12.8***

*   2.4 mg vitamin A/day for 8 weeks
**   60 mg iron/day for 8 weeks
***   Significant change in hemoglobin concentrations (paired t-test)

phytate is high because cereals are the staple food, where little meat is available, and where intake of vitamin C is low due to a lack of or seasonal shortages of fruit or vegetables, conditions that are common in much of the developing world.

Although the frequency of infectious episodes declines as humoral immunity develops (4) and food intake in older children is less influenced by infectious diseases, maintenance of iron stores can be jeopardized by iron losses. Iron in the body is tightly conserved but the risk of schistosomal or hookworm infections increases with age and these parasites can cause chronic bleeding. Iron loss is especially important in school-aged children, in whom the heaviest infestations are likely to occur. Thus infectious diseases, gut parasites, and poor diet combine to deprive children of iron from early infancy, and it is not surprising that 40–50% of children under 14 years of age and women of child-bearing age in developing countries suffer from anemia (1). Children aged 5–14 years and pregnant women are at highest risk of anemia, with estimated prevalences of 48 and 52%, respectively. In general, the prevalence of anemia is highest in southern Asia, although in eastern Africa, the prevalence of anemia in children has been estimated at 75% (24) and in a recent study reported from West Africa, 90% of Gambian infants were reported to have anemia at 12 months of age (25). However, the majority of this anemia is mild anemia and in most people is of little health consequence due to a number of compensatory mechanisms such as increased cardiac output, diversion of blood flow to essential organs and a greater release of oxygen from hemoglobin. Nevertheless, some evidence suggests that mild anemia impairs cognitive capacity in children (26), increases the risk of preterm delivery in pregnancy, and reduces work output in all individuals (27), but the health risks are less than those with severe (hemoglobin [Hb] <70 g/L) or moderate-to-severe (Hb 71–90 g/L) anemia (27, 28). This is not to say that mild ane-

mia is not of public health importance, but the removal of mild anemia may require strategies different to those needed for more severe anemias. It is important to note that the anemia of inflammation is usually mild, normochromic, or normocytic, but occasionally can be microcytic with a normal reticulocyte count (29, 30). It is reported in medical practice that ACI is a common cause of childhood anemia (30). The possibility that inflammation may be a main etiological factor responsible for the initiation and for the continuing presence of anemia in developing countries is the main point to be examined in this chapter.

INFLAMMATORY (ACUTE PHASE) RESPONSE AND IRON METABOLISM

Following an external or internal inflammatory stimulus, the cytokines interleukin-1 (IL-1), tumor necrosis factor-alpha (TNF-α), and IL-6 produced by the innate immune system typically orchestrate the inflammatory response. This is characterized by a specific series of local and systemic effects that are collectively grouped under the name "acute phase response" (APR) (31). Local events include vasodilatation, platelet aggregation, neutrophil chemotaxis, and the release of lysosomal enzymes, histamines, kinins, and oxygen radicals. The systemic events comprise such phenomena as fever, hormonal changes (e.g., activation of the pituitary adrenal system), leukocytosis, thrombocytosis, muscle proteolysis, alterations in carbohydrate, lipid, vitamin, and trace mineral metabolism, and changes in the hepatic synthesis of acute phase proteins (APP) (32). Metabolic changes occur in peripheral tissues and the liver to provide additional nutrients like glucose and amino acids to fuel the activated immune system (33). There are specific sites on the hepatocyte that respond to the cytokines IL-1 and TNF-α and others that respond to IL-6. Over a period of 12–24 hours, the liver responds to cytokine exposure by initiating the hepatic APR with the uptake of amino acids and modulation of gluconeogenesis. IL-1 and TNF-α are also important in exerting profound effects on the progression of the APR. Glucocorticoid production is stimulated by TNF-α, and this both enhances hepatic APP production and diminishes IL-1 synthesis by the macrophage (34). The APR is designed to facilitate both the inflammatory and repair processes, and to protect the organism against the potentially destructive action of inflammatory products (34) (e.g., by limiting cytokine production, neutralizing reactive oxygen species [ROS], inhibiting proteinases, etc.) (35). It should be realized that the APR is not just a response to infection but a broad-based response to many different types of tissue injury (e.g., allergic reaction, thermal damage, hypoxia, surgery, malignancy, and muscular damage following excessive exercise) (36). The functions of APP are still being revealed, but in general they are protective and anti-inflammatory and indicate nonspecifically the presence of inflammation, tissue damage, or endotoxins (37).

With the onset of the inflammatory response, the plasma concentrations of several nutrients, including serum iron, fall rapidly irrespective of nutritional status while a few (e.g., copper) increase (38). In addition, the increase in serum ferritin concentrations was shown to parallel the rapid rise in the APP C-reactive protein (CRP) (39). Both the hypoferremia of infection and the rise in serum ferritin concentrations have recently been shown to be the consequence of induction of hepcidin expression through STAT3 brought about by the action of the inflammatory cytokine IL-6 on hepatocytes (40, 41). Hepcidin is a small polypeptide that can be increased one hundredfold during infections and inflammation, causing a decrease in serum iron levels and contributing to the development of the anemia of inflammation (42). In a mixed group of subjects including those with ACI, iron overload, iron deficiency, and hemochromatosis, urinary hepcidin concentrations strongly correlated with serum ferritin con-

centrations (41). Hepcidin controls plasma iron concentration and tissue distribution of iron by inhibiting intestinal iron absorption, iron recycling by macrophages, and iron mobilization from hepatic stores. Hepcidin acts by inhibiting cellular iron efflux through binding to and inducing the degradation of ferroportin, the sole known cellular iron exporter (43). Any detrimental consequence of these changes in the biomarkers of nutritional status in the short term is probably minimal (44). The changes probably protect the organism from the effects of infection either by conserving nutrients or altering the serum environment to reduce its desirability or the nutritional support it provides to invading pathogens. However, if infection is prolonged or the patient is malnourished at the outset, then a further reduction in the concentration of a circulating nutrient caused by a pathogen may well impair tissue functions, possibly producing or worsening a nutritional deficiency. The resultant deficiency may also impair the body's ability to deal with the infection, as described below.

Iron affects lymphocyte activation and proliferation and how macrophages handle iron. The proliferative phase of lymphocyte activation is an iron-requiring step, as iron is essential for enzymes such as ribonucleotide reductase, which is involved in DNA synthesis. Hence a large number of clinical studies have found reduced T cell function *in vivo* as manifested by impaired skin-test reactions and reduced *in vitro* proliferation of T cells in iron deficient individuals (45). The extent to which mild anemia, the major problem in developing countries (27), impairs lymphocyte proliferation and impairs immune responses is more difficult to ascertain.

The hypoferremia of infection is accompanied by changes in plasma concentrations of several iron-binding proteins **(Table 15.2)** that facilitate the uptake of iron by the reticulo-endothelial system or removal and reutilization of hemoglobin from effete erythrocytes. The regulation of iron

Table 15.2: Changes in some important protein concentrations in plasma and urine accompanying the hypoferremia of inflammation. Modified from references (38, 39, 41, 52).

Protein (units)	Normal range	Production and function	Concentration response in inflammation
Plasma transferrin (g/L) (µmol/L)	1.9–2.58 25–34	Binds and transports iron	Decrease ~30%
Plasma ferritin (µg/L) (nmol/L)	15–250 0.034–0.562	Rise in concentration parallels rise in CRP at start of disease but remains elevated for some time when CRP falls; binds iron in plasma; stores iron in tissue	Rapid increase with onset of inflammation: can rise 30x (6.7 nmol/L).
Plasma lactoferrin (µg/L)	0.91–0.448	Rapid increase in plasma in parallel with increase in white blood cell count; released from granulocytes at sites of inflammation in tissues; transports iron and binds iron especially at low pH in inflammatory lesions	Increase 2–5x
Plasma ceruloplasmin (g/L)	0.155–0.529	Rises slowly over 2–5 days; converts Fe^{2+} to Fe^{3+}	Increases 30–60%
Plasma haptoglobin (g/L) (µmol/L)	0.703–3.79 7.0–37.9	Synthesized by hepatocytes; binds hemoglobin	Increases 2–5x
Urinary hepcidin µg/g creatinine	<10	Rapid increase at onset of inflammation in response to release of IL-6; hepcidin controls plasma iron concentration and tissue distribution of iron by inhibiting intestinal iron absorption, iron recycling by macrophages, and iron mobilization from hepatic stores	Can increase 100x (range 40–900)

metabolism is normally under the control of iron-regulatory proteins (IRP) that bind to sequences on mRNA and protect it from degradation. In iron deficiency, IRP binds to mRNA and promotes the expression of transferrin receptor protein, and ferritin synthesis is repressed. Hence, the utilization and absorption of iron is increased. When iron is adequate, intracellular ferritin synthesis is promoted and iron storage occurs (46). However, in infection the normal control of iron metabolism is reorganized by IL-1, TNF-α, and IL-6, probably through hepcidin. Plasma ferritin levels increase in spite of hypoferremia since ferritin mRNA is sensitive to both iron and cytokines. Rat hepatoma cells exposed to IL-1 and TNF-α doubled the amounts of ferritin released into the medium over 24 and 48 hours (47) and others have reported that TNF-α in particular promoted ferritin translation, resulting in increased iron storage in human monocytic cell lines (48).

It was initially suggested that the hypoferremia of infection protected the host by reducing the iron available for bacterial growth (49). While this may be true for some bacteria, other pathogenic bacteria have powerful siderophores enabling them to compete quite successfully against the iron-binding proteins in the plasma (50). However, hypoferremia may have anti-inflammatory benefits linked to its potential influence on the redox status in the tissues (51). Hypoferremia may protect against the potential prooxidant properties of iron and exacerbation of tissue damage at sites of inflammation (52). In this connection it is interesting to point out that lactoferrin is secreted by neutrophils at sites of inflammation (**Table 15.2**). Lactoferrin has a higher affinity for iron than transferrin and can also bind iron under acid conditions such as those found at sites of inflammation (50, 53). In addition, plasma ascorbate concentrations are reduced in inflammation (54, 55). Vitamin C catalyzes the prooxidant activity of iron (i.e., it converts ferric to ferrous iron), therefore the reduction of both serum vita-

min C and iron concentrations can be considered anti-inflammatory.

Alternatively, *in vitro* studies show that hypoferremia stimulates the effects of IFN-γ on T helper cells and of TNF-α in macrophages with a net effect of increasing cytotoxicity in macrophages (56). In a low iron environment, IFN-γ, TNF-α, IL-1, or lipopolysaccharides (LPS) induce macrophage nitric oxide synthase (NOS) and nitric oxide is central to macrophage-mediated cytotoxicity (57). The mechanisms involved here are clearly complex. Nitric oxide would normally be expected to increase expression of transferrin receptors on macrophages and repress NOS (58, 59). However, recent work suggests that nitric oxide appears to ameliorate rather than potentiate iron sequestration in stimulated macrophages. It is suggested that the major source of iron uptake by stimulated macrophages is phagocytosis of effete erythrocytes, and that iron acquired by the phagocytic route is released more slowly than that from transferrin (60). Hence stimulated macro-phages both store iron and display enhanced NOS activity characteristic of hypoferremia.

Earlier in this section, we indicated that iron was essential for lymphocyte proliferation, but it is also apparent that hypoferremia promotes macrophage cytotoxicity. Does mild anemia benefit the host against infection? There may be no simple answer to this question, and different diseases may pose different demands on host responses. However, there are many reports of adverse consequences following both parenteral and oral iron treatment in environments where there is also a high risk of disease, as in developing countries (10, 61–63) particularly in children with malnutrition (64) and malaria (65, 66). In our own experience with Pakistani infants who received oral iron daily for 3 months, there was evidence of more inflammation in those who received the iron, but this was most obvious in those with the lower plasma retinol concentrations (67). The important role of vitamin A supplements in treating iron deficiency anemia was mentioned earlier, thus no nutrient should be considered on its own. Nevertheless, mild anemia in groups where there is high exposure to infection may be more of an advantage than a disadvantage and caution should be exercised, especially before iron treatment is given.

INFECTIOUS DISEASES, INFECTIONS BY GUT AND OTHER PARASITES AND ANEMIA

As indicated above, anemia can result from a difficulty in absorbing iron through: 1) insufficient dietary iron; 2) poorly bioavailable dietary iron; 3) inflammation; and 4) iron loss. In this section, evidence for the presence of inflammation asso-ciated with common diseases and of the factors responsible for iron losses will be discussed. We have previously shown that variable numbers of apparently healthy children and adults in different populations display evidence of raised APP that serve as markers for sub-clinical inflammation (68). Three of these proteins are particularly useful: CRP, α_1-antichymotrypsin (ACT) and α_1-acid glycoprotein (AGP, also known as

orosomucoid). CRP and ACT are the more acute markers of inflammation, increasing within the first 6 hours of infection, reaching their maximum concentrations within 24 to 48 hours, and usually falling as clinical signs start to disappear (37, 69). Serum AGP concentrations, on the other hand, are much slower to rise and only achieve maximum concentrations 2 to 5 days after infection (37). Thus AGP is a more chronic marker of inflammation than the other two. Using these proteins it is possible to identify persons in an apparently healthy population who may be incubating a disease (raised CRP or ACT and a normal AGP concentration), have recently recovered from a disease (i.e., early convalescence) (raised CRP or ACT and raised AGP), or are in later convalescence (raised AGP only) (68, 70). Where these proteins are increased, they indicate that iron metabolism is disturbed and that the alterations in iron metabolism caused by inflammation may be contributing to the prevalence of anemia in the population. For example, in 418 apparently healthy Indonesian infants (10 months of age) with no inflammation present, mean ferritin concentration was 14.7 µg/L, but in 26% of infants where either or both CRP and AGP were increased, mean serum ferritin was more than doubled **(Table 15.3)** (71). Overall in this population,

Table 15.3: Influence of inflammation on plasma ferritin concentrations in apparently healthy Indonesian infants and "Kenyan adults". Data from Thurnham et al. (70).

Subjects	Plasma ferritin concentrations µg/L			
	No inflammation	Raised acute phase proteins		
		CRP[1]	CRP and AGP	AGP[2]
Indonesian infants*	14.7	32.1	34.3	34.2
Kenyan adults	166	266	1004	309

[1] C-reactive protein
[2] α_1-acid glycoprotein
* Data shown are mean ferritin concentrations (71) and data from Thurnham, et al. (70).

50.2% of infants were anemic (Hb <120 g/L) and the high prevalence of subclinical inflammation in the apparently healthy infants suggests that inflammation in that community is very likely to be linked with the high prevalence of anemia. In contrast, in the apparently healthy Kenyan adults, there was very little anemia in the group, but all the subjects in the study were HIV-1 positive and there were much larger differences in ferritin concentrations between the different subgroups with inflammation.

CAUSE OF ANEMIA–PRIMARILY INFLAMMATION

Malnutrition

Malnutrition as defined by a dietary iron deficiency is obviously a cause of anemia. However, it has also been suggested that there is an increased risk of anemia in an underweight child(72). Growth faltering in childhood is common in developing countries and has been linked to disease (73, 74), thus the issues should be discussed in this chapter.

Impaired intestinal permeability and mucosal injury was shown to be strongly related to growth faltering in apparently healthy Gambian infants (2–15 months of age) (73) and similar results have been observed in underweight but apparently healthy children in many other developing countries (75–79). Malnutrition per se was unlikely to have been responsible for the mucosal damage found in the Gambian children, as the infants were breastfed throughout the study and estimates of food intake could not account for the growth faltering observed. Instead, the authors suggested that the gut injury was due to infection, which in turn would make the gut susceptible to further injury (e.g., by bacterial overgrowth or absorption of bacteria, toxins, etc.), and hence slow to repair (73, 80).

If the etiology of gut injury is infection in underweight but apparently healthy children, then ACI is also likely to be present. This scenario may explain the recent report that being underweight (-2 z-scores weight-for-age) in Ghanian children (odds ratio [OR] 1.83; 1.51–2.21) was a more powerful predictor of anemia than of malaria (OR 1.63; 1.38–2.04) (72). The data were obtained from two large cross-sectional studies in the dry and wet seasons in northern Ghana (n=2,109 and 2,119, respectively) where the incidence of malaria episodes was 2.8 cases/child/year. However, although the data were prevalence data, being underweight represents repeated infections and probably poor gut integrity, whereas malaria was the status at a single point in time. That is, being underweight would be more strongly related to anemia than to malarial infection.

One further point of interest regarding gut per-meability was the observation that iron supplements given to Zambian girls (mean age 10.2 years), as part of a randomized iron or multi-micronutrient (without iron) trial, increased gut injury (P=0.025) (79). The observations were made at a follow-up 10 months later to assess the effect of the interventions. There was no effect of multi-micronutrient supplementation, and no interaction between the interventions. The authors suggest that the finding could be one of the mechanisms explaining the negative effects of medicinal iron supplementation on morbidity found in some other studies.

Diarrheal, respiratory, and febrile disease

Diarrhea is a symptom of many common bacterial and viral infections, including those caused by gut parasites such as *Giardia lamblia, Ascaris lumbricoides*, hookworm species, etc. It is usually not a direct cause of iron loss unless there is extensive damage to the gut mucosa and bloody diarrhea results, as for example in Shigella dysentery. In general, diarrhea results in the loss of water and salts and, as it is caused by infections, it is likely to be accompanied by an inflammatory response.

Any inflammatory response will impair iron metabolism by its effects on iron mobilization and absorption, and the risk of anemia will be related to the frequency, severity, and proximity of the diarrheal episodes. This is illustrated by the studies in Palestinian refugee camps in Syria, Jordan, the West Bank, Gaza Strip, and Lebanon, where between 54 and 75% of children aged 6 to 35 months) were anemic (Hb<110 g/L). The factors associated were poor socioeconomic status and recent diarrheal and febrile illnesses. However, the same children had a 30% greater risk of being anemic if they had fever or diarrhea currently or within the last 14 days, and a 120% greater risk of anemia if they had both symptoms (81).

The presence of elevated markers of inflammation in apparently healthy infants and children is evidence of a recent or a current subclinical infection. Rousham, et al. (82) found elevated plasma ACT concentrations in apparently healthy Bangladeshi preschool children whose mothers reported diarrhea or fever in their child in the previous two weeks. Filteau, et al. (3) found diarrhea in the previous week to be associated with several elevated APP in Ghanaian preschool children, and Panter-Brick, et al. (83) reported that stunting was significantly associated with high plasma ACT concentrations in Nepalese village boys (10–12 years of age) even though morbidity appeared low. Northrop-Clewes et al. (84) reported elevated serum ACT concentrations in >50% apparently-healthy Gambian infants throughout the year and especially high concentrations in the rainy season, when the prevalence of diarrhea, skin diseases, and malaria was particularly high (75). Childhood anemia is a problem in all these communities (72, 85–87).

HIV
Adults get infected with HIV through sexual contact (hetero- and homosexual), intravenous drug use, and transfusions of blood or blood-derived products. Adolescents get the infection by the same routes, although associations with drug use are probably the most frequent. Children get infected most frequently through vertical (mother to fetus) transmission and most of those on delivery (70%). The risk of infection associated with breastfeeding is reported to be 14–30% (88).

Most children infected by their mothers demonstrate no symptoms during the neonatal period, although many will develop the disease in their first year of life. The first clinical symptoms of HIV in the infected child are nonspecific. Fever, generalized lymph node enlargement, persistent diarrheas, recurrent persistent bacterial infections of the upper respiratory tract, sinuses, or ears are common early symptoms in HIV-infected children. As the disease progresses, moderate clinical symptoms become apparent, including anemia (Hb<80 g/L), thrombocytopenia, recurrent or chronic diarrhea, fever for extended periods, bacterial pneumonia, sepsis, meningitis, etc. (88).

Results from the Multistate Adult and Adolescent Spectrum of HIV Disease Surveillance Project found that the incidence of anemia in the US was associated with the clinical stage of disease (89). Baseline prevalence data suggested that anemia (Hb<100g/L) was 1% (men) to 6% (women) in individuals with HIV but not AIDS, and the 1-year incidence of anemia (i.e., new diagnoses 6 to 18 months after baseline) in individuals with HIV but not AIDS was 3.2%, or 12.1% in those with immunologic but not clinical AIDS (<200 CD4 counts/μL). Thus etiology of anemia in HIV/AIDS is probably linked to the generalized inflammation as the disease progresses, together with the frequent opportunistic infections inhibiting absorption and mobilization of any stored iron. In our own data from apparently healthy HIV-1 positive Kenyan adults who had not yet developed clinical signs of AIDS, 21% of women and 10% of men had low Hb (<100 g/L) (unpublished data), but there was already a major impact of subclinical inflammation on plasma ferritin concentrations (**Table 15.3**) (70). These data indicate the rapid effect of inflammation on plasma ferritin concentrations but relatively slower effect on hemoglobin.

Tuberculosis

Tuberculosis (TB) is the most common life-threatening infection in persons infected with HIV and frequently occurs before the onset of severe immunodeficiency. Development of TB is associated with increased HIV-1 viral load, a fall in CD4 lymphocyte counts, and increased mortality. One in every four HIV-1 infected persons in the world is diagnosed with active TB, making TB the most frequent life-threatening co-infection in HIV-1 infected patients. Unlike other opportunistic infections, TB develops throughout the course of HIV-1, and the virological control of HIV-1 replication during dual HIV-1/TB co-infection is less amenable to treatment of TB than other opportunistic infections (90). TB was also reported to be one of the more common abnormalities associated with HIV/AIDS in pediatric Polish patients (88).

Anemia is common among adults with pulmonary TB and HIV infection in sub-Saharan Africa. A study to characterize the factors associated with the pathogenesis of anemia among 370 HIV-positive and 130 HIV-negative adults in Zomba district, Malawi, found that low selenium concentrations, high HIV load, and high IL-6 concentrations were associated with anemia (91). In this study the prevalence of anemia in the HIV-positive and HIV-negative patients was 88 and 77%, respectively (P=0.002), and moderate to severe anemia (Hb <80 g/L) occurred in 30 and 15%, respectively (P=0.001). High concentrations of the pro-inflammatory cytokine IL-6 and HIV load are obviously linked to an inflammatory response but so also may be the low concentrations of serum selenium (92). The high prevalence of anemia in the HIV-negative controls suggests that other factors may be implicated in the etiology of the anemia that were not measured in this study.

Malaria

Despite considerable progress in malaria control over the past decade, malaria remains a serious problem, particularly in sub-Saharan Africa, where about 90% of clinical cases occur. Malaria, either alone or in combination with other diseases, is estimated to kill between 1.1 and 2.7 million people worldwide each year, and over 2,400 million remain at risk (93).

Humans acquire parasites of the genus *Plasmodium* through a mosquito "bite". The parasite passes through a series of asexual stages, which occur successively in the cells of the liver, in the erythrocytes, and transiently free in the plasma. Maturation of the parasite within the red cell is followed by its rupture and is associated with fever and sweating and the liberation of new merozoites that infect new red cells. Sexual forms are eventually formed in the human host, but transfer to another human host must take place through the medium of the mosquito. In the mosquito, the parasite undergoes an equally complicated sexual cycle that involves passage through or development within a number of the invertebrate host's tissues and organs.

The three main species of malaria parasites that infect humans are *Plasmodium falciparum, P. vivax* and *P. malariae*. Of these, *P. falciparum* is by far the most serious and debilitating. A variety of abnormalities in the number, morphology, and function of blood and bone marrow cells may be found in *P. falciparum* and *P. vivax* malaria. In a nonimmune individual, the nature of such abnormalities depends on the time after infection. In others, it is determined by the pattern and intensity of malaria transmission in the area and the extent of host immunity. Severe anemia may occur in children with chronic *falciparum* malaria and low parasitemia, as well as in patients with complicated acute *falciparum* malaria and high parasitemia. However, the mechanisms underlying the anemia in these two situations appear to be different (94).

Inflammation and the parasites' utilization of red cell hemoglobin for growth play major roles in the etiology of anemia in acute uncomplicated malaria. The importance of inflammation was shown in a study of Indian children (2–11 years of age) who had severe, mild, asymptomatic, and no malaria. Mean hemoglobin, ferritin, albumin, and ceruloplasmin concentrations are shown in **Table 15.4** (95). The data show the strong influence of inflammation on the results, and that even asymptomatic malaria was associated with hemoglobin concentrations significantly lower than those associated with no malaria. A serum ferritin concentration <12 µg/L is an indicator of low iron stores but although anemia (Hb <100 g/L) was present in 60 and 92% of the groups with mild and severe malaria, mean ferritin values were 165 and 410 µg/L respectively, indicating that ferritin was behaving as a positive APP in the presence of the malaria infection. In fact, a multiple regression analysis showed that two acute phase markers, ceruloplasmin (positive) and albumin (negative), together with parasite count, explained 59% of the variance in the serum ferritin concen-

trations. Although the percentage of red cells infected in malaria is usually small, anemia probably results from a blockage in the replacement of red cells by inhibition of absorption and mobilization of iron and inhibition of hematopoiesis. In addition, some lysis of uninfected red cells also occurs and although hemoglobin released is bound to haptoglobin or sequestered by macrophages for re-use, replacing lost cells will be inhibited and the anemia will progressively worsen while infection or re-infection continues. In severe malaria, the presence of hematuria can also occur, so blood loss can also contribute to the anemia.

A study done in Tanzanian children also illustrates the influence of inflammation on the development of anemia (96). Acute malaria is an illness whose incidence and severity are largely dependent on age. To gain a better understanding of the inflammatory responses to malaria in children of different ages, 273 Ugandan children (2–120 months of age) presenting acute uncomplicated malaria were monitored at enrolment and

Table 15.4: Biomarkers of iron status and inflammation in Indian children with and without malaria. Data from Das et al. (95).

Biomarkers	No malaria	Malaria cases		
		Asymptomatic	Mild	Severe
Number	50	23	50	50
Age	7.8	7.5	7.7	7.7
Albumin g/L	45.5[a*]	39.3[b]	37[b]	31.3[c]
Ceruloplasmin U/L	197[a]	218[a]	273[b]	311[c]
Hemoglobin g/L	121[a]	99[b]	97[b]	73[c]
Ferritin µg/L	27[a]	39[b]	165[c]	410[d]
Hemoglobin % <100 g/L	18	52	60	92

Unlike superscripts indicate significant differences between group means on the same row. (ANOVA followed by Newman-Keuls test P<0.05).

3 and 7 days later. Younger children had higher geometric mean erythropoietin, TNF-α, and AGP concentrations than older children. Univariate regression analysis revealed that age, serum log(10) erythropoietin concentrations, IL-10/TNF-α ratio, and AGP concentrations were each significantly associated with hemoglobin concentration at baseline. Hemoglobin concentrations were inversely correlated with the log(10) erythropoietin concentrations at all three visits. For the older age groups, higher concentrations of TNF-α were significantly associated with higher IL-10 levels at all three visits, but this relationship was significant only at baseline for younger children (96). IL-10 is an anti-inflammatory and immunosuppressive substance and these data suggest that younger children may regulate IL-10 production in order not to suppress the production of inflammatory cytokines. Younger children are more dependent on innate immunity (i.e., cell-mediated immunity) to protect themselves from invading pathogens. With the development of humoral immunity in the older children, a strong inflammatory response that may damage host tissue as well as the parasite may be contraindicated, hence IL-10 secretion is better matched to the production of TNF-α throughout the duration of the infection.

Systemic inflammation and gut parasites

Evidence of systemic inflammation associated with gut parasites is sparse. Workers have reported that infection of rats with *Schistosoma mansoni* or *Nippostrongylus brasiliensis* led to an increase in serum CRP concentrations coincident with worm passage through the animals' lungs, and a second peak of APP changes seen in *N. brasiliensis* infection at the time of intestinal pathology was greater than that seen during the lung phase (97). However, in 120 Indonesian children (8–11 years of age) chronically infected with the soil-acquired parasites *Ascaris lumbricoides* and *Trichuris trichiura,* plasma concentrations of IL-1, IL-6, TNF-α, and CRP and erythrocyte sedimentation rate (ESR) were all normal both before and 10 days after treatment with albendazole. All children were infected with one of the worms and in 70% of cases with both. Treatment removed all Ascaris, but in 46% of the treatment group (n=27) *Trichuris* remained. Mean white blood cell count was elevated at baseline, and both treatment and placebo groups increased by the same amount over the 10, days suggesting an influence of some external factor and not worm burden. Worm burdens were generally low in the population (*Ascaris* ~2500 eggs/g, *Trichuris* 160 eggs/g) and the data suggest that the intestinal worms had no systemic effects on the hosts (98).

However, the inflammatory markers measured in the study by Karyadi, et al. (98) were mainly markers of acute inflammation. Some workers have found associations between plasma albumin concentration (a slow-reacting negative APP) or ACT (a positive APP (69)) and worm burdens. Low serum albumin concentrations were reported in Egyptian children infected with Ascaris and other parasites (97) and following treatment with pyrantel pamoate (Pfizer) or mebendazole (Janssen) (respectively) serum albumin concentrations rose in *Ascaris*-infected Bangladeshi children (8–11 years of age) (99) and ACT concentrations fell in Bangladeshi children (2–5 years of age) (100). The latter results possibly indicate that there is a low-grade, systemic, inflammatory response in children chronically infected with intestinal parasites. Whether this response is strong enough to influence hemoglobin concentrations needs further investigation, possibly using AGP to measure any inflammation.

CAUSE OF ANEMIA: PRIMARILY BLOOD LOSS

Schistosomiasis

Schistosomiasis is a chronic and debilitating disease which is draining the economic development in much of the tropics, where it is concentrated.

Table 15.5: Distribution and location of parasites causing blood loss in human hosts.

Parasite	Number of persons exposed (x 10^6)	Major locations	Blood loss mL/worm/day*
Ancylostoma duodenale	1277	Global, tropical, and subtropical	0.15
Necator Amerikanus			0.03
Trichuris trichiura	900	Global, tropical, and subtropical	0.005
Schistosoma mansoni	70	Africa, Middle East, S. America	NR
Schistosoma japonicum	95	China and Philippines	NR
Schistosoma haematobium	100	Sub-Saharan Africa	0.11 to 3.8

* Loss of blood in 24 hours calculated from iron in urine of children passing 100 eggs/10 mL urine and assuming 1.85 mg iron is obtained from 5 mL blood (131). NR means not reported.

An estimated 200 million people are infected and another 600 million live in endemic areas **(Table 15.5)**. Sustained heavy infection leads to morbidity, contributes to anemia, and often results in retarded growth and reduced physical and cognitive function in children (101).

Three major species of the trematode blood flukes of the genus *Schistosoma* are associated with blood loss: *S. mansoni, S. japonicum* and *S. haematobium.* The distribution and numbers affected are shown in **Table 15.5**. All species of schistosomes have a two-host life cycle involving a human and a particular species of snail for each of the *Schistosoma* species. Schistosome eggs in the feces or urine of the infested host hatch when they come in contact with fresh water and the larvae find and penetrate the skin of the snail. The larvae multiply asexually in the snail's digestive gland to produce thousands of cercariae, which are released back into fresh water. When a cercaria comes in contact with human skin, it rapidly burrows through the tissue into the blood stream, where it matures. Eventually, the female *S. mansoni* and *S. japonicum* settle in the mesenteric

blood vessels around the intestine, while *S. haematobium* lives in blood vessels around the bladder. Worms are reported to live 3–5 years (102).

Although adult *Schistosoma* flukes feed on blood in the vessels around the bladder and intestine, the anemia caused by schistosomes is mainly due to blood loss caused by the parasite's eggs. Female schistosomes release their eggs into the smallest blood vessels they can reach, where many eggs become wedged. The surface of each egg is co-vered with sharp spines, and these help to cut into the lumen of the gut or bladder as the eggs are forced through the vessel walls. In *S. haematobium* infection, the site of penetration bleeds into the bladder, making the urine pink or even red (hematuria). Typically, however, the color is usually seen in only the last few drops, but the prevalence of urinary hematuria can be used to estimate the prevalence of *S. haematobium.*

The relationship between iron status and degree of infection by *S. haematobium* was studied in 174 schoolchildren from Niger in an area endemic for urinary schistosomiasis. Iron deficiency was defined by a low serum ferritin level combined with either a low transferrin saturation or a high erythrocyte protoporphyrin level, or both. Hematuria and proteinuria were found in 76.4% and 79.9% of the children, respectively, while 95.4% excreted eggs (geometric mean egg count of 31.5 eggs per 10 ml of urine). The prevalences of anemia, iron deficiency, and iron deficiency anemia were 59.7, 47.1, and 57.7%. The hemoglobin level and transferrin saturation decreased significantly when the degree of hematuria increased, while prevalence of anemia and prevalence of iron deficiency increased significantly. The hemoglobin level and the hematocrit were negatively correlated with egg count, while prevalence of anemia increased with increasing egg count. This inverse relationship between degree of infection by *S. haematobium* and iron status shows a deleterious consequence of urinary schistosomiasis for nutrition and hematopoietic status (103).

Hookworm infection

Hookworms are soil-transmitted nematode worms, and it is estimated that 1.3 billion people are affected by them **(Table 15.5)**. Two species are of public health importance, *Ancylostoma duodenale* and *Necator americanus*. Both worms have similar life cycles and habits and eggs from the two species cannot be distinguished when examining feces under a microscope (102). To identify the species it is necessary to either culture the stool and characterize the larvae or expel the worms from the gut using an anthelmintic drug and recover them from the feces. Both methods are time-consuming, difficult and impractical.

The number of hookworm eggs excreted by the infected individual is proportional to the worm burden. However, several factors complicate the relationship. Egg counts are expressed per gram in feces, but precise measurements are difficult to obtain. In a study in rural Kenyan individuals harboring hookworm as well as *A. lumbri-*

coides and *T. trichiura*, there was considerable variation in egg counts from the same stool as well as over the five-day period (104). It is estimated that a mature fertilized female *N. americanus* produces 3,000–6,000 eggs/day, while estimates for *A. duodenale* have been reported at 10,000–20,000 eggs/day, although fecundity is reduced by the presence of other worms. Eggs mature and hatch under warm humid conditions in about five days and can live for several weeks. A life cycle starts when a mature larva on the ground comes in contact with human skin. It penetrates the skin and migrates through the blood to the lungs, where it is coughed up and swallowed. The worms then attach to the walls of the duodenum or jejunum, using sharp "teeth" in its buccal cavity to cut into the tissues. The worm secretes an anticoagulant and feeds on blood and tissue fluids. It may move to a new site several times a day, and each time the anticoagulant causes the site to continue bleeding. The worms may also contribute to anemia by virtue of being sited in the duodenum and jejunum, where most iron is absorbed. Moderate or heavy worm burdens may impair appetite and the anemia may reduce human productivity, thus reducing the quality and quantity of the diet (102).

A study of the epidemiology of iron deficiency anemia (IDA) in 3,595 Zanzibari schoolchildren from Pemba Island found that hookworm infection intensity was the strongest explanatory va-riable for hemoglobin, erythrocyte protoporphyrin, and serum ferritin concentrations (105). It has been estimated that a single *A. duodenale* worm is responsible for a loss of 0.15 mL/day, and an *N. americanus* for a loss of 0.03 mL/day. This fivefold difference in blood loss is supported by epidemiological evidence from another study in Pemba Island. In 525 schoolchildren, where the prevalence of hookworm was 94%, Albonico et al. (106) reported the prevalence of anemia (Hb<110 g/L) and serum low ferritin concentrations (<12 μg/L) were both higher in children with ≥50% *A. duodenale* larvae in the cultured feces (80 and 59) than in those with <50% (60.5 and 33%). However, the relationship between the concentration of hookworm eggs in the feces and the level of anemia varies among study sites even in East Africa, where hookworm anemia is a public health problem, indicating that other factors cannot be ignored in studying the etiology. In general both species are said to occur together, though N. americanus may prevail in the tropics and subtropics, whereas *A. duodenale* tends to be found in cooler and drier climates. Worms are reported to live 2–3 years (102).

Trichuriasis

The other widespread species of intestinal nematode associated with anemia is *T. trichiura,* the whipworm. The parasite is found throughout the tropics and subtropics and it is estimated that 900 million people in the world are infected. The whipworm has a direct, soil-transmitted life cycle, and in warm humid conditions, eggs transported in feces develop and become infectious in 2–3 weeks. Mature eggs are transmitted by contaminated food or by unwashed fingers to the mouth and swallowed. The larva hatches in the gut and penetrates the wall of the large intestine. After several stages of development and maturation, the worm develops a filamentous anterior end that remains embedded in the gut wall, while a thicker posterior end is pushed into the intestinal lumen. The worm secretes a pore-forming protein that is believed to create a syncytial tunnel in the cecal epithelium, which helps to anchor the worm and probably provides a source of nutrition from the host. Heavy infections are associated with damage to the mucosa and its blood vessels and result in chronic colitis, mucosal hemorrhaging, dysentery, and occasionally rectal prolapse (107). Worms are reported to live 1–2 years (102).

Although the worms may consume blood as part of their food, the greatest loss of blood occurs as a result of dysentery and damage to the mucosal lining of cecum (107). The amount of blood lost per worm has been estimated as 0.005 mL/day and therefore only heavy infections will contribute to anemia (102). This is illustrated by a study from Jamaica where 409 school children were identified with *T. trichiura* infection (>1,200 eggs/g feces). Only those children with heavy infections (>10,000 eggs/g feces) had a significantly lower mean hemoglobin concentrations than the rest (115 vs. 121 g/L) and the prevalence of anemia in the heavily infected children was 33%, compared to 11% in the rest (P<0.05) (108). Other workers have reported significantly lower hemoglobin concentrations and more anemia in Panamanian schoolchildren at egg counts of >5000/g, and if the *T. trichiura* was accompanied by hookworm, children were significantly more likely to have signs of anemia than those with no or single infections (109). Other workers have also noted that dual species intensity correlation was consistently strong for *T. trichiura* and *A. lumbricoides* (110, 111), but whether this polyparasitism influences the risk of anemia is not known.

Other gut parasite infections

Approximately 1,500 million people are infected with Ascaris, or about 25 % of the world's population. Ascariasis is concentrated in developing countries with poor sanitation and in tropical areas, where the eggs survive the longest in the environment. An estimated 59 million people are at risk of some morbidity, with 1.5 million children suffering from Ascaris infections that will result in permanent growth retardation, even if the infection is cured (112, 113).

A. lumbricoides, the large intestinal round worm, has both free-living and parasitic stages. During its development in the body of the host, it molts through a series of larval stages and passes successively from the gut to the blood stream, the liver, the lungs, the trachea, and finally, via the pharynx, esophagus, and stomach, back to the intestine again. It matures within the lumen of the intestine and passes its resistant eggs to the outside world in the feces. Fingers or food contaminated with infective feces infect a new or reinfect the original host, so the prevalence of infection rises rapidly with age. School-aged children tend to harbor the heaviest infections of *A. lumbricoides, T. trichiura,* and the schistosomes (102). Polyparasitism is common. For example, on the basis of 203 stool sample examinations in three adjacent villages in northern Bangladesh, the prevalence of *Ascarias, Trichuris,* hookworm, and amoebic infections was estimated as 68, 56, 53 and 19%, respectively. Age-specific prevalence data indicated that approximately 90% of the children were harboring patent *Ascaris* infections by the time they were 4 years old (114). Likewise, in a separate study in southeast Madagascar, fecal examinations revealed prevalences of 78% for *A. lumbricoides,* 38% for *T. trichiura,* 16% for hookworm, and 0.4% for *S. mansoni.* Infection intensity was measured indirectly by fecal egg counts and directly by *A. lumbricoides* expulsion following treatment with pyrantel pamoate (Pfizer). The mean *A. lumbricoides* worm burden for children 5–11 years of age was 19.2 (SD=20.4) worms per child, with a median of 13 worms (n=428) (110).

Infection by *A. lumbricoides* has been linked to low hemoglobin concentrations in Zanzibari (105) and Nepalese (115) children. How this worm causes anemia is uncertain, as the worm feeds on gut contents rather than on blood. Infection is associated with poverty and poor diet and it has been reported to cause anorexia (102, 116). Undoubtedly, worms compete with the host for food, and infestation is linked to poor growth (116, 117). Heavy infection may cause malabsorption of iron, as the worm lives in the duodenum or jejunum, where iron absorption occurs, and low-grade inflammation may contribute to ACI, as discussed earlier.

Diphyllobothrium latum is a species of tape worm that specifically causes pernicious anemia. *D. latum* is relatively uncommon and mostly occurs in Scandinavia among people who eat uncooked fish containing plerocercoid larvae. It can grow to 20 meters in length and when present in the jejunum it selectively absorbs cyanocobalamin, hence depriving the host of vitamin B_{12} (118).

INFLAMMATION AND THE TREATMENT OF ANEMIA

Over the last 50 years or so, there have been many community studies where iron supplements were given to reduce the prevalence of anemia. Frequently, there was little benefit, but in a number of these studies there were adverse consequences that have been summarized elsewhere (61). The adverse reactions to iron increased awareness of avoiding iron supplements in rehabilitating malnourished children who had a high risk of infection (64), but even in apparently healthy persons, iron supplements appeared to increase the prevalence of disease. Infection-induced hypoferremia is a well-recognized phenomenon and withholding iron may both prevent growth of pathogens (119) and be anti-inflammatory by reducing a potential prooxidant (120). The recently discovered hepcidin, which is increased by inflammation and blocks absorption and mobilization of iron, is now known to be responsible for the hypoferremia of infection, and that frequent or chronic infection leads to a reduction in hemoglobin (i.e., ACI) (43). ACI is generally a mild anemia (29) and anemia in the developing world is also mainly mild (27). If anemia in apparently healthy persons in the developing world is mainly due to subclinical inflammation, it explains why supplementation with iron is so ineffective in lowering the prevalence of anemia, as iron does not cure infections.

The iron supplementation study in which parenteral iron dextran or a placebo was given to infants at 2 months in an area of high malaria transmission in Papua New Guinea increased the prevalence of malaria, as judged by parasite and spleen rates at follow-ups at 6 and 12 months compared to those in the placebo group (121). In addition, the same workers also reported that in the placebo group, infants with higher birth hemoglobin levels (and thus higher total body iron content) were significantly more likely to have malaria at follow-up and more likely to be admitted to the hospital with malaria (65). That is, both a high "normal" hemoglobin content and receiving additional iron at 2 months of age increased the risk of malaria severity. There is no doubt that all infants in the study were bitten by malaria-positive mosquitoes during the follow-up period, since the studies were done in an area of high malaria prevalence, but the higher iron status increased the risk of that infection becoming serious.

The studies done in Papua New Guinea also showed that infants appeared to be more seriously affected by malaria when given iron supplements than older children. In a separate study in the same area, prepubescent schoolchildren with hemoglobin levels of 80–120 g/L were randomly assigned to receive either 200 mg ferrous sulfate or a placebo twice daily for 16 weeks. Treatment did not significantly affect parasite rate, parasite density, levels of anti-malarial IgG, spleen size, or the number of reported episodes of suspected malaria during the therapy (122). However, infants are more dependent on innate immunity (i.e., the potential inflammatory response to kill invading parasites) than older schoolchildren who are immune or semi-immune. Neopterin is a marker of cell-mediated immunity, and urinary excretion is high in infancy (123) but decreases markedly over the first two years of life in Tanzanian infants (124). Furthermore, pro- and anti-inflammatory cytokines appear to be delicately balanced to produce a more powerful inflammatory response in younger children (96). Thus additional dietary iron given to infants exposed to frequent infections may upset this delicate balance.

Vitamin A supplements have been shown to have hematopoietic properties in children and adults in the absence of additional iron (12–15). It is also now widely accepted that vitamin A supplements in many countries have consistently reduced mortality, overall by 23% (125–127). It is very likely that a reduction in mortality is due to a reduction in morbidity, and certainly the smaller supplementation studies in patients with serious measles showed a reduction in morbidity and a shortening in recovery times (128, 129). If mild anemia in the developing world is mainly due to subclinical inflammation, then providing vitamin A supplements should reduce some of the inflammation and enable iron mobilization to restore hematopoiesis (18). However, hematopoiesis can only occur when dietary iron or iron stores are available, thus in communities or groups where hookworms, schistosomes, and/or whipworms are serious problems, vitamin A alone may have minimal effects on anemia in the absence of added dietary iron.

The international community's increasing awareness of the importance of infection in the etiology of anemia (2) and the recent adverse effects of oral iron supplements in Zanzibar, where malaria and infectious disease are highly prevalent (66), has forced the international community to recognize that iron supplements must be given with caution (130). However, these latest announcements do not appear to have capitalized on the potential importance of vitamin A when supplementing with iron. We previously showed that when iron was given to Pakistani preschool children in a non-malarious area, there was little evidence of increased morbidity as a result of the iron supplement, except in those children with the poorest vitamin A status. In the latter group, there were significantly higher concentrations of the APP ACT postintervention (67). That is, the risk of adverse consequences to iron supplements may be modified by vitamin A status, and it would seem prudent that future iron interventions be preceded by vitamin A supplements with or without anthelminthic treatment according to local conditions.

RESEARCH PRIORITIES

The extent to which inflammation is associated with and responsible for anemia in developing countries is currently not known. One difficulty is the time lag between the hypoferremic state caused by disease and a reduction in hemoglobin. The APP, CRP, and AGP are clinically robust markers of inflammation that will indicate the nature of disease pressures on an apparently healthy population. We suggest that to improve our understanding of why iron supplements are sometime ineffective in communities where there is anemia, the acute phase proteins CRP and AGP should be monitored before and after iron supplementation.

A field-friendly assay kit, similar to those made by HemoCue, is now available for CRP. Similar field-friendly techniques and machines need to be developed to measure serum AGP and urinary hepcidin concentrations.

CDC/WHO (2) recommended serum ferritin concentrations should be used to measure iron status and to measure the impact of iron intervention in populations. However, as ferritin is increased by the APR, the working group recommended that at least one APP be measured together with ferritin. We suggest CRP and AGP should both be included with ferritin measurement, as two APP are more informative than one to interpret plasma retinol concentrations.

There is a need to determine whether worms like *Ascaris* contribute to anemia through inflammation. AGP is a good biomarker of chronic inflammation, but it does not seem to have been used to determine whether intestinal parasites cause chronic inflammation that might influence iron absorption and iron mobilization in the host.

There is evidence that intestinal parasites produce a local inflammatory response in intestinal cells (not discussed in this chapter). Work needs to be done to determine whether hepcidin is produced locally in the gut.

REFERENCES

1. World Health Organization. Iron deficiency anaemia: assessment, prevention and control. A guide for programme managers. Geneva: WHO, 2001. [Distribution no. 01.3]
2. World Health Organization, Center for Disease Control. Assessing the iron status of populations. Geneva: WHO, 2004:1–31.
3. Filteau SM, Morris SS, Raynes JG, et al. Vitamin A supplementation, morbidity, and serum acute-phase proteins in young Ghanaian children. Am J Clin Nutr 1995;62:434–8.
4. Sepulveda J, Willett W, Munoz A. Malnutrition

and diarrhea. A longitudinal study among urban Mexican children. Am J Epidemiol 1988; 127:365–76.
5. Miller M, Humphrey JH, Johnson EJ, Marinda E, Brookmeyer R, Katz J. Why do children become vitamin A deficient? J Nutr 2002;132:2867S–80S.
6. Beisel WR. Trace elements in infectious processes. Med Clin North Am 1976;60:831–49.
7. Beresford CH, Neale RJ, Brooks OG. Iron absorption and pyrexia. Lancet 1971;1:568–72.
8. Bender-Gotze C, Ludwig U, Schafer KH, et al. "Cytochemische Knochenmarksbefunde und diag-

nostische $^{95}Fe^{2+}$ Absorption wahrend des akuten and chronischen Infecter in Kinderalter." Monatssch Kinderheilkd (in German) 1976;124:305–7.

9. Weber J, Werre JM, Julius HW, Marx JJM. Decreased iron absorption in patients with active rheumatoid arthritis, with and without iron deficiency. Ann Rheum Dis 1988;47:404–9.

10. Hershko C, Peto TEA, Weatherall DJ. Iron and infection. BMJ 1988;296:660–4.

11. Hess SY, Thurnham DI, Hurrell RF. Influence of provitamin A carotenoids on iron, zinc and vitamin A status. Washington, DC: International Food Policy Research Institute, HarvestPlus Technical Monographs 6. 2005:1–28.

12. Muhilal, Permeisih D, Idjradinata YR, Muherdiyantiningsih, Karyadi D. Vitamin A-fortified monosodium glutamate and health, growth, and survival of children: a controlled field trial. Am J Clin Nutr 1987;48:1271–6.

13. Mejia LA, Chew F. Hematological effects of supplementing anemic children with vitamin A alone and in combination with iron. Am J Clin Nutr 1988;48:595–600.

14. Mwanri L, Worsley A, Ryan P, Masika J. Supplemental vitamin A improves anemia and growth in anemic school children in Tanzania. J Nutr 2000;130:2691–6.

15. Suharno D, West CE, Muhilal, Karyadi D, Hautvast JGAJ. Supplementation with vitamin A and iron for nutritional anaemia in pregnant women in West Java, Indonesia. Lancet 1993;342:1325–8.

16. Gamble MV, Palafox NA, Dancheck B, Ricks MO, Briand K, Semba RD. Relationship of vitamin A deficiency, iron deficiency, and inflammation to anemia among preschool children in the Republic of the Marshall Islands. Eur J Clin Nutr 2004;58:1396–401.

17. Cusick SL, Tielsch JM, Ramsan M, et al. Short-term effects of vitamin A and antimalarial treatment on erythropoiesis in severely anemic Zanzibari preschool children. Am J Clin Nutr 2005;82:406–12.

18. Thurnham DI. Vitamin A, iron and haematopoiesis. Lancet 1993;342:1312–3.

19. Hallberg L, Brune M, Rossander L. Iron absorption in man: ascorbic acid and dose-dependent inhibition by phytate. Am J Clin Nutr 1989;49:140–4.

20. Bates CJ, Fleming M, Paul AA, Black AE, Mandel AR. Folate status and its relation to vitamin C in healthy elderly men and women. Age Ageing 1980;9:241–8.

21. Powers HJ, Bates CJ. Micronutrient deficiencies in the aetiology of anaemia in a rural area in The Gambia. Trans R Soc Trop Med Hyg 1987;81:421–5.

22. Saarinen UM, Siimes MA. Developmental changes in red blood cell counts and indices of infants after exclusion of iron deficiency by laboratory criteria and continuous iron supplementation. J Pediatr 1978;92:412–6.

23. Rowland MGM, Cole TJ, Whitehead RG. A quantitative study into the role of infection in determining nutritional status in Gambian village children. Brit J Nutr 1977;37:441–50.

24. DeMaeyer EM, Adiels-Tegman M. The prevalence of anemia in the world. World Health Stat Q 1985;38:302–16.

25. Darboe MK, Thurnham DI, Morgan G, et al. Effectiveness of the new IVACG early high-dose vitamin A supplementation scheme compared to the standard WHO protocol: a randomised controlled trial in Gambian mothers and infants. Lancet 2007 (in press).

26. Black MM, Baqui AH, Zaman A, et al. Iron and zinc supplementation promote motor development and exploratory behavior among Bangladeshi infants. Am J Clin Nutr 2004;80:903–10.

27. Stoltzfus RJ. Rethinking anaemia surveillance. Lancet 1997;349:1764–6.

28. Ghattas H, Fulford T, Prentice A. Effect of moderate anaemia on later mortality in rural African children. Lancet 2003;361:2048–50.

29. Means RT Jr. The anaemia of infection. Baillieres Best Pract Res Clin Haematol 2000;13:151–62.

30. Abshire TC. The anemia of inflammation. A common cause of childhood anemia. Pediatr Clin North Am 1996;43:623–37.

31. Baxendale JH, Gauldie J. The acute phase response. Immunol Today 1994;15:74–80.

32. Van Leeuwen MA, Van Rijswijk MH. Acute phase proteins in the monitoring of inflammatory disorders. Baillieres Best Pract Res Clin Rheumatol 1994;8:531–54.

33. Grimble RF. Dietary manipulation of the inflammatory response. Proc Nutr Soc 1992;51:285–94.

34. Steel DM, Whitehead AS. The major acute phase reactants: C-reactive protein, serum amyloid P component and serum amyloid A protein. Immunol Today 1994;15:81–8.

35. Tilg H, Dinarello CA, Mier JW. IL-6 and APPs: anti-inflammatory and immunosuppressive mediators. Immunol Today 1997;18:428–32.

36. Cannon JG, Meydani SN, Fielding RA et al. Acute phase response in exercise. II. Associations between vitamin E, cytokines, and muscle proteolysis. Am J Physiol 1991;260:R1235–R40.

37. Fleck A, Myers MA. Diagnostic and prognostic significance of acute phase proteins. In: Gordon AH, Koj A, eds. The acute phase response to injury and infection. Amsterdam: Elsevier Scientific Publishers, 1985:249–71.

38. Thurnham DI, Northrop-Clewes CA. Effects of infection on nutritional and immune status. In: Hughes DA, Darlington LG, Bendich A, eds. Diet and human immune function. Totowa, NJ: Humana Press, 2004:35–64.

39. Feelders RA, Vreugdenhil G, Eggermont AMM, Kuiper-Kramer PA, van Eijk HG, Swaak AJG. Regulation of iron metabolism in the acute-phase response: interferon-g and tumor necrosis factor-a induce hypoferraemia, ferritin production and a decrease in circulating transferrin receptors in cancer patients. Eur J Clin Invest 1998;28:520–7.

40. Wrighting DM, Andrews NC. Interleukin-6 induces hepcidin expression through STAT3. Blood 2006;108:3204–9.

41. Nemeth E, Valore EV, Territo M, Schiller G, Lichtenstein A, Ganz T. Hepcidin, a putative mediator of anemia of inflammation, is a type II acute-phase protein. Blood 2003;101:2462–3.

42. Ganz T. Hepcidin, a key regulator of iron metabolism and mediator of anemia of inflammation. Blood 2003;102:783–8.

43. Nemeth E, Ganz T. Regulation of iron metabolism by hepcidin. Ann Rev Nutr 2006;26:323–42.

44. Beisel WR. Infection-induced depression of serum retinol – a component of the acute phase response or a consequence? Am J Clin Nutr 1998;68:993–4.

45. Brock J. Iron and immunity. J Nutr Immunol 1993;2:47–106.

46. Hesketh JE, Vasconcelos MH, Bermano G. Regulatory signals in messenger RNA: determinants of nutrient-gene interaction and metabolic compartmentation. Brit J Nutr 1998;80:307–21.

47. Tran TN, Eubanks SK, Shaffer KJ, Zhou CYJ, Linder MC. Secretion of ferritin by rat hepatoma cells and its regulation by inflammatory cytokines and iron. Blood 1997;90:4979–86.

48. Fahmy M, Young SP. Modulation of iron metabolism in monocyte cell line U937 by inflammatory cytokines: changes in transferrin uptake, iron handling and ferritin mRNA. Biochem J 1993;296:175–81.

49. Weinberg ED. Iron withholding: a defense against infection and neoplasia. Physiol Rev 1984;64:65–102.

50. Bullen JJ. The significance of iron in infection. Rev Infect Dis 1981;3:1127–38.

51. Thurnham DI. Micronutrients and immune function: some recent developments. J Clin Pathol 1997;50:887–91.

52. Thurnham DI. Antioxidants and prooxidants in malnourished populations. Proc Nutr Soc 1990;48:247–59.

53. Baynes RD, Bezwoda W, Bothwell TH, Khan Q, Mansoor N. The non-immune inflammatory response: serial changes in plasma iron, iron-binding capacity, lactoferrin, ferritin and C-reactive protein. Scand J Clin Lab Invest 1986;46:695–704.

54. Ross MA, Crosley LK, Brown KM, et al. Plasma concentrations of carotenoids and antioxidant vitamins in Scottish males: influences of smoking. Eur J Clin Nutr 1995;49:861–5.

55. Vallance P, Hume R, Weyers E. Reassessment of changes in leucocyte and serum ascorbic acid

after acute myocardial infarction. Br Heart J 1978;40:684–9.

56. Weiss G, Wachter H, Fuchs D. Linkage of cell-mediated immunity to iron metabolism. Immunol Today 1995;16:495–500.

57. Moncada S, Palmer RMJ, Higgs EA. Nitric oxide physiology, pathophysiology and pharmacology. Pharmacol Rev 1991;43:109–42.

58. Domachowske JB, Rafferty SP, Singhania N, Mardiney M, Malech HL. Nitric oxide alters the expression of G-globulin, H-ferritin, and transferrin receptor in human K562 cells at the posttranscriptional level. Blood 1996;88:2980–8.

59. Rouault TA, Klausner RD. Iron-sulfur clusters as biosensors of oxidants and iron. Trends Biochem Sci 1996;21:174–7.

60. Brock JH, Mulero V. Cellular and molecular aspects of iron and immune function. Proc Nutr Soc 2000;59:537–40.

61. Tomkins A, Watson, F. Malnutrition and infection – a review. Mason J B, ed. . 1989. Lavenham, Suffolk; The Lavenham Press Ltd., 1993:1–136.

62. Murray MJ, Murray AB, Murray MB, Murray CJ. The adverse effect of iron repletion on the course of certain infections. BMJ 1978;2:1113–5.

63. Oppenheimer SJ. Iron and its relation to immunity and infectious disease. J Nutr 2001;131:616–35.

64. McFarlane H, Reddy S, Adcock KJ, Adeshina H, Cooke AR, Akene J. Immunity, transferrin and survival in kwashiorkor. BMJ 1970;4:268–70.

65. Oppenheimer SJ. Iron and malaria. Parasitol Today 1989;5:77–9.

66. Sazawal S, Black RE, Ramsan M, et al. Effects of routine prophylactic supplementation with iron and folic acid on admission to hospital and mortality in preschool children in a high malaria transmission setting: community-based, randomised, placebo-controlled trial. Lancet 2006;367:133–43.

67. Northrop-Clewes CA, McCloone UJ, Paracha PI, Thurnham DI. Influence of iron supplementation on markers of infection in Pakistani infants. Proc Nutr Soc 1994;153:264 (abstr).

68. Thurnham DI, McCabe GP, Northrop-Clewes CA, Nestel P. Effect of subclinical infection on plasma retinol concentrations and assessment of prevalence of vitamin A deficiency: meta-analysis. Lancet 2003;362:2052–8.

69. Calvin J, Neale G, Fotherby KJ, Price CP. The relative merits of acute phase proteins in the recognition of inflammatory conditions. Ann Clin Biochem 1988;25:60–6.

70. Thurnham DI, Mburu ASW, Mwaniki DL, de Wagt A. Micronutrients in childhood and the influence of subclinical inflammation. Proc Nutr Soc 2005;64:502–9.

71. Wieringa FT, Dijkhuizen MA, West CE, Northrop-Clewes CA, Muhilal. Estimation of the effect of the acute phase response on indicators of micronutrient status in Indonesian infants. J Nutr 2002;132:3061–6.

72. Ehrhardt S, Burchard GD, Mantel C, et al. Malaria, anemia, and malnutrition in African children – defining intervention priorities. J Inf Dis 2006;194:108–14.

73. Lunn PG, Northrop-Clewes CA, Downes RM. Intestinal permeability, mucosal injury and growth faltering in Gambian infants. Lancet 1991;338:907–10.

74. Briend A, Hasan KZ, Azis KMA, Hoque BA. Are diarrhoeal control programmes likely to reduce childhood malnutrition? Observations from rural Bangladesh. Lancet 1989;2:319–22.

75. Thurnham DI, Northrop-Clewes CA, McCullough FSW, Das BS, Lunn PG. Innate immunity, gut integrity and vitamin A in Gambian and Indian infants. J Inf Dis 2000;182:23S–8S.

76. Northrop-Clewes CA, Lunn PG, Wongworapat K, Kaewvichit R, Khamboonruang C. Intestinal permeability, mucosal damage and Strongyloides stercoralis infection. J Med Microbiol 1993;38:303 (abstr).

77. McCullough FSW, Northrop-Clewes CA, Thurnham DI. The effect of vitamin A on epithelial integrity. Proc Nutr Soc 1999;58:289–93.

78. Goto R, Panter-Brick C, Northrop-Clewes CA, Manahdhar R, Tuladhar NR. Poor intestinal permeability in mildly stunted Nepali children: associations with weaning practices and Giardia lamblia infection. Brit J Nutr 2002;88:141–9.

79. Nchito M, Friis H, Michaelsen KF, Mubila L, Olsen A. Iron supplementation increases small intestine permeability in primary schoolchildren in Lusaka, Zambia. Trans R Soc Trop Med Hyg 2006;100:791–4.

80. Campbell DI, Elia M, Lunn PG. Growth faltering in rural Gambian infants is associated with impaired small intestinal barrier function, leading to endotoxemia and systemic inflammation. J Nutr 2003;133:1332–8.

81. Hassan K, Sullivan KM, Yip R, Woodruff BA. Factors associated with anemia in refugee children. J Nutr 1997;127:2194–8.

82. Rousham EK, Northrop-Clewes CA, Lunn PG. Maternal reports of child illness and the biochemical status of the child: the use of morbidity interview in rural Bangladesh. Br J Nutr 1998;80:451–6.

83. Panter-Brick C, Lunn PG, Baker R, Todd A. Elevated acute-phase protein in stunted Nepali children reporting low morbidity: different rural and urban profiles. Br J Nutr 2001;85:125–31.

84. Northrop-Clewes CA, Lunn PG, Downes RM. Seasonal fluctuations in vitamin A status and health indicators in Gambian infants. Proc Nutr Soc 1994;53:144 (abstr).

85. Abdalla SH. Iron and folate status in Gambian children with malaria. Ann Trop Paediatr 1990;10:265–72.

86. Tielsch JM, Khatry SK, Stoltzfus RJ, et al. Effect of routine prophylactic supplementation with iron and folic acid on preschool child mortality in southern Nepal: community-based, cluster-randomised, placebo-controlled trial. Lancet 2006;367:144–52.

87. Ahmed F. Anaemia in Bangladesh: a review of prevalence and aetiology. Public Health Nutr 2000;3:385–93.

88. Dobosz S, Marczynska M. The most common pathologic syndromes in HIV-infected children. HIV AIDS Rev 2004;3:51–3.

89. Sullivan PS, Hanson DL, Chu SY, Jones JL, Ward JW. Epidemiology of anemia in human immunodeficiency virus (HIV)-infected persons: results from the Multistate Adult and Adolescent Spectrum of HIV Disease Surveillance Project. Blood 1998;19:301–8.

90. Kizza HM, Rodriguez B, Quinones-Mateu M, et al. Persistent replication of human immunodeficiency virus type 1 despite treatment of pulmonary tuberculosis in dually infected subjects. Clin Diagn Lab Immunol 2005;12:1298–304.

91. van Lettow M, West CE, van Der Meer JWM, Wieringa FT, Semba RD. Low plasma selenium concentrations, high plasma human immunodeficiency virus load and high interleukin-6 concentrations are risk factors associated with anemia in adults presenting with pulmonary tuberculosis in Zomba district, Malawi. Eur J Clin Nutr 2005;59:526–32.

92. Maehira F, Miyagi I, Eguchi Y. Selenium regulates transcription factor NF-kB activation during the acute phase reaction. Clin Chim Acta 2003;334:163–71.

93. World Health Organization Expert Committee on Malaria. 20th Report. Geneva: WHO, 2000. [Technical Report Series no 892].

94. Wickramasinghe SN, Abdalla SH. Blood and bone marrow changes in malaria. Baillieres Best Pract Res Clin Haematol 2000;13:277–99.

95. Das BS, Thurnham DI, Das DB. Influence of malaria on markers of iron status in children: implications for interpreting iron status in malaria-endemic communities. Br J Nutr 1997;78:751–60.

96. Nussenblatt V, Mukasa G, Metzger A, Ndeezi G, Garrett E, Semba RD. Anemia and interleukin-10, tumor necrosis factor alpha, and erythropoietin levels among children with acute, uncomplicated Plasmodium falciparum malaria. Clin Diagn Lab Immunol 2001;8:1164–70.

97. Stadnyk AW, Gauldie J. The acute phase protein response during parasitic infection. Immunoparasit Today 1991;7:A7–12.

98. Karyadi E, Gross R, Sastroamidjojo S, Dillon D, Richards AL, Sutanto I. Anthelminthic treatment raises plasma iron levels but does not decrease the acute-phase response in Jakarta school children. SE Asian J Trop Med Publ Hlth 1996;27:742–53.

99. Northrop CA, Lunn PG, Wainwright M, Evans J. Plasma albumin concentrations and intestinal permeability in Bangladeshi children infected with

Ascaris lumbricoides. Trans R Soc Trop Med Hyg 1987;81:811–5.

100. Northrop-Clewes CA, Rousham EK, Mascie-Taylor CG, Lunn PG. Anthelmintic treatment of rural Bangladeshi children: effect on host physiology, growth and biochemical status. Am J Clin Nutr 2001;73:53–60.

101. Utzinger J, Singer BJ, Bergquist R, Xiao SH, Tanner M. Sustainable schistosomiasis control – the way forward. Lancet 2006;362:1932–4.

102. Hall A, Drake L, Bundy D. Public health measures to control helminth infections. In: Ramakrishanan U, ed. Nutritional anemias. Boca Raton, FL: CRC Press 2000:215–39.

103. Prual A, Daouda H, Develoux M, Sellin B, Gallan P, Hercberg S. Consequences of Schistosoma haematobium infection on the iron status of school-children in Niger. Am J Trop Med Hyg 1992;47:291–7.

104. Hall A. Quantitative variability of nematode egg counts in faeces: a study among rural Kenyans. Trans R Soc Trop Med Hyg 1981;75:682–7.

105. Stoltzfus RJ, Chwaya HM, Tielsch JM, Schulze KJ, Albonico M, Savioli L. Epidemiology of iron deficiency anemia in Zanzibari school children: the importance of hookworms. Am J Clin Nutr 1997;65:153–9.

106. Albonico M, Stoltzfus MC, Savioli L, et al. Epidemiological evidence for a differential effect of hookworm species, Ancylostoma duodenale or Necator americanus, on iron status of children. Int J Epidemiol 1998;27:530–7.

107. Drake L, Korchev Y, Bachford L et al. The major secreted product of the whipworm, Trichuris, is a pore-forming protein. Philos Trans R Soc Lond B Biol Sci 1994;257:255–61.

108. Ramdath DD, Simeon DT, Wong MS, Grantham-McGregor SM. Iron status of school-children with varying intensities of Trichuris trichiura infection. Parasitol 1995;110:347–51.

109. Robertson LJ, Crompton DW, Sanjur D, Nesheim MC. Haemoglobin concentrations and concomitant infections of hookworm and Trichuris trichiura in Panamanian primary schoolchildren. Trans R Soc Trop Med Hyg 1992;86:654–6.

110. Kightlinger LK, Seed JR, Kightlinger MB. The epidemiology of Ascaris lumbricoides, Trichuris trichiura, and hookworm in children in the Ranomafana rainforest, Madagascar. J Parasitol 1995;82:159–69.

111. Holland CV, Asaolu SO, Crompton DW, Stoddart RC, Macdonald R, Torimiro SE. The epidemiology of Ascaris lumbricoides and other soil-transmitted helminths in primary school children from Ile-Ife, Nigeria. Parasitology 1989;99:275–85.

112. Crompton DW. How much human helminthiasis is there in the world? J Parasitol 1999;85:397–403.

113. de Silva NR, Chan MS, Bundy DA. Morbidity and mortality due to ascariasis: re-estimation and sensitivity analysis of global numbers at risk. Trop Med Int Health 1997;2:519–28.

114. Martin J, Keymer A, Isherwood RJ, Wainwright SM. The prevalence and intensity of Ascaris lumbricoides infections in Moslem children from northern Bangladesh. Trans R Soc Trop Med Hyg 1983;77:702–6.

115. Curtale F, Tilden R, Muhilal., Vaidya Y, Pokhrel RP, Guerra R. Intestinal helminths and risk of anaemia among Nepalese children. Panminerva Med 1993;35:159–66.

116. Crompton DW, Nesheim MC. Nutritional impact of intestinal helminthiasis during the human life cycle. Ann Rev Nutr 2002;22:35–59.

117. Jalal F, Nesheim MC, Zulkarmain A, Diva S, Habicht J-P. Serum retinol concentrations in children are affected by food sources of β-carotene, fat intake and anthelmintic drug treatment. Am J Clin Nutr 1998;68:623–9.

118. von Bonsdorff B, Gordin R. Castle's test (with vitamin B12 and normal gastric juice) in the ileum in patients with genuine and patients with tapeworm pernicious anaemia. Acta Med Scand 1980; 208:193–7.

119. Weinberg ED. Iron and susceptibility to infectious disease. Science 1974;184:952–6.

120. Thurnham DI. An overview of interactions between micronutrients and of micronutrients with drugs, genes and immune mechanisms. Nutr Res Rev 2004;17:211–40.

121. Oppenheimer SJ, Gibson FD, MacFarlane SBJ, et al. Iron supplementation increases prevalence and effects of malaria: report on clinical studies in Papua New Guinea. Trans R Soc Trop Med Hyg 1986;80:603–12.

122. Harvey PWJ, Heywood PF, Nesheim MC, et al. The effect of iron therapy on malaria infection in Papua New Guinean school children. Amer J Trop Med Hyg 1989;40:12–8.

123. Wachter H, Fuchs D, Hausen A, Reibnegger G, Werner ER. Neopterin as a marker for activation of cellular immunity: immunological basis and clinical application. Adv Clin Chem 1989;27:81–141.

124. Reibnegger G, Fuchs D, Hausen A. The dependence of cell-mediated immune activation in malaria on age and endemicity. Trans R Soc Trop Med Hyg 1987;81:729–33.

125. Glasziou PP, Mackerras DEM. Vitamin A supplementation in infectious diseases: a meta-analysis. BMJ 1993;306:366–70.

126. Fawzi WW, Chalmers TC, Herrera MG, Mosteller F. Vitamin A supplementation and child mortality. A meta-analysis. J Am Med Assoc 1993;269:898–903.

127. Beaton GH, Martorell R, Aronson KJ, et al. Effectiveness of vitamin A supplementation in the control of young child morbidity and mortality in developing countries. Geneva: WHO, 1993.

128. Hussey GD, Klein M. A randomized, controlled trial of vitamin A in children with severe measles. N Engl J Med 1990;323:160–4.

129. Barclay AJG, Foster A, Sommer A. Vitamin A supplements and mortality related to measles: a randomised clinical trial. BMJ 1987;294:294–6.

130. World Health Organization, United Nations Children's Fund. Iron supplementation of young children in regions where malaria transmission is intense and infectious disease is highly prevalent. Geneva: WHO, 2006.

131. Stephenson LS, Latham MC, Kurz KM, Miller D, Kinoti SN, Oduori ML. Urinary iron loss and physical fitness of Kenyan children with urinary schistosomiasis. Am J Trop Med Hyg 1985;34:322–30.

16

Making programs for controlling anemia more successful

Saskia de Pee[1,2]

Martin W. Bloem[1,4]

Regina Moench-Pfanner[3]

Richard D. Semba[4]

[1]World Food Programme (WFP), Rome, Italy
[2]Helen Keller International, New York, USA
[3]Global Alliance for Improved Nutrition (GAIN), Geneva, Switzerland
[4]Johns Hopkins Bloomberg School of Public Health, Baltimore, USA
Contact: sdepee@compuserve.com

SASKIA DE PEE
Saskia obtained her PhD in Nutrition from Wageningen University in the Netherlands. She is affiliated to the World Food Program, Helen Keller International, and Wageningen University. Saskia focuses on the interaction between programs and science and her areas of expertise are micronutrient deficiencies, health and nutrition in the context of urbanization, economic crisis and globalization, complimentary feeding, and the development, implementation, monitoring and evaluation of programs.

MARTIN W. BLOEM
Martin has a MD from the University of Utrecht and a PhD from the University of Maastricht, both in the Netherlands. He is currently the Chief of Nutrition Services for the World Food Programme United Nations in Rome, Italy. Martin also holds the position of Adjunct Associate Professor at the Johns Hopkins Bloomberg School of Public Health, Baltimore, and the Friedman School of Nutrition Science and Policy at Tufts University, both in the USA, and consults widely to a number of organizations. His special interest is in micronutrient deficiencies, especially vitamin A and iron, and emergency feeding. He has earned wide recognition for his innovative approach to nutrition research, which combines scientific analysis with real-world pragmatic applications.

REGINA MOENCH-PFANNER
Regina is a Fulbright Scholar and has a PhD in International Nutrition from the University of Bonn, Germany. She is currently the Senior Manager responsible for GAIN's global food fortification program. Regina has spent more than 20 years working in the field of relief assistance and international development and has provided technical consultancies in food and nutrition programs for a number of international organizations including WHO, WFP, and UNHCR.

RICHARD SEMBA
Richard obtained his MD from Stanford University and MPH from Johns Hopkins University, both in the USA. He is currently Professor of Ophthalmology at the Johns Hopkins School of Medicine, and holds joint appointments in International Health and in Molecular Microbiology and Immunology in the Johns Hopkins Bloomberg School of Public Health. Richard has conducted research in anemia in different populations around the world and is currently studying the role of hepcidin and other factors in the pathogenesis of anemia of chronic inflammation. He has published widely and served on the editorial boards of the Journal of Nutrition and Nutrition.

INTRODUCTION

The 1990 World Summit for Children set goals for eliminating micronutrient deficiencies (**Figure 16.1**). Before then, in developed countries, iron and folic acid supplements were given to pregnant women, salt was iodized, and vitamin A fortification of margarine and dairy products had already been widespread for several decades. However, the prevalence of deficiencies in developing countries, and in particular their severe consequences, in developing countries had only recently been recognized. Whereas clinical signs (goiter due to iodine deficiency, xerophthalmia due to vitamin A deficiency, and pallor due to severe anemia) were known, the impact of deficiencies at a level that did not (yet) lead to overt recognizable clinical signs had only just been realized.

For vitamin A, the impact on child survival, as intensively studied by trials in the 1980s and 90s (1), mobilized substantial support for fighting vitamin A deficiency. For iodine deficiency, the impact on IQ points was the trigger for substantial support. For iron deficiency and anemia, the impact on productivity and pregnancy outcome was regarded as the primary negative consequence. Knowledge about the impact of iron deficiency on mental development increased somewhat later, hence combating iron deficiency

anemia in young children was not among the World Summit Goals accepted in 1990 (**Figure 16.1**).

More than a decade later substantial progress has been made in combating vitamin A deficiency. While the deficiency is widespread and has serious consequences, there is an underlying trend of improvement. Many countries are providing high-dose vitamin A capsules twice a year to children aged 6–59 mo., many countries are fortifying one or more foods with vitamin A (e.g., margarine, oil, and sugar), and dietary diversification as well as hygiene and health are being promoted.

Similar, or even greater, progress has been made in combating iodine deficiency disorders. While iodized oil was at first used, initially by injection and later orally the iodization of salt and the accompanying awareness campaigns substantially reduced the prevalence of iodine deficiency disorders. The key issues to be improved for iodized salt are distribution and marketing in remote areas, and quality control of iodine content (2).

Figure 16.2 shows the percentage of countries reporting high coverage (>60%) for vitamin A capsule distribution, iodized salt use and iron

---

1990 World Summit Goals for Reduction of Micronutrient Deficiencies

1. Reduction of iron deficiency anemia in women by one third of the 1990 levels;

2. Virtual elimination of iodine deficiency disorders;

3. Virtual elimination of vitamin A deficiency and its consequences, including blindness.

Figure 16.1: Goals of the 1990 World Summit for Children for reducing micronutrient deficiencies. These goals were to be achieved by the year 2000.

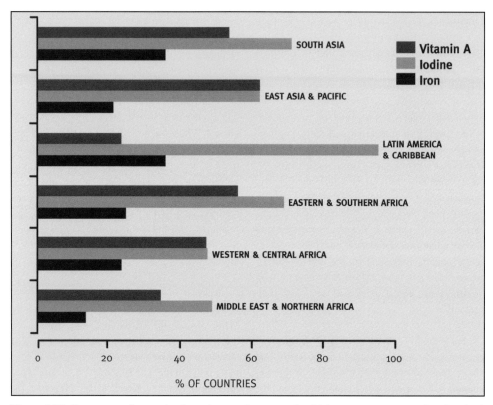

Figure 16.2: Percentage of countries in various regions reporting high program coverage for vitamin A supplementation (>60% of children 6–59 months of age receiving capsules), iodine fortification (>60% of households using salt with at least 15 ppm iodine), and iron supplementation (>60% of pregnant women receiving supplements). Regions are as defined by UNICEF. Reproduced with permission from Mason et al (2).

supplementation for pregnant women. Control of Iodine Deficiency Disorders (IDD) through the use of iodized salt is most widespread (40–80% of countries reporting high coverage, i.e. >60% of households), closely followed by VAC distribution among underfives (20–50% with high coverage). With regard to the latter, it should be noted that Latin American countries have made great progress by fortifying sugar (2) rather than distributing VAC, thus if this were taken into account, the percentage of high coverage for control of vitamin A deficiency disorders (VADD) would be higher. The proportion of countries reporting high iron supplement coverage for pregnant women was lowest, ranging from 10–30%. Although there are various sources of iron supple-

ments, the fact that the number of iron tablets supplied by UNICEF to developing countries in 2000 was only enough for 3% of all pregnant women in these countries (2) indicates that the percentage of countries with high coverage may be closer to 10% than to 30%.

It is important to note that these coverage data do not take compliance into account. The reported low proportion of countries with high coverage of iron supplements is inline with the fact that the prevalence of anemia among pregnant women over the past 20–30 years has not declined in any region of the world (2). Furthermore, as the iron supplement coverage of pregnant women is already so low, coverage among young children is even lower.

This chapter discusses the lack of progress in controlling iron deficiency and anemia, particularly compared with IDD and VADD, and how this could be remedied.

WHY ARE IRON DEFICIENCY AND ANEMIA CONTROL LAGGING BEHIND?

A number of papers have dealt with the question of why iron deficiency and anemia control are not implemented on a much larger scale. Some have focused on what would be needed to implement the preferred approach, i.e. the improved distribution of iron folate supplements to pregnant women, in order to increase coverage as well as compliance (3, 4). Others have evaluated alternative supplements, dosing frequencies, etc. in order to improve compliance and hence impact (5). And others took a more comprehensive approach that specifically assessed what should be communicated to whom in order to gain momentum for the control of iron deficiency anemia (6, 7).

Yip assessed the key components of an action program for controlling iron deficiency. He stated that iron supplementation can be regarded as one of the best-studied areas of nutrition research, from molecular to population level, and therefore this research has provided effective information on what needs to be done. However, that the mechanisms are lacking at country and global levels to ensure that effective measures are implemented. That situation is largely due, he says, to the fact that operational components of controlling iron deficiency anemia are less well developed in comparison to Research and Development (R&D), and that neither of these is well coordinated with communication. Communication in this regard encompasses the effort to generate political support and funding, as well as to encourage families and communities to accept better nutrition practices through health education and promotion (7). A balanced program with interconnected components is required to reduce iron deficiency anemia effectively.

Communication for the control of iron deficiency and anemia is more challenging than for the control of VADD and IDD, as can easily be concluded from a comparison of websites on anemia, for example those of UNICEF, WHO, GAIN, WFP, MI and USAID. The consequences of iron deficiency and anemia emphasized, the approaches advocated, etc. vary considerably from one website to another. These discrepancies are due to the fact that the strategy for controlling iron deficiency and anemia is not the same for every situation, needs to involve various sectors, and is therefore essentially different from the control of VADD and IDD, which are both much more 'bullet-oriented' approaches that respectively emphasize the use of vitamin A capsules and iodized salt.

Vitamin A capsule distribution is regarded as a strategy that must be in place until dietary strategies (e.g., fortification, biofortified crops, and increased intake of foods naturally rich in vitamin A) provide enough vitamin A. Salt iodization, however, must continue because there are very few sources of iodine in food, as most iodine has been leached from the soil. Vitamin A capsule distribution only reaches specific target groups (6–59 mo. old children and women shortly after delivery), and is a medical approach where a high-dose capsule is provided to a child every 4–6 mo., to women within 8 weeks of delivery, and in case of specific medical conditions (measles, treatment of acute malnutrition, etc.). Because of the long interval between doses, a medical approach is appropriate and can be implemented in collaboration with the health sector. Fortifying salt with iodine is a food-based approach, which is highly suitable for regularly (at least a few times per week) supplying a small amount of a micronutrient in a way that does not involve changing dietary habits.

Below we discuss the aspects of iron deficiency and anemia control which have complicated communication, as well as the design and implementation of programs to alleviate their burden and how these could be improved or approached differently.

1. ANEMIA VS. IRON DEFICIENCY

Problem: Anemia is not only due to iron deficiency and iron deficiency does not always lead to anemia.

Background: For this reason, there has been a long, ongoing debate on what the goal should be: just reducing iron deficiency and iron deficiency anemia, or also reducing anemia due to other causes, such as malaria, helminth infestation, other micronutrient deficiencies, etc. Since an effective approach requires knowledge of anemia's primary causes, gathering knowledge on this is prioritized and often no action is taken until these are clear.

Solution: Focusing on the following facts should facilitate decision-making on which programs to implement:

- Over 2 billion people are anemic and the estimated number of people affected by iron deficiency is even higher (8). Therefore, it is unlikely that any population is affected by anemia that is not to some extent due to iron deficiency, nor that only iron deficiency underlies the anemia observed.
- Iron needs during infancy and pregnancy are so high that it is virtually impossible for these to be met through diet alone. Only when the diet of infants and pregnant women contains a considerable amount of fortified foods and heme-iron from animal foods, and the infant starts life, and the woman pregnancy, with good iron stores, might their needs be met through diet alone. Thus, iron deficiency in

these age groups is almost guaranteed, also because one third of the world population suffer from iron deficiency, most of whom are less likely to suffer from iron deficiency than infants and pregnant women.

Thus, the question is not whether intervening with iron, multi-micronutrients and/or infection control will have an impact on iron deficiency and anemia, but rather which strategy is most effective. Instead of determining the precise extent to which each factor plays a role, action should be taken to address the causes that are assumed most important, while concurrently monitoring the impact of these measures on iron deficiency and anemia in the population, in order to adjust and fine-tune the program. The rationale for this is that doing nothing does more harm than not treating all cases because some causes are not yet known.

2. NUTRITION, HEALTH, DEVELOPMENT OR ECONOMIC CONSEQUENCES

Problem: For a long time, iron supplementation was promoted as a means to prevent and treat anemia, a largely medical term that did not speak to the minds of policymakers and governments concerned with stimulating economic growth etc.

Background: Anemia was described as a state where not enough oxygen was transported through the body and people suffering from anemia were described as more easily tired (lethargic), less productive at work, with lower achievement at school, and severe anemia increased the risk of maternal mortality. This description was mainly geared to nutritionists and medical professionals. However, the consequences for children's current and future mental capacity, a nation's development, as well as economic consequences, were not sufficiently advocated in various sectors such as economics, early child development, education, etc.

Solution: Emphasizing the fact that damage done by iron deficiency to a young child's mental capacity cannot be reversed later in life (9, 10) and quantifying the loss of GDP when iron deficiency and anemia are left untreated (11) should be the key messages to mobilize action across a wide range of sectors for combating iron deficiency and anemia. As mentioned above, IDD control really went to scale when the impact on IQ became apparent and a relatively simple solution was at hand in the form of iodized salt. The beneficial impact of iron on a child's mental capacity is therefore surely a good argument to advocate iron deficiency control, but the solution should also be well thought through (see below).

3. MEDICAL VS. FOOD-BASED, PUBLIC-HEALTH APPROACH

Problem: When anemia is regarded as a medical problem, solutions will focus on a medical approach. This implies identifying the precise cause for each population before taking action, giving a high dosage of nutrients that is sufficient to treat rather than to prevent anemia, and giving messages focused on treating a perceived or assumed problem.

Background: As mentioned under point 1, because iron deficiency and anemia are so widespread, existence of the problem can be assumed and action should therefore be taken accordingly. However, at the same time it is difficult at an individual level because most people who suffer from anemia or iron deficiency are not aware of it, and parents are likewise not aware that their children are anemic. Therefore, they are less likely to take, or provide, supplements for a long period of time, because they think taking those supplements should result in a noticeable improvement of their condition and will hence only take them till they feel better. The case of vitamin A deficiency, which puts children at greater risk of morbidity and mortality, is different because taking a vitamin A capsule twice per year is perceived as being similar to immunization.

Solution: Because one third of the world population suffers from iron deficiency and anemia, primarily because of an inadequate diet, a food-based approach that aims at increasing the whole population's intake of iron and other micronutrients and focusing particularly on the groups most at risk makes the most sense. Such an increased intake should be sustained for a long period of time and should be considered as a way of promoting good health and protecting cognitive development and it should be realized that the costs to the individual and society of not doing so are very high. In addition, by increasing everyone's intake of iron, using a food-based approach, women will enter pregnancy with higher stores which will reduce the gap between needs and intake during pregnancy. The biggest challenge for a food-based approach is to find a way of increasing intake sufficiently among the most at-risk groups: young children and pregnant women. The best way to assure consumption of an adequate amount of micronutrients is by adding fortificants to an individual's bowl of food, a strategy known as home-fortification (12, 13).

4. FEW SUCCESSFUL EXPERIENCES DESCRIBED

Problem: The experiences with iron and folic acid supplementation during pregnancy are mixed and decision-makers therefore seem to think twice before embarking on new iron deficiency anemia control programs for pregnant women and/or young children. Because of this, there are few successful program experiences described, especially for young children.

Background: Most research on iron deficiency and anemia has been conducted by academic institutions and thus focused on gaining new knowledge about the technical feasibility of interventions (an innovative process), rather than focusing on operational feasibility (7). The consequence seems to be that those implementing the programs wait for the scientists to conclude what is best, whereas the scientists go on to improve possible interventions and test new preparations, dosing schemes, combinations of micronutrients, etc. At the same time, programs often do not place enough emphasis on monitoring and evaluation, and are hence not doing a good job in communicating successes and lessons learned.

Solution: There should be a greater link between the R&D community and those implementing programs to ensure greater investment in defining the operational feasibility of promising interventions and to monitor and evaluate their implementation thoroughly (7). These programs should be implemented on a sufficiently large scale. Too often relatively small projects are implemented, and conclusions shared, that are not suitable for upscaling to an entire province or country.

5. COMMUNICATING AND INTERPRETING NEW RESEARCH FINDINGS AND EXCEPTIONS

Problem: New research findings and reports on cases that showed no or a negative benefit of iron or multi-micronutrient supplementation often lead to conclusions that these supplements should be withheld from everyone because of the possible risk of negative consequences.

Background: Scrimshaw has listed the following misconceptions that impede the implementation of programs for preventing iron deficiency (14):

• The myth that iron deficiency is more difficult to prevent than iodine and VA deficiencies. This is largely based on the fact that few successful programs have so far been implemented for iron deficiency control as compared with the control of vitamin A and iodine deficiencies.
• The myth that iron supplementation can increase the severity of infections. Three papers

have reviewed the evidence in this regard and concluded that only very young children (<2 mo.), severely malnourished children with clinical complications, and children in areas where malaria is highly endemic and without good malaria control, should not receive high doses of iron (>10 mg/d) as supplements (15–17). Fortified foods can be provided to children in areas with high malaria endemicity. There is not enough evidence at present to know whether home fortificants, most of which provide 10 – 12.5 mg iron mixed with one meal, are safe in areas with high malaria endemicity and it has therefore been recommended that these are only provided under carefully controlled circumstances (i.e. good malaria control etc., see ref. 17). The increase of diarrhea among children that received iron was too small to be of clinical significance (16).

• The assumption that thalassemias and other hemoglobinopathies are contraindications to iron supplementation. In some regions of the world, anemia is complicated by thalassemia and hemoglobinopathies (18). In severe cases of thalassemia, there may be iron overload. Routine iron supplementation during pregnancy in areas with a high prevalence of thalassemia and hemoglobinopathies results in widely varying hematologic responses (19). Pregnant women who are homozygous for Hb E do not benefit from iron supplementation, but this routine intervention does not appear to cause iron overload, and routine iron supplementation appears to be safe for women who are Hb E carriers (19). The authors are not aware of reports on complications arising from routine iron supplementation durin pregnancy that are related to thalassemia and hemoglobinopathies in the population.

• The idea that screening is required before supplementation because of the prevalence of hemochromatosis. Homozygotes for hemochromatosis have a very low prevalence (<0.5%) and the gene for the common form of hemochromatosis is only prevalent in populations with ancestral origins in Northern Europe. With regard to the risk of iron overload in hemochromatosis sufferers, Sean Lynch has said: "I do not for a moment believe that the theoretical risk of iron overload is a reason to withhold iron from people at risk for iron deficiency living in developing countries" (personal communication).

- The finding that iron fortification and supplementation could increase the risk of heart disease and cancer. A possible relationship between iron status and the risk of cardiovascular disease and cancer has been the subject of a number of recent observational studies. As yet, there is no firm evidence that such a relationship exists, nor that it would be a causal relationship (20, 21).

Solution: It is most important not to lose sight of the very widespread prevalence of iron deficiency and anemia, of the severe consequences, and the underlying cause of a deficient diet. Whereas research findings should be thoroughly examined and their applicability to the situation among different populations evaluated, they should lead to fine-tuning and better implementation of iron deficiency and anemia control programs, rather than to a halt of programs when that means that the majority of the population is left untreated because of a small increased risk for a minority. This situation has recently occurred in response to the finding of higher mortality among children in a highly malaria endemic area when supplemented with iron in the absence of malaria control measures (22). That the increased risk was small, that those findings were not observed in an area where malaria transmission was controlled using treated bed nets and treatment of suspected cases, and that malaria was very highly endemic in the area (23), did not receive much emphasis in the discussions that followed on the publication of the findings.

CONCLUSION

Thus, in summary, because iron deficiency and anemia are so prevalent and the consequences for individuals and populations so severe, the focus should be on implementing control programs. Advocacy for these programs should focus on the benefits for early child development and hence success later in life, also for the population as a whole, and on the increase in productivity and thus economic benefit for the nation. The programs should preferably promote a food-based approach, including fortifying staple foods and condiments that are consumed by the entire population, as well as home-fortificants for specific target groups that are unlikely to have all their needs met by fortified foods alone. A food-based approach is preferred because it is more sustainable and less perceived as treatment for a condition that should be perceived considered as needing treatment. A food-based approach can also be used in areas of high malaria endemicity where supplements are not recommended in the absence of a good malaria control and prevention program. Where large scale programs are implemented, assessing their coverage, compliance and effectiveness in reducing iron deficiency and anemia among the population is essential.

The good news is that there is growing momentum for programs to control iron deficiency and anemia because the severe consequences of leaving the conditions untreated are becoming increasingly clear. This in turn stimulates operations-oriented research and suggestions, and sparks new initiatives such as the Global Alliance for Improved Nutrition (GAIN) and the Flour Fortification Initiative (FFI) that aim to increase fortification and focus on public-private partnerships, the Iron Deficiency Program Advisory Service (IDPAS) that collects information on iron deficiency and its control and makes this information readily available on its website. In addition, the change in conceptual thinking (using a life-cycle approach), realizing the need for a well-balanced diet with sufficient vitamins and minerals, and the development of new strategies for ensuring an adequate intake, such as home fortification, also creates further opportunities and new approaches.

REFERENCES

1.   Beaton GH, Martorell R, Aronson KJ, et al. Effectiveness of vitamin A supplementation in the control of young child morbidity and mortality in developing countries. In: ACC/SCN State of the Art Series Nutrition Policy Discussion Paper, No 13, Geneva: ACC/SCN, 1993.

2.   Mason JB, Lotfi M, Dalmiya N, Sethuraman K, Deitchler M. The micronutrient report: current progress and trends in the control of vitamin A, iron, and iodine deficiencies. Micronutrient Initiative, International Development Research Centre, Ottawa, Canada. 2001. Internet: www.micronutrient.org/resources/publications/The %20Micronutrient%20Report.htm (accessed 1 Feb 2007).

3.   Galloway R, McGuire J. Determinants of compliance with iron supplementation: supplies, side effects, or psychology? Soc Sci Med 1994; 39 (3): 381--90.

4.   Schultink W, van der Ree M, Matulessi P, Gross R. Low compliance with an iron-supplementation program: a study among pregnant women in Jakarta, Indonesia. Am J Clin Nutr 1993; 57 (2): 135-9.

5.   Beard JL. Effectiveness and strategies of iron supplementation during pregnancy. Am J Clin Nutr 2000; 71:1288S-94S.

6.   Manoff Group. Summary of advocacy research and key approaches to advocacy for iron deficiency.Internet: http://www.idpas.org/pdf/630SummaryofAdvocacy.pdf. Accessed 1 Feb 2007.

7.   Yip R. Prevention and control of iron deficiency: Policy and strategy issues. J Nutr 2002; 132:802S-805S.

8.   Stoltzfus RJ. Defining iron-deficiency anemia in public health terms: a time for reflection. J Nutr 2001; 131: 565S-567S.

9.   Lozoff B, Jimenez E, Wolf AW. Long-term developmental outcome of infants with iron deficiency. N Engl J Med 1991; 325 (10): 687-94.

10.   Lozoff B, Jimenez E, Smith JB. Double burden of iron deficiency in infancy and low socioeconomic status: a longitudinal analysis of cognitive test scores to age 19 years. Arch Pediatr Adolesc Med 2006; 160 (11): 1108-13.

11.   Horton S. The Economics of Nutritional Interventions. In: Semba RD, Bloem MW. Nutrition and health in developing countries. Totowa NJ: Humana Press Inc, 2001.

12.   Nestel P, Briend A, de Benoist B, et al. Complementary food supplements to achieve micronutrient adequacy for infants and young children. J Pediatr Gastroenter Nutr 2003; 36: 316-28.

13.   Zlotkin SH, Schauer C, Christofides A, Sharieff W, Tondeur MC, Hyder SMZ. Micronutrient sprinkles to control childhood anaemia. A simple powdered sachet may be the key to addressing a global problem. PLoS Medicine 2005; 2 (7): e1. Internet: www.plosmedicine.org

14.   Scrimshaw NS. The global threat of hidden hunger. Presentation. United Nations University. 2000. Internet: www.idpas.org, document nr 2243. Accessed on 1 Feb 2007.

15.   Oppenheimer SJ. Iron and its relation to immunity and infectious disease. J Nutr 2001; 131 (2S-2): 616S--635S.

16.   Gera T, Sachdev HP. Effect of iron supplementation on incidence of infectious illness in children: systematic review. BMJ 2002; 325 (7373): 1142-51.

17. WHO. Iron supplementation of young children in regions where malaria transmission is intense and infectious disease highly prevalent. 2006. Internet: http://www.who.int/child-adolescenthealth/New_Publications/CHILD_HEALTH/WHO_statement_iron.pdf. Accessed on 1 Feb 2007.

18. Thurlow RA, Winichagoon P, Green T, et al. Only a small proportion in northeast Thai schoolchildren is associated with iron deficiency. Am J Clin Nutr 2005; 82 (2): 380–7.

19. Sanchaisuriya K, Fucharoen S, Ratanasiri T, et al. Effect of the maternal β^E-globin gene on hematologic responses to iron supplementation during pregnancy. Am J Clin Nutr 2007; 85 (2): 474–9.

20. Derstine JL, Murray-Kolb LE, Yu-Poth S, Hargrove RL, Kris-Etherton PM, Beard JL. Iron status in association with cardiovascular disease risk in 3 controlled feeding studies. Am J Clin Nutr 2003; 77 (1): 56–62.

21. Kelly C. Can excess iron increase the risk for coronary heart disease and cancer? Nutr Bull 2002; 27:165–79.

22. Sazawal S, Black RE, Ramsan M, et al. Effects of routine prophylactic supplementation with iron and folic acid on admission to hospital and mortality in preschool children in a high malaria transmission setting: community-based, randomized, placebo-controlled trial. Lancet 2006; 367 (9505): 133–43.

23. English M, Snow RW. Editorial. Iron and folic acid supplementation and malaria risk. Lancet 2006; 367 (9505): 90–1.

17

Successful approaches: Sprinkles

Stanley H. Zlotkin

Melody Tondeur

Sprinkles Global Health Initiative, Division of Gastroenterology, Hepatology and Nutrition,
Hospital for Sick Children, Toronto, Canada
Contact: stanley.zlotkin@sickkids.ca

STANLEY ZLOTKIN
Stanley obtained his MD degree from McMaster University, Canada and his PhD in Nutritional Sciences from the University of Toronto, Canada. He is the Founder and President of the Sprinkles Global Health Initiative at the Hospital for Sick Children in Toronto, Canada, as well as a Professor in the Department of Pediatrics at the University of Toronto, and Head of the Division of Gastroenterology, Hepatology and Nutrition at the Hospital for Sick Children. Stanley is known internationally for his work on knowledge translation and as a successful social entrepreneur, and was awarded the Order of Canada, the highest civilian honor, for his international work to improve the lives of children globally.

MELODY TONDEUR
Melody has a MSc from the University of Toronto, Canada. Her graduate research on iron bioavailability was conducted in rural Ghana. Her main professional interest is contributing to improving the health and nutrition of vulnerable populations in underdeveloped countries. Melody is currently working for the Sprinkles Global Health Initiative at the Hospital for Sick Children in Toronto where she is involved in program development, research, field operations management, and partner relationships.

INTRODUCTION

Iron deficiency remains the most common preventable micronutrient deficiency despite continued global initiatives for its control. Recent WHO/UNICEF estimates suggest that the number of children with iron deficiency and anemia is greater than 750 million (1). The many risk factors that contribute to iron deficiency anemia (IDA) in children are low birth weight, early cord clamping, maternal anemia, gastrointestinal blood loss due to infection (*Helicobactor pylori* and helminth infections), limited access to iron rich foods, and other nutritional deficiencies that impede the incorporation of iron into hemoglobin. The most significant negative consequences of IDA in children less than 2 years of age are impairments in motor and mental development, which may be irreversible later in life (2). Historically, the problem of IDA in children largely disappeared in North America when commercial foods fortified with iron and other essential micronutrients became available for children (3). Although specific groups of infants and children still remain at risk (e.g., infants born prematurely), generally the low prevalence of iron deficiency found in the West is recognized as a successful public health accomplishment. The use of commercially fortified food has had limited success in underdeveloped countries, where store-bought foods are not widely available or affordable, especially for young children.

Current INACG/WHO/UNICEF recommendations (4) are to provide daily iron supplementation to all infants with normal birth weight in the first year of life starting at 6 months of age in regions where the prevalence of anemia is below 40% and where iron fortified complementary foods are not widely used. In areas where the prevalence of anemia is at least 40% or above, it is recommended to continue supplementation until 24 months of age. However, few options exist for supplementing iron to infants and young children. For the past 150 years or more, oral ferrous sulfate syrups have been the primary strategy to control IDA in infants and young children (5). However, adherence is often limited due to a combination of factors: the syrup has an unpleasant metallic aftertaste, leaves dark stains on teeth, and high doses cause abdominal discomfort (6). Furthermore, there are technical disadvantages associated with the use of liquid iron preparations such as short shelf life, high transportation costs due to the weight of the bottles, and difficulty in accurately dispensing the drops, especially among illiterate populations, as the caregiver is required to measure a decimal volume from a dropper (7, 8).

Despite UNICEF's goal to reduce the prevalence of anemia (including iron deficiency) by one third by 2010 and the ongoing work of the UN Standing Committee on Nutrition and others to meet this goal, attempts to decrease the prevalence of anemia in infants and young children have had limited success. The root cause of the ineffectiveness of many programs has been an inability to develop a sustainable framework to reach the most vulnerable populations with appropriate and cost-effective solutions. This article describes each stage in the development of the Sprinkles intervention for the control of anemia and micronutrient deficiencies in infants and young children.

THE APPROACH

Our research group at the Hospital for Sick Children and University of Toronto, in Toronto, Canada, conceived of the strategy of home fortification with Sprinkles, single-dose sachets containing micronutrients in a powder form. Sprinkles are easily mixed onto any food prepared in the household. The idea of home fortification was presented in 1996, when a group of international experts determined that the prevention of childhood IDA was a UNICEF priority, yet available interventions (syrup and drops) were not effective (8). The Sprinkles concept was based on the principle that targeted food fortification has been successful in the West and was inspired by a legacy at the Hospital for Sick Children, where Pablum (the first fortified infant cereal) was invented in 1929 to control the epidemic of rickets which was rampant in Canada at that time.

In Sprinkles, the iron (ferrous fumarate) is encapsulated within a thin lipid layer to prevent the iron from interacting with food, thereby limiting changes to the taste, color, or texture of the food. Caregivers are instructed to add the entire contents of one sachet daily to any semi-solid food prepared for their infant or young child in the household, immediately before serving. Other essential micronutrients including zinc, iodine, vitamins C, D and A, and folic acid may be added to Sprinkles sachets.

SUMMARY OF RESEARCH EVIDENCE

Initially, *in vitro* dissolution studies were conducted to demonstrate that the lipid encapsulation would dissolve at the low pH of the stomach, leaving the iron available for absorption (unpublished observations, S. Zlotkin et al, 1998). Then, to evaluate the efficacy, bioavailability, acceptability, and safety of Sprinkles, community-based clinical trials were conducted in several regions ranging from Northern Canada to Asia, Africa, and Latin America involving both anemic and non-anemic infants and young children. In addition, studies and pilot projects were conducted to generate data on effectiveness. Findings from other research groups using Sprinkles are also included in this publication.

Efficacy and bioavailability

For the efficacy studies described below, details on study location, sample size, age group, length of intervention, eligibility criteria, micronutrient formulations, and outcome measures are described in **Table 17.1**.

The first efficacy study involved only anemic children and demonstrated that Sprinkles achieved a similar cure rate as compared to the reference standard, iron drops (9). Fifty-eight percent of children who received Sprinkles went from an anemic (Hb<100 g/L) to a non-anemic state (Hb⩾100 g/L) in 2 months. Given that the study took place during the wet season, when malaria transmission is high, the anemia cure rate of close to 60% was considered very successful. Children who were treated for anemia in this study were included in a maintenance phase study for 6 months to determine whether continued intake of Sprinkles was needed to sustain their non-anemic status. Results showed that in most children who had been successfully treated for anemia, further intervention was not needed. At 12 months post-intervention, 77% of children remained non-anemic (10).

In an effort to reproduce the efficacy of Sprinkles among this population, another study was conducted in the same area during the dry season, when malarial transmission is lower. This study demonstrated that Sprinkles (with or without added zinc) were efficacious to treat anemia with an average cure rate of 69% (11). Elsewhere, in non-malaria endemic areas, it was observed that: 1) 91% of 62 children aged 1 to 6 years who had anemia raised their hemoglobin to above 125 g/L after receiving Sprinkles for two months in Bolivia (unpublished, J. Cataudella et al, 2001); and 2) among 70 anemic young children aged 12–24 months (with very little hookworm infestation) given Sprinkles for 2 months in Bangladesh, mean hemoglobin increased from 97 g/L to 113 g/L (12).

To determine the bioavailability of the microencapsulated iron and zinc in Sprinkles, stable-isotope studies were conducted. It was

Table 17.1: Randomized community-based trials on sprinkles.

Study	Location	Sample size, n	Age group	Length of intervention	Eligibility criteria	Intervention groups — Group	Intervention groups — Micronutrient formulation	Outcome measures — Baseline	Outcome measures — End	Additional measures
Zlotkin et al. 2001 (9)	Ghana	557	6–18 mo	2 mo (60 Sprinkles sachets), daily intake	Hb 70–99 g/L	Sprinkles	80 mg Fe, 50 mg vit C	Hb, sFt², malaria, anthropometry	Hb, sFt, anthropometry	Adherence, side effects, ease of use
						Iron drops	40 mg Fe as FS¹			
Zlotkin et al. 2003 (10)	Ghana	437	8–20 mo	6 mo, daily intake	Hb ≥100 g/L	Sprinkles – vit A	40 mg Fe, 50 mg vit C, 600 µg vit A	Hb, sFt, serum retinol, malaria, anthropometry.	Hb, sFt, serum retinol, anthropometry	Adherence, side effects, ease of use, Hb status of non-anemics at 12 mo postintervention
						Sprinkles	40 mg Fe, 50 mg vit C			
						Iron drops	12.5 mg Fe as FS			
						Sprinkles placebo	n/a			
Zlotkin et al. 2003 (11)	Ghana	304	6–18 mo	2 mo (60 Sprinkles sachets), daily intake	Hb 70–99 g/L	Sprinkles – Zn	80 mg Fe, 50 mg vit C, 10 mg Zn	Hb, sFt, plasma Zn, anthropometry	Hb, sFt, plasma Zn, malaria, anthropometry	Adherence, side effects, ease of use
						Sprinkles	80 mg Fe, 50 mg vit C			
Sharieff et al. 2006 (11a)	Pakistan	75	6–12 mo	2 mo (60 Sprinkles sachets), daily intake	History of ≥1 episode of diarrhea in preceding 2 wk	Sprinkles – probiotics	30 mg Fe, 5 mg Zn, 50 mg vit C, 300 µg vit A, 7.5 µg vit D, 150 µg folic acid plus L. acidophilus	Anthropometry	Hb, sFt	Longitudinal prevalence of diarrhea, morbidity indicators
						Sprinkles	30 mg Fe, 5 mg Zn, 50 mg vit C, 300 µg vit A, 7.5 µg vit D, 150 µg folic acid			
						Sprinkles placebo	n/a			
Christofides et al. 2006 (15)	Ghana	133	6–18 mo	2 mo (60 Sprinkles sachets), daily intake	Hb 70–99 g/L	Sprinkles – FF³ 12.5	12.5 mg Fe, 5 mg Zn, 50 mg vit C, 300 µg vit A, 7.5 µg vit D, 160 µg folic acid	Hb, sFt, CRP, sTfR³, malaria, anthropometry	Hb, sFt, CRP, sTfR, anthropometry	Adherence, side effects, ease of use, Hb status at wk 3
						Sprinkles – FF 20	20 mg Fe, 5 mg Zn, 50 mg vit C, 300 µg vit A, 7.5 µg vit D, 160 µg folic acid			
						Sprinkles – FF 30	30 mg Fe, 5mg Zn, 50 mg vit C, 300 µg vit A, 7.5 µg vit D, 160 µg folic acid			
						Sprinkles – FP 20	20 mg Fe as FP⁴, 5 mg Zn, 50 mg vit C, 300 µg vit A, 7.5 µg vit D, 160 µg folic acid			
						Iron drops	15 mg as FS			

Study	Country	n	Age	Duration/regimen	Hb criteria	Group	Composition	Outcomes	Outcomes	Other
Hyder et al. 2005, 2007 (12, 27)	Bangladesh	136	12–24 mo	2 mo with different administration regimen	Hb 70–109 g/L	Sprinkles – daily	12.5 mg Fe, 5 mg Zn, 50 mg vit C, 300 μg vit A, 150 μg folic acid	Hb, sFt, sTfR, anthropometry	Hb, sFt, sTfR, anthropometry	Adherence, side effects, acceptability
						Sprinkles – once weekly	30 mg Fe, 5 mg Zn, 50 mg vit C, 300 μg vit A, 150 μg folic acid			
Ip et al. 2005 (22)	Bangladesh	362	6–24 mo	60 Sprinkles sachets over a different time period	Hb ≥70 g/L	Sprinkles – daily, 2 mo	12.5 mg Fe, 5 mg Zn, 50 mg vit C, 300 μg vit A, 160 μg folic acid	Hb, anthropometry	Hb, anthropometry	Adherence, Acceptability, Hb status of nonanemics at 6 mo post-intervention
						Sprinkles – flexible, 3 mo	Same as above			
						Sprinkles – flexible, 4 mo	Same as above			
Giovannini et al. 2006 (17)	Cambodia	204	6 mo	12 mo, daily	Hb ≥70 g/L	Sprinkles – multiple	12.5 mg Fe, 5 mg Zn, 50 mg vit A, 300 μg vit C, 7.5 μg vit D, 150 μg folic acid	Hb, sFt, CRP, anthropometry, malaria	Hb, sFt, CRP, anthropometry, malaria	Adherence, side effects, acceptability
						Sprinkles – folic acid	12.5 mg Fe, 150 μg folic acid			
						Sprinkles placebo	n/a			
Hirve et al. 2007 (16)	India	432	6–18 mo	2 mo (60 Sprinkles sachets), daily intake	Hb 70–100 g/L	Sprinkles – FF12.5	12.5 mg Fe, 5 mg Zn, 50 mg vit C, 300 μg vit A, 7.5 μg vit D, 160 μg folic acid	Hb, sFt, anthropometry	Hb, sFt, anthropometry	Adherence, side effects, concurrent illnesses, ease of use, Hb status at wk 3
						Sprinkles – FF20	20 mg Fe, 5 mg Zn, 50 mg vit C, 300 μg vit A, 7.5 μg vit D, 160 μg folic acid			
						Sprinkles – FF30	30 mg Fe, 5 mg Zn, 50 mg vit C, 300 μg vit A, 7.5 μg vit D, 160 μg folic acid			
						Sprinkles – FP20	20 mg Fe as FP, 5mg Zn, 50 mg vit C, 300 μg vit A, 7.5μg vit D, 160 μg folic acid			
						Iron drops	20 mg as FS (ferrous glycine drops)			

[1] ferrous sulphate · [2] serum ferritin · [3] ferrous fumarate · [4] C-reactive protein
[5] soluble transferrin receptor · [6] ferric pyrophosphate
Note: In all studies outlined above, severely anemic infants (Hb<70 g/L) were excluded. To be included in the studies, all infants were required to be ingesting at least one weaning food daily in addition to breastmilk. The form of iron in Sprinkles is microencapsulated ferrous fumarate.

demonstrated that both the iron and zinc in Sprinkles are adequately absorbed and that infants with IDA absorb iron from Sprinkles about twice as efficiently as iron deficient or non-anemic infants (13, 14). Geometric mean absorption from two doses of iron from Sprinkles (30 mg vs. 45 mg) was 8.3% (range: 2.9–17.8%) in infants with anemia and 4.5% (range: 1.1–10.6%) in infants without anemia (13). Geometric mean absorption from two doses of zinc from Sprinkles (5 mg vs. 10 mg) was ~6–7% in a mixed population of anemic and non-anemic young children (14). Based on these data, further studies were carried out to determine the most appropriate dose of iron to include in a Sprinkles sachet for program settings and the most appropriate duration of intervention. A dose-response study was first conducted in rural Ghana to compare the hemoglobin response in anemic children to iron drops containing 15 mg of iron as ferrous sulfate, or to Sprinkles containing either 12.5, 20, or 30 mg of iron as ferrous fumarate or 20 mg of iron as micronized ferric pyrophosphate (15). After 2 months of intervention, the prevalence of anemia in all groups dropped to less than 45%, with no difference between the groups. Because there was no observed dose effect on hemoglobin concentration and the 12.5 mg iron dose was efficacious in increasing hemoglobin concentration, it was concluded that a 12.5 mg iron dose (as recommended by WHO) (4) would be sufficient for program settings when using Sprinkles. After that trial, a subsequent study was conducted using 12.5 mg iron to investigate the optimal duration of the Sprinkles intervention to control anemia in a mixed population of anemic and nonanemic children. Sprinkles were given daily for either 2, 3, or 4 months. At the end of the intervention, there were no differences in anemia prevalence between groups (unpublished, S. Owusu-Agyei et al, 2003). In addition, adherence was found to be as high as 88% and did not vary between groups. Thus, it was concluded that 12.5 mg of iron given as Sprinkles for 2 months was adequate for anemia reduction. The follow-up data among the children found non-anemic at the end of the intervention showed a significant increase in anemia prevalence in all groups after 8 and 12 months post-intervention, which provided evidence that the intervention at this level of iron (12.5 mg) should be repeated more than once per year. Similar to the study conducted in Ghana, a dose-response study was conducted in India to compare the hemoglobin response to Sprinkles containing different amounts of iron (12.5, 20 and 30 mg per sachet) with the standard treatment, iron drops. After 2 months of intervention, hemoglobin concentration rose significantly in all groups with no differences between groups (16).

In the only double-blind placebo-controlled study published to date, two different formulations of Sprinkles (containing 12.5 mg iron with or without 5 mg zinc) were compared to a Sprinkles placebo. Outcomes included anemia, iron status and growth. Sprinkles were given daily for 12 months starting at 6 months of age. Findings demonstrated that Sprinkles were effective in preventing and treating anemia. Anemia cure rate was found to be ~53.5% in both groups receiving Sprinkles and 22% in the placebo group (17). The incidence of iron deficiency increased about fourfold in the placebo group and did not change in the two groups receiving Sprinkles. There were no differences in growth patterns among the three study groups.

Additional research was conducted in Ghana to compare the efficacy and acceptability of three types of micronutrient interventions added to complementary foods prepared in the home. Sprinkles, Nutritabs (crushable tablets), or Nutributter (a peanut butter spread) was to be given daily to children from 6 to 12 months of age. Results indicated that all of the interventions were well accepted and had a similar effect on iron status. Compliance was similar among the groups (18). Nutributter was the only intervention to increase the rate of growth in infants.

Effectiveness and program experience

Several larger-scale studies were conducted to gather data on effectiveness. The first large-scale distribution program using Sprinkles was conducted from 2001–2004 in Mongolia to explore the feasibility and acceptability of Sprinkles through program implementation and evaluation. Results demonstrated that distributing Sprinkles in partnership with a non-governmental organization is programmatically feasible (19, 20). Sprinkles including iron and vitamin D were used in over 15,000 children, 6 months to 3 years of age. Within program areas, the prevalence of anemia (Hb<115 g/L) decreased from 46% at baseline to 25% at the final survey. Moreover, the prevalence of vitamin D rickets significantly decreased from 43% to 33%. Sprinkles were well accepted by the target population and caregivers, and no cultural barriers were identified that would inhibit the use of Sprinkles. More recently, a project was conducted among Pakistani children and Afghan refugee children in Northern Pakistan. Sprinkles were found to be successful in reducing the prevalence of anemia in young children from 86 to 51% within a 2-month period. They were also found to be highly acceptable with a measured compliance rate of 73% (21). In Bangladesh, Sprinkles were found to be highly acceptable in an effectiveness trial which examined three administration models, including a flexible dosing schedule (22). In that study, overall anemia prevalence was reduced from 77% to 38% and mean compliance to the intervention was over 88%. In addition to community-based programs, the role of Sprinkles is being evaluated in the area of humanitarian aid. To date, Sprinkles have been successfully used in emergency settings in Indonesia and in Haiti (23).

Operational research studies were carried out in Benin and in Vietnam to evaluate the effectiveness of iron pots versus Sprinkles for infants (24). In Benin, after 6 months of supplementation with Sprinkles, the prevalence of anemia decreased by 38% and prevalence of IDA decreased by 28%. In Vietnam, the cure rate of anemia was 96% and the prevalence of low iron stores fell from 44% to 23% after 6 months of supplementation with Sprinkles. The effectiveness of Sprinkles was also assessed in reducing anemia in children 6 to 20 months of age in Haiti. The intervention was given for 2 months along with fortified wheat-soy blend (WSB) distributed through a maternal and child health and nutrition (MCHN) program. Anemia prevalence dropped from 53% to 29% in the children receiving Sprinkles along with the WSB whereas it increased from 37% to 45% in the children receiving WSB alone without Sprinkles (25). It was concluded that Sprinkles given for 2 months were effective in improving hemoglobin levels and reducing anemia in populations with high anemia prevalence. From this trial, it was also shown that it is feasible: 1) to distribute Sprinkles along with the monthly take-home food rations provided by the MCHN program; and 2) to ensure their appropriate use after just one training session (26). In addition, Sprinkles were well accepted and appreciated by mothers.

Acceptability and adherence

To determine acceptability and adherence to the intervention, caregivers were asked about their perception of their infants' response to Sprinkles, whether it changed the taste, color or consistency of the food to which it was added, and if there were any perceived side effects. Side effects recorded included the incidence of diarrhea, constipation, general discomfort, and/or darkening of the stools. Invariably, the response to Sprinkles has been positive. No appreciable change in the food to which Sprinkles was added has been reported and Sprinkles were reported to be easy to use. The only consistently reported side effect was darkening of the infant's stool, which is expected since most of the iron is excreted in stool. The average number of Sprinkles sachets consumed per child out of the total assigned during our trials was ~70% (range: 50–100%). These data suggest that Sprinkles were well accepted in the communities that received the intervention.

In a recently conducted study in Bangladesh, using a four-point measurement scale, 60% of the mothers "extremely liked," 30% "liked," and the remaining 10% "somewhat liked" the Sprinkles intervention; no one disliked Sprinkles. Major reasons cited for liking Sprinkles included ease in mixing Sprinkles with complementary food and that their use promoted the appropriate introduction of complementary foods, since Sprinkles could only be used if complementary foods were used (27). A study was also undertaken to assess the acceptability of Sprinkles among Chinese mothers in large urban and smaller pre-urban centers. Using the facilities of the ACNeilsen, Sprinkles were delivered to a total of 1,386 homes with children between 6 months and 5 years of age. After 4 weeks of usage, mothers found Sprinkles very easy to use and perceived health benefits in their children who had received Sprinkles. The overall conclusion was that Sprinkles were well accepted in this population.

Iron toxicity and safety

Since iron is toxic if too much is ingested, it is important to assess the safety of an intervention which provides iron supplements for a prolonged period of time. Safety is of particular concerns in the non-anemic recipients of an iron intervention aimed at preventing anemia. Symptoms of iron toxicity occur when intake is between 20 and 60 mg iron per kilogram of body weight (28). A young child would need to consume many Sprinkles sachets (~20) to reach toxicity levels. Single-dose packaging, the bland taste of the Sprinkles powder, and distribution of a limited supply are deterrents to accidental overdosing. A further advantage of single-dose packaging is that no special measuring or handling is required. Risk of overdose is therefore less compared to liquid iron preparations, which are distributed in multiple dose bottles. These liquid preparations, can be inadvertently and easily consumed in their entirety thus leading to severe toxicity.

Table 17.2: Pharmacokinetics of microencapsulated versus non-microencapsulated formulations. Based on (30–32)

Compound	Cmax[1]	Tmax[2]
1) **Digoxin (0.76 mg)**		
Microencapsulated	2.0 ± 0.5 nmol/L	3.3 ± 0.6
Nonencapsulated	4.7 ± 1.1 nmol/L	1.1 ± 0.4
2) **Venlafaxine**		
150 mg encapsulated	149 ± 79 ng/mL	5.4 ± 1.1
75 mg nonencapsulated	225 ± 86 ng/mL	2.0 ± 0.7
3) **O-demethylvenlafaxine**		
150 mg encapsulated	260 ± 109 ng/mL	9.0 ± 2.6
75 mg nonencapsulated	290 ± 117 ng/mL	3.1 ± 1.5
4) **Alpha-tocopherol (5,000 IU)**		
Microencapsulated	3.29 ± 0.13 µg/mL	76.8 ± 8.9
Oil form	4.07 ± 0.19 µg/mL	73.1 ± 14.1

[1]Peak serum concentration

[2]Time to peak serum concentration (hours)

Table 17.3: Pharmacokinetics upon ingestion with and without food. Based on (31).

Compound	Cmax[1]	Tmax[2]
Digoxin microencapsulated		
Fasting	2.0 ± 0.5	3.3 ± 0.6
Postprandial	1.0 ± 0.3	3.9 ± 1.7
Digoxin nonencapsulated		
Fasting	4.7 ± 1.1	1.1 ± 0.4
Postprandial	2.7 ± 0.5	1.4 ± 0.9

[1]Peak serum concentration (nmol/L)
[2]Time to peak serum concentration (hours)

In two small trials conducted to date, it was demonstrated that Sprinkles were safe for the prevention of anemia. One of the trials was a multicenter randomized controlled trial, which was conducted in non-anemic young children in Northern Canada. After receiving Sprinkles or a placebo for 6 months, no differences in serum ferritin concentration (all values were within the normal range) or adverse effects were found (29). In addition, growth was not impaired by the use of Sprinkles. The other trial involved non-anemic children who were given Sprinkles either weekly or daily for a 13-week period during meals served in a kindergarten in Northern China. At the end of the intervention, none of the children who had received Sprinkles had elevated serum ferritin levels (30).

The impact of iron on enhancing the severity of infections, both parasitic (malaria) and bacterial, remains an important but unresolved issue. It is postulated that if rapid absorption of iron (e.g., from an iron supplement) exceeds the transferrin binding capacity, there is the possibility of free (non-transferrin bound) iron enhancing pathogen (parasite or bacteria) proliferation. It is well known that the form and dose of iron will impact the rate of absorption. For example, the most water soluble forms of iron (e.g., ferrous sulfate) are absorbed more quickly than those that are less water soluble (e.g., ferrous fumarate). In addition, there is evidence that the peak serum iron level of the same iron source is directly related to the dose and that the higher the dose is, the higher the peak serum iron level will be. Microencapsulation will also impact the rate of absorption. Traditionally, microencapsulation has been used in the pharmaceutical industry for two reasons: 1) to mask the taste of a strong tasting chemical; and 2) to slow the release of a drug into the bloodstream. It has long been determined that sustained-release forms of drugs (or nutrients) have different absorption kinetics (and characteristics) than regular forms. Absorption kinetics can be examined by comparing the peak serum concentration (Cmax) with and without encapsulation. Results of such studies have shown the microencapsulated form of a drug or nutrient to have significantly reduced and delayed Cmax (**Table 17.2**) (31–33). The study by Bergdahl, et al. (32) also examined the effect of giving the drug with or without food and demonstrated that, not surprisingly, Cmax tended to be higher when the drug was given in a fasting state (**Table 17.3**).

The iron in Sprinkles is in the form of microencapsulated ferrous fumarate. The microencapsulate (an edible vegetable-based lipid) masks the taste of the iron and prevents interactions between the iron and the food to which it is added, thereby preventing undesirable color changes. We have not directly compared Cmax of ferrous sulfate drops (or other iron interventions containing ferrous sulfate) with that of encapsulated ferrous fumarate (as is used in Sprinkles) at a similar dose. However, we recently compared iron provided as Sprinkles (with food) with iron provided as a tablet (without food) in adults and demonstrated that the Cmax was higher with the tablet (unpublished, B. Hartman-Craven et al, 2006). It is noteworthy that Middleton, et al. (34) compared ferrous sulfate (in tablet form) to encapsulated ferrous fumarate at the same dose in six healthy adults and found that Cmax for ferrous sulfate was about 60 mcg/100 mL versus 20 mcg/100 mL for encapsulated ferrous fumarate. Therefore, based on the experimental evidence available in the literature as well as our own data showing different absorption characteristics of iron given with and without food, we postulate that the dynamics of iron absorption are different with Sprinkles (added to food and containing microencapsulated ferrous fumarate) compared to ferrous sulfate products (given with or without food). We would therefore predict a lower Cmax with Sprinkles. Thus, in terms of safety, if higher Cmax for iron increases susceptibility to infection, fortified foods (including Sprinkles) appear to be a safer alternative. More studies on this topic are warranted.

SPRINKLES FORMULATION DEVELOPMENT

Two standard formulations have been developed: a nutritional anemia formulation (**Table 17.4**) and a complete micronutrient formulation (**Table 17.5**). In addition to iron, the nutritional anemia formulation includes ascorbic acid to enhance iron absorption, folic acid to prevent megaloblastic anemia, and zinc and vitamin A to enhance immune status. The level of nutrients used in the formulations is based on bioavailability and dose-response studies using Sprinkles as well as the

Recommended Nutrient Intakes (RNI) published by WHO (2002) (35) and the Dietary Reference Intakes of the Institute of Medicine in the US (28). The doses of micronutrient in these formulations do not exceed the Tolerable Upper Intake Level (UL) set by the Institute (i.e., the highest level of a nutrient that is likely to pose no risk of adverse health effects to 98% of a population and refers to total intake of a nutrient from food, fortified food, and supplements) (28).

ADVANTAGES OF SPRINKLES

The Sprinkles intervention has many advantages (**Table 17.6**). One of the greatest benefits of the Sprinkles concept is that it can be easily incorporated into currently recommended complementary feeding practices for infants after 6 months of age. In many underdeveloped countries, poor weaning practices are common, such as prolonged exclusive breastfeeding, delayed introduction of semi-solid foods, and feeding of poor quality complementary foods with low iron content and bioavailability (36). Aside from providing iron and other essential micronutrients, the Sprinkles intervention can contribute to healthy weaning practices through the concurrent promotion of appropriate feeding practices, since Sprinkles can only be used with complementary foods.

COST-EFFECTIVENESS OF THE SPRINKLES INTERVENTION

The cost-effectiveness of a Sprinkles intervention in Pakistan was recently published (37). Pakistan was chosen because of its high rates of anemia (50– 90% depending on the population group) and high longitudinal prevalence of diarrhea in children (10– 20%). The infant mortality rate is also very high (83 per 1,000) and the per capita GDP is low. In the Pakistan model, Sprinkles containing zinc and iron were found to be cost-effective. The estimated cost per DALY

Table 17.4: Composition of nutritional anemia formulation Sprinkles.

Micronutrient	Amount
Iron	12.5 mg
Zinc	5 mg
Folic acid	160 µg
Vitamin A	300 µg RE
Vitamin C	30 mg

saved was $12.20 (US), and cost per death averted was $406. There are also cognitive benefits associated with the prevention of iron deficiency anemia, which, when translated into academic achievement and ultimate adult employment are estimated to be $37 gained for each $1 spent.

ENSURING A SUSTAINABLE SUPPLY

As the results of the first studies showing the efficacy of Sprinkles were becoming available, the

Table 17.5: Composition of multi-micronutrient formulation Sprinkles.

Micronutrient	Amount
Vitamin A	400 µg RE
Vitamin C	30 mg
Vitamin D	5 µg
Vitamin E	5 mg TE
Vitamin B$_1$	0.5 mg
Vitamin B$_2$	0.5 mg
Vitamin B$_6$	0.5 mg
Vitamin B$_{12}$	0.9 µg
Folic acid	150 µg
Niacin	6 mg
Iron	12.5 mg
Zinc	4.1 mg
Copper	0.56 mg
Iodine	90 µg

need for a reliable high quality supply became apparent. In 2000, the H.J. Heinz Company of Pittsburgh expressed an interest in the Sprinkles program as a component of their corporate social responsibility program. Since 2001, the H.J. Heinz Company has provided support and expertise in evaluation of consumer needs and a supply of Sprinkles for research, while the H.J. Heinz Foundation has provided financial support for research activities. Through a formal process of technology transfer, local country-specific Sprinkles production has been encouraged. Currently approved independent manufacturers are supporting Sprinkles production in Guyana, Pakistan, Bangladesh, Indonesia, India, and Canada.

SCALING UP FOR COUNTRYWIDE DISTRIBUTION

For Sprinkles, the scale-up process involves the identification of sustainable methods of distribution that are able to reach and provide Sprinkles to the most vulnerable populations in underdeveloped countries. While taking Sprinkles from small-scale research projects to larger-scale programs, we quickly realized that our research group did not have the necessary funding, experience, or personnel needed to influence health policy, develop a social marketing strategy, or maintain a distribution network at a countrywide level. We have thus partnered with organizations that specialize in each of these areas to help achieve our goal of sustainable distribution. Examples of these organizations include PSI for social marketing in Haiti, SMC for social marketing in Bangladesh, and Greenstar for social marketing in Pakistan.

SPRINKLES IN OTHER AGE GROUPS

Research and development of Sprinkles for pregnant and lactating women, another group at risk, was launched in 2004. Studies in pregnant and lactating women are underway in Bangladesh, Kyrgyzstan, Mexico, and Canada. It is hoped that Sprinkles for pregnant and lactating women will follow the same path as Sprinkles for children by providing an evidence-based, cost-effective approach to treat and prevent anemia, a major cause of morbidity and mortality in women in developing countries.

CONCLUSION

Each stage in the evolution of the Sprinkles intervention for young children has been evaluated in a controlled manner. It has been determined that the use of Sprinkles does not appreciably change the taste or color of the food to which it is added; it has been shown that anemia rates decrease with the use of Sprinkles; and it has been documented that the acceptability of Sprinkles among caregivers who use Sprinkles in their homes is high. Finally, through various partnerships, successful models to scale up the intervention for country-wide use have been developed. The challenge for the future is to advocate for the adoption of Sprinkles in nutrition policies of underdeveloped countries to allow the distribution of Sprinkles to vulnerable populations.

Table 17.6: Advantages of the Sprinkles intervention.

1	Sprinkles can provide the Recommended Nutrient Intake (RNI) of micronutrients to each child.
2	In addition to iron, essential micronutrients such as vitamins A, C and D, folic acid, iodine, and zinc can be added to the sachets to prevent and treat micronutrient deficiencies and improve overall nutritional status.
3	Lipid encapsulation of the iron prevents it from interacting with food and masks its taste, thus there are minimal changes to the taste, color, or texture of the food to which Sprinkles are added. Encapsulation may also reduce gastrointestinal discomfort and interaction of iron with other nutrients.
4	The sachets are easy to use and convenient. No special measuring utensils or handling is required and they can be given with any meal during the day. One does not have to be literate to learn how to use them.
5	The use of Sprinkles does not require any change in food practices as it can be mixed with homemade foods. They do not conflict with breastfeeding and can help promote the timely transition from exclusive breastfeeding to complementary foods at 6 months of age as recommended by WHO.
6	Sprinkles are a food-based rather than a medical intervention and thus can be easily incorporated into any feeding schedule.
7	The potential for overdose is unlikely because numerous individual sachets would have to be opened and ingested for this to occur (an infant would need to consume approximately 20 sachets to reach toxicity levels).
8	The sachets are lightweight and thus are simple to store, transport and distribute. Sprinkles have a long shelf-life (2 years), even in hot or humid conditions.
9	The cost of Sprinkles is not excessive (US$0.015 to 0.035 per sachet depending on volume produced and site of production). The packaging of Sprinkles is attractive and thus is easily accepted.

ACKNOWLEDGMENTS

We gratefully acknowledge the generous financial support of the H.J. Heinz Company Foundation. Without this support, we would not have been able to accomplish our numerous research goals in support of improving the nutrition of vulnerable populations worldwide.

In addition, funding agencies including the Canadian International Development Agency (CIDA), the Canadian Institutes of Health Research (CIHR), the Inter-American Development Bank (IADB), Health Canada, the International Atomic Energy Agency (IAEA), the Micronutrient Initiative (MI), and the United States Agency for International Development (USAID) are gratefully acknowledged for their support of the Sprinkles Global Health Initiative at the Hospital for Sick Children, Toronto, Canada.

Grateful thanks are expressed to our research affiliates and program partners around the world without whom none of the research projects on Sprinkles would have been possible.

REFERENCES

1. United Nations Children's Fund. Delivering essential micronutrients: iron. Available from: http://www.unicef.org/nutrition/index_iron.html, 2003. (accessed in August 2006).
2. Grantham-McGregor S, Ani C. A review of studies on the effect of iron deficiency on cognitive development in children. J Nutr 2001;131:649S–666S; discussion 666S–668S.
3. Ramakrishnan U, Yip R. Experiences and challenges in industrialized countries: control of iron deficiency in industrialized countries. J Nutr 2002;132:820S–4S.
4. Stoltzfus RJ, Dreyfuss ML. Guidelines for the use of iron supplements to prevent and treat iron deficiency anemia. Washington, DC: INACG/WHO/UNICEF, 1998.
5. Andrews NC. Disorders of iron metabolism. N Engl J Med 1999;341:1986–95.
6. Galloway R, McGuire J. Determinants of compliance with iron supplementation: supplies, side effects, or psychology? Soc Sci Med 1994;39:381–90.
7. DeMaeyer EM, Dallman P, Gurney JM, Hallberg L, Sood SK, Srikantia SG. Preventing and controlling iron deficiency anaemia through primary health care: a guide for health administrators and programme managers. Geneva: World Health Organization, 1989.
8. Nestel P, Alnwick D. Iron/multi-micronutrient supplements for young children. Summary and conclusions of consultation held at UNICEF. August 19–20, 1996. Copenhagen. Washington, DC: ILSI, 1997.
9. Zlotkin S, Arthur P, Antwi KY, Yeung G. Treatment of anemia with microencapsulated ferrous fumarate plus ascorbic acid supplied as sprinkles to complementary (weaning) foods. Am J Clin Nutr 2001;74:791–5.
10. Zlotkin S, Antwi KY, Schauer C, Yeung G. Use of microencapsulated iron(II) fumarate sprinkles to prevent recurrence of anaemia in infants and young children at high risk. Bull World Health Organ 2003;81:108–15.
11. Zlotkin S, Arthur P, Schauer C, Antwi KY, Yeung G, Piekarz A. Home-fortification with iron and zinc sprinkles or iron sprinkles alone successfully treats anemia in infants and young children. J Nutr 2003;133:1075–80.
11a. Sharieff W, Bhutta Z, Schauer C, Tomlinson G, Zlotkin S. Micronutrients (including zinc) reduce diarrhoea in children: the Pakistan Sprinkles Diarrhoea Study. Arch Dis Child 2006;91:573-9.

12. Hyder Z, Haseen F, Rahman M, Tondeur MC, Zlotkin SH. Effect of daily versus once weekly home fortification with sprinkles on haematological and iron status among young children in rural Bangladesh. Food Nutr Bull 2007 (In press).

13. Tondeur MC, Schauer CS, Christofides AL, et al. Determination of iron absorption from intrinsically labeled microencapsulated ferrous fumarate (sprinkles) in infants with different iron and hematologic status by using a dual-stable-isotope method. Am J Clin Nutr 2004;80:1436–44.

14. Zlotkin SH, Schauer C, Owusu Agyei S, et al. Demonstrating zinc and iron bioavailability from intrinsically labeled microencapsulated ferrous fumarate and zinc gluconate Sprinkles in young children. J Nutr 2006;136:920–5.

15. Christofides A, Asante KP, Schauer C, Sharieff W, Owusu Agyei S, Zlotkin S. Multi-micronutrient Sprinkles including a low dose of iron provided as microencapsulated ferrous fumarate improves haematologic indices in anaemic children: a randomized clinical trial. Mater Child Nutr 2006;2:169–180.

16. Hirve S., Bhave S, Bavdekar A, et al. Low dose of Sprinkles–an innovative approach to treat iron deficiency anemia in infants and young children. Indian Pediatr 2007 (in press).

17. Giovannini M, Sala D, Usuelli M, et al. Double-blind, placebo-controlled trial comparing effects of supplementation with two different combinations of micronutrients delivered as sprinkles on growth, anemia, and iron deficiency in cambodian infants. J Pediatr Gastroenterol Nutr 2006;42:306–12.

18. Adu-Afarwuah S, Lartey A, Brown KH, Zlotkin S, Dewey KG. Randomized comparison of 3 types of micronutrient supplements in Ghanaian infants. FASEB J 2006;20(4, Part 1): 557(abstr).

19. Colleen Emary and SM Ziauddin Hyder. Sprinkles: Home-based fortification in Mongolia. Issue Theme: Anaemia. In: Nutrition Issue 3, December 2006:9-11

20. Nyamsuren M, Emary C, Bat G, Gerein S, Zlotkin S, Chan M. Integrated programming, including homebased fortification using 'Sprinkles', is an effective strategy for addressing anaemia in Mongolian children. Proceedings of the International Nutritional Anemia Consultative Group Symposium; November 18, 2004; Lima, Peru. Washington, DC: ILSI Research Foundation,2004 (abstr).

21. Khan E, Hyder SM, Tondeur MC, Raza S, Ahmed Khan N, Zlotkin S. Home fortification with Sprinkles to reduce childhood anemia: lessons learned in North West Frontier Province, Pakistan. Pak J Med Res 2006;45:35–40.

22. Ip H, Hyder SM, Haseen F, Rahman M, Zlotkin SH. The effectiveness of flexible administration of Sprinkles in anemic and non-anemic infants and young children in rural Bangladesh. Proceedings of the Federation of American Societies for Experimental Biology (FASEB). San Diego,, 2005 (abstr).

23. De Pee S, Moench-Pfanner R, Martini E, Zlotkin S, Darton-Hill I, Bloem MW. Home-fortification in emergency response and transition programming: Experiences in Aceh and Nias, Indonesia. Food Nutr Bull 2007 (In Press).

24. Berti PR, Zlotkin S, FitzGerald S, et al. The efficacy of iron pots and steel pots in reducing prevalence of anaemia in Vietnam. International Nutritional Anemia Consultative Group Symposium. November 18, 2004, Lima, Peru. Washington, DC: ILSI Research Foundation,2004 (abstr).

25. Menon P, Ruel MT, Loechl CU, Arimond M, Habicht J, Pelto G. Micronutrient Sprinkles are effective at reducing anemia among children 6–24 months in rural Haiti. FASEB J 2006;20(4, Part 1):556 (abstr).

26. Loechl CU, Arimond M, Menon P, Ruel MT, Pelto G, Habicht J. Feasibility of distributing micronutrient Sprinkles along with take-home food aid rations in rural Haiti. FASEB J 2006;20(4, Part 1): 612-3(abstr).

27. Hyder SMZ, Haseen F, Ip H, Zlotkin S. Acceptability of Sprinkles in rural Bangladesh: a new home fortification approach to deliver micronutrients among young children. Proceedings of the Federation of American Societies for Experimental Biology (FASEB). San Diego, 2005 (abstr).

28. National Academy of Sciences, Institute of Medicine, Food and Nutrition Board. Dietary

Reference Intakes for vitamin A, vitamin K, arsenic, boron, chromium, copper, iodine, iron, manganese, molybdenum, nickel, silicon, vanadium and zinc. Washington, DC: National Academy Press, 2001.

29. Christofides A, Schauer C, Sharieff W, Zlotkin SH. Acceptability of micronutrient sprinkles: a new food-based approach for delivering iron to First Nations and Inuit children in Northern Canada. Chronic Dis Can 2005;26:114–20.

30. Sharieff W, Yin SA, Wu M, et al. Short-term daily or weekly administration of micronutrient Sprinkles has high compliance and does not cause iron overload in Chinese schoolchildren: a cluster-randomised trial. Public Health Nutr 2006;9:336–44.

31. Baldi A, Bontempo V, Cheli F, Carli S, Sgoifo Rossi C, Dell'Orto V. Relative bioavailability of vitamin E in dairy cows following intraruminal administration of three different preparations of DL-alpha-tocopheryl acetate. Vet Res 1997;28:517–24.

32. Bergdahl B, Bogentoft C, Jonsson UE, Magnusson JO. Fasting and postprandial absorption of digoxin from a microencapsulated formulation. Eur J Clin Pharmacol 1983;25:207–10.

33. Olver JS, Burrows GD, Norman TR. The treatment of depression with different formulations of venlafaxine: a comparative analysis. Hum Psychopharmacol 2004;19:9-16.

34. Middleton EJ, Nagy E, Morrison AB. Studies on the absorption of orally administered iron from sustained-release preparations. New Eng J Med 1966;274:136–9.

35. World Health Organization. Recommended Nutrient Intakes. Joint FAO/WHO Expert Consultation. Vitamin and mineral requirements in human nutrition. Geneva: World Health Organization, 2002.

36. Gibson RS, Ferguson EL, Lehrfeld J. Complementary foods for infant feeding in developing countries: their nutrient adequacy and improvement. Eur J Clin Nutr 1998;52:764–70.

37. Sharieff W, Horton SE, Zlotkin S. Economic gains of a home fortification program: evaluation of "Sprinkles" from the provider's perspective. Can J Public Health 2006;97:20–3.

18

Safety of interventions to reduce nutritional anemias

Klaus Schümann[1]   Noel W. Solomons[2]

[1]*Central Institute for Nutrition and Food Research, Technical University of Munich, Freising, Germany*
[2]*Center for Studies of Sensory Impairment, Aging and Metabolism, Guatemala City, Guatemala*
Contact: kschuemann@schuemann-muc.de

KLAUS SCHÜMANN
Klaus obtained his MD from the Free University in Berlin, Germany. He is currently Senior Researcher and Professor for Pharmacology and Toxicology at the Central Institute for Nutrition and Food Research at the Technical University in Munich, Germany. He has participated in a number of committees, including membership of the Task Force on Upper Safe Levels for Vitamins and Minerals of the European Commission, and is a member of the Task Force on Chronic Diseases of the IUNS, as well as being on the scientific advisory board of a range of publications.

NOEL W. SOLOMONS
Noel obtained his MD from Harvard Medical School, USA. He is the Program Director for Central America of the Centre for Studies of Sensory Impairment, Aging and Metabolism (CeSSIAM), which he cofounded in 1985 and is also CeSSIAM's Senior Scientist and Scientific Director. Noel's scientific interests are the physiology of trace element absorption, assessment of micronutrient status, nutrition and non-communicable diseases, and gerontological nutrition. He is a consultant to many organizations and universities, is author of over 500 publications, serves on the editorial board of 11 scientific publications, and is an active member of many nutrition committees. Noel has also won numerous awards for his work.

INTRODUCTION

As the contributions to this manual amply illustrate, nutritional anemia represents a public health problem of vast magnitude worldwide, depriving sufferers of physical endurance, cognitive function, immune defenses, and maximal vitality; it merits a vigorous public health campaign to reduce its prevalence. Anemia is defined as a state of reduced hemoglobin concentration, reduced number of circulating erythrocytes in the blood, or both. In the developing world, it is caused by a lack of essential constituents of hemoglobin or erythrocytes. Iron deficiency, for example, accounts for approximately half of the anemias arising in developing countries (1). The other half is non-iron-deficiency anemia, which was proposed to be due to lack of copper, zinc, folate, or vitamins A, B_2, B_{12}, or C (2). Such anemia-related deficiencies can be due to blood losses, to deficient supply of the constituents, to wastage from the body, or to impaired utilization. Besides deficiency states, anemia can have other origins such as anemia of chronic diseases (3) or anemia due to hemoglobinopathies. The scope of deficient nutrients and the different causes of deficiency require different interventions to correct them, and we shall discuss that here.

A venerable admonition from the Hippocratic medicine tradition states: *Primum non nocere* (first, do no harm). Unfortunately, there are certain safety issues and concerns for the very measures instituted to combat nutritional anemia. These arise because adverse consequences, and even toxic effects, can result from excess exposure to the vitamins and minerals directly or indirectly involved in nutritional anemia. Moreover, because specific individuals or subgroups within a population can habitually receive excessive exposure to micronutrients in supplements or fortified foods (or have idiosyncratic reactions to other measures involved in public health control of anemia), there is potential harm to some of those who are reached by an intervention to control nutritional anemias. Protecting the pub-

lic's health, therefore, involves both reducing the risk of nutritional anemia and exempting individuals in the population from adverse consequences of these interventions.

STANDARDS OF SAFETY FOR THERAPEUTIC AND PUBLIC HEALTH INTERVENTIONS

Whether as a practitioner in a clinical engagement with an anemic subject or as a public health authority in an anemia-endemic society, certain standards to guarantee the safety of therapeutic or prophylactic interventions must be maintained.

Supplementation

Nutrient supplements may contain more than the physiological daily requirements for a nutrient, in particular for iron. Issues of quality control in manufacturing and dosing are important. For vitamins, overages are routinely included in the formulation of supplements at the time of their manufacture so that the specified dosage will be present on the expiration date of the shelf life. Therapeutic supplementation aims to level out existing imbalances with pathogenic consequences, such as severe iron deficiency that exceeds the compensating capacity of homoeostasis. The problem with iron supplementation is to avoid new imbalances that may arise from iron-induced corrosive effects or oxidative damage in the different compartments, from the interaction of iron homoeostasis with inflammatory responses, or from iron-related imbalances in the equilibrium between hosts and pathogens, as was observed with malaria in the Pemba trial (4). Accuracy in delivery is even more important, as an unintended overdosing, such as occurred with a liquid preparation of retinyl palmitate in Assam, India (5), can threaten lives and damage the reputation of intervention programs.

Fortification

When exogenous nutrients are placed into food, the variation across a population in the consumption of the fortified items comes into play. There can be a tenfold variance in the amount of a product, such as cooking oil or sugar, between the highest and lowest consumers in a population. The work by Quinlivan and Gregory (6) on folic acid intakes in the USA since the 1998 institution of mandatory folic acid fortification of the food supply illustrates the phenomenon of sequestration of extreme habitually elevated intakes. Security concerns would militate that the fortification level should provide a safe exposure for the upper distribution of consumers.

Dietary diversification

Interventions related to promoting foods as the source of nutrients are not without potential safety issues. Nutritional anemias can be combated by increased consumption of food items rich in hematinic nutrients. Such interventions, however, might encourage a dietary pattern that is less healthful, by increasing higher intake of foods promoting chronic disease risk. Distorted intakes of red meat as a natural source of bioavailable iron could increase the risk of colon cancer and the host of diseases associated with saturated fat exposure.

Consequences of universal nutrient distribution and considerations for targeted distribution through screening

Toxicology and risk assessment have long viewed environmental exposure issues in terms of the range of ambient exposures in a population as illustrated in **Figure 18.1** (7–9). Changing only the mean level of exposure in the population as a whole may not make a significant contribution to public health. Within a population with a distribution in which a certain percentage has intakes above some upper acceptable levels, gains for public health can only be made by reducing the intake of that fraction with unacceptably high intakes. Efforts to reduce the risk of deficiency of an entire population are ineffective unless they control excess exposures. Conversely, efforts that control excess exposures – but also decrease

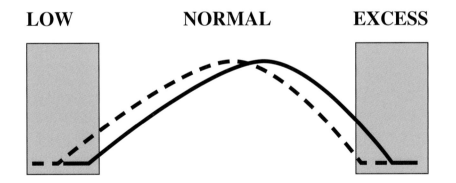

LOW   **NORMAL**   **EXCESS**

Figure 18.1: A mean shift of values to the right (i.e., to higher intakes in the whole population) reduces the deficient fraction as intended. However, at the same time, a mean shift to the right increases the fraction with excessive intakes, when the distribution of intakes remains unaltered. To avoid this effect, supplementation should be targeted to the deficient fraction of the population. For fortification, food matrices that are consumed at relatively constant amounts (e.g., salt, sugar, spices, condiments, or food staples that are consumed in large and, therefore, close to constant quantities) are preferable over others with elastic consumption. This helps to avoid uncontrolled shifts in micronutrient intake due to altered consumption of the matrix.

intakes of individuals with normative exposures – may be inefficient and also produce untoward effects on the lower end of the distribution.

The group with below adequate intake is the inherent target of any micronutrient intervention program. If the effort is aimed at raising the mean intake of the population, it may be both inefficient (spreading around resources where they are not needed) and ineffective (not targeting those most in need of exposure to the nutrient), and at the same time harmful (by pushing some of those at the upper end of the distribution to an even higher habitual intake) **(Figure 18.1)**.

It may be concluded that nutrient interventions are inherently safest when they find a way to target those who are most in need, and remove them from the danger zone of low intakes, as compared to those that distribute nutrients to everyone in the population as a way to reach those with need. Influencing the mean exposure only benefits the public health goal, if it successfully removes the population in the inadequacy risk group from that status without producing additional excessive exposure at the opposite end of the distribution.

Policy makers and public health officials must be uncompromising with the principle that fortification programs must be safe for all consumers. This runs into an obvious mathematical constraint when the range of intakes in a population is wide. Allen, et al. (10) note: "The price of making an intervention for nutritional anemia more effective and efficient is often to make it less safe. Conversely, making such interventions safer may exact a high price on effectiveness and efficiency. The primacy is on the safety side; hence, the challenge for policy and program is to maximize the safety and effectiveness of interventions in the most culturally-acceptable and economic manner possible." The inevitable logical consequence of the aforementioned phenomenon will be a need to develop diagnostic assessment and monitoring in conjunction with population-wide interventions. This will require the development of inexpensive, culturally acceptable, and sustainable measures to obtain and utilize information on the intake and status of individuals and populations.

SAFETY OF INTERVENTIONS TO ADDRESS IRON-DEFICIENCY AND IRON DEFICIENCY ANEMIA

Role in nutritional anemias

Three chapters of this Manual (11–13) amply discuss the biological and physiological issues associated with the role of iron and the transport of oxygen to tissues via hemoglobin in the red cells. The reduction of circulating red cell mass with insufficient oxygen transport capacity is termed anemia. When unavailability of iron to produce erythrocytes is the basis of the reduction in hemoglobin synthesis and the hypoproliferation of red cells, we are dealing with an iron deficiency anemia (IDA), a form that can be treated or prevented by iron intake. However, by virtue of its own physicochemical characteristics and biological interactions, iron presents a series of challenges to its safe application.

TOXIC AND ADVERSE EFFECTS OF IRON

Acute iron toxicity

To put this section on high dose iron toxicity into a nutritional perspective, we remind the reader that the usual nutritional supplement dose for a 70-kg adult is 30–60 mg iron, at most 120 mg during pregnancy. The usual dose for a child is 2 mg iron/kg of body weight. This is far below the intakes that may cause acute iron toxicity. Even intestinal side effects are usually not seen after oral intake of 30–60 mg iron. However, the subsequent sections are useful to understand the toxic potential of iron. Thus, very high oral iron exposures are needed to produce shock in humans (19, 20), and are relevant to therapy and prophylaxis only in the context of acciden-tal overdose. Young children are especially at risk (20) as they may accidentally ingest high iron doses in relation to body weight.

Acute iron toxicity in animals

LD_{50} values for Fe(II)-sulphate, -succinate and -gluconate after oral administration in mice are 560, 320 and 230 mg iron/kg body weight, respectively. Likewise, the impact on growth of male rats after oral application of 50 and 100 mg iron/kg body weight for 12 weeks showed a rank order of Fe(II)-sulphate > succinate > fumarate > gluconate (14). Similar investigations were per-formed to rank emetic impact and gastrointestinal damage from oral iron in cats and rabbits (15). Such ranking shows that the toxic impact varies among different iron species, in parallel to their relative bioavailability. The implication of animal studies for humans is problematic, however, as considerable differences in the quantitative aspect of iron kinetics have been found among humans, rats, and mice (and even between different stains of mice), with no qualitative differences noted (16–18).

Acute iron toxicity in humans

Ingestion of acute overdoses of oral iron prepara-tions causes mucosal erosion in the stomach and intestine. Blood-containing vomit and diarrhea are the first symptoms, followed by a "silent interval" of up to 24 hours. Gastrointestinal stric-tures are the long-term sequelae of intestinal dam-age, and may require surgical intervention. In the course of acute iron intoxication, large amounts of absorbed iron may produce shock symptoms by arteriolar dilatation, capillary leakage, and heart failure, leading to symptoms of shock. An oral dose of 180–300 mg iron/kg body weight can be lethal in humans; oral doses below 10–20 mg iron/kg body weight not only do not cause acute systemic toxicity, but represent a no observed adverse effects level (NOAEL) (14).

ADVERSE CONSEQUENCES ASSOCIATED WITH ORAL IRON INTAKE

Of more germane interest are the doses of iron to which an individual may be exposed on a daily basis from the combination of foods, fortificants in the diet, and nutrient supplements. The Insti-tute of Medicine of the National Academies (USA) sets a series of tolerable upper intake lev-els (UL) in its Dietary Reference Intakes (21), defined as "the highest level of daily nutrient intake that is likely to pose no risk of adverse health effects to almost all individuals in a spe-cific life stage group." It applies to chronic daily use. The European Union established a task force to determine similarly defined ULs for that region (22). With respect to the safety of regular con-sumption of iron, the European body failed to find sufficient scientific basis to develop a UL for this element. The North American Food and Nutrition Board, however, established age-related ULs for this mineral as shown in **Table 18.1** (21). They are 40 mg/day for the younger age groups down to infancy and 45 mg/day for adults. The criterion was gastrointestinal irritation, which has been criticized as an erroneous basis for reference to the chronic dietary setting (23).

Intestinal side effects of oral iron preparations

As recognized in the DRI (21), oral iron prepara-tions frequently cause nausea, vomiting, and epi-gastric discomfort at therapeutic dose levels (24–28). These effects are due to mucosal irrita-tion and to altered gastrointestinal motility and depend on the free iron concentration in the lumen (29). At increasing doses, an increased fraction of patients is affected (30). The lowest observed adverse effects level (LOAEL) for upper intestinal irritations at single doses was estimated to be between 50 (24) and 60 mg iron (26). More recent data suggest that even 80 mg iron does not increase intestinal side effects in pregnant women beyond the usual discomfort associated with pregnancy (31). Oral iron intake

Table 18.1: Tolerable Upper Levels of Intake (ULs) from the US-Canada Dietary Reference Intakes (DRI) and the European Food Safety Authority (EFSA) for nutrients of interest in selected age-groups from the US-Canada Dietary Reference Intakes. DRI 1998 (134), DRI 2001 (21), EFSA 2006 (22).

Nutrient	Infant	Preschool child (1–3 y)	School child (9–13 y)[1] (11–14)[2]	Adults
Iron	40 mg n.d.	40 mg n.d.	40 mg n.d.	45 mg n.d.
Folic acid[3]	n.d. n.d.	300 µg 200	600 µg 600	1000 µg 1000 µg
Vit A[4]	600 µg n.d.	600 µg 800	1700 µg 2000	3000 µg 3000
Zinc	4/5 mg[5] n.d.	7 mg 7 mg	23 mg 18 mg	40 mg 25 mg
Copper	n.d. n.d.	1 mg 1 mg	5 mg 4 mg	10 mg 5 mg

n.d. = not determined
[1] Age-range set for US-Canada schoolchild population in the DRI
[2] Age-range set for European school child population by the EFSA
[3] Refers to folate from fortification sources or supplements
[4] As preformed vitamin A, excluding any contribution from provitamin A carotenoids
[5] 4 mg/day up to 6 months, and 5 mg/day from 6 to 12 months of age.

mately 6% of therapeutic iron administrations, and seem less dose-dependent.

Iron and atherogenic effects

Observations on the correlation between dietary iron intake and the risk for acute myocardial infarction (AMI) are controversial. Due to the impact of inflammation on ferritin expression and to contradictory findings among different trials, a dose-response relationship for these effects has not been firmly established (21, 23, 32). Heme iron's putative atherogenic role is confounded by concomitant meat consumption and, thus, also by cholesterol intake effects. The assessment of iron intake by 4-day recall suggests that the risk for AMI increases by 5% (33) or 8.4% (34) with each additional milligram of ingested iron. Estimation of total iron intake over the preceding year correlated poorly with AMI risk (35), whereas intake of heme iron correlated significantly (35, 36).

Iron and inflammation

Iron supplementation also increased indices of oxidative stress and inflammation *in vivo*, such as thiobarbituric acid reactive substances (TBARS) in rats (37). In humans, breath alkanes responded to a single oral dose of 10 mg iron (38). Plasma TBARS were elevated in the plasma from pregnant women after oral intake of 60 mg iron/day (39), and luminal exposure to 80 mg iron as ferrous sulfate increased TBARS content in the human duodenal lumen (40). Moreover, the acute phase protein, antichymotrypsin, was increased in the serum after daily supplementation of 20 mg iron/day for 8 weeks in Guatemalan children (41). To select those oxidative and inflammatory responses that respond to oral iron supplementation in a systematic manner, we investigated the kinetics of changes in 23 biomarkers over time after intake of 120 mg iron/day for 7 days in three volunteers. Circulating interleukin-4 (IL-4) and tumor necrosis factor-alpha (TNF-α) increased during the first 2 days of the trial; urinary TBARS responded on days 4–6 after the beginning of the iron supplementation. Urinary 8-hydroxyguanosine (8-OHG) or F2-isoprostane (F2-IsoP) responded in two of three subjects on days 4 and 5, respectively. These responses were not of the magnitude seen in pathological conditions; they were, however, considerably elevated over the baseline state (42), showing that iron intake causes responses in oxidative biomarkers in healthy adult humans.

Iron-induced oxidative stress participated in the pathophysiology of inflammatory bowel disease (43) and rheumatoid arthritis (44) in animal experiments. Moreover, systemic inflammation induces catabolic responses in intermediary metabolism (45), which have been suggested as a cause of early growth retardation (46) observed in iron-replete infants supplemented with iron (47, 48).

Iron and bacterial infections in humans

The effect of iron on human infections reflects the ambiguity of a nutrient that is needed by the pathogen as well as for host-defence mechanisms. In 1928, McKay (49) reported that iron supplementation reduced respiratory and gastrointestinal infections in London infants by 50%. By contrast, Barry and Reeve (50) observed *E. coli* sepsis in 2% of Polynesian neonates that had received 250 mg iron dextran parenterally at birth as compared to a prevalence of 0.2% after discontinuation of this practice. In parallel, neonatal *E. coli* meningitis prevalence increased after parenteral iron administration in New Zealand (51). The bacteriostatic activity of serum from these neonates on *E. coli in vitro* was reduced, suggesting excessive free iron concentrations as a putative underlying cause (52). Hyperferremia after intravenous iron dextran administration seems to last 2–3 days (53). Moreover, neonates show high iron saturation and an impaired immune status (54). Thus, parenteral iron administration in the neonatal period is contraindicated (55).

However, oral iron supplementation is mostly beneficial. Thus, in iron-deficient children with reduced growth, oral iron supplementation reduced infection prevalence (56, 57) in line with the early observations of McKay. In a number of studies, iron administration improved iron status without negative impact on the prevalence of infection (58–60). In line with these observations, a systematic review on iron supplementation and infection found no evidence for increased prevalences in non-malaria areas, with the exception of diarrhea (61). This underscores the nonabsorbed fraction of supplemented oral iron having a negative impact in the gut lumen and increasing prevalence of diarrhea, whereas parenteral iron administration to neonates seems to increase the risk of *E. coli* sepsis and meningitis.

Therapeutic interventions

Treatment of iron deficiency anemia

Therapeutic iron supplementation employs what might be considered high oral doses, such as of 50–400 mg iron/day or cumulative parenteral administration of 250 mg iron/week. The effects on preexisting disease symptoms such as iron deficiency anemia and its consequences (62) can be individually monitored and iron doses should be continuously geared to a changing demand.

Treatment of geohelminth infections

As geohelminths do more harm than iron deficiency anemia alone, the net health impact of anthelmintic treatment is likely to go beyond that of iron supplementation. Reduction of worm load limits competitive consumption of nutrients by helminths, reduces impairment of the host's nutrient absorption, and reduces metabolic alterations caused by the infection (63). It has been suggested that the host's utilization of iron may be constrained by infection, inflammation, and/or deficiencies in other micronutrients (64). In Zanzibari children aged 6–71 months, iron supplementation improved iron status and reduced severe anemia but did not alleviate growth retardation or mild anemia. Anthelmintic treatment in the same study, by contrast, also reduced mild anemia in children under 24 months of age, reduced wasting in children under 30 months of age, and increased appetite (65). Thus, effective treatment of iron deficiency in the course of helminth infection requires anthelmintic treatment and iron supplementation simultaneously, and also has additive effects in the control of maternal anemia during pregnancy without signs of malformation. Based on such findings, the U.S. Food and Drug Administration (FDA) approved the use of albendazole in pregnancy when the potential benefit exceeds the risk, though this compound was shown to be teratogenic in some animal species (66). Mebendazole and albendazole are approved for use in children over 12 months of age (67). Both drugs are generally well tolerated. High-dose therapy may lead to abdominal pain, headache, fever, fatigue, leukopenia, and thrombocytopenia. Patients with hepatic damage require reduced doses. In hookworm infections use of albendazole seems superior to use of mebendazole (66).

Soil-transmitted helminth infections should be treated with albendazole, leomisole, mebendazole, or pyrantel, the latter costing less than $0.03 (USD) for a single dose. Treatment of a child with schistosomiasis with praziquantel is effective in 85% of cases, reducing fecal and urinary egg excretion by 90% (68). The treatment is estimated to cost between $0.30 and $1.00 USD (69).

Prophylactic interventions

Prophylactic supplementation with iron
In contrast to therapeutic situations, large scale public health oral iron supplementation aims primarily to prevent iron deficiency in high risk populations, such as infants 6–24 months of age or women of childbearing age. At any given point in time, a fraction of such populations will be iron deficient and anemic. This has led to international consensus recommendations for supplementation programs at the population level, notably for two subgroups: pregnant women; and infants and toddlers 6–24 months of age (70).

Gestational supplementation
The most venerable nutrient supplementation program in public health has been the prenatal distribution of the hematinic combination of iron and folic acid, generally as a combined tablet. The traditional dosage was a daily dose of 120 mg of iron and 200 µg of folic acid, and this practice remains widespread in developing countries today. This is despite the revision of recommendations in 1998 (70) to a formulation of 60 mg of iron and 200 µg folic acid and a later further adjustment to 400 µg. Concerns for cost, compliance, and safety motivated some professionals to explore intermittent, as opposed to daily, dosing of prenatal hematinics (71). Many comparisons of efficacy of weekly vs. daily iron-folate supplementation have been conducted (72), but few with a view to their comparative safety.

A Mexico City experience
A recent prospective randomized trial among pregnant women in Mexico City addressed the relative safety of two gestational supplementation regimens in terms of hemoconcentration, low birth weight, and premature delivery (39). Sixty pregnant women received a daily supplement tablet of 60 mg of iron, 200 µg of folic acid, and 1 µg of vitamin B_{12} from their twentieth gestational week onwards, whereas 60 women consumed two tablets (with twice the nutrients) only on one day per week over the same interval. Efficacy for preventing low hemoglobin at delivery was equivalent for both hematinic regimens. Side effects of nausea, heartburn, and constipation were higher in the daily supplement group. Treatment assignment per se was not associated with

the adverse pregnancy outcomes. Daily supplementation, however, was associated with a greater number of women with excessively elevated hemoglobin, of >145 g/L (adjusted for altitude) after 8–16 weeks of supplementation; within this sub-group ($n=25$ after 16 weeks of supplementation), moreover, the relative risk of low birth weight and prematurity was over 6 times greater than in women with lower hemoglobin (P<0.05). The safety concern derives from the observation that an altered process in the physiology of red cell circulation mediating poor neonatal outcomes is associated with the recommended prenatal regimen, at least in this high altitude location (2240 m above sea level).

Young child supplementation

Thus, according to current WHO recommendations (70), anemia prevalences of over 40% in infants aged 6–24 months require intervention. For these anemic children such intervention has a "therapeutic" character as they try to "cure" a preexisting deficiency. However, these interventions lack monitoring of the therapeutic success and there is no dose adaptation to changes in demand.

The other fraction without iron deficiency obviously has had a sufficient iron supply so far. For them the intervention is prophylactic and aims to prevent future deficiency with the same doses used for the iron-deficient fraction. These children receive iron until they become too old to belong to the high risk group. These iron adequate children run an increased risk of imbalances caused by excess iron, such as impaired growth (47, 48) or dying from malaria (4,73). In these children, the functional compartments such as the red cells (erythron) and tissue enzymes are adequately supplied with iron; any extra iron can contribute to oxidative stress in the gut lumen or, if absorbed, can increase the labile iron pool (LIP) in the cells, add to excess iron in the serum, and may foster growth and thriving of pathogens in all these compartments.

Iron-supplementation in malaria-endemic areas

Approximately 700,000 children under 5 years of age die from malaria each year worldwide (74). Concerns have long been raised about untoward interactions of iron administration in malaria areas. The first prospective study on the impact of iron on infectious outcome (79) reported 13 malaria attacks after iron supplementation ($n=71$), as compared to only one ($n=67$) in the control group. Oral iron intervention in school children and adults increased the prevalence of malaria (80–82), whereas iron deficiency seemed to protect against it (83). Other trials, though, did not support the notion of any relationship of iron status to malaria susceptibility (84–87). Analysis of the iron impact on malaria transmission and clinical presentation is confounded by the complex interaction between vector, environment, and host (87), as well as by thalassemia and sickle cell anemia (88, 89). Such confounders may, at least in part, explain the controversial outcome of different studies. Moreover, malaria provoked by iron may have a promoting effect on other infections (89, 92). Thus, in oral (84) and parenteral iron intervention (90, 91) in Tanzania and New Guinea, clinical malaria went along with increased prevalence of pneumonia.

This situation prompted a large-scale iron intervention trial in infants in Pemba, Zanzibar, a holoendemic area for malaria (4). It engaged a total of 32,155 infants aged 1–35 months and investigated the impacts on death rates and hospital admission of daily supplementation with 12.5 mg iron plus 50 µg folic acid, or 10 mg zinc/day, or 12.5 mg iron, 50 µg folic acid and 10 mg zinc/day compared to a placebo. These doses follow current international recommendations (70). The two endpoints were supplemented by careful post-mortem interviews. Extra staff took shifts in the five hospitals on the island to fill out questionnaires and do a malaria parasite count in blood smears whenever a study participant was admitted to hospital. A substudy enrolled 3,175 children and obtained baseline data on anthropometry plus hemoglobin, erythrocyte zinc protoporphyrin, and a routine malaria parasite count at baseline.

Both iron-containing treatment groups showed a 12% higher rate of serious events leading to clinic admission, death, or both. Moreover, there was a higher incidence of serious adverse effects (relative risk 1.31) and death due to infection-related causes apart from malaria (relative risk 1.61). These occurrences forced discontinuation of the study at midterm of the scheduled duration. In the substudy group, the baseline prevalence of anemia and iron deficiency was 57% and 75%, respectively. Iron deficiency and anemia at baseline reduced the rate of malaria-related adverse effects in groups receiving iron. The prevalence of anemia had dropped a nonsignificant 42% after 12 months of iron supplementation. Among iron-treated children with initial iron deficiency, a reduced risk for malaria-related adverse effects as compared to a placebo was observed.

A concurrent field trial with a parallel protocol was conducted in the lowlands of Nepal (75), and was also curtailed prior to the predetermined duration, largely in relation to the events in Zanzibar. It confirmed the efficacy of the 12.5 mg iron and folic acid daily intervention to reduce anemia rates. In this non-malaria environment, iron administration produced no increased risk of death, but it reduced neither morbidity or mortality in relation to placebo.

These combined results challenge current recommendations that infants 6–24 months of age in areas with anemia prevalences >40% should generally receive iron and folic acid at the dose level used in this study (70). The data obtained here rather recommends restriction of iron supplementation to iron deficient infants in malaria-endemic areas. So, as a bottom line, iron supplementation targeted to iron deficient children reduced anemia

prevalence and, thus, has a role in the maintenance of normal motor and cognitive development. However, in children with neither iron deficiency nor IDA, iron administration increased the risk of hospital admission and death in a malaria-endemic area. This flags a research need to develop and test adequate and economic procedures for large-scale iron status determination in the field (76-78).

Fortification with iron

Food fortification
Fortifying foods with iron is currently conducted in an increasingly wider array of formats, from the traditional fortification of staple foods in the diet, to the addition of iron to drinking water and beverages, to increased development of iron fortified commercial products. Fortified condiments such as fish sauces (93) and even table salt have been developed through advances in food technology (94). For young children, iron fortified infant formula and complementary foods have long been common (95), as are an increasing number of "foodlet" innovations (96), fortified condiments (Sprinkles) (97), or spreads (98) for discretionary fortification of weaning diets in the home.

Iron fortification of staple foods
With respect to staple foods, fortification of cereal grains with iron is mandated in a large number of nations in both the developed and developing world. The levels of addition are in the range of 20–50 mg per kg, depending on the iron-fortification compound. The WHO guidelines (10) provide detailed information on a procedure that can be used for deciding the Feasible Fortification Level (FFL) for each nutrient added in mass fortification programs based on safety and technological and cost constraints. This is particularly applicable for appropriate planning of addition of iron and other micronutrients to dietary staples such as flour and grains. Commer-

cial foods fortified with iron can also become part of population interventions, as when purchased and distributed by charitable non-governmental organizations. Here the WHO guidelines for market-driven foods (10) are also relevant. They suggest that no more than 3 mg of fortificant iron be added to a 50 g serving portion of a solid food or a 250 mL draught of beverage, contributing a maximum of 22% of the daily iron needs from a diet with high bioavailability.

The benefit from iron fortification depends on the quantity of the added iron, but even more on its bioavailability, which, in turn, depends on the composition of food ligands and on the choice of the iron source. Vegetarian diets were estimated to limit iron availability to an absorption rate of 2.5%, whereas bioavailability in diets of developed countries containing meat and fish is up to 10 times higher (99). The impact of the iron source is also considerable. Ferrous sulphate is estimated to have a bioavailability between 2% and 12% (100), whereas that of elemental iron is at best half of that (101) and its biological impact doubtful (102). Absorption from ferrous bisglycinate and NaFeEDTA, in contrast, is two to three times higher than that of ferrous fumarate and ferrous sulphate in flour (103, 104). Moreover, the fit between fortificant and fortified food matrix needs to be considered. For example NaFeEDTA or EDTA alone affects the viscosity of wheat flour dough, and ferrous sulphate causes undesirable changes in the sensory properties of wheat flour when added in larger amounts. The maximum levels compatible with tortillas produced from fortified nixtamalized corn flour were 30 mg/kg for ferrous fumarate and 15 mg/kg for ferrous bisclycinate and NaFeEDTA. Hence, in this situation one cannot improve net iron uptake simply by increasing the concentration of the fortificant Cost issues are an additional concern. For a similar biological impact one needed to invest four times more with NaFeEDTA and seven times more with ferrous bisglycinate than with ferrous fumarate at 2002 price levels. Nevertheless, these more expensive fortificants remain interesting for multiple food fortification when problems of interaction and cost issues are more complex (102). Iron bisglycinate (105) and NaFeEDTA (106) are more expensive, but they have relatively greater absorption efficiency in the context of inhibitory substances in the diet.

NaFeEDTA is not metabolized in humans. Its absorption rate is low and its urinary excretion is rapid (106). On this basis, the Joint Expert Committee on Food Additives (JECFA) recommends a maximal exposure of 2.5 mg per kilogram of body weight per day. When consumed below this JECFA threshold, its use is safe. An issue can arise, however, with infants and preschool children, in whom the 2.5 mg/kg maximum dosage does not allow the delivery of their full iron requirements from the NaFeEDTA compound.

The discretionary fortified foods such as condiment sauces have a much wider variation in consumption and, thus, of derived iron than from the bulkier staple grains and their products. The intraindividual variation in salt intake within populations is wide (107). Similarly wide-ranging dosages of iron could be derived from fish sauces and other condiment foods, depending on individual tastes and tolerances. In both cases, the total chronic individual iron intake increases at the upper extremes of habitual consumption of salt and sauce, but neither is likely to contribute >50% of recommended iron intakes at currently used fortification levels. Unintended increases in sodium exposure, however, could be a safety concern for such interventions with iron-fortified seasoning products; hence, care must be taken in the education and promotion of condiment vehicles of micronutrients.

Iron fortification of infant formulas and complementary foods

Unlike staple foods, which contribute only a fraction of the individual's daily iron needs, fortified infant formulas and complementary foods provide up to 100% of a day's intake. To the extent that consumption by the young child would be limited by the total energy content, such foods must be formulated with an appropriate iron density and bioavailability. Related to the effects of iron on intestinal microflora, concern has been raised about increased diarrheal risk with ingestion of iron fortified formula. The published findings around this concern are contradictory and inconsistent, exemplified by diametrically opposite findings published within a 2-year period from the same research institute in Chile (58, 108). Additional research supports excess diarrhea with iron fortification of complementary foods (109).

With respect to iron density of complementary foods, Brown and Dewey (110) suggest that it is one of the "problem nutrients" which cannot achieve the combinations of density and bioavailability unless provided by meats, or iron-fortifying compounds. When it comes to fortifying complementary foods, the iron requirements are in such rapid transition from 6 months to 24 months of age, that two different fortification densities, lower for the toddlers, are required to avoid overexposure for the older age group (111). Foodlet supplements to fortify foods for young children have proven to be effective in improving iron status (98, 112, 113) in field trials, but long-term behavior in their use, and safety margins, have yet to be examined. Remaining is the potential of overconsumption of iron in foodlet scenarios, because they are discretionary and independent of the energy density of the food, eliminating the satiety constraints seen with prefortified complementary foods (95).

Biofortification

The "Green Revolution" has so far prevented mass starvation of the increasing world population by supplying enough carbohydrates for energy procurement. Reduced food crop diversity, however, has impaired the access to micronutrients that was supplied by pulses, fruits, or vegetables before monocultures of energy-supplying food staples became predominant. Biofortification (i.e., genetic modification of energy rich food crops such as rice, wheat, maize, sweet potatoes, and cassava) uses systematic plant breeding or genetic techniques to develop micronutrient rich staple foods. In contrast to supplementation and traditional food fortification, this approach avoids the need for centralized processing and the complex logistics that go along with it. Thus, conventional breeding of rice varieties with high iron content is systematically performed (e.g., in the China National Rice Research Institute) (114). Prerequisite for successful biofortification is, however, that the soil contains enough trace elements, in our case iron, which may require iron fertilization to avoid soil depletion (115). Haas, et al. (116) demonstrated the efficacy of a high-iron rice to improve iron status in Filipino women with marginal iron status.

To increase iron intake and availability with iron-rich rice, Lucca, et al. explored multiple strategies; these included trying 1) to increase the iron content in the edible parts of the crop; 2) to decrease the amount of antinutrients that reduce bioavailability; and 3) to increase the amount of food ligands that increase iron bioavailability (117). In this approach, iron content was doubled by introduction of a ferritin gene from *Phaseolus vulgaris* (117), in parallel to the earlier introduction of soybean ferritin, which tripled iron content in rice (118). Assuming a consumption of 300 g of rice daily (119), this modification would increase daily iron intake from 3 to up to 6 to 9 mg, which goes at least half the way towards an RDA of 15 mg/day for women of reproductive age (21). However, the probably low bioavailability of ferritin iron is a justified concern regarding this approach (120). An alternative to ferritin is the introduction of genes that improve iron uptake from the soil (114). The extra 3–6 mg iron/day that is ingested daily with such food staples does not seem to pose much risk in iron deficient populations. Questions to be asked before implementation would be whether selection of micronutri-ent-rich varieties will affect consumer safety, crop yields, or acceptability to farmers or consumers. Will the micronutrient content be high enough and will it be bioavailable? Conventional plant breeding and selection to optimize micronutrient content and availability as pursued by for example HarvestPlus seems like the less controversial alternative, as genetically modified plants may raise a lot of ecological problems which are beyond the scope of this text.

Dietary diversification

Encouraging populations to diversify their diets so as to include richer sources of certain widely deficient micronutrients is an intervention strategy with relevance in the discussion of iron. Interventions to encourage home- and school-gardening often tout the iron content of the horticultural items cultivated and consumed (125). Because of the comparably low iron content and bioavailability in fruits and vegetables, consumers are generally safe from any iron excess. Other interventions have included the promotion of greater meat consumption, as through small ruminant husbandry (126) or subsidizing meat purchase (127) as well as in poultry and fish farming (e.g., in Vietnam) (128). Excessive iron consumption is again unlikely, and the safeness of the intervention relies on the sanitary issues relating the sources of meat and any long-range consequences for chronic diseases associated with high meat intakes.

Delayed umbilical cord clamping

With regards to increasing the iron reserve of the neonate, delayed clamping of the umbilical cord is an effective prophylactic measure. It increases iron endowment of the child at birth by 50% as compared to immediate clamping. This resulted in higher blood flow to vital organs in the first week after birth and less anemia in term infants at 2 months of age (129). Thus, it permits longer periods of breastfeeding, as iron fortified milk

is not required as early. Fewer transfusions for anemia and less intraventricular hemorrhages and no differences in other outcomes were found in a systematic review of the literature (130). Two minutes' delay in clamping along with iron-fortified complementary food protected infants from iron-deficiency before 6 months of age (131) and reduced the prevalence of late-onset sepsis and intracranial hemorrhages in infants of very low birth weight (132). A systematic review showed significantly higher hemoglobin values at 2–3 months after delayed cord clamping in children from developing and industrialized countries, which were more marked when mothers were anemic (133). On the negative side, meta-analysis showed an increased risk of hyperbilirubinanemia in 12% of the children, but none of the nine studies reported a need for phototherapy or exchange transfusion (133). No polycytemia or significant hyperbilirubinemia was found in another meta-analysis (132)

SAFETY OF INTERVENTIONS TO TREAT MEGALOBLASTIC ANEMIA CAUSED BY VITAMIN B$_{12}$ AND FOLIC ACID DEFICIENCIES

Vitamin B$_{12}$

Role of vitamin B$_{12}$

Vitamin B$_{12}$ is required for the recycling of a critical nucleotide base (deoxy-thymidine), essential for the rapid synthesis of DNA during cell replication, and hence is indispensable for the proliferation of all of the hematological cell lines in the bone marrow. The absence of vitamin B$_{12}$ allows progenitor cells to enlarge, but not to divide into generations of daughter cells, leading to a hypoproliferative anemia with giant, immature, macrocytic red cells in the circulation (megaloblastosis).

Toxicity and adverse effects of vitamin B$_{12}$

Vitamin B$_{12}$ is remarkable for its high safety margin. The Dietary Reference Intakes panel of the Institute of Medicine (USA) and the EU Scientific Committee on Food were both unable to identify any adverse effects from vitamin B_{12} at any level of intake from foods or supplements (22, 134).

Therapeutic interventions

The traditional treatment for vitamin B_{12} deficiency megaloblastic anemia is a single intramuscular dose of parenteral cyanocobalamin in the order of 1000 µg. The safety concern is not with the cyanocobalamin, but with contemporary issues surrounding parenteral injections in this era of blood-borne viral infections such as HIV and hepatitis (135). Conditions to assure sterile hypodermic needles and their safe handling and destruction are paramount. Alternatively, doses of 1000–2000 µg/day of an oral cobalamin have been found to be as effective as parenteral dosages in correcting vitamin B_{12} deficiency (136), depending on underlying causes of the deficiency.

Prophylactic interventions

Prophylactic supplementation of vitamin B_{12} as a policy measure is virtually unknown. RDA levels of the vitamin are contained in the multiple micronutrient combination that was recommended for distribution in reproductive age and pregnant women (137).

Vitamin B_{12} fortification is practiced. Vitamin B_{12} is added to staples and also to commercial products. Because of its low toxicity, the WHO guidelines for fortification do not address the toxicity aspects of this vitamin (10)

Folic acid

Role of folate

Folate has both a primary and secondary relationship with nutritional anemias. Severe folate deficiency due to a folate poor diet or to conditions that interfere with its absorption or utilization (138) produces suppression of bone marrow proliferation as part of a macrocytic anemia. Where iron deficiency is the central problem, the restoration of adequate iron nutriture would produce a reticulocyte response for rapid replenishing of a normal red cell mass. The requirements for synthesis of new DNA bases for rapid cell proliferation place additional demands for folic acid, such that iron supplements have conventionally been combined with a adjunctive dosage of folic acid (70).

The recent recommendations for daily intake of this vitamin (139) are no longer based on its hematological function, supporting the proliferation of the bone marrow elements, but based at a higher level for the prevention of neural tube birth defects (140). Consistent intake at recommended levels is more than sufficient for hematological needs.

Toxicity and adverse effects of folic acid and folates

Adverse consequences have been associated with or attributed to excessive intakes of folic acid. The Institute of Medicine (134) and the EU Scientific Committee on Food have established ULs (**Table 18.1**) of 1,000 µg/day for adults. The major concern for high intakes of folic acid is the potential for masking an underlying vitamin B_{12} deficiency, correcting the hematological defect and delaying diagnosis until neurological manifestations develop (141, 142), but this is less of an eventuality in young populations. Acute intake of folic acid of 266 µg or more in a meal produced a detectable rise in circulating concentrations of "unmetabolized" folic acid in adult volunteers (143,); it would be expected that the smaller the body size, the higher the concentration rise would be, as was demonstrated in infants from the same laboratory (144). The theoretical consideration regarding circulatory exposure to unmetabolized folic acid (pteroylglutamic acid) is that it is a totally unphysiological form, never found in foods, diets, or the circulation. The cellular uptake and metabolism of this species has unpredictable implications for normal metabolism of the native folate pool. The observations by Troen, et al. (145) that exposure to unmetabolized folic acid produces immunosuppression, especially in older individuals, signal a clear note of caution.

Therapeutic interventions

With the detection of a case of macrocytic anemia due to folate deficiency, a restorative course of folic acid is indicated. A daily supplementation course in doses of 500–5,000 µg can be given, depending upon the local availability of folic acid preparations. It is prudent, also, to provide the therapy for vitamin B_{12} (above) concurrently. The safety margin for the use of up to 5 mg of folic acid as treatment for anemia is favorable.

Prophylactic interventions

Supplementation of folic acid has been instituted primarily in a targeted manner to groups at risk of neural tube defects; for this purpose, it is used in a dose of 400 µg, which is itself innocuous, for the respective conditions both alone (prophylaxis against neurotubal defects) or in combination with iron (70) or iron and other micronutrients (prenatals) (137). The results of the trial in Pemba (4) strongly argue against routine supplementation with iron and folic acid in populations with high rates of malaria. Folic acid at a dose of 50 µg/day may interfere with the first-line anti-malaria treatment used in Pemba, which consisted of the antifolate combination of sulfadoxine and pyrimethamine. Concomitant folate exposure may cause a significant delay in parasite clearance (146). Such inhibitory influence of malaria treatment by folic acid supplementation may need to be considered, though recovery from malaria episodes did not seem to differ from those in the placebo group (4).

Folic acid fortification of foods is widely practiced. The WHO consultancy specifies 1.3 mg/kg of edible foodstuff as the maximal addition for fortification of staples. For fortified commer-cial food items, which can be employed in distributions by government or non-governmental organization as an intervention to the benefit of individuals or groups within a population, the WHO document (10) recommends a maximum of 27 µg of folic acid per 40 kcal serving of product.

The USA has mandated fortification of breakfast cereals and grain products at a level of 140 µg/100 g flour since 1998. Overages of up to 190 µg/100 g (+36%) have been documented (147). In Chile, the fortification specifications are 220 µg/100 g of wheat flour, and average folic acid levels in bread sampled in that country were 202 µg/100 g; Chilean women were found to receive, on average, 220 µg of folic acid daily from fortification sources (148).

SAFETY OF INTERVENTIONS TO ADDRESS HYPOVITAMINOSIS A AND HYPORIBOFLAVINOSIS

Vitamin A

Role of vitamin A

Vitamin A deficiency is not a cause per se of nutritional anemia. Therefore, vitamin A interventions would not be considered as primary tools to alleviate nutritional anemia. Any direct influence of vitamin A deficiency on the renal hormonal maintenance of erythropoietin has recently been discounted (149). However, vitamin A adequacy has been shown to act as an adjuvant to optimize the utilization of iron to support the human erythron (150). In this secondary context, the safety of how we conduct public health interventions with vitamin A is germane to the topic.

Toxicity and adverse effects of vitamin A

Acute intakes of immense doses of preformed vitamin A, as might be obtained by dining on polar bear liver, produce dramatic and life-threatening manifestations of acute intoxication such as hepatic failure, increased intracranial pressure (*pseudotumor cerebri*), convulsions, and coma. It has been demonstrated, however, that the high-dose supplements administered to infants in the first semester of life, currently recommended in the context of offspring of HIV-seropositive mothers (151), do not produce bulging of the fontanel (152).

In terms of the chronic setting, total vitamin A exposure should be limited to a cumulative dosage that maintains a hepatic vitamin A concentration of <300 µg/g, which is considered the threshold of toxicity. Regular daily consumption of 30 mg of vitamin A in the retinoid form is associated with chronic toxicity including liver fibrosis, ascites, and scaly dermatitis (153).

The UL set by the Dietary Reference Intakes (21) and EU SCF (22) is at 10,000 IU (3,030 µg) daily as retinol. This seems to be the threshold value for an unacceptable risk for teratogenesis, with the production of diverse birth defects. Interestingly, the extrapolation for the UL for males and the youngest and oldest female age groups (**Table 18.1**) is based on this risk of birth defects, despite no possible involvement of vitamin A exposure with reproductive biology in these groups. There is increasing interest in the possibility that bone mineral loss and risk of osteoporotic fractures befalls chronic consumers of half of this daily dose. The current data are conflicting and not yet consistent (153), but with the rapid aging of populations around the world, efforts to resolve the bone health aspect should be redoubled.

Sustained high intakes of β-carotene (a provitamin A carotenoid) produce a yellow-orange discoloration of skin (carotenodermia), which is dermatologically innocuous. It has been used in the suppression of acute porphyria episodes in continuous daily doses of 180 mg with absolute safety to patients with this disorder (154). Some disquieting observations about the safety of iso-lated β-carotene in supplements in the 30–50 mg daily range come from two primary prevention intervention trials to reduce the risk of lung cancer development in cohorts with exceptional high susceptibility (tobacco smokers, asbestos workers) (155, 156). Both trials were stopped early when the contrary finding of an increased risk of death was observed.

Prophylactic vitamin A supplementation
As a vitamin A supplement is part of the regimen for intensive rehabilitation of children with severe protein-energy malnutrition (PEM) (157), in situations in which a child might have multiple hospital readmissions, strict records need to be carefully kept to prevent repeated vitamin A supplementation at intervals of less than 6 months. It is no longer officially recommended that high dose supplements of vitamin A be given postpartum to lactating women to support milk vitamin A. If dosing were mistimed and delivered beyond the 42-day window after delivery, it could produce inadvertent damage to a new conceptus in the mother's womb (153). Allen and Haskell (158), moreover, concluded that international recommendations for periodic high-dose vitamin A could exceed the US-Canada UL criteria for vitamin A, but would remain short of the no observed adverse effect level (NOAEL) upon which the tolerable limit was established.

Prophylactic vitamin A food fortification
The WHO consultancy does not specify a safety limit level for fortification of staple foods with vitamin A. In Zambia and most of the countries of the Central American Isthmus, refined sugar is fortified with vitamin A (159). Edible oil is the staple food vehicle for vitamin A in the Philippines, Morocco, Mali, Uganda, and Yemen. It has also been added to margarines and ghees in Asia and cereal flours and grain meals in Latin America. It has been suggested that fortification of a staple food with vitamin A be designed to provide at least 15% of the daily vita-

min A needs for the target group, but should usually not exceed 30% (159).

For fortified commercial food items, the WHO document (10) recommends a maximum vitamin A addition of 60 µg per 40 kcal of serving. The issues of safety relate to the segment of the population (the extreme outliers) whose dietary habits would lead to a habitual high consumption of the fortification vehicle (or whose high exposures come from food sources and self supplementation but are complemented by additional intake from public health fortification). The risk profile of the population should be carefully estimated, and repeatedly updated, during the lifetime of the public fortification program.

Prophylactic vitamin A biofortification
A new and emerging thrust in public health micronutrient interventions is biofortification. Its promotion is coordinated by the HarvestPlus initiative (160). This involves developing genetic varieties, either through conventional crossbreeding or genetic modification (161, 162). Provitamin A-rich varieties of carrots (163) and sweet potatoes (164) have been developed. The exposure to these food forms of β-carotenes should be safe across the population. Given the aforementioned theoretical considerations on GMO safety (123, 124), the security of any provitamin A rich (or even retinoid rich) plant varieties introduced for human consumption would have to be monitored long-term for any adverse consequence (e.g., from genetic manipulations).

Riboflavin

Role of riboflavin
Ariboflavinosis, like hypovitaminosis A, is not a cause per se of nutritional anemia, and as such, riboflavin interventions would not be considered a primary tool to alleviate nutritional anemia. As is the case with vitamin A, however, riboflavin is an adjunctive or supportive nutrient to maximize the iron-mediated repletion of a full red cell mass (165).

Toxicity and adverse effects of riboflavin
In its Dietary Reference Intakes (21) the Institute of Medicine states that "no adverse effects associated with riboflavin consumption from foods or supplements have been reported." For this reason, no UL was assigned. Oral doses of ~2 mg daily have been employed to treat persons with ariboflavinosis, this being considered a safe dosage.

Riboflavin interventions
Riboflavin would enter into consideration as a public health intervention only in the context of its addition to multimicronutrient supplements (below) and in fortification of staple cereals. It is typically added at a concentration of up to ~200 mg per kilogram of cereal flours. Given its high margin of safety, no risk considerations for vitamin B_2 are pertinent for any type of exposure from interventions to improve nutritional status of a population.

SAFTEY OF COPPER INTERVENTIONS

Role of copper
Severe copper deficiency produces a hypochromic microcytic anemia, mimicking iron deficiency anemia in its histological and clinical characteristics (166). Primary human copper deficiency is rarely seen, occurring almost exclusively in infants and young children subsisting on low-copper, milk-based formulas or in adults on total enteral or parenteral nutrition with insufficient copper delivery. Copper deficiency anemia is not a public health problem. Copper interventions are hardly in the armamentarium of measures against nutritional anemias. However, a secondary copper deficiency anemia could be related to interventions with zinc at levels in excess of its tolerable limits (167).

Toxicity and adverse effects of copper

Copper is a strong emetic, provoking nausea and vomiting when ingested in even low amounts. Araya, et al. (168) found that copper concentrations in household drinking water in excess of 4 mg/L for women and 6 mg/L for men produced increased incidence of gastrointestinal symptoms. The Dietary Reference Intakes (21) identify an UL for copper of 10 mg for adults, whereas the EU convention places it at 5 mg (22). The chronic excess intake of copper has been associated with abnormal elevation of LDL cholesterol (169), and this response was taken into consideration for setting the UL. It has recently been shown in Chile, however, that 2 months of exposure to drinking water with 10 mg/L of copper resulted in transient alterations in liver enzymes (amino transferases) in health volunteers (170).

By virtue of its emetic properties, accidental or intentional overdoses of gram amounts of copper salts are generally rejected by the intense vomiting they produce. However, individuals have succeeded in committing suicide by ingesting gram doses of copper, death being caused by acute hepatic failure, massive hemolytic anemia or both (171). Chronic copper ingestion from copper and bronze cooking utensils, the so-called Indian childhood cirrhosis, has been associated with hepatic fibrosis (172).

Oral copper therapy

Copper deficiency anemia has been successfully treated with daily doses of copper as cupric sulfate of 1– 2 mg/day in adults and in young children; doses of up to 9 mg/day in divided doses are safe and tolerable in adults (173). Situations in which high-dose zinc was given for therapeutic or prophylactic reasons, such as a notable trial of micronutrients to prevent age-related macular degeneration (174), included 2 mg of copper in the formulation to prevent the distortion of copper nutriture by zinc.

THE SAFETY OF MULTIPLE MICRO-NUTRIENT INTERVENTIONS IN THE CONTEXT OF ANEMIA PREVENTION AND MITIGATION

In the 1990s, a conceptual and policy shift occurred in which the development of isolated vertical programs for each of the micronutrients of primary public health interest was criticized as antithetical to integrated health service delivery. Moreover, based on the assumption that nutrient deficiencies occurred in combination, programs to deliver multiple micronutrients were devised (175, 176). When introduced as a concept, the universal delivery of daily recommended doses of essential micronutrients as part of prophylactic care for the reproductive period of women in deprived conditions was considered to be inherently safe and innocuous (137, 177). Experience from field trials with multimicronutrient combinations in gestation have revealed surprising and unexpected findings that bear on the safety of the practice. At two sites in the rural, lowland plains of Nepal, pregnant women were randomized in a field trial to receive iron-folate prenatal supplements or a more comprehensive multivitamin-mineral supplement throughout the middle and latter stages of gestation (178, 179). Birth weight was improved with the multimicronutrient treatments as compared to the control regimens. However, a pooled analysis of the data from the two trials revealed what the authors termed a "worrisome finding" of a statistically significant increase in perinatal (36%) and neonatal (52%) mortality (180) selectively in the multiple micronutrient assignment groups.

The field trial by Fawzi, et al. in Dar es Salaam, Tanzania (181–184) has the particular focus of risks and benefits for the infant-mother dyad in the context of maternal seropositivity for HIV. In this situation, the multiple vitamin-mineral preparations did not contain iron. The positive experience was that supplementation of multivitamins delayed the progression of HIV. In contrast, the multiple micronutrient intervention containing vitamin A annihilated the positive effects of multivitamins for mothers and their babies (181–184). The IRIS trials (112) added micronutrients in the RDA range to iron without any obvious positive or negative effect on health, though laboratory parameters for the added micronutrients improved. Clearly, both biological and nutrient-nutrient interactions may be at play at the basis of the partially contradictory effects emanating from large multiple micronutrient supplementation trials in reproductive settings and in infants. Moreover, it is precisely the combination of several nutrients that complicates attribution of positive or negative health consequences to specific combinations of circumstances or micronutrients. More information on this subject seems desirable.

NUTRITIONAL ANEMIA OF SEVERE PROTEIN-ENERGY MALNUTRITION (PEM)

A type of nutritional anemia occurs in protein-energy malnutrition (PEM). It is generally seen only in clinically severe and metabolically disordered situations with edema (185). Although children with severe PEM commonly have multiple micronutrient deficiencies, the low hemoglobin levels were early attributed to a redistribution of iron from the red cell compartment to the bone marrow and storage sites of the body as part of an adaptive process of protein conservation (186). Oxygen consumption is low with the inactivity and low body mass of extreme malnutrition, whereas amino acids in the red cells are of greater immediate use for vital organs such as the brain, kidneys, and heart. In children treated for PEM in hospital and with initially high ferritins, iron is mobilized from the storage pool to new red cells (187). It has been postulated (188) and later demonstrated (189) that oxidative stress is a central pathophysiological mechanism in edematous PEM. This provides additional theoretical basis

for avoiding administration of iron, which is a strong oxidizing substance, in such patients.

In the latter part of the 1990s, a number of groups pointed out an apparent deterioration in the general success of treatment of PEM and rising in-hospital mortality (190, 191), which remobilized investigative interest in the clinical management of the deficiency disease. In 1999, WHO and the Nestlé Foundation published a manual for standardized care of severe PEM (192). There are a number of phases in the rehabilitation of PEM (193), and during the resuscitation and induction of recovery phases, the WHO regimen excludes iron supplementation (192, 194). Supplementation with vitamin B_{12} and copper is begun early in the treatment course, and once recuperation from PEM is advanced and spontaneous hematological recovery has not occurred, oral iron can then safely treat the component of the anemia related to lack of body reserves of iron.

CONCLUSIONS

Current evidence and relative degrees of safety concerns among measures directed at control or correction of nutritional anemia

The evidence is firm and conclusive that treatment or fortification with vitamin B_{12}, food fortification with riboflavin, and treatment or prophylaxis with routine anthelmintic drugs are innocuous in almost any and all instances. With strict adherence to WHO guidelines for rehabilitation of PEM (192), including delayed introduction of iron supplements to the regimen, maximal survival with resolution of the anemia of severe malnutrition should be achieved. Finally, safety experience with EDTA as an additive has allayed prior concerns about NaFeEDTA as a fortificant.

Rising above the threshold of inherent and universal safety are issues relating to delayed cord clamping in delivery, therapy for schistosomiasis, as well as folic acid supplementation and fortification. With delayed cord clamping, one must weigh the demonstrable advantages of higher early-life iron stores and prolonged exclusive breast milk adequacy against any risk of distracted attention to neonatal emergencies such as apnea and asphyxia, and the consequent 12% increase in risk for bilirubin elevations, some of which may require light therapy.

Folic acid exposure is not inherently safe. Currently, the lowest effective doses are not routinely used in supplements, but rather what is available on the pharmaceutical marketplace, which ranges from 100 to 5000 µg tablets. As few as 266 µg of folic acid produce measurable increases in unmetabolized folate. A theoretical disadvantage of including folic acid in the recommended public health regimen to prevent anemia (70) arises in malarial areas, where this vitamin may neutralize the efficacy of concomitant treatment with antimalarial drugs by interfering with folate metabolism in the parasite.

Finally, public health programs for provision of additional iron as a direct measure for iron deficiency anemia and of additional vitamin A as an indirect measure to improve iron utilization raise the most serious concerns among nutritional anemia interventions. With respect to iron supplementation, the Pemba study (4) was posited as a test of the safety of following the international recommendations for iron supplementation in populations of young children with a >40% prevalence of anemia with 12.5 mg of iron and 50 µg of folic acid (70). Disquieting adverse effects were observed. Heterogeneous populations vary widely in iron status and in the prevalence of malaria, HIV, and other chronic diseases. Some arguments state that iron exposure within these groups must be adjusted and only given to those with need for iron and after control of infections, in which case targeted delivery must be considered as an alternative to en masse distribution. Such focalized delivery of iron raises the

specter of a need for screening individuals for their current iron status and infected state, and monitoring both as treatments are administered. This is an area where the inclusion of new safety guidelines presents challenges related to the cost and sustainability of safely addressing this form of nutritional anemia.

With respect to iron fortification, reliance on the assumption that the human homeostatic mechanisms to limit excess absorption and accumulation of iron are hermetic (195) can no longer be justified, due to revelations about porous regulation of iron uptake in young organisms (196) and adults (197). For populations in which only small subsegments have a risk of iron deficiency, such as in industrialized nations, universal fortification of a staple food may move more individuals to an upper extreme of iron status, rather than make any antideficiency impact. Moreover, both in industrialized countries and increasingly in developing nations, introduction of fortified commercial foods is combined with iron fortification of a major staple, increasing individuals' chances of consuming multiple different iron-fortified commercial foods and beverages.

The WHO statement (198) offers the message that the concerns raised by the experience in Pemba do not cross over to the naturally occurring iron or iron used to fortify foods and beverages. Insofar as single-meal intakes of foods fortified in the home with Sprinkles (97), spreads (98), or foodlets (112) deliver a bolus intake of 10–12.5 mg of iron, the exposure conditions are too closely analogous to Pemba's supplementation scenario to firmly accept a qualitative distinction. This is an area of concern worthy of targeted research. Related is the situation with infant formula or fortified weaning foods, where a single vehicle is the source of virtually all iron for an infant. Child-to-child variation in caloric intake will produce a concomitant variation in iron consumption, such that such products must hedge their fortification levels based on safety considerations for the upper extreme of daily consumption from the single sources (110).

Concern for interventions bringing excessive vitamin A exposure to at least some section of populations arises with the multiplicity of its sources in the diet (periodic supplementation plus daily fortification in a staple, plus commercial foods fortified with the vitamin). This concern comes into perspective as increasing evidence appears of adverse effects on bone health from prolonged consumption of vitamin A in the range of 2 RDA intakes. The safety concerns of promoting animal sources of iron from organ or muscle (red) meat for young children do not relate so much to any excess burden of iron accumulation, but rather to the high content of vitamin A in mammalian liver, and its concentration of heavy metals and organic residues from the environment.

Finally, since increased neonatal and perinatal mortality has befallen the offspring of Nepalese mothers receiving routine multiple micronutrient supplementation while pregnant (180), even while improving average birth weight, the assumption of safety for RDA levels of vitamins and minerals in combination for reproductive age women has been placed on hold.

Recommendations for a research agenda for safety in interventions for nutritional anemias

- Research on the relative safety of supplement level doses of iron as tablets or elixirs (supplement presentation) or in fortifying foods (Sprinkles, spreads, foodlets) in areas endemic for malaria and other intracellular infections.
- Developmental research on low-cost and culturally acceptable diagnostic screening procedures that could rapidly and accurately differentiate those with iron deficiency from those who are iron replete. Such research would span the continuum from development of the test kits (77) to application in the field to economic sustainability.
- Further research on the consequences of raising circulating levels of unmetabolized folic acid after bolus doses from supplements and fortified foods.
- Elucidate the nature of the paradoxical adverse pregnancy and neonatal outcomes upon supplementing certain combinations of multiple micronutrients.

REFERENCES

1. Stoltzfus RJ. Defining iron-deficiency anemia in public health terms. A time for reflection. J Nutr 2001;131:565S–67S
2. Allen LH, Rosado JL, Casterline JE, Lopez P, Munoz E, Garcia OP, et al. Lack of hemoglobin response to iron supplementation in anemic Mexican preschoolers with multiple micronutrient deficiencies. Am J Clin Nutr 2000;71:1485–97.
3. Weiss G, Goodnough LT. Anemia of chronic disease. New Engl J Med 2005;352:1011–23.

4. Sazawal S, Black RE, Ramsan M, Chwaya HM, Stoltzfus RJ, Dutta A, et al. Effects of routine prophylactic supplementation with iron and folic acid on admission to hospital and mortality in preschool children in a high malaria transmission setting: community-based, randomised, placebo-controlled trial. Lancet 2006;367:133–43.
5. Mudur G. Deaths trigger fresh controversy over vitamin A programme in India. BMJ 2001; 323:1206.

6. Quinlivan EP, Gregory JF III. Effect of food fortification on folic acid intake in the United States. Am J Clin Nutr 2003;77:221–5.

7. Leventhal A, Kaluski DN. A national survey as a basis for public health policy. A case study with folic acid. Public Health Rev 2005;29:153–7.

8. Rubingh CM, Kruizinga AG, Hulshof KF, Brussaard JH. Validation and sensitivity analysis of probabilistic models of dietary exposure in micronutrients: an example based on vitamin B_6. Food Addit Contam 2003:20(Suppl 1): 50S–60S.

9. Tressou J, Crepet A, Bertail P, Feinberg MH, Leblanc JC. Probabilistic exposure assessment to food chemicals based on extreme value theory: application to heavy metals from fish and sea products. Food Chem Toxicol 2004;42:1349–58.

10. Allen LH, de Benoist B, Dary O, Hurrell R. Guidelines on food fortification with micronutrients. Geneva: WHO, 2006.

11. Lynch S. Iron metabolism. In: Kraemer K, Zimmermann MB, eds. Nutritional anemia. Basel: SIGHT AND LIFE Press, 2007 (this volume).

12. Hurrell R, Egli I. Bioavailability of iron forms and enhancers. In: Kraemer K, Zimmermann MB, eds. Nutritional anemia. Basel: SIGHT AND LIFE Press, 2007 (this volume).

13. Gleason G, Scrimshaw NS. Functional consequences of anemia. In: Kraemer K, Zimmermann MB, eds. Nutritional anemia. Basel: SIGHT AND LIFE Press, 2007 (this volume).

14. Ellenham MJ, Barceloux DG. Iron. In: Medical toxicology. New York: Elsevier, 1988:1023–30.

15. Berenbaum MC, Child KJ, Davis KL, Sharpe HM, Tomich EG. Animal and human studies on ferrous fumarate, an oral hematinic. Blood 1960;15:540–550.

16. Whittsker P, Dunkel VC, Bucci TJ, Kusewitt DF, Warbritton A, Wolf GL. Genome-linked toxicity responses to dietary iron overload. Toxicol Pathol 1997;25:556–64.

17. Fleming RE, Holden CC, Tomatsu S, Waheed A, Brunt EM, Britton RS, et al. Mouse strain differences determine severity of iron accumulation in Hfe knockout model of hereditary hemochromatosis. Proc Natl Acad Sci U S A 2001:98:2707–11.

18. Lebeau A, Frank J, Biesalski HK, Weiss G, Srai SK, Simpson RJ, et al. Long-term sequelae of HFE deletion in C57BL/6 x 129/O1a mice, an animal model for hereditary haemochromatosis. Eur J Clin Invest 2002;32:603–12.

19. Engle JP, Polin KS, Stile IL. Acute iron intoxication: treatment controversies. Drug Intell Clin Pharm 1987;21:153–9.

20. Anderson AC. Iron poisoning in children. Curr Opin Pediatr 1994;6:289–94.

21. Institute of Medicine, Food and Nutrition Board. Dietary Reference Intakes for vitamin A, vitamin K, arsenic, boron, chromium, copper, iodine, iron, manganese, molybdenum, nickel, silicon, vanadium and zinc. Washington, DC: National Academy Press, 2001.

22. Scientific Committtee on Food, European Food Safety Authority. Tolerable upper intake levels for vitamins and minerals. Parma: European Commission, 2006.

23. Schümann K, Borch-Iohnsen B, Hentze MW, Marx JJ. Tolerable upper intakes for dietary iron set by the US Food and Nutrition Board. Am J Clin Nutr 2002;76:499–500 (letter).

24. Brock C, Curry H, Hanna C, Knipfer M, Taylor L. Adverse effects of iron supplementation: a comparative trial of a wax-matrix iron preparation and conventional ferrous sulfate tablets. Clin Ther 1985;7:568–73.

25. Coplin M, Schuette S, Leichtmann G, Lasher B. Tolerability of iron: a comparison of bis-glycino iron II and ferrous sulphate. Clin Ther 1991;13:606–12.

26. Frykman E, Bystrom M, Jansson U, Edberg A, Hansen T. Side effects of iron supplements in blood donors: superior tolerance of heme iron. J Lab Clin Med 1994;123: 561–4.

27. Ganzoni AM, Töndung G, Rhymer K. Orale Eisenmedikation. [Medicanal iron]. Dtsch Med Wochenschr 1974;99:1175–8 (in German).

28. Liguori L. Iron protein succinylate in the treatment of iron deficiency: controlled, double-blind, multicenter clinical trial on over 1,000 patients. Int J Clin Pharmacol Ther Toxicol 1993;31:103–23.

29. Cook JD, Carriaga M, Kahn SG, Schack W, Skikne BS. Gastric delivery system for iron supplementation. Lancet 1990;336:1136–9.

30. Reddaiah VP, Raj PP, Ramachandran K, Nath LM, Sood SK, Madan N, et al. Supplementary iron dose in pregnancy anemia prophylaxis. Indian J Pediatr 1989;56:109–14.

31. Milman N, Byg KE, Bergholt T, Eriksen L. Side effect of oral iron prophylaxis in pregnancy – myth or reality? Acta Haematol 2006;115:53–7.

32. Schümann K. Toxicological aspects of iron. Forum Nutr 2003;56:51-3.

33. Salonen JT, Nyyssönen K, Korpela H, Tuomilehto J, Seppänen R, Salonen R. High stored iron levels are associated with excess risk of myocardial infarction in eastern Finnish men. Circulation 1992;86;803–11.

34. Tuomainen TP, Punnonen K, Nyyssönen K, Salonen JT. Association between body iron stores and the risk of acute myocardial infarction in men. Circulation 1998;97:1461–6.

35. Klipstein-Grobusch K, Koster JF, Grobbee DE, Lindemans J, Boeing H, Hofman A, et al. Serum ferritin and risk of myocardial infarction in the elderly: the Rotterdam study. Am J Clin Nutr 1999;69:1231–6.

36. Ascherio A, Willett WC, Rimm EB, Giovannucci EL, Stampfer MJ. Dietary iron intake and risk of coronary disease among men. Circulation 1994;89:969–74.

37. Knutson MD, Walter PB, Ames BN, Viteri FE. Both iron deficiency and daily iron supplementation increase lipid peroxidation in rats. J Nutr 2000;130:621–8.

38. Knutson MD, Walter PB, Mendoza C, Ames BN, Viteri FE. Effects of daily oral iron supplementation on iron status and lipid peroxidation in women. FASEB J 1999;13:698.

39. Casanueva E, Viteri FE, Mares-Galindo M, Meza-Camacho C, Loria A, Schnaas L, et al. Weekly iron as a safe alternative to daily supplementation for nonanemic pregnant women. Arch Med Res. 2006;37:674–82.

40. Troost FJ, Brummer RJM, Haenen GR, Bast A, van Haaften RI, Evelo CT, et al. Gene expression in human small intestinal mucosa in vivo is mediated by iron-induced oxidative stress. Physiol Genomics 2006;25:242–249.

41. Rosales FJ, Kang Y Pfeiffer B, Rau A, Romero-Abal M-E, Erhardt JG, et al. Twice the recommended daily allowance of iron is associated with an increase in plasma α-1 antichymotrypsin concentration in Guatemalan school-aged children. Nutr Res 2004;24:875-87.

42. Schümann K, Kroll S, Weiss G, Frank J, Biesalski HK, Daniel H, et al. Monitoring of hematological, inflammatory and oxidative reactions of acute oral iron exposure in human volunteers: preliminary screening for selection of potentially-responsive biomarkers. Toxicology 2005;212:10–23.

43. Seril DN, Liao J, Ho KL, Warsi A, Yang CS, Yang GY. Dietary iron supplementation enhances DSS-induced colitis and associated colorectal carcinoma development in mice. Dig Dis. Sci 2002;47:1266–78.

44. Telfer JF, Brock JH. Expression of ferritin, transferrin receptor and non-specific resistance associated macrophage proteins 1 and 2 (Nramp 1 and Nramp 2) in the human rheumatoid synovium. Ann Rheum Dis 2002;61:741–4.

45. Keusch GT, Farthing MJ. Nutrition and infection. Ann Rev Nutr 1986;6:131-54.

46. Solomons NW, Mazariegos M, Brown KH, Klasing K. The underprivileged, developing country child: environmental contamination and growth resisted. Nutr Rev 1993;61 327–32.

47. Majumdar I, Paul P, Talib VH, Ranga S. The effect of iron therapy on growth of iron-replete and iron-deplete children. J Trop Pediatr 2003;49:84–8.

48. Idjradinata P, Watkins WE, Pollitt E. Adverse effects of iron supplementation on weight gain of iron-replete young children. Lancet 1994;343:1252–4.

49. MacKay HM. Anemia in infancy; its prevalence and prevention. Arch Dis Child 1928;3:117–47.

50. Barry DMJ, Reeve AW. Increased incidence of gram-negative neonatal sepsis with intramuscular iron administration. Pediatrics 1977;60 908–12.

51. Farmer K, Becroft DMO. Administration of parenteral iron to newborn infants. Arch Dis Child 1976;51:500–1.

52. Becroft DMO, Dix MR, Farmer K.

Intramuscular iron-dextran and susceptibility of neonates to bacterial infections. Arch Dis Child 1977;52:778–81.

53. Kanakakorn K, Cavill I, Jacobs A. The metabolism of intravenously administered iron-dextran. Br J Haematol 1973;25:637–43.

54. Saarinen UM, Siimes MA. Developmental changes in serum iron, total iron-binding capacity, and transferrin saturation in infancy. J Pediatr 1977;91:875-7.

55: Oppenheimer SJ. Iron and its relation to immunity and infectious disease. J Nutr 2001;131:616S–35S.

56: Chwang LC, Soemantri AG, Pollitt E. Iron supplementation and physical growth of rural Indonesian children. Am J Clin Nutr 1988;47:496–501.

57. Angeles IT, Schultink WJ, Matulessi P, Gross R, Sastroamidjojo S. Decreased rate of stunting among anemic Indonesian preschool children with iron supplementation. Am J Clin Nutr 1993;58:339–42.

58. Heresi G, Pizarro F, Olivares M, Cayazzo M, Hertrampf E, Walter T, et al. Effect of supplementation with an iron-fortified milk on incidence of diarrhea and respiratory infection in urban-resident infants. Scand J Infect Dis 1995;27:385-9.

59. Power HM, Heese HD, Beatty DW, Hughes J, Dempster WS. Iron fortification of infant milk formula: the effect on iron status and immune function. Ann Trop Paediatr 1991;11:57–66.

60. Hemminki E, Nemet K, Horvath M, Malin M, Schuler D, Hollan S. Impact of iron fortification of milk formulas on infant growth and health. Nutr Res 1995;15:491–503.

61. Gera T, Sachdev HPS. Effect of iron supplementation on incidence of infectious illness in children: systematic review. BMJ 2002;325:1142–52.

62. Fleming AF. Iron deficiency in the tropics. Clin Haematol 1982;11:365–88.

63. Schultz MG. Ascariasis: nutritional implications. Rev Infect Dis 1982;4:815–9.

64. Gilgen DD; Mascie-Taylor CG, Rosetta LL. Intestinal helminth infections, anaemia and labour productivity of female tea pluckers in Bangladesh. Trop Med Int Health 2001;6:449–57.

65. Stoltzfus RJ, Chwang HM, Montresor A, Tielsch JM, Jape JK, Albonico M, et al. Low dose daily iron supplementation improves iron status and appetite, but not anemia, whereas quarterly anthelmintic treatment improves growth, appetite and anemia in Zanzibari preschool children. J Nutr 2004;134:348–356.

66. 32nd ed. In: Parfill K, ed. Martindale: The complete drug reference. London: Pharmaceutical Press, 1999:96–105.

67. Bradley M, Horton J. Assessing the risk of benzimidazole therapy during pregnancy. Trans R Soc Trop Med Hyg 2001;95:72–3.

68. Sin MA, Suttorp N. Intestinale Nematoden [Intestinal nematodes] 16th ed. In: Dietel M, Suttorp N, Zeitz M, eds. Harrisons Innere Medizin [Harrison's Principles of Internal Medicine], vol 1.. Berlin: ABW Wissenschaftsverlag, 2005:1349–52.

69: Montresor A, Crompton DWT, Gyorhos TW, Savioli L. Helminth control in school aged children. A guide for managers of control programmes. Geneva: WHO 2002.

70. Stoltzfus RJ, Dreyfuss ML. Guidelines for the use of iron supplements to prevent and treat iron deficiency anemia. Washington, DC: ILSI Press, 1998.

71. Viteri FE. Iron supplementation for the control of iron deficiency in populations at risk. Nutr Rev 1997;55:195–209.

72. Cavalli-Sforza T. Effectiveness of weekly iron-folic acid supplementation to prevent and control anemia among women of reproductive age in three Asian countries: development of the master protocol and implementation plan. Nutr Rev 2005;63 (12 Pt 2):77S–80S.

73. Smith AW, Hendrickse RG, Harrison C, Hayes RJ, Greenwood BM. The effects on malaria of treatment of iron-deficiency anaemia with oral iron in Gambian children. Ann Trop Paediatr 9:17–23.

74. Snow RW, Craig M, Deichmann U, Marsh K. Estimating mortality, morbidity and disability due to malaria among African non-pregnant population. Bull World Health Organ 1999;77:624–40.

75. Tielsch JM, Khatry SK, Stoltzfus RJ, Katz J, LeClerq SC, Adhikari R, et al. Effects of routine prophylactic supplementation with iron and folic acid

on preschool child mortality in southern Nepal: community-based, cluster-randomised, placebo-controlled trial. Lancet 2006;367:144–52.
76. Olivares M, Walter T, Cook JD Hertrampf E, Pizarro. Usefulness of serum transferrin receptor and serum ferritin in diagnosis of iron deficiency in infancy. Am J Clin Nutr 2000;72:1191–5.
77. Erhardt JG, Estes JE, Pfeiffer CM, Biesalski HK, Craft NE. Combined measurement of ferritin, soluble transferrin receptor, retinal binding protein, and C-reactive protein by an inexpensive, sensitive and simple sandwich enzyme-linked immunoab-sorbed assay technique. J Nutr 2004;134:3127–32.
78. Berger J, Dyck JL, Galan P, Aplogan A, Schneider D, Traissac P, et al. Effect of daily iron supplementation on iron status, cell-mediated immunity and incidence of infections in 6-36 month old Togolese children. Eur J Clin Nutr 2000;54:29–35.
79. Murray MJ, Murray AB, Murray MB, Murray CJ. The adverse effect of iron repletion on the course of certain infections. BM J 1978;2:1113–5.
80 Smith AW, Hendrickse RG, Harrison C, Hayes RJ, Greenwood BM. The effects on malaria of treatment of iron-deficiency anaemia with oral iron in Gambian children. Ann Trop Paediatr 1989;9:17–23.
81. Adam Z. Iron supplementation and malaria. A randomized placebo controlled field trial in rural Ethiopia [doctoral thesis]. London: University of London; 1996.
82. Bates CJ, Powers HJ, Lamb WH, Gelman W, Webb E. Effects of supplementary vitamins and iron on malaria incidence in rural Gambian children. Trans R Soc Trop Med Hyg 1987;81:286–91.
83. Nyakeriga AM, Troye-Blomberg M, Dorfman JR, Alexander ND, Back R, Kortok M, et al. Iron deficiency and malaria among children living on the coast of Kenya. J Inf Dis 2004;190:439-47.
84. Van den Hombergh I, Dalderop E, Smit Y. Does iron therapy benefit children with severe malaria-associated anamia? A clinical trial with 12 weeks supplementation of oral iron in young children from the Turiani Division, Tanzania. J Trop Pediatr 1996;42:220–7.
85. Verhoef H, West CE, Nzyoko SM, de Vogel S, van der Valk R, et al. Intermittent administration of iron and sulfadoxine-pyrimethamine to control

anaemia in Kenyan children: a randomised controlled trial. Lancet 2002;360:908–14.
86. Desai MR, Mei JV, Kariuki SK, Wannemuehler KA, Phillips-Howard PA, Nahlen BL, et al. Randomized, controlled trial of daily iron supplementation and intermittent sulfadoxine-pyrimethamine for the treatment of mild childhood anemia in Western Kenya. J Infect Dis 2003;187:658–66.
87. Mebrahtu T, Stoltzfus RJ, Chwaya HM, Jape JK, Savioli L, Montresor A, et al. Low-dose iron supplementation for 12 months does not increase the prevalence of malarial infection for density of parasites in young Zanzibari children. J Nutr 2004;134:3037–41.
88. Oppenheimer SJ. Iron and its relation to immunity and infectious disease. J Nutr 2001;131:616S–35S.
89. Allen SJ, O'Donnell A, Alexander ND, Alpers MP, Peto TE, Clegg JB, et al. Alpha+-Thalassemia protects children against disease caused by other infections as well as malaria. Proc Natl Acad Sci U S A 1997;94:14736–41.
90. Oppenheimer SJ, Hendrickse RG, MacFarlane SB, Moody JB, Harrison C, Alpers M, et al. Iron and infection in infancy – report of field studies in Papua New Guinea: 2. Protocol and description of cohort. Ann Trop Paediatr 1984;4:145–53.
91. Oppenheimer SJ, MacFarlane SB, Moody JB, Bunari O, Williams TE, Harrison C, et al. Iron and infection in infancy – report of field studies in Papua New Guinea: 1. Demographic description and pilot surveys. Ann Trop Paediatr 1984;4:135–43.
92. Alonso PL, Lindsay SW, Armstrong JR, Conteh M, Hill AG, David PH, et al. The effect of insecticide-treated bed nets on mortality of Gambian children. Lancet 1991;337:1499–1502.
93. Van Thuy P, Berger J, Nakanishi Y, Khan NC, Lynch S, Dixon P. The use of NaFeEDTA-fortified fish sauce is an effective tool for controlling iron deficiency in women of childbearing age in rural Vietnam. J Nutr 2005;135:2596–601.
94. Wegmuller R, Camara F, Zimmermann MB, Adou P, Hurrell RF. Salt dual-fortified with iodine and micronized ground ferric pyrophosphate affects iron status but not hemoglobin in children in Cote d'Ivoire. J Nutr 2006;136:1814-20.

95. Nestel P, Briend A, de Benoist B, Decker E, Ferguson E, Fontaine O, et al. Complementary food supplements to achieve micronutrient adequacy for infants and young children. J Pediatr Gastroenterol Nutr 2003;36:316–28.

96. Perez-Exposito AB, Villalpando S, Rivera JA, Griffin IJ, Abrams SA. Ferrous sulfate is more bioavailable among preschoolers than other forms of iron in a milk-based weaning food distributed by PROGRESA, a national program in Mexico. J Nutr 2005;135:64–9.

97. Zlotkin SH, Christofides AL, Hyder SM, Schauer CS, Tondeur MC, Sharieff W. Controlling iron deficiency anemia through the use of home-fortified complementary foods. Indian J Pediatr 2004;71:1015–9.

98. Lopriore C, Branca F. Strategies to fight anaemia and growth retardation in Saharawi refugee children. Rome: European Commission Humanitarian Office (ECHO), Comitato Internazionale per lo Sviluppo dei Popoli (CISP), Istituto Nazionale di Ricerca per gli Alimenti e la Nutrizione (INRAN), 2001.

99. Hallberg L. Factors influencing the efficacy of iron fortification and the selection of fortification vehicles. In: Clydesdale FM, Weiner KL, eds. Iron fortification of foods. New York: Academic Press, 1985:7–28.

100. Hallberg L, Hulthen L, Garby L. Iron stores in man in relation to diet and iron requirement. Eur J Clin Nutr 1998;52:623–31.

101. Hurrell R. Preventing iron deficiency through food fortification. Nutr Rev 2002;55:210–22.

102. Dary O. Staple food fortification with iron: a multifactorial decision. Nutr Rev 2002;60: 34S–41.

103 Layrisse M, Garcia-Casal MN, Solano L, Baron MA, Arguelle F, Llovery D, et al. Iron bioavailability in humans from breakfasts enriched with bis-glycine chelate, phytates and polyphenols. J Nutr 2000;130:2195–9.

104. Davidsson L, Dimitriou T, Boy E, Walczyk T, Hurrell R. Iron bioavailability from iron-fortified Guatemalan meals based on corn tortillas and black bean paste. Am J Clin Nutr 2002;75: 535–9.

105. Bovell-Benjamin AC, Viteri FE, Allen LH. Iron absorption from ferrous bisglycinate and ferric tris-glycinate in whole maize is regulated by iron status. Am J Clin Nutr 2000;71:1563–9.

106. Heimbach J, Rieth S, Mohamedshah F, Slesinski R, Samuel-Fernando P, Sheehan T, et al. Safety assessment of iron EDTA [sodium iron (Fe(3+)) ethylenediaminetetraacetic acid]: summary of toxicological, fortification and exposure data. Food Chem Toxicol 2000;38:99–111.

107. Melse-Boonstra A, Rexwinkel H, Bulux J, Solomons NW, West CE. Comparison of three methods for estimating daily individual discretionary salt intake: 24 hour recall, duplicate-portion method, and urinary lithium-labelled household salt excretion. Eur J Clin Nutr 1999;53:281–7.

108. Brunser O, Espinoza J, Araya M, Pacheco I, Cruchet S. Chronic iron intake and diarrhoeal disease in infants. A field study in a less-developed country. Eur J Clin Nutr 1993;47:317–26.

109. Dewey KG, Domellof M, Cohen RJ, Landa Rivera L, Hernell O, Lonnerdal B. Iron supplementation affects growth and morbidity of breast-fed infants: results of a randomized trial in Sweden and Honduras. J Nutr 2002;132:3249–55.

110. Dewey KG, Brown KH. Update on technical issues concerning complementary feeding of young children in developing countries and implications for intervention programs. Food Nutr Bull 2003;24:5–28.

111. Dewey KG. Nutrient composition of fortified complementary foods: should age-specific micronutrient content and ration sizes be recommended. J Nutr 2003;133:2950S–2S.

112. Smuts CM, Lombard CJ, Benade AJ, Dhansay MA, Berger J, Hop le T, et al; International Research on Infant Supplementation (IRIS) Study Group. Efficacy of a foodlet-based multiple micronutrient supplement for preventing growth faltering, anemia, and micronutrient deficiency of infants: the four country IRIS trial pooled data analysis. J Nutr 2005;135:631S–8S.

113. Sharieff W, Yin SA, Wu M, Yang Q, Schauer C, Tomlinson G, Zlotkin S. Short-term daily or weekly administration of micronutrient Sprinkles has high compliance and does not cause iron overload in Chinese schoolchildren: a cluster-randomised trial.

Public Health Nutr 2006; 9:336–44.

114. Meng F, Wei Y, Yang X. Iron content and bioavailability in rice. J Trace Elem Med Biol 2005;18:333–8.

115. Welch RM. Biotechnology, biofortification, and global health. Food Nutr Bull 2005;26:419–21.

116. Haas JD, Beard JL, Murray-Kolb LE, del Mundo AM, Felix A, Gregorio GB. Iron-biofortified rice improves the iron stores of nonanemic Filipino women. J Nutr 2005;135:2823–30.

117. Lucca P, Hurrell R, Potrykus I. Fighting iron-deficiency anemia with iron-rich rice. J Am Coll Nutr 2002;21:184S–90S.

118. Goto F, Yoshihara T, Shigemoto N, Toki S, Takaiwa F. Iron fortification on rice seed by the soybean ferritin gene. Nat Biotechnol 199;17:282–6.

119. International Rice Research Institute. Rice Almanac. Manila: IRRI, 1993.

120. Skikne B, Fonzo D, Lynch SR, Cook JD. Bovine ferritin iron bioavailability in man. Eur J Clin Invest 1997;27:228–33.

121. Graham RD, Welch RM, Bouis HE. Addressing micronutrient malnutrition through enhancing the nutritional quality of staple foods: principles, perspectives and knowledge gaps. Adv Agron 2001;70:77-142.

122. Chassy BM. Food safety evaluation of crops produced through biotechnology. J Am Coll Nutr 2002;21:166S–73S.

123. Poulsen LK. Allergy assessment of foods or ingredients derived from biotechnology, gene-modified organisms, or novel foods. Mol Nutr Food Res 2004;48:413–23.

124. Haslberger AG. Need for an "integrated safety assessment" of GMOs, linking food safety and environmental considerations. J Agric Food Chem 2006;54:3173–80.

125. Miura S, Kunii O, Wakai S. Home gardening in urban poor communities of the Philippines. Int J Food Sci Nutr 2003 54:77–88.

126. Grillenberger M, Neumann CG, Murphy SP, Bwibo NO, Weiss RE, Jiang L, et al. Intake of micronutrients high in animal-source foods is associated with better growth in rural Kenyan school children. Br J Nutr 2006;95:379 90.

127. Krebs NF, Westcott JE, Butler N, Robinson C, Bell M, Hambidge KM. Meat as a first complementary food for breastfed infants: feasibility and impact on zinc intake and status. J Pediatr Gastroenterol Nutr 2006;42:207–14.

128. Nguyen ND, Allen JR, Peat JK, Beal P, Webster BH, Gaskin KJ. Iron status of young Vietnamese children in Australia. J Paediatr Child Health 2004;40:424–9.

129. Mercer J, Erickson-Owens D. Delayed cord clamping increases infants' iron stores. Lancet. 2006;367:1956–8.

130. Rabe H, Reynolds G, Diaz-Rossello J. Early versus delayed umbilical cord clamping in preterm infants. Cochrane Database Syst Rev 2004;(4):CD003248.

131. Chaparro CM, Neufeld LM, Tena Alavez G, Eguia-Liz Cedillo R, Dewey KG. Effect of timing of umbilical cord clamping on iron status in Mexican infants: a randomised controlled trial. Lancet 2006;367:1997–2004.

132. Mercer JS. Current best evidence: a review of the literature on umbilical cord clamping. J Midwifery Womens Health 2001;46:402–14.

133. van Rheenen P, Brabin BJ. Late umbilical cord-clamping as an intervention for reducing iron deficiency anaemia in term infants in developing and industrialised countries: a systematic review. Ann Trop Paediatr 2004;24:3–16.

134. Institute of Medicine, Food and Nutrition Board. Dietary Reference Intakes for thiamine, riboflavin, niacin, vitamin B_6, folate, vitamin B_{12}, pantothenic acid, biotin and choline. Washington, DC: National Academy Press, 1998.

135. Hoelscher M, Riedner G, Hemed Y, Wagner HU, Korte R, von Sonnenburg F. Estimating the number of HIV transmissions through reused syringes and needles in the Mbeya Region, Tanzania. AIDS 1994;8:1609–15.

136. Vidal-Alaball J, Butler CC, Cannings-John R, Goringe A, Hood K, McCaddon A, et al. Oral vitamin B_{12} versus intramuscular vitamin B_{12} for vitamin B_{12} deficiency. Cochrane Database Syst Rev 2005;(3):CD004655.

137. UNICEF/United Nations University/World

Health Organization Study Team. Multiple micronutrient supplementation during pregnancy (MMSDP): efficacy trials. Report of a meeting held on March 4-8, 2002 at the Center for International Child Health, Institute of Child Health, London. London: CICH, 2002.

138. Herbert V. The five possible causes of all nutrient deficiency: illustrated by deficiencies of vitamin B_{12}. Am J Clin Nutr 1973;26:77–86.

139. World Health Organization/Food and Agricultural Organization. Human vitamin and mineral requirements. Geneva: WHO, 2004.

140. Czeizel AE, Dudas I. Prevention of the first occurrence of neural-tube defects by periconceptional vitamin supplementation. N Engl J Med 1992;327:1832–5.

141. Mills JL. Fortification of foods with folic acid – how much is enough? N Engl J Med 2000;342:1442–5.

142. Hirsch S, de la Maza P, Barrera G, Gattas V, Petermann M, Bunout D. The Chilean flour folic acid fortification program reduces serum homocysteine levels and masks vitamin B-12 deficiency in elderly people. J Nutr 2002;132:289–91.

143. Kelly P, McPartlin J, Goggins M, Weir DG, Scott JM. Unmetabolized folic acid in serum: acute studies in subjects consuming fortified food and supplements. Am J Clin Nutr 1997;65:1790–5.

144. Sweeney MR, McPartlin J, Weir DG, Daly S, Pentieva K, Daly L, Scott JM. Evidence of unmetabolised folic acid in cord blood of newborn and serum of 4-day-old infants. Br J Nutr 2005;94:727–30.

145. Troen AM, Mitchell B, Sorensen B, Werner, Johnston A, Wood B, et al. Unmetabolized folic acid in plasma is associated with reduced natural killer cell cytotoxicity among postmenopausal women. J Nutr 2006;136:189–194.

146. Carter JY, Loolpapit MP, Lema O, Tome JL, Nagelkerke NJ, Watkins WM. Reduction of the efficacy of antifolate antimalarial therapy by folic acid supplementation. Am J Trop Med Hyg 2005;73:166–70.

147. Choumenkovitch SF, Selhub J, Wilson PW, Rader JI, Rosenberg IH, Jacques PF. Folic acid intake from fortification in United States exceeds predictions. J Nutr 2002;132:2792–8.

148. Hertrampf E, Cortes F, Erickson JD, Cayazzo M, Freire W, Bailey LB, et al. Consumption of folic acid-fortified bread improves folate status in women of reproductive age in Chile. J Nutr 2003;133:3166–9.

149. Cusick SE, Tielsch JM, Ramsan M, Jape JK, Sazawal S, Black RE, et al. Short-term effects of vitamin A and antimalarial treatment on erythropoiesis in severely anemic Zanzibari preschool children. Am J Clin Nutr 2005;82:406–12.

150. Semba RD, Bloem MW. The anemia of vitamin A deficiency: epidemiology and pathogenesis. Eur J Clin Nutr 2002;56:271-81.

151. Sommer A (rapporteur). Innocenti micronutrient research report #1. Sight & Life Newsletter 2005(3):13–8.

152. Baqui AH, de Francisco A, Arifeen SE, Siddique AK, Sack RB. Bulging fontanelle after supplementation with 25,000 IU of vitamin A in infancy using immunization contacts. Acta Paediatr 1995;84:863–6.

153. Solomons NW. Vitamin A. In: Bowman BA, Russell RM, eds. Present knowledge in nutrition. 9th ed. Washington, DC: ILSI Press, 2006:157–183.

154. Mathews-Roth MM. Carotenoids in erythropoietic protoporphyria and other photosensitivity diseases. Ann N Y Acad Sci 1993;691:127–38.

155. Alpha-Tocopherol Carotene Cancer Prevention Study Group. The effect of vitamin E and carotene on the incidence of lung cancer and other cancers in male smokers. N Engl J Med 1994;330:1029–35.

156. Omenn GS, Goodman GE, Thornquist MD, Balmes J, Cullen MR, Glass A, et al. Effects of a combination of carotene and vitamin A on lung cancer and cardiovascular disease. N Engl J Med 1996;334:1150–5.

157. Ashworth A, Chopra M, McCoy D, Sanders D, Jackson D, Karaolis N, et al. WHO guidelines for management of severe malnutrition in rural South African hospitals: effect on case fatality and the influence of operational factors. Lancet 2004;363:1110–5.

158. Allen LH, Haskell M. Estimating the potential for vitamin A toxicity in women and young children. J Nutr 2002;132:2907S–19S.

159. Dary O, Mora JO; International Vitamin A Consultative Group. Food fortification to reduce vitamin A deficiency: International Vitamin A Consultative Group recommendations. J Nutr 2002;132:2927S–33S.

160. Nestel P, Bouis HE, Meenakshi JV, Pfeiffer W. Biofortification of staple food crops. J Nutr 2006;136:1064–7.

161. Sautter C, Poletti S, Zhang P, Gruissem W. Biofortification of essential nutritional compounds and trace elements in rice and cassava. Proc Nutr Soc 2006;65:153–9.

162. Khush GS. The promise of biotechnology in addressing current nutritional problems in developing countries. Food Nutr Bull 2002;23:354–7.

163. Surles RL, Weng N, Simon PW, Tanumihardjo SA. Carotenoid profiles and consumer sensory evaluation of specialty carrots (*Daucus carota*, L.) of various colors. J Agric Food Chem 2004;52:3417–21.

164. van Jaarsveld PJ, Faber M, Tanumihardjo SA, Nestel P, Lombard CJ, Benade AJ. Beta-carotene-rich orange-fleshed sweet potato improves the vitamin A status of primary school children assessed with the modified-relative-dose-response test. Am J Clin Nutr 2005;81:1080–7.

165. Powers HJ. Riboflavin (vitamin B-2) and health. Am J Clin Nutr 2003;77:1352–60.

166. Zlotkin S, Arthur P, Schauer C, Antwi KY, Yeung G, Piekarz A. Home-fortification with iron and zinc sprinkles or iron sprinkles alone successfully treats anemia in infants and young children. J Nutr 2003;133:1075–80.

167. Hoffman HN 2nd, Phyliky RL, Fleming CR. Zinc-induced copper deficiency. Gastroenterology 1988;94:508–12.

168. Araya M, Olivares M, Pizarro F, Llanos A, Figueroa G, Uauy R. Community-based randomized double-blind study of gastrointestinal effects and copper exposure in drinking water. Environ Health Perspect 2004;112:1068–73.

169. Medeiros DM, Milton A, Brunett E, Stacy L. Copper supplementation effects on indicators of copper status and serum cholesterol in adult males. Biol Trace Elem Res 1991;30:19–35.

170. Araya M, Olivares M, Pizarro F, Mendez MA, Gonzalez M, Uauy R. Supplementing copper at the upper level of the adult dietary recommended intake induces detectable but transient changes in healthy adults. J Nutr 2005;135:2367–71.

171. Chuttani HK, Gupta PS, Gulati S, Gupta DN. Acute copper sulfate poisoning. Am J Med 1965;39:849–54.

172. Barceloux DG. Copper. J Toxicol Clin Toxicol 1999;37:217–30.

173. Gregg XT, Reddy V, Prchal JT. Copper deficiency masquerading as myelodysplastic syndrome. Blood 2002;100:1493–5.

174. Age-Related Eye Disease Study Research Group. A randomized, placebo-controlled clinical trial of high-dose supplementation with vitamins C and E, beta-carotene, and zinc of age-related macular degeneration and vision: AREDS report no. 8. Arch Ophthalmol 2001;119:1417–36.

175. Bienz D, Cori H, Hornig D. Adequate dosing of micronutrients for different age groups in the life cycle. Food Nutr Bull 2003;24(3 Suppl):7S–-15S.

176. Gross R, Solomons NW. Multiple micronutrient deficiencies: future research needs. Food Nutr Bull 2003;24(3 Suppl):42S–53S.

177. Gross R. Micronutrient supplementation throughout the life cycle. New York: UNICEF, 2001.

178. Christian P, Khatry SK, Katz J, Pradhan EK, LeClerq SC, Shrestha SR, et al. Effects of alternative maternal micronutrient supplements on low birth weight in rural Nepal: double blind randomised community trial. BMJ 2003; 326:571.

179. Osrin D, Vaidya A, Shrestha Y, Baniya RB, Manandhar DS, Adhikari RK, et al. Effects of antenatal multiple micronutrient supplementation on birthweight and gestational duration in Nepal: double-blind, randomised controlled trial. Lancet 2005;365:955-62.

180. Christian P, Osrin D, Manandhar DS, Khatry SK, de L Costello AM, West KP Jr. Antenatal micronutrient supplements in Nepal. Lancet 2005;366:711-2 (letter).

181. Fawzi WW, Msamanga GI, Spiegelman D, Wei R, Kapiga S, Villamor E, et al. A randomized trial of multivitamin supplements and HIV disease progression and mortality. N Engl J Med 2004;351:23-32.

182. Fawzi WW, Msamanga GI, Hunter D, Renjifo

B, Antelman G, Bang H, et al. Randomized trial of vitamin supplements in relation to transmission of HIV-1 through breastfeeding and early child mortality. AIDS 2002;16:1935-44.

183. Villamor E, Saathoff E, Manji K, Msamanga G, Hunter DJ, Fawzi WW. Vitamin supplements, socioeconomic status, and morbidity events as predictors of wasting in HIV-infected women from Tanzania. Am J Clin Nutr 2005;82:857-65.

184. Villamor E, Fawzi WW. Effects of vitamin A supplementation on immune responses and correlation with clinical outcomes. Clin Microbiol Rev 2005;18:446-64.

185. Viteri FE, Torun B. Protein energy malnutrition. In: Warren KS, Mahmoud AA, eds. Tropical and geographic medicine. Philadelphia: McGraw-Hill, 1990:531–546.

186. Viteri FE, Alvarado JE, Luthringer DG, Wood RP 2nd. Hematological changes in protein calorie malnutrition. Vitam Horm 1968;26:573–618.

187. Caballero B, Solomons NW, Batres R, Torun B. Homeostatic mechanisms in the utilization of exogenous iron in children recovering from severe malnutrition. J Pediatr Gastroenterol Nutr 1985;4:97–102.

188. Golden MH, Ramdath D. Free radicals in the pathogenesis of kwashiorkor. Proc Nutr Soc 1987;46:53–68.

189. Manary MJ, Leeuwenburgh C, Heinecke JW. Increased oxidative stress in kwashiorkor. J Pediatr 2000;137:421–4.

190. Schofield C, Ashworth A. Why have mortality rates for severe malnutrition remained so high? Bull World Health Org 1996;74:223–9.

191. Prudhon C, Golden MH, Briend A, Mary JY. A model to standardise mortality of severely malnourished children using nutritional status on admission to therapeutic feeding centres. Eur J Clin Nutr 1997;51:771–7.

192. World Health Organization. Management of severe malnutrition: A Manual for physicians and other senior health workers. Geneva: WHO, 1999.

193. Solomons NW. Rehabilitating the severely malnourished infant and child. J Am Diet Assoc 1985;85:28–36, 39.

194. Karaolis N, Jackson D, Ashworth A, Sanders D, Sogaula N, McCoy D, et al. WHO guidelines for severe malnutrition: are they feasible in rural African hospitals? Arch Dis Child. 2006 May 2.

195. Hallberg L, Hulten L, Gramatkovski E. Iron absorption from the whole diet in men: how effective is the regulation of iron absorption? Am J Clin Nutr 1997;66:347–56.

196. Kelleher SL, Lönnerdal B. Zinc supplementation reduces iron absorption through age-dependent changes in small intestine iron transporter expressed in suckling rat pups. J Nutr 2006;136:1185–91.

197. Fleming DJ, Tucker KL, Jacques PF, Dallal GE, Wilson PW, Wood RJ. Dietary factors associated with the risk of high iron stores in the elderly Framingham Heart Study cohort. Am J Clin Nutr 2002;76:1375–84.

198. World Health Organization. Iron supplementation of young children in regions where malaria transmission is intense and infectious disease highly prevalent. Geneva: WHO, 2006.

19

The importance and limitations of food fortification for the management of nutritional anemias[1]

Omar Dary

A2Z Project, Academy for Educational Development, Washington, DC, USA.
Contact: odary@aed.org

OMAR DARY

Omar has a PhD in Biochemistry from the University of California, Riverside. He is currently the Food Fortification Specialist of A2Z: The USAID Micronutrient Program and advises on design, policy, implementation, food control, monitoring, evaluation, and regulation of food fortification programs. Omar has provided technical assistance to more than 30 countries around the world and has served as a consultant to many organizations including UNICEF, WHO, PAHO, GAIN, and MI. He is on the Steering Committees of the Micronutrient Forum and IZiNCG.

---

[1] From A2Z/The USAID Micronutrient and Child Blindness Project, Washington DC.

INTRODUCTION

The customary diet of populations in developing countries (1) and population subgroups in developed countries (2) does not have the adequate micronutrient balance to satisfy the requirement of one or more nutrients. This occurs due to economic[2], cultural[3] or physiological[4] reasons, making the addition of micronutrients an appropriate intervention. Two approaches can be used for this purpose: dietary supplementation and food fortification.

A dietary supplement is a product which requires a voluntary and educated decision for consumption. Supplements are highly dense in vitamins and minerals to provide large amounts of nutrients in one or few doses. The formulation of dietary supplements can be tailored to the requirements of specific population groups. They may also deliver adequate amounts of micronutrients and the interactions of micronutrients and absorption inhibitors—mainly for iron, zinc, copper, and calcium—can be diminished (3). Supplementation programs often have a disadvantage of low population coverage and acceptance.

A fortified food can be defined as an edible product (staple food, processed food, condiment, or product for special groups) manufactured by the food industry with a nutritional composition that is enhanced by the addition of vitamins and minerals. The WHO Guidelines for food fortification (4) distinguishes three approaches to food fortification: mass, targeted, and market-driven. Mass fortification refers to the addition of micronutrients to edible products that are consumed regularly by the general public, such as cereals, oils and vegetable fats, milk, and condiments. Targeted fortification refers to the fortification of foods designed for specific population subgroups, such as complementary weaning foods for infants, foods for institutional programs aimed at schoolchildren or preschoolers, and foods used under emergency situations. Market-driven fortification refers to a situation in which a food manufacturer takes the initiative to add one or more micronutrients to processed foods in order to increase sales and profits.

Adding micronutrients in each type of fortification approach requires different guidelines. In any case, the objective is to provide the intended benefit for the target population while avoiding potential risks associated with excessive micronutrient intake to individuals who consume the fortified products in large amounts. That means the micronutrient content is limited to prevent individuals from surpassing the Tolerable Upper Intake Level (UL)[5]. Other restrictions result from negative interactions with the food matrices and the need to minimize the additional cost (4,6). Because of this, the supply of some micronutrients, mainly through mass fortification, may be insufficient, especially for individuals in the most at risk groups. The advantage of mass fortification, however, is that population coverage is large.

Targeted fortification has an intermediate position between dietary supplementation and mass fortification. While it can deliver high

[2] Little access to good quality and nutritious foods, e.g.

[3] Strict vegetarianism or diet largely based on starchy or refined foods, e.g.

[4] Low gastric capacity in small children, larger nutritional requirements during pregnancy or lactation, or reduced intestinal absorption in the elderly, e.g.

[5] The Tolerable Upper Intake Level (UL) is the highest average daily nutrient intake level unlikely to pose risk of adverse effects to almost all apparently healthy individuals in an age- and sex-specific group (5).

amounts of micronutrients, the population coverage is restricted and some undesirable interactions between micronutrients and other diet ingredients may still occur. With targeted fortification, the limitations due to sensorial changes in the food matrix are less restrictive than with mass fortification.

The importance of market-driven fortification in developing countries is still uncertain because of the generally low accessibility of these foods to the poor and to rural groups. Another disadvantage is the potential risk of providing excessive intakes to some consumers. Thus, the balance of the micronutrient content to the energy density in the food is increasingly being recommended as the guideline to determine the micronutrient amounts for this type of fortification (2, 4).

Lastly, it is important to recognize the concept of household fortification. This term identifies the consumption of dietary supplements (usually in powder forms) mixed with foods during meals. In this case, the conditions that are established are similar to those of targeted fortification (i.e., probably high micronutrient intake), but limited population coverage, still with possible negative interactions between the minerals and the ingredients of the diet.

This chapter discusses food fortification to address nutritional anemia. Two population groups are especially vulnerable to anemia: children younger than 24 months of age and women of reproductive age. The former group should receive special attention and products, such as complementary foods (targeted fortification) and age specific dietary supplements. Therefore, fortification for young children is not included here.

This chapter focuses on the use of food fortification to manage nutritional anemia in women of reproductive age, although it also describes a few studies that assessed biological impact in school-age children.

JUSTIFYING AND DESIGNING MASS FORTIFICATION

Cost of correcting micronutrient deficiencies

Nutritional anemia is only one of the consequences of micronutrient deficiencies, but is usually the most difficult to overcome. Nutritional anemias have been usually associated with deficiency of iron. While this may be the case, the status of vitamins A, B_2, B_6, B_{12}, and folate must also be adequate for the synthesis of hemoglobin (7). Because hemoglobin is carried by red blood cells, many other nutrients that ensure cell replication, growth and maintenance are also needed, including those participating in energy metabolism (vitamins B_1, B_2, and niacin), in protein and nucleic acid synthesis (vitamins B_2, B_6, B_{12}, niacin, and folate), in genetic modulation (vitamins A and D, and iodine), and in the protection against oxidation (vitamins C and E, magnesium, selenium, and zinc) (8,9). A sufficient supply of essential amino acids, fatty acids, and metabolic energy is also necessary. Supplying additional iron would reduce anemia only if iron is very deficient and only up to the point where another factor becomes rate limiting. In the case of poor societies, other factors – both nutritional and environmental – could be present (10). Therefore, management of nutritional anemia requires good general nutrition conditions and the improvement of the status of many micronutrients, not just iron.

Table 19.1 lists the current cost to supply the estimated average requirement (EAR)[6] of nutrients

---

[6] Estimated average requirement (EAR) is the average (median) daily nutrient intake level estimated to meet the needs of half the healthy individuals in a particular age and gender group. These are the dietary parameters recommended to assess and plan population-based interventions (5).

Table 19.1: Calculated costs to provide one estimated average requirement (EAR) to women of reproductive age through food fortification.

Micronutrient	Fortificant	Micronutrient in fortificant (proportion)	Fortificant price ($/kg)[1]	Micronutrient loss before consumption (%)	EAR[2] (mg/day)	Cost to supply EAR ($/year)[3]
Vitamin B$_1$	Thiamin mononitrate	0.81	25.00	30	0.9	0.013
Vitamin B$_2$	Riboflavin	1.00	38.00	15	0.9	0.014
Niacin	Niacinamide	0.99	10.00	10	11	0.045
Vitamin B$_6$	Pyridoxine	0.82	31.00	15	1.1	0.017
Vitamin B$_{12}$	Vitamin B$_{12}$ 0.1 % WS	0.001	42.00	15	0.002	0.035
Folate	Folic acid	1.00	90.00	30	0.188	0.008
Vitamin A	Retinyl palmitate (oil)	0.51	70.00	30	0.357	0.023
	Retinyl palmitate (dry)	0.075	40.00	30	0.357	0.090
Iron	NaFeEDTA	0.13	6.50	0	9.4–14.1[4]	0.172–0.257
	Ferrous bisglycinate	0.20	25.00	0	9.4–14.1	0.429–0.643
	Ferrous fumarate	0.32	7.05	0	14.1–28.2	0.113–0.227
	Ferrous sulfate (dry)	0.32	2.60	0	14.1–28.2	0.042–0.084
	Micronized ferric pyrophosphate	0.25	9.10	0	20.1–40.3	0.267–0.535
	Electrolytic iron	0.97	4.50	0	21.6–43.2	0.037–0.073
	Hydrogen reduced iron	0.96	3.25	0	28.2–56.4	0.035–0.070
	Encapsulated ferrous sulfate	0.16	13.00	0	14.1–28.2	0.418–0.836
Zinc	Zinc oxide	0.80	3.35	0	4.1–8.2	0.006–0.013
Iodine	Potassium iodate	0.59	20.00	15	0.107	0.002
Calcium	Calcium carbonate	0.40	2.70	0	833	2.105
Vitamin C	Ascorbic acid (fine powder)	1.00	11.20	60	37	0.242

to women of reproductive age through food fortification. Cost varies from the least expensive nutrient, iodine ($0.002 per year), to the most expensive, calcium ($2.105 per year). The higher cost of calcium is mainly due to the large amounts of the mineral needed. Costs of iron, vitamin C, and vitamin A follow after calcium. These costs are estimated also taking into consideration the expected micronutrient losses during production, distribution, storage, and food preparation. The costs are also adjusted to consider the estimated physiological biovailabilities. Iron costs range from $0.035 to $0.836 per year, depending on the iron compound and the diet characteristics. The cost of vitamin C is approximately $0.242 per year, and the cost of vitamin A can vary from $0.023 per year to $0.090 per year. The cost of combining all the other micronutrients listed in the table is lower than $0.150 per year.

Under typical conditions (excluding calcium and vitamin C[7]), it is estimated that a woman can receive her entire yearly requirement of micronutrients through food fortification activities with an annual investment of $0.35 to $1.00. The type of iron and vitamin A compounds determine the variation in costs. This investment would be lower if we consider that food fortification aims to cover the gaps between a person's nutritional needs and their usual diet. This means that food

fortification could be the most favorable and cost-effective strategy among micronutrient interventions. However, as described below, many factors can hinder the potential use and efficacy of food fortification.

In mass fortification under formal industrial settings (large factories), approximately 80–90% of the cost corresponds to the purchase of micronutrient compounds (13, 14). Thus, the cost of the fortificants is a proxy estimation of the overall cost of mass fortification. Such a generalization is valid neither for small operations nor rice, which is fortified by using micronutrient coated or artificial kernels. In the latter case, 50–90% of the cost is associated with production of the fortified kernels.

With supplements, the cost of the micronutrients represents 10–40% of the overall cost. If one assumes that each supplement cost $0.02, and that a weekly delivery may require 50% higher doses than the daily scheme to compensate for lower absorption, then daily and weekly schemes would need annual investments to manufacture the product in the order of $7.30 and $2.00, respectively. The cost of the weekly scheme is attractive if it were biologically efficacious. Recent evidence suggests that this is indeed the case, at least for some micronutrients (15), which

---

[7] Calcium because of the relatively large amounts needed, and vitamin C because the high loss during storage and during food preparation is usually not included in most mass-food fortification cases.

Table 19.1

[1] Vitamin information provided by DSM, the Netherlands; most mineral information by Paul Lohmann, Germany; NaFeEDTA by Akzo Nobel Chemicals, Singapore; and ferrous bisglycinate as in the market.

[2] All micronutrients, except iron, as specified in Allen (4). Folate expressed in Dietary Folate Equivalents (i.e., 1 mg folic acid=1.7 mg DFE), and EAR of vitamin B_{12} divided by two because of higher bioavailability of the synthetic form. Iron values for diets with 10% and 5% iron bioavailability were estimated from the Institute of Medicine of the USA (5), dividing the absorbed iron need (1.4 mg/day) by 0.10 and 0.05, respectively. EAR values for each iron compound are approximations based on their relative biovailabilities as compared with ferrous sulfate.

[3] Cost=(EAR x 365) x (fortificant price x (1 + (% loss/100)) / (micronutrient proportion x 10^6).

[4] First figure is an approximation for a diet whose general mineral bioavailability is intermediate (10% for dietary iron), the second figure corresponds to a diet of low mineral bioavailability (5% for dietary iron). EAR for electrolytic and hydrogen reduced irons are estimated as 65% and 50% as ferrous sulfate, respectively, following data of relative bioavailability (11). EAR for micronized ferric pyrophosphate was estimated as 70% that of ferrous sulfate (12).

justifies further attention to this strategy. Dietary supplementation requires a distribution system, while one is usually already operative in the case of mass fortification. Creating this new system may be a very expensive and challenging task. Therefore, the absence of cost due to distribution, rather than the cost of the fortificants, demarcates the main advantage of mass fortification over supplementation and the other fortification approaches.

Vehicle selection

The low cost of using mass fortification over supplementation or targeted fortification holds true only in industrial settings, where only few acceptable developed factories produce the foods. That means that the main criterion for mass fortification is that the fortification vehicle should be produced by formal and centralized industries. Otherwise, the economic advantages of this intervention might be significantly reduced or even lost. These advantages include the fast pace and low cost for implementation, the production following good manufacturing practices, the easy distribution and control of the micronutrient mixes, and the feasibility of the essential regulatory enforcement by the government. The above consideration is contrary to the common paradigm that a widely consumed food, regardless of the system of production and trade, such as staple cereals and salt, is a suitable fortification vehicle. In many instances, results of biological efficacy of fortification projects implemented in small operations, under strictly controlled and subsidized schemes, are used as evidence of the feasibility of this practice. The fact that biological impact depends on the quality and amount of the added micronutrients and not on the mechanism of delivery, and that operational success under controlled conditions does not predict program viability, is often overlooked. Hence, it is important to recognize that the social penetration of a mass fortification program is determined by the extent to which the centrally-produced foods are distributed, and by the amount of products that are accessible and affordable to the at risk population.

Table 19.2 presents some characteristics of ongoing mass fortification programs. Two of these characteristics are essential in predicting the feasibility of a mass fortification program: 1) high dilution factor of the fortificant (source of micronutrients) in the food; and 2) low cost expressed in relative terms to the price increase of the commodity. If these two conditions are met, the chance of introducing a mass fortification program improves and the risk of noncompliance is reduced. Except for fish/soy sauces fortified with NaFeEDTA, which show a dilution factor in the hundreds and not in the thousands, the other fortification examples included in the table fulfill the mentioned requirements.

Fish and soy sauce fortification is being introduced in Vietnam and China (16), respectively, but the establishment of real mass fortification programs has not as yet been demonstrated. It is possible that, in the absence of a very strong governmental pressure, this fortification effort may end as a "market-driven" fortification of a few brands, or end as targeted fortification sponsored by institutions outside of the food industry. The same restrictions may hinder the introduction of mass fortification of rice using micronutrient coated or artificial kernels; the dilution factor is 1:100 to 1:200 (17) and the raise in price is between 3 and 6%. A very small number of countries have rice mills in a position to produce rice under such conditions. The failure of fortification efforts with vitamin A of monosodium glutamate in the Philippines and Indonesia in the 1970s may provide an example of how real this threat is. The project, although biologically efficacious, collapsed a few months after initiation because of product discoloration in Indonesia, and because the price increase was too large to favor acceptance of the product by the consumers in the Philippines (18).

The maximum dilution factor possible in mass fortification depends on the physical weight and volume of the fortificants, their proportional

Table 19.2: Comparison of dilution factors, and costs of existing mass fortification programs.

Food	Micronutrients and average contents (mg/kg)	Grams of fortificant per 1000 kg or L	Dilution factor fortificant: food+fortificant	Fortificant cost ($/1000 kg or L)	Food price ($/kg or L)	Price increase due to fortification
Salt	Iodine (40)	75	1:13,333	1.36	0.20	0.7%
Oil	Vitamin A (20)	40	1:25,000	2.75	0.50	0.5%
Sugar	Vitamin A (15)	200	1:5,000	8.00	0.40	2.0%
Milk	Vitamin A (0.6), Vitamin D (0.01) Folic acid (0.2) Iron (bisglycinate) (10) Zinc (7.0)	75	1:13,333	1.50	0.60	0.2%
Low extraction wheat flour	Vitamin B$_1$ (6), Vitamin B$_2$ (5) Niacin (60), Folic acid (2) Iron (ferrous fumarate) (45)	250	1:4,000	2.17	0.40	0.5%
Low extraction wheat flour[1]	Vitamin B$_1$ (6), Vitamin B$_2$ (5) Niacin (60), Vitamin B$_6$ (6) Vitamin B$_{12}$ (0.01), Vitamin A (2) Folic acid (2), Zinc (30) Iron (ferrous fumarate) (45)	400	1:2,500	4.00	0.40	1.0%
Fish/soy sauce	Iron (NaFeEDTA) (500)	3,846	1:260	25.00	1.00	2.5%

[1] Some African countries have proposed using a formula like this, while Jordan and the Palestinian territories have already introduced the same micronutrients, but at around one half of the amounts shown here, because of the large consumption of wheat flour in those countries, and the use of ferrous sulfate as the iron source.

content of micronutrients, and the selected micronutrient content for the fortified food. For example, in the case of sugar fortification with vitamin A, the maximum possible dilution factor to produce fortified sugar with a content of 15 mg/kg, using an encapsulated compound of vitamin A that contains this nutrient at 7.5% (w/w, weight per weight), is 1:5,000 (i.e., 200 g of fortificant per 1,000 kg of fortified sugar). This means that one part of the compound containing vitamin A is present for each 5,000 parts of fortified sugar. However, this dilution factor may be too large to make a homogeneous product. Thus, the vitamin A compound is diluted first to 1:5, to reduce the dilution factor to 1:1,000 (i.e., 1 kg of fortificant premix per 1,000 kg of fortified sugar). Nevertheless, dilution factors lower than 1:1,000 may be very cumbersome for the staple industries to implement, because large volumes and weights are difficult to handle, store, distribute and dilute.

Design of the fortification formulation

Annex D of the WHO Guidelines on food fortification (4) describes a procedure to estimate the micronutrient content in mass fortification. In brief, the model is based on the determination of a Feasible Fortification Level (FFL). The FFL is the maximum content of micronutrient that can be added and still remain compatible with the food matrix; it increases the price of food within an acceptable value; and it provides the greatest number of at risk individuals with an adequate intake without causing an unacceptable risk of excessive intake in the population at large. A mass fortification program can be constituted by more than one food vehicle. Then, the FFL for each micronutrient and food should be estimated in cumulative sequence, starting with the food with the largest market penetration. An alternative approach is to make a combined analysis of all foods that are being considered as part of the program. In either case, the objective is to reduce the risk of excessive intakes for those individuals who consume these foods in large quantities and at the same time to provide as much micronutrients as possible to

the population at risk. As a consequence, the maximum content of micronutrients in mass fortification is determined by those individuals who eat the food vehicles in the largest quantities (i.e., the upper 5–10%). This can result in a situation in which important portions of the population at nutritional risk may still not receive sufficient additional intakes to fulfill their nutritional gaps. Thus, complementary measures may still be needed. This circumstance affects mainly those micronutrients with UL values near to the EAR values, such as folic acid, vitamin A, iron, iodine and calcium. These nutrients coincidentally are among the micronutrients whose intake should be raised among poorer populations.

For nutrients without recognized UL values, the FFL may be higher than necessary to satisfy the nutritional gap of most of the population. In this case, the content of those micronutrients can be much lower than the FFL, without compromising the supply to ample sectors of the population.

Table 19.3 shows that for iron fortification of flours, the factor that limits the content of iron is of a technological nature, namely the incompatibility between the iron compounds and the food matrices. Addition of iron must be low to prevent undesirable changes in the sensorial properties of the flours. Thus, ferrous sulfate, which is water soluble and highly reactive, can be added in amounts around 25 mg/kg of iron in a low extraction wheat flour (highly refined, and low in fats). Less reactive iron compounds, such as ferrous fumarate and elemental iron of different types, are usually incorporated in amounts of 50 mg/kg of iron. However, in high extraction flours (whole or unrefined flours), the content of any type of iron is lower because of the presence of fats and other substances that cause rancidity and changes in color.

The addition of NaFeEDTA to bakery refined flour is still under investigation after a study reported interference of bread making by the EDTA moiety (19). Even though NaFeEDTA was

Table 19.3: Technical restrictions in the addition of iron reduce the estimated bioefficacy of fortified flours for women of reproductive age.

Iron compounds	Low extraction flour in an intermediate bioavailable diet (10%) for dietary iron)			High extraction flour in a low biovailable diet (5% for dietary iron)		
	Possible iron content (mg/kg)	Approximate EAR and RNI for women (mg/day)[1]	% EAR and RNI supplied in 100 g/day flour consumption	Possible iron content (mg/kg)	Approxiamte EAR and RNI for women (mg/day)	% EAR and RNI supplied in 100 g/day flour consumption
NaFeEDTA	-	-	-	20	14.1 and 29.4	14 and 7
Ferrous fumarate	45	14.1 and 29.4	32 and 15	25	28.2 and 58.8	9 and 4
Ferrous sulfate (dry)	25	14.1 and 29.4	18 and 9	-	-	-
Electrolytic iron	50	21.6 and 45.0	23 and 11	40	43.2 and 90.0	9 and 4
Hydrogen reduced iron	50	28.2 and 58.8	18 and 8	40	56.4 and 117.6	7 and 3

[1] EAR and RNI values for electrolytic and hydrogen reduced irons are estimated as 65% and 50% as ferrous sulfate, respectively, following data of relative bioavailability (11).

found to be compatible with flour destined for making bread, the amount of iron from this source would be restricted to around 35 mg/kg, considering that currently the maximum recommended intake of iron from NaFeEDTA is 0.2 mg iron/kg body weight per day (20). This maximum iron content from NaFeEDTA is estimated assuming 400 g/day as the largest flour consumption by a 70 kg person. Due to the better bioavailability, 35 mg/kg iron content from NaFeEDTA would provide a larger proportion of the EAR to women than 45 mg/kg of iron from ferrous fumarate in a diet low in iron absorption inhibitors (37% EAR against 32% EAR, respectively, when flour consumption is 100 g/day). However the cost would double, from $1/MT[8] to $2/MT.

Data in **Table 19.3** shows that with the amounts of iron incorporated into flour, and when flour consumption is 100 g/day, the additional intake of this nutrient can be from 18–32% of women's EAR (or from 8–15% RNI[9]) using refined flours, and from 7–14% EAR (or from 3–7% RNI) using unrefined flours. The modest increments of additional iron intake from fortified unrefined flours raise doubts over the usefulness of fortifying these flours with iron. Similarly, iron fortification of other foods that would be consumed with meals rich in iron inhibitors may have low efficacy or would have low cost effectiveness because of the large quantities of iron that would be needed.

Nevertheless, flours can also carry many other micronutrients, and their role in improving one's nutritional status is potentially much higher than that for iron, as illustrated in **Table 19.4**. Flour consumption of 100 g/day of fortified refined flour is able to provide 70–100% EAR (60–85% RNI) of folate, vitamin B_{12}, and zinc; and 55–65% EAR (40–55% RNI) of vitamin A and all the other vitamins of the B complex. Similar intakes of vitamins A, and B_{12} and folate are obtained through the consumption of fortified unrefined flours. These flours provide lower amounts (15–45% EAR, or 10–35% RNI) of zinc and other vitamins of the B complex than the refined flours. This difference is expected given the lower addition of these nutrients in the fortification profile of unrefined flours. Because unrefined flours maintain important amounts of those micronutrients, the need for addition of micronutrients is smaller.

Assessing the potential nutritional implications

The WHO Guidelines on food fortification (4) suggest that the potential benefit of food fortification programs can be estimated by examining which proportion of the population moves from below to above the corresponding EAR values. It is not only difficult, but also rare, to estimate the distribution profile of EAR in populations from the usual diet. As a proxy, the calculation of the additional EAR obtained from fortified foods may be useful. In theory, the magnitude of the biological impact would correlate with the proportion of the additional EAR that is supplied. As a convention, it may be accepted that if a food provides at least 20% or 40% EAR[10], this food

---

[8] MT=metric ton=1,000 kg.

[9] Recommended nutrient intake (RNI) refers to the daily intake which meets the nutrient requirements of almost all apparently healthy individuals (97.5%) in an age- and sex-specific population group. It is set at the estimated average requirement plus 2 standard deviations (5).

[10] This is similar to the recommendation given by the Codex Alimentarius (21) for nutrition claims, which specifies that if a food is a "source" of a specific nutrient if it supplies 15% of the Codex Nutrient Reference Values (NRV), which are similar to the Recommended Nutrient Intakes (RNI), per usual serving. In order to qualify as being "high" in a specific nutrient, a food product must contain twice as much of the nutrient as the "source" does. Excluding iron, the EAR values are approximately 80% of the corresponding RNI values.

Table 19.4: Cost and additional supply of micronutrients in fortified flours for women of reproductive age (assuming consumption of 100 g/day).

Micronutrient	Fortificant	Low extraction flour in an intermediate bioavailable diet (10% for dietary iron)			High extraction flour in a low bioavailable diet (5% for dietary iron)		
		Nutrient content (mg/kg)	Cost ($/MT)[1]	% EAR and RNI supplied [2]	Nutrient content (mg/kg)	Cost ($/MT)	% EAR and RNI supplied
Vitamin B$_1$	Thiamin mononitrate	6.0	0.19	67 and 55	2.0	0.06	22 and 18
Vitamin B$_2$	Riboflavin	5.0	0.19	56 and 45	4.0	0.15	44 and 36
Niacin	Niacinamide	60	0.61	55 and 43	15	0.15	14 and 11
Vitamin B$_6$	Pyridoxine	6.0	0.23	55 and 46	5.0	0.19	45 and 38
Vitamin B$_{12}$	Vitamin B$_{12}$ 0.1% WS	0.01	0.42	100 and 83	0.01	0.42	100 and 83
Folate	Folic acid	2.0	0.20	106 and 85	2.0	0.20	106 and 85
Vitamin A	Retinyl palmitate (dry)	2.0	1.07	56 and 40	2.0	1.07	56 and 40
Iron	NaFeEDTA	-	-	-	20	1.00	14 and 7
	Ferrous fumarate	45	0.99	32 and 15	25	0.55	9 and 4
	Ferrous sulfate (dry)	25	0.20	18 and 9	-	-	-
	Electrolytic iron	50	0.23	23 and 11	40	0.19	9 and 4
	Hydrogen reduced iron	50	0.17	18 and 9	40	0.13	7 and 3
Zinc	Zinc oxide	30	0.15	73 and 61	20	0.08	24 and 20

[1] Cost = (micronutrient content in food x fortificant price) / (micronutrient proportion in fortificant x 1000)

[2] % RNI (or % EAR) = [(micronutrient content x food consumption) x (1 – % loss/100) / (1000 x RNI – or EAR –)] x 100. First value corresponds to EAR and second to RNI, when wheat flour consumption is 100 g/day.

could be considered as a "good" or an "excellent" source of the micronutrient, respectively. The importance of mass fortification as a public health program could be estimated by the absolute and relative number of individuals from the at risk groups whose consumptions reach those categories.

If the cost were disregarded, the most promising source of iron in refined flours is ferrous fumarate. Consumption of fortified wheat flour in amounts of about 125 g/day would provide 40% EAR (although only 19% RNI) to women of reproductive age. This iron compound may be replaced with electrolytic iron (type A-131) or ferrous sulfate if the consumption of flour is nearly or higher than 225 g/day. The only advantage of ferrous sulfate over the electrolytic iron is that it can be easily identified in the fortified flour. It is very difficult to guarantee that electrolytic iron (A-131) and not any other elemental iron of much lower bioavailability is being used (11, 22). The countries of Central America selected ferrous fumarate as the iron source to fortify wheat flour, not only because it has a good bioavailability (19), but also as a practical solution to guarantee that the flour contains a good iron compound.

In the case of unrefined flour, probably the only justifiable source of iron is NaFeEDTA, because of the potential to improve absorption of iron from other sources. However, the daily flour consumption should be larger than 150 g/day to supply at least 20% EAR (around 10% RNI) of iron to women of reproductive age.

How much additional iron is needed to have a biological impact?

All the prior considerations do not answer the question of how much additional iron is needed to obtain biological effects. **Table 19.5** attempts to respond to that query. The table summarizes published data of several efficacy and effectiveness studies on iron fortification interventions.

The study with refined wheat flour in Sri Lanka (25) failed to reduce the anemia prevalence in women of reproductive age, after two years of supplying a daily average of 12.5 mg of electrolytic (A-131) or reduced iron. This outcome can be easily explained by the small additional percent of EAR (22–29%), or RNI (11–14%), in a diet high in iron absorption inhibitors. Although this study could not determine serum ferritin, similar work in Bangladesh, supplying wheat flour fortified with reduced iron to 6–15 year old children for six months (30), found no changes in anemia. There were also no differences in serum ferritin and serum transferrin receptors between the experimental and the control groups. The experimental group had an additional intake of 6.6 mg/day of iron (25% EAR, or 20% RNI), and 300 mg/day of vitamin A (75% EAR). The prevalence of low retinol levels (<0.7 μmol/L or 20 μg/dL) changed from 13.6 to 7.4% in the experimental group, and from 15.4 to 22.5% in the control group. This result proved that wheat flour was a good fortification vehicle for vitamin A, but not for iron, especially within a population whose diet has low iron bioavailability.

Zimmermann and colleagues (26) recently published the results of an iron efficacy study that used snacks made with refined flour (40%), butter and margarine (25%), and sugar (22%). The snack was given to 18–50 year old Thai women six days a week over 35 weeks. The iron dose averaged 12–14 mg/day (estimated 46–92% EAR or 22–44% RNI, depending on the iron compound). The group treated with ferrous sulfate (92% EAR or 44% RNI) had a reduction of the anemia rate from 18 to 12%. The other iron compounds, electrolytic (A-131) and hydrogen reduced, did not produce a significant change in anemia rates. Nevertheless, both ferrous sulfate (92% EAR or 44% RNI) and the electrolytic iron (60% EAR or 29% RNI) improved iron stores measured by changes in serum ferritin and serum transferrin receptor. This study showed that both ferrous sulfate and electrolytic iron are absorbed and able to improve iron status. The effect correlated well with the proportions of EAR that were supplied. Here, it is important to point out that this treatment was applied in a diet free of iron absorption inhibitors, because the snack was given separately from meals.

Thuy et al. (27) reported an iron efficacy study using fish sauce fortified with NaFeEDTA in Vietnam. Women of reproductive age received 10 mg/day of iron (71% EAR or 34% RNI) over six months. The experimental group showed reduction in iron deficiency and iron deficiency anemia, but the change in total anemia prevalence was reported as not significant compared with the control group. A similar study conducted with soy sauce in China (31) reported reduction in anemia in all members of the family. However, low serum ferritin levels (<12 µg/L) were highly prevalent in all groups even after the period of treatment. This result, together with the relative low additional intake of iron (4 mg/day), makes the results of this study difficult to interpret.

The findings in Vietnam can be explained in several ways. First, the anemia may have been related to multiple factors other than iron deficiency, and hence the reduction was not as large as expected. Second, the period of exposure to the higher iron intake may have been too short. Finally, the iron dose may have been insufficient. The response of serum ferritin rules out infection as a reason for the lack of response. The period of exposure was likely adequate because a steady-state situation to a new intake of iron was reached during that period (32). In addition to the presence of multiple micronutrient deficiency, the most probable explanation for the lack of anemia reduction was that the additional intake of iron (71% EAR or 34% RNI) was still insufficient to reduce anemia in this population, although it was sufficient to start improving iron status. The results were comparable to the study using snacks that were fortified with electrolytic iron (60% EAR or 29% RNI) in Thailand.

An efficacy trial performed on school-age children of Morocco succeeded in demonstrating anemia reduction associated with the additional intake of iron, given as micronized ferric pyrophosphate in salt (28). Although the additional intakes of iron were similar to those in the studies made with women (7–18 g/day), given the lower iron requirements of the school-age children, it was determined that a larger biological supply of iron was reached: around 138% EAR (or 112% RNI).

Wegmüller et al. (29), from the same research group, made a similar study in Ivory Coast. However, in this case, anemia prevalence was not reduced. The authors attributed this outcome to the concomitant presence of malaria, and also probably to vitamin B_2 deficiency. However, this result can also be explained by the lower proportion of EAR supplied in this intervention trial: 65% versus 138% in Morocco (or 52% versus 112% RNI, respectively). It is interesting to note, that despite lack of response in anemia or iron deficiency anemia, iron stores were improved in the group of children receiving additional amounts of iron in Ivory Coast. This is a similar response to the women in Thailand who increased iron intake by 60% EAR (or 29% RNI) through the consumption of an iron fortified snack (26).

Data presented in **Table 19.5** suggest that, regardless of the fortified food and the iron compound used, the reduction of iron deficiency and iron deficiency anemia depends on the magnitude of the bioavailable iron. Obviously, the necessary amount of iron is influenced by the initial nutritional gap found in the population. In the studies reviewed, at least an additional intake equivalent to 60% EAR of iron was required to improve iron stores, and at least 90% EAR was needed to decrease nutritional anemia. Nevertheless, caution is needed to extrapolate this association to other populations, especially considering that anemia is caused by a multitude of factors and nutritional status varies widely in populations.

Table 19.5: Comparison of biological impact of iron fortification interventions (efficacy and effectiveness).

Food (country)	Target group	Iron compound	Additional intake of iron (mg/day)	Approx. EAR and RNI (mg/day)[1]	Additional % EAR and RNI	Anemia change[2] (%)	IDA[3] or (iron stores)[4] (%)	Iron content in food (mg/kg)	Dilution factor
Refined wheat flour (Sri Lanka)[a]	Women 32 ± 9 y, 2 years	Electrolytic (A-131)	12.5	43.4 and 90.0	29 and 14	27 to 24	No data	66	1:15,151
		Reduced	12.5	56.4 and 117.6	22 and 11	39 to 39	No data	66	1:14,545
		Control	0	-		30 to 32	No data	-	
		Ferrous sulfate		14.1 and 29.4	92 and 44	18 to 12[(**)]c	(34 to 7)[(**)]	562	1:569
Snack made with refined wheat flour (Thailand)[b]	Women 18–50 y, 6 days/wk, 35 wks	Electrolytic (A-131)	12–14	21.6 and 45.0	60 and 29	26 to 21[(*)]	(28 to 11)[(**)]	562	1:1,725
		Hydrogen reduced		28.1 and 58.8	46 and 22	20 to 18[(*)]	(30 to 21)[(*)]	562	1:1,708
		Control	0	-	0	19 to 20[(*)]	(39 to 30)[(*)]	-	-
Fish sauce (Vietnam)[d]	Women 17-49 y, 6 days/wk, 6 mos	NaFeEDTA	10	14.1 and 29.4	71 and 34	100 to 66.2	70 to 20** (70 to 33)*	1,000	1:130
		Control	0	-	-	100 to 89	69 to 58 (69 to 65)		

Food (country)	Target group	Iron compound	Additional intake of iron (mg/day)	Approx. EAR and RNI (mg/day)[1]	Additional % EAR and RNI	Anemia change[2] (%)	IDA[3] or (iron stores)[4] (%)	Iron content in food (mg/kg)	Dilution factor
Salt (Morocco)[e]	Children 6–15 y, 10 mos	Micr. ferric pyrophosph.	18	13 and 16	138 and 112	60 to 13**	30 to 5** (52 to 9)**	2,000	1:125
		Control	0	-	0	55 to 43	34 to 30 (55 to 57)	-	-
Salt (Ivory Coast)[f]	Children 5–15 y, 6 mos	Micr. ferric pyrophosph.	8.4	13 and 16	65 and 52	42 to 47	42 to 23* (58 to 28)**	3,000	1:83
		Control	0	-	0	62 to 62	62 to 38* (38 to 25)	-	-

[1] Using the WHO recommendations (4), and assuming iron bioavailability values as follows: ferrous sulfate: 10% in the snack made with refined flour and consumed separately from meals; electrolytic and hydrogen reduced irons in the snack estimated as 65% and 50% of ferrous sulfate, respectively, following data of relative bioavailability (11). Electrolytic and reduced iron of wheat flour consumed in meals estimated as 32% and 25% of ferrous sulfate in the snack, respectively. Ferric pyrophosphate bioavailability in salt was assumed as 34% of ferrous sulfate, based on a diet around 5% iron bioavailability (23), and that ferric pyrophosphate is around 70% as bioavailable as ferrous sulfate (12). NaFeEDTA bioavailability as 10% in fish sauce consumed with meals (24).

[2] Using the conventional WHO/FAO cut-off points for each age group.

[3] IDA = iron deficiency anemia.

[4] Serum ferritin concentration <15 µg/L (30 µg/L for Ivory Coast; 12 µg/L for Vietnam) or serum transferrin receptor concentration >8.5 mg/L.

[a] Data for calculations obtained from Nestel et al. (25), and assuming a diet 5% bioavailable for iron.

[b] Data for the calculations obtained from Zimmermann et al. (26), and assuming a diet 10% bioavailable for iron.

[c] Asterisks denote statistical difference from baseline: * P <0.02, ** P <0.001. Data belonging to the same group by logistic regression at P <0.05 are symbolized by: (*) and (**).

[d] Data for the calculations obtained from Thuy et al. (27), and assuming a diet 10% bioavailable for iron.

[e] Data for the calculations obtained from Zimmermann et al. (28), and assuming a diet 10% bioavailable for iron, and ferric pyrophosphate 70% as bioavailable as ferrous sulfate.

[f] Data for the calculations obtained from Wegmüller et al. (29) and assumptions same as above.

The analysis made illustrates the difficulty in improving iron status by means of iron fortification of flours, because the low amounts of bioavailable iron that are supplied (18–32% EAR in refined flours, and 7–14% EAR in unrefined flours), when flour consumption is around 100 g/day (see **Table 19.4**).

Information in **Table 19.5** is also useful to identify which types of food fortification were used in the studies. These examples cannot be classified as mass fortification, because the level of iron is very high, and consequently the dilution factor is very low. Thus, the iron contents were: snack with 652 mg/kg from different iron sources (26); fish sauce with 1,000 mg/kg iron from NaFeEDTA (27); and salt fortified with 2,000–3,000 mg/kg iron from micronized pyrophosphate (28, 29).

The estimated dilution factor for the snack was 1:569 to 1:1708, depending on the iron source. This figure, compared with the dilution factor of 1:14,545 or 1:15,151 of wheat flour fortified with iron (25), clearly shows that the snack was a special food and not one of mass fortification. The high content of iron and the special way that the product should be manufactured (highly processed food) makes this product an example of targeted fortification. Similarly, the other products included in **Table 19.5** should be manufactured by a reduced number of industries, under strict supervision, well packaged and labeled, and aimed at specific target groups. Under the usual rules of production and trade, these products cannot compete with the unfortified alternatives, not only because the relative difference in the cost is high, but also because of the complexities of handling large volumes of premixes and the low dilution factors. Nevertheless, these studies opened the possibility of effectively using target

fortification as a valid strategy to reduce iron deficiency in poor communities.

Basic parameters for control and enforcement
The success of any micronutrient intervention depends on ensuring that the target populations receive the micronutrients in the amount and quality that are needed. Therefore, quality control and assurance actions by the producers, and inspection and enforcement by the public sector, is required to ensure that food fortification complies with expected standards (33, 34). In order to meet these requirements, it is important to establish values of reference and compliance criteria. This subject is frequently neglected and standards and regulations commonly do not reflect the realities of the fortification practice, both in terms of the variation process and the normal decay of vitamins during storage and distribution. Conflicts between the food industry and the public sector may arise when the public sector attempts to enforce unreasonable standards (33). **Table 19.6** introduces the basic production and regulatory parameters that can be used as reference for factory and legal compliance for fortified wheat flour of low extraction, when daily consumption pattern is from 50–200 g/day. In food production factories, the average content of each micronutrient in foods is calculated by adding the selected fortification content to the intrinsic content of the nutrient in the unfortified product. An acceptable range around the average should be estimated by means of subtracting and adding two coefficients of variation of the fortification process operating satisfactorily; those are the minimum and the maximum contents, respectively. In liquids, the variation of the fortification process is around 10%, but in solids it fluctuates between 12 and 30%, depending on the particle size, fluidity, and the relative amount of the added fortificant. The

---

[11] It is not equivalent to shelf life, which is the period that the food keeps the expected sensorial properties and it is safe to be consumed. Marketing time is the period that goes between manufacturing and purchasing of the product by the consumer. The marketing time might be much shorter than the shelf life.

Table 19.6: Basic parameters for food control and enforcement as applied to refined wheat flour fortified with several micronutrients.[1]

Micronutrient	Selected fortification content (mg/kg)	Intrinsic content (mg/kg)	Marketing losses (%)	C.V. of process (%)	Production parameters (mg/kg)			Regulatory parameters (mg/kg)	
					Minimum[2]	Average[3]	Maximum[4]	Legal minimum[5]	Tolerable maximum[6]
Vitamin B$_1$	6	0.6	15%	25%	3.3	6.6	9.9	3.0	N.A.
Vitamin B$_2$	5	0.5	10%	25%	2.7	5.5	8.3	2.5	N.A.
Niacin	60	10	5%	12%	53	70	87	50	N.A.
Vitamin B$_6$	6	0.4	10%	25%	3.2	6.4	9.6	3.0	N.A.
Vitamin B$_{12}$	0.01	0	10%	25%	0.005	0.010	0.015	0.005	N.A.
Folate	2	0.2	30%	25%	1.1	2.2	3.3	1.0	4.0
Vitamin A	2	0.0	30%	25%	1.0	2.0	3.0	0.8	3
Iron (total)	45	10	0%	12%	42	55	68	40	70
Iron (from fumarate)	45	0	0%	12%	34	45	56	30	60
Zinc	30	10	0%	12%	30	40	50	30	50

[1] This example is applicable when daily consumption pattern is from 50–200 g/day. If consumption is larger, fortification levels should be reduced.
[2] Minimum (mg/kg) = average x [1 - (2 x C.V. of fortification process (%)/100)]
[3] Average (mg/kg) = selected fortification content + intrinsic content
[4] Maximum (mg/kg) = average x [1 + (2 x C.V. of fortification process (%)/100)]
[5] Legal minimum (mg/kg) = minimum (mg/kg) x (1-marketing loss/100), and rounded.
[6] The Maximum Tolerable Level is the rounded value of the factory maximum. In the case of micronutrients whose Tolerable Upper Limit of Intake is not specified or very large, the regulation might be simplified by avoiding the inclusion of this parameter; i.e., non-applicable (N.A.).

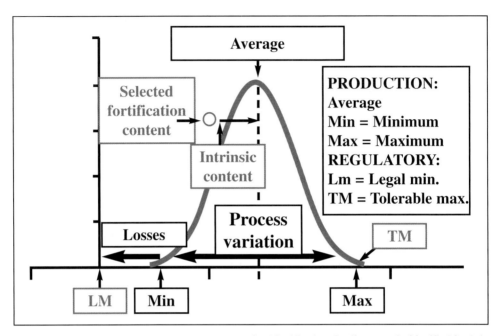

Figure 19.1: Production and regulatory parameters on food fortification. Quality control of fortified foods in factories aims to keep the micronutrient levels as near as possible to the **average** content (the selected fortification content plus the intrinsic content of the same micronutrient in the unfortified food), but always inside a range limited by the **minimum** (content calculated by reducing the average content by two coefficient of variation of the fortification process) and the **maximum** (content calculated by increasing the average content by two coefficient of variation of the fortification process). The regulatory parameters appear in the standards and on food labels, and support enforcement; they are the **legal minimum** (the minimum micronutrient content in the fortified food, which is calculated by reducing the usual losses of the micronutrient during normal conditions of distribution and storage within the marketing time of the food vehicle) and the **Maximum Tolerable Level** (the micronutrient content that coincides with the accepted maximum content at factories). The Maximum Tolerable Level may be excepted for micronutrients with very large or unspecified UL values of intake (figure modified from [4]).

acceptable ranges of fortification variation should be estimated for each food vehicle and for each micronutrient added.

In food standards, the expected rate of degradation of the vitamins in the product stored under acceptable conditions, within the usual marketing time[ll] of the fortified food, should be subtracted from the factory minimum. The calculated value is in turn the legal minimum. In the case of those micronutrients whose intake is limited because of safety concerns, a tolerable maximum is also used. The value of this parameter should coincide with the factory maximum. Nutrients without UL recommendation may not present a tolerable maximum in order to simplify enforcement of the standards. Data in **Table 19.6** shows that it is normal to expect the tolerable maxima to be two to four times the value of the legal minima.

Figure 19.1 illustrates the relative position, in terms of nutrient content, of all the production and regulatory parameters described above. In practice, quality control and inspection cannot be done for each one of the added micronutrients to the food, and most of the times only one of them is used as the indicator. However, for this system to work properly, the micronutrient mixes and premixes should be certified. Experience has shown that mixes and premixes should also be included in standards and regulations (35). They also need to be supervised by the government authorities, because their quality determines the entire program's success. To estimate the content of micronutrients in the premix, one needs only multiply the selected fortification content of the fortified food by the estimated dilution factor. In turn, the calculated value becomes the minimum content of the micronutrients in the premix. Manufacturers of mixes and premixes may decide to add an overage (additional amounts to compensate for the expected losses) to guarantee compliance with the minimum content until the date of useful life that is claimed for mixes and premixes. Following the procedure described above, there is no need to calculate overages for the fortified food.

Certification of mixes and premixes is required not only for the micronutrient amounts but also for the quality. Poor quality vitamins degrade much more rapidly than high quality ones. In the case of minerals, especially elemental iron, the relative bioavailability depends not only on the type and quality, but also in the specific manufacturer (11, 22). Microbiological safety is another parameter to be checked in the micronutrient mixes and premixes.

All types of food fortification should follow official standards, and compliance should be monitored by the government. Fortification outside the range of the standards should never be permitted, as consumers do not have control over the additional micronutrient intakes. In the case of mass fortification, the very wide coverage of the intervention demands that standards should be followed strictly. In most countries, mass fortification is triggered by compulsory governmental regulations, although application of these may be limited only to the industrially manufactured foods and not to the domestically produced options.

CONCLUSIONS

Food fortification and dietary supplementation are alternative and complementary delivery systems that can increase the intake of micronutrients deficient in the diet. Efficacy depends on the amount and quality of the supplied micronutrients, regardless of the type of intervention. In the case of food fortification, the presence of absorption inhibitors in the diet, especially those based on plant foods (36–38) increases the necessary amounts of minerals (iron, zinc, copper, and calcium) to be delivered. Dietary supplements have the advantage of being able to supply sufficient quantities of micronutrients in amounts tailored to target groups, but their disadvantages are low coverage and high cost. Mass fortification, when used under industrial settings, has the advantage of wide coverage and low cost, but the disadvantage that micronutrient intakes may be insufficient to bridge the nutritional gap of at risk subgroups of the population. Targeted fortification has an intermediate position between dietary supplementation and mass fortification; the mentioned constraints of mass fortification are less limiting, but coverage is lower and cost is much higher than in mass fortification. Market-driven fortification may have epidemiological influence only in Western societies, where the consumption of processed foods provides a large proportion of the dietary energy. This fortification strategy, without proper regulations, may increase the risk of providing excessive micronutrient intakes.

Correction of nutritional anemia in developing countries requires not only iron but also the intake of many other vitamins and minerals. The latter nutrients can be effective and efficiently incorporated into mass fortification.

Iron fortification is a very difficult, complex and expensive endeavor. Efficacy and effectiveness trials have shown that it is necessary to supply large amounts of iron in the meals of most developing country diets to obtain a beneficial biological response in communities affected by nutritional anemias. It may also be necessary to give the treatment independently from meals, especially when the diet is rich in iron absorption inhibitors. The high iron density in the food vehicles of the demonstrated successful fortification trials discussed here makes these products examples of targeted fortification rather than mass fortification. These kinds of products, as well as dietary supplements, appear to be a reasonable way to proceed to reduce iron deficiency anemia in developing countries. Funding such strategies and making them permanent and sustainable remains a challenge.

In developing countries, mass fortification may still be the most cost-effective strategy to bridge the nutritional gap for essential micronutrients other than iron. Iron fortification may work as well, if the diet is not rich in iron absorption inhibitors. However, it is important to emphasize that the technological feasibility of mass fortification is linked to foods produced by centralized and adequately developed industries. It involves using large dilution factors of the fortificant in the food, and the sensorial changes, micronutrient segregation, vitamin deterioration, and price increase should be kept within reasonable limits. The presence of reliable government supervision is usually essential to guarantee product quality. It is also critical to keep in mind the fact that the public health significance of mass fortification depends on the extent of the consumption of the industrially produced food by the population, as well as the frequency and amount of consumption by individuals. If those conditions are not fulfilled, then targeted fortification and dietary supplementation may be adequate alternatives.

Any type of food fortification should be government regulated and supervised. Inspection should be based on sensible standards that reflect variation of the process, and micronutrient decay during the marketing time of the food and when storage conditions are adequate. Factories should also implement quality control and auditing procedures, based on checking one or very few micronutrients. In order that such a system works, the quality of the micronutrient mixes and premixes must be certified.

ACKNOWLEDGMENTS

I would like to thank Shama Patel, A2Z intern and a graduate student of the Public Health Program at Emory University, who during the summer of 2006, helped me to gather recent information about the effective use of food fortification.

I also thank Hector Cori (DSM), Wolfgang Vogl (Paul Lohmann) and Geoff Smith (Akzo Nobel) for providing recent prices of fortificant compounds, and Penelope Nestel and Juan Pablo Peña-Rosas for critical comments to an original version of this article.

REFERENCES

1. Dary O, Mora JO. Food fortification: (b) Developing countries. In: Caballero B, Allen L, Prentice A, eds. Encyclopedia of human nutrition. New York: Elsevier, 2006.

2. Flynn A, Moreiras O, Stehle P, Fletcher RJ, Müller DJG, Rolland Valérie. Vitamins and minerals: a model for safe addition to foods. Eur J Nutr 2003;42:118–30.

3. Hallberg L, Bjorn-Rasmussen E, Ekenved G, Garby L, Rossander L, Plee-hachinda R, Suwanik R, Arvidsson B. Absorption from iron tablets given with different types of meals. Scand J Haematol 1978;21:215–24.

4. Allen LH, de Benoist B, Dary O, Hurrell R. Guidelines on food fortification with micronutrients. Geneva: WHO/FAO, 2006.

5. Institute of Medicine. Dietary reference intakes. Washington, D.C.: National Academy Press, 2001.

6. Allen LH. New approaches for designing and evaluating food fortification programs. J Nutr 2006;136:1055–8.

7. Fishman SM, Christian P, West KP. The role of vitamins in the prevention and control of anaemia. Public Health Nutr 2000;3:125–50.

8. Ramakrishnan U. Nutritional anemias. Boca Raton: CRC Press, 2001.

9. Lucock M, Yates Z. Folic acid – vitamin and panacea or genetic time bomb? Nat Review Genet 2005;6:235–40.

10. Stoltzfus RJ. Defining iron-deficiency anemia in public health terms: a time for reflection. J Nutr 2001;131:565S–7S.

11. Hoppe M, Hulthén L, Hallberg L. The relative bioavailability in humans of elemental iron powders for use in food fortification. Eur J Nutr 2006;45:37–44.

12. Wegmüller R, Zimmermann MB, Moretti D, Arnold M, Langhans W, Hurrell RF. Particle size reduction and encapsulation affect the bioavailability of ferric pyrophosphate in rats. J Nutr 2004;134:3301–4.

13. Mora JO, Dary O, Chinchilla D, Arroyave G. Vitamin A sugar fortification in Central America.

Experience and lessons learned. Washington, D.C.: MOST/US Agency for International Development (AID), 2000. [http://www.mostproject.org/PDF/sugarlessonsEnglish.pdf]

14. Nestel P, Nalubola R. Manual for wheat flour fortification with iron, part 1. Washington D.C.:MOST/US AID, 2000. [http://www.mostproject.org/PDF/1.pdf]

15. Cavalli-Sforza T, Berger J, Smitasiri S, Viteri F. Weekly iron-folic acid supplementation of women of reproductive age: Impact, overview, lessons learned, expansion plans, and contributions toward achievement of the millennium development goals. Nutr Rev 2005;63:152S–8S.

16. Lynch SR. The impact of iron fortification on nutritional anemia. Best Pract Res Clin Haematol 2005;18:333–46.

17. Moretti D, Lee T-C, Zimmermann MB, Nuessli J, Hurrell RF. Development and evaluation of iron-fortified extruded rice grains. J Food Sci 2005;70:330S–6S.

18. Dary O, Mora JO. Food fortification to reduce vitamin A deficiency: International vitamin A Consultative Group recommendations. J Nutr 2002;132:2927S–33S.

19. Dary O. Lessons learned with iron fortification in Central America. Nutr Rev 2002;60:30S–3S.

20. WHO. Evaluation of certain food additives and contaminants. Fifty-third report of the Joint Organization. Geneva: WHO, 2000. [WHO Technical Series No. 896.]

21. Codex Alimentarius Commission. Guidelines for use of nutrition claims. Rome: FAO, 1997. [Joint FAO/WHO Food Standards Program, CAC/GL 23–1997; revised 2004.]

22. Hurrell R, Bothwell T, Cook JD, Dary O, Davidsson L, Fairweather-Tait S, Hallberg L, Lynch S, Rosado J, Walter T, Whittaker P. The usefulness of elemental iron for cereal flour fortification: a SUSTAIN Task Force report. Sharing United States Technology to Aid in the Improvement of Nutrition. Nutr Rev 2002;60:391–406.

23. Zimmermann MB, Zeder C, Chaouki N, Saad Am, Torresani T, Hurrell RF. Dual fortification of salt with iodine and microencapsulated iron: a randomized, double-blind, controlled trial in Moroccan schoolchildren. Am J Clin Nutr 2003;77:425–32.

24. Fidler MC, Davidsson L, Walczyk T, Hurrell RF. Iron absorption from fish sauce and soy sauce fortified with sodium iron EDTA. Am J Clin Nutr 2003;78:274–8.

25. Nestel P, Nalubola R, Sivakaneshan R, Wickramasinghe AR, Atukorala S, Wickramanayake T. The use of iron-fortified wheat flour to reduce anemia among the estate population in Sri Lanka. Int J Vitam Nutr Res 2004;74(1):35–51.

26. Zimmermann MB, Winichagoon P, Gowachirapant S, Hess SY, Harrington M, Chavasit V, Lynch SR, Hurrell RF. Comparison of the efficacy of wheat-based snacks fortified with ferrous sulfate, electrolytic iron, or hydrogen-reduced elemental iron randomized, double-blind, controlled trial in Thai women. Am J Clin Nutr 2005;82:1276–82.

27. Thuy PV, Berger J, Davidsson L, Khan NC, Lam NT, Cook JD, Hurrell RF, Khoi HH. Regular consumption of NaFeEDTA-fortified fish sauce improves iron status and reduces the prevalence of anemia in anemic Vietnamese women. Am J Clin Nutr 2003;78:284–90.

28. Zimmermann MB, Wegmueller R, Zeder C, Chaouki N, Rohner F, Saïssi M, Torresani T, Hurrell RF. Dual fortification of salt with iodine and micronized ferric pyrophosphate: a randomized, double-blind, controlled trial. Am J Clin Nutr 2004;80:952–9.

29. Wegmüller R, Camara F, Zimmermann MB, Adou P, Hurrell RF. Salt dual-fortified with iodine and micronized ground ferric pyrophosphate affects iron status but not hemoglobin in children in Cote d'Ivoire. J Nutr 2006;136:1814–20.

30. Rahman AS, Wahed MA, Alam MS, Ahmed T, Ahmed F, Quaiyum MA, Sack DA. Randomized,

double-blind controlled trial of wheat flour (chapatti) fortified with vitamin A and iron in improving vitamin A and iron status in healthy, school aged children in rural Bangladesh. In: MOST: Wheat flour fortification program in Bangladesh. Final Report. Washington, D.C.: Most, 2003. [http://www.mostproject.org/PDF/Fn1%20 Bangladesh%20Rpt.PDF]

31. Chen J, Zhao X, Zhang X, Yin S, Piao J, Huo J, Yu B, Qu N, Lu Q, Wang S, Chen C. Studies on the effectiveness of NaFeEDTA-fortified soy sauce in controlling iron deficiency: a population-based intervention trial. Food Nutr Bull 2005; 26(2):177–86.

32. Hallberg L, Hulten L, Gramatkovski E. Iron absorption from the whole diet in men: How effective is the regulation of iron absorption? Am J Clin Nutr 1997;66:347–56.

33. Dary O, Martinez C, Guamuch M. Sugar fortification with vitamin A in Guatemala: the program's successes and pitfalls. In: Freire WB, ed. Nutrition and an active life. Washington DC: Pan American Health Organization, 2005.

34. Sullivan KM, Houston R, Gorstein J, Cervinskas J. Monitoring universal salt iodization programs. Ottawa: UNICEF/PAMM/M/ICC-IDD/WHO, 1995.

35. Pan American Health Organization. Code of practice for food premix operations. FCH/NU/66-04. Washington DC: Pan American Health Organization, 2006.

36. Bothwell TH, Pirzio-Biroli G, Finch CA. Iron absorption. I. Factors influencing absorption. J Lab Clin Med 1958;51(1):24–36.

37. Hallberg L. Bioavailability of dietary iron in man. Annu Rev Nutr 1981;1:123–47.

38. Moretti D, Zimmermann MB, Wegmuller R, Walczyk T, Zeder C, Hurrell RF. Iron status and food matrix strongly affect the relative bioavailability of ferric pyrophosphate in humans. Am J Clin Nutr 2006;83:632–8.

20

Food-based approaches for combating iron deficiency

Brian Thompson

Food and Agriculture Organization (FAO), Rome, Italy
Contact: brian.thompson@fao.org

BRIAN THOMPSON
Brian has an MSc in Human Nutrition from the London School of Hygiene and Tropical Medicine, UK and has 25 years of international development experience as a nutritionist. He is a Senior Nutrition Officer of the FAO's Household Food Security and Community Nutrition Group of the Nutrition and Consumer Protection Division where he advises member countries on the development and implementation of strategies and plans of action for improving food security and nutritional wellbeing. Brian is an advocate for the adoption of socially constructive development policies.

INTRODUCTION

Iron deficiency is a serious and widespread public health problem. The scale and magnitude of the problem combined with the functional impact such deficiencies have on the quality of life, both physiologically and socioeconomically, require the urgent adoption of known and effective measures. However, the focus of development practitioners on their own narrow area of interest or expertise, be it health care or food, has prevented the realization of a truly comprehensive approach being taken to tackle this critical problem. This chapter is an effort to correct this imbalance and to place food-based approaches back into the center of the debate and to encourage their adoption on a broader scale as a matter of priority.

Micronutrient deficiencies exist in both developing as well as developed countries and may be considered as "hidden hunger." In developing countries they exist in the context of food insecurity, where meeting overall energy needs and dietary diversity continues to be the major challenge. Consequently, efforts to reduce micronutrient malnutrition need to be placed in the context that an estimated 854 million people are hungry (1), 20 million children under the age of 5 suffer from severe malnutrition, and around 1 million children die due to malnutrition each year.

The underlying causes of such high levels of malnutrition, including the high levels of micronutrient deficiencies, are poverty and insufficient agricultural development, which lead to food insecurity at national and household levels. To address these causes, FAO is placing emphasis on actions that promote an increase in the supply, access, and consumption of an adequate quantity, quality, and variety of foods for all population groups. By promoting and supporting sustainable food-based programs and strategies to improve nutrition, FAO is seeking to resolve the micronutrient deficiency problems of developing coun-

tries through increasing the consumption of an adequate and varied diet in combination with the use of supplements and fortification strategies rather than through the use of supplements or fortification strategies alone. This is in keeping with the right to food, a concept whose achievement means that all people should be able to gain access to a varied diet consisting of a variety of foods that provide all the energy and macro- and micronutrients sufficient to achieve a healthy and productive life.

DEFINITIONS AND TERMINOLOGY

Iron has several vital functions in the body. It serves as a carrier of oxygen to the tissues from the lungs by red blood cell hemoglobin, as a carrier of electrons within cells, and as an integrated part of important enzyme systems in various tissues. Iron is reversibly stored within the liver as ferritin and hemosiderin and is transported between different compartments in the body by the protein transferrin. Hemoglobin (Hb), mean cell volume (MCV), transferrin saturation (TSAT), serum ferritin (SF), transferrin receptor (TfR), total iron binding capacity (TIBC), and erythrocyte protoporphyrin (EP) are measurements commonly used when investigating iron status. However, the sensitivity and specificity of these indicators is unclear and a combination of these indicators is sometimes used.

Iron deficiency may be defined as an absence of iron stores combined with signs of iron-deficient erythropoiesis (the making of red blood cells) implying there is an insufficient supply of iron to various tissues. This occurs at a serum ferritin level <15 μg/L. Under these conditions, an insufficient amount of iron is delivered to transferrin, the circulating transport protein for iron, resulting in a reduction in transferrin saturation. Formation of hemoglobin is reduced resulting in a reduction in mean corpuscular hemoglobin. The concentration of transferrin in plasma increases in an effort to compensate. Iron deficiency may be classified according to serum ferritin concentration with depleted iron stores (SF<24 ng/mL), mild iron deficiency (SF=18–24 ng/mL) and severe iron deficiency (SF<12 ng/mL).

Nutritional anemia is a condition in which the hemoglobin content of blood is lower than normal as a result of a deficiency of one or more essential nutrients. Because anemia is the most common indicator used to screen for iron deficiency, the terms anemia, iron deficiency, and iron deficiency anemia are sometimes incorrectly used interchangeably. However, there are cases where a person may not be anemic but is mildly or moderately iron deficient and consequently may be functionally impaired.

Iron deficiency anemia (IDA) is the most common nutritional cause of anemia and occurs when there is an inadequate amount of red blood cells caused by lack of iron. The prevalence of iron deficiency anemia is therefore less frequent than iron deficiency. Iron deficiency anemia is a rather imprecise concept and has no immediate physiologic meaning. Cut-offs may vary but WHO defines children under 5 years of age and pregnant women living at sea level as anemic if their hemoglobin concentration is <11 g/dL, non-pregnant women as anemic if Hb <12 g/dL, and men as anemic if Hb <13 g/dL. Mild-moderate anemia is Hb 7–10.9 g/dL, and severe anemia is Hb <7 g/dL. The main benefit of using cut-offs is to allow comparisons to be made between population groups. IDA is not normally symptomatic until hemoglobin level is about 8 g/dL or lower.

Recommended Nutrient Intakes (RNI) is the daily intake which meets the nutrient requirements of almost all (97.5%) apparently healthy individuals in an age and sex-specific population group based on an estimated average nutrient requirement (EAR) plus two standard deviations.

A requirement is an intake level which meets specified criteria of adequacy while preventing risk of deficit or excess.

Vitamins and minerals are referred to as **micronutrients** because the body needs them in very small quantities for growth, development, and maintenance.

A **food-based strategy** has the goal of improving nutrition through increasing the availability and consumption of a nutritionally adequate micronutrient rich diet made up of a variety of available foods.

Food-based dietary guidelines (FBDGs) recognize that people eat food, not nutrients, and focus on giving simple practical advice on the appropriate combination of foods that can meet nutrient requirements rather than on how each specific nutrient is provided in adequate amounts.

Food security is a situation that exists when all people, at all times, have physical, social and economic access to sufficient, safe, and nutritious food that meets their dietary needs and food preferences for an active and healthy life.

REQUIREMENTS

Iron is required to replace basal losses, losses due to menstruation, and for growth. Losses from the skin and the interior surfaces of the body are estimated at 14 μg/kg body weight/day with a non-menstruating 55-kg woman losing about 0.8 mg iron and a 70-kg man about 1 mg iron/day. Menstrual losses range from 0.48–1.90 mg/day. Requirements to allow for growth up to 18 years years of age range from 0.23–0.60 mg/day depending on age and sex. By adding up these estimates we may calculate that total absolute iron requirements at the 50th percentile ranges from 0.46–1.68 mg/day and iron requirements at the 95th percentile ranges from 0.63–3.27 mg/day.

Requirements for iron vary depending on age, physiological status, growth rate, degree of physical maturity, body composition, and activity level. Increased requirements are also noted in patients with malaria, congenital hemoglobinopathies, and other causes of hemolysis. Iron requirements in relation to energy intake are highest during the last trimester of pregnancy, during the weaning period, and in adolescents. As explained below, it is only possible to meet these high requirements if the diet has a consistently high content of meat and foods rich in ascorbic acid.

Iron is present in foods in two forms, as heme iron, which is derived from flesh foods (meats, poultry, and fish), and as non-heme iron, which is the inorganic form present in plant foods such as cereals, pulses, legumes, grains, nuts, and vegetables. Heme iron is well absorbed with an average absorption of heme iron from meat-containing meals of around 25%, ranging from about 40% during iron deficiency to about 10% when iron stores are replete. Non-heme iron has a lower rate of absorption (2–10%), depending on the balance between iron absorption inhibitors and iron absorption enhancers present in the diet. Consequently, the amount of iron absorbed not only depends on the iron content of the meal but, and to a marked degree, on the composition of the meal (i.e., the balance among all factors enhancing and inhibiting the absorption of iron).

Reducing substances (i.e., substances that keep iron in the ferrous form) need to be present for iron to be absorbed. These enhancing factors include ascorbic and citric acids found in certain fruit juices, fruits, potatoes, and certain vegetables; cysteine-containing peptides found in meat, chicken, fish, and other seafood; and ethanol and fermentation products like vegetables, soy sauce, etc., which enhance the absorption of both heme and non-heme iron. Other foods contain factors (ligands) that strongly bind ferrous ions and inhibit absorption. These inhibiting factors (phy-

tates, polyphenols, calcium, and phosphate) are found in bran products, bread made from high extraction flour, breakfast cereals, oats, rice (especially unpolished rice), pasta products, cocoa, nuts, soya beans, and peas; iron-binding phenolic compounds (e.g., tea, coffee, cocoa, certain spices, certain vegetables, and most red wines); calcium (e.g., milk, cheese); and soy proteins. In infant foods containing soy proteins, the inhibiting effect can be overcome by the addition of sufficient amounts of ascorbic acid. Consumption of betel leaves, common in areas of Asia, also has a marked negative effect on iron absorption. However, again the addition of certain vegetables or fruits containing ascorbic acid can double or triple iron absorption thereby counteracting many of the effects of these inhibitors depending on the other properties of the meal. As the effect is so marked, this may be considered as one of vitamin C's physiological roles. Each meal should preferably contain at least 25 mg of ascorbic acid and possibly more if the meal contains many inhibitors of iron absorption.

Bioavailability of meals with a similar content of iron, energy, protein, fat, etc. can vary more than tenfold. Just the addition of certain spices (e.g., oregano) or a cup of tea may reduce the bioavailability by one-half or more. Therefore to translate physiological iron requirements into recommendations for dietary iron intakes, the bioavailability of iron (i.e., its absorption for utilization by the body) in different diets therefore need to be calculated. A study on the bioavailability of different Indian diets found 1.7–1.8% of iron was absorbed from millet-based diets, 3.5–4.0% in wheat-based diets, and 8.3–10.3% from rice-based diets. Other studies from South East Asia show absorption rates can rise significantly from less than 5% to more than 15% if animal products and vitamin C are amply provided. Recommended Nutrient Intakes (RNI's) for iron at four levels of dietary iron bioavailability (5, 10, 12 and 15%) and are given in **Table 20.1**. In nonpathological states the Recommended

Table 20.1: Recommended nutrient intakes for iron (i) from meals with bioavailability 5-15%. From (2).

Age	15% bioavailability *mg/day*	12% bioavailability *mg/day*	10% bioavailability *mg/day*	5% bioavailability *mg/day*
0–6 months	(k)	(k)	(k)	(k)
7–1 months	[6] (l)	[8] (l)	[9] (l)	[19] (l)
1–3 years	4	5	6	12
4–6 years	4	5	6	13
7–9 years	6	7	9	18
Males 10–18 years	10 (10-14 yrs)	12 (10-14 yrs)	15 (10-14 yrs)	29 (10-14 yrs)
	12 (15-18 yrs)	16 (15-18 yrs)	19 (15-18 yrs)	38 (15-18 yrs)
Females 10–18 years	9 (10-14 yrs) (m)	12 (10-14 yrs) (m)	14 (10-14 yrs) (m)	28 (10-14 yrs) (m)
	22 (10-14 yrs)	28 (10-14 yrs)	33 (10-14 yrs)	65 (10-14 yrs)
	21 (15-18 yrs)	26 (15-18 yrs)	31 (15-18 yrs)	62 (15-18 yrs)
Males 19+ years	9	11	14	27
Females:				
19–50 years pre-menopausal	20	24	29	59
51+ years menopausal	8	9	11	23
Pregnancy:				
First trimester	(n)	(n)	(n)	(n)
Second trimester	(n)	(n)	(n)	(n)
Third trimester	(n)	(n)	(n)	(n)
Lactation:				
0–3 months	10	12	15	30
4–6 months	10	12	15	30
7–12months	10	12	15	30

(i) Iron absorption can be significantly enhanced when each meal contains a minimum of 25 mg of vitamin C, assuming three meals per day. This is especially true if there are iron absorption inhibitors in the diet such as phytate or tannins.

(k) Neonatal iron stores are sufficient to meet the iron requirement for the first six months in full term infants. Premature infants and low birth weight infants require additional iron.

(l) Bioavailability of dietary iron during this period varies greatly.

(m) Non-menstruating adolescents.

(n) It is recommended that iron supplements be given to all pregnant women because of the difficulties in correctly evaluating iron status in pregnancy. In the non-anaemic pregnant woman, daily supplements of 100 mg of iron (e.g., ferrous sulphate) given during the second half of pregnancy are adequate. In anaemic women higher doses are usually required.

Nutrient Intake (RNI) for men ranges from 9 mg in diets with high bioavailability to 27 mg in diets where bioavailability is only 5%. For menopausal women the range is similar, although levels are slightly lower (20 mg) due to variation in body size. In premenopausal women aged between 19 and 50 the recommended intake is 59 mg (2).

In summary, the amount of dietary iron absorbed is mainly determined by the amount of body stores of iron (absorption rates increase when body stores are depleted and decrease as iron stores are replenished), and by the properties of the meal as determined by the amount of heme and non-heme iron in the meal, food preparation practices in terms of cooking time and temperature, and the presence of enhancing dietary factors such as meat peptides and vitamin C, and inhibiting dietary factors such as phytates and calcium (e.g., milk, cheese), all of which affect bioavailability.

PREVALENCE OF IRON DEFICIENCY ANEMIA

Iron deficiency and iron deficiency anemia are worldwide public health problems. Over 2 billion people – over 30% of the world's population – are anemic, many due to iron deficiency, which is frequently exacerbated by infectious diseases particularly in resource-poor areas of low income countries. Malaria, hookworm, schistosomiasis, HIV/AIDS, and other infections such as tuberculosis are particularly important factors contributing to the high prevalence of anemia in some areas. Low levels of plasma iron, folate, zinc, and vitamins B_{12} and A have also been shown to be associated with anemia.

The latest preliminary estimate figures from WHO on the prevalence of iron deficiency anemia by age group and region show the highest prevalence is found in infants, children, adoles-

cents, and women of childbearing age, especially pregnant women (preschool aged children: 47.6%; non-pregnant women: 30.3%; pregnant women: 41.6%). Among children the determinants of iron deficiency anemia are age (the younger the child, the higher the risk with the weaning period in infants being especially critical because of the very high iron requirements in relation to energy requirements), sex (males are at higher risk), weight and height (stunted and underweight children are at greater risk), and plasma retinol levels (higher levels lower the risk of IDA). Among pregnant women the determinants are age, gravida, and stage of gestation with women below 20 years of age, those who have been pregnant before, and those in their second and third trimester being more prone to deficiency. Among lactating women the determinants are period of lactation and vitamin A status.

Africa has the highest prevalence rates of anemia in preschool children (65.4%), nonpregnant women (44.7%), and pregnant women (55%). Asia has the highest number of cases of anemia with about half of the world's anemic women living in the Indian Subcontinent, the majority of whom develop anemia during pregnancies. In India, the National Family Health Survey (1998–1999) (3) showed anemia prevalence of 82% in expectant mothers, 74% in children under 3 years of age, 52% in married woman 15–49 years of age, and more than 50% in adolescents. The Indian Counsel of Medical Research (ICMR) (4) reported that 62% of expectant mothers suffered from anemia, of whom 9% had severe anemia defined as Hb <8 g/dL.

In many developing countries, anemia rates in children are high (above 50%) and the severity of anemia is marked. In many cases this is due to low availability of dietary iron rather than low intakes, as 90% of the total dietary supply in many of these countries comes from plants, which contain non-heme iron that is poorly absorbed. Prevalence among vegetarians and in those reliant on cereal or tuber foods is significantly higher than in omnivore populations. Further disaggregation shows agroecological and country and urban/rural differences, the variation in iron status in different populations being mainly related to variations in the diet.

EFFECTS OF IRON DEFICIENCY AND OF IRON DEFICIENCY ANEMIA

Iron deficiency and iron deficiency anemias have a significant impact on human welfare both at the level of the individual and for the economic development of a country. At the individual level, iron deficiency has several negative effects on important functions of the body. Deficiency can slow growth, hinder physical and mental development, and reduce the ability of the body to maintain itself. It is associated with impaired immune response, lowered resistance to infection and increased morbidity and mortality rates, adverse pregnancy outcome, and reduced school performance. Growth faltering is associated with IDA, and the Body Mass Index (BMI) is positively correlated with hemoglobin concentration.

Iron nutrition is of great importance for the adequate development of the brain and iron deficiency has serious consequences for cognitive, psychomotor, physical and mental development of children. There is a relationship even with mild iron deficiency and brain development and there are functional defects affecting learning and behavior that cannot be reversed by giving iron later on. Infants with iron deficiency anemia (IDA) may have reduced interaction with the physical and social world and become "functionally isolated," which impedes their cognitive development. Studies have found indicators of iron status associated with a number of cognitive abilities in young school children, and with

information processing and level of cognitive development in adult women. Several structures in the brain have high iron content, with iron continuing to accumulate throughout the 20–30 year period of brain growth. There appears to be a relationship between iron deficiency and brain function and between iron deficiency and attention, memory, and learning in infants and small children (5). Administration of iron to nonanemic but iron deficient adolescent girls improved verbal learning and memory (6). These cognitive effects are a strong argument for the more active and effective combating of iron deficiency, especially in women up through the period of adolescence and into early adulthood prior to and during pregnancy, and for infants and children.

Iron deficiency negatively influences the body's normal immunological defense mechanisms against infection. The cell-mediated immunologic response of T lymphocytes is im-paired as a result of a reduction in the formation of these cells. This in turn is due to reduced DNA synthesis that is dependent on the function of the radionuclide reductase, which requires iron for its function. Iron deficiency also impairs the phagocytosis and killing of bacteria by neutrophil leukocytes, with probable involvement of the iron sulfur enzyme NADPH oxidase and cytochrome b, a heme enzyme. Administration of iron reverses these changes within 4–7 days. Anemia increases the dangers of lead poisoning, particularly among young children.

Iron deficiency anemia during pregnancy increases maternal hemorrhages and maternal morbidity and mortality rates. Women with a low hematocrit of <37% had twice the risk of a premature birth as women with a hematocrit between 41% and 44% (7, 8).

Iron deficiency reduces the physical capacity to do work, which seems to be less related to the degree of anemia than to the impaired oxidative metabolism in the muscles due to the lack of iron-containing rate-limiting enzymes for oxidative metabolism. This reduced ability to do work can be reversed with iron administration. Studies of adolescent girls show that iron deficiency without anemia is associated with reduced physical endurance and changes in mood and ability to concentrate. A study showed a re-duction in maximum oxygen consumption in iron deficient nonanemic woman unrelated to the decreased oxygen transport capacity of the blood (9).

Since the highest prevalence is found in infants, children, adolescents, and women of childbearing age, the burden falls not just on the individual but on society as a whole. The debilitating consequences include loss of human capital and reduced work capacity and therefore of productivity in adults. In economic terms, the World Bank and the US Agency for International Development (USAID) estimated iron deficiency cost the country of India about 5% of its GNP annually (10) in the mid-1990s.

DETERMINING FACTORS

Worldwide the most common cause of iron deficiency is nutritional iron deficiency. Does this imply that the normal diet cannot cover physiological iron requirements? For many years nutritionists have assumed that all nutrients can be obtained from a diet containing a variety of foods drawn from a variety of sources. It has been thought that if people had access to a sufficient quantity and variety of foods, then they would meet their nutritional needs. This still may be true, but despite increases in the availability of a wide variety of foods in almost every country in the world, the continued existence of micronutrient deficiencies, including iron deficiency anemia, throws this general assumption into question. Why have improved food supplies not necessarily resulted in adequate vitamin and mineral intakes?

Factors that determine iron deficiency anemia include overall low incomes and poverty that result in low overall food intakes and poor monotonous diets low in micronutrient content. These may be compounded by a lack of understanding of the value of a varied diet and the importance of foods rich in micronutrients as well as the role of dietary inhibitors and enhancers that interfere with the absorption of iron. Illness and infections such as malaria, tuberculosis, and HIV/AIDS are also contributing factors.

Poor dietary intake both in terms of total quantity of food and of micronutrient rich food are often the major cause of micronutrient malnutrition. Virtually all traditional dietary patterns can satisfy the nutritional needs of population groups so long as the capacity to produce and purchase food is not limited for example by socio-economic conditions or cultural practices that restrict the choice of foods. The erosion of these practices due to changing lifestyles and modernization can lead to unhealthy food choices, and the protection and promotion of those diets that can provide the nutrients we require need our continued support.

The most affected population groups in need of improved nutrition generally include vulnerable resource-poor subsistence farmers and landless laborers whose main food supplies come directly from the land and who often have restricted access to fortified foods due to low purchasing power and undeveloped distribution channels. Those who are physiologically vulnerable include those groups with special dietary problems or nutritional needs, including women of childbearing age, pregnant and lactating women, young children and famine-affected populations, who may lack access to a diet that is sufficient in quantity or quality to provide adequate levels of iron. Special attention is needed to meet the food and nutrition needs of both these vulnerable groups.

Iron requirements also tend to be difficult to meet, and replenishment remains challenging for those severely deficient. Low bioavailability of iron in cereal- and tuber-based diets is one of the main causes of iron deficiency anemia in low income countries, as they contain high amounts of polyphenols (tannins) and phytates that inhibit iron absorption. A number of practical actions and interventions that can reduce these effects are presented below.

A number of potential dietary sources need to be urgently promoted including many leafy vegetables and legumes that contain important quantities of iron, with special emphasis on increasing the consumption of animal products that are high in bioavailable iron and in iron absorption enhancers. In Kenya, a study showed that meat intake in children under 3 years of age was positively related to hemoglobin, suggesting low meat intakes are an important cause of anemia in this age group (11).

The addition of small quantities of particular foods to a cereal- or tuber-based diet increases the nutrient density considerably. The addition of legumes can slightly improve the iron content of cereal- and tuber-based diets. However, the bioavailability of this non-heme iron source is low. Therefore, it is not possible to meet the recommended levels of iron from staple-based diets unless some meat, poultry, or fish is included. Adding 50 g of meat, poultry, or fish increases total iron content as well as the amount of bioavailable iron. Variations in bioavailability of iron (mg/1000 kcal) with meal composition for each of the four basic staple diets of white rice, corn tortilla, refined couscous, and potato have been calculated and are presented in **Table 20.2**.

Under ideal conditions of food access and availability, food diversity should satisfy micronutrient and energy needs of the general population. Unfortunately, for many people in the world, access to a variety of micronutrient rich foods is not possible. As demonstrated in the analysis of typical staple-based diets, micronutrient rich foods including small amount of flesh foods and a variety of plant foods (vegetables and fruits) are needed daily. This may not be realistic at present for many communities living under conditions of poverty. Food fortification and food supplementation are important alternatives that complement food-based approaches to satisfy the nutritional needs of people in developing and developed countries.

Poor monotonous diets deficient in one micronutrient are also likely to be deficient in other micronutrients, as well as in other important foods such as fat and protein that further reduce absorption of what nutrients have been ingested, and of energy. Population groups consuming such diets are known to have multiple micronutrient deficiencies.

At the same time, increasing the consumption of a greater variety of plant foods, especially of fruits and vegetables, will provide most of the missing vitamins and minerals. In addition, a number of plant-based nutrients or phytochemicals will be consumed and there is emerging evidence on the health benefits from food phytochemicals. This double benefit of consuming a variety of foods could play a major role in offsetting what is called the double burden of malnutrition.

INTERVENTION PROGRAMS

Intervention programs to overcome and prevent micronutrient deficiencies are generally considered under four main strategies:

- Dietary enhancement and diversification
- Food fortification including biofortification
- Vitamin and mineral supplementation
- Global public health and disease control measures.

Table 20.2: Variation in iron (mg/1000 kcals) with meal composition (white rice, corn tortilla, refined couscous and potato). From (2).

	Rice 598g Veg oil 25g	Rice 590g Veg oil 25g Carrots 21g	Rice 570g Veg oil 25g Carrots 21g Oranges 60g	Rice 483g Veg oil 25g Carrots 21g Oranges 60g Lentils 95g	Rice 477g Veg oil 25g Carrots 21g Oranges 60g Beef 55g	Rice 468g Veg oil 25g Carrots 21g Oranges 60g Beef 55g Spinach raw 50g	Rice 428g Veg oil 25g Carrots 21g Oranges 60g Beef 55g Lentils 45g Spinach raw 50g
Iron (mg)	1.2	1.3	1.3	4.3	2.8	4.1	5,6
	Tortilla 368g Veg oil 20g	Tortilla 363g Veg oil 20g Carrots 21g	Tortilla 351g Veg oil 20g Carrots 21g Oranges 60g	Tortilla 314g Veg oil 20g Carrots 21g Oranges 60g Lentils 71g	Tortilla 297g Veg oil 20g Carrots 21g Oranges 60g Beef 55g	Tortilla 292g Veg oil 20g Carrots 21g Oranges 60g Beef 55g Spinach raw 50g	Tortilla 266g Veg oil 20g Carrots 21g Oranges 60g Beef 55g Spinach raw 50g Black beans 45g
Iron (mg)	5.2	5.2	5.1	6.9	6.0	7.3	7.9
	Couscous 697g Veg oil 25g	Couscous 690g Veg oil 25g	Couscous 665g Veg oil 25g Carrots 21g Oranges 60g	Couscous 590g Veg oil 25g Carrots 21g Oranges 60g Lentils70g	Couscous 555g Veg oil 25g Carrots 21g Oranges 60g Beef 55g	Couscous 546g Veg oil 25g Carrots 21g Oranges 60g Beef 55g Spinach raw 50g	Couscous 493g Veg oil 25g Carrots 21g Oranges 60g Beef 55g Spinach raw 50g Black beans 45g
Iron (mg)	2.6	2.8	2.7	4.7	3.9	5.3	6.0
	Potato 907g Veg oil 25g	Potato 895g Veg oil 25g Carrots 21g	Potato 865g Veg oil 25g Carrots 21g Oranges 60g	Potato 770g Veg oil 25g Carrots 21g Oranges 60g Lentils 70g	Potato 723g Veg oil 25g Carrots 21g Oranges 60g Beef 55g	Potato 710g Veg oil 25g Carrots 21g Oranges 60g Beef 55g Spinach raw 50g	Potato 649g Veg oil 25g Carrots 21g Oranges 60g Beef 55g Lentils 45g Spinach raw 50g
Iron (mg)	.8	2.9	2.9	4.9	4.1	5.4	6.7

A comprehensive intervention program combining elements from these strategies is consi-dered the most effective way to prevent deficiencies. To determine the most appropriate mix, a situation analysis should first be conducted on the magnitude, prevalence, and distribution of deficiencies, food consumption levels including the intake of micronutrients, and food habits and attitudes of vulnerable groups, including socioeconomic data to identify major constraints and opportunities.

The most successful approach to increasing consumption of micronutrient rich foods is likely to be a combined strategy that addresses both increased production (supply) and increased consumption (demand) of food. The special needs of particular groups such as children and women of childbearing age require particular attention. Food-based intervention programs, dietary enhancement and diversification, and food fortification including biofortification play a critical role in alleviating micronutrient malnutrition. Food-based strategies focus on improving the availability of, access to, and consumption of vitamin and mineral rich foods. Benefits of such food-based strategies include not only improved intakes of specific nutrients but also improved overall diets and health status.

Government policies and regulations can influence the availability and price of micronutrient rich foods. Vitamin and mineral deficiencies can be reduced with relatively small investments in agriculture, education, and public health. National agricultural planning strategies such as crop diversification to promote micronutrient rich crops, agroforestry, and the promotion of traditional and wild foods can have an impact on the availability of micronutrient foods. Regulations that prohibit urban gardening or which reduce the availability or sale of fresh foods by street vendors can reduce the availability of micronutrient foods. Examining the profitability of producing, processing, and marketing such foods and reviewing the impact of policies on micronutrient

status are important steps in planning food-based strategies.

Policies, intervention programs and activities at the international, national, and community level are required to effectively alleviate micronutrient deficiencies. These efforts include:

1) Increasing the overall quantity of foods consumed by those most vulnerable to deficiencies and at the same time
2) Diversifying their diets with focus on micronutrient rich sources of food including animal products, vitamin C, fruit and vegetables;
3) Better managing and controlling dietary inhibitors (e.g., phytates) and enhancers (e.g., vitamin C);
4) Processing, preservation, and preparation practices that retain micronutrient availability including for example the use of iron cooking pots and improved drying techniques to reduce losses as well as the seasonal variation in availability;
5) Nutrition education;
6) Food quality and safety issues with implications for public health and disease control measures to reduce nutrient losses by the body and to maximize the potential of fruit and vegetables as high value commodities for income generation;
7) Fortification including biofortification; and
8) Supplementation.

Strategies to promote dietary diversification within the implementation of food-based approaches include:

1. Increasing overall food intakes
Micronutrient deficiencies are closely associated with poverty, food insecurity, and undernutrition and are common in those groups whose overall food intakes are not sufficient to meet nutritional requirements. Seldom is only one nutrient deficient. If a deficiency for one micronutrient exists

it is likely that multiple deficiencies are also present. For those with inadequate food intakes, increasing overall food consumption provides several essential micronutrients thereby simultaneously addressing a combination of deficiency problems. In addition, physiological interactions between vitamins and minerals enhance the body's ability to absorb and utilize essential micronutrients. Consequently, intervention programs need to as a first priority to ensure that overall food supplies are adequate through increasing the production, availability, access to, and consumption of an adequate and nutritious diet, especially by those who are hungry and food insecure and most vulnerable to deficiencies.

By doing so, food-based strategies address the root causes of micronutrient malnutrition and assist communities and households to adequately feed and nourish themselves in both the short and long term. Stimulating the small scale agricultural sector can produce overall long-term economic benefits for those groups dependent upon agriculture for their livelihoods and for the economy as a whole, thereby encouraging sustainable development.

2. Increasing consumption of micronutrient rich foods

Most traditional diets and food habits provide a range of nutrients that are able to meet the nutritional requirements of most groups. However, those physiologically challenged such as the sick, young children, and pregnant and lactating women may require larger amounts of micronutrient rich foods to meet their increased needs. For those affected by relatively abrupt changes in lifestyle, for example due to civil disruption, migration, urbanization and modernization, traditional food practices may not be easy to maintain resulting in imbalanced and inadequate diets. Where iron deficiency is widely prevalent, the usual diet often does not provide enough bioavailable iron. Under such circumstances, promoting the increased consumption of micronutrient rich

foods is key to good health and nutrition. The promotion of dietary improvement/diversification with a focus on improving the intake of bioavailable iron through greater consumption of animal products, fruit and vegetables, especially those rich in vitamin C, is the only intervention that can lead to self-sustained success in improving iron status. Neither supplementation nor fortification can be effective on its own. Promoting consumption of micronutrient rich foods fosters better overall health for all members of society, provides sustainable improvements by encouraging market solutions and long-term behavioral changes among high risk groups and is often linked to income earning activities.

Efforts to address both increased production (supply) and increased consumption (demand) of food need to be undertaken simultaneously. At the district and national levels, implementation of large scale commercial livestock and vegetable and fruit production can provide micronutrient foods at reasonable prices. The objective is to provide micronutrient rich foods at reasonable prices through effective and competitive markets and distribution channels which can lower consumer prices without reducing producer prices. This will serve predominantly the urban and non-food-producing rural areas. Commercial oil seed production and red palm oil for example can increase the availability of low cost dietary fat crucial for the absorption of fat soluble vitamins (A, D, E and K) and of other micronutrients, including iron.

At the community level, small-scale community or home fruit and vegetable gardens can play a significant role in increasing production of micronutrient rich foods. Production of fish, poultry and small animals such as guinea pigs, rabbits, and goats are excellent sources of highly bioavailable essential micronutrients such as vitamin A, iron, and zinc. The production of animal foods at the local level may permit communities to access foods which otherwise are not available because of their high costs. These types of projects also need some support from local governments or non-governmental organizations to overcome the cost constraints of program implementation, including the training of producers. Horticultural programs and agricultural extension workers can encourage the production of animals, milk and dairy products, legumes, green leafy vegetables, and fruits. These projects should lead to increased production and consumption of micronutrient rich foods at the household level.

A micronutrient and health program in Malawi targeted to women used revolving funds to increase household access to animal food sources through a small animal (poultry, rabbits, guinea fowl, and goats) husbandry program. Over 10,000 households participated in the World Vision program which included an education component on the nutritional benefits of animal food consumption. Over a 4-year period, anemia rates in pregnant women fell from 59% to 42% and in children under 5 years of age from 84% to 66% (12). It is clear that if production gains are to be reflected in increased intakes, community participation, the involvement of women, and consumer education are essential elements. In Indonesia among adolescent girls given iron rich foods 6 times a week for 6 months, Helen Keller International found anemia was significantly reduced and concluded that foods naturally rich in iron increase hemoglobin concentration among anemic Indonesian adolescents (13).

Improving the micronutrient content of soils and in plants and improved agricultural practices can improve the composition of plant foods and enhance yields. Current agricultural practices can improve the micronutrient content of foods through correcting soil quality and pH and increasing soil mineral content depleted by erosion and poor soil conservation. Long-term food-based solutions to micronutrient deficiencies will require improvement of agricultural practices, seed quality, and plant breeding (by means of a classical selection process or genetic modifica-tion). Plant breeding through conventional methods or with genetic modification (biofortification) can increase the micronutrient content of staple and other crops and may play a significant role in combating iron deficiency anemia.

The success of such projects requires a good knowledge and understanding of local conditions as well as the involvement of women and the community in general. These are key elements for supporting, achieving, and sustaining beneficial nutritional change at the household level. Educational efforts need to be directed towards securing appropriate distribution within the family, considering the needs of the most vulnerable members, especially infants and young children. Separate food-based dietary guidelines (FBDG) for vulnerable groups, such as pregnant and lactating women, children, and the elderly, should be developed.

Foods that are rich sources of iron include:
- oysters
- liver
- lean red meat (especially beef)
- poultry, dark red meat
- lamb, pork, shellfish
- tuna, salmon
- iron fortified cereals
- eggs (especially egg yolks)
- whole grains: wheat, millet, oats, brown rice
- legumes: lima beans, soybeans, dried beansand peas, kidney beans
- seeds: almonds, Brazil nuts
- dried fruits: prunes, raisins, apricots
- vegetables: broccoli, spinach, kale, collards, asparagus, dandelion greens

Efficacy issues

It is argued that in order to generate greater interest as well as resources for implementing food-based approaches, the contributions that such interventions can make compared with other interventions such as supplementation and fortification need to be better quantified and more information generated to demonstrate their efficacy. However, evaluations of the efficacy of food-based aproaches are lacking in the literature partly because of the complexity of the interventions, the wide variety of food components contained in food, the large number of inputs, outcomes and confounding factors, the range of intermediary components and short and long term impacts that present difficulties for study design. While evaluation of the nutritional impact and cost benefit of food-based approaches in combating micronutrient deficiencies is a research priority, there are compelling reasons for supporting the wider implementation of a food-based approach.

3. Management and control of inhibitors and enhancers

Improved food preparation and cooking methods and the modification of consumption practices to increase dietary enhancers and eliminate inhibitors of absorption can safeguard the amounts of micronutrients that are available and maximize their uptake by the body. Practical interventions to reduce dietary inhibitors and increase iron absorption facilitators include:

- Ensuring dietary intakes of oils and fats, vitamin A, and of ascorbic acid are adequate for enhancing absorption of micronutrients
- Fermentation and germination for the enzymatic hydrolysis of phytates in cereals and legumes
- Promoting nonenzymatic methods of reducing phytic acid content
- Encouraging home processing techniques like malting
- Avoiding drinking tea or coffee within 2 hours of eating meals
- Reducing the use of tamarind as a souring agent and instead using tomato or lime juice in order to facilitate non-heme iron absorption

- Adopting food to food fortification practices whereby dietary inhibitors (e.g., phytates) and enhancers (e.g., vitamin C) are better managed and controlled.

The bioavailability of non-heme iron rises to a level similar to that of meat products when consumed with a significant source (25 mg) of vitamin C in the same meal. In Nigeria the incorporation of baobab fruit pulp drink in the diet of children 6–8 years old for a 3-month period significantly increased hemoglobin from 10.85 to 12.92 g/dL and decreased the number of individuals with SF<12 mcg/L from 65% to 23%. The study concluded that the high vitamin C content of the baobab which provided 60 mg of ascorbate per day promoted the absorption of iron (14).

Reducing phytates and tannins by oxidation with polyphenol oxidases, enzymes found in many fruits and vegetables, increases the bioavailability of iron. Incubation of cereals with fruit extracts such as banana can be done at the household level to increase the bioavailability of iron and may be encouraged as part of a food-based strategy to prevent iron deficiency anemia. Fermentation for a couple of days (sourdough fermentation) almost completely degrades the phytate of wheat bran and increases the bioavailability of iron in bread made from whole-wheat flour. Calcium inhibits iron absorption and so the practical solution for overcoming the negative effects of calcium on iron absorption is to increase iron intake, increase its bioavailability, and avoid the intake of foods rich in calcium and foods rich in iron at the same meal.

4. Processing, preservation and preparation to maintain micronutrient availability

Fruit and vegetables are perishable products and the reduction of postharvest losses and prevention of wastage through improved processing and handling and by adopting simple methods of storage practices may considerably increase availability throughout the year. By improving methods of processing and preservation of surplus foods produced during the peak season, further losses may be reduced leading to greater year-round availability of these foods, improving nutritive value, acceptability and shelf life, and thereby improving consumption. Local food preservation and processing facilities should therefore be strongly promoted. At the household level, the promotion of effective cooking methods and practical ways of preserving foods (solar drying of seasonal micronutrient rich foods such as papaya, grapes, mangoes, peaches, tomatoes, and apricots) may significantly increase the access to bioavailable micronutrient rich foods. At the commercial level, grading, packing, transport, and marketing practices can reduce losses, stimulate economic growth, and generate income.

Food preparation and dietary practices need also to be improved in efforts to combat iron deficiency. For example, it is important that vegetables rich in vitamin C, folate, and other water-soluble or heat-labile vitamins be minimally cooked in small amounts of water. For iron bioavailability, it is essential to reduce the intake of inhibitors of iron absorption and to increase the intake of enhancers of absorption in a given meal. It is re-commended to increase the intake of germinated seeds, fermented cereals, heat-processed cereals, meats, and fruits and vegetables rich in vitamin C, and to encourage the consumption of tea, coffee, chocolate, or herbal teas at times other than with meals. This advice for meal preparation is particularly important for people who consume a high proportion of cereal and tubers and who are also most at risk for micronutrient deficiencies.

Cast iron pots and cookware can also be a source of significant quantities of dietary iron. Encouraging the use of cooking in iron pots has been shown to improve iron status. In Ethiopia, Malawi, and Brazil the use of cast iron cooking pots has been observed to increase the amount of iron in the diet and thereby reduce iron deficiency anemia (15).

5. Consumer education for behavioral change

Communication techniques can be used to help bring about changes in eating practices at the household level. As incomes rise, people often reduce breastfeeding, stop gathering wild foods, and eat fewer green leafy vegetables. Such nutritionally beneficial traditional practices are under threat of erosion from factors related to urbanization and modernization and need to be protected and supported by education campaigns and communication strategies that aim to preserve such positive traditional practices. This is especially the case for those foods which may be available but are not consumed in sufficient quantities to prevent deficiencies or perhaps not at all by some vulnerable groups. Mothers and others who directly influence food production, food purchasing, food preparation and child feeding behavior may be specifically targeted by such programs.

Intervention programs should always be accompanied by a public nutrition education and promotion program to encourage improved food consumption. Advice for a healthy diet should provide both a quantitative and qualitative description of the diet for it to be understood by individuals, and information on both size and number of servings per day should be provided. Quantitative aspects include the estimation of the amount of nutrients in foods and their bioavailability in the form they are actually consumed. Qualitative aspects relate to the biological utilization of nutrients in the food as consumed and the potential for modifying the balance between food enhancers and inhibitors.

A healthy diet can be attained in more than one way because of the wide variety of foods which can be combined. The development of food-based dietary guidelines (FBDGs) by FAO and WHO (16, 17) recognizes this and, noting that there are economic constraints which limit food supply at the household level, focuses on the combination of foods that can meet nutrient requirements rather than on how each specific nutrient is provided in adequate amounts. FBDGs are based on the fact that people eat food, not nutrients. The approach is first to define the significant diet-related public health problems in a community and to evaluate the adequacy of the diet by comparing the information available on dietary intake with Recommended Nutrient Intakes (RNIs). Food-based dietary guidelines can then be prepared that indicate what aspects of the diet could be modified to improve nutrition. Such FBDGs would need to take into account dietary patterns, the ecological, socioeconomic and cultural factors, and the biological and physical environment in which the targeted population live.

Nutritional status can be improved significantly by educating households on food preparation practices which minimize the consumption of inhibitors of iron absorption, for example, the fermentation of phytate-containing grains before the baking of breads to enhance iron absorption. The consumption of ascorbic acid preferably through foods rich in vitamin C along with foods rich in iron enhances absorption. The tannins contained in tea and coffee when taken with meals strongly inhibit iron absorption and education programs need to highlight this.

At the household level appropriate food distribution within the family must be considered to ensure that children and women receive adequate food with high micronutrient density. Household food distribution must be considered when establishing general dietary guidelines and addressing the needs of vulnerable groups in the community. In addition, education detailing the appropriate storage and processing of foods to prevent micronutrient losses at the household level is important.

6. Quality assurance – food quality and safety issues

Improving the quality and safety of food has obvious benefits for health and for business. The importance of improving public health as an intervention strategy to reduce nutrient losses by the body is clear and safe, good quality food makes an important contribution to that. Information campaigns may raise awareness of the health problems that can arise from improper food storage and handling practices. On the business side, fruit and vegetables are valuable commodities with high potential for income generation. Processed and marketed foods need to be quality assured to compete in the market place and this aspect often needs further support in the area of laws and regulations and on food quality control to ensure required standards are enforced.

7. Food fortification

Food fortification is the addition of nutrients at levels higher than those found in the original food. Increasing the micronutrient content of staple and other crops through biofortification has been referred to above. Biofortification enhances the nutritive value of foods using modern tools of biotechnology. Food fortification has a role in meeting iron, folate, iodine, and zinc needs and is recommended when dietary iron is insufficient or the dietary iron is of poor bioavailability, which is the reality for most people in the developing world and for vulnerable population groups in the developed world.

Because staple foods around the world provide predominantly non-heme iron sources of low bioavailability, the traditionally eaten staple foods represent an excellent vehicle for iron fortification. Examples of foods which have been fortified are wheat flour, corn (maize) flour, rice, salt, sugar, cookies, curry powder, fish sauce, and soy sauce. However, even with foods fortified with iron, the consumption of iron absorption enhancers should always be promoted to get the best out of the food consumed.

Fortified foods as part of food aid protect the nutritional status of vulnerable groups and victims of emergencies but under normal circumstances, fortified foods may not be widely available to the poorest and more isolated populations. Community-based approaches to fortification, for example using rural hammer mills, may be a useful way of reaching these rural populations. In Malawi, maize is being fortified with iron as well as with B vitamins, folate, zinc, and vitamin A. However, dietary diversification programs are of critical importance and should always be promoted.

Fortification of food with iron and other micronutrients is considered a valid technology and strategy for adoption as part of a food-based approach when and where existing food supplies and limited access fail to provide adequate levels of the respective nutrients in the diet, and where the fortified food is highly likely to be accessible to the target population. In such cases, fortification of food is seen as a valuable adjunct program to ongoing nutrition improvement programs. In FAO's view, fortification is not an alternative to the overall goal of improving nutrition through the consumption of a nutritionally adequate diet made up from a variety of available foods.

8. Supplementation

Supplementation refers to periodic administration of pharmacological preparations of nutrients as capsules, tablets, or by injection. Supplementation is necessary as a short-term emergency measure to reverse clinical signs or for prevention in groups at risk. Nutritional supplementation should be restricted to vulnerable groups which cannot meet their nutrient needs through food (women of childbearing age, infants and young children, elderly people, low socioeconomic groups, displaced people, refugees, and populations experiencing other emergency situations). Iron supplementation is used to control and prevent iron deficiency anemia in pregnant women and appears to be essential during the second half of pregnancy. However, there is some concern about possible

negative effects of iron supplementation in that it may be toxic at high doses. It can cause diarrhea and other abdominal symptoms, and for newborns and in highly malaria-endemic areas it may increase the morbidity of infectious disease and reduce linear growth in iron-replete infants. Some studies suggest that iron negatively affects zinc status and that zinc and iron interact when administered together in therapeutic doses and thus should be supplemented independently to avoid this interaction. However, evidence is mixed.

CURRENT AND PLANNED ACTIVITIES

Achieving food security for all is at the heart of FAO's efforts to ensure that people have regular access to enough high quality food to lead active and healthy lives. FAO has been leading efforts ensuring that agriculture, particularly in the developing world, can help meet the demand for healthy food and develop food production systems that are both economically and environmentally sustainable. Promoting the production and consumption of fruits and vegetables, and animal foods (fish and poultry) that are rich in micronutrients is central to FAO's efforts to eradicate hunger, alleviate poverty, and raise levels of nutrition and standards of living.

FAO advocates for and promotes the consumption of healthy diets and acknowledges the important role that dietary diversity can play in improving health and generating incomes for poor population groups. To enhance food and nutrition security in rural households, FAO promotes the production of vegetables and fruits, as well as animal foods (fish ponds and animal husbandry) in home, community and school gardens. Home and school gardening are frequently linked with school feeding programs, nutrition education, and promotional campaigns to encourage consumption of micronutrient rich foods. Owing to the rapid rise in the world's urban populations, FAO promotes urban gardening and agriculture as part of its Food for the Cities program to make available fresh micronutrient rich food and offer a means of self-employment and income generation for poor urban families.

Food and nutrition education play a vital role in FAO activities aimed at promoting healthy dietary intake. There is ample evidence to show that programs aimed at food and dietary diversification, such as home gardening and horticultural programs, are most effective when they are combined with promotional and educational activities (18, 19). Nutrition education in schools and the promotion of healthy eating is important as children's food habits and dietary patterns are formed when they are young, but it is equally necessary to reach adults and parents with clear messages that promote healthy food choices, food preparation and consumption. FAO promotes the development of national food-based dietary guidelines and provides technical assistance in the development and implementation of nutrition education programs and campaigns in communities and schools. Educational materials that promote the production and consumption of a variety of healthy foods, including indigenous ones, can be found on FAO's Food and Nutrition website at: *http://www.fao.org/ag/agn/sitemap_en.stm.*

Additional materials are available on the inter-departmental website on school gardens at: *http://www.fao.org/schoolgarden/* and FAO's Education for Rural People Tool Kit: *http://www.fao.org/SD/ERP/ERPtktoolkit_en.htm.*

Key initiatives through which FAO, in collaboration with governments, partners in the UN community, NGOs, and civil society, promotes the production and consumption of micronutrient rich foods and healthy diets include:

School Gardens for Better Education and Nutrition

School garden programs have the potential to improve education of rural children and their families by making it more relevant to local needs. They enhance the quality of education and can serve as an outdoor laboratory for practical learning across a broad range of subjects. With wider community involvement, they can also address nutritional deficiencies by supplementing school feeding and adding nutritional value to school meals. Foods produced within school gardens focus on easy to grow micronutrient rich vegetables and fruits, as well as animal foods, such as chickens and rabbits. A key function of school gardens is to encourage children to stay in school and to acquire a range of knowledge and skills, an aspect which is especially important in countries with a high prevalence of HIV and AIDS and a growing number of orphans. School gardens, in both urban and rural settings, can provide school children with hands-on experience in food production and natural resource management, as well as a focus for education on good nutrition and healthy eating. New skills and techniques that students acquire in the school garden can be taken home to their family farms or household gardens. For their full potential to be realized, school gardens are best developed within the context of a carefully designed, comprehensive national program which leaves ample room for local adaptation and promotes the full engagement of local communities. FAO collaborates with WFP's Food for Education Program, UNICEF, national and international NGOs, as well as community-based organization in the promotion and establishment of school gardens for children's better learning and nutrition worldwide. See FAO's school garden website: *http://www.fao.org/schoolgarden/.*

Global Fruit and Vegetable Initiative for Health

A recently published WHO/FAO report (20) recommends as a population-wide intake goal the consumption of a minimum of 400 g of fruit and vegetables per day (excluding potatoes and other starchy tubers) for the prevention of chronic diseases such as heart disease, cancer, diabetes, and obesity, as well as for the prevention and alleviation of several micronutrient deficiencies, especially in less developed countries.

Recognizing the increasing scientific evidence that low fruit and vegetable intake is a key risk factor for several noncommunicable diseases and plays an important role in the prevention and alleviation of micronutrient deficiencies, WHO and FAO launched a joint fruit and vegetable promotion initiative in Rio de Janeiro in November 2003. The overall goal of this initiative is to strengthen, promote, and protect health in the context of a healthy diet by guiding the development of sustainable actions at community, national and global levels that, when taken together, will lead to reduced risk of chronic diseases through increased fruit and vegetable consumption. The WHO/FAO Global Fruit and Vegetable Initiative for Health (GlobFaV) seeks to maximize synergies between WHO's global work on diet, physical activity, and health, and FAO's programs on nutrition, food security, and the horticultural supply chain. In concert with other UN agencies, the initiative will support national programs in developing countries involving coalitions of stakeholders ranging from ministries of agriculture, health and transport, to farmers, extension services, schools, and the food industry. See the WHO/FAO Global Fruit and Vegetable Initiative for Health at: *http://www.fao.org/ag/magazine/0606sp2.htm* and the framework document developed at the Kobe workshop at: *http://www.fao.org/ag/magazine/FAO-WHO-FV.pdf*

International Fruit and Vegetable Alliance
An International Fruit and Vegetable Alliance (IFAVA) has called for increasing fruit and vegetable consumption in order to help stem the rise of obesity and chronic diseases arguing that this should be a primary goal within a health, food and agricultural policy. Health authorities in many countries support the "5 a day" campaign that encourages people to eat at least five servings of fruits and vegetables daily. The reason why fruit and vegetables are so beneficial is because of their array of compounds. In addition to vitamins, minerals and trace elements, fiber, and some food energy, fruit and vegetables also contain antioxidants and many other complex plant components (called phytochemicals). It appears that the benefits stem not only from the individual components, but also from the interactions between these components. Dietary supplements containing isolated vitamins or minerals do not appear to have the same beneficial effects as fruit and vegetables themselves. Indeed, in some studies, supplements caused more harm than good. FAO is able to provide advice on strategies for increasing the production, availability, processing, preservation, and consumption of micronutrient rich foods.

Nutrition-Friendly Schools Initiative
Based on the understanding that effectively addressing the increasing global burden of malnutrition (both undernutrition and obesity and related chronic diseases), requires common policy options, the Nutrition-Friendly Schools Initiative (NFSI) has been developed as a follow-up to the WHO Expert Meeting on Childhood Obesity in Kobe, in 2005. The main aim of the NFSI is to provide a framework for designing integrated school-based interventions that address all forms of malnutrition that affect school-age children, building on the ongoing work of various agencies and partners, including the UNESCO coordinated FRESH Initiative (Focusing Resources on Effective School Health), Child-Friendly Schools (UNICEF), Essential Package (UNICEF/WFP), Health Promoting Schools (WHO), and Food and Nutrition Education Programs (FAO). The NFSI applies the concept and principles of the Baby-Friendly Hospital Initiative.

Improving the nutritional status of school-age children is an effective investment for the future generation. Preschools and schools offer many opportunities to promote healthy diets and physical activity for children and are also a potential access point for engaging parents and community members in preventing child malnutrition in all its forms (i.e., undernutrition, micronutrient deficiencies, and obesity and other nutrition-related chronic diseases). The universality of the school setting for gaining access to children makes it highly relevant to global efforts to combat the increasing public health problems of nutrition-related ill health. The NFSI framework is currently being pilot-tested in 30 countries around the world prior to its official release.

CONCLUSIONS

Iron deficiency and iron deficiency anemia are serious and widespread public health problems. Their global scale and magnitude, combined with their damaging physiological socioeconomic effects, require the urgent adoption of known and effective measures to tackle this critical problem.

With the knowledge that the intake of foods rich in iron increase hemoglobin concentration and reduce the prevalence of anemia significantly, much focus has been placed on iron fortification and supplementation programs rather than on increasing food consumption and improving and diversifying diets. This is partly because governments, international agencies, and donors have considered both fortification and supplementation programs attractive for their apparent simplicity and cost-effectiveness. However, in practice many such programs are proving to be difficult to manage, more costly than expected to implement, and less effective than promised.

As these programs have had little reported success in reducing anemia, interest is turning to food-based approaches that have higher potential

for achieving far-reaching and long-lasting benefits for the control of iron deficiency. Food-based approaches aim to improve nutrition through increasing the availability and consumption of a nutritionally adequate and micronutrient rich diet made up from a variety of available foods. Food-based approaches are recognized as an essential part of an urgently needed more comprehensive strategy to combat iron and other micronutrient deficiencies.

There are a number of actions that may be taken by international agencies, governments, line ministries of agriculture, health, education, industry and the private sector, communities and households themselves that are feasible and practical and that will increase the consumption and bioavailability of iron. As food-based strategies aim to improve the quality of the overall diet by increasing the availability and consumption of a wider range of foods, they address multiple nutrient deficiencies simultaneously. By so doing, food-based strategies are preventive, cost-effective, and sustainable. They also encourage popular demand for safe, wholesome food, and foster the development of sustainable agriculture that has positive knock-on effects for the rural economy.

The strategies proposed to promote dietary diversity need strong community-level commitment and their successful implementation requires advocacy to obtain community acceptance of and political support for programs. Involving local people in program assessment, analysis, and actions will facilitate community acceptance. The support of local authorities and government may facilitate the implementation of such projects because these actions require economic resources, which sometimes are beyond the reach of the most needy.

Success also depends upon well financed food-based initiatives at the international level. FAO can provide technical assistance to governments in concert with international agencies, non-governmental organizations, and public and private institutions and the food industry to support planned and ongoing government food-based programs for meeting a broad spectrum of micronutrient needs, including iron. By adopting food-based strategies on a broader scale as a matter of priority, we will have a balanced, more comprehensive approach that has the greatest potential for overcoming not only iron but also other micronutrient deficiencies.

Work in pursuit of this strategy includes continuing efforts to ensure that dietary diversification, food fortification, supplementation, and public health measures are taken comprehensively to combat iron deficiency, specifically:

- Increase overall food intakes of those who are food insecure through support for enhanced food production, availability, processing, preservation, and consumption.
- Increase the consumption of micronutrient rich foods that meet dietary needs and food preferences.
- Explore ways to increase financial investments in food-based initiatives at the country level including by better quantifying the contribution that such interventions can make to demonstrate their efficacy.
- Draw up a list of best practices that households can adopt to prevent iron deficiency anemia (IDA) based on local Trials of Improved Practices (TIPs) and design a communication strategy for affecting behavioral change
- Research on the amounts of phytates and iron-binding polyphenols in food, condiments, and spices and in common meals and their usual variations in composition in order to make realistic recommendations about changes in meal composition, taking into consideration the effect of such changes on other nutrients (e.g., vitamin A).
- Evaluate the nutritive value of diets not only on energy and protein adequacy but also on micronutrient density.
- Explore home fortification of weaning foods.

REFERENCES

1. Food and Agriculture Organization of the United Nations. The state of food insecurity. Washington, DC: FAO, 2006.
2. Food and Agriculture Organization of the United Nations, World Health Organization. Human vitamin and mineral requirements. Report of a joint FAO/WHO expert consultation, Bangkok, Thailand. Rome: FAO, 2002.
3. International Institute for Population Sciences. National Family Health Survey-2. Anemia among women and children. Mumbai: IIPS, 2000.
4. Nair MK. Iron absorption and its implications in the control of iron deficiency anaemia. Nutrition News 1999;20(2):1–4.

5. Scrimshaw NS. Functional consequences of iron deficiency in human populations. J Nutr Sci Vitaminol (Tokyo) 1984;30:47–63.
6. Bruner AB, Joffe A, Duggan AK, Casella JF, Brandt J. Randomised study of cognitive defects of iron supplementation in non-anaemic iron-deficient adolescent girls. Lancet 1996;348:992–6.
7. Lieberman E, Ryan KJ, Monson RR, Schoenbaum SC. Association of maternal hematocrit with premature labor. Am J Obstet Gynecol 1988;159:107–14.
8. Garn SM, Ridella SA, Petzold AS, Falkner F. Maternal hemologic levels and pregnancy outcomes. Semin Perinatol 1981;5:155–62.

9.   Zhu YI, Haas JD. Iron depletion without anemia and physical performance in young women. Am
J Clin Nutr 1997;66:334–41.

10. Sanghvi TG. Economic rationale for investing
in micronutrient programs. A policy brief based on
new analyses. Office of Nutrition, Bureau for
Research and Development, United States Agency
for International Development. Washington, DC:
USAID 1996.

11. Neumann C, Long J, Weiss R, Murphy S, Liang
J, Gewa C, et al. Predictors of anemia in rural
Kenyan children: malaria, infection, vitamin B12
and A, and meat intake. Report of the 2004 INACG
Symposium; 2004 Nov 18; Lima, Peru. Washington,
DC: ILSI, 2005 (abstr Th67).

12. Namarika R, Yiannakis M, Main B, Siekmans
K. Small animal revolving fund addresses iron defi-
ciency anaeia in Malawi. Report of the 2004 INACG
Symposium; 2004 Nov 18; Lima, Peru. Washington,
DC: ILSI, 2005 (abstr Th34).

13. Sari M, de Pee S, Yip R, Martini E, Sugiatmi,
Soekarjo D, et al. Foods naturally rich in iron
increase hemoglobin concentration in anemic
Indonesian adolescents. Report of the 2004 INACG
Symposium; 2004 Nov 18; Lima, Peru. Washington,
DC: ILSI, 2005 (abstr Th30).

14. Nnam NM. Baobab fruit pulp (Adansonia digita-
ta L.) improves iron status in Nigerian children. Report
of the 2004 INACG Symposium; 2004 Nov 18; Lima,
Peru. Washington, DC: ILSI, 2005 (abstr Th90).

15. Berti PR, Zlotkin S, Hoang MA, FitzGerald S,
Tuan T, Sharieff W, et al. The efficacy of iron and

steel pots in reducing prevalence of anaemia in
Vietnam: report of midline findings. Report of the
2004 INACG Symposium; 2004 Nov 18; Lima,
Peru. Washington, DC: ILSI, 2005 (abstr Th20).

16. World Health Organization, Food and
Agriculture Organization of the United Nations.
Preparation and use of food-based dietary guide-
lines. Report of a joint FAO/WHO consultation,
Nicosia, Cyprus. Geneva: WHO Nutrition
Programme, 1996.

17. Food and Agriculture Organization of the
United Nations, International Life Sciences
Institute. Preventing micronutrient malnutrition: a
guide to food-based approaches. Washington, DC:
ILSI Press, 1997.

18. Ruel MT, Levin CE. Assessing the potential for
food-based strategies to reduce vitamin A and iron
deficiencies: a review of recent evidence.
Washington DC: International Food Policy Research
Institute, 2000. [Food Consumption and Nutrition
Division Discussion Paper, No. 92]

19. Faber M, Phungula AS, Venter SL, Dhansay
MA, Benade AJ. Home gardens focusing on the production of yellow and dark-green leafy vegetables
increase the serum retinol concentrations of 2–5-y-
old children in South Africa. Am J Clin Nutr
2002;76:1048–54.

20. World Health Organization. Diet, nutrition, and
the prevention of chronic diseases. Report of a joint
FAO/WHO Expert Consultation. Geneva: WHO,
2003. [Who Technical Report Series, No. 916]

21

Global perspectives: accelerating progress on preventing and controlling nutritional anemia

Ian Darnton-Hill[1]   Neal Paragas[2]   Tommaso Cavalli-Sforza[3]

[1]Nutrition Section, UNICEF, New York, USA
[2]Institute of Human Nutrition, Columbia University, New York, USA
[3]Nutrition and Food Safety, the Western Pacific Regional office of WHO, Manila, Philippines
Contact: idarntonhill@unicef.org

IAN DARNTON-HILL
Ian obtained his MD from the University of Adelaide in Australia and is a Fellow of the Australasian Faculty of Public Health Medicine. He is currently Acting Chief, Nutrition Section, and Senior Advisor, Child Survival and Nutrition, for UNICEF and also holds academic appointments in Australia and the USA. Ian has over 30 years of experience, working across the world in public health interventions, health policy, and the analysis of programs and has over 100 publications to his name. His special interest is in the prevention and control of micronutrient malnutrition and he regularly serves on UN Technical Expert and other Committees, including chairing the Micronutrient Working Group of the UN Standing Committee on Nutrition.

NEAL PARAGAS
Neal obtained his BS in Botany from the University of Washington, Seattle, USA. His appreciation of the plant-human interaction led him to join the Institute of Human Nutrition PhD program at Columbia University, New York, USA, where he is currently a pre-doctoral fellow working on elucidating alternate pathways of iron transport.

TOMMASO CAVALLI-SFORZA
Tommaso obtained his MD and specializations in Nutrition and Dietetics, as well as Psychiatry, from the University of Milan, Italy, and an MSc in Human Nutrition from the London School of Hygiene and Tropical Medicine. He is currently the Regional Adviser in Nutrition and Food Safety at the WHO Regional Office for the Western Pacific, based in Manila, Philippines. Tommaso has 30 years of experience in public health, nutrition, noncommunicable diseases (NCD), and food safety in Italy, many Asian and Pacific countries, and some African countries. His areas of particular interests include the prevention of anemia, IDD and other micronutrient deficiencies, obesity prevention and control, promotion of infant and young child feeding, school health, and development/implementation of national plans of action for nutrition. Tommaso has over 70 publications to his name.

INTRODUCTION

It is clear from the preceding chapters that nutritional anemias, including especially iron deficiency anemia, are currently the greatest global nutritional problem. They mainly affect women and children and represent a significant constraint to many nations' chances of improved public health and economic development. While there has been little documented success in addressing the problem at a public health level in less affluent countries, there is, nevertheless, many years of programmatic experience and a vast amount of science behind the complex picture of iron metabolism (1–3). What remains surprising, as we will see below, is how much is still unknown, and how many new areas continue to emerge from the ongoing research, both basic and programmatic. This chapter examines global perspectives and poses the question as to why there has been so little progress at the public health level in poorer countries in addressing nutritional anemia. It reviews from earlier chapters: 1) the present magnitude of the problem; 2) how it is currently being addressed; 3) some lessons learned from years of experience; and then suggests some ways forward.

Although the data are relatively poor, it seems likely that in the first decade of the UN's goal to reduce iron deficiency by a third, a goal endorsed by a large number of national leaders (4), virtually no measurable progress was made (1, 2). Some reasons for this failure will be suggested in this chapter. Before that, in reference to the magnitude of the problem, we draw on chapter one by WHO (5), noting there are virtually no global prevalence figures for other nutritional anemias besides iron deficiency, and even these are based on prevalence data of low hemoglobin (Hb) values. In areas such as that described in 2003 in the Pemba district of Zanzibar in Tanzania, an area of high, continuous transmission of malaria, it is clear that, in infants and young children, approximately half of the anemia is caused by malaria,

although there are concomitant iron deficiencies and other nutritional deficiencies (6, 7). This is different from the profile in, say, Nepal where there is little malaria and the high levels of anemia are likely to be mainly due to poor nutrition, particularly, but not exclusively, of iron (8). High levels of other nutritional deficiencies often occur in poor quality diets, usually along with inhibiting factors such as phytates, high parasite loads, and socio-cultural factors (including poverty and gender discrimination), all of which contribute to the high levels of anemia seen in poorer populations (9, 10). It has recently been noted in the Lancet's early childhood development series that at least 200 million of those under five fail to reach their cognitive and socio-emotional development due to undernutrition, including iron deficiency, and inadequate stimulation (11).

Nutritional anemias should also be seen as a reflection of inequities, and hence poverty alleviation activities must become a fundamental nutrition intervention. The diets of the poor are characterized more by poor quality than quantity, although the latter is often the case in many chronic, and especially acute, emergency situations. The diets of the poor have a low energy density and poor availability of important micronutrients, for example, iron, vitamin A and zinc (12, 13). The bioavailability of these micronutrients is also poor, but other factors in these diets compound the issue, such as the often high phytate and fiber levels, and low access to ascorbic acid-containing foods. This makes them even less bioavailable (14).

The rest of the chapter reviews the ways of addressing the problem; some of the lessons learned from the considerable country experience (rarely well evaluated or documented); a review of some of the current science that may inform progress; and suggestions for exactly how this might be achieved. While several program inter-

ventions have mainly been shown to be efficacious, not all have proven to be effective on a
large scale. It seems likely that part of any
improved impact will be secured by addressing
areas such as female education, which are not
always seen as an anemia intervention, and sepa-
rating out more clearly therapeutic and preventive
approaches, although there will be a good deal of
overlap at times, for example, the recommended
supplementation with iron supplements from two
months onward in low birth weight infants (15,
16). Other broader approaches will be the fortification of staple foods and condiments, promotion
of animal-source foods in poor diets, a focus on
poverty alleviation, as well as addressing the
other causes of nutritional anemias by, for example, multimicronutrient home fortification.

REVIEW OF THE MAGNITUDE OF THE PROBLEM

The current estimates of prevalence

As indicated in the first chapter, nutritional anemias, largely due to iron deficiency, remain the
major nutritional problem facing the poorer
nations. Even in more affluent countries anemia
remains a significant problem in certain, usually
disadvantaged, groups. The recent WHO estimates give prevalence data for preschool age children and nonpregnant and pregnant women,
according to information available with pre-spec-
ified criteria (5). For infants and young children,
the range is from 3.4% in North America to nearly
two thirds (65.4%) in Africa. In women, the range
is 7.6% in North America to 44.7% in Africa
(nonpregnant), and for pregnant women, 4.7 to
55%. However, individual studies have identified
far higher prevalence in infants and women, especially in South Asia, that shows, for example,
84.9% of pregnant women anemic (<110 g/L)
with 13.1% having severe anemia (<70 g/L). In
India, adolescent girls have levels of 90.1% with
7.1% having severe anemia in the 16 Districts
surveyed (17).

The current estimates of burden

The disability adjusted life years (DALYs) – an
expression of years of life lost and years lived
with disability – provide an overall estimate of the
magnitude of economic losses in a population due
to disease (18). Other indirect social and health
consequences of impaired fitness and vitality are
difficult to estimate and are often not considered,
although they may well be relevant to nutritional
anemias. For example, among resource poor societies the premature death of a mother and the
lower income generating capacity of iron deficient and anemic workers translate into greater
rates of disease and overall undernutrition (16).

Anemia impairs individual growth and development as well as family, community, and
national socioeconomic development. The negative impact on national development can be estimated from the number of individuals affected in
various age and gender categories; the severity of
the deficiency; and the duration and consequences of the condition. The economic implications of such conditions include the costs incurred
by the public and private sectors in treating anemia; the consequences for the society of increased
maternal mortality and decreased productivity;
and the long term negative consequences of
impaired mental development on human capital
formation (16). Based on estimates of iron deficiency anemia as a risk factor for mortality, when
added to its direct sequelae, the total attributed
global burden amounts to 841,000 deaths and
35,057,000 DALYs (19). The authors note the
great majority of this disease burden derives from
anemia in pregnancy and early childhood and is
borne by women and children in Asia and Africa.

The economic costs of anemia due to cognitive delays in children, lower productivity in
adults, and premature births have been estimated
by Ross and Horton (20), among others. They
suggest that the median value of productivity
losses due to iron deficiency is about $4 (US) per
capita or 0.9% of GDP. On a per capita basis,

losses are greatest in rich countries where wages are higher, even though iron deficiency is less widespread. Nevertheless the estimated cost to South Asia, where the prevalence of anemia is highest, is estimated to be around $5 billion annually. It has also been calculated that the productivity of adult anemic agricultural workers (or other heavy manual labor) is reduced by 1.5% for every 1% decrease in hemoglobin concentration below established thresholds of safe health (21). Eliminating severe anemia in pregnancy has been estimated potentially to reduce the maternal disease burden by 13% (22).

There is also increasing information about the cost effectiveness of some interventions in addressing nutritional anemia, in particular iron deficiency and iron deficiency anemia. Economic growth is emerging as the new paradigm for why iron deficiency anemia prevention and control programs should be funded, as independent bodies such as the Copenhagen Consensus and other economists repeatedly identify iron supplementation, and probably fortification, as cost effective interventions (23–25). Chapter three by Alderman and Horton ably demonstrates this (24) and the heavy costs of iron deficiency (other nutritional anemias being unlikely to be common enough to have an economic impact). Particularly in the case of iron deficiency anemia, benefits can derive from both cost reductions and from enhanced productivity. Alderman and Horton conclude that nutritional anemia is associated with a significant health burden, even before information from studies in young girls and the likely benefits of improved pregnancy outcomes and intergenerational effects are considered (24).

Problems in defining anemia and its causes

It is surprising how little is known about iron metabolism and other nutritional anemias at the most basic level and about public health interventions, especially when one considers that enrichment of flour and bread with iron has been in place in the USA for over 60 years (26), and antenatal supplementation for even longer. Dietary iron uptake and metabolism continues to attract serious scientific attention and each new advance appears to make the picture even more complex, although the chapter by Lynch (3) in this volume offers considerable clarity.

Total body iron stores are regulated solely by the absorption of iron and the continuous loss through the sloughing of epidermal tissue and menses. Current data indicate that total body iron balance is achieved by regulating uptake of dietary iron, since the loss of iron is not regulated and there is no known excretion process. Therefore, the regulation of iron movement into and out of intestinal mucosal cells is the leading factor contributing to the body's global iron status. Iron absorption is decreased in iron replete mammals and is increased when iron stores are low. When the body is iron loaded, iron accumulates in the intestinal enterocytes and is gradually lost during the normal recycling of intestinal mucosa (27). Therefore iron export is thought to play the critical role in the regulation of iron absorption and total iron status.

Dietary heme iron is the more absorbable form of iron. Heme iron is typically absorbed in the proximal duodenum. Recently an intestinal heme transporter has been identified (28) that mediates the heme uptake in a temperature dependent and saturable manner. The discovery echoes the earlier one by Lynch et al. (29) that heme iron is more efficiently absorbed than inorganic iron from the diet. Trafficking of iron loaded dietary heme represents the most important source of iron (30, 31). The bioavailability of iron is regulated by the dietary contents such as phytates, animal foods (heme and nonheme iron), calcium, and ascorbic acid, all of which influence the amount of iron the enterocytes will absorb.

In the regulation of dietary iron uptake, intestinal iron absorption is currently understood to be controlled by three stimuli (32) all of which have potential implications in public health programs to prevent and control nutritional anemias. The first is known as "mucosal block" and is characterized by the inhibition of enterocytes to absorb iron for several days after a large bolus of iron has been delivered (33). Mucosal block occurs in systemic iron deficiency most probably because the enterocyte is led to believe that iron requirements have been met. The second stimulus to control iron balance is the "stores regulator" which responds to total body iron (34). The molecular mechanism has not been clearly elucidated but it most likely involves saturation of circulating transferrin (Tf). The third regulatory system is the "erythropoietic regulator" which modulates intestinal iron absorption independent of body iron (34). Hepcidin, a new player in the iron trafficking field, appears to play the major role in this mechanism.

Hepcidin, a recently elucidated systemic iron regulatory peptide, operates as the key to the mucosal gate (35). Hepcidin is secreted by the liver and excreted through the kidneys. In experiments where mice receive a bolus of iron, hepcidin gene expression increases, which suggests it plays a compensatory response in order to limit iron absorption (36). Hepcidin is presumed to be a negative regulator of intestinal iron absorption from the diet with its major role being the ultimate regulator of iron homeostasis (37). It also plays an essential role in regulating iron transport through both placental and intestinal barriers. These studies in mice identifying the role of hepcidin also exhibit many of the same features as the anemia of inflammation (38) caused by infection, inflammatory disorders, malignancies, and trauma. The transgenic mice displayed sequestration of iron in the macrophages, iron restricted erythropoiesis, and low hemoglobin concentrations, all characteristics indistinguishable from the anemia of inflammation. These important findings have the potential to treat anemia of inflammation by controlling endogenous hep-

cidin. In addition, mutations in hepcidin have been documented in humans with hemochromatosis, thus confirming hepcidin's role as the master regulator of dietary iron uptake (39). Overall, hepcidin has shed a new light on the importance of genetics in the process of dietary iron metabolism and its subsequent effect on nutritional anemia.

The implications of this greater understanding of factors in the control and prevention of nutritional anemias for public health interventions are still being evaluated but are likely to be important. For example, if populations have high levels of infection they will also have high levels of hepcidin. This may block the uptake of iron present in the diet from fortification and supplementation (40). However, hepcidin has not been shown to effect dietary heme uptake, which lends support to the promotion of animal-source foods in poor diets. It is becoming more apparent that treatment strategies encompass all the health concerns of a population: Nutritional anemia can only be completely addressed if other diseases are concurrently treated.

One of the likely reasons for the apparent failure to reduce the prevalence of anemia is the fact that many programs have been designed with the assumption that the only cause of anemia is iron deficiency. Projections of prevalence derived from the hemoglobin concentration alone do not allow the contribution of iron deficiency in anemia to be estimated, and ignore the role of other causes. In regions of Africa (in particular) where malaria is holoendemic, half of the cases of anemia will be due to malaria rather than nutritional causes (41). Consequently, mortality due to severe malarial anemia in such populations of children is greater than that due to iron deficiency anemia (42).

The main causes of anemia are: dietary iron deficiency; infectious diseases such as malaria, hookworm infections, schistosomiasis,

HIV/AIDS, and tuberculosis as well as other chronic diseases including almost any inflammatory illness which lasts several months or longer, and some malignancies; deficiencies of other key micronutrients including folate, vitamin B_{12}, vitamins C and A, protein, copper, and other minerals; or inherited conditions that affect red blood cells, such as thalassemia; severe acute hemorrhage (e.g., occurring in childbirth), chronic losses (e.g., in peptic ulcer); and trauma (16).

In order to plan effective interventions in combating both iron deficiency and anemia, and properly monitor their impact, better information is needed not only on the iron status of populations, but also on other causes of anemia (43). It is possible, for example, to have functional iron deficiency even when adequate iron stores are present if the normal physiological systems for transporting iron to target tissues are impaired. This occurs most commonly by cytokines released during inflammation caused by infectious diseases (44). Iron supplementation or fortification will have little benefit in such circumstances. Deficiencies in other nutrients such as vitamin A may also cause a functional iron deficiency even when iron stores are adequate (45, 46). Apparent iron sufficiency may also be misleading. For example, supplementation of workers in Indonesia and elsewhere improved work capacity even in those not anemic (47).

One of the main reasons for the lack of information on the causes of anemia is the fact that only hemoglobin or hematocrit tests can be routinely performed in field settings, while more precise, multiple biochemical tests of iron status and other potential deficiencies are usually only conducted in resource adequate countries or under special research or survey conditions. Advances in laboratory methods that allow the determination of causes of anemia at low cost, either in the field or later in a laboratory, without refrigeration of samples (e.g., the use of dried spots of blood or serum), would greatly contribute to the assessment of the causes of anemia in populations and allow interventions to be planned more appropriately.

In the absence of information on the causes of anemia, the proportion of iron deficiency as a cause of nutritional anemia can only be indirectly estimated. For example, the relative proportion of anemia due to iron deficiency increases as the prevalence of anemia increases. Up to a prevalence of iron deficiency anemia of 40%, the prevalence of iron deficiency will be about two or 2.5 times that of anemia (16, 48). In a normal population 2.5% would be expected to be below the WHO cutoffs. Hence, iron deficiency anemia would be considered a public health problem only when the prevalence of low hemoglobin concentration (as defined by WHO) exceeds 5% of the population. The prevalence of iron deficiency anemia in a population is therefore a statistical rather than physiological concept, although it reflects that proportion of the population which has iron deficient erythropoiesis (16).

Anemia risk at different times of the life cycle
Normal hemoglobin distributions vary with age and gender, at the different stages of pregnancy, and with altitude and smoking (49). There is also a genetic influence (50) which may have programmatic implications, such as hemoglobinopathies which may provide up to 90% protection against death due to malaria (51). In the United States, for example, individuals of African extraction have hemoglobin values five to 10 g/L lower than those of European origin. This difference is not related to iron deficiency (52). The correct interpretation of hemoglobin or hematocrit values, therefore, requires the consideration of modulating factors in selecting appropriate cutoff values.

Risk of iron deficiency and anemia varies throughout the life course, with several periods of greater vulnerability. This variation is due to changes in iron stores, level of intake, and needs in relation to growth or iron losses. In general, children aged from six months to five years of age and women of childbearing age, especially during pregnancy, are the most vulnerable groups. Substantial amounts of iron are deposited in the placenta and fetus during pregnancy. Overall, iron balance is increased during pregnancy, when iron absorption is increased and menstruation stops. Pregnant women may still not absorb sufficient additional iron, however, and the risk of iron deficiency increases. While lactation results in loss of iron via breast milk, and iron deficient pregnant women are likely to remain deficient during lactation, lactational amenorrhea more than compensates for iron lost through breast milk (16).

Severe anemia in pregnancy is defined as hemoglobin <70 g/L and requires medical treatment. Very severe anemia is defined as hemoglobin <40 g/L. Very severe anemia in pregnant women is a medical emergency due to the risk of congestive heart failure and greatly increases maternal death rates (16). Criteria for age-related normal hemoglobin and hematocrit levels have been developed and updated (53, 54). Criteria for stages of pregnancy, and adjustment factors for altitude and smoking are also available. For populations of African origin, achieving a similar screening performance (sensitivity and specificity) requires a hemoglobin criterion that is 10 g/L lower (48).

Full term infants are normally born with adequate iron stores in the liver and hematopoietic tissue, because of destruction of fetal red blood cells soon after birth. This leads to deposition of iron in these tissues, especially if the cord is ligated after it stops pulsating, with a cord clamping delay of two minutes increasing the iron stores at six months by 27–47 mg (55). However, infants born to anemic women have a greater risk of being anemic themselves. Breast milk is relatively low in iron, although the iron in breast milk is much better absorbed than that in cows' milk, and iron deficiency (although apparently not ane-

mia) upregulates iron absorption in breastfed infants (56). Iron deficiency commonly develops after six months of age if complementary foods do not provide sufficient absorbable iron, even for exclusively breastfed infants (16).

Iron requirements on a body weight basis are proportional to growth velocity. Accordingly, iron deficiency is most common in infancy, the preschool years and during puberty, as well as in women in their reproductive years (due to the physiological losses of menstruation). Following menarche, adolescent females often do not consume sufficient available iron to offset menstrual losses (a further reason why adolescent pregnancies are to be avoided). As a result, a peak in the prevalence of iron deficiency frequently occurs among females during adolescence. In areas with a high prevalence of hookworm infestation, school-aged children as well as adults can develop significant iron deficiency. Another peak may occur in old age, when diets frequently deteriorate in quality and quantity (16). About one third of the anemia found in older adults is thought to be due to nutritional anemias (iron, folate, B_{12} deficiencies) (57).

Other causes of anemia
The fact that the etiology of anemia is multifactorial has the programmatic implication that different etiologies will need differing interventions since they will not respond in a similar manner to say, any one treatment of a particular nutritional anemia. Distinguishing other anemias, such as anemia of malaria (42, 58), inflammation (previously referred to as anemia of chronic disease) (59), and HIV/AIDS (60), from nutritional anemia remains difficult. Not only does additional iron not increase hematopoiesis in most cases of non-nutritional anemia, it also might be detrimental by enhancing the viral and bacterial infection that led to the anemia in the first place (61). Nevertheless, a review by Gera and Sachdev (62) finds that iron supplementation has no apparent harmful effect on the overall

incidence of infectious illnesses in children (though it slightly increases the risk of developing diarrhea), but probably not on the incidence of malaria (6).

Anemia of inflammation

Anemia of inflammation is a condition of impaired iron utilization where functional iron (hemoglobin) is low but tissue iron (such as in storage) is normal or high. It is characterized by adequate reticuloendothelial iron stores but reduced concentrations of serum iron, transferrin, and total iron binding capacity; normal or raised ferritin; and high erythrocyte sedimentation rate (59). The mechanism behind anemia of inflammation is thought to be a result of blunted erythropoietin response per level of hemoglobin. Anemia of inflammation is seen in a wide range of chronic malignant, autoimmune, leukemic, inflammatory, and infectious disease conditions. These diseases lead to slightly shortened red blood cell life span and an isolation of iron in inflammatory cells (macrophages) that result in a decrease in the amount of iron available to make red blood cells. In the presence of these effects, a low to moderate grade anemia occurs.

Malaria

Plasmodium falciparum malaria causes anemia by the hemolysis of red blood cells and the compounding suppression of erythropoiesis. Data indicate that treating anemia due to malaria with iron and folic acid can cause increased mortality in children in malarious areas if the malaria is not also aggressively treated (7). It has been concluded that in regions with high levels of malaria transmission, malaria control must be primary to the iron status of the child (61, 63). However, micronutrient deficiencies, especially nutritional anemia, also allow the infection to progress more rapidly. Adequate iron status in the individual is required for a robust immune response and it would appear that low dose iron supplementation

for 12 months does not increase the prevalence of malarial infection or density of parasites (6).

There is a need for more disaggregated global figures to define clearly other nutritional anemias besides those caused by iron deficiency, and other nutritional deficiencies in general from those due to thalassemia, infectious disease, dysentery, helminths, and anemia of inflammation. One practical application might be a mapping of the commonest causes which would have a public health utility, especially to countries with the most widespread and severe anemia, as they often also have the most limited resources. Such a mapping would allow such limited resources to be prioritized and allocated effectively (15) by helping to select the most appropriate intervention; For example, iron supplementation will have little impact where the main cause is malaria. A few mapping projects have had some effectiveness in addressing the need to disaggregate global figures of anemia and other conditions that lead to anemia, especially malaria (64–67), but a lack of agreement on terminology and prevalence make them currently less helpful to public health recommendations than might be expected. The need for global maps to be updated and coordinated to reflect current technology has been noted (68). Given that the recent conclusions of the WHO Expert Consultation on prevention and control of iron deficiency in infants and young children in malaria endemic areas effectively gives recommendations that are different for anemic infants and children in malaria "endemic" areas, this defining of endemic areas becomes even more important (61, 63).

HIV

Anemia is a common hematologic complication in human immunodeficiency virus (HIV) infected patients caused by concomitant infections, neoplasms, or drug treatment (60). The causes of HIV related anemia are multifactorial: directly affecting the bone marrow stromal cell or causing cytokine secretion, leading to decreased production of red blood cells and other bone marrow elements; acquisition of chronic parvovirus B_{19} infection leading to decreased red blood cell production; indirect effects due to adverse reaction to medication, opportunistic infections, neoplasms, alterations in the components of normal erythropoiesis; bone marrow function impaired by secondary infections; renal insufficiency leading to erythropoietin production; and other conditions, such as hemolysis and gastrointestinal bleeding. Nutritional causes, apart from poor diets, include nutritional abnormalities stemming from anorexia, malabsorption, or metabolic disorders.

Unexplained anemia

Even when taking into account all known causes of anemia, a large proportion of anemia in many high risk populations remains unexplained. This has been found for the older population in the USA (57) and Europe, and the conundrum exists for other groups such as pregnant women in Bangladesh (not a lot of iron deficiency or malaria, but a very high prevalence of anemia). A large proportion of anemia remains following multimicronutrient supplementation in young children and cannot all be attributed to anemia of chronic inflammation. Unexplained anemia is a "diagnosis" of exclusion, and after identifying nutritional anemias, anemia of inflammation, malaria and other infections, and renal disease, there remains a large proportion of unexplained anemia about which little is known. Further analysis of this large and uncharacterized anemic population in both developed and undeveloped countries deserves closer analysis and novel strategies to address this unexplained anemia need to be developed.

ADDRESSING THE PROBLEM

There is general agreement that progress on treating iron deficiency and iron deficiency anemia has been unimpressive (1, 2). There are inadequate data to assess progress, or otherwise, on other nutritional anemias, although anemia associated with HIV has almost certainly increased. The anemia of malaria may have decreased over the last year or so since treated bed nets are now more widely used but this remains to be confirmed as the epidemiology of malaria prevalence changes due to increased resources for prevention and treatment, urbanization, and global climate change (67). More worryingly, based on trends observed over the last 20 years, there is no reason to think anemia or iron deficiency anemia is likely to decrease in the coming decade (19). Why the progress has been so poor is the implicit theme of this chapter; Of equal importance, is how to move ahead. The ways in which iron is delivered, through improved diets, supplementation and different modes of fortification, are addressed in detail by de Pee, Bloem, Moench-Pfanner and Semba in chapter 16 (69). Such strategies in the prevention and control of iron deficiency in children have been recently and succinctly reviewed by Lynch, Stoltzfus and Rawat for WHO (70).

One of the frequent criticisms of anemia programs is that the public health approach is undermined by a clinical or medicalized addressing of the problem (71). Consequently, supplementation with an iron sulphate/folic acid combination has become the norm (although the currently recommended daily dose of 120 mg of iron for pregnant women is likely to be unnecessarily high). Questions about the wisdom of including folic acid supplementation in malaria endemic areas are currently being raised since they interfere with antimalarials (58). The identified problems with antenatal formulations have been poor compliance (for a variety of reasons), poor availability and logistics, as well as inadequate programmatic support, political commitment, and insufficient service delivery (72). Because the supplements are usually distributed by health systems, if these are dysfunctional or understaffed (73), as they often are in many poor areas in which anemia prevalence is usually highest, then there is an immediate difficulty.

Although young children in developing countries have extremely high rates of anemia and a number of countries have policies on iron supplementation, these are rarely implemented. This is for a variety of reasons including difficulty in the use and transport of iron syrups, concerns with safety, staining of teeth, and so on. In infants and children, folate deficiency is rarely a cause of anemia. Thus, in malaria-endemic areas, folic acid should probably not be included in multimicronutrient formulations since the addition of folic acid makes little sense and may be a disadvantage in malaria-endemic areas using folate antagonist antimalarial drugs.

Screening for programmatic purposes should be considered for anemia prevalence of between 5–20% and in areas of high malaria endemicity (61). Prevalence within this range suggests more appropriate interventions would be those based on dietary modifications, provision of iron fortified foods, targeted iron supplementation, and control of infections. Severe prevalence of anemia (>40%) justifies universal iron supplementation in virtually all settings without screening individuals. When the prevalence of iron deficiency anemia reaches the 20–30% level in the age-gender group under evaluation, it is likely to be more effective, and possibly more efficient, to provide universal supplementation to that entire group rather than to screen for individual case management purposes. A decision analysis using the US national survey data reached a similar conclusion (74). Anemia response to treatment for malaria must be considered, along with treatment of hookworm, in areas with a known incidence of these conditions (16, 61). In spite of the reservations of the WHO Expert Consultation, it does seem likely that low dose iron supplementation does not increase the prevalence of malaria infection or parasite density (6). It also seems likely that the iron in multimicronutrient home fortifica-

tion formulations will not increase morbidity, but there is insufficient current evidence to be absolutely sure of this. In the meantime, the Report of the WHO Expert Consultation recommendations confirm that because "iron deficiency has adverse effects on child health and development... provision of additional iron to infants and young children who are iron deficient should be a public health priority." (61). Several reports and reviews emphasize the importance of adequate iron stores in the development of infants and young children (75, 76). The same necessity to avoid iron deficiency and nutritional anemia applies also to women of reproductive age, preferably before they become pregnant.

There have been sporadic attempts, through social marketing, to have poor clients buy iron/folic acid supplements. These have rarely been sustainable, although there are some promising current experiences in several Asian countries, for example, Cambodia, the Philippines and Vietnam (77). It is, however, unlikely to be a useful approach for the very poorest and most marginalized, where supplementation remains the option of choice (e.g., in Lao PDR). Iron fortification has been an important contributor to improved iron status and, most likely, B vitamins in industrialized countries (78) and, probably, Latin America (79) although the chemical and physical form of iron used in national fortification programs has been questioned as to efficacy (41). As has recently been noted with magnesium sulphate (a cheap drug for use in preeclampsia) "even when low cost, effective treatments exist, drug availability for many common health problems remains poor in many settings, limiting progress towards achieving the millennium development goals." (80). Add to this the apparent lack of conviction in health workers regarding the usefulness of the intervention, and other barriers such as unaffordable primary user fees, distance from health system clinics, and the not infrequent abusive treatment by healthcare providers (81–83). In fact, some health workers when questioned thought that iron supplements might actually be harmful by increasing the amount of blood and size of fetus, with the attendant risks in marginalized areas distant from obstetric care (personal observation in Indonesia and Zambia, Darnton-Hill 1997).

Public and private sector in the prevention of anemia

Chief among the constraints in the fight against anemia and other micronutrient deficiencies is the limited willingness of governments (and donors) to invest sufficiently in order to improve diets and reduce social inequities. This is because such action requires large, long term investments to improve the supply, distribution, and consumption of animal and vegetable foods, and needs, especially to target those who are in greatest need. Similarly, health systems in the countries most affected are seriously under resourced (73). These factors involve not only problems of access and related cost, since the highest undernutrition rates are usually found among those in remote rural areas who are more difficult to reach, but also because those living in remote rural communities are usually peripheral to the concerns of the urban political class. It is therefore important to keep the government's responsibility to provide for the good health and nutritional status of its people on the national planning agenda, and to emphasize that a nation's development and economy strongly depend upon maximizing the potential of its population. It is clear, however, that this is a complex task which requires various parts of society to collaborate in order to succeed. Important partners besides national government include local governments, the private food and health sectors, the media, consumers' associations, and community organizations. The benefits to national economic development of improving the population's nutritional status, especially micronutrient status, are now well established (84, 85).

The role that the food and health industries can play in improving the nutritional status of a population is important for all the key strategies, from efforts to improve the supply, distribution, and consumption of animal and vegetable food, to fortification and supplementation. Reduction in rates of anemia and other micronutrient deficiencies are more likely to be achieved through a combination of the three key approaches of dietary improvement, supplementation and fortification, while also aiming to reduce social inequities (given that nutritional anemias are most often a consequence of poverty). Fortification can offer a partial solution in the medium and long term, but this requires: wheat or other food producers to work with the pharmaceutical companies in producing micronutrient mixes; consumers and the public health community to put pressure on government to adopt legislation and regulations on voluntary or mandatory fortification of foods; and effective communication of the importance of this approach through the media and schools in order for people to know that they should demand it. There is a great deal of attention currently focused on expanding fortification to developing and transitional economies (14, 41, 86, 87). This seems likely to be the most cost-effective approach (24, 88).

Likewise, supplementation programs should be seen as an opportunity also to promote improved diets, since supplementation is a perhaps less sustainable means of helping address deficiencies due to inadequate food intake and/or other factors. In comparing four weekly iron and folic acid supplementation programs in Cambodia, for example, the most successful one included (in addition to weekly iron and folic acid supplements), vitamin A capsules and deworming tablets taken every six months; the program attempted also to address water quality and sanitation problems, and the fact that children often go to school without breakfast (77).

In many developing countries, the private health and nongovernmental sectors may have multiple advantages in delivering health care interventions such as micronutrient supplementation over poorly resourced government services. Such advantages include the existence of better functioning facilities – (and in some places, the only clinics available); A better image, including among the poor, and the (often undeserved) reputation for providing better health care; A drugs and supplements distribution network and the interest in ensuring it functions well; the ability to advertise their products and services. Nevertheless, governments must still be held responsible for the wellbeing of the very poorest whom the World Bank, amongst others, has identified as being at particular disadvantage in an increasingly globalized world (89).

In the Philippines the involvement of the pharmaceutical company producing the new weekly iron and folic acid supplements meant a comprehensive and well managed approach to social marketing, assessing changes in people's perceptions of anemia and of the new supplements, monitoring sales, understanding problems with distribution of the new product and how they could be corrected, and eventually a national launch of the product, with a marketing strategy that was reassessed and corrected after time. The government health services, on the other hand, have a large network of experienced staff in regular contact with their public and the opportunity to develop complementary strategies with other government and nongovernment structures, such as schools, workplaces, and municipalities. The dialogue between the health ministries and the food industry now taking place in many countries also offers the opportunity to integrate the prevention of chronic diseases by limiting the consumption of foods high in fat, sugar, and salt, with the prevention of micronutrient deficiencies through the promotion of diets rich in fruits and vegetables, and fortification.

Countries where government and mass organizations both work closely with communities offer a great opportunity for synergistic approaches to supplementation. A good example in Asia is Vietnam, where the collaboration of the Women's Union with the government health services permits a combination of the sales of weekly iron and folic acid supplements to non-pregnant women and the distribution of the same kind of supplements (with a higher dose of iron), at no cost, through the health services when pregnancy starts (90). Half the profit of the sales goes to a revolving fund, one quarter to the woman selling the supplements, and the rest to social marketing activities to further promote sales. This integration of agencies with different functions can achieve the level of investment and continuity that is essential for a successful lifecycle approach in the prevention of anemia. Particularly important is the role of schools, especially where school attendance is still high in the adolescent years. Teachers can discuss anemia with students, explain causes, consequences and how it can be effectively prevented through diet and intermittent supplementation. They can also supervise the intake of supplements until the habit of taking them is well established. Starting weekly supplements from the time of menstruation helps to establish a clear link between blood loss and increased iron needs.

For women of reproductive age and schoolchildren a weekly dose of iron and folic acid, possibly combined with vitamin A and other nutrients for which there is evidence of widespread deficiency, can be a good way of providing additional iron and selected other micronutrients in doses known to be sufficient to maintain satisfactory concentrations of nutrients in the blood and red blood cells and produce positive outcomes, while avoiding excessive intake (77, 91, 92). The evidence of the effectiveness and feasibility of this approach is presently being reviewed for a WHO consultation. Projects that have aimed for long-term supplementation (one year or longer) have achieved reductions in anemia rates in nonpregnant women often greater than 50%, in millions of school age children and adolescents, in Cambodia (93), India (94), and Malaysia (95), as well as in nonpregnant and pregnant women of reproductive age in Vietnam (96). Of the Vietnamese women who took the weekly supplements for six months before conception and continued during pregnancy with a double dose of iron, no woman had iron deficiency anemia or iron deficiency in the first and second trimester, when anemia is associated with low birth weight and preterm delivery. The doses used in these projects varied from 60 to 120 mg of iron per week (in most cases as ferrous sulphate) and from 0.5 to 3.5 mg of folic acid per week.

The other group at high risk of anemia that has been largely neglected by prevention programs is that of infants and young children. The challenge here is to achieve diets that are adequate in nutrients and energy, considering the limitations imposed by multiple factors such as the small size of the stomach of children of this age, and the higher cost and more limited availability of foods that are rich in micronutrients and protein. Solutions here include the adoption of models of food combinations for complementary feeding of infants and young children, which aim to optimize diets, while considering the various limiting factors (such as nutrient and energy requirements, types of food available, their nutrient density, their cost and affordability by the families whose children are at high risk of undernutrition) (97). In adults, as noted, iron homeostasis is primarily controlled through regulatory changes in iron absorption; However there is relatively less understanding of mechanisms that regulate iron absorption in infants (98).

The use of home based fortification, with the use of micronutrient powders that are colorless, odorless, and tasteless, and can be mixed in with homemade gruel, (the "Sprinkles" described by Zlotkin and Tondeur in this volume) and dispersible multimicronutrient tablets as proposed by Gross (99), can be an effective additional measure to supplement diets during the critical period when requirement of iron and other micronutrients are particularly high. There is evidence that six months of supplementation at the doses used by Zlotkin and colleagues in various countries, with a frequency of a few doses per week (the optimal frequency differed in different studies), may provide sufficient additional micronutrients to compensate for dietary deficiencies that are difficult to remedy through dietary changes in the first two years of life. The efficacy of these multimicronutrient powders has been well established and increasing experience with effectiveness is now being documented (99, 100), including in emergencies (69).

It has been established that even in industrial countries iron balance can be maintained in pregnancy only when there are adequate iron stores at the start of pregnancy (88), although the need for prophylactic iron during pregnancy in women who are iron replete and not anemic, remains uncertain (101). There is strong evidence of an association between maternal hemoglobin concentration in the first part of pregnancy and birth weight, as well as between maternal hemoglobin concentration and preterm birth (102). Severe maternal anemia (<70 g/L) has been shown to be associated with birth weights 200–400 g lower than in women with higher (>100 g/L) hemoglobin values (16). The problem is that, in most countries, pregnant women receive supplementation only during pregnancy, and this starts, in most cases, in the second trimester, or even later. This has led to the introduction of the concept of preventive supplementation with iron and folic acid, and more recently, to trials with iron, folic acid, and other micronutrients, starting before pregnancy which aims to ensure that women are not anemic and have good iron and folate status by the time pregnancy begins (71).

The role of diet based interventions in addressing nutritional anemia has not been clearly elucidated, especially in the areas of adequacy of breastfeeding in anemic women, premature infants, and other possible circumstances. There is some interesting work, for example, from the Pune Maternal Nutrition study where the intake of micronutrient rich foods in rural Indian mothers was found to be positively associated with the size of their babies at birth (103). The most important role that dietary based approaches, including fortified foods and fortified complementary foods, have in combating nutritional anemia may well be in supplying other micronutrients related to anemia (104). Vitamin A and cobalamin both play a critical role in the cause of nutritional anemia. For example, women who are strict vegetarians have been shown to have children born with cobalamin deficiency and cobalamin deficiencies lead to anemia. The propensity of infants born to mothers with low cobalamin intake to become deficient suggests that cobalamin status during infancy is critically dependent on fetal cobalamin accumulation and, thereby, maternal cobalamin status in pregnancy (105). Vitamin A deficiency is also one of many factors that contribute to anemia by negatively influencing hemoglobin metabolism (see West 2007 in this volume). Since vitamin A has a global influence on the body's metabolism, it is not surprising that there are many potential mechanisms by which a deficiency could cause anemia. Three general categories of mechanism have been identified: modulation of erythropoiesis; modulation of immunity to infectious diseases and anemia of infection; and modulation of iron metabolism (45).

Limited availability, accessibility and intake of animal source foods at the household level, and lack of knowledge about their value in the diet and role in health, contribute to poor diet quality. Poor diet quality has a profound impact on the spectrum of necessary micronutrients that play a helpful role in the movement of iron through the body. Animal source foods have the potential to be a sustainable food based approach to micronutrient deficiencies, are energy dense and offer an excellent source of high quality protein (14). While fortification and use of supplements play an important role in preventing and combating micronutrient deficiencies, micronutrient deficiencies are often multiple and coupled with macronutrient deficiencies due to inadequate quantities of food and to inaccessibility, which supplements or fortification will not address. There is a higher risk of inadequate intakes of vitamin B_{12}, riboflavin, vitamin A, and bioavailable iron and zinc in a diet consisting of plant based foods where animal source foods are low (106). Thus, inclusion of animal source foods, even in modest amounts in the diet together with plant based foods, has the potential to handle multiple deficiencies (107). Poverty and lack of availability and accessibility are the main reasons for the minimal amounts or absence of meat and other animal foods in the diet. In addition, there are potential economic benefits associated with animal ownership in poor communities (14).

Historically, food fortification programs were designed to replace micronutrients in processed foods, to introduce micronutrients in substitute foods, or to correct deficiencies in populations (87). There have been numerous successes and failures in fortifying foods with iron. These depend on many factors, especially the form of the iron used (which has been not infrequently inappropriate), and these experiences have guided the most recent and successful iron fortification programs. (41). However, commercially fortified foods are not always available or affordable to those most at risk, so other delivery mechanisms such as multimicronutrients (99, 100) that act as fortificants added to the meal, are also necessary. Fortifying flour, usually with iron and B vitamins, sometimes with zinc and occasionally vitamin A, is, as an approach to improving health, extremely cost-effective (86) but its success depends greatly upon being carried out properly (41, 108). Estimates by the Flour Fortification Initiative (FFI) suggest that fortifying flour with iron has the potential to increase national IQ by 5%, increase national GDP by 2%, and eliminate 60,000 deaths in pregnant women every year (86). Fortifying with folic acid can also significantly reduce the 200,000 cases of neural tube defects such as spina bifida found annually in newborn babies, and so represents the main reason for adding folic acid to iron fortification programs.

Targeted fortification has been an important tool in industrialized countries with the addition of micronutrients to foods consumed by specific groups of the population, such as fortified infant formulas, infant cereals, and foods as a part of social welfare programs (109). WHO/UNICEF/INACG guidelines state that children aged six to 24 months should be supplemented with 2 mg of iron per kg of body weight to meet the RDA of 8 mg (15). Getting these levels into complementary foods is a challenge, since safety concerns must also be addressed. Where fortified complementary cereals are not available, are too costly for most families, or are unacceptable, in-home fortification may be an effective alternative. However, this still may need to be subsidized.

As noted above, one of the under utilized mechanisms to prevent and control nutritional anemias is the use of sociopolitical measures to reduce inequities. Nutritional anemias, especially those related to iron (but arguably all of them), are conditions of poverty. This is largely because diets of those living in poverty are low in available iron and in foods of animal origin, combined with inhibiting factors such as phytates, fiber, high intakes of tea in some cultures and so on (107). In addition, there are high rates of disease, and poor access to treatment and care. A further factor is that micronutrient deficiencies affect women and children more, even if intrahousehold distribution does not generally discriminate against girls (apart from in South Asia where it has been documented, and where it is likely to be a factor in the higher rates of anemia in these populations (10)).

SOME LESSONS LEARNED AND THE WAY FORWARD

One purpose of this chapter is to ask why so little progress has been made, especially with iron deficiency anemia, and to suggest ways forward by looking at the lessons learned. One way of doing this might be to consider and address identified constraints and facilitating factors. These can be broadly grouped as sociocultural factors (poverty, gender discrimination); delivery factors (targeting, supplementation, fortification, and food based approaches); systems (health systems, private sector marketing, logistics); and the end user (accessibility, compliance).

In view of the very limited success of iron/folic acid supplementation given to pregnant women via antenatal clinics in the past 30 years, it is important to adopt alternative approaches to the prevention of anemia. These should begin before pregnancy, ideally in adolescence. Iron supplementation is traditionally seen as therapeutic and is taken on doctor's prescription, rather than as a preventive supplement available from nonmedical providers. Other factors, such as confusing messages, are described in a review of supplementation experiences by Yip (110) and in chapter 16 (69). Consumers, particularly women of reproductive age, and the medical profession need to see nutritional anemia as a potential problem throughout much of life. It therefore needs to be addressed by, for example, fortification or weekly iron and other micronutrient supplement consumption as part of a normal routine to avoid risking the ill effects of iron deficiency and anemia. The effectiveness studies described earlier demonstrate how, in three Asian countries, a mindset change in women of reproductive age is feasible when social marketing and community mobilization accompany affordable supplements which are available from local providers (77). The same group has described the lessons learned with regard to what makes supplementation programs successful, including improved logistics, better compliance, and the involvement of multiple stakeholders. Nevertheless, Yip (110), in the review of iron supplementation country-level experience, emphasizes the need to consider iron supplementation as just one part of a comprehensive strategy to prevent iron deficiency.

Integrated community approaches combining iron and folic acid supplementation with other interventions such as mass deworming, health education, improved water and sanitation, as well as with other micronutrients such as vitamin A or multiple micronutrients (where these are known to be lacking), are likely to lead to considerably greater success, especially where there are multiple causes of anemia. A similar rationale for including other micronutrients (13) is stimulating a great deal of work on the impact of antenatal and even prenatal, supplementation with multimicronutrients. While reducing micronutrient deficiencies and nutritional anemia, it is likely that early multimicronutrient supplementation has a positive effect on reducing the incidence of low birth weight (111). The cost of preventive supplementation with weekly iron and folic acid has been estimated to be as low as $1 per targeted woman per year, for example, in India (94) and Vietnam (90); A very small price for reducing the prevalence of anemia and neural tube defects by half, and one that governments and individuals have been willing to pay. The cost-effectiveness of iron fortification, depending on accessibility, is thought to be even higher (24, 88). Either way, a comprehensive, multiple intervention approach is considered most likely to be necessary for sustainable success.

Perhaps the most important step in moving forwards is to rethink a couple of positions and secure widespread acceptance and clarity for them. If the impact which can be achieved is clear, then funding is likely to follow. First and most important of these is to be clear about what is causing the nutritional anemia in question. If 50% of the anemia in children is due to malaria,

then treating with iron supplementation will not help, and in fact may have a negative impact (7). However, if an integrated approach is taken by treating the malaria, associated infections, and iron then survival is likely to be higher (7). Likewise if other limited micronutrients, for example, folate, vitamin A, etc. are a partial cause of the anemia, then unless these are treated the anemia is unlikely to respond. This suggests a role for multimicronutrient supplements that have proven efficacy (12, 100, 111) and have increasing promise of effectiveness, especially in emergencies (112). The key issue for policy, as noted by Alderman and Horton in chapter three, is not that policy makers have been unaware of the costs of deficiency, but rather that there are difficulties in finding cost-effective interventions which reduce iron deficiency.

Compliance is an issue in many settings, especially when the supplements are of poor quality and taste. They are also likely to cause stomach upset and blackened stools (melena) although various behaviors can reduce this, for example, by taking the tablets with food (72). There is evidence that improving the taste and appearance of the supplement/tablets will improve compliance but this then has cost issues (69, 77) which may not be sustainable for poorly resourced health clinics. Galloway and McGuire (72) have argued that blaming compliance is a form of victim blaming and that logistical problems are a greater constraint. Mason et al. (2) have pointed out that the number of iron/folic acid tablets handled by UNICEF is entirely inadequate to the size of the problem (reflecting lack of demand in countries, or, more optimistically, countries budgeting for their own supplies). Nevertheless the flow of supplements to rural centers is poor, and investigations have shown problems at all levels in ordering and supply, and then distribution to the individual. Consequently, there needs to be a realistic assessment of both accessibility and availability of iron and other relevant micronutrients, whether they are being delivered as supplements, by fortification, or other channels, including poverty reduction programs. This may include assessment of the viability of health systems, feasibility of social marketing and the reach of health education.

CONCLUSION

The WHO Expert Consultation on the prevention and control of iron deficiency in infants and young children in malaria endemic areas concluded that adequate iron status is necessary for the optimal growth and development of young children and should be ensured. Equally, adequate iron status is necessary for the health and even survival of pregnant women, as well as for the prevalence of adequate birth weight infants, thus ensuring all the positive longer term health and development outcomes that follow. The Copenhagen Consensus has attributed high cost-effectiveness to iron and other micronutrient programs (23). There is now considerable evidence that not addressing iron deficiency and other anemias will cost countries up to 2% of their GNP, and impair the intellectual development of their children and future productivity. The international and national health partners need to get firmly behind these statements, so that consistent measures and approaches reinforce one another. Iron deficiency and other anemias must be repositioned as an economic intervention that will increase the economic wellbeing of poor countries and reduce inequities. As has been noted by a WHO background chapter "… the evidence strongly suggests that under a 'business as usual' scenario, the prevalence of iron deficiency anemia will not decrease over the next decade (19)."

There is virtually a complete consensus that any programs designed to prevent and control the nutritional anemias must be multipronged and include improved social conditions by poverty alleviation measures, as well as the more direct measures of fortification, supplementation, and improved health care. Poverty and inequity reduction programs, while not frequently thought of as an anemia prevention activity, are in fact likely to be essential since iron deficiency anemia and other anemias differentially affect the poor, especially women and children. Clearly, countries should not wait until all aspects of a comprehensive program are in place, as each measure will individually have an impact. They must, however, be prepared for a more limited impact until all intervention modalities are addressed. Innovative interventions such as multimicronutrients, weekly dosing, "slow release" supplements, and improved forms of iron with high bioavailability should all be brought to a quick consensus and, where the evidence base supports it, into mainstream programs.

There is a degree of inertia in continuing programs that have been shown to be relatively ineffective. These should be modified appropriately since they are diverting resources and produce a sense of pessimism. Industrialized countries have been able largely to solve the problem, although pockets of disadvantaged groups remain. The integrated approaches used in these countries should be widely implemented and appropriately tailored to a country's concerns and resources. Donor funds should be specifically addressed to nutritional interventions, including preventing and controlling nutritional anemias. Private sector interventions need to be encouraged where they reach a large portion of the populations, fortification needs to become self-sustaining where there are adequate markets, and government spending and investment in the health (and nutrition) sectors, should increase. For example, African governments should allocate at least 15% of government budgets to the public health sectors, as agreed in Abuja in 2001. At the very least there should be mandatory iron and folic acid (usually with other B vitamins) fortification of some widely consumed foods in all countries; supplementation or home fortification for selected population groups, particularly pregnant and lactating women (whose needs cannot be met by fortification), weaning age children, and geographically vulnerable or ethnically disadvantaged groups; and broader poverty alleviation programs. It also appears that deworming should be given a higher priority.

There are encouraging signs: increased consensus on ways to move forward; increased funding since it has been recognized that most of the millennium development goals will not be reached without addressing many of the factors that also result in anemia such as gender parity, hunger and undernutrition, malaria and HIV, and education. As many larger countries experience economic growth, the reduction of iron deficiency and other nutritional anemias will become both an engine and outcome of this improved position. In other struggling countries, public health interventions that affect the life cycle of a child and his or her potential, such as adequate micronutrient status and health, need to be actively fostered as a cost-effective investment in the future.

REFERENCES

1.   Adamson P. MI/UNICEF. Vitamins & mineral deficiency: a global progress report. Ottawa: Micronutrient Initiative, 2003.

2.   Mason J, Deitchler M, Mathys E, Winichagoon P, Tuazon MA. Lessons from successful micronutrient programs. Part 3: Program impact. Food and Nutrition Bulletin 2004;25:53–78.

3.   Lynch S. Iron Metabolism. In: Kraemer K, Zimmermann MB, eds. Nutritional anemia. Basel: SIGHT AND LIFE Press, 2007.

4.   UNICEF. World Summit for Children. New York: UN, 1990.

5.   McLean E, Cogwell M, Egli I, de Benoist B, Wojdyla D. Nutritional anemia. In: Kraemer K, Zimmermann MB, eds. Nutritional anemia. Basel: SIGHT AND LIFE Press, 2007.

6.   Mebrahtu T, Stoltzfus RJ, Chwaya HM, et al. Low-dose daily iron supplementation for 12 months does not increase the prevalence of malarial infection or density of parasites in young Zanzibari children. J Nutr 2004;134:3037–41.

7.   Sazawal S, Black RE, Ramsan M, et al. Effects of routine prophylactic supplementation with iron and folic acid on admission to hospital and mortality in preschool children in a high malaria transmission setting: community-based, randomised, place-bo-controlled trial. Lancet 2006;367:133–43.

8.   Tielsch JM, Khatry SK, Stoltzfus RJ, et al. Effect of routine prophylactic supplementation with iron and folic acid on preschool child mortality in southern Nepal: community-based, cluster-randomised, place-bo-controlled trial. Lancet 2006;367:144–52.

9.   Smitasiri S, Solon FS. Implementing preventive iron-folic acid supplementation among women of reproductive age in some Western Pacific countries: possibilities and challenges. Nutr Rev 2005;63:S81–6.

10.   Darnton-Hill I, Webb P, Harvey PW, et al. Micronutrient deficiencies and gender: social and economic costs. Am J Clin Nutr 2005;81:1198S–1205S.

11.   Jolly R. Early childhood development: the global challenge. Lancet 2007;369:8–9.

12.   Rivera JA, Hotz C, Gonzalez-Cossio T, Neufeld L, Garcia-Guerra A. The effect of micronutrient deficiencies on child growth: a review of results from community-based supplementation trials. J Nutr. 2003;133:4010S–4020S.

13.   Huffman SL, Baker J, Shumann J, Zehner, ER. The case for promoting multiple vitamin/mineral supplements for women of reproductive age in developing countries. Linkages Project. Washington, DC: Academy for Educational Development, 1998.

14.   Allen LH. Interventions for micronutrient defi-

ciency control in developing countries: past, present and future. J Nutr 2003;133:3875S–3878S.

15. Stoltzfus R, Dreyfus ML. Guidelines for the use of iron supplements to prevent and treat iron deficiency anemia. In: INACG/WHO/UNICEF, Washington, DC: ILSI Press, 1998.

16. WHO/UNICEF/UNU. Iron deficiency anaemia: assessment, prevention, and control. A guide for programme managers. Geneva: World Health Organization, 2001.

17. Toteja GS, Singh P, Dhillon BS, et al. Prevalence of anemia among pregnant women and adolescent girls in 16 districts of India. Food Nutr Bull 2006;27:311–5.

18. Murray CJ, Lopez AD. Global comparative assessments in the health sector. In: Geneva WHO, ed., 1994.

19. Stoltzfus R, Mullany L, Black RE. Iron deficiency anemia. In: Ezzati M, Rodgers A, Murray CJL ed. Comparative quantification of health risks: The global and regional burden of disease attributable to selected major risk factors. Geneva: WHO, 2004:163–209.

20. Ross JS, Horton S. Economic consequences of iron deficiency. Ottawa: Micronutrient Initiative, 1998.

21. Levin HM, Pollitt E, Galloway R, McGuire J. Micronutrient deficiency disorders. Washington, DC: World Bank, 1993.

22. Behrman JR, Rosenzweig MR. The Returns to Increasing Body Weight. Penn Institute for Economic Research, 2001.

23. Copenhagen Consensus. How to spend $50 million to make the World a better place. Copenhagen Consensus Center, 2004.

24. Alderman H, Horton S. The economics of addressing nutritional anemia. In: Kraemer K, Zimmermann MB, eds. Nutritional anemia. Basel: SIGHT AND LIFE Press, 2007.

25. Baltussen R, Knai C, Sharan M. Iron fortification and iron supplementation are cost-effective interventions to reduce iron deficiency in four subregions of the world. J Nutr 2004;134:2678–84.

26. Bishai D, Nalubola PR. The history of food fortification in the United States: its relevance for current fortification efforts in developing countries.

Economic Development and Cultural Change, 2002:37–53.

27. Lombard M, Chua E, O'Toole P. Regulation of intestinal non-haem iron absorption. Gut 1997;40:435–9.

28. Shayeghi M, Latunde-Dada GO, Oakhill JS, et al. Identification of an intestinal heme transporter. Cell 2005;122:789–801.

29. Lynch SR, Skikne BS, Cook JD. Food iron absorption in idiopathic hemochromatosis. Blood 1989;74:2187–93.

30. Andrews NC. Understanding heme transport. N Engl J Med 2005;353:2508–9.

31. Fleming RE, Bacon BR. Orchestration of iron homeostasis. N Engl J Med 2005;352:1741–4.

32. Donovan A, Andrews NC. The molecular regulation of iron metabolism. Hematol J 2004;5:373–80.

33. Hahn PF, Bale WF, Ross JF, Balfour WM, Whipple GH. Radioactive iron absorption by gastrointestinal tract: influence of anemia, anoxia, and antecedent feeding distribution in growing dogs. Journal of Experimental Medicine, 1943:169–188.

34. Finch C. Regulators of iron balance in humans. Blood 1994;84:1697–702.

35. Leong WI, Lonnerdal B. Hepcidin, the recently identified peptide that appears to regulate iron absorption. J Nutr 2004;134:1–4.

36. Pigeon C, Ilyin G, Courselaud B, et al. A new mouse liver-specific gene, encoding a protein homologous to human antimicrobial peptide hepcidin, is overexpressed during iron overload. J Biol Chem 2001;276:7811–9.

37. Nicolas G, Bennoun M, Porteu A, et al. Severe iron deficiency anemia in transgenic mice expressing liver hepcidin. Proc Natl Acad Sci U S A 2002;99:4596–601.

38. Roy CN, Mak HH, Akpan I, Losyev G, Zurakowski D, Andrews NC. Hepcidin antimicrobial peptide transgenic mice exhibit features of the anemia of inflammation. Blood 2007.

39. Roetto A, Papanikolaou G, Politou M, et al. Mutant antimicrobial peptide hepcidin is associated with severe juvenile hemochromatosis. Nat Genet 2003;33:21–2.

40. Hurrell R, Egli I. Bioavailability of iron forms and enhancers. In: Kraemer K, Zimmermann MB, eds. Nutritional anemia. Basel: SIGHT AND LIFE Press, 2007.

41. WHO/FAO. Guidelines on food fortification with micronutrients for the control of micronutrient malnutrition. Geneva: World Health Organization, 2006.

42. Brabin B, Prinsen-Geerligs P, Verhoeff F, Kazembe P. Anaemia prevention for reduction of mortality in mothers and children. Trans R Soc Trop Med Hyg 2003;97:36–8.

43. WHO/CDC. Assessing the iron status of populations. Joint World Health Organization/Centers for Disease Control and Prevention technical consultation on the assessment of iron status at the population level. Geneva: WHO/CDC, 2004.

44. Andrews NC. Anemia of inflammation: the cytokine-hepcidin link. J Clin Invest 2004;113:1251–3.

45. Semba RD, Bloem MW. The anemia of vitamin A deficiency: epidemiology and pathogenesis. Eur J Clin Nutr 2002;56:271–81.

46. West KP, Sommer A. Vitamin A. In: Kraemer K, Zimmermann MB, eds. Nutritional anemia. Basel: SIGHT AND LIFE Press, 2007.

47. Haas JD, Brownlie T 4th. Iron deficiency and reduced work capacity: a critical review of the research to determine a causal relationship. J Nutr 2001;131:676S–688S; discussion 688S–690S.

48. Yip R, Stoltzfus R, Simmons WK. Assessment of the prevalence and the nature of iron deficiency for populations: the utility of comparing hemoglobin distributions. In: Hallberg LA, ed. Iron nutrition in health and disease: John Libbey and Company Ltd, 1996:31–48.

49. Chanarin I, Rothman D. Further observations on the relation between iron and folate status in pregnancy. Br Med J 1971;2:81–4.

50. de Carvalho Rondo PH, Rodrigues PR, Curti ML. Haemoglobin variants and anaemia among preschool/school children in north-east Brazil. Trans R Soc Trop Med Hyg 2005;99:844–7.

51. Pasvol G. Does alpha+-thalassaemia protect against malaria? PLoS Med 2006;3:e235.

52. Perry GS, Byers T, Yip R, Margen S. Iron nutrition does not account for the hemoglobin differences between blacks and whites. J Nutr 1992;122:1417–24.

53. Summary of a report on assessment of the iron nutritional status of the United States population. Expert Scientific Working Group. Am J Clin Nutr 1985;42:1318–30.

54. WHO/UNICEF/UNU. Iron deficiency anaemia: assessment, prevention and control. A guide for programme managers. Geneva: World Health Organisation, 2001.

55. Chaparro CM, Neufeld LM, Tena Alavez G, Eguia-Liz Cedillo R, Dewey KG. Effect of timing of umbilical cord clamping on iron status in Mexican infants: a randomised controlled trial. Lancet 2006;367:1997–2004.

56. Hicks PD, Zavaleta N, Chen Z, Abrams SA, Lonnerdal B. Iron deficiency, but not anemia, upregulates iron absorption in breast-fed peruvian infants. J Nutr 2006;136:2435–8.

57. Guralnik JM, Eisenstaedt RS, Ferrucci L, Klein HG, Woodman RC. Prevalence of anemia in persons 65 years and older in the United States: evidence for a high rate of unexplained anemia. Blood 2004;104:2263–8.

58. English M, Snow RW. Iron and folic acid supplementation and malaria risk. Lancet 2006;367:90–1.

59. Fitzsimons EJ, Brock JH. The anaemia of chronic disease. BMJ 2001;322:811–2.

60. Moore RD. Human immunodeficiency virus infection, anemia, and survival. Clin Infect Dis 1999;29:44–9.

61. WHO. Conclusions of the Expert Consultation on prevention and control of iron deficiency in infants and young children in malaria endemic areas. Lyon: UNESCO Centre for Trace Elements, 2006:1–19.

62. Gera T, Sachdev HP. Effect of iron supplementation on incidence of infectious illness in children: systematic review. BMJ 2002;325:1142.

63. UNICEF/WHO. Meeting on the prevention and control of iron deficiency in infants and young children: programmatic aspects. UNICEF(ESARO). Nairobi: UNICEF (ESARO), 2006.

64. WHO Global Health Atlas. Internet: http://globalatlas.who.int.

65. MARA/ARMA (Mapping Malaria Risk in Africa). http://www.mara.org.za.

66. Malaria Atlas Project. Internet: http://www.map.ox.ac.uk/.

67. Hay SI, Snow RW. The Malaria Atlas Project: Developing Global Maps of Malaria Risk. PLoS Med 2006;3:e473.

68. Hay SI, Guerra CA, Tatem AJ, Noor AM, Snow RW. The global distribution and population at risk of malaria: past, present, and future. Lancet Infect Dis 2004;4:327–36.

69. de Pee S, Bloem M, Moench-Pfanner R, Semba R. Strategies to fight nutritional anemia. In: Kraemer K, Zimmermann MB, eds. Nutritional anemia. Basel: SIGHT AND LIFE Press, 2007.

70. Lynch S, Stoltzfus R, Rawat. Critical review of strategies to prevent and control iron deficiencies in children. Background paper for the WHO Expert Consultation on prevention and control of iron deficiency in infants and young children in malaria endemic areas. WHO/UNESCO Centre for Trace Elements, 2006:1–19.

71. Viteri FE, Berger J. Importance of pre-pregnancy and pregnancy iron status: can long-term weekly preventive iron and folic acid supplementation achieve desirable and safe status? Nutr Rev 2005;63:65S–76S.

72. Galloway R, McGuire J. Determinants of compliance with iron supplementation: supplies, side effects, or psychology? Soc Sci Med 1994;39:381–90.

73. UN Millennium project. Who's got the power? Transforming health systems for women and children. Task Force on Child Health and Maternal Health. New York: UN, 2005.

74. Binkin NJ Yip R. When is anemia screening of value in detecting iron deficiency? In: Hercberg S, Galan P, Dupin H, eds. Recent knowledge on iron and folate deficiencies in the world. Paris: INSERM, 1990:137–146.

75. Olney DK, Pollitt E, Kariger PK, et al. Combined iron and folic acid supplementation with or without zinc reduces time to walking unassisted among Zanzibari infants 5- to 11-mo old. J Nutr 2006;136:2427–34.

76. Lozoff B, Jimenez E, Smith JB. Double burden of iron deficiency in infancy and low socioeconomic status: a longitudinal analysis of cognitive test scores to age 19 years. Arch Pediatr Adolesc Med 2006;160:1108–13.

77. Cavalli-Sforza T, Berger J, Smitasiri S, Viteri F. Weekly iron-folic acid supplementation of women of reproductive age: impact overview, lessons learned, expansion plans, and contributions toward achievement of the millennium development goals. Nutr Rev 2005;63:S152–8.

78. Bishai D, Nalubola PR. The history of food fortification in the United States: its relevance for current fortification efforts in developing countries. Economic Development and Cultural Change 2002;51:37–53

79. Darnton-Hill I, Mora JO, Weinstein H, Wilbur S, Nalubola PR. Iron and folate fortification in the Americas to prevent and control micronutrient malnutrition: an analysis. Nutr Rev 1999;57:25–31.

80. Sevene E, Lewin S, Mariano A, et al. System and market failures: the unavailability of magnesium sulphate for the treatment of eclampsia and pre-eclampsia in Mozambique and Zimbabwe. BMJ 2005;331:765–9.

81. Gilson L, McIntyre D. Removing user fees for primary care in Africa: the need for careful action. BMJ 2005;331:762–5.

82. Doherty T, Chopra M, Nkonki L, Jackson D, Greiner T. Effect of the HIV epidemic on infant feeding in South Africa: "When they see me coming with the tins they laugh at me". Bull World Health Organ 2006;84:90–6.

83. Brikci N, Philips M. User fees or equity funds in low-income countries. Lancet 2007;369:10–1.

84. Sachs J. Report of the Commission on Macroeconomic and Health. WHO Commission on Macroeconomics and Health. Macroeconomics and health: investing in health for economic development. Geneva: World Health Organization, 2001.

85. Hunt JM. The potential impact of reducing global malnutrition on poverty reduction and economic development Asia Pac J Clin Nutr 2005;14:10–38.

86. FFI. The Flour Fortification Initiative. A pub-

lic-private-civic initiative investment in each nation. httpl/www.sph.emory.edu/wheatflour/.

87. Allen LH. New approaches for designing and evaluating food fortification programs. J Nutr 2006;136:1055–8.

88. Bothwell TH. Iron requirements in pregnancy and strategies to meet them. Am J Clin Nutr 2000;72:257S–264S.

89. The World Bank. Equity and development. Washington, DC: The World Bank, 2006.

90. Khan NC, Thanh HT, Berger J, et al. Community mobilization and social marketing to promote weekly iron-folic acid supplementation: a new approach toward controlling anemia among women of reproductive age in Vietnam. Nutr Rev 2005;63:S87–94.

91. Norsworthy B, Skeaff CM, Adank C, Green TJ. Effects of once-a-week or daily folic acid supplementation on red blood cell folate concentrations in women. Eur J Clin Nutr 2004;58:548–54.

92. Martinez-de Villarreal LE, Limon-Benavides C, Valdez-Leal R, Sanchez-Pena MA, Villarreal-Perez JZ. Impact of weekly administration of folic acid on folic acid blood levels. Salud Publica Mex 2001;43:103–7.

93. Longfils P, Heang UK, Soeng H, Sinuon M. Weekly iron and folic acid supplementation as a tool to reduce anemia among primary school children in Cambodia. Nutr Rev 2005;63:S139–45.

94. Dwivedi A, Schultink W. Reducing anaemia among Indian adolescent girls through once-weekly supplementation with iron and folic acid. Standing Committee on Nutrition of the UN System: SCN News. Geneva: World Health Organization, 2006:19–23.

95. Tee ES, Kandiah M, Awin N, et al. School-administered weekly iron-folate supplements improve hemoglobin and ferritin concentrations in Malaysian adolescent girls. Am J Clin Nutr 1999;69:1249–56.

96. Berger J, Thanh HT, Cavalli-Sforza T, et al. Community mobilization and social marketing to promote weekly iron-folic acid supplementation in women of reproductive age in Vietnam: impact on anemia and iron status. Nutr Rev 2005;63:S95–108.

97. Ferguson EL, Darmon N, Fahmida U, Fitriyanti S, Harper TB, Premachandra IM. Design of optimal food-based complementary feeding recommendations and identification of key "problem nutrients" using goal programming. J Nutr 2006;136:2399–404.

98. Kelleher SL. Effects of age and mineral intake on the regulation of iron absorption in infants. J Pediatr 2006;149:S69–73.

99. Allen L, Shrimpton R. The International Research on Infant Supplementation study: implications for programs and further research. J Nutr 2005;135:666S–669S.

100. Zlotkin S, Tondeur MC. Successful approaches-Sprinkles. In: Kraemer K, Zimmermann MB, eds. Nutritional anemia. Basel: SIGHT AND LIFE Press, 2007.

101. Cogswell ME, Parvanta I, Ickes L, Yip R, Brittenham GM. Iron supplementation during pregnancy, anemia, and birth weight: a randomized controlled trial. Am J Clin Nutr 2003;78:773–81.

102. Rasmussen K. Is There a Causal Relationship between Iron Deficiency or Iron-Deficiency Anemia and Weight at Birth, Length of Gestation and Perinatal Mortality? J Nutr 2001;131:590S–601S; discussion 601S–603S.

103. Rao S, Yajnik CS, Kanade A, et al. Intake of micronutrient-rich foods in rural Indian mothers is associated with the size of their babies at birth: Pune Maternal Nutrition Study. J Nutr 2001;131:1217–24.

104. Steiger G. Why nutritional anemia needs a holistic approach. Nutriview 2005;4:9–10.

105. Bjorke Monsen AL, Ueland PM, Vollset SE, et al. Determinants of cobalamin status in newborns. Pediatrics 2001;108:624–30.

106. Murphy SP, Allen LH. Nutritional importance of animal source foods. J Nutr 2003;133:3932S–3935S.

107. Demment MW, Young MM, Sensenig RL. Providing micronutrients through food-based solutions: a key to human and national development. J Nutr 2003;133:3879S–3885S.

108. Dary O. Technical Aspects of Food Fortification. In: Kraemer K, Zimmermann MB, eds. Nutritional anemia. Basel: SIGHT AND LIFE Press, 2007.

109. Dary O, Freire W, Kim S. Iron compounds for food fortification: guidelines for Latin America and the Caribbean 2002. Nutr Rev 2002;60:S50–61.

110. Yip R. Iron supplementation: country level experiences and lessons learned. J Nutr 2002;132:859S–61S.

111. SCN/WHO/UNICEF. Multiple micronutrient supplementation compared to iron/folic acid supplementation among presumably HIV-negative women during pregnancy: An SCN/WHO/UNICEF meeting to review results of randomised controlled trials. Geneva: World Health Organization, 2006.

112. de Pee S, Moench-Pfanner R, Martini E, Zlotkin S, Darnton, Hill I, Bloem M. Home-fortification in emergency response and transition programming: experiences in Aceh and Nias, Indonesia. Food Nutr Bull 2007 (In press).

22

Conclusions and research agenda

Klaus Kraemer[1]   Elisabeth Stoecklin[2]   Jane Badham[3]

[1]SIGHT AND LIFE, Basel, Switzerland
[2]R&D Human Nutrition and Health, DSM Nutritional Products Ltd, Kaiseraugst, Switzerland
[3]JB Consultancy, Health Communication and Strategy Consultants, Johannesburg, South Africa
Contact: klaus.kraemer@sightandlife.org

KLAUS KRAEMER

Klaus obtained his doctorate in nutritional sciences from the University of Giessen, Germany. He is currently Secretary General of SIGHT AND LIFE, a humanitarian initiative of DSM involved with a number of activities to ensure a sustainable and significant improvement in human nutrition, health, and wellbeing. Klaus has over 20 years of research experience in the field of health and safety of vitamins, minerals, carotenoids, and nutraceuticals. He serves on several professional societies dedicated to nutrition, vitamins, and antioxidants, has published many scientific articles, and coedited four books.

ELISABETH STOECKLIN

Elisabeth obtained her MD from the University of Basel, Switzerland, and then spent some time at the University of Stanford in the USA working on pre-clinical and clinical aspects of research with many well-known institutions, universities, and companies in the USA, Germany, and Switzerland. She initially specialized in pathology and immunopathology but has a special interest in molecular biology. She currently works for DSM as Senior Scientist in the R&D Centre for Human Nutrition and Health where she is responsible for investigating the role of vitamins in human nutrition and health with regard to new opportunities and benefits for the future.

JANE BADHAM

Jane is a dietitian with an MSc in Nutrition from North West University, Potchefstroom Campus, South Africa. She is currently the Managing Director of JB Consultancy, a health communication and strategy company that advises the pharmaceutical industry, food industry, humanitarian organizations, and the media. Jane is also the CEO of the 5-a-Day for Better Health TRUST in South Africa that promotes the increased consumption of vegetables and fruit. She serves on the Board of Directors of the International Fruit and Vegetable Alliance (IFAVA) as well as being part of the organizing team of the African Nutrition Leadership Program (ANLP).

INTRODUCTION

The United Nations' goal of reducing by one-third the prevalence of anemia by 2010 is unlikely to be met. Nutritional anemia remains common in many countries of the world and its eradication through effective interventions must be a priority for attention and action. Anemia impairs individual growth and development, as well as family, community, and national socioeconomic development. There has unfortunately been little documented success in addressing the problem at a public health level over the last decades, although there is now a great deal of programmatic experience and a vast and growing amount of scientific data and new information on iron metabolism and the role of other nutrients in the etiology of nutritional anemia. However, much is still unknown and many new areas requiring attention and research continue to emerge.

This final chapter aims to summarize some of the conclusions drawn from the previous chapters in this volume, draw attention to the unchanged magnitude of the problem and its resulting economic implications, and determine the crucial points for going forward in addressing nutritional anemia by specifying critical factors for future research related to micronutrients and identifying key components that ensure that programs and interventions really work.

DIMENSION OF THE PROBLEM

Previously, global estimates on the prevalence of anemia did not include nationally representative data from China, which accounts for ~20% of the world's population. In this volume, new global estimates on anemia prevalence for preschool children and nonpregnant and pregnant women have been released, compiled by the World Health Organization (WHO) for its Vitamin and Mineral Nutrition Information System (VMNIS).

Surveys included in the database assessed anemia by measuring hemoglobin using standard methodology and excluded those that used clinical signs to confirm anemia prevalence. Only representative data from countries were included in the analysis and adjusted for WHO cut-offs (Hb <110 g/L for preschool children and pregnant women and Hb <120 g/L for nonpregnant women). For preschool children and women, national surveys cover a large proportion of the population and the data suggest that the global burden of anemia is high, although the proportion of severe anemia still remains unknown. The analysis suggests that almost 50% of preschool children are affected worldwide, with the highest rates in Africa (64.6%) and Asia (47.7%). This number amounts to almost 300 million children under 5 years of age. The anemia prevalence is 41.8% in pregnant women and 30.2% in nonpregnant women. Globally, 818 million women (pregnant and nonpregnant) and children under 5 years of age are affected by anemia. Individual studies from South Asia point to far higher prevalence numbers in pregnant women and adolescent girls.

Four key messages can be concluded from the analysis:

1. More countries should assess anemia prevalence more precisely at the national level and also determine the degree of severity of anemia.
2. Countries should assess iron deficiency in more detail, as it is uncertain how much anemia is due to iron deficiency and how much is due to other causes. It is important to distinguish between anemia due to nutritional causes and anemia as a result of chronic endemic infections, (e.g., malaria, helminth infections, and HIV/AIDS).
3. Subclinical inflammation may be very common in apparently healthy people, and may lead to misclassification of anemia.

4. More comparative evaluation of the advantages and disadvantages of currently available methods for the measurement of iron status (ferritin, sTfR and indicators of infection/inflammation) is required, in addition to reducing the costs of these analyses while maintaining their accuracy.

Weakness and fatigue have long been associated with iron deficiency anemia only. More recent research however points to functional consequences even before the clinical onset of anemia. Longitudinal studies caution that chronic iron deficiency in infancy permanently retards cognitive, motor, and socioemotional development. This is an especially grave concern as more than 200 million children under 5 years of age, mostly living in South Asia and sub-Saharan Africa, fail to reach their cognitive and socioemotional development potential due to malnutrition, including iron and iodine deficiency and inadequate stimulation. These children are likely to fail at school, miss their income potential, and thus remain in the poverty trap. There is consensus among a broad range of scientists from academia and UN agencies that global and national priority should be given to the prevention of even mild anemia in infants and young children because of the risk of impaired intellectual development. Also of concern is the fact that amongst breastfed infants, only about 50% of their iron requirement during the first 6 months can be obtained from breast milk, indicating a need for early supplementation for all infants.

In the past, the wide-ranging consequences of iron deficiency and anemia have primarily been dealt with as a medical problem, rather than emphasizing the mental and economic consequences. The economic gain from reducing any micronutrient deficiency comes from both cost reduction and from enhanced productivity. This includes reduced mortality, reduced health care costs, reduced morbidity, improved productivity, and intergenerational benefits through improved health. It is clear that anemia at all stages of the life cycle is associated with a significant health burden and has a potentially large negative impact on productivity and hence also income and gross domestic product (GDP) loss; current estimates are as high as $50 billion (US). The total loss per capita due to physical as well as cognitive losses amounts to billions annually and is considerable when compared to the modest costs of decreasing nutritional anemia.

We have derived five key findings from the analysis:

1. Iron interventions in adults have been shown to have productivity impacts of around 5% in light manual labor and as high as 17% in heavy manual labor.
2. It can be inferred that anemia potentially reduces adult earnings (due to its cognitive effects) by 2.5%.
3. Iron fortification is one of the most attractive public health interventions, as seen in the cost per disability-adjusted life year (DALY) saved or in the cost-benefit ratio. The cost per person per year for fortification is in the range of $0.10–1.00 with a cost-benefit ratio of:1:6 (physical benefits to adults) or as high as 1:9 (including estimated cognitive benefits to children).
4. Supplementation costs per person are around $2.00–5.00 but are five times more costly than fortification in DALY terms and it is noted that the results of large-scale programs have to date been disappointing.
5. More research urgently needs to be done to quantify the economic loss of mental retardation due to iron deficiency anemia.

CRITICAL POINTS IN ANEMIA RESEARCH RELATED TO MICRONUTRIENTS

There is no easy solution to overcoming the global scourge of anemia. The etiology of anemia is complex and multifactorial and there appears to be a clear role for multiple micronutrients (vitamins and minerals) in nutritional anemia prevention as well as generally improved nutrition and health. The challenge is to create optimal combinations of micronutrients that will work best together and even synergize each other. No single intervention will revert or prevent anemia in any population. However, there is still limited scientific information about multiple micronutrients in the prevention of nutritional anemia. Moreover, the findings from these clinical studies remain controversial and some need to be interpreted with caution.

Several factors have to be considered when planning future intervention studies with fortified food or supplements in populations with impaired nutritional status and health:

1. Nutritional factors

The impact of the composition of the habitual diet including micro- and macronutrients should be evaluated with priority. A poor quality diet, often due to limited intake of animal source food as well as fruits and vegetables, is one of the main causes of multiple micronutrient deficiencies which do not occur in isolation, but rather concurrently. Furthermore, poor bioavailability of nutrients and diets high in plant-based food containing constituents such as phytates and polyphenols limits the absorption of iron and other trace elements.

2. Health environment and non-nutritional factors

Infectious diseases such as malaria, tuberculosis, HIV/AIDS, parasitic infections, and certain chronic inflammations are other factors that contribute to anemia and impair nutritional and health status. It is therefore important to take the total health environment into account and to control and/or treat any underlying disease. An integrated intervention approach that considers each population group's epidemiological, socioeconomic, and cultural context is required.

3. Target population

The most vulnerable segments of the population are pregnant and lactating women, infants, young children, and adolescent girls. Infancy is the age group in which micronutrient deficiencies start and progress with potentially severe consequences later in life, yet poor nutrition starts in utero. Thus, adequate nutrition and health status should receive high priority during both pregnancy and infancy. The message is clear: a life cycle approach is required, taking the diverse requirements of the different target populations into account.

4. Recommended intake and composition of micronutrients

For efficacy of interventions, the optimal dose and composition of micronutrients is still unknown. The potential risks of interactions have to be taken into account when food fortification or supplementation programs are initiated, especially when directed to population groups with a generally poor nutritional status. The interactions between various micronutrients (e.g., iron, zinc, and other minerals, and antinutritional factors inhibiting iron absorption) appear to be especially important. Different combinations and doses as well as new delivery forms of micronutrients still need to be investigated.

5. Deliveries through the health system

It is also important to take into account existing prevention programs such as high dose vitamin A, iron/folic acid supplementation, and parasitic disease and malaria control. These programs have to be integrated and monitored carefully in new clinical trials.

6. Duration

Long-term outcomes and effectiveness is not yet fully defined with regard to nutrition, health, and general wellbeing and should receive priority. Endpoints of short- and long-term studies vary considerably. Functional outcomes as true indicators of the effects are needed and should be addressed as endpoints in studies.

MAKING PROGRAMS AND INTERVENTIONS WORK

Scientific knowledge relating to interventions has expanded beyond iron and now a range of other nutrients (such as vitamin A and multiple micronutrients) as well as infectious disease and parasitic infestation are being considered. In addition, it is now recognized that interventions don't always turn out the way we had hoped; consider the results showing possible negative effects in malaria-endemic areas. So too it has been learned that food-based strategies such as biofortification and dietary diversification are also important. It would seem, that although often a specific angle is emphasized or an approach advocated, the key message should be that all the recognized and documented causes and intervention approaches must work together and that supplementation, fortification (food and home), biofortification, food-based approaches, and public health measures have to be viewed and practiced as complementary to one another. For the long-term success and sustainability of nutritional anemia control programs, all the factors and options must be viewed together as a whole and be adjusted to suit the specific local conditions and requirements. Controlling iron deficiency anemia is different from controlling other recognized deficiencies such as VADD and IDD, where "bullet orientated" approaches of capsules and fortification, respectively, seem to have worked.

It is a sobering statistic that in the year 2000, the number of iron supplements supplied by UNICEF to developing countries was only enough for 3% of all pregnant women in those countries – and that is before one considers compliance. This highlights the view that a key hindrance to achieving the global goals is the fact that operational components of controlling iron deficiency anemia are less well developed in comparison to research and development efforts, and that neither of these are generally linked to communication, which includes political advocacy, funding, motivation for acceptance of better nutrition practices, health education, and promotion. In fact, the greatest challenge probably does not lie in the need for more scientific research, although there are still many unanswered questions and areas for new or renewed focus, but rather in communicating and interpreting the research findings and exceptions so as to fine tune programs.

Advocacy communication needs to focus on the benefits throughout the life cycle and the associated impact of interventions on improving productivity, which ultimately lead to the economic uplift of both individuals and countries. Emphasizing the fact that the damage to intellectual development caused by iron deficiency in early childhood cannot be reversed later in life and quantifying the loss of GDP when iron deficiency is left untreated should be the key messages to mobilize action across a wide range of sectors for the eradication of iron deficiency and anemia. What we need are effective bridges between science and technology, service providers and political as well as financial decision makers. The problem is not the lack of knowledge about tailored solutions but rather a lack of clear political and financial commitment to undertake interventions to match the magnitude of the problem. The problem is clearly described. What remains is to accept the challenge and accelerate the action.

INDEX

5-L-oxoproline (5-OP) 221, 222

A1-acid glycoprotein (AGP) 39, 41, 239, 244, 250

a1-antichymotrypsin (ACT) 239, 241, 244, 249, 290

abdominal symptoms 353

absorption, enhancers 16, 78, 89, 90, 91, 201, 202, 340, 350, 352

absorption, inhibitors 16, 68, 78, 89, 90, 202, 204, 206, 208, 233, 324, 334, 340, 345, 352, 386

absorption, intestinal iron 46, 62, 236, 363

absorption, of iron 17, 65, 69, 70, 81, 83-86, 88, 90, 91, 102, 106, 137, 142, 148, 206, 234, 248, 250, 278, 362, 365, 371

acute myocardial infarction (AMI) 290

acute phase proteins (APP) 235, 236, 239, 241, 243, 244, 249, 250

adipose tissue 161, 164, 219

AIDS see HIV/AIDS

Albion Laboratories 87

alpha-tocopherol see also vitamin E 156, 158-167, 170-175, 276

amino acids see also cysteine, methionine, chelates 62, 82, 87, 104, 114, 157, 191, 222, 224, 340

Ancylostoma duodenale 245, 246

anemia, and infection 3, 11, 14, 16, 17, 26, 27, 38-41, 49, 51-54, 71, 92, 105, 106, 134, 137, 146-148, 156, 218, 222, 232-250, 262, 264, 270, 277, 278, 291-294, 298, 304, 305, 327, 342, 343, 344, 363, 365, 367, 368, 372, 384, 386

anemia, and mortality 3, 5, 11, 14, 23, 25, 49, 53, 172, 190, 219, 224, 343, 361, 363, 366,

anemia, and productivity 21, 23, 25, 51, 246, 259, 344, 361, 362, 375, 385, 387

anemia, brassica- 192

anemia, folate deficiency- 114, 165

anemia, hemolytic- 156, 165, 168, 302

anemia, hyperbilirubi- 297

anemia, in pregnancy 3-11, 39, 46-50, 66, 67, 124, 136, 143, 200, 235, 260, 292, 339, 341-343, 349, 361, 362, 365, 384

anemia, iron deficiency 11, 14, 20, 22, 46, 48, 49, 52-54, 88, 91, 157, 167, 200, 206, 240, 246, 259, 261-263, 270, 279, 288, 291, 304, 327, 329, 334, 339, 342-345, 356, 360-376, 385, 387

anemia, macrocytic- 112, 113, 121, 205, 217, 298, 299

anemia, maternal- 25, 292, 371

anemia, megaloblastic- 112-114, 117, 121, 124, 128, 165, 220, 297, 298

anemia, microcytic- 101, 121, 205, 220, 225, 235, 301

anemia, normocytic- 121, 205, 235

anemia, nutritional 11, 15-33, 39-42, 99, 133-148, 278, 279, 286, 288, 303, 317, 333, 360-375, 384, 386, 387

anemia, of chronic disease see anemia of inflammation

anemia, of infection 147, 148

anemia, of inflammation 70, 189, 193, 236, 258, 363, 366, 367

anemia, of malaria 3, 11, 26, 92, 134, 137, 147, 156, 200, 232, 233, 238, 240, 241-243, 360, 363, 365-367, 374, 384, 386

anemia, pernicious 126, 265, 248

anemia, prevalence of 2, 3-11

anemia, sickle cell- 156, 165, 167, 168, 169, 170, 232

anemia, sideroblastic- 112

anemia, vitamin B$_{12}$ deficiency- 156

anorexia nervosa 216, 219, 220, 234, 248, 367

anthelmintic treatment 26, 246, 291, 292, 303

antichymotrypsin see also a1-antichymotrypsin 239, 290

antioxidant 102, 156-161, 165-174, 191, 192, 220, 222, 224, 355